Sharing the **Land,** Sharing a **Future**

PERCEPTIONS ON TRUTH AND RECONCILIATION

ISSN 2371-347X

SHARING THE **LAND,**
SHARING A **FUTURE**

Edited by Katherine A.H. Graham
and David Newhouse

UNIVERSITY OF MANITOBA PRESS

Sharing the Land, Sharing a Future:
The Legacy of the Royal Commission on Aboriginal Peoples
© The Authors 2021

25   24   23   22   21   1   2   3   4   5

University of Manitoba Press
Winnipeg, Manitoba, Canada
Treaty 1 Territory
uofmpress.ca

Cataloguing data available from Library and Archives Canada
Perceptions on Truth and Reconciliation, ISSN 2371-347X ; 4
ISBN 978-0-88755-868-9 (PAPER)
ISBN 978-0-88755-870-2 (PDF)
ISBN 978-0-88755-869-6 (EPUB)
ISBN 978-0-88755-917-4 (BOUND)

Cover and interior design by Vincent Design

Printed in Canada

The University of Manitoba Press acknowledges the financial support for
its publication program provided by the Government of Canada through
the Canada Book Fund, the Canada Council for the Arts, the Manitoba
Department of Sport, Culture, and Heritage, the Manitoba Arts Council,
and the Manitoba Book Publishing Tax Credit.

Funded by the Government of Canada | Canadä

CONTENTS

PART 3 : POWERFUL COMMUNITIES, HEALTHY COMMUNITIES

FOREWORD

"WE ARE ALL HERE TO STAY": THE SHARING THE LAND, SHARING A FUTURE FORUM MARKING THE TWENTIETH ANNIVERSARY OF RCAP

Marlene Brant Castellano and Frederic Wien
Co-Chairs of the Oversight Committee for Sharing the Land, Sharing a Future

The concluding volume of the report of the Royal Commission on Aboriginal Peoples (RCAP) (1996) was titled *Renewal: A Twenty-Year Commitment*. The report anticipated that, if the agenda for institutional change and investment mapped out by RCAP was launched immediately, then benefits would accrue to Aboriginal peoples and the nation as a whole. Within ten years, levels of social well-being, reduction in costs of dependency, and increased productivity would visibly offset expenditures. By the twentieth year, there would be a net dividend to Canada as a result of the equitable participation of healthy, educated, empowered Aboriginal nations.

As the twentieth anniversary of RCAP approached, the RCAP body of work had almost disappeared from public view. The enormous legacy of information assembled in published reports, research studies, intervenor briefs from NGOs, Aboriginal organizations and communities, and transcripts of extensive public hearings was inaccessible, lodged in digital archives incompatible with current software. Most recommendations had been ignored.

The report of the Truth and Reconciliation Commission (TRC) in 2015 acknowledged that RCAP had set out a bold new path to change the very foundation of Canada's relationship with Aboriginal peoples and declared that "the country has a rare second chance to seize a lost opportunity for reconciliation." The TRC report frequently cited RCAP documents to add clarity and depth to its own analysis, and the calls to action (CTA) echoed many of the recommendations made two decades earlier, including CTA 45 for a new Royal Proclamation to be developed jointly by the government of Canada and Aboriginal peoples, reaffirming a nation-to-nation relationship based on principles of mutual recognition and respect and shared responsibility.

By 2015, conversations involving former staff of and contributors to RCAP had already begun, to the effect that "we should do something to mark the anniversary." Widespread public response to the TRC calls to action was evident in the political arena, civil society organizations, media coverage, and engagement of Aboriginal and settler citizens in respectful dialogue. The notion of an event that would honour RCAP's legacy and add momentum to reconciliation began to take shape.

In July 2015, a group of volunteers assembled at Queen's University to plan what became a national forum on reconciliation, marking the twentieth anniversary of RCAP. An Oversight Committee was formed with representation from Indigenous organizations, academia, and other parts of civil society. The committee provided guidance on all aspects of the forum program as well as on financial and administrative matters. The composition of the committee is found in the appendix of this publication.

We received important administrative support from Queen's University through its School of Policy Studies and from the University of Manitoba through its National Centre for Truth and Reconciliation. Financial contributions were provided by these universities and by Dalhousie University, the Canadian Institutes of Health Research, the Social Sciences and Humanities Research Council, and the Federation for the Humanities and Social Sciences. The lead donor was Indigenous and Northern Affairs Canada.

In organizing the 2016 RCAP forum, we were impressed with the interest in and support for RCAP that exist not only in Aboriginal organizations but also among people active in discourse on Indigenous policies and services. The impact of the commission has been more profound than is commonly recognized. In addition to concrete steps such as apologies and settlements for residential schools and High Arctic relocations, RCAP argued strongly for important ideas that have since been more broadly accepted, such as the inherent right of Indigenous peoples to govern themselves, the concept of three orders of government in Canada, and the principle that comprehensive land claim agreements should not extinguish Indigenous rights to the land. The federal government has also come to see the logic of creating two departments, one to address urgent issues in Indigenous services and the other to structure far-reaching changes in Crown-Indigenous relations.

We were interested in examining the impacts of RCAP over the past twenty years. We also wanted to consider the priorities and approaches needed to sustain movement toward reconciliation in light of changes in areas such as demographics, court decisions, and economic development. In addition to the speakers featured on the forum program, we commissioned a number of background papers. They make up the bulk of this volume and will be properly introduced by the co-editors, Katherine Graham and David Newhouse.

To our delight, we discovered that Library and Archives Canada (LAC) was interested in the RCAP database in the context of its own response to the TRC calls to action, particularly as they relate to history and education. A joint approach from the Centre for Truth and Reconciliation and the RCAP forum organizers resulted in a commitment by LAC to migrate the entire RCAP data collection to contemporary software on an accelerated schedule for public release on the LAC website. The availability of the RCAP information in an accessible and searchable format was announced at the national forum on reconciliation on 3 November 2016.

There is hope that Canada might finally be coming to grips with what is required to renew (some would say create for the first time) a mutually beneficial relationship between Indigenous and settler peoples. RCAP and the themes that it addressed are still current. This volume brings to bear the varied perspectives of contemporary authors and forum presenters as a contribution to the ongoing search for a new relationship based on the principles of recognition, respect, responsibility, and sharing.

INTRODUCTION
CHARTING A WAY FORWARD

Katherine A.H. Graham and David Newhouse

In November 2016, a group of 150 people from major sectors of Canadian society gathered in Winnipeg to determine how the lessons learned from the twenty years since the release of the final report of the Royal Commission on Aboriginal Peoples (RCAP) could inform the process of reconciliation. In many respects, the calls to action (CTA) of the Truth and Reconciliation Commission (TRC) mirrored those of the 1996 RCAP report. The consensus of those in attendance was that Canada has lost a generation of effort in building a new relationship with and improving the lives of Indigenous peoples. The major recommendations for building a new relationship with and making a large-scale effort to improve the lives of Indigenous peoples were not followed. The 2015 release of the TRC report has produced, as of the time of writing, a modicum of goodwill among many governments to make and foster changes that will improve the situation. The challenge going forward is to animate this goodwill and build upon the developing Indigenous institutional and governance foundation so that the gains are not lost and indeed are expanded.

The forum reinforced the need for developing a new relationship between Indigenous peoples and Canada based on the fundamental principles that RCAP set out: recognition, respect, sharing, and responsibility. These principles are intended to guide our actions with each other. Recognition asks that we see each other as partners now living on this land, that we respect each other's laws and institutions, and that we cooperate for mutual benefit. Respect asks us to look again at each other, to act in ways that enhance our dignity as human beings, and to build a high regard for Indigenous culture and heritage into Canadian culture. Sharing asks us to enjoy equitably the benefits of Canada's lands and resources. And responsibility asks us to act with honesty and good faith in our treatment of each other. Acting with recognition and respect means that the relationship ought to be informed as much by Indigenous theory as by Western political theory. The Two-Row Wampum and the Medicine Circle bring these ideas into the political forum as important contributions to the ongoing discussion about the nature of the relationship. The foundation of the new relationship should be nation to nation and nation to Crown.

THE TWENTY-FIRST-CENTURY CONTEXT

Context matters. There are significant differences when comparing Indigenous peoples and their relationships of the 1960s with those of the 2020s. The RCAP forum took place on the eve of the 150th anniversary of Canadian Confederation. Canada itself has changed since it celebrated its centenary in 1967. Yet the "Indian problem" remains potent in the eyes of decision makers. Moving forward requires that we address the policy legacy based on the ideas of civilization and assimilation. Indigenous peoples were not directly involved in the historical policy conversation, described by RCAP as a soliloquy.[1] They were policy objects to be acted on at will by a Canada that believed it knew what was best for them. In the 1970s, as a result of activism surrounding the 1969 White Paper on Indian Policy,[2] the policy conversation started to shift as Indigenous peoples became directly involved as policy actors rather than just policy objects. Inuit were similarly regarded as policy objects, at least until their assertion of land rights and their engagement with the federal government on land claims and visions of governance beginning in the 1970s. Métis were not recognized as a distinct people in Canadian public policy as late as the time of RCAP. That has changed, largely as a result of the courts. The current context makes a difference in shaping the way forward.

Treating Indigenous peoples in a respectful way that recognizes them as important political actors and indeed sees them as one of the founders of Canada is important. The existence of acknowledged Indigenous rights under Section 35 of the Constitution, and the conception of Canada as a land subject to multiple sovereignties, are fundamental to our collective future, to Canada's self-image as a peaceful, multicultural, and plurinational state that works. The work of Confederation will not be complete until Indigenous peoples believe that the deal with Canada is fair and just. Canada is a nation that consists of Indigenous peoples and immigrant-settlers trying to work out how to live well here together. As former Supreme Court Justice Antonio Lamer wrote in the *Delgamuukw* decision, "let us face it, we are all here to stay."[3] Indigenous peoples are important to the future of Canada and, as the scholarship of the past two decades shows us, to its past.

Canada's relationship with its original inhabitants is different in 2020 from the time of the White Paper on Indian Policy in 1969. Indigenous peoples' struggles in the process of constitutional patriation, the visions of the future expressed during the RCAP process, and the quest for modern treaties, accords, and recognition of a genuine treaty relationship have led to a time when Indigenous peoples are engaging in all aspects of Canadian life both as individuals and as political actors. As a result of the TRC report, Canadian institutions are starting to explore ways in which to ensure that they engage Indigenous peoples meaningfully.

There are those who argue that the relationship between Indigenous peoples and Canada is still a settler-colonial relationship since Indigenous governance is not a fully realized aspiration, treaties are not yet fully implemented, jurisdictions over Indigenous lands and waters are not recognized, and the economic, social, and health conditions of Indigenous peoples remain poorer than those of other Canadians. These views were strongly and eloquently expressed at the RCAP forum. But significant change has occurred.

The past half-century, in our view, has provided some foundational elements that can enable things to change rapidly. The RCAP report and the TRC point the way forward. An examination of the process that produced both reports gives some insight into the changes of the past half-century. The 1966 *Survey of the Contemporary Indians of Canada* (commonly known as the Hawthorn Report) was produced by University of British Columbia professors without guidance or input from Indigenous peoples.[4] That report is noteworthy for two reasons: it documented the gap in socio-economic status between Indigenous people and the general Canadian population, and it made recommendations to alleviate this situation, focused on shifting the policy paradigm from direct federal programming and the Indian Act to a concept of "citizens plus" in which Status Indians should have acknowledged special rights as charter members of Canada but also receive services from the federal and provincial governments in a manner similar to the general population. This notion of citizens plus strongly influenced the 1969 White Paper.

The 1996 RCAP report was produced by a seven-person commission, the majority of whom were Indigenous and guided a group of Indigenous and non-Indigenous researchers through an arduous Indigenous community-based project that represented the voices of Indigenous peoples, largely absent from the Hawthorn Report. The commission also conducted extensive hearings in all parts of Canada and reviewed a significant number of briefs submitted by intervenors. The RCAP report presented a very different prescription for moving forward in a good way, based on the four fundamental principles to guide our relationship and a vision of Indigenous nationhood, with re-emergent Indigenous nations being recognized as sovereign in their own domains but also essential parts of a new Canadian partnership.

Similarly, the Truth and Reconciliation Commission consisted of three individuals whose stature was beyond repute. They were the centre of a network of public and private testimonies over an eight-year period about residential school experiences and impacts. The TRC set out ten principles of reconciliation and ninety-four calls to action in its final report. In doing so, it looked beyond the borders of Canada to the United Nations Declaration on the Rights of Indigenous Peoples (UNDRIP). Fundamental is the conception of reconciliation and a positive future based on an understanding that "all Canadians ... as Treaty peoples share responsibility for establishing and maintaining mutually respectful relationships."[5]

The fundamental lesson of the past half-century, and particularly since the tabling of the RCAP final report in 1996, is that ignoring Indigenous peoples' voices in the national discussion about the way forward is sheer folly and leads to suboptimal results. Indigenous peoples through their representative organizations and local governments and service organizations must be directly involved in all discussions about their participation in the Canadian federation and aimed at improving their lives as Indigenous individuals, communities, and nations.

We must not ignore the absolute determination of Indigenous peoples to survive and thrive within the Canadian state and to reclaim a place of respect and dignity among the new peoples of this land. For more than half a century, Indigenous peoples have used a wide variety of means to ensure their survival as distinct societies with rights to self-determination. Worldwide, these rights have been defined in the UNDRIP, which now forms a framework for discussions within settler-colonial nation-states and a basis for the measurement of progress toward lives of dignity.

The situation will not change much until the distinctiveness of Indigenous peoples is recognized and built into the foundation of Canada. RCAP found that the experiences of Indigenous peoples in Canada's urban centres were profoundly unhappy except when there was support for Indigenous cultures, languages, knowledges, and self-determination. The same could be said for all Indigenous peoples. The restoration of jurisdiction over lands and waters is also important as a foundational element of the development and good functioning of Indigenous communities and economies.

Improving the quality of life for Indigenous peoples will take special efforts and public expenditures. But so does maintaining the existing system and paying for its effects. The cost of doing nothing is higher than the cost of doing the right thing. The RCAP twenty-year plan to improve the quality of life was not implemented. Numerous studies have demonstrated the economic benefits to be achieved from public expenditures on Indigenous education, social services, community infrastructure, cultural and language support, and economic development. What is seen as important is also seen as too costly, and the results are seen as coming too slowly.

We know that government policies developed without the involvement and input of Indigenous peoples do not produce good results. We heard from the forum that Indigenous peoples want governments to do something specific: that is, to recognize their nations, governments, communities, and institutions as legitimate parts of the Canadian fabric. They want to be recognized as distinct social, cultural, and political communities. They want the capacity to develop their own policies and programs, communities, and economies in their own ways to meet the needs that they have identified. It is not surprising that the official record of the RCAP forum is entitled *Hear Our Voice*.

We also know that, when Indigenous peoples take charge of their own lives, build their own nations and communities, and exercise their own stewardship over their lands and waters, their lives and the lives of those around them improve.

THE TASK BEFORE US

The task before Canada is huge and requires the collective effort of Canadians, First Nations, Métis, and Inuit acting on the four principles articulated by RCAP. The forum discussed the most important actions to take over the next two decades. It set out three areas of priority for action: building new national institutions, fostering vibrant communities, and improving education. These priorities are linked. There is no choice between one or the other.

A nation-to-nation and nation-to-Crown relationship requires the recognition of First Nations, Métis, and Inuit peoples as nations with governments and a rethinking of the institutions of governance to ensure that they have powers and jurisdictions clearly articulated and built into the governing structure of Canada. It means transforming the ad hoc structures and arrangements that have emerged and replacing them with well-designed and substantive new arrangements. It means treating Indigenous peoples as important partners in Confederation rather than a problem for policy makers to solve. Creating a just society means bringing Indigenous peoples into the body politic as Indigenous peoples with a distinct set of rights.

Community is the centre of Indigenous life. Taking steps to support the development of vibrant Indigenous communities to ensure equity of life conditions between Indigenous and non-Indigenous peoples is an important aspect of creating a just society. Although there are many vibrant Indigenous communities, there are also many that struggle with housing, community infrastructure, health, education, and employment, and the lives of Indigenous peoples are unsatisfactory. Fostering vibrant communities means developing a long-term framework of support and moving from the program approach to one that provides resources and decision-making authority over their use in responding to the unique needs and circumstances of each community. Communities are developed on the ground. The Kelowna Accord is a model that has great potential to make a difference. It tied all parties to the accord to long-term commitments and accountability for actions.

Education is the key institution in which the knowledge of one generation is transmitted to another. For most of the past century, the formal education system was used as a means to attempt to transform Indigenous peoples into Europeans and the means to inform non-Indigenous

Canadians about Indigenous peoples. Today the education system needs to be reformed to educate non-Indigenous Canadians about the truths of Canadian Indigenous history and to educate Indigenous peoples about their own cultures, languages, and knowledges.

The three areas are broad and will require enormous creativity, energy, and innovation. However, as we have pointed out, there is a foundation that can be strengthened and built upon. Although there is growing public support for action to improve the life circumstances of Indigenous peoples, support for institutional reform of the type deemed necessary by Indigenous peoples is soft.

A key element underlying all of these tasks is the need for a new fiscal/financial relationship between Indigenous nations and Canada. Effective governance requires a stable and predictable source of resources, both financial and human. Governance without a commitment to resource sharing as a source of funding becomes program administration, and the relationship of dependence continues. The fact that the Royal Commission prepared a multi-year plan to implement its recommendations is little known. That plan is still relevant to those actively engaged in Indigenous policy, and it has some elements that might reduce the natural fear of the unknown as we embark on necessary institutional reform.

THE LEADERS' COMMENTS

Five of the national leaders spoke at the forum setting out their ideas about what constitutes a nation-to-nation relationship and how to achieve it.

National Chief Perry Bellegarde of the Assembly of First Nations (AFN) focused his remarks on the state of relations twenty years after the RCAP report. He asserted the inherent rights of Indigenous peoples and treaties as underlying our relationship: "Nations make treaties, treaties do not make nations."[6] Ours is a nation-to-nation relationship that has yet to be fully realized as a result of the colonial and assimilationist policies of Canadian governments and the continuing challenges for Indigenous peoples in reaffirming their nationhood and self-determination. Chief Bellegarde assessed the current progress, from the AFN perspective, in working with the federal and provincial/territorial governments to achieve positive change. Although he acknowledged some positive developments, he noted that the fundamental step for First Nations is to move beyond the strictures of the Indian Act and to assert their own existing jurisdiction.

Natan Obed, president of the Inuit Tapiriit Kanatami (ITK), spoke of the importance for Inuit of an Inuit-to-Crown relationship as distinct from a nation-to-nation relationship. He focused on the specific place of Inuit in Canada and within the Constitution. He noted that, as a result of Inuit co-management of 35 percent of Canada's land mass and over 50 percent of its coastline, Inuit enable Canada to assert its Arctic sovereignty. Despite this and the firm commitment of Inuit to Canada, he called on the federal government to recognize the nature of the Inuit-to-Crown relationship by working with Inuit respectfully to deal with the many challenges that they and the Arctic face.

Clément Chartier, president of the Métis National Council (MNC), also talked about the distinctiveness of the Métis people, with no treaty except the Manitoba Act of 1870. The lack of formal recognition of Métis as a people by governments and others has made the realization of a nation-to-nation relationship challenging but important. He spoke of the RCAP process and final report as key for Métis to articulate their vision of themselves as a nation and their aspirations for the future, only for Métis to be largely forgotten in the official federal response to RCAP.[7] In the twenty intervening years, judicial decisions have enabled Métis to make major gains in being recognized and having their rights affirmed. The goal now is to work with the federal government to implement the recent renewal of a nation-to-nation relationship between Canada and the Métis Nation.

Francyne Joe, president of the Native Women's Association of Canada (NWAC), spoke of the contribution of RCAP to giving voice to Indigenous women and explicitly acknowledging that eradicating the gender discrimination embedded in the past colonial relationship is essential for all to move forward. She spoke of the sacred inheritance of women and of the central role that women play in leadership, both through tradition and in times of practical need. Yet women are still struggling to be heard and included in discussions of nation-to-nation relationships.

National Chief Robert Bertrand of the Congress of Aboriginal Peoples (CAP) focused on the legacy of RCAP for Indigenous people living off-reserve and in urban areas. He spoke of the unfinished business of governance as it relates to urban Indigenous people and of the continued need for initiatives that address the disparities in circumstances between those represented by CAP and others. He emphasized the challenges of housing, even though it is a fundamental human right. He encouraged all governments to honour the principles articulated by RCAP and to work cooperatively with Indigenous organizations to create solutions for Indigenous people in need.

INDIGENOUS POLICY THEN AND NOW

Minister of Indigenous and Northern Affairs Carolyn Bennett also spoke at the forum. She spoke of the bold vision of First Nations, Métis, and Inuit as sovereign nations within Canada, asserted by the Royal Commission and its scathing characterization of the life circumstances of many Indigenous people. She reflected on her sense of déjà vu when reading the government's 1998 response to RCAP, *Gathering Strength: Canada's Aboriginal Action Plan*, quoting its statement that "reconciliation is an ongoing process. In renewing our partnership, we must ensure that the mistakes which marked our past relationships are not repeated."[8] She spoke of the need for consultation, communication, and investment to provide equitable services to Indigenous peoples compared with others in the Canadian population.

It is well known that Prime Minister Justin Trudeau has made progress on Indigenous relations and issues a public priority for his government. As he famously wrote in 2015 in the original mandate letters to all ministers, "no relationship is more important to me than the one with Indigenous peoples."[9] Over its mandate and particularly in the years since the RCAP forum, the government of Canada has initiated some important structural changes and policy statements intended to reflect this priority.

As of the 2019 federal budget, the government earmarked over $21 billion in expenditures on infrastructure, health, child welfare, and capacity-building support for Indigenous peoples.[10] In part, this reflects the removal of the 2 percent cap on Indigenous program funding, which had been in place since the early 1990s and contributed to ever-increasing impoverishment of Indigenous services.

In 2017, the government split the Department of Indigenous and Northern Affairs in two, creating the Department of Crown-Indigenous Relations to steward the new relationship and the Department of Indigenous Services to provide support for the delivery of services.

As the government noted, this split was influenced by the recommendations of RCAP twenty years earlier.[11] Also in 2017, the federal government was generally applauded for its announced intention to create an Indigenous Languages Act to promote and sustain Indigenous languages. It was followed by the promulgation of Ten Principles regarding the government of Canada's relationship with Indigenous peoples. Among these principles is the recognition that Section 35 of the Constitution contains "a full box of (Indigenous) rights" and that there are unique rights, interests, and circumstances of First Nations, the Métis Nation, and Inuit.[12] Finally, the prime minister announced a Recognition and Implementation of Rights Framework in February 2018, seeking implementation of the framework before October 2019. The government was unable to realize its initial intention for a broad piece of legislation to implement this framework according to its original self-imposed deadline of October 2019. This deadline was seen as inadequate in providing the necessary time for consultation and "getting it right" by some First Nations. In light of this, the federal government has focused on new initiatives and relationships on a sector-by-sector basis, for example in education.

This announcement was met by criticism from Indigenous leaders and others who argued that the framework had not been developed in partnership with Indigenous peoples. Critics have argued that the foundations of the framework are based on a colonial paradigm;[13] that the framework ignores key issues such as fiscal relationships and the roles of provincial and territorial governments; and that the proposed time frame for implementation is precipitous. At our time of writing, the minister of Crown-Indigenous relations acknowledged imperfections in the process of developing the framework if not its alleged colonial paradigm and limited scope. "We want to get this right," she stated, "and with your help ... I know we can."[14]

To be sure, there have been other federal policy developments and responses. But they are not among the most significant and illustrate the severe challenges that the government of Canada faces as it confronts the power of Canada's colonial past. As was noted earlier, the RCAP forum was told that public support for institutional reform is relatively weak. Despite efforts by the government to "educate" the public service about our true history and the fundamentals of reconciliation, there are significant drags on changing the culture of the public service, including resistance to change and the competing demands on public servants' time and priorities. Civil society organizations might be supportive, but generally their resources are limited. Finally, the private sector, particularly the natural resource sector, has relationships with First Nations, Métis, and Inuit people, organizations, and governments that go beyond any common definition of complex.

The policy challenge for the government of Canada (and indeed for other governments in Canada) is to acknowledge Indigenous sovereignties and their attendant jurisdictions and to work with First Nations, Métis, and Inuit to reform institutions and create new ones that reflect the four principles articulated by RCAP. Education about the benefits of doing so and about the costs to us all of doing nothing is an essential element of this task.

THE FORUM PAPERS

The forum Steering Committee commissioned a series of papers on five themes: the nation-to-nation relationship, closing the gap, youth and citizen engagement, powerful and healthy communities, and moving to action. These papers formed the basis of workshops and addresses. The Steering Committee also asked leaders of national Indigenous organizations to present their views on what they believed was the way forward.

The commissioned papers and addresses by the national leaders were collected and edited for this volume. They represent the best thinking on the way forward as of November 2016. The papers demonstrate the challenges before us and present us with directions.

We start with the fundamental idea of the nation-to-nation relationship. Mark Dockstator, president of the First Nations University of Canada, reminded us that we have a shared past and a shared future. He presented a model of the historical relationship between Indigenous peoples and Canadian settler society grounded in two Indigenous ideas: the Guswentah, or Two-Row Wampum, and the Medicine Circle. He emphasized the importance of considering the relationship from various perspectives—citizens, citizens plus, citizens minus, and dual/sovereign citizens—in pursuit of a balance between Indigenous and Canadian societies.

In Chapter 1, Frances Abele, Erin Alexiuk, Satsan (Herb George), and Catherine MacQuarrie review the RCAP recommendations for a nation-to-nation relationship and note the barriers that have prevented further discussion on and implementation of such a relationship. They cite the small population size of First Nations and the lack of collaborative policy and agenda-setting mechanisms such as those that led to the Kelowna Accord as important barriers to change. They argue that the public service needs to adopt a mindset similar to that which Canada uses in international development.

Yvonne Boyer, Josée Lavoie, Derek Kornelsen, and Jeff Reading set out in Chapter 2 how a new nation-to-nation relationship would work in the area of health. They argue for a national First Nations, Métis, and Inuit health policy informed by the First Nations Health Authority established in British Columbia and based on the policy idea of reciprocal accountability.

Moving to the development of powerful communities, healthy communities, in Chapter 11 Jo-ann Archibald (Q'um Q'um Xiiem) and Jan Hare review developments in Indigenous education over the past two decades, pointing out the improvement in local control of Indigenous education and the development of new educational approaches incorporating and based on Indigenous knowledge. They argue for improved funding for Indigenous education across all jurisdictions and the development of Indigenous educational legislation that addresses jurisdictional and funding issues for all Indigenous students. Urban and Métis students need particular attention.

In Chapter 12, Jennifer Dockstator and her collaborators report on the lessons derived from the Poverty Action Research Project, a five-year project involving five First Nations focused on improving community wellness through local community economic development initiatives. Alleviating poverty was found to require a multi-sector approach grounded first and foremost in Indigenous understandings of community wellness.

Wanda Wuttunnee, Frederic Wien, and David Newhouse examine in Chapter 13 the conditions necessary for the development of sustainable Indigenous economies. They argue that, though there is a foundation of Aboriginal rights that provides some degree of certainty about access to lands and natural resources, there needs to be widespread recognition of the diversity of Indigenous opinion on what constitutes a sustainable and healthy community as well as improved support for Indigenous education and business activity.

In Chapter 14, Caroline Tait and her colleagues reflect on the journey toward Indigenous wellness over the past two decades, addressing the central issues of intergenerational trauma, addiction and mental illness, and increasing use of Indigenous holistic models of healing and wellness.

They highlight the need for collaborative approaches in knowledge generation such as those of the Aboriginal Healing Foundation and the Institute of Indigenous Peoples' Health.

In Chapter 15, Carrie Bourassa, Eric Oleson, Sibyl Diver, and Janet McElhaney examine the legacy of colonialism and racism in the delivery of health care to Indigenous peoples. They identify that Indigenous-centred principles such as cultural safety and Indigenous self-determination, among others, as important elements in improving care.

In Chapter 16, Cindy Blackstock describes and analyzes the history and impact of discriminatory and failed government child-care policies upon Indigenous families and communities. Her research advocates for child-care policy reform that would affirm First Nations jurisdictions and provide equitable and flexible funding for comprehensive culturally based programs tackling poverty, housing, and health.

Jonathan Dewar writes in Chapter 17 of the need for artists to be part of the process of reconciliation, not to create exhibits that showcase Indigenous pain but to engage with communities to make art that promotes and facilitates healing. Healing comes from engagement in making art. Dewar recommends the development of policies that support community engagement rather than community exhibition.

Recognizing that the way forward will require the engagement of citizenship, in Chapter 18 Lynne Davis and Chris Hiller analyze the significant challenges of mobilizing Indigenous and non-Indigenous peoples for reconciliation. Their research indicates that issues such as land, treaties, and sovereignty, central to Indigenous relationship building, are largely absent from non-Indigenous discussion of reconciliation. They see a need to create new dialogical spaces where Indigenous ideas can be discussed and actions developed from them.

In Chapter 19, Aaron Franks reflects on the ways in which the academic research community can be restructured and mobilized in support of a new relationship. He suggests that SSHRC support the greater Indigenous research autonomy as well as the continued development of Indigenous knowledge systems.

In Chapter 20, Daniel Salée and Carol Lévesque analyze the policy tools (commissions of inquiry and consultation) that Canada has used to implement the recommendations of RCAP and address issues. Canada, they argue, has been strategic in choosing the areas of engagement and selective about the tools used to engage Indigenous peoples in the process of policy development. It has had much success in the area of education but less in the area of Indigenous governance. This engagement has not resulted in a reconfiguration of state power relationships and the outcomes that Indigenous peoples want, particularly in the area of nation-to-nation relationships.

CONCLUSIONS

First Nations, Métis, and Inuit participants in Sharing the Land, Sharing a Future made it clear that they have diverse but concrete ideas about healing their communities and developing new relationships with non-Indigenous governments.

First, the most effective thing needed to speed up progress is re-establishing themselves as nations. The first RCAP principle, recognition, captures much of the dialogue at the forum related to this critical political project. As the commission pointed out, "mutual recognition has three major facets: equality, co-existence and self-government."[15] A decolonized institutional framework for all three Indigenous groups would be a key manifestation of the concept of recognition. For First Nations, it would replace the nineteenth-century Indian Act; for Métis and Inuit, it would require new institutions enshrined in law. Canadian governments at all levels and other institutions need to listen respectfully to ideas for a new relationship, recognizing that there might be different approaches. Respectful listening is the necessary foundation for achieving a better future that adheres to the four RCAP principles.

Second, a commitment to reduce the gap between Indigenous peoples and Canadians to ensure healthier and more vibrant communities for all Indigenous peoples, and especially the youth who will become tomorrow's leaders, is needed. If we do not invest in our youth—allowing them to educate us as we help to illuminate their traditional ways and languages and prepare them for the future—then we risk losing another generation and with it our best chance to advance good relations and develop a shared responsibility for the future.

Third, a commitment to widespread education of Canadians is the only way to eradicate ignorance about Indigenous peoples—their histories, communities, challenges, aspirations, and beliefs. Education enables change. Indigenous nationhood is not a threat to Canada. Ignorance is.

We should all remember that Canada was founded on the principle of being a federation with multiple sovereignties. Recognizing the sovereignties of First Nations, Inuit, and Métis does not violate the Constitution. Recognizing the sovereignties of Indigenous peoples is essential to their continued growth.

NOTES

1   Graham, Dittburner, and Abele, *Soliloquy and Dialogue*.
2   Minister of Indian Affairs and Northern Development, *Statement of the Government of Canada on Indian Policy*.
3   *Delgamuukw v. British Columbia*, [1997] 3 S.C.R. 1010.
4   Hawthorn, *Survey of the Contemporary Indians of Canada*.
5   Truth and Reconciliation Commission 2015, Principle 6, 4.
6   CBC News, "Treaty 4 Commemoration."
7   Minister of Indian Affairs and Northern Development, *Gathering Strength*.
8   Minister of Indian Affairs and Northern Development, *Gathering Strength*, 4.
9   Office of the Prime Minister of Canada, "Statement by the Prime Minister."
10 Government of Canada, *Budget 2019*, Chapter 3.
11 Office of the Prime Minister of Canada, "New Ministers to Support the Renewed Relationship with Indigenous Peoples."
12 Justice Canada, "Principles Respecting the Government of Canada's Relationship with Indigenous Peoples."
13 King and Pasternak, "Canada's Emerging Rights Framework."
14 Quoted in Shepherd and McCurry, "Ottawa Must Talk to Canadians."
15 Royal Commission on Aboriginal Peoples, *Looking Forward, Looking Back*, 646.

REFERENCES

CBC News. "Treaty 4 Commemoration Honours Past, Looks Toward the Future." 13 September 2016. https://www.cbc.ca/news/canada/saskatchewan/treaty-4-renewal-fort-quappelle-1.3761153.

Government of Canada. Budget 2019. Chapter 3. 19 March 2019. https://www.budget.ca/2019/docs/plan/chap-03-en.html..

Graham, Katherine, Carolyn Dittburner, and Frances Abele. *Soliloquy and Dialogue: Overview of Major Trends in Public Policy Relating to Aboriginal Peoples*. Ottawa: Minister of Public Works and Government Services Canada, 1996.

Hawthorn, H.B., ed. *Survey of the Contemporary Indians of Canada*. Ottawa: Department of Indian Affairs and Northern Development, 1966.

Justice Canada. "Principles Respecting the Government of Canada's Relationship with Indigenous Peoples." 2018. https://www.justice.gc.ca/eng/csj-sjc/principles-principes.html.

King, Hayden, and Shiri Pasternak. "Canada's Emerging Rights Framework: A Critical Analysis." Yellowhead Institute Special Report, 5 June 2018. https://yellowheadinstitute.org/wp-content/uploads/2018/06/yi-rights-report-june-2018-final-5.4.pdf.

Minister of Indian Affairs and Northern Development. *Statement of the Government of Canada on Indian Policy*. Ottawa: Indian and Northern Affairs Canada, 1969.

——. *Gathering Strength—Canada's Aboriginal Action Plan*. Ottawa: Indian and Northern Affairs Canada, 1998.

Office of Prime Minister of Canada. "Statement by the Prime Minister of Canada After Delivering a Speech to the Assembly of First Nations Special Chiefs." 8 December 2015. https://pm.gc.ca/en/news/statements/2015/12/08/statement-prime-minister-canada-after-delivering-speech-assembly-first.

——. "New Ministers to Support the Renewed Relationship with Indigenous Peoples." 28 August 2017. https://pm.gc.ca/eng/news/2017/08/28/new-ministers-support-renewed-relationship-indigenous-peoples.

Royal Commission on Aboriginal Peoples (RCAP). *Report of the Royal Commission on Aboriginal Peoples, Vol. 1: Looking Forward, Looking Back*. Ottawa: Indian and Northern Affairs Canada, 1996.

Shepherd, Robert, and Pamela McCurry. "Ottawa Must Talk to Canadians about Nation-to-Nation Agenda." Policy Options, 31 October 2018. http://policyoptions.irpp.org/magazines/october-2018/ottawa-must-talk-to-canadians-about-nation-to-nation-agenda/.

PART 1

SETTING THE SCENE FOR A NEW NATION-TO-NATION RELATIONSHIP

CHAPTER 1
COMPLETING CONFEDERATION:
THE NECESSARY FOUNDATION

Frances Abele, Erin Alexiuk, Satsan (Herb George), and Catherine MacQuarrie

The work of the Royal Commission on Aboriginal Peoples (RCAP, 1991–96) was undertaken at a difficult time in Indigenous-Canadian[1] relations. As Indigenous activists of the time saw, the negotiations leading to the patriation of the Canadian Constitution in 1982 provided an opportunity to register significant changes. Their political efforts and the support of allies led to the inclusion of "existing aboriginal and treaty rights" in Section 35, a provision for a process to specify the nature of these rights in Section 37, and, in Section 25 of the Charter of Rights and Freedoms, a guarantee that the Charter would not "abrogate or derogate from any aboriginal, treaty or other rights."[2] Although these provisions marked important gains in entrenching Indigenous peoples' rights in the Constitution Act, they were seen by all parties as incomplete.

After 1982, however, the First Ministers' Conferences mandated in Section 37 and all attempts to reach consensus among Indigenous peoples and Canadian government leaders on the meaning of the phrase "existing aboriginal and treaty rights" faltered. Conflicts over jurisdiction, constitutional wrangling, and legal action on the meaning and effect of Section 35 became bitter battles. A handful of comprehensive land claims (modern treaties) were negotiated between 1984 and 1993, but most remained mired in protracted negotiations. First Nations communities continued to labour under the administrative strictures of the Indian Act. Many fought the Crown to make good on the promises of historical treaties. Long-standing, dire social and economic disparities in the conditions in Indigenous communities remained. And protests had sprung up in various corners of the land, sometimes leading to violent conflicts. The siege at Kanesatake/Oka in the summer of 1990 over land rights was marked by deteriorating relationships between the provincial and federal governments and Mohawk activists, and ultimately, one death.[3] Reportedly, the siege at Kanesatake was the event that finally convinced the federal cabinet to act on an earlier promise to appoint a Royal Commission to inquire into Indigenous-Crown relations.[4]

If the conflict at Kanesatake was the spark, the failure of the referendum on the Charlottetown Accord in 1992 was the wind that kept the fire burning. The Charlottetown Accord reflected consensus among federal, provincial, territorial, and Indigenous leaders on the inherent right to self-government and other key matters. The consensus was reflected in an agreement among those engaged in the national discussion that included numerous other reform provisions concerning the balance of federal and provincial powers, recognition of Quebec as a distinct society, parliamentary institutions, and other provisions. RCAP weighed in on the national Charlottetown debate with a 1992 commentary, *The Right to Aboriginal Self-Government and the Constitution*. In this document, the commissioners observed that the right to self-government was becoming accepted, and they proposed four possible constitutional clauses that would explicitly identify the right to Aboriginal self-government as a constitutional right.[5] Reportedly, this argument was accepted by the drafters of the Charlottetown Accord. In 1993, the commission released a second commentary, *Partners in Confederation: Aboriginal Peoples, Self-Government, and the Constitution*, which argued that "there are persuasive grounds for believing that this provision [Section 35] includes an inherent right of self-government";[6] in this case, a constitutional amendment would not be required.

In any event, constitutional amendment was not forthcoming; the Charlottetown Accord was rejected in a national referendum in 1992. Many observers commented that, whatever the merits of its individual parts, there was sufficient variety in the accord to give too many voters a reason to decline the package. It was evident that, though conceptual progress in renovating Indigenous-Canadian relations had been made, particularly among political leaders and activists, other measures were needed to institutionalize change.

The commissioners found ground for hope in this complex landscape. They set out a new interpretation of Canadian history inclusive of Indigenous history and the history of Indigenous-Canadian relations and an ambitious, detailed agenda for renewing those relations. The underlying theme was the vital importance of self-determination and self-reliance to the achievement of better lives and better relationships within Canada for Indigenous peoples.[7] Fully 54 of the 440 recommendations deal with governance, spanning matters of Constitution and Parliament, legal frameworks, jurisdictional arrangements, machinery of government, citizenship, financing, and professional and institutional capacity, among others.

In this chapter, we review certain features of the analysis put forward by the Royal Commission, consider what has changed in Indigenous-Canadian relations since 1996, and offer some observations on the pathways to self-determination that lie ahead. We are interested in delineating the necessary foundation that will permit the just completion of Confederation.

RCAP'S VISION

The final report of the Royal Commission on Aboriginal Peoples provided important—and still relevant—insights into the meaning of sovereignty and the distinctions between self-determination and self-government. For the commission, Indigenous sovereignty, as heard from witnesses, is an "inherent attribute, flowing from sources within a people or nation rather than from external sources such as international law."[8] The commissioners noted that Indigenous sovereignty in Canada is recognized and given effect by the various formal alliances and treaties that had been made between First Nations and European powers over time.[9] It is a relational rather than an exclusionary concept. The inherent principle of or right to self-determination flows from this sovereignty, with the exercise of the constitutional right to self-government being one of the paths to express self-determination.[10] These came to be known as "Section 35 rights."

As a fundamental starting point, the commission held that Section 35 rights acknowledge the *pre-existence* of the right to self-determination.

It found that, in core areas of jurisdiction, Aboriginal people are free to implement the right through "self-starting initiatives, without the need for agreements with the federal and provincial governments."[11] However, the commission also concluded that, because the rights are acknowledged within the Canadian Constitution, they can operate only within the sphere of sovereignty defined by it (including the application of the Charter of Rights and Freedoms to their citizens). This required that their implementation—at least in part—would result from negotiated agreements with other governments, particularly where rights and interests might overlap (concurrent spheres of jurisdiction) and in the "interest of reciprocal recognition and the avoidance of litigation."[12]

RCAP offered a useful distinction between core jurisdiction and peripheral jurisdiction. The commission defined core jurisdictions as matters that "are vital to the life and welfare of a particular Aboriginal people, its culture and identity; do not have a major impact on adjacent jurisdictions; and are not otherwise the object of transcendent federal or provincial concern." These jurisdictions are non-negotiable. There is a need for negotiations with other governments on peripheral jurisdictions—those that significantly affect other jurisdictions or are a matter of concern for provincial or federal governments.[13]

THE EXPRESSION AND EXERCISE OF THE INHERENT RIGHT

The Royal Commission also found that the existence of Section 35 effectively establishes a third order of government within Canada, although implementation of the third order would be dependent on the reconstitution of effective self-governing nations. The commission further recommended that the government of Canada formally recognize and help to bring about the implementation of self-governing rights through legislation, an act that would also provide the mechanism for it to vacate its legislative authority and responsibility under Section 91(24) of the Constitution.[14] In the event of any conflict between Indigenous law and federal law within a concurrent sphere of jurisdiction, "the Aboriginal law will take priority, except where the federal law satisfies the *Sparrow* standard."[15]

Short of the vision of fully reconstituted nations exercising self-government from defined land bases, RCAP anticipated that a variety of arrangements might be necessary to give *expression* to the right to self-determination given the diversity of peoples and cultures, historical experiences of colonialism, where they made their homes, and their visions of governance. In the diversity of presentations received from Inuit, Métis, and First Nations representatives across the land, RCAP saw that the visions of Indigenous peoples embraced two main goals: greater authority over lands and peoples and greater control over matters affecting a particular nation—especially its culture, identity, and collective well-being "wherever they happen to be located."[16] RCAP saw these ideas as complementary rather than contradictory and thus built into its models of self-determination the potential for a range of approaches, including service delivery by a nation to those living outside its boundaries or self-determination by a nation's citizens living dispersed throughout a region or within an urban centre. The commission suggested that this latter situation be dealt with by "community of interest governments" to which people living dispersed throughout other jurisdictions may voluntarily associate for a limited set of governing purposes.[17]

ONLY NATIONS CAN EXERCISE THE INHERENT RIGHT

In regard to an Aboriginal order of government *exercising* the right to self-determination, the Royal Commission found that the right was vested in Indigenous nations, not small communities or individuals living in urban centres. Even if a measure of power was ultimately exercised at the local level, only the people of the nation as a whole could negotiate and conclude treaties relating to the inherent right.[18]

This was as much a matter of practical implementation as a philosophical or legal view. The commission said that in order for governments to be effective they require three basic things: legitimacy, power, and resources.[19] It defined a nation as "a sizeable body of Aboriginal people with a shared sense of national identity that constitutes the predominant population in a certain territory or collection of territories." Within this definition, three important concepts were at play: "collective sense of identity, size as a matter of capacity, and territorial predominance."[20]

While recognizing that the imposition of the Indian Act and other colonial policies over more than a century had led many Indigenous peoples— First Nations in particular—to identify strongly with local communities and community administrations, the commission stated that band administration is little more than self-administration (being within the aegis of federal control over decision making); it is not self-government.[21] Furthermore, "community level governments will generally continue to be poor, weak and isolated unless they form part of larger governmental structures."[22] The commission understood the factor of territorial predominance to be fundamental: "To hold a right of self-determination an Aboriginal group must constitute a majority of the permanent population in a certain territory or collection of territories."[23] This was seen as an important element for determining geographical boundaries of power and appropriate structures of government.

Accordingly, a number of the Royal Commission's recommendations were directed at Indigenous peoples themselves, urging them to begin the process of rebuilding nations, including establishing citizenship and new governing structures. Interestingly, despite declaring that Indigenous peoples are entitled to identify their own national units, the commission also recommended that the federal government put in place a process for "identifying Aboriginal groups entitled to exercise the right of self-determination as nations" (Recommendation 2.3.3).[24] Not so surprisingly, given that colonial administration has undermined the capacity of peoples to be self-determining, the commission also recommended that the Canadian government put in place various institutional and other supports needed to build and maintain modern Indigenous governments, including division of the Department of Indian Affairs and Northern Development. The commission also foresaw the need to foster education and crucial skills in government and economic self-reliance.

NEW NATION-TO-NATION RELATIONSHIPS

In regard to economic self-reliance, the Royal Commission called for "a fundamentally new fiscal arrangement" for Indigenous governments, one not based on the current practices under the Indian Act whereby the Canadian government determines priority spending and amounts, how funds may be spent, and where accountability for spending is primarily to the minister of Indian affairs rather than to the citizens of Indigenous governments.[25]

Recommendations 2.3.17 to 2.3.26 lay out a comprehensive framework for financing Indigenous governments, not unlike the type of fiscal arrangements that currently exist between the federal and provincial levels of government. Here the commission provided important details about taxation, land use and development, economic investments, financial settlements arising out of land claims, and what should or should not be included as a direct source of funding for Aboriginal governments. Furthermore, negotiated fiscal agreements among the three orders of government were envisioned. They should meet five key objectives: self-reliance, equity, efficiency, accountability, and harmonization.[26]

To effect the creation of a new nation-to-nation relationship and the implementation of the inherent right to self-determination in particular, the commission recommended a variety of legislative and other actions: a new Royal Proclamation, framework legislation on the inherent right as well as recognition of nations, a Canada-wide framework to guide a new fiscal relationship, and the creation of guiding and supporting institutions. Twenty years later, almost none of these things had happened. But much has happened to give some effect to the RCAP vision in some parts of the country. Perhaps its reflection on the following presaged the events to come: "Self-government is not a machine to be turned on or off. It is an organic process, growing out of the people as a tree grows from the earth, shaped by their circumstances and responsive to their needs. Like a tree growing, it cannot be rushed or twisted to fit a particular mould."[27]

TWENTY YEARS SINCE RCAP'S REPORT: WHAT HAS CHANGED?

In a chapter of this length, it is impossible to trace fully the Royal Commission's influence on constitutional jurisprudence, federal policy, or estimation of Indigenous peoples of the terrain of negotiation that lies before them. Nor is it possible, when considering these matters, to separate the influence of the commission's analysis from other, interacting forces for change. We point to four significant factors for change, with some reflections on what they might mean for the future.

SECTION 35: FROM AN EMPTY BOX TO A FULL BOX OF RIGHTS

When Section 35 was included in the Constitution Act, 1982, many viewed the phrase "existing aboriginal and treaty rights" metaphorically as an "empty box" of rights, a placeholder clause awaiting the negotiations and federal and provincial "concessions" that would determine its contents. The empty box view was disputed by the Indigenous leadership of the time, and indeed, three constitutional conferences and several Supreme Court decisions later, the box has been found to be nearly full. The long march through the courts has transformed the constitutional and legal landscape of Indigenous-Crown relations in Canada.[28]

Without aiming to explain or explore all of the developments in jurisprudence over the past twenty years, we would like to highlight a few signal decisions that have strengthened the foundations for new relationships between Indigenous nations and the Crown. These changes provide a framework for reconciliation through Section 35 based on recognition and protection.[29]

As a result of its timing, *R. v. Sparrow* (1990) dominated the legal context for commissioners and staff during the commission's deliberations. For the first time in Canadian jurisprudence, this decision asserted that there was a burden of proof on the Crown to justify negative infringements on Section 35 rights, outlining what came to be known as the Sparrow Test.[30] A year after the release of the Royal Commission's final report, *Delgamuukw and Gisdayway v. British Columbia* (1997) provided clarity concerning the definition and content of Aboriginal title in relation to self-government, describing Aboriginal title as a right to the land itself that includes a right to decide how that land is to be used.[31]

Subsequent cases provided guidance and strengthened what was established through *Delgamuukw and Gisdayway*. Notably, the British Columbia Supreme Court decision in *Campbell* (2000) marked the first explicit constitutional recognition of the inherent right to self-government and clarified that negotiations are not necessary to implement self-governance. Then, in the mid-2000s, the Supreme Court of Canada's *Haida* (2004) and *Mikisew Cree* (2005) decisions clarified, developed, and expanded the new relationship and process of reconciliation introduced in *Delgamuukw and Gisdayway*. These decisions include a procedural component (the duty to consult) and a substantive component (the duty to accommodate), applicable in areas without treaty but where Indigenous title has been proven or is asserted.[32] More recently, the *Tsilhqot'in* (2014) decision declared approximately 1,700 square kilometres in central British Columbia to be Tsilhqot'in title lands. The court also took an unprecedented step by requiring consent with respect to potential infringements on title lands and consideration of the dual perspectives at play: that is, "the dual perspectives of the common law and of the Aboriginal group bear equal weight in evaluating a claim for Aboriginal title."[33] The court also strongly recommended that the Crown seek consent even before title is proven.[34] Where *Sparrow* provided a procedure for justifying infringement on Section 35 rights, the *Tsilhqot'in* decision clarified that Section 35 *recognizes, affirms,* and *protects* rights and that consultation and accommodation should drive negotiations toward reconciliation. Accordingly, the threshold for infringing on Section 35 rights is now remarkably high, and, in the *Tsilhqot'in* case, the BC Forest Act failed to apply on Tsilhqot'in title lands.[35] The burden has thus shifted to the Crown to bring its laws, regulations, and policies into line with Aboriginal title.

Métis peoples have also turned to the court system to establish and define their rights under Section 35. Three key decisions since 2003 (two within the past few years) are laying the groundwork for the exercise of Métis rights across the country. In addition to establishing traditional harvesting rights, *R. v. Powley* (2003) laid out the legal test for determining who is Métis (for the purposes of Section 35).[36] *Manitoba Metis Federation v. Canada* (2013), in which the majority held that a promised land grant to Métis children of the Red River Settlement in the late 1800s had been improperly implemented, set the stage for new Metis land settlements in Manitoba at least. And finally—but most significantly for Métis peoples—the 2016 decision of the Supreme Court in *Daniels* closed the jurisdictional responsibility gap in which Métis peoples have been trapped for the past 150 years. The court determined Métis and Non-Status Indians to be "Indians" under Section 91(24) of the Constitution.[37] This was not, as some worried, a case of creating a new "Indian" identity for the Métis. Instead, it put policy and legislative responsibility for them squarely in the lap of the federal government (as with Inuit in 1939), finally making it clear which order of government Métis peoples can turn to for policy redress.[38]

ADVANCES IN LAND CLAIMS AND SELF-GOVERNMENT AGREEMENTS
In 1991, when the Royal Commission began its work, just three comprehensive land claims agreements had been negotiated, and only one "self-government" agreement had been concluded.[39] Four more comprehensive land claims agreements were reached while the commission deliberated, including the umbrella Yukon Comprehensive Claims Agreement, which led over time to the completion of self-government agreements for almost all of the signatory First Nations, and the Nunavut Agreement. Following the Nunavut Agreement, the Northwest Territories was divided to create Nunavut and a new Northwest Territories. Inuit in Nunavut chose to create a public government (one not ethnically exclusive) to complement the powers affirmed in their land claim agreement. There are now thirty-two agreements being implemented for land settlements, self-government, or both (see Tables 1.1–1.3).

The year before the Royal Commission tabled its final report, the federal cabinet adopted the Inherent Right Policy (1995), recognizing self-government as a constitutionally protected right under Section 35. This had an immediate impact on the Nisga'a negotiations, leading to a land agreement in 2000 that included self-government provisions, and it had a similar effect on all subsequent negotiations.

In different ways, all of the comprehensive land claim and self-government agreements provide constitutionally protected space under Section 35 from which to exercise self-government and frame new relationships with other governments.[40] Land claim agreements remove settlement lands from exclusive federal jurisdiction. They are lands owned exclusively by the Indigenous signatories, thus subject to the concurrent jurisdictions of all three orders of government (federal, provincial/territorial, and Indigenous) as set out in the land claim agreement. With the exception of specified transitional measures, the Indian Act no longer applies to individuals who are part of the collectivities who have signed land claim agreements. The status of Indigenous peoples as "Indians" under Section 91(24) is not altered. In addition, because land claim agreements are protected as treaties under Section 35, federal powers under Section 91(24) are constrained. New Aboriginal governments derive their authorities from the modern treaties and not the Indian Act.[41]

Importantly, land claim agreements also include the cession of most traditional lands, certainty of ownership over those lands selected by Indigenous signatories, large cash settlements providing capital for future building, co-management boards, and a variety of other governance provisions. Although the basic principle is similar, there are important differences, even among the four agreements of Inuit Nunangat, the Inuit homelands (discussed further in the next section).

TABLE 1.1. COMPLETED COMPREHENSIVE LAND CLAIM AGREEMENTS

AGREEMENT	EFFECTIVE DATE
James Bay and Northern Quebec Agreement	1977
Northeastern Quebec Agreement	1978
Inuvialuit Final Agreement	1984
Gwich'in Comprehensive Land Claim Agreement	1992
Sahtu Dene and Metis Comprehensive Land Claim Agreement	1994
Nunavik Inuit Land Claims Agreement	2008
Eeyou Marine Region Land Claims Agreement	2012

TABLE 1.2. COMPLETED COMPREHENSIVE LAND CLAIM WITH SELF-GOVERNMENT AGREEMENTS

AGREEMENT	EFFECTIVE DATE
Council for Yukon Indians Umbrella Final and Self-Government	1977
Agreements (Eleven Total)	
Vuntut Gwitch'in First Nation (1993)	
First Nation of Nacho Nyak Dun (1993)	
Champagne and Aishihik First Nations (1993)	
Teslin Tlingit Council (1993)	
Little Salmon/Carmacks (1997)	
Selkirk First Nations (1997)	
Tr'ondëk Hwëch'in (1998)	1993–2006

AGREEMENT	EFFECTIVE DATE
Ta'an Kwach'an Council (2002)	
Kluane First Nation (2004)	
Kwanlin Dun First Nation (2005)	
Carcross/Tagish First Nation (2006)	
Nunavut Land Claims Agreement	1993
Nisga'a Final Agreement	2000
Labrador Inuit Land Claims Agreement	2005
Tłı ch Land Claims Agreement and Self-Government Agreement	2005
Tsawwassen Final Agreement	2009
Maa-nulth Final Agreement	2011
Tla'amin Final Agreement	2016
Sahtu Dene and Metis Comprehensive Land Claim Agreement (1994)	
Déline Self-Government Agreement (2016)	2016

TABLE 1.3. STAND-ALONE SELF-GOVERNMENT AGREEMENTS

AGREEMENT	EFFECTIVE DATE
Sechelt Indian Band Self-Government Act	1986
Mi'kmaq Education Agreement (sectoral agreement— education)	1997
Westbank First Nation Self-Government Agreement	2005
Sioux Valley Dakota Nation Governance Agreement	2015

Of the ninety-nine open self-government and comprehensive land claim negotiation tables across the country, over half are in British Columbia.[42] The independent BC Treaty Commission (BCTC) reports that 105 current or former Indian Act bands in the province have completed or are participating in treaty negotiations and that nearly half (95 of 200) have chosen not to engage with the BCTC process.[43] Although many Indian Act bands are negotiating independently, some have chosen to negotiate together with the Crown, with the result that the 105 Indian Act bands involved in the BCTC process are represented by sixty-five First Nations at the treaty tables. A structure unique to this province, the British Columbia Treaty Commission was established in 1992 to facilitate treaty negotiations among Canada, British Columbia, and First Nations in the province. It allocates funding to support First Nations with negotiation costs and works to educate the public regarding treaty negotiations.[44] Only four agreements have been completed under this process.[45] Seven First Nations are in the process of negotiating toward final agreements. The remaining fifty First Nations are still at much earlier stages of negotiation. The treaty process itself has not been updated to reflect jurisprudence since its inception twenty-five years ago.

Neither British Columbia's mandate nor Canada's key frameworks for its negotiating positions—the Comprehensive Land Claims Policy and the Approach to the Implementation of the Inherent Right—have been formally updated to reflect changes in jurisprudence or precedents set in other agreements in the past twenty years. In 2014, Canada released an interim Comprehensive Land Claims Policy,[46] intended as a starting point for dialogue, and appointed Ministerial Special Representative Douglas Eyford to lead engagement on renewing the policy.[47] However, this process has yet to produce a final policy update.[48]

POLICY INSTRUMENTS

Some First Nations still under the Indian Act are choosing a step-wise path to becoming more self-determining. Two pieces of opt-in legislation demonstrate this approach. First, the First Nations Land Management Act (FNLMA), introduced in 1999, delegates certain land management responsibilities under the Indian Act to band councils. As of 2017, there are currently thirty-six First Nations operating under the FNLMA and fifty-eight more that are working toward it.[49] The FNLMA eliminates the need to seek ministerial approval under the Indian Act on decisions related to lands, thereby freeing up time and money for other self-governance activities.[50]

Second, the First Nations Fiscal Management Act (FNFMA), introduced in 2006, is intended to enhance the ability of First Nations to promote economic development and collect property tax. Since it came into force, eighty-seven First Nations have opted in and are currently collecting tax through the FNFMA.[51] A further 197 are in the process of opting in.[52] The First Nations Tax Commission, established through the FNFMA, provides assistance in drafting taxation laws and bylaws and provides training for First Nations tax administrators.

Of the other policy instruments introduced after the Royal Commission on Aboriginal Peoples reported, the First Nations Governance Act (FNGA), introduced in 2002, has been a notable failure. Intended to recognize the inherent right to self-government and transform the relationship with the Crown, it was met with widespread suspicion and criticism. Critics focused on both the efficacy of the consultation process and the content of the FNGA, largely concluding that it was yet another iteration of federal colonial policy—of reform from above without regard for the necessity of democratic process to lead transformation.[53]

It is also worth noting the Kelowna Accord (2005), a ten-year plan developed to implement and evaluate strategies to equalize the standard of living of Indigenous peoples with other Canadians. Although it was never implemented, the inclusive process used to reach the accord is still largely regarded as setting a high standard for consultative policy making. The substance of the accord itself, abandoned by the newly elected Harper Conservative government in 2006, marks a missed opportunity to reset Indigenous-Crown relations in Canada.[54]

DEMOGRAPHIC CHANGE

In the twenty years since the Royal Commission reported, a new generation has grown to adulthood, and a generation of Elders has passed on. The following table provides a snapshot of the significant demographic changes that have taken place in the past twenty years, without reference to the numerous statistical indicators of progress or lack thereof in education, income, employment, health, or myriad other issues that complicate the landscape for governments—Indigenous and non-Indigenous alike. The number of Canadians who report identifying as Aboriginal has grown from 2.6 percent of the general population to 4.2 percent. It is a young population. Aboriginal children aged fourteen and under made up 28 percent of the total Aboriginal population and 7 percent of all children in Canada. It is also a mobile and increasingly urban population. In 1996, 49 percent of people who identified as First Nations, Métis, or Inuit lived in urban centres. In the 2011 National Household Survey, that number had grown to 56 percent.[55]

TABLE 1.4. ABORIGINAL IDENTITY IN CANADA FROM 1996 TO 2016

POPULATION

CHARACTERISTIC	1996	2001	2006	2011*	2016
Canadian population	28,528,125	29,639,035	31,241,030	32,852,320	35,151,728
Aboriginal identity*	799,010	976,305	1,172,790	1,400,685	1,673,785
Métis single identity	210,190	292,305	389,780	451,795	587,545
Inuk (Inuit) single identity	41,080	45,075	50,480	59,440	65,025
On-reserve Aboriginal identity	–	286,080	308,490	324,780	326,786
Non-reserve Aboriginal identity	–	690,225	864,295	1,075,910	–
Urban Aboriginal identity	–	494,095	623,470	–	–
Rural Aboriginal identity	–	196,130	240,825	–	–

* All subgroups that comprise this figure are not included in the table. We report Aboriginal identity—that is, how individuals who responded to the census identified themselves—rather than Aboriginal descent.

THE NEXT TWENTY YEARS: DIVERGING PATHS TO SELF-DETERMINATION

A SHIFT IN THE BALANCE OF POWER

The Royal Commission's vision of a nation-to-nation relationship founded on Indigenous self-determination has not been realized. Many of the 440 specific recommendations have not been acted on or have seen only partial implementation. What the commission did achieve was to give authoritative voice to a new interpretation of Canadian history, with Indigenous-Crown relations at its centre, and lay the base for a new national consensus on the fundamental way forward. This new vision, which has received rhetorical endorsement from the current federal government, includes truth telling and mutual responsibility for reforming Confederation on the basis of consent and cooperation.

The commission envisioned renewed relationships based on "mutual recognition, mutual respect, sharing and mutual responsibility."[56] Most significant to our time was its assertion—now borne out by and further detailed in numerous court decisions—that Section 35 is a rather full box of rights indeed: rights that Indigenous peoples can assert and define for themselves how best to exercise and that other governments must recognize and find ways to accommodate. The political balance of power has shifted dramatically, although the ramifications are only starting to be realized. The Indigenous-Crown relationship has gained further "mutuality" through the growing number of significant modern treaties and land settlements. Collectively, modern treaties affect nearly half of Canada's lands, waters, and resources.[57]

Inuit have concluded modern treaties with the Crown that encompass multiple communities and land titles within four different provincial or territorial jurisdictions, each treaty creating somewhat different governance arrangements. In Nunatsiavut, the modern treaty included the usual comprehensive land claim provisions (a cash and land settlement), but it also established the Nunatsiavut government, responsible to and serving Inuit beneficiaries in Labrador and elsewhere in Canada. In Nunavik, the Makivik Corporation has represented the interests for forty years of the Inuit of northern Quebec, who are also served by the public institutions of the Kativik Regional Government and the Kativik Regional School Board. Nunavut is the new territory created by the Nunavut Agreement, with a public government serving all residents of Nunavut, coexisting in Nunavut with the treaty-holding organization, Nunavut Tunngavik Incorporated, and a number of co-management boards. In the Northwest Territories, Inuvialuit have managed their lands and capital through the Inuvialuit Regional Corporation and co-management boards.

All of these new governments are coping with growing pains—a high demand for skilled employees; huge demands on leaders and resources to respond to social, demographic, and corporate pressures; and strong desires of citizens for governments that operate in their own languages and according to their own ways. In all parts of Inuit Nunangat, these are still distant goals. There is an acute shortage of Inuit who can staff the new governments, compounding the difficulty of the task of redesigning these governance forms so that they have a reasonable degree of continuity with Inuit traditions while maintaining their effectiveness in contemporary politics and administration. This remains an enormous challenge.

For First Nations, the evolution of self-determination is as divergent as the many different cultures and languages that exist within their territories. A handful of First Nations are well on the way to being fully self-governing, having achieved agreements with other orders of government; dozens more are at some stage of negotiation. Those with modern treaties, in common with Inuit, share the challenges of nation building and development of effective and culturally appropriate forms of administration. The modern treaty-holding organizations have formed the Land Claims Agreement Coalition to address common problems and development issues. It is evident that relations among Canadian governments and Inuit, Métis, and First Nations party to modern treaties are defined by those treaties—and by Section 35 rights. The treaty-holding organizations require of Canadian governments that those governments ensure that the treaties form the bases for all bureaucratic and political initiatives toward them and their lands, something unevenly achieved at the moment.

SELF-GOVERNMENT AGREEMENTS ARE ONLY A BEGINNING, NOT AN END

Even assuming the successful conclusion of modern treaties, the path of implementation is not always smooth. The hard work of building and resourcing internal capacity to deliver on new roles and responsibilities is in addition to the effort needed to hold the Crown to its commitments. The minister's special representative on the renewal of comprehensive land claims provides only the latest in a line of assessments criticizing the government's record on treaty implementation.[58] As more than one wag has quipped, treaties are like marriages—signalling only the start of a relationship that requires tending, continued negotiation, and compromise over the long haul. As Eyford notes, "successful treaty implementation is part of an ongoing and collaborative relationship."[59]

Recent research indicates that a self-government and/or comprehensive land claims agreement increases community well-being.[60] However, these are early studies. Examining the James Bay and Northern Quebec Agreement (JBNQA), a full thirty-five years after its signing, Papillon explains the difficulties in determining whether reported improvements in quality of life and well-being are causally linked to such agreements. Accordingly, Papillon concludes that key lessons from the JBNQA lie neither in its content, though still very important, nor in the marginal socio-economic improvements experienced in Cree and Inuit communities that might have still occurred in the absence of the treaty. Instead, key lessons are to be found in how the Cree of Eeyou Istchee and Inuit of Nunavik leveraged legal and institutional foundations provided by treaty implementation to consolidate their cultural and political identities; increase political autonomy, expertise, and capacity at multiple scales of governance; and formalize intergovernmental agreements and relations with Quebec and Canada, among other things.[61] Tracking the outcomes of modern treaties is an area of study that deserves much more time and attention and could provide useful insights important to all of the parties concerned—including those at the early stages of choosing their future paths.

CLEARING NEW PATHS: MÉTIS PEOPLES AND URBAN INDIGENOUS POPULATIONS

For Métis, the path to a renewed relationship based on self-determination is only starting to clear. The Manitoba Metis Federation and Daniels decisions open a new world of possibilities for negotiation with the Crown, yet it remains to be seen whether they will result in the set of circumstances that RCAP thought was necessary for exercising full self-determination, with "territorial predominance" being a key factor. Most Métis now live dispersed throughout the general population of Canada. They have well-established networks of associations, however, that form the basis of "community of interest governments," as RCAP envisioned. Whether

Métis can achieve more will be largely influenced by their success in negotiations and by Métis themselves: through creative negotiation proposals, by managing the difficult internal dialogue to define citizenship and confirm representative governments, as well as by developing capable governing institutions.[62]

In this chapter, we have not looked at the urban Indigenous population, composed of Inuit, Métis, and First Nation peoples, who may be Status (Registered with the DIA) or non-Status. The *Daniels* decision provided some clarity about federal responsibility for Non-Status Indians, too, but again this is only the beginning of a new path for all of the parties, the end point of which is still uncertain. In regard to the exercise of self-determination for urban Indigenous populations in general, the continued rapid growth in these populations and the concomitant opportunities and pressures make this a significant and complex topic worth further study and discussion by all orders of government.

We now turn our attention to First Nations still governed under the Indian Act, where we find the clearest potential and perhaps the greatest need for new nation-to-nation relationships.

A NEW PATH: OPPORTUNITIES FOR TRANSITIONAL GOVERNANCE

Twenty years after RCAP, the majority of First Nations continue as administrative subjects to that "ill-fitting boot," the Indian Act.[63] Perhaps the most need, and the most opportunity for renewed relationships, lie here. The eighth generation has been born under the brutal reality of this oppressive law. In earlier times, the Indian Act was an instrument of direct assimilation and very successful in achieving what it was designed to do: First Nations were removed from traditional lands, settlements expanded, and the resulting developments supported European political and economic progress. Today, although its most egregiously oppressive features have been moderated, the act still draws time and initiative from community leaders who cannot be their own agents of change but must rely on the attention, approval, and resources of others.

The Crown still determines policy priorities, program criteria, funding levels, and operational requirements of each band administration.[64] Still too much of this is designed and delivered in bureaucratic silos, resulting in overlap, duplication, gaps, and stretched capacity across myriad issues with which band councils must deal. The Indian Act and its bureaucratic implementation were designed to oppress, and they continue to suppress, First Nations. This is evident in the ongoing yawning gap between the quality of life that First Nations "enjoy" versus other Canadians.[65]

It is a mistake, however, to label all Indian Act First Nations communities as unsuccessful or problematic. Examples of economic, social, cultural, or other success exist across the country. If one accepts the Community Well-Being Index[66] as an indicator of progress, then First Nations communities experience a range of well-being—from very high to the notably tragic and dire situations of extreme poverty and poor physical and mental health. This raises a question: why are some communities successful and others not? For successful communities, extensive personal experience tells us that their success has been achieved partly because of local histories and partly because of dogged persistence, ingenuity, business savvy, and occasional policy or economic opportunities. Having the option to allay some of the more problematic features of the Indian Act, through instruments such as the FNLMA and FNFMA, has undoubtedly helped too. But the fact is that Canada lacks the longitudinal research on and evidence of "what works" in developing First Nations, and it has yet to apply a supportive and integrated approach to development in its administration of First Nations communities.[67]

CUTTING THEIR OWN PATH

At the current pace of self-government negotiations, it is not practical to expect that this is the only path to lasting change. Nor does it need to be. As RCAP asserted and is now established in jurisprudence, First Nations have a full box of rights that they can use to begin to set themselves on the path to self-determination.

Exercising this full box of constitutional and legally enforceable Section 35 rights requires understanding them as the basis for what we call "transformational governance." They must first be defined by Indigenous peoples who have a major challenge ahead to determine how they will choose to exercise those rights and bring clarity and detail to what must be recognized, accommodated, or otherwise dealt with by other governments and other Canadians.

Transformational governance encompasses not only understanding, defining, and asserting Section 35 rights but also all of the work that needs to go into responsibly exercising governing powers: from engaging and involving community members in setting a new direction, determining priorities, and agreeing on political structures to making a transitional plan, drafting laws, and building the capacities of institutions to implement those laws. Transformational governance requires a new government-to-government relationship. This is what we need to do.

It is not an all-or-nothing proposition. As with the step-wise development currently under way in some communities, First Nations can choose to begin by exercising their rights in a core jurisdiction of prime importance to them—whether lands and resources, culture and language, or education. The important thing is that they begin to do so.

In our view, it begins with band councils—elected members and staff—that learn to master the Indian Act, in the sense of putting it in its place. The energies of community leadership must be liberated from "serving the machine"—the endless round of reporting and record keeping and proposal writing required by funders, particularly but not exclusively the Department of Indigenous Affairs, in order to have time and energy for meaningful discussion, developing policy, planning, and implementing a different future. Moving from Indian Act administration toward self-government entails a change of focus away from small-scale or protracted negotiations with the Crown in right of the provincial or federal government and toward exercising the jurisdictional rights and title to traditional lands that exist now. Some of the best experience and governing capacity will be gained on the job in the actual exercise of jurisdiction.[68]

The process of mastery must begin with community dialogue and education. From *Delgamuukw and Gisdayway* through to *Tsilhqot'in*, the Supreme Court has consistently stated that Aboriginal rights and title are communally and collectively held by the people and that their consent is required to take action.[69] Similarly, Indigenous thinkers have consistently advanced this understanding.[70] As a first step, First Nations must overcome the widespread lack of understanding regarding the inherent right to self-government and of the relationship implied by the duty to consult and accommodate. They can become drivers of reconciliation and movement toward transitional governance. Education and dialogue are also required among First Nations about the realities of the Indian Act: the multi-generational impact that it has had and continues to have on their ability to be masters in their own houses. The need to heal and reconcile is as important for communities and nations as it is for individuals. Leaders will face many challenges in re-engaging their people, who have been robbed of a sense of agency by the colonial experience, but this must be where change starts. Part of this process will be served by further research on why the Indian Act is not the right form of governance going forward and, more importantly, on the strategies that will help First Nations to get out from under it.

A note is needed here to acknowledge RCAP's strong view that the inherent right is vested only at the level of nations and can only be exercised by nations. Unfortunately, Canada's willingness in the past twenty years to enter into self-government agreements with so many small communities has waylaid that vision, at least insofar as it would be impossible to change course suddenly. Of the ten comprehensive claims and self-government agreements and stand-alone self-government agreements completed by First Nations, seven were signed by individual communities, of which only two had a population of over 1,000 people (Sioux Valley Dakota Nation and Sliammon First Nation).[71] Of the ninety-nine open negotiations, nearly half are being negotiated with groups representing 1,000 people or fewer.[72]

From a practical governance perspective, nation building is still to be wished for—not least because of the strength that comes with numbers and shared resources. We expect that, as communities work to gain mastery over their own destinies, they will also build the confidence to delegate and share powers and responsibilities with others, for the greater good.

GOVERNMENTS AND OTHERS AS SUPPORTIVE ENABLERS

Although we see the shift to self-determination being driven primarily by the people themselves, federal and provincial governments should play a key supporting role. For example, the *Tsilhqot'in* decision clarifies that Aboriginal title can arise either through declaration by the courts or through *agreement with the Crown*.[73] If the history of Indigenous-Crown relations teaches us anything, then it is this: as much as the Crown must honour its promises, it cannot have more than an enabling and accommodating role in Indigenous social, political, and economic development. This is not a call for benign neglect. Rather, we urge federal, provincial, and territorial governments—at the political and bureaucratic levels—to embark on their own critical self-examinations of where their policies and actions continue to maintain the colonial mindset and hinder progress for Indigenous peoples and the creation of better long-term relationships between Indigenous and other Canadians.

At the political level, this means setting a new tone—as many are now doing—and consistently aligning actions with avowals of reconciliation and new relationships. It means reframing the relationship from one that must be constricted, limited, and "managed" in the short term to one that is accommodating and acknowledges the ongoing nature of the relationship as well as the equal importance and value of the lives of Indigenous peoples to other Canadians within their jurisdiction. It means developing and maintaining the kinds of collaborative policy-making and agenda-setting relationships that the Kelowna Accord showed us are possible. Although RCAP's recommendations for a new Royal Proclamation, framework legislation, and other legal instruments might ultimately be useful for cementing agreements, they are not essential to getting on with renewed relationships characterized by RCAP's four principles: recognition, respect, sharing, and responsibility.

Public servants can start with developing their professional responsibility to understand the historical and legal realities of the relationship and of the day-to-day challenges of their Indigenous counterparts. They need to adopt a supportive development mindset not unlike the approach that Canadians proudly extend to developing countries. They need to ask themselves some questions. Where can they combine and streamline program and service delivery to make things simpler and more effective for recipients? Where can they support or get out of the way of communities setting their own priorities? Which funding models and approaches can they design to support local priorities and capacity building? And how can they practically restructure accountability relationships to be accountable to local communities rather than to a minister in Ottawa?

Finally, governments, universities, and Indigenous governments and institutions themselves need to invest in training and support for self-governance through consistently funded, Indigenous-led institutions and other mechanisms that support the ongoing development of Indigenous governments no matter what their starting points.

Some of the institutions recommended by RCAP came into being (e.g., the National Centre for First Nations Governance [now the Centre for First Nations Governance] and the First Nations Information Governance Centre), whereas others were never implemented (e.g., the Aboriginal Lands and Treaties Tribunal). The Aboriginal Healing Foundation was established in 1998, providing funding for work to heal the effects of residential schooling, until funding was withdrawn in 2009. The FNFMA established three institutions that support the fiscal aspects of self-government: the First Nations Tax Commission, the First Nations Financial Management Board, and the First Nations Finance Authority. Associations such as AFOA Canada (formerly the Aboriginal Financial Officers Association, a national association of financial officers and senior administrators who work in First Nations government and band administration) were established to help professionalize band administration. Some universities now offer programs in Indigenous governance and administration. Given the task at hand and the diversity of needs, however, including for Inuit and Métis (whose needs are largely unmet in the above list of institutions), much more needs to be done.

CONCLUSION

Canada is a test case for a grand notion—the notion that dissimilar peoples can share lands, resources, power and dreams while respecting and sustaining their differences. The story of Canada is the story of many such peoples, trying and failing and trying again, to live together in peace and harmony.

But there cannot be peace or harmony unless there is justice.[74]

We end where RCAP began twenty-five years ago—with a hopeful vision for reconciliation and renewed relationships. Although not all of the recommendations came to pass as the commissioners might have hoped, progress is being made, and there are stronger foundations from which Indigenous peoples and other Canadians can continue the hard work of forging a better future together. The fundamental nation-to-nation framework for reconfiguring Indigenous-Canadian relations offered by RCAP is now widely accepted—explicitly by the current prime minister and at least one other political party and implicitly in many legal and practical respects. Shared understanding of the implications of Section 35 reflects the RCAP arguments and jurisprudence following *Sparrow* rather than the restrictive empty box meaning imputed by some during constitutional negotiations.

Without minimizing the strife and conflict that continue to exist in many quarters of our society, we are encouraged by a generally more positive political climate in many regions and by seeing the burgeoning awareness of Canadians of the compelling reasons for change and the need for continued progress in Indigenous-Canadian relations. This is thanks in no small part to the tremendously difficult and courageous work of all who participated in the Truth and Reconciliation Commission and who continue to carry the banner for truth and reconciliation. The importance of these efforts to renewing the relationship cannot be underestimated. The path ahead will not always be over easy terrain, and it is still a long one for many, but the direction is clear.

NOTES

We are grateful to Paul Chartrand, Brian Crane, Larry Innes, Stephanie Irlbacher Fox, George Kinloch, Kent McNeil, Peter Usher, and Graham White for their generous help in making this a much better chapter, though remaining errors belong to us. For expert research assistance, we warmly thank Zachary Smith and Andrew Swift. The authors of this chapter are founders of the Transformational Governance Project, a collaboration that aims to support First Nations working their ways out from under the Indian Act. For more information, contact Frances Abele, Professor, School of Public Policy and Administration, Carleton University; Erin Alexiuk, PhD Candidate, School of Environment, Resources, and Sustainability, University of Waterloo; Satsan (Herb George), Wet'suwet'en Hereditary Chief, Senior Associate, First Nations Governance Centre; and/or Catherine MacQuarrie, Project Manager, Transforming Indian Act Governance Project.

1 The terms "Aboriginal people" and "Aboriginal peoples" were standard twenty years and more ago; in this chapter, recognizing the significance of the United Nations Declaration on the Rights of Indigenous Peoples and increasingly common usage, we refer to "Indigenous people" and "Indigenous peoples," except where doing so would be anachronistic.

2 The full clause reads thus:

The guarantee in this Charter of certain rights and freedoms shall not be construed as to abrogate or derogate from any aboriginal, treaty or other rights or freedoms that pertain to the aboriginal peoples of Canada including

(a) any rights or freedoms that have been recognized by the Royal Proclamation of October 7, 1763; and

(b) any rights or freedoms that now exist by way of land claims agreements or may be so acquired.

3 Goodleaf, *Entering the War Zone: A Mohawk Perspective on Resisting Invasions*; York and Pindera, *People of the Pines*.

4 The idea of appointing a Royal Commission on Aboriginal issues was floated by Prime Minister Brian Mulroney during the Meech Lake Accord discussions in 1987 as a means of dealing with Aboriginal issues that had been intractable and not resolved in "the Quebec round"—the agreement to constitutional recognition of Quebec as a distinct society. See Delacourt, "PM Hints He Will Create Native Panel"; Peach, "The Power of a Single Feather," 30.

5 Royal Commission on Aboriginal Peoples (RCAP), *The Right of Aboriginal Self-Government and the Constitution*.

6   RCAP, *Partners in Confederation*, vi.

7   RCAP, *Volume 2: Restructuring the Relationship*, 1. "If one theme dominates, it is that Aboriginal peoples must have room to exercise their autonomy and structure their own solutions."

8   RCAP, *Volume 2: Restructuring the Relationship*, 107.

9   RCAP, *Volume 2: Restructuring the Relationship*, 183.

10   RCAP, *Volume 2: Restructuring the Relationship*, 106, 156.

11   RCAP, *Volume 2: Restructuring the Relationship*, 203.

12   RCAP, *Volume 2: Restructuring the Relationship*, 202–03.

13   RCAP, *Volume 2: Restructuring the Relationship*, 202–03.

14   RCAP, *Volume 2: Restructuring the Relationship*, 298.

15   RCAP, *Volume 2: Restructuring the Relationship*, 204. *R. v. Sparrow*, [1990] 1 S.C.R. 1075, established rules to restrict uninhibited infringement of Aboriginal rights. The infringement is acceptable only if it serves a valid legislative objective with as little infringement as possible to affect the desired result, if it provides fair compensation, and if Aboriginal groups have been consulted.

16   RCAP, *Volume 2: Restructuring the Relationship*, 134. In 1996, 49 percent of people who identified as First Nations, Métis, or Inuit lived in urban centres. In the 2011 census, that number had grown to 56 percent. Indigenous and Northern Affairs Canada (INAC), *Urban Indigenous Peoples*.

17   RCAP, *Volume 2: Restructuring the Relationship*, 262. Because of the limited space here, we set aside further discussion of urban governance. The issues are complex and increasingly so.

18   RCAP, *Volume 2: Restructuring the Relationship*, 223.

19   RCAP, *Volume 2: Restructuring the Relationship*, 156.

20   RCAP, *Volume 2: Restructuring the Relationship*, 169.

21   RCAP, *Volume 2: Restructuring the Relationship*, 269.

22   RCAP, *Volume 2: Restructuring the Relationship*, 224.

23   RCAP, *Volume 2: Restructuring the Relationship*, 170.

24   RCAP, *Volume 2: Restructuring the Relationship*, 175.

25   RCAP, *Volume 2: Restructuring the Relationship*, 271.

26   RCAP, *Volume 2: Restructuring the Relationship*, 293.

27   RCAP, *Volume 2: Restructuring the Relationship*, 203.

28   See Asch, *Aboriginal and Treaty Rights in Canada*, and Asch, *On Being Here to Stay*; Foster, Raven, and Webber, eds., *Let Right Be Done*; McNeil, "Aboriginal Governments and the Canadian Charter of Rights and Freedoms"; and Newman, *The Duty to Consult: New Relationships with Aboriginal Peoples* for legal overviews.

29   These developments build on the 1973 *Calder* decision, which initiated the resulting decades of case law regarding Aboriginal title and rights in Canada and strengthened political will for reopening treaty negotiations. See Godlewska and Webber, "The *Calder* Decision"; Scholtz, *Negotiating Claims*.

30   Moralleto, *The Crown's Constitutional Duty*.

31   McNeil, "The Jurisdiction of Inherent Right in Aboriginal Governments." In the 1997 decision widely referred to as *Delgamuukw v. British Columbia*, we acknowledge the contributions of the Gitxsan and Wet'suwet'en Nations to the case and therefore use the full title, *Delgamuukw and Gisdayway v. British Columbia*.

32   Newman, *The Duty to Consult*.

33   *Tsilhqot'in Nation v. British Columbia*, 2014 SCC 44, para. 14.

34 See *Tsilhqot'in Nation v. British Columbia*, para. 97. For a different view of this decision and preceding jurisprudence, see McCrossan, "Contaminating and Collapsing Indigenous Space"; McCrossan and Ladner, "Eliminating Indigenous Jurisdictions."

35 See *Tsilhqot'in Nation v. British Columbia*, 2014 SCC 44, para. 116.

36 See *R. v. Powley*, 2 S.C.R. 207, 2003 SCC 43, para. 12.

37 See *Daniels v. Canada (Indian Affairs and Northern Development)*, 2016 SCC 12, para. 15.

38 Supreme Court of Canada Reference whether "Indians" includes "Eskimos," [1939] S.C.R. 104 1939-04-05. *A Matter of National and Constitutional Import: Report of the Minister's Special Representative on Reconciliation with Metis: Section 35 Metis Rights and the Manitoba Metis Federation Decision* was released in August 2016. Its seventeen recommendations include that Canada should create a framework for negotiating and addressing Métis rights, establish a Métis-specific claims process, review policies affecting Métis, and provide stable funding for some of the country's largest Métis "governments."

39 The Sechelt Indian Band Self-Government Act (1986) was the first in Canada to remove several provisions of the Indian Act. The act was twenty years in the making, during which the band envisioned, and obtained, legislation that enabled certain self-government abilities while maintaining a relationship with the federal government prior to the constitutional protection of self-government. See Etkins, "The Sechelt Indian Band."

40 Section 91(24) of the Constitution Act, 1982, assigns "Indians and the Lands reserved for Indians" to federal jurisdiction.

41 For a broader discussion of jurisprudence on this point and the vesting of democratic governing authority in collectivities, see McNeil, "Aboriginal Title and Indigenous Governance."

42 INAC, "Comprehensive Land Claim and Self-Government Negotiation Tables."

43 BCTC, *Treaty Commission Annual Report*.

44 BCTC, "About us."

45 One of the four, the Yale First Nation Final Agreement, was initialled in 2010. However, Yale First Nation released a letter in early 2016 stating its decision not to proceed with implementation. See its press release at http://media.wix.com/ugd/6896ba_04f7889773c8491c8b91dba8a060966c.pdf.

46 INAC, "Renewing the Federal Comprehensive Land Claims Policy."

47 Eyford, "A New Direction."

48 See INAC, "Renewing the Federal Comprehensive Land Claims Policy."

49 INAC, "First Nations Land Management."

50 Alcantara, "Reduce Transaction Costs?"; Warkentin, "Study of Land Management and Sustainable Economic Development."

51 FNTC, "First Nations with Property Tax Jurisdiction," and "First Natons Tax Commission."

52 FNTC, "First Nations with Property Tax Jurisdiction," and "First Natons Tax Commission."

53 See, for example, Cassidy, "The First Nations Governance Act: A Legacy of Loss"; Cornell, Jorgensen, and Kalt. "The First Nations Governance Act: Implications of Research Findings"; and Ladner and Orsini, "The Persistence of Paradigm Paralysis."

54 Poelzer and Coates, *From Treaty Peoples to Treaty Nation*.

55 Statistics Canada data from censuses and the 2011 National Household Survey (NHS). Prior to 2011, demographic, socio-economic, and housing data were collected through the national long-form census. In 2011, a switch was made to the voluntary NHS, making year-over-year comparisons difficult. With respect to Indigenous peoples, the NHS lacked breadth and depth compared to a census (especially its lack of metropolitan statistics).

Note that Table 1.4 includes long-form census data prior to 2011 and from 2016 and NHS data in 2011.

56 RCAP, *Volume 1: Looking Forward, Looking Back*, 645.

57 Land Claims Agreements Coalition (LCAC). "Modern Treaties Benefit All Canadians," n.d.

58 Eyford, "A New Direction"; see also Canada 1985.

59 Eyford, "A New Direction," 78.

60 Pendakur and Pendakur, "An Analysis of the Socio-Economic Outcomes," 19.

61 Papillon, "Aboriginal Quality of Life under a Modern Treaty."

62 For further discussion, see Chartrand, "Defining the 'Métis' of Canada," and "Citizenship Rights and Aboriginal Rights in Canada."

63 Abele, "Like an Ill-Fitting Boot."

64 A recent BC Court of Appeal decision, *Louie v. Louie BCCA 247* (2015) affirmed the strict limitations on power and authority vested in band councils through s. 2(3) of the Indian Act, which constrains decision-making powers in the absence of related bylaws or laws often subject to ministerial approval.

65 See, for example, Anaya, *Report of the Special Rapporteur on the Rights of Indigenous Peoples*.

66 Aboriginal Affairs and Northern Development Canada (AANDC), "The Community Well-Being Index."

67 See, for example, in the United States, *The Harvard Project on Indian Economic Development*, http://hpaied.org/.

68 Warkentin, "Study of Land Management and Sustainable Economic Development"

69 See *Delgamuukw v. British Columbia*, [1997] 3 S.C.R. 1010, para. 115, and *Tsilhqot'in Nation v. British Columbia*, 2014 SCC 44, paras. 74, 75.

70 Borrows, *Recovering Canada* and Borrows, *Canada's Indigenous Constitution*; Val Napoleon, "Thinking about Indigenous Legal Orders."

71 INAC, "General Briefing Note on Canada's Self-Government."

72 INAC, "Urban Indigenous Peoples."

73 *Tsilhqot'in Nation v. British Columbia*, 2014 SCC 44, paras. 89–90.

74 *Highlights from the Final Report of the Royal Commission on Aboriginal Peoples: People to People, Nation to Nation*, https://www.aadnc-aandc.gc.ca/eng/1100100014597/1100100014637.

REFERENCES

Abele, Frances. "Like an Ill-Fitting Boot: Government, Governance, and Management Systems in the Contemporary *Indian Act*." Prepared for the National Centre for First Nations Governance, 25 June 2007. http://fngovernance.org/ncfng_research/frances_able.pdf.

Aboriginal Affairs and Northern Development Canada (AANDC). "The Community Well-Being Index: Well-Being in First Nations Communities, 1981–2011." 2 April 2015. https://www.aadnc-aandc.gc.ca/eng/1345816651029/1345816742083#chp7.

Alcantara, Christopher. "Reduce Transaction Costs? Yes. Strengthen Property Rights? Maybe: The First Nations Land Management Act and Economic Development on Canadian Indian Reserves." *Public Choice* 132, nos. 3–4 (2007): 421–32.

Anaya, James. *Report of the Special Rapporteur on the Rights of Indigenous Peoples: The Situation of Indigenous Peoples in Canada*. New York: United Nations General

Assembly, 2014.

Asch, Michael. *Aboriginal and Treaty Rights in Canada: Essays on Law, Equality and Respect to Difference.* Vancouver: UBC Press, 1997.

——. *On Being Here to Stay: Treaties and Aboriginal Rights in Canada.* Toronto: University of Toronto Press, 2014.

Borrows, John. *Recovering Canada: The Resurgence of Indigenous Law.* Toronto: University of Toronto Press, 2002.

——. *Canada's Indigenous Constitution.* Toronto: University of Toronto Press, 2010.

British Columbia Treaty Commission (BCTC). "About Us." 2016a. http://www.bctreaty.ca/about-us.

——. *Treaty Commission Annual Report 2016.* 2016b. http://www.bctreaty.ca/sites/default/files/BCTC-AR2016-WEB.pdf.

Campbell et al. v. AG BC/AG Cda and Nisga'a Nation et al. 2000 BCSC 1123.

Canada. Task Force to Review Comprehensive Claims Policy. *Living Treaties, Lasting Agreements: Report of the Task Force to Review Comprehensive Claims Policy.* Ottawa: Department of Indian Affairs and Northern Development. 1985.

Canada. *A Matter of National and Constitutional Import: Report of the Minister's Special Representative on Reconciliation with Metis: Section 35 Metis Rights and the Manitoba Metis Federation Decision.* Special Representative: Thomas Isaac. Ottawa: Department of Indigenous and Northern Affairs. 2016.

Cassidy, Frank. "The First Nations Governance Act: A Legacy of Loss." *Policy Options,* 1 April 2003. http://policyoptions.irpp.org magazines/big-ideas/the-first-nations-governance-act-a-legacy-of-los.

Chartrand, Paul L.A.H. "Defining the 'Métis' of Canada: A Principled Approach to Crown-Aboriginal Relations." In *Métis-Crown Relations: Rights, Identity, Jurisdiction, and Governance,* edited by Frederica Wilson and Melanie Mallet, 27–70. Toronto: Irwin Law, 2008.

——. "Citizenship Rights and Aboriginal Rights in Canada: From 'Citizens Plus' to 'Citizens Plural.'" In *The Ties that Bind: Accommodating Diversity in Canada and the European Union,* edited by John Erik Fossum, Johanne Poirier, and Paul Magnette, 129–54. Brussels: Peter Lang, 2009.

The Constitution Act. Part I Canadian Charter of Rights and Freedoms, 1982.

The Constitution Act. Schedule B to the Canada Act 1982 (UK), 1982, c. 11.

Cornell, Stephen, Miriam Jorgensen, and Joseph Kalt. "The First Nations Governance Act: Implications of Research Findings from the United States and Canada." Prepared for the Office of the British Columbia Regional Vice-Chief, Assembly of First Nations, July 2002. http://www.nni.arizona.edu/pubs/AFN02Report.pdf.

Daniels v. Canada (Indian Affairs and Northern Development), 2016 SCC 12.

Delacourt, Susan. "PM Hints He Will Create Native Panel." *Globe and Mail,* 12 April 1991, A4.

Delgamuukw v. British Columbia, [1997] 3 S.C.R. 1010.

Etkins, Carol E. "The Sechelt Indian Band: An Analysis of a New Form of Native Self Government." *Canadian Journal of Native Studies* 8, no.1 (1988): 73–105.

Eyford, Douglas R. "A New Direction, Advancing Aboriginal and Treaty Rights." Report of the ministerial special representative on renewal of the comprehensive land claims policy, Indigenous and Northern Affairs Canada, 2 April 2015. https://www.aadnc-aandc.gc.ca/eng/1426169199009/1426169236218.

First Nations Tax Commission (FNTC). "First Nations with Property Tax Jurisdiction." 2016a. http://fntc.ca/property-tax-fns/.

———. "First Nations Tax Commission." 2016b. http://fntc.ca.

Foster, Hamar E.B., Heather Raven, and Jeremy Webber, eds. *Let Right Be Done: Aboriginal Title, the Calder Case, and the Future of Indigenous Rights, Law, and Society.* Vancouver: UBC Press, 2007.

Godlewska, Christina, and Jeremy Webber. "The Calder Decision, Aboriginal Title, Treaties, and the Nisga'a." In *Let Right Be Done: Aboriginal Title, the Calder Case, and the Future of Indigenous Rights, Law, and Society,* edited by Hamar E.B. Foster, Heather Raven, and Jeremy Webber, 1–33. Vancouver: UBC Press, 2007.

Goodleaf, Donna Kahenrakwas. *Entering the War Zone: A Mohawk Perspective on Resisting Invasions.* Penticton, BC: Theytus Books, 1995.

Indigenous and Northern Affairs Canada (INAC). "Comprehensive Land Claim and Self-Government Negotiation Tables." 2 June 2014a. http://www.aadnc-aandc.gc.ca/eng/1346782327802/1346782485058.

———. "First Nations Land Management—Operational and Developmental First Nations." 23 May 2014b. https://www.aadnc-aandc.gc.ca/eng/1327165048269/1327165134401.

———. "Renewing the Federal Comprehensive Land Claims Policy." 2 April 2015. https://www.aadnc-aandc.gc.ca/eng/1405693409911/1405693617207.

———. "General Briefing Note on Canada's Self-Government and Comprehensive Land Claims Policies and the Status of Negotiations." 16 August 2016a. https://www.aadnc-aandc.gc.ca/eng/1373385502190/1373385561540#s2-9.

———. "Urban Indigenous Peoples." 1 September 2016b. https://www.aadnc-aandc.gc.ca/eng/1100100014265/1369225120949.

Ladner, Kiera, and Michael Orsini. "The Persistence of Paradigm Paralysis: The First Nations Governance Act as the Continuation of Colonial Policy." In *Canada: The State of the Federation 2003, Reconfiguring Aboriginal-State Relations,* edited by Michael Murphy, 185–203. Montreal and Kingston: McGill-Queen's University Press, 2003.

Land Claims Agreements Coalition (LCAC). "Modern Treaties Benefit All Canadians." N.d. http://www.landclaimscoalition.ca.

Louie v. Louie. BCCA 247. 2015.

Manitoba Metis Federation Inc. v. Canada (Attorney General), 2013 SCC 14, [2013] 1 S.C.R. 623.

McCrossan, Michael. "Contaminating and Collapsing Indigenous Space: Judicial Narratives of Canadian Territoriality." *Settler Colonial Studies* 5, no. 1 (2015): 20–39.

McCrossan, Michael, and Kiera Ladner. "Eliminating Indigenous Jurisdictions: Federalism, the Supreme Court of Canada, and Territorial Rationalities of Power." *Canadian Journal of Political Science* 49, no. 3 (2016): 411–31.

McNeil, Kent. "Aboriginal Governments and the Canadian Charter of Rights and Freedoms." *Osgoode Hall Law Journal* 34 (1996): 61–99.

———. "The Jurisdiction of Inherent Right in Aboriginal Governments." Prepared for the National Centre for First Nations Governance, 11 October 2007. http://fngovernance.org/ncfng_research/kent_mcneil.pdf.

———. "Aboriginal Title and Indigenous Governance: Identifying the Holders of Rights and Authority." All Papers 264. 2016. http://digitalcommons.osgoode.yorku.ca/all_papers/264.

Mikisew Cree First Nation v. Canada (Minister of Canadian Heritage), 2005 SCC 69, [2005] 3 S.C.R. 388.

Morellato, M. *The Crown's Constitutional Duty to Consult and Accommodate Aboriginal and Treaty Rights.* Ottawa: National Centre for First Nations Governance, 2008.

Napoleon, Val. "Thinking about Indigenous Legal Orders." In *Dialogues on Human Rights and Legal Pluralism,* edited by R. Provost and C. Sheppard, 229–46. Ius Gentium: Comparative Perspectives on Law and Justice 17. Dordrecht: Springer, 2013.

Newman, Dwight G. *The Duty to Consult: New Relationships with Aboriginal Peoples*. Saskatoon: Purich Publishing, 2009.

Papillon, Martin. "Aboriginal Quality of Life under a Modern Treaty: Lessons from the Experience of the Cree Nation of Eeyou Istchee and the Inuit of Nunavik." *IRPP Choices* 14, no. 9 (2008). http://irpp.org/research-studies/choices-vol14-no9/.

Peach, Ian. "The Power of a Single Feather: Meech Lake, Indigenous Resistance and the Evolution of Indigenous Politics in Canada." *Review of Constitutional Studies* 16, no. 1 (2011): 30.

Pendakur, Krishna, and Ravi Pendakur. "An Analysis of the Socio-Economic Outcomes of Aboriginal Peoples Living in Communities Associated with Self-Government Agreements, 1991–2011." Evaluation, Performance Measurement and Review Branch of Aboriginal Affairs and Northern Development Canada (AANDC), 2015.

Poelzer, Greg, and Ken Coates. *From Treaty Peoples to Treaty Nation: A Road Map for All Canadians*. Vancouver: UBC Press, 2015.

R. v. Powley, [2003] 2 S.C.R. 207, 2003 SCC 43.

R. v. Sparrow, [1990] 1 S.C.R. 1075.

Royal Commission on Aboriginal Peoples (RCAP). *The Right of Aboriginal Self-Government and the Constitution: A Commentary*. Ottawa: Minister of Supply and Services, February 1992.

——. *Partners in Confederation: Aboriginal Peoples, Self-Government, and the Constitution*. Ottawa: Supply and Services, 1993.

——. *Volume 1: Looking Forward, Looking Back*. Ottawa: Minister of Supply and Services, 1996a. https://qspace.library.queensu.ca/bitstream/1974/6874/5/RRCAP1_combined.pdf.

——. *Volume 2: Restructuring the Relationship*. Ottawa: Minister of Supply and Services, 1996b. https://qspace.library.queensu.ca/bitstream/1974/6874/4/RRCAP2_combined.pdf.

Scholtz, Christa. *Negotiating Claims: The Emergence of Indigenous Land Claim Negotiation Policies in Australia, Canada, New Zealand, and the United States*. New York: Routledge, 2006.

Supreme Court of Canada Reference Whether "Indians" Includes "Eskimos," [1939] S.C.R. 104 1939-04-05.

Thalassa Research. *Nation to Nation: Indian Nation–Crown Relations in Canada*. Prepared for the Royal Commission on Aboriginal Peoples, 1 December 1994. http://data2.archives. ca/rcap/pdf/rcap-169.pdf.

Tsilhqot'in Nation v. British Columbia, 2014 SCC 44.

Warkentin, Chris. "Study of Land Management and Sustainable Economic Development on First Nations Reserve Lands: Report of the Standing Committee on Aboriginal Affairs and Northern Development." March 2014. http://www.parl.gc.ca/content/ hoc/Committee/412/AANO/Reports/RP6482573/AANOrp04/aanorp04-e.pdf.

York, Geoffrey, and Loreen Pindera. *People of the Pines: The Warriors and the Legacy of Oka*. Toronto: Little Brown, 1991.

CHAPTER 2

TWENTY YEARS LATER:
THE RCAP LEGACY IN INDIGENOUS HEALTH SYSTEM GOVERNANCE— WHAT ABOUT THE NEXT TWENTY?

Yvonne Boyer, Josée Lavoie, Derek Kornelsen, and Jeff Reading

In November 1996, the Royal Commission on Aboriginal Peoples (RCAP)[1] published its final landmark report, which provided for the first time detailed community insights into a multitude of long-standing issues prevalent and problematic within the relationship among Indigenous peoples, other Canadians, and governments in Canada. The 4,000-page, five-volume report based on extensive consultation with Indigenous peoples provided a blueprint for a new relationship, one based on reclaiming self-governance by exerting autonomy over factors that determine health, including social, political, cultural, economic, and spiritual affairs. The report's recommendations addressed a wide scope of health issues for which implementation still remains preliminary, fragmented, ineffective, or simply absent. The purpose of this chapter is to discuss the progress made to date on key RCAP health-related recommendations. The following sections discuss recommendations while highlighting areas of progress and ongoing shortcomings and disconnects. The last section, which we call "Moving Forward," provides a framework that will lead to a healthier future via legal and policy options and that supports the report of the Truth and Reconciliation Commission of Canada (2015)[2] and the United Nations Declaration on the Rights of Indigenous Peoples.[3] The framework that we propose calls for action and implementation in Indigenous communities, governments, civil society, and relevant institutions.

RCAP THEN AND NOW

In the following section, we review specific recommendations made by RCAP and note government progress made on them. Ten key recommendations are grouped into four main areas:
- government oversight, recognition, and jurisdiction;
- self-government, integration, and responsiveness;
- inclusiveness of all services; and
- valuing Indigenous cultures, knowledges, and practices.

GOVERNMENT OVERSIGHT,
RECOGNITION OF JURISDICTION, AND OBLIGATIONS

In this section, we discuss three recommendations related to the federal government's role in providing national leadership with regard to federal, provincial, and territorial obligations to First Nations, Métis, and Inuit in health care. Our review of RCAP recommendations singled out three specific recommendations:
- Federal, provincial and territorial governments, and Aboriginal governments and organizations, must support the assumption of responsibility for planning health and social services by regional Aboriginal agencies and councils where these now operate, and the formation of regional Aboriginal planning.[4]
- Aboriginal organizations, regional planning and administrative bodies and community governments currently administering health and social services transform current programs and services into more holistic delivery systems that integrate or co-ordinate separate services. Aboriginal, federal, provincial and territorial governments incorporate in funding agreements plans for capital development and operating costs of a network of healing lodges.[5]
- Federal, provincial and territorial governments should commit themselves to providing the necessary funding, consistent with their juris-

dictional responsibilities, to implement a co-ordinated and comprehensive human resources development strategy; to train 10,000 Aboriginal professionals over a 10-year period in health and social services.[6]

A number of interrelated themes emerge from these recommendations, namely an explicit acknowledgement of federal, provincial, and territorial jurisdiction; the need for federal, provincial, and territorial governments to give space to and invest in holistic health-informed healing lodges; and a commitment to train 10,000 First Nation, Métis, and Inuit health and social services professionals. A discussion of each follows.

An Explicit Acknowledgement of Federal, Provincial, and Territorial Jurisdiction

Little to no progress has been made on clarifying jurisdictional obligations. At the national level, the Aboriginal health policy framework that existed in 1996 remains largely untouched. A review by Lavoie and colleagues of all federal and provincial health legislation and policies containing Indigenous-specific content shows that what exists in Canada was then and remains a patchwork, marred by inconsistencies and numerous gaps.[7] There are significant gaps at the federal level. Indeed, the federal government's position to date has been that federal services are provided for humanitarian reasons and as a matter of policy only. Obligations stemming from constitutionally protected Aboriginal and treaty rights have clearly been ignored.[8] As a result, federal, provincial, and territorial jurisdictional debates continue, perpetuating delays and gaps in services identified in RCAP reports.[9]

This is especially true for First Nations. Jordan Rivers was a child with complex medical needs because of a rare neuromuscular disorder that could not be managed from his home in Norway House First Nation. Although his physician and family agreed to discharge him to a specialized foster home facility near his home reserve, Jordan was left to live the remainder of his life in a hospital while federal and provincial government officials argued for over two years about which level of government should pay for the specialized home care that he needed in order to be discharged, the transportation costs, and even tiny items such as a showerhead.[10] The case received national attention and resulted in the adoption of Jordan's Principle[11] by the federal and provincial governments across Canada.[12] On 26 January 2016, the Canadian Human

Rights Tribunal ordered the federal government to take measures to adopt fully Jordan's Principle. On 6 July 2016, the federal government committed to investing $382 million to implement a broader application. Although this is a positive advance, the federal government continues to limit the application of Jordan's Principle to on-reserve children with disabilities or short-term conditions.[13]

Jurisdictional gaps have also been documented for First Nations adults seeking care in a variety of settings, leading to delays in access and negative outcomes. To date, the federal government continues to define its obligations to First Nations as limited to complementing what the provinces offer and as a "payor of last resort."[14] No province has clearly defined its area of jurisdiction in regard to First Nations. At the federal level, programs are defined nationally and implemented across the provinces in spite of provincial variations in the provision of services.

Following the Romanow Commission in 2002, which highlighted issues of jurisdictional debate as a priority, Indigenous regional planning processes emerged in British Columbia (the First Nations Health Authority) and Manitoba (the Intergovernmental Committee on Manitoba First Nations' Health).

The Manitoba table brings together high-level government officials from all relevant federal departments (regional representatives of the First Nations and Inuit Health Branch of Health Canada, Indigenous and Northern Affairs) and provincial departments (finance, health, Aboriginal affairs, social services, etc.) and the Assembly of Manitoba Chiefs. Although this table has commissioned numerous studies, it has yet to address effectively systems-level jurisdictional barriers to care, largely because appointees remain accountable to their own department and government rather than to a cross-jurisdictional objective and are not empowered to resolve issues that demand a flexible understanding of their department's obligations.

The BC First Nations Health Authority, in contrast, is empowered to address systems-level jurisdictional issues as they apply to First Nations and as they emerge in the province. Subsequent to extensive tripartite discussions among BC First Nations leaders and the governments of British Columbia and Canada, in October 2013 the First Nations Health Authority took responsibility for all functions previously shouldered by the First Nations and Inuit Health Branch of Health Canada (FNIHB) in British Columbia. This transfer of responsibility has resulted in new relationships between First Nations and provincial or regional health authorities and a culture of problem solving. This new relationship is supported by an enabling infrastructure, and it seems to be a positive and concrete step forward that might have found inspiration in the RCAP report of 1996. In other provinces, tripartite discussions continue.

In the case of Métis, the long-awaited Supreme Court of Canada decision in *Daniels* (2016) held that Métis are "Indians" under Section 91(24) of the Constitution Act, 1982. The same decision includes Non-Status Indians previously not recognized under that section. The implications for federal responsibility for health care for Métis and Non-Status Indians are under discussion and will be determined in the future.

For Inuit, Métis jurisdictional issues are somewhat less ambiguous. For those who live in Nunangat (Nunatsiavut in Labrador, Nunavik in northern Quebec, Nunavut and Inuvialuit in the Northwest Territories), jurisdictional responsibilities are better defined. Inuit from Inuvialuit or Nunavut who must travel to provincial jurisdictions (mainly Edmonton, Winnipeg, Ottawa, and Montreal) to access health care have the costs of their care paid by the territory of residence. Although some support exists in these cities for accommodations and access to care, the transition from northern communities to southern urban settings is often difficult, especially when long-term or permanent relocation is required. For Inuit living in Winnipeg, for example, the Manitoba Inuit Association advocates for more culturally appropriate health services. At the time of writing, there is no clear funding pathway for Inuit organizations providing services in southern cities.

TRC Call to Action (CTA) 20 confirms the requirement for jurisdictional clarity: "In order to address the jurisdictional disputes concerning Aboriginal people who do not reside on reserves, we call upon the federal government to recognize, respect, and address the distinct health needs of the Métis, Inuit, and off-reserve Aboriginal peoples."[15] Twenty years after RCAP, it is disheartening to see similar themes reiterated in the TRC recommendations, acknowledging that what little progress has been made is uneven and generally taking much longer than anticipated.

The Need for Federal, Provincial, and Territorial Governments to
Invest in Holistic Health-Informed Healing Lodges
Culturally appropriate mental health and healing services remain in their
infancy on reserves, across the North, and in many urban centres. Services
that exist on reserves are severely underfunded[16] and, as a result, underdeveloped and focused on crisis intervention instead of prevention and
healing. The Aboriginal Healing Foundation, created in 1999 as a result
of RCAP, was defunded in 2014. The foundation played a pivotal role in
funding healing initiatives across Canada. These initiatives were funded,
however, on a competitive basis, as projects.[17] It is unclear whether any of
these projects has reached sustainability and might continue.

We note that the Truth and Reconciliation Commission called in CTA
21 for investments in Aboriginal healing centres, just like RCAP had:
"We call upon the federal government to provide sustainable funding
for existing and new Aboriginal healing centres to address the physical,
mental, emotional, and spiritual harms caused by residential schools,
and to ensure that the funding of healing centres in Nunavut and the
Northwest Territories is a priority."[18] Clearly, the Indigenous community
is reaching out for safe spaces for health and healing. We hope that this
recommendation will result in tangible long-term commitments, resulting in long-term community-based programs, rather than short-term
projects. This would be an innovation.

Indigenizing the Health and Social Care Workforce
Following ten years of intractable action or inaction, the federal government committed $100 million over five years (2005–10) to the creation of
an Aboriginal Health Human Resources Initiative (AHHRI) to enhance the
Indian and Inuit Health Careers Program (IIHCP). The objective was *to lay*
the foundation for longer-term systemic changes in the creation, demand,
and supply of supportive working environments for Aboriginal health
human resources.[19] Expenditures in the programs totalled approximately
$102 million over five years (2005–10). A study by Lecompte showed that
the number of Indigenous health professionals rose from 8,840 in 1996 to
21,805 in 2006 (for a net gain of 11,965).[20] It is noteworthy that this progress was achieved before implementation of the AHHRI.

The AHHRI has since promoted health careers at career days and
science fairs and funded 2,594 Indigenous students (2006–12) through
the Indspire bursaries and scholarships program designed to support

studies in the health professions. To date, it appears that Statistics Canada and the Canadian Institute of Health Information keep statistics on progress on increasing the number of Indigenous health providers.

SELF-GOVERNMENT, INTEGRATION, REPRESENTATION, AND RESPONSIVENESS

The RCAP reports highlighted two (3.3.2 and 3.3.3) recommendations related to self-government: "Governments [must] recognize that the health of a people is a matter of vital concern to its life, welfare, identity and culture and is therefore a core area for the exercise of self-government by Aboriginal nations. Governments [must] act promptly to (a) conclude agreements recognizing their respective jurisdictions in areas touching directly on Aboriginal health; (b) agree on appropriate arrangements for funding health services under Aboriginal jurisdiction [RCAP recommendations apply generally to all Aboriginal peoples including Inuit, Métis, and First Nations]; and (c) establish a framework, until institutions of Aboriginal self-government exist."[21] To date, mechanisms put in place to support self-determination have been limited to First Nations living on reserves and to Inuit living in their traditional territories. Métis, Non-Status Indians, and those living outside their traditional territories have been systematically excluded despite a growing population of First Nations, Métis, and Inuit calling urban centres home for substantial periods of time.[22]

Administrative mechanisms that provide avenues for some level of self-determination (which more closely resembles self-administration) continue to perpetuate jurisdictional fragmentation by separating health from other services and by creating barriers for service integration and adaptation. Recent research findings suggest that regimes of accountability that emerged in the mid-1990s, on the heels of the RCAP recommendations, have made matters worse, resulting in decreased responsiveness in services,[23] in part associated with a decrease in on-reserve per capita funding over time.[24]

An exception is British Columbia, where unprecedented and substantial progress has been made through the transfer of funding and functions previously shouldered by the FNIHB. Yet, even in that case, First Nations secured increased control over existing health services, but the funding provided was largely based on historical expenditures, rather than needs, and cannot support services that match recognized clinical guidelines in a number of key areas, including dental care.

RESPONSIVENESS OF ALL SERVICES

The health-care systems in place to serve the needs of Indigenous peoples include federal, provincial, and territorial services and Indigenous-controlled services. Our review highlights two recommendations that speak to these specific issues.

> Aboriginal, federal, provincial and territorial governments must acknowledge the determinants of health found in Aboriginal traditions and health sciences and endorse the fundamental importance of:
>
> · holism, that is, attention to whole persons in their total environment;
> · equity, that is, equitable access to the means of achieving health and equality of outcomes in health status;
> · control by Aboriginal peoples of the lifestyle choices, institutional services and environmental conditions that support health; and
> · diversity, that is, an accommodation of the cultures and histories of First Nations, Inuit and Métis people that make them distinctive within Canadian society and that distinguish them from one another.[25]

> Non-Aboriginal service agencies and institutions involved in the delivery of health or social services to Aboriginal peoples, and professional associations, unions, and other organizations in a position to influence the delivery of health or social services to Aboriginal peoples undertake a systematic examination to determine how they can encourage and support the development of Aboriginal health and social service systems, and improve the appropriateness and effectiveness of mainstream services to Aboriginal peoples; engage representatives of Aboriginal communities and organizations in conducting such an examination.[26]

Racism in health care continues to be reported, perpetuating frustration, distrust, delayed access to responsive care, poor outcomes, and at times tragedies.[27] Brian Sinclair died in the Emergency Department of the Health Sciences Centre in Winnipeg in September 2008. He had recently seen a family physician at a Winnipeg Regional Health Authority's primary care clinic. The physician had referred him to the

Health Sciences Centre, where he was ignored by staff and security for thirty-four hours and died of complications from a readily treatable bladder infection.[28] This case apparently exemplifies racial discrimination in the health-care system in Canada.

There has been increased attention paid over the past twenty years since the RCAP report to the importance of culturally safe care and, increasingly, trauma-informed care in order to meet the health-care needs of Canadians.[29] Although this attention has not necessarily resulted in an overall improvement in health services, we note modest progress. For example, the Provincial Health Services Authority in British Columbia created an Indigenous Cultural Safety program to increase Indigenous-specific knowledge, enhance individual self-awareness, and strengthen skills for any professional working directly or indirectly with Indigenous peoples.[30] Introduced in 2011, this program had trained 10,000 professionals by the end of 2014. Manitoba and Ontario are in the process of adapting the program to their own contexts. Emerging evidence from a study that used the program as an intervention with health professionals providing health services to Indigenous and non-Indigenous peoples living in marginalized circumstances indicates that the program is effective in transforming practice and ensuring better outcomes in non-profit health-care organizations.[31] It is unclear whether these findings can be generalized to the broader health-care community.

VALUING INDIGENOUS CULTURES, KNOWLEDGES, AND PRACTICES
As highlighted by RCAP, Western educational institutions and professional organizations play a key role in perpetuating or addressing the conditions that promote the marginalization of Indigenous peoples at all levels of Canadian society, including in health care. Furthermore, the same institutions actively displace and devalue Indigenous knowledges and traditional healing practices. We identified three relevant recommendations:

- Post-secondary educational institutions involved in the training of health and social services professionals, and professional associations involved in regulating and licensing these professions, should collaborate with Aboriginal organizations and governments to develop a more effective approach to training and licensing that recognizes the importance and legitimacy of Aboriginal knowledge and experience.[32] Governments, health authorities and traditional practitioners should

co-operate to protect and extend the practices of traditional healing
and explore their application to contemporary Aboriginal health and
healing problems.[33]

- Non-Aboriginal educational institutions and professional associations involved in the health and social services fields must sensitize
practitioners to the existence of traditional medicine and healing
practices, the possibilities for co-operation and collaboration, and
the importance of recognizing, affirming and respecting traditional
practices and practitioners.[34]

- Aboriginal traditional healers and bio-medical practitioners should
strive actively to enhance mutual respect through dialogue and . . .
explore areas of possible sharing and collaboration.[35]

Similar recommendations were reiterated by the TRC calls to action:

23. We call upon all levels of government to: i. Increase the number
of Aboriginal professionals working in the health-care field.
ii. Ensure the retention of Aboriginal health-care providers
in Aboriginal communities. iii. Provide cultural competency
training for all health-care professionals.

24. We call upon medical and nursing schools in Canada to require
all students to take a course dealing with Aboriginal health
issues, including the history and legacy of residential schools,
the United Nations Declaration on the Rights of Indigenous
Peoples, Treaties and Aboriginal rights, and Indigenous teachings and practices. This will require skills-based training in
intercultural competency, conflict resolution, human rights,
and anti-racism.[36]

Although integrating Western and traditional practices has been
discussed for decades, at least in some settings,[37] no progress has been
made to facilitate this integration at the policy level. A handful of clinics across Canada currently operate with integrated models of service
delivery. More clinics have hired Elders to improve cultural safety and
provide counselling services. In all cases that we are aware of, funding
remains an ongoing issue.

Some legislation exists to protect Indigenous healing practices from
the encroachment of other legislation. For example, the Yukon Act[38]
and the Ontario Regulated Health Professions Act[39] require the respect

of traditional Indigenous practitioners and healing practices. Other legislation requires the recognition of Indigenous traditional midwifery practices.[40] Finally, British Columbia, Alberta, Saskatchewan, Manitoba, Ontario, New Brunswick, and Prince Edward Island have adopted tobacco-control legislation that does not apply to the use of tobacco for ceremonial purposes.[41] It is difficult to assess whether at least some of these legislated provisions emerged as a result of RCAP. It is noteworthy that some preceded it.

The Truth and Reconciliation Commission made a specific call to action on traditional healing: "22. We call upon those who can effect change within the Canadian health-care system to recognize the value of Aboriginal healing practices and use them in the treatment of Aboriginal patients in collaboration with Aboriginal healers and Elders where requested by Aboriginal patients."[42] Overall, the progress made on integrating Indigenous and Western health and medical knowledge is dismal.

KEY MESSAGES AND NEXT STEPS

To date, little progress has been made to operationalize nine of the ten RCAP recommendations discussed above. A notable exception is the progress made in the training of Indigenous health-care professionals, although statistics are lacking to assess the magnitude of the progress.

In 2010, after three years of contesting the process, Canada finally expressed support for the United Nations Declaration on the Rights of Indigenous Peoples (UNDRIP). This was followed by a full commitment to implementation of the UNDRIP in May 2016 by the Liberal government of Justin Trudeau. We note from the UNDRIP two resolutions (Articles 23 and 24.1) that echo some of the themes discussed above:

> Indigenous peoples have the right to determine and develop priorities and strategies for exercising their right to development. In particular, indigenous peoples have the right to be actively involved in developing and determining health, housing and other economic and social programmes affecting them and, as far as possible, to administer such programmes through their own institutions.[43]

> Indigenous peoples have the right to their traditional medicines and to maintain their health practices, including the conservation of their vital medicinal plants, animals and minerals. Indigenous

individuals also have the right to access, without any discrimination, all social and health services.[44]

Canada's commitment to UNDRIP, and to reaffirming its relationship
with First Nations, Métis, and Inuit, give us some confidence that the TRC
resolutions might be seriously considered and implemented.

MOVING FORWARD

As we have noted from the above review, the RCAP recommendations
have been either partially implemented or not implemented at all. The
disproportionate burdens of ill health experienced by First Nations, Métis,
and Inuit continue to be attributed to an uncoordinated and a fragmented
health-care system. This system is rooted in laws and public policies that
have created jurisdictional gaps resulting in prolonged disputes among
federal, provincial, and Indigenous governments about who is responsible
for First Nations, Métis, and Inuit health care. The recent *Daniels*[45] decision confirmed that Métis and Non-Status Indians are considered Indians
within Section 91(24) of the Constitution Act, 1982, but the parameters
of this classification have not been determined. Government responsibilities might be revised in the years to come. Our observation is that the
legislative and policy vacuum in which the federal government operates
in regard to First Nations, Métis, and Inuit health obligations is the most
significant barrier to moving forward. This vacuum is related to a lack of
federal leadership in integrating Indigenous aspirations, many of which
are supported by Supreme Court rulings, into policies.

RECIPROCAL ACCOUNTABILITY

Generally, the continued failure of federal and provincial governments
to fulfill obligations articulated by RCAP, the UNDRIP, and the TRC, as
well as Indigenous peoples in Canada, demonstrates that colonial governments remain unaccountable to the Indigenous peoples whom they are
obligated to serve. The "legislative and policy vacuum" noted above can
be ameliorated in part by introducing formal accountability frameworks
that entrench the relevant governments' accountability to the Indigenous
peoples working to achieve more responsive and effective care for their
communities. In this regard, our key recommendation is to forward the
concept of *mutual accountability* or *reciprocal accountability* as a way to
entrench nation-to-nation relationships between Indigenous peoples and

Canadian governments and to underwrite meaningfully the obligations inherent in this relationship, thus enabling the improvement of health services for Indigenous peoples in Canada.

The concept of reciprocal accountability has been defined as a process that "two (or multiple) partners agree to be held responsible for the commitments that they have voluntarily made to each other. It relies on trust and partnership around shared agendas rather than on hard sanctions for non-compliance to encourage the behaviour change needed to meet commitments. It is supported by evidence that is collected and shared among all partners."[46] In keeping with this vision, leading Indigenous organizations in Canada have called for a shift to reciprocal accountability and the equal partnership that it entails. According to the Native Women's Association of Canada (NWAC), the goal is healthy communities, and an accountability model "based on governments working in full partnership with First Nations, Metis and Inuit peoples of Canada" is the required means.[47] Similarly, the Assembly of First Nations (AFN) has stated that "combining efforts to lead toward enhanced mutual accountability for the results of program spending and support development toward increased First Nations responsibility and control" is necessary in order to bring general funding and service delivery up to the standards enjoyed by members of the broader Canadian society. More specifically, the AFN has proposed a First Nations Health Reporting Framework (FNHRF) as part of a "transformative plan to close the gap in health outcomes between Canadian People and Aboriginal Peoples." Reciprocal accountability is a core feature of this proposal: "The FNHRF is being built on the concept of reciprocal accountability, specifically recognizing that there exists a severe imbalance of power between First Nations and the FPT [federal, provincial, and territorial] governments. The FNHRF by way of taking control over the measurement of the performance of FPT governments in their success to meet their stated objectives will enable First Nations to use evidence to support future negotiations to ensure that First Nations interests are identified as priorities."[48]

Finally, the BC First Nations Health Authority (FNHA)[49] has been developed by First Nations for First Nations. It provides health service delivery for First Nations living in British Columbia. The FNHA identifies reciprocal accountability with government funders as essential to "the success of this new health governance arrangement."[50] It lists nine

principles that guide reciprocal accountability:
- clear roles and responsibilities for the partners;
- clear performance expectations;
- balanced expectations based on capacities;
- credible reporting;
- reasonable review and adjustment;
- ethics;
- community level;
- regional level; and
- provincial/national level.

Nevertheless, although reciprocal accountability is a core feature of the new fiscal arrangement between British Columbia's First Nations Health Authority and government funders, and despite significant endorsement by other Indigenous organizations and governments such as the AFN and NWAC, reciprocal accountability frameworks remain underdeveloped and underimplemented.

A key barrier to moving forward with reciprocal accountability frameworks appears to be the entrenched colonial practice of maintaining a "top-down" or "guardian and ward" approach.[51] In Canadian health-care systems, this approach is evident within the funding agreements themselves and places service providers in unworkable situations. The patient relies on the service provider to offer responsive and effective care, yet the service provider is accountable not to the patient but to federal and provincial funders through transfer or contribution agreements. Greater autonomy and influence at the local level to define and implement health-care needs and solutions and to set reporting metrics must be key features of any reciprocal accountability framework, thus allowing service providers to remain meaningfully accountable to their patients. Where the guardian and ward approach remains entrenched, the system lacks transparency and works against the development of the trust-based and equal partnerships necessary for a workable reciprocal accountability framework. That is, the top-down approach stands as a barrier to an improved health status for Indigenous peoples because it does not allow for the creation of the kinds of relationships among funders, practitioners, and communities conducive to the open communication and priority setting necessary for effective, responsive care that meets the needs of patients as *they* articulate them. To shift effectively to reciprocal accountability, it would ideally pervade relations at all levels—from high-level organizational agreements on strategic policies, funding, and governance to community-level partnerships, agreements, and projects to the space in between that extends to reciprocal accountability between health professionals and clients' relational care.

FIDUCIARY OBLIGATIONS

If accountability frameworks are to adhere to the commitments to self-determination as outlined in the various TRC calls to action and the articles in the UNDRIP, it is key that Indigenous perspectives on reciprocal accountability contribute significantly to our understanding of the concept. In this regard, Kornelsen and colleagues have argued that an examination of the history and practice of fiduciary obligations can create the necessary space for Indigenous perspectives on reciprocal accountability: "A consideration of Indigenous perspectives on reciprocity and accountability is an essential yet mainly overlooked component of the development of effective and appropriate accountability models between Indigenous peoples and state-based funders."[52] Since the beginning of the British assertion of sovereignty, the guiding principles of fiduciary law have governed Crown-Indigenous relations.[53] This fiduciary obligation is formed in several ways, through the Royal Proclamation of 1763 and the historical protective relationship between Indigenous peoples in Canada and the state;[54] through the protective language of the early treaties that is rooted in the *sui generis* relationship; and through the constitutionally entrenched protections of Aboriginal and treaty rights and subsequent case law[55] that further define and solidify these fiduciary obligations.

As Brian Slattery poignantly explains,

> the Crown has a general fiduciary duty toward native people to protect them in the enjoyment of their aboriginal rights and in particular in the possession and use of their lands. This general fiduciary duty has its origins in the Crown's historical commitment to protect native peoples from the inroads of British settlers, in return for a native undertaking to renounce the use of force to defend themselves and to accept instead the protection of the Crown as its subjects. In offering its protection, the Crown was animated less by philanthropy or moral sentiment than by the need to establish peaceful relationships with peoples whose friendship was a source of military and economic advantage, and

whose enmity was a threat to the security and prosperity of the colonies. The sources of the general fiduciary duty do not lie, then, in a paternalistic concern to protect a "weaker" or "primitive" people, as has sometimes been suggested, but rather in the necessity of persuading native peoples, at a time when they still had considerable military capacities, that their rights would be better protected by reliance on the Crown than by self-help.[56]

Given these origins of the fiduciary relationship between Indigenous peoples and the Crown, it is crucial to recognize that Indigenous peoples and conceptual frameworks were key to the development of the concept itself. The late Mohawk scholar Patricia Monture provides an insightful analysis of how the idea of "treaty philosophy" ought to inform understandings of the fiduciary relationship.[57] This perspective emphasizes the relational processes necessary to maintain good relations or trust and mutual respect between sovereign entities rather than stipulating particular static rights. Treaties require a commitment to ongoing interaction and ceremony as means to nurture the relationships and to enable sensitivity to the needs of each party such that responsibilities could become apparent and the relationships could be sustained for future generations.[58] As a result, practices of treaty making between sovereign entities work to establish and maintain an "ethical community, that is, [a] community within which promises are kept."[59] This general ideal of treaty making as reflecting the building and maintenance of relationships of mutual trust, reciprocity, and respect is ubiquitous in Indigenous scholarship on the topic.[60]

However, as a result of historical and ongoing colonial practices and the resultant disparity in power between the Crown and Indigenous nations, current practice regarding fiduciary relationships is generally vulnerable to the Crown's discretion and potential abuse. The Supreme Court is clear that, when a beneficiary relies on a fiduciary, the fiduciary carries a certain amount of discretion when discharging its duties. There are strict guidelines that govern the discretionary behaviour of the fiduciary. Certain positive duties are imposed on the federal government because of this fiduciary relationship. Core elements include the Crown's duty to provide full disclosure of its actions so as not to compromise Aboriginal or treaty rights and the requirement that the Crown refrain from acting in conflict of interest situations or benefiting from its role as fiduciary. Case law provides that, if there is any possibility of infringement on Aboriginal or treaty rights, meaningful consultation is required, and justification must be advanced to account for such infringement.

THE DISCONNECT

Fiduciary law principles are also strict in relation to conflict of interest situations: fiduciaries must not act in a conflict of interest situation, must not benefit from their positions, must provide full disclosure of their actions, and must not compromise their beneficiaries' interests.[61]

The conflict of interest principles appear to be an oxymoron, however, when one examines the government's actions in matters affecting Indigenous peoples. For example, the Crown has unilaterally decided what to do with the lands, interests, and assets of its Indigenous beneficiaries. The Crown derives its resources from the land base obtained through treaties and land surrenders and from taxes and then uses its virtually unlimited resources to oppose Indigenous court challenges to its powers, thereby benefitting from its position. By so doing, it literally converts its position from fiduciary to discretionary beneficiary of its own position and power.[62]

The same analogy could be used in relation to health policy. The Non-Insured Health Benefits policy distributes health-care resources to First Nations under the Indian Act. The Canadian government states that this is done through policy and not because of any perceived legal obligation. An example of discretionary power that the fiduciary has over the beneficiary is seen in this policy, for a number of unilateral decisions have been made that adversely affect the health of First Nations.[63] Moreover, in the Canadian Human Rights Tribunal First Nations child welfare case, the federal government spent over $3 million in its unsuccessful attempts to have the case dismissed between 2007 and 2016. It argued that First Nations child welfare services should not be compared with those delivered to others in Canada and that this funding is not a service and therefore exempt from the Canadian Human Rights Act.[64] In September 2016, the Canadian Human Rights Tribunal issued a second compliance order to compel the federal government to rectify immediately funding formulas to ensure that First Nations children who live on reserves have access to health services on the same terms as all other Canadians.[65] It appears that the Canadian Human Rights Tribunal does not carry legal force other than repeating its orders while the federal government chooses to listen or ignore its voice.

A disconnect in health-care status clearly exists between the government and First Nations, Métis, and Inuit. This disconnect cannot be relied on to justify or maintain the status quo in relation to poor health status unless it is also without the acknowledgement that such continuance is the result of (1) a disregard for existing constitutionally protected Aboriginal and treaty rights to health, (2) a breach of the Crown's fiduciary obligations, (3) a discriminatory exercise of discretion, and (4) a conflict-of-interest position from which the federal government continues to benefit.[66]

The federal government cannot continue to maintain reasonably that health services provided to First Nations, Métis, and Inuit are "voluntary" and provided for "humanitarian reasons" and as a matter of policy. Such a characterization is a discriminatory reading of Canada's commitments to provide the highest attainable standard of physical and mental health to *all* residents of Canada and to facilitate reasonable access to health services without financial or other barriers based on need.

The federal government recognizes and affirms its unique constitutional obligations to First Nations, Métis and Inuit but fails to implement them according to certain existing Aboriginal and treaty rights—including access to health care. Instead, Canada's health policies and guidelines affecting Indigenous health should be examined to ensure that they no longer reflect the outdated wardship model of Crown-Indigenous relations but reflect the fiduciary relationship that the Supreme Court of Canada has stated properly characterizes Crown-Indigenous relations.

CONCLUSION AND RECOMMENDATIONS

The 1996 RCAP report provided a detailed assessment of long-standing issues prevalent and problematic in the relationship between Indigenous peoples and other Canadians. The report provided a blueprint for a new relationship based on reclaiming self-governance by exerting autonomy over factors that determine health, including social, political, cultural, economic, and spiritual affairs. The RCAP recommendations addressed a wide array of health issues for which implementation still remains preliminary, fragmented, ineffective, or simply absent. We believe that the operationalization of the RCAP, TRC, and UNDRIP recommendations requires the adoption of a national and enabling First Nations, Métis, and Inuit health policy inclusive of the following overarching principles: Recognizing and implementing the constitutional protections of Aboriginal and treaty rights to health; inherent Indigenous rights to health; and Crown/Indigenous fiduciary obligations. The RCAP report made a credible evidence-based case that supported the belief that Indigenous peoples could reclaim the management of their own affairs in a context of mutual trust and respect for the constitutional entrenchment of Aboriginal rights. Regrettably, twenty years have elapsed, and very little has changed, as reflected in the strikingly similar calls to action from the Truth and Reconciliation Commission. RCAP repeatedly stated that Crown-Indigenous relationships are based not on the doctrine of discovery, *terra nullius,* or other nonsensical colonial justifications for the theft of lands and lives but on inherent Aboriginal rights and the treaty-making process, and they do not entail the relinquishing of inherent rights or treaty rights.[67]

Moreover, the fact that inherent Aboriginal and negotiated treaty rights are entrenched in the supreme law of Canada through Section 35 of the Constitution Act, 1982 is confirmation of the recognition of these inherent Aboriginal rights and the treaty-making process between nations. The sovereignty of the nations signing the treaties is indicative of the ability of the parties to be self-determining and the recognition of a distinct legal order *sui generis* in nature. A key distinction is noted:

> While the *Canada Health Act* is geared to distributing health care to all Canadians equally, Aboriginal peoples argue that their constitutional difference is relevant to the just distribution of health rights and entitlements. Treatment of Aboriginal people as merely "other peoples" ignores their constitutional rights and creates inequality of services. The Supreme Court recognizes the constitutional supremacy of these rights and has provided guiding principles for the legislature, governments and courts. Aboriginal and treaty rights are remarkable sets of rights that recognize Aboriginal people as distinct rights bearing holders of unique customs, practices and traditions. Moreover, these rights are constitutionally entrenched in the Supreme Law of Canada.[68]

For true accountability in health care, it is critical that recognition of these rights shapes the Crown-Indigenous relationships in health-care funding. In the drafting of many contribution agreements, legislation and applicable documents clearly state that there is to be no interference with

Aboriginal and treaty rights as protected by the Constitution Act, 1982. In fact, this non-interference clause is entrenched in the Constitution through Section 25: "The guarantee in this Charter of certain rights and freedoms shall not be construed so as to abrogate or derogate from any aboriginal, treaty or other rights or freedoms that pertain to the aboriginal peoples of Canada."[69]

The First Nations Health Authority includes Aboriginal and treaty rights and the ensuing fiduciary obligations in its directives for a community engagement process that outlines the standards for a new health governance relationship based on reciprocal accountability in Directive 6:

- Not impact on Aboriginal Title and Rights or the treaty rights of First Nations, and be without prejudice to any self-government agreements or court proceedings.
- Not impact on the fiduciary duty of the Crown.
- Not impact on existing federal funding agreement[s] with individual First Nations, unless First Nations want the agreements to change.[70]

Although reciprocal accountability is seen to be a critical component of an Aboriginal and treaty rights legal analysis, Kornelsen and colleagues observe that "this kind of language is ubiquitous in funding agreements and policy statements, [and] it has yet to be meaningfully operationalized in accountability frameworks."[71]

Canada's health policies and guidelines affecting First Nations, Métis, and Inuit must be examined to ensure that they no longer reflect the outdated wardship model of Crown-Indigenous relations but reflect the fiduciary relationship that the Supreme Court of Canada has stated properly characterizes Crown-Indigenous relations. In light of constitutional reform and judicial interpretation of constitutionally protected Aboriginal and treaty rights, lawmakers and policy makers should be compelled to accept the existence and implementation of Aboriginal and treaty rights to health in Canada. Therefore: Reciprocal accountability agreements that establish commitments to relationship-building amongst all stakeholders (round tables, etc.) as a means to ensuring the *process of reciprocity, trust-building, transparency* are a key focus rather than simply focusing on adding a bi-directional arrow to existing models. Reciprocal accountability means mutually shared responsibility among all of the partners, ranging from the community level (First Nations, Métis, or Inuit) to the provincial or regional level (provincial governments, inclusive of health authorities) to the national level (federal governments) to realize collective goals. It consists of the recognition that each party is "responsible for the effective operation of their part of the health system recognizing that the space occupied by each is interdependent and interconnected."[72] It also echoes the language of patient-centred care, which has gained currency in the health-care literature over the past decade. In this regard, the First Nations Health Authority stands as an innovative, perhaps radical, development that appears to be constructed in ways that can encourage the development of effective mutual accountability frameworks and effective, responsive care.

Reciprocal accountability is seen to be a critical component of an Aboriginal and treaty rights legal analysis.[73] To implement reciprocal accountability effectively within a new legal and fiduciary framework, the perimeters of jurisdiction can be redrawn in a unified federal policy based on catchment areas (including treaty catchments) rather than provincial boundaries:[74] "To be effective, the reoriented conceptual framework needs to be committed to the creation of Aboriginal and treaty rights catchment areas pertaining to policy, program, and delivery, rather than relying on existing provincial and territorial schemes.... Such catchment areas can best resolve the complex issue of First Nation ethics, privacy, consent, and related issues of First Nation representivity."[75] The restructuring of health care with the implementation of catchments can offer a natural clarity and a solution-driven answer to the jurisdictional bickering and quagmire that we have seen in the past twenty or more years.

Canada celebrated its 150th birthday in 2017, and the need to move forward has never been greater. We must move toward reconciliation to avoid repeating mistakes that would commission yet another report in the future with yet more calls to action. Thus, we recommend immediate implementation of the RCAP calls to action. An action plan should be initiated in partnership with Indigenous peoples, with an urgent mandate to blueprint the architecture of the unfinished business of Confederation, that being the elimination of inequality in health and well-being for Indigenous peoples and their descendants.

NOTES

1   In this chapter, we prefer using the term "Indigenous peoples." We will use the term "Aboriginal," however, when citing historical documents that use this term.

2   Truth and Reconciliation Commission of Canada (TRC), "Honouring the Truth, Reconciling for the Future."

3   TRC, "Honouring the Truth, Reconciling for the Future." Canada's commitment to enacting the TRC calls to action includes implementation of the UNDRIP as follows: "We call upon federal, provincial, territorial, and municipal governments to fully adopt and implement the *United Nations Declaration on the Rights of Indigenous Peoples* as the framework for reconciliation" (Article 43), and "we call upon the Government of Canada to develop a national action plan, strategies, and other concrete measures to achieve the goals of the *United Nations Declaration on the Rights of Indigenous Peoples*" (Article 44).

4   Royal Commission on Aboriginal Peoples (RCAP), *Report of the Royal Commission on Aboriginal Peoples*, Vol. 3, 237.

5   RCAP, *Report of the Royal Commission on Aboriginal Peoples*, Vol. 3, 224.

6   RCAP, *Report of the Royal Commission on Aboriginal Peoples*, Vol. 3, 246.

7   Lavoie et al., "Aboriginal Health Policies in Canada."

8   Boyer, *Moving Aboriginal Health Forward.*

9   RCAP, *Report of the Royal Commission on Aboriginal Peoples*, Volumes 1–5.

10   MacDonald and Attaran, "Jordan's Principle, Governments' Paralysis."

11   Jordan's Principle is a child-first principle used in Canada to resolve jurisdictional disputes within and between governments regarding payment for government services provided to First Nations children.

12   Jordan's Principle Working Group 2015.

13   See "First Nations Child and Family Caring Society of Canada," 2016, https://fncaringsociety.com/jordans-principle.

14   For instance, clients who have dental coverage under another plan or program must submit their claims to their other payers first. See www.hc-sc.gc.ca/fniah-spnia/nihb-ssna/benefit-prestation/newsletter-bulletin-eng.php.

15   TRC, "Honouring the Truth," 3.

16   Lavoie et al., "The Evaluation of the First Nations and Inuit Health Transfer Policy."

17   Lavoie et al., "The Evaluation of the First Nations and Inuit Health Transfer Policy."

18   TRC, "Honouring the Truth," 3.

19   Evaluation Directorate, *Evaluation of the First Nations.*

20   Lecompte, "Aboriginal Health Human Resources."

21   RCAP, Vol. 3: *Gathering Strength*, 632.

22   Lavoie et al., "Missing Pathways to Self-Governance."

23   Lavoie et al., "Negotiating Barriers, Navigating the Maze."

24   Lavoie, "A Comparative Financial Analysis."

25   RCAP, Vol. 3: *Gathering Strength*, 209.

26   RCAP, Vol. 3: *Gathering Strength*, 268.

27   Jordan's Principle Working Group, "Without Denial, Delay, or Disruption."

28   Lavallee, "Honoring Jordan."

29   Brascoupé and Waters, "Cultural Safety"; Browne, Varcoe, and Fridkin, "Addressing Trauma, Violence and Pain"; Browne et al., "Closing the Health Equity Gap"; Diffey and Lavallee, "Is Cultural Safety Enough?"

30 See BC Provincial Health Services Authority, San'yas Indigenous Cultural Safety Training, http://www.sanyas.ca/home.

31 Browne, Varcoe, and Walthen, "Innovative Responses to Structural Violence."

32 RCAP, *Vol. 3: Gathering Strength*, 260.

33 RCAP, *Vol. 3: Gathering Strength*, 266.

34 RCAP, Vol. 3: Gathering Strength, 268.

35 RCAP, *Vol. 3: Gathering Strength*, 337.

36 TRC, "Honouring the Truth," 3.

37 Gregory, "An Exploration of the Contact between Nurses and Indian Elders"; Young, Ingram, and Swartz, "A Cree Healer"; Young, Ingram, and Swartz, *Cry of the Eagle*.

38 Bill C-39, The Yukon Act (LS-422E) 2002.

39 Regulated Health Professions Act, 1991, S.O. 1991, c. 18.

40 Midwifery Act, 1991, S.O. 1991, c. 31.

41 Tobacco Reduction Act, S.A. 2005, c. T-3.8; The Tobacco Control Act, S.A. 2001, c. T-14; The Non-Smokers Health Protection Act, R.S.C. 1985, c. 15; Smoke-Free Ontario Act, S.O. 1994, c. 10.

42 TRC, "Honouring the Truth," 3.

43 UNDRIP 2007, Article 23.

44 UNDRIP 2007, Article 24.1.

45 *Daniels v. Canada (Indian Affairs and Northern Development)*, 2016 SCC 12 [Daniels].

46 OECD n.d.; for the full report, see Steer, Wathne, and Driscoll, "Mutual Accountability at the Country Level."

47 Native Women's Association of Canada (NWAC), "Accountability for Results from an Aboriginal Women's Perspective."

48 Assembly of First Nations (AFN), "The Development of a First Nations Health Reporting Framework."

49 The FNHA is an Indigenous-led health service organization responsible for planning, designing, funding, and managing the delivery of health programs and services for First Nations people living in British Columbia. For more information, see the FNHA website, http://www.fnha.ca.

50 FNHA, "British Columbia First Nation Perspectives," 6.

51 The guardian and ward approach was brought into Canadian law in the early 1800s and described "Indians" as "wards" incapable of making decisions on their own. It therefore followed that the federal government was their guardian in a position to make decisions on their behalf. This concept was replaced in law in 1982 by the Guerin decision, which changed this approach to a legally enforceable fiduciary obligation. Unfortunately, the guardian and ward theory still underpins much policy affecting Indigenous peoples today. See Aboriginal Peoples Television Network (APTN), "Northern Ontario Doctors Rebel over Health Canada Rules"; Boyer, "First Nations, Métis and Inuit Health and the Law," 337.

52 Kornelsen et al., "Reciprocal Accountability and Fiduciary Duty."

53 Rotman, *Parallel Paths*, 4.

54 Royal Proclamation of 1763, R.S.C. 1985, App. II, No. 1 [Royal Proclamation]. See also *R. v. Sparrow*, [1990] 1 S.C.R. 1075, [1990] 3 C.N.L.R. 160 at 177; *Delgamuukw v. British Columbia*, [1997] 3 S.C.R. 1010, [1998] 1 C.N.L.R. 14 (SCC), reversing in part (1993) 10 D.L.R. (4th) 470, [1993] 5 C.N.L.R. 1 (BCCA), varying in part [1991] 3 W.W.R. 97, [1991] 5 C.N.L.R. 1 (BCSC) at para. 200 per La Forest, J.

55 *Calder v. British Columbia* (Attorney General), [1973] S.C.R. 313, 34 D.L.R. (3d) 145, 7 C.N.L.C. 91; Guerin v. R., [1984] 2 S.C.R. 335, [1985] 1 C.N.L.R. 120, and subsequent decisions.

56 Slattery, "Understanding Aboriginal Rights," 762.

57 Monture, "The Experience of Fiduciary Relationships."

58 Little Bear, "Aboriginal Paradigms"; Miller, Compact, Contract, Covenant; Simpson, *Dancing on Our Turtle's Back*.

59 Asch, *On Being Here to Stay*.

60 See also Alfred, *Peace, Power, and Righteousness*; Borrows, *Canada's Indigenous Constitution*; Henderson, "*Ayukpachi*:EmpoweringAboriginal Thought"; and Miller, *Compact, Contract, Covenant*.

61 Rotman, *Parallel Paths*, 180.

62 As McNeil notes, "how any infringement of Aboriginal rights can accommodate the Crown's fiduciary duty is somewhat of a puzzle, as it seems to violate the basic principle that a fiduciary is bound to act in the best interests of the person(s) to whom the duty is owed." McNeil, "Section 91(24) Powers, the Inherent Right of Self-Government, and Canada's Fiduciary Obligations," 319.

63 Health Canada, First Nations and Inuit Health Branch (FNIHB), Medical Transportation Policy Framework. See also *Child Welfare Funding Case: Timeline of Procedural Delays*, https://fncaringsociety.com/sites/default/files/Procedural%20Diagram%202007-2016.pdf.

64 *Information Sheet: The Canadian Human Rights Tribunal on First Nations Child Welfare* (Docket: T1340/7708), January 2016, https://fncaringsociety.com/sites/default/files/Tribunal%20Briefing%20Note%20January%202016.pdf.

65 See CBC News, "Federal Government Failing to Comply with Ruling."

66 Boyer, "Aboriginal Health."

67 Boyer, *Moving Aboriginal Health Forward*.

68 Boyer, *Moving Aboriginal Health Forward*, 167.

69 Constitution Act, 1982, Being Schedule B to the Canada Act 1982 (UK), 1982, c. 11, s. 25.

70 See the website of the First Nations Health Authority, http://www.fnha.ca/about/fnha-overview/directives.

71 Kornelsen et al., "Reciprocal Accountability and Fiduciary Duty," 20–21.

72 *British Columbia First Nations Perspectives on a New Health Governance Arrangement: Consensus Paper*, http://www.fnha.ca/Documents/FNHC_Consensus_Paper.pdf.

73 Kornelsen et al., "Reciprocal Accountability and Fiduciary Duty."

74 Henderson, "First Nations Conceptual Frameworks," 9–10.

75 Henderson, "First Nations Conceptual Frameworks," 9–10.

REFERENCES

Aboriginal Peoples Television Network (APTN). "Northern Ontario Doctors Rebel over Health Canada Rules that Breach First Nation Patient's Privacy." APTN National News, 7 October 2016. http://aptn.ca/news/2016/10/07/northern-ontario-doctors-rebel-over-health-canada-rules-that-breach-first-nation-patients-privacy/.

Alfred, Taiaiake. *Peace, Power, and Righteousness: An Indigenous Manifesto*. 2nd ed. Don Mills: Oxford University Press, 2009.

Asch, Michael. On Being Here to Stay: *Treaties and Aboriginal Rights in Canada*. Toronto: University of Toronto Press, 2014.

Assembly of First Nations (AFN). "The Development of a First Nations Health Reporting Framework." 2006. An unpublished paper.

Borrows, John. *Canada's Indigenous Constitution*. Toronto: University of Toronto Press, 2010.

Boyer, Yvonne. "Aboriginal Health: The Crown's Fiduciary Obligations." Discussion Paper Series 2, National Aboriginal Health Organization and Native Law Centre of Canada, May 2004.

———. "First Nations, Métis and Inuit Health and the Law: A Framework for the Future." PhD diss., University of Ottawa, 2011.

———. *Moving Aboriginal Health Forward: Discarding Canada's Legal Barriers*. Saskatoon: Purich Publishing, 2014.

Brascoupé, Simon, and Catherine Waters. "Cultural Safety: Exploring the Applicability of the Concept of Cultural Safety to Aboriginal Health and Community Wellness." *Journal of Aboriginal Health* 5, no. 2 (2009): 6–41.

Browne, Annette J., Colleen Varcoe, and Alycia Fridkin. "Addressing Trauma, Violence and Pain: Research on Health Services for Women at the Intersections of History and Economics." In *Health Inequities in Canada: Intersectional Frameworks and Practices*, edited by Jo-Anne Lee and Olena Hankivsky, 401–23. Vancouver: UBC Press, 2011.

Browne, Annette J., Colleen Varcoe, and Nadine C. Walthen. "Innovative Responses to Structural Violence among Vulnerable Populations: Integrating Trauma- and Violence-Informed Care into Routine Primary Health Care Practices." Paper presented at the National Conference on Health and Domestic Violence, Washington, DC, 21 March 2015. https://nchdv.confex.com/nchdv/2015/webprogram/Paper11434.html.

Browne, Annette J., et al. "Closing the Health Equity Gap: Evidence-Based Strategies for Primary Health Care Organizations." *International Journal for Equity Health* 11, no. 59 (2012): n. pag. doi:10.1186/1475-9276-11-59.

CBC News. "Federal Government Failing to Comply with Ruling on First Nations Child Welfare: Tribunal." 15 September 2016. http://www.cbc.ca/news/politics/human-rights-tribunal-failing-to-comply-1.3764233.

Diffey, Linda, and Barry Lavallee. "Is Cultural Safety Enough? Confronting Racism to Address Inequities in Indigenous Health." *Office of Educational and Faculty Development News* [University of Manitoba], 2016. Conference paper, 1–4.

Evaluation Directorate. *Evaluation of the First Nations and Inuit Health Human Resources Program 2008–09 to 2012–13*. Ottawa: Health Canada and Public Health Agency of Canada, 2013.

First Nations Health Authority (FNHA). "British Columbia First Nation Perspectives on a New Health Governance Arrangment." 2011. http://fnhc.ca/pdf/FNHC_Consensus_Paper_-_WEB.pdf.

Gregory, David. "An Exploration of the Contact between Nurses and Indian Elders/Traditional Healers on Indian Reserves and Health Centers in Manitoba." In *Health Care Issues in the Canadian North*, edited by D. Young, 39–44. Edmonton: Boreal Institute for Northern Studies, 1988.

Health Canada. First Nations and Inuit Health Branch (FNIHB). *Medical Transportation Policy Framework*. Ottawa: FNIHB, 2005.

Henderson, Sákéj. "Ayukpachi: Empowering Aboriginal Thought." In *Reclaiming Indigenous Voice and Vision*, edited by Marie Battiste, 248–78. Vancouver: UBC Press, 2000.

———. "First Nations Conceptual Frameworks and Applied Models on Ethics, Privacy, and Consent in Health Research and Information." First Nations Centre, National Aboriginal Health Organization, 2006.

Jordan's Principle Working Group. "Without Denial, Delay, or Disruption: Ensuring First Nations Children's Access to Equitable Services through Jordan's Principle." Assembly of First Nations, 2015.

Kornelsen, Derek, Yvonne Boyer, Josée Lavoie, and Judith Dwyer. "Reciprocal Accountability and Fiduciary Duty: Implications for Indigenous Health in Canada, Australia and New Zealand." *Australian Indigenous Law Review* 19, no. 2 (2015-16): 17-33.

Lavallee, Trudy L. "Honoring Jordan: Putting First Nations Children First and Funding Fights Second." *Paediatrics and Child Health* 10, no. 9 (2005): 527-29.

Lavoie, Josée G. "A Comparative Financial Analysis of the 2003-04 and 2009-10 Health Care Expenditures for First Nations in Manitoba." Winnipeg, Manitoba: Centre for Aboriginal Health Research, 2014.

Lavoie, Josée G., Laverne Gervais, Odile Bergeron, and Ginnette Thomas. "Aboriginal Health Policies in Canada: The Policy Synthesis Project." Prince George, BC: National Collaborating Centre for Aboriginal Health, 2013.

Lavoie, Josée G., et al. "The Evaluation of the First Nations and Inuit Health Transfer Policy." *International Journal of Aboriginal Health* 8, no. 2 (2005): 18-22.

Lavoie, Josée G., et al. "Negotiating Barriers, Navigating the Maze: First Nation People's Experiences of Medical Relocation." *Canadian Public Administration* 58, no. 2 (2015a): 295-314.

Lavoie, Josée G., et al. "Missing Pathways to Self-Governance: Aboriginal Health Policy in British Columbia." International Indigenous Policy Journal 6, no. 1 (2015b): n. pag. doi:10.18584/iipj.2015.6.1.2.

Lecompte, Emily. "Aboriginal Health Human Resources: A Matter of Health." *International Journal of Aboriginal Health* 8, no. 2 (2012): 16-22.

Little Bear, Leroy. "Aboriginal Paradigms: Implications for Relationships to Land and Treaty Making." In *Advancing Aboriginal Claims: Visions/Strategies/Directions*, edited by Kerry Wilkins, 26-38. Saskatoon: Purich Publishing, 2004.

MacDonald, Noni, and Amir Attaran. "Jordan's Principle, Governments' Paralysis." CMAJ 177, no. 4 (2007): n. pag. doi:10.1503/cmaj.070950.

McNeil, Kent. "Section 91(24) Powers, the Inherent Right of Self-Government, and Canada's Fiduciary Obligations." Paper presented at the Canadian Aboriginal Law Conference, Vancouver, December 2002.

Miller, J.R. Compact, Contract, *Covenant: Aboriginal Treaty-Making in Canada.* Toronto: University of Toronto Press, 2009.

Monture, Patricia. "The Experience of Fiduciary Relationships: Canada's First Nations and the Crown." In *In Whom We Trust: A Forum on Fiduciary Relationships*, edited by Law Commission of Canada and Association of Iroquois and Allied Indians, Part 2 Alexandria NSW, Australia Law Commission of Canada, 2002.

Native Women's Association of Canada (NWAC). "Accountability for Results from an Aboriginal Women's Perspective." 2005.

Organization for Economic Cooperation and Development (OECD). *Mutual Accountability: Emerging Good Practice.* N.d. https://www.oecd.org/dac/effectiveness/49656340.pdf.

Rotman, L.I. *Parallel Paths: Fiduciary Doctrine and the Crown-Native Relationship in Canada.* Toronto: University of Toronto Press, 1996.

Royal Commission on Aboriginal Peoples (RCAP). *Report of the Royal Commission on Aboriginal Peoples, Vol. 1: Looking Forward, Looking Back.* Ottawa: Canada Communication Group Publishing, 1996a.

——. *Report of the Royal Commission on Aboriginal Peoples, Vol. 2: Restructuring the Relationship.* Ottawa: Canada Communication Group Publishing, 1996b.

——. *Report of the Royal Commission on Aboriginal Peoples, Vol. 3: Gathering Strength.* Ottawa: Canada Communication Group Publishing, 1996c.

——. *Report of the Royal Commission on Aboriginal Peoples, Vol. 4: Perspectives and Realities.* Ottawa: Canada Communication Group Publishing, 1996d.

———. *Report of the Royal Commission on Aboriginal Peoples, Vol. 5: A Twenty-Year Commitment.* Ottawa: Canada Communication Group Publishing, 1996e.

Simpson, Leanne. *Dancing on Our Turtle's Back: Stories of Nishnaabeg Re-Creation, Resurgence and a New Emergence.* Winnipeg: Arbeiter Ring Publishing, 2011.

Slattery, Brian. "Understanding Aboriginal Rights." *Canadian Bar Review* 66, no. 4 (1987): 727–83.

Steer, Liesbet, Cecilie Wathne, and Ruth Driscoll. "Mutual Accountability at the Country Level: A Concept and Emerging Good Practice Paper." Overseas Development Institute (ODI), OECD, 2008.

Truth and Reconciliation Commission of Canada (TRC). "Honouring the Truth, Reconciling for the Future: Summary of the Final Report of the Truth and Reconciliation Commission of Canada." 2015. www.trc.ca.

Young, David E., Grant Ingram, and Lise Swartz. "A Cree Healer Attempts to Improve the Competitive Position of Native Medicine." *Arctic Medical Research* 47, supplement 1 (1988): 313–16.

———. *Cry of the Eagle: Encounters with a Cree Healer.* Toronto: University of Toronto Press, 1989.

LEGISLATION

Bill C-39, The Yukon Act (LS-422E) 2002.

Constitution Act, 1982, Being Schedule B to the Canada Act 1982 (UK), 1982, c. 11, s. 25.

Midwifery Act, 1991, S.O. 1991, c. 31.

The Non-Smokers Health Protection Act, R.S.C. 1985, c. 15.

Regulated Health Professions Act, 1991, S.O. 1991, c. 18.

Smoke-Free Ontario Act, S.O. 1994, c. 10.

Royal Proclamation of 1763, R.S.C. 1985, App. II, No. 1.

The Tobacco Reduction Act, S.A. 2005, c. T-3.8.

The Tobacco Control Act, S.A. 2001, c. T-14.

PART 2

CREATING THE VISION FOR A NEW NATION-TO-NATION RELATIONSHIP

CHAPTER 3
ADDRESS BY RENÉ DUSSAULT[1]

Co-Chair, Royal Commission on Aboriginal Peoples

First of all, to say as we say in Quebec, *bonjour tout le monde*. Hello everybody. I would like to recognize three of my fellow commissioners who are present, Mary Sillett, Viola Robinson, and Peter Meekison. Also, thank you to the organizers of the conference, both Marlene Brant Castellano and Frederic Wien. It wouldn't have happened without their hard work and dedication. Thank you.

It's my pleasure to be with you on this occasion, to acknowledge and celebrate the renewal of the information legacy of the Royal Commission on Aboriginal Peoples. I think if the commission had been created today, we would have talked about "Indigenous peoples," but then it was the Royal Commission on Aboriginal Peoples.

When we published our final report the 21st of November 1996, we called on governments and the Canadian people to make a twenty-year commitment to fundamental change in the relationship with Aboriginal peoples. We argued that the tragically flawed relationship that had become entrenched for over more than a century had inflicted great cost on Aboriginal peoples themselves and great losses on Canadian society as a whole. We proposed that transformative change was possible and that, within twenty years, strategic investments and support of self-determination would result in transformative change.

To put it bluntly, that hasn't happened as we imagined. Twenty years after the publication of the RCAP report, it remains just as urgent that Canada re-examine the foundations of its relationship with Aboriginal peoples. Twenty years, or even a century, appears to be a short period of time in relation to history. But for those people who lived their lives—those Aboriginal peoples who now live their lives in communities and in cities—twenty years is an awfully long time.

In 2015, the Truth and Reconciliation Commission acknowledged that the RCAP report urged Canadians to begin a national process of reconciliation that would have set the country on a bold new path. By and large, apart from being readily welcomed into the courts, where the report dramatically influenced the development of Aboriginal law over the past twenty years, much of what RCAP had to say was ignored. There are exceptions. But the fundamental one—that we change the relationship—hasn't happened yet.

Now, with the work of the Truth and Reconciliation Commission stimulating a new conversation, Canada has a rare second chance to seize the opportunity for reconciliation, a renewed, mutually respectful reconciliation between people.

I would like to remind you that ten years after the publication of the RCAP report in 2006, there was a conference like this one in Saskatoon. I had an opportunity to talk about the vision of the Royal Commission on Aboriginal Peoples or about what I called the "soul" of the report. It could appear strange to talk about the soul of a report, but when you put aside the technicalities (and they are very important because they are the main obstacle to attaining progress) what is left is the vision and the "soul" of the new relationship.

I wanted to convey at that time—and I'm quoting from what I said ten years ago—that, "to the extent that it addresses the fundamental covenant for a relationship between Canada and Aboriginal peoples, development of the national policy of reconciliation is something which we could all be proud of. It is a central facet of Canada's heritage, and the Royal Commission proposed it be developed with the full participation of the federal government, the provinces and territories, and Aboriginal peoples." In short, RCAP goes purposely to the fabric of what Canada is and could be.

I applaud the initiative of Library and Archives Canada in making available, in a publicly accessible format, the RCAP publications, hearing transcripts, research reports, and intervenor briefs. Our final report distills our findings and recommendations on a comprehensive set of issues. The supplementary documents reveal how we arrived at those conclusions. The process of how we fulfilled our mandate is described in Appendix C, volume 5, of our final report.

The commission's hearings were fundamental to illuminating important issues and the vision and initiative of people at the grassroots—pointing to a way forward. Presentations and briefs by Aboriginal and non-Aboriginal organizations revealed the readiness for a new relationship and the obstacles to achieving it. Community-based research explored political and economic development in communities and the resurgence of traditional knowledge and cultures. Research by Aboriginal and non-Aboriginal experts examined law and policy in the Canadian context and the possibility for structural change.

As I've already said, the realities of Aboriginal life have not changed significantly in the past twenty years. The calls to action urged by the Truth and Reconciliation Commission repeatedly echo the analysis and recommendations of the RCAP report and special publications. The avenues to reconciliation mapped by RCAP remain largely unexplored and untested.

I believe that the body of work of the Royal Commission on Aboriginal Peoples represents the wisdom of Aboriginal and non-Aboriginal people of goodwill, responding to the challenge of living together with justice and respect. I hope that the RCAP legacy will come to be known and belong to successive generations of Canadians, both Aboriginal and non-Aboriginal, Indigenous and non-Indigenous peoples, helping to share a common future. Many thanks to the organizers and supporters of Sharing the Land, Sharing a Future, and for making this, in quotes, "historic moment" possible.

NOTES

1   René Dussault, address to Sharing the Land, Sharing a Future: A National Forum on Reconciliation, Winnipeg, 2–4 November 2016.

CHAPTER 4

ADDRESS BY GEORGES ERASMUS[1]

Co-Chair, Royal Commission on Aboriginal Peoples

Unfortunately, I will not be able to attend this conference on Sharing the Land, Sharing the Future,[2] which is a celebration twenty years later of the Royal Commission on Aboriginal Peoples. My situation just does not allow me to attend this wonderful conference.

I want to send greetings to everybody that's going to be there, and I wish you a wonderful conference. I feel a bit of regret that I will not be able to see commissioners and staff who worked with me during the RCAP process. I must say it was a wonderful experience in my life. It was very intense, hard work.

I remember being up at four and five o'clock in the morning going through copies of the next chapters that we were going to deal with in our meetings—combing through every last little word. What a wonderful team we had as commissioners, and the staff, to me, were absolutely wonderful. So I want to send thanks to all the commissioners and staff who are there in Winnipeg.

I want also to recognize the work that was done by the Truth and Reconciliation Commission. I've looked at your report and followed your work, obviously, and attended a few of the events. I want to thank you for the work that you've done, and obviously it's going to carry on. The reconciliation work that needs to be done is extremely important.

In relation to the impact of the Royal Commission on Aboriginal Peoples twenty years later, the question is whether it is still relevant. Should it just be forgotten, should it be like another report, gathering dust? I find that it is still amazingly current; it is still fundamentally important.

One of my recent jobs was for twelve years being the chief negotiator of the Dehcho here in the Northwest Territories. And it's amazing how often, even at that table, the work of the Royal Commission played a role there. For instance, one of the impacts we had two years ago was that the alternatives to extinguishment we had recommended for the comprehensive claims process all of a sudden were fully implemented. We had had a partial implementation previously. The Dehcho up here had fought to find a way to have an agreement that did not extinguish their rights, but unfortunately it had a release at the end of it, and that particular right was actually extinguished.

A couple of years ago the Stephen Harper government said "we're doing a review on comprehensive claims, do you have any suggestions for changes?" And that was one of the areas we participated in, wanting to get rid of the back-end release. We wanted to have a complete, unadulterated recognition clause that had been recommended by the Royal Commission on Aboriginal Peoples. Lo and behold, the government actually recognized it, and we put it into the Dehcho agreement.

So the RCAP report continues to be a living document. There are many examples of how it impacts everyday life. With the current federal government now saying they're prepared to do something, I think it's very important for Canadians and Aboriginal people to participate in that, because what I've learned by being in politics most of my life is that politicians only move when they have no option.

I have not seen very often genuine leadership from the hearts and from the ethics of politicians. Usually, their goal is to get re-elected. Aboriginal policies, Indigenous policies, have never really been an election issue. Even though Canadians have always supported Canadian governments to do more and to do the right thing, it's never been an election issue. You're not going to lose an election, usually, because you haven't implemented an Aboriginal issue.

My experience has been you need to force and strong-arm governments. You have to cajole if that's going to work. You have to sweet-talk them if that's necessary, but if not then you need to take to the streets, and you need to get the support of Canadians. The more support you can get, the better it is.

We had to do that back in the '70s when we wanted a comprehensive claims policy that had both land and governance included in it. After many years of effort, we ended up with a policy that had both governance and land.

So I think that the document is still relevant—its major recommendations for land, governance, dealing with social issues, dealing with young people now, so that we have Aboriginal people who are participating fully in Canadian society. It can still be implemented. It still is as relevant today as it was when we printed it twenty years ago.

I wish you a wonderful conference, and I look forward to the results of this gathering. Thank you. *Mahsi cho*. Good luck.

NOTES

1   The editors gratefully acknowledge the contribution of Dr. Michael DeGagné, president of Nipissing University, for arranging and conducting the interview with Georges Erasmus and for his permission to include these remarks in this volume.

2   Georges Erasmus, video address to Sharing the Land, Sharing a Future: A National Forum on Reconciliation, Winnipeg, 2–4 November 2016.

CHAPTER 5

ADDRESS BY PERRY BELLEGARDE[1]

National Chief, Assembly of First Nations

I am very happy to be here, and I acknowledge the Creator for another beautiful day. To all my relatives, I greet you all in a humble, respectful way. I acknowledge the Treaty 1 territory whose ancestral lands we gather on and the homeland of our Métis brothers and sisters in this territory.

After twenty years, what's happened? What are the next steps here in 2016 and beyond?

In your title, Sharing the Land, Sharing a Future, it really comes down to that. I start off by noting that we Indigenous peoples are about 4.5 percent of Canada's 35 million people. We have 634 First Nations right across Canada, a million and a half people, but we say we're not ethnic minorities, we are Indigenous peoples.

As Indigenous peoples, we have one of the most important rights, and that's the inherent right to self-determination. We say "nations make treaties, treaties do not make nations." We have inherent rights, Aboriginal rights, and we have treaty rights. One of the most fundamental rights is that right to self-determination.

We have the five requirements for that right to be recognized. We have our own lands; we have our own laws; we have our own languages; we have our own identifiable peoples; and [we have] our own identifiable forms of government. Because of that inherent right, we're able to [engage] in a nation-to-nation relationship with the Crown. When we look at it, though, we've never had [the treaties] honoured or implemented according to the spirit and intent, so there's work to do in that area.

The Royal Commission on Aboriginal Peoples twenty years ago did a monumental piece of work. But we were trained as Indigenous peoples not only to go to RCAP. Start with the Hawthorn Report, then get into the Penner Report, then get into the RCAP Report and now the TRC Report. Those four reports over the years, in some way, shape or have formed policy and legislation that affects Indigenous peoples and Indigenous rights in Canada.

What do we mean by nation to nation?

I apply it to myself at Little Black Bear, where I grew up, a member of the Cree Nation or Cree Assiniboine. We put the Creator on top, then the people. Because of the *Corbière* decision,[2] everybody on and off reserve gets to vote at Little Black Bear for the chief and council. Little Black Bear belongs to the File Hills Agency, five reserves that work together. We belong to a tribal council—eleven reserves that work together—the File Hills Qu'Appelle Tribal Council.

So Little Black Bear, File Hills Agency, FHQ Tribal Council, and then Little Black Bear belong to the Federation of Saskatchewan Indian Nations, seventy-four reserves working together in Saskatchewan. Little Black Bear [also] belongs to the Assembly of First Nations. Six hundred and thirty-four First Nations. AFN's on the bottom, it's not on [the] top. Little Black Bear entered into treaty in 1874, September 15th, on that very special land at Fort Qu'Appelle. We're part of the Cree Assiniboine Nation. There's your constant on that side. That happened in 1874—Treaty Number 4.

The dialogue and discussion and debate now among ourselves is "what is the vehicle that will take us beyond this Indian Act that was put in place in 1876?" I'm talking about my own personal experience, what I know from years spent with our Elders and our old people, their teachings.

What's constant for us? Your nationhood and the treaty, those are the constants.

Why are they constants? Because of that sanctity of contract, that sanctity of agreement. When our old people entered into treaty, it was through ceremony. It's a covenant with the Creator and all of our grandmothers and grandfathers. I'm a believer in treaty areas coming together.

So how do we move beyond the Indian Act? Exert First Nations laws and First Nations jurisdiction. Are we organized by nations now? Some are moving down that road. How do you get back to your nationhood status as the Ojibwe Anishinaabeg Nations, Anishinaabemowin, the Haudenosaunee, the Blackfoot Confederacy, the Mohawk peoples, the Mi'kmaq peoples, the Dene peoples? Those are our nations and our treaty territories.

There are trends now moving across Canada getting toward what I just described. We have an opportunity here in Canada with this government. You can see it reflected in the Throne Speech of last year and reflected in this Liberal government in terms of priorities going forward. We influenced that. We did our job in terms of advocacy and making sure our priorities are front and centre on the agenda. Now there are five priorities that this prime minister is going to work on collaboration with Indigenous peoples.

Number one, the [National] Inquiry [into Missing and Murdered Indigenous Women and Girls]. We pushed for the inquiry, and we see that happening. I say this as well: you don't have to wait two years for the recommendations to come from this inquiry. Federal governments, provincial governments, big cities, even some First Nations governments can make investments in daycare and safe shelters and wellness shelters—all of the above. Budget for it, and prioritize it accordingly right now.

Number two, the government said they will implement all the TRC calls to action. The prime minister said this to the chiefs-in-assembly last December. He said all ninety-four of the TRC's calls to action will be honoured and implemented. There is one that really stands out for me, and that's the United Nations Declaration on the Rights of Indigenous Peoples. We were all very pleased when Canada went to the United Nations and Minister [Carolyn] Bennett and Minister Jody Wilson-Raybould said we will accept the UN declaration without qualification. But then in July Minister Jody Wilson-Raybould came to the AFN Annual General Assembly and said something different, that it's going to be problematic to implement the UN declaration in Canada's constitutional context. You could hear the gasp in the room. How can Canada on one hand say "without qualification" and then have the minister of justice, the attorney general of Canada, say it's going to be difficult to implement? We're saying we've got to find common ground—that balance—because it is the pathway for reconciliation in Canada. We held up Rachel Notley in Alberta when she said Alberta's going to find ways to implement the UN declaration. That's one premier showing leadership. Then you have Romeo Saganash's Private Member's Bill [C-262] on the UN declaration, which is a framework. It can be done. The UN declaration is very important. The right to self-determination is in there. The UN declaration is a very important pathway to reconciliation.

The third piece is lifting the 2 percent funding cap and work[ing] toward long-term, sustainable, predictable funding. Those are the words of the prime minister. That 2 percent funding cap never kept up with inflation. It's not based on needs, not based on total membership or population. It was a cap on growth, it was a cap on opportunity, a cap on potential. That's supposed to be gone. The Liberals put $8.4 billion [for Indigenous people, programs, and services] in the last federal budget—unprecedented. The prime minister's vision and our vision [are] large, and the minister of Indian affairs' vision is large. But the government bureaucracy's vision is small. They still have ineffective and inefficient policies and programs for getting that money out. That's what we've got to fix. We've got a fiscal MOU with Minister Carolyn Bennett, working toward long-term, sustainable, predictable funding. Proper inflationary adjustments and proper escalators are part of that. We have INAC sitting with us, but we need Treasury Board, not just INAC. Our relationship is with the Crown. TRC recommendations go to the Crown [and] all the different departments.

Investment in education was the fourth commitment, to make sure that our young ones are able to walk in both worlds, to make sure that they get strong math and science, literacy and numeracy, strong schools, proper infrastructure, good teacher salaries on one hand, but equally important are investments in languages and our ceremonies and our traditions—who we are. Our young ones walk in both worlds, and they have to walk in both worlds. Our Elders always told us [to] walk in balance. You know who you are, where you come from, and that's important. Because, after years of residential schools, I don't just say cultural genocide, I say it's genocide. You wonder why our young ones are looking at suicide? There [are many] factors [to] that, but part of it is identity loss [and] language loss. Then, on top of that, the poverty [and] the overcrowded housing. Getting the pride back is essential and supporting two systems of education. It's not only on reserve now. Portability rights, [the] portability of services and programs—50 percent of our people reside off the reserves. You have to look at both strategies going forward.

The fifth commitment: a federal law review. Review all these laws that were unilaterally imposed—C-38, C-45, C-51, C-26, C-10—which impact on inherent rights and treaty rights in a negative way and don't respect our jurisdiction. We've also said it's not just the federal law review. It's got to be policy as well because there are four policies that still remain in effect that are based on termination of rights, not recognition of rights and title. There's the Comprehensive Claims policy—it's outdated. The Specific Claims policy is outdated. The Additions to Reserve policy is outdated. And the Inherent Right to Self-Government policy is totally outdated. So it's a federal law and policy review because the judicial branch of government is saying very clearly through 234 Supreme Court wins regarding treaty and Aboriginal rights—the *Tsilhqot'in* case, the *Williams* case, and so on, all these cases are saying this. But the legislative [branch] and the executive branch of government do not keep up with what the judicial branch is saying.

Five commitments from the prime minister to our chiefs-in-assembly. Out of the five, you could say three of them are moving, but two aren't: the TRC ninety-four calls to action really aren't moving, and the federal law and policy review is not moving. We're hoping that, within the next month and a half, there'll be an announcement from the Liberal government that there's a plan and process for those.

Two other things are a priority. One is the revitalization and the rejuvenation of our Indigenous languages. At one time, there were over 300 Indigenous languages prior to contact on Turtle Island. We have fifty-eight left. We have to focus on the revitalization of our languages. No more should they be in the shadow of English and French. No more should we be accepting the myth that this great country called Canada was founded just on two founding nations. No more, and so the same with languages. If you want reconciliation, it's important that we work toward the rejuvenation and revitalization of our Indigenous languages. That's one of the key elements [of] the inherent right to self-determination. We can't do our ceremonies in English. You have to do it in Cree, you have to do it in Blackfoot, you have to do it in Ojibwe, you have to do it in Mi'kmaq.

I went to a Mohawk longhouse, a ceremony, and I've been to a potlatch ceremony, and I sundanced for the last thirty years. When we talk about unity and how you can bring about unity among so many different nations, it's ceremony. I'll go to your ceremonies, you come to our ceremonies.

Languages are vital. If this government would spend just a small fraction of the resources, human and financial, as they spent in terminating our languages, we'd have progress. So that's another big focus: language. Studies have shown that, when a young First Nations person is fluent in their language, they're more successful in school and therefore more successful in life. Even that piece is an investment in success, in human capital, [in the] revitalization of our Indigenous languages.

The seventh priority is processes to move beyond the Indian Act. [There are] ninety-five self-government tables right now that Indian Affairs funds. Treaty 3 has been united for many, many years [in] saying "we want to engage the Crown now for treaty implementation [and] treaty enforcement." Treaty 3 is working together. A tribal council can't do this work. A provincial-territorial organization, a PTO can't do this work. AFN can't do this work. Treaty territories can do this work—our nations. So Treaty 3 is working together.

Treaty 9 in northern Ontario is working together. Treaty 4, where I'm from, is working together. It's the only collectively held reserve in Canada. All thirty-four First Nations that entered into that treaty work together; they're looking at a process. We even had the governor general come out this past September, because September 15th, 1874, is when we entered into treaty. Every September we have a Treaty 4 gathering.

We're all treaty people. To the lawyers, our ancestors don't understand those words *cede, surrender,* and *relinquish.* We said we'd share to the depth of a plow. We'll share the land. That principle of peaceful coexistence, the mutual respect between our peoples, we'll always put that at the forefront.

Treaty 4, Treaty 3, Treaty 9, the Robinson Huron Treaties, and other ones. People think there are no treaties in British Columbia. Well, there are treaties in British Columbia. The Douglas Treaties on Vancouver Island want to work together to look at treaty implementation, treaty enforcement, and moving beyond the Indian Act. There are certain nations that want to get together, like the Mi'kmaq Nation in Nova Scotia, who are looking at ways to move beyond the Indian Act. Nation to nation, treaty territories, moving beyond the Indian Act—that's the federal landscape.

Internationally, in 2017, what's going to happen? Internationally, there's the UN Declaration on the Rights of Indigenous Peoples and all the work at the United Nations. And internationally, there's a very important person we're trying to get to come to Canada: Pope Francis. Why? Two reasons. The Catholic Church is the only church that has not formally apologized to the survivors of the residential schools. We want that apology to be made. The second reason is we want him to make the declaration that the doctrine of discovery and that concept of *terra nullius* are illegal and racist doctrines. That's the push. It's about your theme, Sharing the Land. Little Black Bear First Nation is defined by the government as federal Crown land set aside for the use and benefit of Indians. I don't believe that, but that's how it's defined. First Nations are on 0.2 percent of the land base in Canada; 99.8 percent has been taken up for settlement already. So it's very important for the pope to come because that doctrine of discovery is how the Crown gained title to the land.

We have lots of work to do on reconciliation at the international level, including Foreign Protection and Promotion Agreements, the Trans Pacific Partnership, and the Foreign Investor Protector Agreement (FIPA) and all the international trade agreements. It is offensive to Indigenous peoples when Canada goes to the world and says "Canada's open for business. We have oil, coal, potash, and uranium. We have timber, we have water." From an Indigenous person's perspective, if we're not involved in any way, shape, or form meaningful when these international treaties are made, it is completely disrespectful. Even on the international file, there's ongoing work on all those streams.

Provincially, I meet with the premiers. We can't ignore the provinces. Education, health care, and social services were offloaded to the provinces in 1961. I meet the premiers, and here are the points I raise:

- Number one, premiers, you've got to meet with the chiefs and leadership in your respective boundaries on a regular basis. Establish a bilateral process, call it whatever you want—intergovernmental affairs, tier-one, tier-two process—I don't care what you call it, but establish that process to build relationships. Here in Manitoba, the sixty-six chiefs should be meeting with the premier here and cabinet on a regular basis. Same thing in every province.
- Number two, on the education system, change your curriculums. That's in RCAP, that's in [the] TRC. Teach about residential schools so that every school, from kindergarten to grade twelve, public school, catholic school, all the school systems teach the impacts of the residential schools. Treaty and Aboriginal rights should be taught. Teach the impacts of the Indian Act. All these things have to be taught in the school system, and schools have a role to play in the revitalization of Indigenous languages.

I hold up the Northwest Territories. They're the only territory or province that recognizes Indigenous languages as founding languages. The eleven Dene languages in [the] NWT are recognized as founding languages. That should be happening in every other province, especially in the year of reconciliation.

Then we talk to the premiers about the economy. If you want economic certainty and economic stability, then establish the tables to include Indigenous peoples. Before you build anything, you build a respectful relationship with Indigenous peoples. That way you'll prevent the lawsuit blockades and prevent the other kinds of blockades if you involve Indigenous peoples in a respectful way. If you don't, there will be conflict.

I also ask them to do this simple policy change: before they issue a licence or permit to any industry operating in the provincial boundaries, that company, that CEO, that chairman of the board [had] better demonstrate that they have a plan to include Indigenous peoples for procurement, for employment opportunities, for revenue sharing, and, if they don't, don't issue them a licence or permit. This will create strategic partnerships.

The last piece on the premiers is that they have different intergovernmental affairs processes. [There's the] federal, provincial, territorial, [and] Indigenous leaders' process which Minister Bennett chairs currently with the Ontario government, and we attend. Then there's the Council of the Federation, where the premiers meet on an annual basis. Then there are first ministers' meetings where the prime minister chairs. There are three intergovernmental affairs processes. [The] AFN puts forward our priorities and advocates for action.

One important example is child and family services, child welfare. It's a priority of Minister Bennett. It's a priority because the Canadian Human Rights Tribunal made the determination that there is discrimination and racism when it comes to child care on reserve. That has to be fixed. A motion was passed in Parliament. It's going to happen.

But that's one piece of the problem. We've got to have the provincial systems fixed as well. We also have to have First Nations jurisdiction recognized for looking after our children. I told the chiefs, if you don't want the provincial Child and Family Services Act applying to you, then create your own piece of legislation and occupy the field. If we don't start occupying the field in terms of our own laws and our own jurisdiction, then other governments will still have their acts applied, whether it be a federal piece of legislation or a provincial piece of legislation. Occupy the field, and create your own laws. Create your own Child and Family Services Act. Occupy the field. Create your own First Nations Matrimonial Real Property Act, and occupy the field. Occupy the field, because if you don't other legislation will apply.

Fix the provincial systems for children—we have 40,000 children, Aboriginal children, First Nations children, in care—not acceptable. That's linked to missing and murdered Indigenous girls. It's linked to child exploitation. It's linked to so many things. So fix the system on and off reserve. I've said to the premiers I'm not going to come to these meetings anymore just for a photo opportunity and nothing gets done. Let's get something done. So we're going to focus on children, focus on overhauling and fixing the child welfare systems. There should be announcements in every province soon that there's a process on reserve and there's a plan and collaboration of work off reserve. That's child and family services.

There are other issues like revenue sharing, but my message to the premiers and to the federal government is that, wherever there's a table, we need Indigenous voices there. We can't be excluded anymore. We need to be involved. Our numbers are counted in those fiscal transfers to the provinces, transfers for established programs (EPF) and other transfers. Our numbers are used, so where are we? How are we involved in every province and territory as Indigenous peoples? Do we have Indigenous peoples on the health-care boards? Do we have Indigenous peoples on all the school boards? There is work to do.

So, friends and relatives, I wanted to give a little bit of an overview in terms of what's going on locally, regionally, nationally, and internationally. Our efforts as Indigenous peoples again are going to strive toward self-determination. Going forward now, there's a movement that on July 1st we're going to mark 150 years of Canada. Then on July 2nd we're going to get together and say what are the next 150 years going to look like? How are the next 150 years going to be shaped and framed for our children and grandchildren so that there really is a country that's respectful of diversity? That there really is a country that's respectful of the Indigenous peoples' contribution to this land and this country? It's our children and grandchildren that are going to write that story. I think it's going to be a great story. Thank you.

NOTES

1   Perry Bellegarde, address to Sharing the Land, Sharing a Future: A National Forum on Reconciliation, Winnipeg, 2–4 November 2016.

2   *Corbière v. Canada (Minister of Indian and Northern Affairs)*, [1999] 2 SCR 203.

CHAPTER 6
ADDRESS BY NATAN OBED[1]

President, Inuit Tapiriit Kanatami

Nakumiik, everyone, I'm Natan Obed. I'm the president of Inuit Tapiriit Kanatami, a national representational organization for Canada's 60,000 Inuit. I wanted to first recognize the elected leaders in the room and our Elders but also the commissioners for the Royal Commission on Aboriginal Peoples, specifically in relation to Inuit Mary Sillett. I want to thank her for the contributions she has made over her lifetime to advance Inuit issues. She's also a former president of Inuit Tapiriit Kanatami. At the time, it was called the Inuit Tapirisat of Canada.

So I want to recognize not only Mary but all of you who have done work on the advancement of Indigenous peoples in this country. It is a long and hard road and one that requires not only intellect and dedication but also a sense of eternal optimism that just about no other people in any other profession have to have in order to keep going.

I want to start with a bit of a story because I want to talk a little bit about what drives us to keep going and why we are still fighting in the way that we are. I grew up in Labrador in what is now Nunatsiavut. I was raised by a single mother of three with an older sister and a younger brother. We grew up in poverty. We had nothing for most of my childhood, and I was enriched by my community and also by the love from my mother. But we struggled, and whenever my mother got a little bit of money you would think that she would be thinking about rent or food for the next two weeks or clothes for us, paying the heat, things like that. But when you're in poverty and you're a parent—and this is something I've sort of understood over time—in that moment you want to show your love for your kids. You want to give them something that they don't usually have.

And so in the moment where she would get a little bit of money, often we would go to the store, and we would get an ice cream cone, or we would get a small treat, or perhaps she would get me a hockey stick that she knew that I really wanted. I relate that to this because I feel like with the work that we do, every ten years or so, there's a big initiative. There is something that gives us hope, and so for people who have been marginalized in Canada, [who rarely] see the end of the tunnel, and all we see is poverty and inequity, there come along these times, these periods of hope. Still we live with immense challenges in our communities.

Our median income in Inuit Nunangat is $60,000 less than non-Inuit who live in Inuit Nunangat. But for the Royal Commission on Aboriginal Peoples, or for the Kelowna process, or for [the] Truth and Reconciliation Commission, we gathered together. We talked about what we can do. We imagined a new future. But in the same way, we also knew in the back[s] of our minds that what is going to come perhaps isn't what we need.

We live in the moment sometimes, and I think [this is] why people are here in this room. It's not because I think that you believe that we somehow can change all of what needs to be changed in the next year. It's just this recognition that we keep moving on and that we take what we can get. We are excited about the fact that we still have optimism, even though we know that the challenges sometimes are so much larger than we can overcome ourselves. In many ways, I am that person who is trying to provide for people, all the while knowing that the resources that we have at hand are not the resources that we need to have a successful, sustainable, loving society with all the things that we know we want to give to all of our people. But we still have to move on.

And so when I look at the twenty-year commitment—and this is the literal book that is on the shelf, right—[I look] at the Inuit Tapiriit Kanatami office. When I went to university, I studied the Labrador land claim process, and so I first went through this set of books at the ITK library in 1999, all five volumes of the RCAP report. But what have we done as a society? What have governments done? What changes have been made because of the Royal Commission? I would imagine that, in an evaluation context, there are many things that have happened that would not have happened without the commission. The very fact that these volumes exist [means that] students can go through and read them in their complexity, in their eloquent way that they've described the reality of that time, and the recommendations about how our society moves forward, and how reconciliation happens, and how our self-determination happens will stand the test of time.

A lot of the work that I've done in my career as an advocate for Inuit in thinking about the creation of poverty reduction strategies in Nunavut, or suicide prevention strategies on the Nunavut and national levels, has taken the long view. Perhaps in some time there will be an awakening. We will think not just in the present but also of all the things that we've cumulatively done, bringing them all together and understanding the amount of time, effort, patience, and knowledge that's contained within them, and we will use all of the assets that we have to move forward.

There's amnesia within our government structures, and it isn't just in the federal government or our provinces or territories. It is also within our Indigenous organizations and people's lives. The cumulative efforts of entire organizations for three to five years can be wiped out by a next round of politicians or a politician that comes in and just isn't interested or ha[s] an alternative view. If you think about how we're going to move forward with the Truth and Reconciliation Commission, or the implementation of the UN Declaration on the Rights of Indigenous Peoples, or the mandate of this federal Liberal government, we have to somehow break that cycle of amnesia, of planned obsolescence of our work and our toil.

I was a part of the Kelowna process, the year and a half that led up to the Kelowna Accord. It was my job to convene a number of the Inuit-specific policy discussions on housing, on the relationship, on a number of different things that then would ultimately make up some of the components of [the] Kelowna [Accord]. A lot of people questioned me at the time, saying "It's not worth my time, I'm not going to fly for two days and go to a meeting for a day and go back home, and I'm not going to spend a week of my life to talk about something that I know isn't going to make a difference." It was my job to say "No, it's going to make a difference. It's different this time. Yes, RCAP has been on a shelf, but perhaps this is a time when we can revive some of those principles or those recommendations, and we can incorporate them into [the] Kelowna [Accord] and this new relationship, and I believe in Prime Minister Martin. I know that this is different, this is a different time." And that's how I got a lot of Inuit from the four Inuit regions, from across Inuit Nunangat, our Canadian Arctic, into the room to discuss policy issues with that government at that time.

These were people who had already gone through a similar process and given their time and provided the same perspective a decade before. Here we are a decade later, and I'm calling on my Inuit leadership across Inuit Nunangat now in my role as president to say "You should believe in this new government. This is a point in time that is exciting, that is going to change our reality forever." In my head, I'm thinking "If this time things don't go the way that we want them to, a lot of the things that have been promised to us—and not things that I put in the prime minister's mouth or the minister of Indigenous and northern affairs—all link into a lifetime of work by people who want to move our societies forward." I think it's lost on a lot of the leaders in this country that they're not the first people to pretend that they care about Indigenous people.

It becomes a part of a political process that they feel that they can come in and be our saviours or to change this relationship but not necessarily understand that we have been working in a patient, thoughtful, generous way with all levels of government for a very long time with virtually nothing to show for it.

I recognize that, when my father was growing up, it was not something to be proud of to be Indigenous, that [many] people who were Indigenous who could pass themselves off as non-Indigenous were quiet. Perhaps they didn't want to be mocked and ridiculed about the colour of their skin or their customs or their language, and so today I'm very happy to see the pride that Indigenous people have in Canada, the fact that we can go into any room or into any institution and be respected for who we are without having to feel as though, when we walk into that room, we're going to be disrespected. The fact that we hope for respect and that we expect it is something new, and we should acknowledge it.

There's still massive racism in this country, and it's something that we still have to fight against. But the fact that we expect equality, that we expect that when we walk into any room we'll be treated as a human being, that's actually something that's pretty new.

I do want to recognize that we're not in the place that we were. But at the same time, we have never really been successful in achieving what we need to do for our societies: education, housing, health care, governance, implementation of land claim agreements, and infrastructure. These are all things that we have been working toward. In our community histories in Inuit Nunangat, there's never been a time where we have housing sustainability or housing equity. We have 40 percent overcrowding in our regions. We have a 35 percent core housing need for our regions compared to 12 percent of all Canadians. We have a graduation rate that is much lower than all of Canada. We have less than 30 percent of our people that have a grade twelve education between the ages of twenty-five and sixty-four, compared to 65 percent for non-Indigenous Canadians. We have a tuberculosis rate that is still 250 times the rate of all others that are born in Canada. We have massive social inequity, and we are in a situation now where we have evidence.

We've worked through these challenges. We have calls to action, we have recommendations in the Royal Commission on Aboriginal Peoples report, we have supposedly a renewed relationship with this federal government. For Inuit, we've called for a renewed Inuit-to-Crown relationship which is different [from] the nation-to-nation [relationship]. The prime minister has used Inuit-to-Crown, but it has not stuck.

We are a small component of the Indigenous population in Canada, but we have a very specific place, and we have a specific place within the Constitution. If you think about our small size of 60,000 [people], but then you think about the space Inuit occupy, we co-manage 35 percent of Canada's land mass and over 50 percent of its coastline. We are the reason why Canada can assert that it is an Arctic nation. We provide sovereignty to Canada in the human sense. These are not small contributions. So, no matter how many people we have or how few people we have, social equity should be for everyone.

In the path to governance in this renewed relationship, the national Indigenous leaders met with the prime minister in December of last year. The prime minister asked the question "How do we create success?" I thought that it was a genuine question, and so I answered that it is going to be through a structured relationship because there are Liberal platform promises, priorities of this federal government; there are also priorities of Inuit Tapiriit Kanatami, the national representational body for Canadian Inuit. Luckily, there's a large space in the middle where our priorities overlap.

So what do partners do? They work together on shared priorities, but they have to do it in a structured way. So what's missing from this new supposed relationship is a structured relationship. We still have a federal government that is dictating to Indigenous people what success looks like, how we'll get there, and how much money it will take. It doesn't have to be that way, and the country will be better for it if there was a true partnership.

In January of this year, I wrote a letter to the prime minister and outlined an Inuit-to-Crown Partnership Committee which would have four senior cabinet ministers from the federal side and our four land claim presidents on our side. I would be a part of that as well, and the prime minister could come in once a year. So it would be a committee to set a shared agenda, to work through the issues as they come, to direct the work, and also to evaluate and be responsible for the outcomes of the work.

There's no answer and no counteroffer from the federal government about that proposal.[2] This is supposedly [a] new relationship. What is the new relationship? Let's figure it out. Almost a year has passed now since that letter was sent, and there has not been one discussion about what Inuit looked at as a draft proposal, no dialogue. So is that how partners interact with one another? No, it is not, or if it is that's a very dysfunctional relationship.

The key point here is that, before we achieve shared success, we need to have a structure in place that understands the relationship that we have but also respects us as people and respects the UN Declaration on the Rights of Indigenous Peoples, respects our constitutional status, [and] respects our land claim agreements that we have with Canada. That would create an environment in which we could then work together, and it doesn't matter which government is in power, there would be this relationship that is expected and normal.

Right now we're still working in the ways that we've always worked, with the federal system. We are at the pleasure of whatever ideas that the federal government has about how we come to meetings, when we're asked to leave the room, what policies are going to affect us, and what the legislative agenda and process [are]. We're playing in the margins still when the rhetoric of this new government talks about us being partners. We all know in this room what that means when we think about it in our own personal lives, and I think with the challenges now we need to respect what that means from an institutional perspective.

I'll close just by talking a bit about the resiliency of Indigenous people and specifically Inuit. We've been through a lot. If you think about the last forty to fifty years, we're just getting around to the concept that the land that we've lived in from time immemorial isn't necessarily ours and that we would then have to do land use and occupancy studies to even get to the point to then go through comprehensive land claim agreements with the government of Canada.

Then we had to explain to our people that our land is not necessarily owned by us, that it's something called "Aboriginal title to our land," which is a lower standard of ownership. We had to explain that we don't actually own any of the resources beneath our lands and [that] we have to negotiate for even percentages of investment or profit from projects that happen on our territories. We had to explain that we only recently were allowed the opportunity to work toward self-government.

We have always, throughout this process, believed in Canada. We savoured "Canadians First, First Canadians." This is a slogan that Jose Kusugak made famous in our world around the year 2002 [or] 2003, and it's something that our people believe in. We're proud Canadians. Imagine the resiliency that takes to still say that we're proud Canadians—with all the things that have happened to us, the marginalized [role] that we play within the society, and the fact that we didn't do anything to deserve the treatment that we've received from successive governments and from institutions over the past 150 years or 400 years.

So moving forward the challenge here is to take these commitments and all those things that have come from those commitments and to imagine them as one line. Imagine them as resources that we can use—that are not political in nature, that don't have expiry dates. Imagine a new world in which Indigenous people have the respect of the country. Also imagine that, when we say things like new partnerships or respecting land claim agreements or treaties, we actually mean them in a policy sense, in a governmental sense, not in the sympathetic, ad hoc, political way that we often hear in the rhetoric today. Inuit are here, wanting to work through all these challenges, not wanting to ignore our past. Inuit hope that there's the courage and determination and practicality from our partners to create this new reality. *Nakumiik.*

NOTES

1   Natan Obed, address to Sharing the Land, Sharing a Future: A National Forum on Reconciliation, Winnipeg, 2–4 November 2016.

2   Four months after this address, on 9 February 2017, a Declaration on Inuit-to-Crown Partnership was signed by the prime minister, along with the Inuit Tapiriit Kanatami, the Inuvialuit Regional Corporation, the Makivik Corporation, the Nunatsiavut Government, and Nunavut Tunngavik Incorporated. The text of the declaration can be found at https://pm.gc.ca/eng/news/2017/02/09/inuit-nunangat-declaration-inuit-Crown-partnership.

CHAPTER 7
ADDRESS BY CLÉMENT CHARTIER[1]

President, Métis National Council

I'm pleased to have the opportunity to interact on this twentieth anniversary of the Royal Commission's report. I was involved in it to varying degrees, and I believe it's important that this conference is taking place in the homeland of the Indigenous people here, including the historical Métis Nation, and I thank Marlene Brant Castellano and Fred Wien.

In any event, nation to nation, it means a lot to me, it means a lot to the people I represent, the historical Métis Nation, and that is a fact. We are a distinct people. We are a nation. We have a distinct homeland which is basically the prairie provinces, and it extends into Ontario, British Columbia, and [the] Northwest Territories and part of the northern United States. We have a flag that's 200 years old, first flown in the battle of Seven Oaks, which is now within the city of Winnipeg, on June 19th, 1816.

We have customs, traditions, clothing, foods, the Michif language, and so we have all the attributes that make a nation a nation or a people a people. Not only do we have the political consciousness, [but] we also had, and I think continue to have, the will to fight for what rightfully belongs to us.

We've done this of course in the late 1800s on the battlefields of Duck Lake, Batoche, Fish Creek, and of course in the setting up of the first provisional government of the Métis Nation here at the Red River in 1869–70, then at Batoche in 1885. Unfortunately, the military might of Canada and Great Britain was just too much for us, and of course our leader was subsequently tried and hanged on November 16th, 1885.

Having said that, the Canadian government in its wisdom, or lack of it, treated us as individuals as opposed to a collective. No treaties other than the Manitoba Act and negotiations with the Métis, no treaties with us, no collective approach. I think they did that to break our military strength and our political strength and our desire to continue our existence as a distinct people.

Of course, they didn't succeed. What they did succeed at, though, was putting in a process under their legislative regime which dispossessed us of our lands and resources. I won't get into that because it will just take too long. I just want to give you that background.

So with that we've endured now decades of being ignored, not forgotten. They didn't forget about us; they just ignored us. Because they know who we are, and they know what we can do and what we're capable of. So it was a period of ignorance or being ignored, whatever the verb is. In any event, we didn't just sit back and do nothing. Our people continued organizing in their homes and their communities, and in the 1920s, again, our political resurgence came about, and by the late 1960s, early 1970s, we again became a fairly strong force, at least in our own eyes, in terms of the Indigenous political movement in Canada.

Also in the late 1970s, we also went to the ballot box election system, and today we do have that system. We have our governments. We don't refer to ourselves as an organization. We're not a national Indigenous organization. We are—and the Métis National Council is—the government of the Métis Nation. In this province, the Manitoba Metis Federation is the government of the Métis living within this geographic area. After 1870, the provincial boundaries were created, and they basically carved up our homeland. They dissected us into what we now know as provinces. We have five governing members from Ontario to British Columbia, which together form the Métis National Council, again the government of the Métis Nation.

In 1981, along with other Indigenous peoples, we did pursue having our rights recognized and entrenched in Canada's Constitution. That came about because of politics, not because Canada really wanted to give us anything. It's because the prime minister of the day didn't have the support of eight provinces and turned to the public, including the Indigenous peoples, and we gave our support on certain conditions.

The then leader of the Native Council of Canada, Harry Daniels, was instrumental in ensuring that the Métis were mentioned, that the Métis were included in the guarantees that were promised to be put into Canada's Constitution. Hence you have, as you know, the definition of Aboriginal peoples being the First Nations, Inuit, and Métis peoples. That was a big breakthrough for us.

There was a promise of a constitutional conference to be held within one year of patriation, and that conference did take place [in] March of 1983, and again we were at a place where the Métis Nation had to retrench to get our rightful place at that constitutional table. We did through political action and also legal action because we sought an injunction against the prime minister calling the conference because the Métis people were no longer invited—because we were no longer part of the Native Council of Canada, now known as the Congress of Aboriginal Peoples. We got our accommodation, and we've been there ever since.

When it came to the Royal Commission on Aboriginal Peoples, we played, I believe, a fairly instrumental role in bringing forward the aspirations of the Métis Nation. I believe we had a fair hearing before the commission. We have no complaints about the access to the commission and the willingness of the Royal Commission to listen to us and to the positions that we took forward.

In fact, the commission did meet with the Métis Nation leadership in Saskatoon, in western Canada. It then met in Ottawa with the other Métis, whoever those were, because they had to deal with everyone. That was a reality because there are Métis, people of mixed ancestry outside of the historical Métis Nation, who refer to themselves as Métis because they are of mixed ancestry and don't necessarily fit in with any other Indigenous nation.

We were engaged in [the constitutional] process, and during the '80s we were actually heavily engaged. We attended all four [constitutional] conferences. Just a little footnote of history: I believe I'm the last remaining active politician who signed the 1983 constitutional amendments back in the day, so I've been around for a little while. Some people think [it's been] much too long, but that was the only success that we had during that constitutional process in the 1980s. In 1992, we did negotiate a side deal for the Métis Nation known as the Métis Nation Accord, which would have accommodated our land rights negotiations and our self-government negotiations. Part of the taxes we paid were going to be given to us to run our governments. So things were in place, and also [there was] an agreement that Section 91(24) of the Constitution would be amended to include all Indigenous peoples, and there were many, many amendments to the Constitution itself which would have recognized the inherent right of self-government and so on and so forth. It was a tremendous breakthrough for Indigenous people but for the Métis Nation specifically. Unfortunately, it fell with the October 1992 referendum.

Stepping back to 1983, when we went into the constitutional conference process, we said "We're going to go there not on the basis of Section 35," which recognizes Aboriginal rights and title. But that's a lesser right, at least in my view, than the right of self-determination as peoples. We went there on the basis that as a people, as a nation, we have the right to a land base and self-government, and we said that at the end of the day, if that fails, we'll fall back on Section 35. And so, with the failure of the 1992 conference, we did fall back on Section 35, and we did start defending our people as they were charged and appearing in front of the courts, and to date that has been fairly successful.

I want to go to RCAP and its final report in 1996. The chapter "Métis Perspectives" has been very useful to us. First of all, it's a great educational tool. It adequately describes our people, our history, very, very well. We've been using that in every court case that we've gone to in terms of our hunting and fishing rights. We always put it as evidence, and our experts speak to it as well. So it's been helpful in educating the courts, and it's helpful in establishing evidence that leads to the recognition of our rights. It's also been helpful in policy and political discussions. It's been a useful document.

Unfortunately, when the federal government came with its response to the Royal Commission, I believe it's called *Gathering Strength*, again the Métis were invisible. We weren't there, and of course our then leadership raised a hue and cry. Minister Goodale, who was then federal interlocutor for Métis and Non-Status Indians, went to cabinet and got a financial allocation of $8 or $9 million to deal with the Métis and the RCAP report.

We were able, through that process, to begin a consultation with our people, to come up with a definition of who are the citizens of the Métis Nation. This was very helpful. After several years of consultations, in the fall of 2002, we did come up with the criteria of who is eligible to be registered as a citizen of the Métis Nation. A year later the Supreme Court of Canada, in the *Powley* decision,[2] came up also with criteria which were fairly close. The only difference was [that] in *Powley* it's acceptance by the Métis community. In our criteria, it's acceptance by the Métis Nation. Because of the way that courts have been unfolding, the [Métis] community and the Métis Nation may mean two different things. Of course, the Métis Nation is a community, but there may be other Métis communities out there, something which the courts are grappling with at this particular time.

Out of that also came a test case fund. We initially received $200,000 a year; then it went up to $300,000. Then of course we had Harper, and then we had zero thousand after that. But in any event we were able to fight some of these cases in the courts, and we've had success. In *Powley*, it says that Métis are full-fledged, rights-bearing Aboriginal people. There is no hierarchy in rights. Métis rights are no greater than First Nations or Inuit rights or vice versa. Métis rights flow from the Métis people themselves. They're not inherited rights from their Indian forebears, and basically it's a good decision [that] sets a test for those who purport to have Section 35 rights.

We've had several cases on the Prairies, in Saskatchewan and Manitoba particularly, where the test has easily been met. In the Maritimes and in Quebec, that test thus far has not been met. There is the *Corneau* appeal in the Court of Appeal of Quebec, to be heard in December, where they're putting forward the Métis defence, and we'll see where that takes us [regarding the land rights of Métis in Quebec]. Being Métis is more than being of mixed ancestry, and it's a good thing that the court has recognized that.

So we come to the Martin era. Up until then, not much was happening in terms of the RCAP report other than the $8 or $9 million that was allocated to us. Prime Minister Martin did open up a significant space. We had a process of about a year and a half, leading to the Kelowna Accord. Again the Métis Nation was a big winner, not in terms of the amount of monies at the end of the day, but it was the recognition of our people. Also, we agreed to look at a Métis Nation economic development institute, an institute on excellence in education, and a housing authority, among other things. But of course, again, we had the federal election, and the potential progress that could have been made under Kelowna was wiped away.

At the time, Paul Martin did say that the government would move forward on the basis that Métis were also included under Section 91(24), again without any sort of amendment. So we were looking at some significant progress. Then we had of course the Harper government that came in. We lost momentum. We did sign with the Harper government a Métis Nation protocol. We had a Métis economic development symposium process. So, on economic development, we did make some progress [but] not too much.

The Supreme Court of Canada [during] the intervening years was sort of the friend of the Métis, if I can call it that. The justices had the *Cunningham* case in 2011 where they said that the Métis Nation has the right to determine its own citizenship.[3] Based on litigation by the Manitoba Metis Federation in 2013, they ruled that the action of the federal government between 1870 and 1880, or thereabouts, did not fulfill the honour of the Crown regarding the promise of 1.4 million acres to the Métis individuals in the province of Manitoba. They are now renegotiating that. Of course, we had *Daniels* in April of this year, where they said that Non-Status Indians and Métis fall within the purview of Section 91(24).[4]

Now we have the government of Mr. Trudeau, and they have a fairly good Métis policy that is being put into place. I just want to read that policy. It says "Canada must complete the unfinished work of Confederation by establishing a renewed nation-to-nation relationship with the Métis Nation, based on trust, respect and cooperation for mutual benefit. A Liberal government will work in partnership with the Métis Nation on a nation-to-nation basis to further Métis self-government,"[5] and there's a lot more to it than that.

We have met with the prime minister, and currently the Métis Nation is looking at having a Crown–Métis Nation summit with the prime minister, hopefully by the end of December. We did table a framework for reconciliation of Métis Section 35 rights, and we're still negotiating that framework. It's been a year in the making. The only difference between this government and the previous one [is that] under Minister Chuck Strahl we negotiated our Métis Nation protocol in less than forty-eight hours. This time we're going on quite a number of months, but in any event we believe we will move forward.

On intergovernmental forums, there needs to be a structural approach, as Natan Obed has said. We have to go forward on a distinctions-based approach, First Nations, Inuit, and Métis Nation. We can't get solutions unless we isolate what it is that we, as distinct peoples, are seeking and what we want to negotiate.

We've been dealing with the Council of the Federation and under them the Aboriginal Affairs Working Group since 2009. Of course, in addition to the Métis National Council, the Assembly of First Nations, and Inuit Tapiriit Kanatami, we have the Congress of Aboriginal Peoples [CAP] and the Native Women's Association of Canada [NWAC] at the table. We all bring different perspectives. We [the Métis Nation] don't refer to ourselves as an organization but as a government. I've been pushing for respectful language with the prime minister, with the premiers, and with the ministers that, when they refer to us in the future, it's "national representatives of Indigenous governments and organizations."

Intergovernmental meetings [and] intergovernmental relations should be with the national representatives of Indigenous governments. Where it's not an intergovernmental meeting, then it should be again "national representatives of Indigenous governments and organizations." In these cases, CAP and [the] Native Women's Association of Canada should be there as well to address their issues that they advocate for.

NWAC has done excellent work over the years and I believe will continue to do excellent work. I fully support NWAC as we move forward on this nation-to-nation and government-to-government basis.

We're having that kind of discussion, and in terms of the Métis Nation, this new federal-provincial-territorial-Indigenous forum, we're saying [that], unless governments respect it in the terms of reference which are being fought for by some people, unless they respect us as governments, the Métis Nation is not going to the table, because we have to make a stand somewhere. We can't be going on 1970s thinking. We have to be going with what is there today.

In conclusion, in terms of the Métis Nation, many obstacles still face us. We need to take political action and be disruptive if necessary to the integrity of our nation. [What is] foremost is our historical nation, our homeland, and we are going to be taking some strict and hard decisions on that. We need to protect the integrity of our people and our nation, and one of the things that I'm pressing forward is the adoption of a constitution which sets out our governance.

I'm also pushing that by 2020, which is the 150th anniversary of the Métis negotiating our homeland into Confederation, we establish our head of government and our national assembly here at the Red River and that we then have an embassy in Ottawa. Basically, we want to ensure that our rights are not only recognized but [also that] our people, our nation, and our citizenship [are] part of the three orders of government in this country. We'll continue to push that, and we're saying now "Let's not worry about being disruptive. Let's not worry about stepping on people's toes." [That includes] some of the people currently within the Métis National Council.

We're going to move forward. I believe that the work that was done by the Royal Commission on Aboriginal Peoples has been helpful to us on this road to recognition of our nation and of our inherent right to self-government and of our place in this great country. Thank you.

NOTES

1   Clément Chartier, address to Sharing the Land, Sharing a Future: A National Forum on Reconciliation, Winnipeg, 2–4 November 2016.

2   *R.v.Powley*, 2003, SCC.

3   *Alberta (Aboriginal Affairs and Northen Development) v. Cunningham*, 2011, SCC.

4   *Daniels v. Canada (Indian Affairs and Northern Development)*, 2016, SCC.

5   Métis Nation, "What the Parties Are Saying," 2015, http://www.Métisnation.org/media/631404/election-platforms.pdf.

CHAPTER 8
ADDRESS BY ROBERT BERTRAND[1]

National Chief, Congress of Aboriginal Peoples

Dear leaders, Elders, representatives, fellow panellists, and guests, my name is Robert Bertrand, and I'm the national chief of the Congress of Aboriginal Peoples or CAP. *J'aimerais reconnaître le territoire du Traité No. 1 et de la nation Métis représentée par la Fédération des Métis du Manitoba pour lequel nous sommes tous actuellement privilégiés de nous rencontrer ici ce matin.*

I would like also to thank Marlene [Brant] Castellano and Frederic Wien of the RCAP 20 Oversight Cmmittee for reaching out to our organization and inviting us to speak to you today on CAP's perspective on the twentieth anniversary of the Royal Commission on Aboriginal Peoples. I would also like to acknowledge Mr. Ernie Blais, the president of CAP's provincial affiliate here in Manitoba, the Indigenous Peoples Alliance of Manitoba, for attending the forum with me today.

The Congress of Aboriginal Peoples, or CAP, is one of the five national Aboriginal representative organizations recognized by the government of Canada. Founded in 1971 as the Native Council of Canada, the organization was originally established to represent the interests of Métis and Non-Status Indians. Reorganized and renamed in 1993, CAP has extended its constituency to include off-reserve Status and Non-Status Indians, Métis, and southern Inuit people and serves as the national voice for its provincial and territorial affiliate organizations.

The final RCAP report states that, "in urban centres, Aboriginal people from many nations form a minority of the population. They're not 'nations' in the way we define it, but they want a measure of self-government nevertheless—especially in relation to education, health care, economic development and protection of their culture."[2] This in many ways defines the mandate of the Congress of Aboriginal Peoples.

In reading through the RCAP report, a distinct sense of déjà vu sets in regarding current Indigenous issues, in particular when the report addresses Indigenous peoples living off reserve. Aboriginal people leave home to improve their education, look for work, or escape family violence. If they have troubles, they may find urban services difficult to penetrate, alien in spirit, and perhaps racist. Many make successful transitions, but others fall into the cracks between cultures, whether they are isolated, unemployed, or underserved. The RCAP report also notes that almost half of all the Aboriginal peoples in Canada live in urban areas. Many Canadians will find these facts surprising, and governments certainly appear to have given little thought in policy and program decisions. Whereas the report cites that in 1996 half of the Indigenous people live off reserve, today's statistics estimate that over 70 percent do so.

The Royal Commission on Aboriginal Peoples was a necessary journey into the very heart of the relationship between Indigenous people, the government of Canada, and the culture of the nation as a whole. Lasting four years, from 1992 to 1996, and culminating in a final report of 4,000 pages, with an astounding 440 recommendations, RCAP not only opened the door on the fractured state of the Indigenous people's relationship with the government, [but] it also became a benchmark that provided Indigenous organizations with the foundation from which they could build their own mandates and vision in regard to reconciliation, advocacy, and government engagement.

En nous penchant sur le CRPA plus tard, il serait facile de s'attarder au nombre de recommandations qui sont restées lettres mortes. RCAP Co-Chair Mr. Georges Erasmus proposed that there should be a comprehensive strategy over twenty years to restore social, economic, and political health to Aboriginal peoples and rebuild the relationship with all Canadians. A sense of irony cannot be lost when we hear this and stop to ask ourselves, "Has it been twenty years already?"

The complete restoration of social, economic, and political health to Indigenous peoples is still an ongoing daily issue. Our people are recorded as being represented as the worst in every socio-economic indicator according to StatsCan: the poorest, the unhealthiest, the most unemployed and underemployed, the highest incarceration rates, the highest [incidences of] family and domestic violence, and the list goes on and on.

In addition, the fundamental right of self-governance amongst our Indigenous people still needs to be addressed as a whole-of-government approach so that all sectors are addressed in negotiated agreements. As the RCAP report states, the right to self-government cannot be taken away, it cannot be given, it exists, it's inherent. It's already recognized and confirmed by Section 35 of the Constitution.

While it remains a well-worn cliché, we can either look at the current situation of Indigenous people in Canada as a glass being either half empty or half full. The theme of this RCAP anniversary is Sharing the Land, Sharing a Future: Realizing the Promise, Facing the Challenge of Reconciliation. Two words from this theme stand out to me as ones that inextricably represent the seeds that RCAP has continued to sow over the last twenty years: future and reconciliation.

There have been a number of important steps towards a mutually beneficial reconciliation between Indigenous peoples and government that work towards repairing the fractured fabric of our people caused by the devastating ripple effect of the residential school system. First and foremost are the ninety-four calls to action, as recommended by the Truth and Reconciliation Commission [TRC] of Canada. Senator Murray Sinclair, speaking in his previous role as the chair of the TRC, stated that "reconciliation is not an Aboriginal problem, it's a Canadian one. Reconciliation requires a new vision, based on a commitment to mutual respect be developed."[3]

The TRC's calls to action place the lens of responsibility and stewardship on each and every one of us to take up our own initiative, whether it's on a national level or in a classroom in an elementary school in Gloucester, Ontario. *Le travail entrepris par la CVR poursuit l'héritage du CRPA et rappelle à tous les Canadiens que le défi de la réconciliation que nous voulons relever devrait être très bien accueilli.*

The Missing and Murdered Indigenous Women and Girls Inquiry has long been overdue. There is perhaps no other issue facing Indigenous people that encapsulates the damage inflicted upon them by the residential school system, the Sixties Scoop, and systemic racism. I wish the commissioners of the National Inquiry into Missing and Murdered

Indigenous Women the very best in their endeavour to tackle this vicious cycle. CAP supports you completely.

The United Nations Declaration on the Rights of Indigenous Peoples is another effective tool for governments to exercise their obligations to engage and consult with Indigenous organizations. As I've stated before, CAP represents the needs of off-reserve and Non-Status Indians, Métis, and southern Inuit people. The challenge of reconciliation and the realization of promise took further shape for our people earlier this year when CAP won a historic victory with the *Daniels* decision by the Supreme Court of Canada.[4]

Seventeen years ago our former leader, the late Harry Daniels, along with CAP, went to court to force the federal government to acknowledge that Métis and Non-Status Indians are indeed Indians under Section 91(24) of the Constitution and that [the] government has a fiduciary responsibility to them. The congress launched this case, paid for it every step of the way, and pushed it through every level of the court process, and I'm very pleased to state that on April 14th, 2016, we finally won. It took the *Daniels* decision to end the judicial limbo of Métis and Non-Status Indians. Before *Daniels*, we were stuck with the provinces and the federal government passing the buck as to who[m] should we deal with and who has the fiduciary responsibility. The decision has enormous practical utility for our people.

I've given you a brief overview of the *Daniels* case because the road to reconciliation with the Indigenous people whom I advocate for could not happen until this main dispute about the federal responsibility was addressed. We've gathered here this morning to discuss Indigenous communities in a new relationship. There is a wide range of such communities located across the country in urban, rural, and remote areas, all with their own differences and similarities. Between each of them, however, lies a fundamental commonality. These communities represent, in their own way, a home.

While it would not be possible to discuss each of the recommendations proposed by RCAP to date, there is one issue that the Congress of Aboriginal Peoples has continued to strongly advocate for, and one that I feel is a necessary stepping stone for all Indigenous people. It is a basic human right that should be accorded to every person in Canada: housing. We cannot enjoy a good quality of life and contribute to society without having a safe place to lay our heads at night and to raise our families. A home should be a place of welcome and stability. *Un endroit où trouver du confort après une dure journée de travail, ou une mauvaise journée à l'école.*

Housing is a fundamental human right. Safe and affordable housing has always been a top priority at CAP. During its time with the Aboriginal [Affairs] Working Group [AAWG, with provincial and territorial governments], CAP pushed hard and was ultimately successful in establishing a separate working group table at the AAWG to address the rampant housing issues affecting off-reserve Indigenous peoples. We will continue our work on housing with the recently implemented Federal-Provincial-Territorial Indigenous Forum.

This past September, with the generous cooperation of the Canada Mortgage and Housing Corporation (CMHC), CAP undertook a day-long national symposium exclusively devoted to housing. Ultimately, safe and affordable housing gives a person dignity, security, and a sense of confidence and self-worth. The welfare of our people from a social, cultural, and economic perspective depends on it. CAP is encouraged by the inclusion of $21.9 billion for social infrastructure, including housing, homelessness, and early learning and child care in the government of Canada's fall economic statement of 2016. We hope that these key issues of policy development include all Indigenous people, whether they live in urban, rural, or remote areas, and we will continue to push them on it.

Back in 1996, the commissioners of RCAP stated "we directed our consultation to one overriding question: what are the foundations of a fair and honourable relationship between the aboriginal and non-aboriginal people of Canada?"[5] Twenty years on, the answer to this is for the governments to honour their commitments to Indigenous people for open and mutual engagement and consultation on all policy issues. Federal, provincial, and territorial governments and national Indigenous organizations must cooperate in order to create solutions for our people now.

Nous sommes tous concernés par ceci. We truly do share the land and share a future together, and it should include every single one of us so that, when we all meet here again in twenty years, we will be able to set aside the time to not only discuss the challenges ahead but [also] to celebrate the accomplishment that we've achieved in the name of reconciliation. *Merci beaucoup, miigwech,* thank you.

NOTES

1   Robert Bertrand, address to Sharing the Land, Sharing a Future: A National Forum on Reconciliation, Winnipeg, 2–4 November 2016.

2   Indigenous and Northern Affairs Canada, "Highlights from the Royal Commission on Aboriginal Peoples," September 2010, http://www.aadnc-aandc.gc.ca/eng/110010001 4597/1100100014637.

3   The Hon. Murray Sinclair, "The Current," CBC Radio. Posted 2 June 2015.

4   *Daniels v. Canada (Indian Affairs and Northern Development)*, 2016, SCC.

5   Indigenous and Northern Affairs Canada, "Highlights from the Royal Commission on Aboriginal Peoples."

CHAPTER 9
ADDRESS BY FRANCYNE JOE[1]

President, Native Women's Association of Canada (NWAC)

Wa'iht, good morning. Thank you for the opportunity to speak with you today. First, I'd like to acknowledge that we are meeting on the traditional lands of the Anishinaabe people of Treaty 1 and the homeland of the Métis Nation. I would also like to thank the organizers for bringing us together to discuss a new relationship between Canadian Indigenous women and the federal government for the future.

When I look around the room, I see many leaders. I want to acknowledge each of you for the important work that you do on behalf of Indigenous people. My comments will be framed based on the NWAC's responsibility to represent the issues of priority to Indigenous women in Canada today and which we have been doing ... since 1974. A fundamental premise of our work is that the civil, political, cultural, social, and economic rights of Indigenous peoples cannot be realized without identifying the needs, responding to the injustices, and ensuring full engagement of Indigenous women.

"The time to act is now" has been the rallying cry since the inception of the Royal Commission on Aboriginal Peoples [RCAP] in 1991. For Indigenous women, the time to act has been embedded in our roles as mothers, grandmothers, and aunties. In 2014, MP Romeo Saganash, when calling for an Inquiry into Missing and Murdered Indigenous Women, described Indigenous women as follows: "In many Indigenous cultures and societies, we are taught to honour women as life givers, as knowledge keepers, as storytellers, as medicine women, as word carriers, as community members and human beings, and colonialism has impacted negatively on these values."[2]

Part of reconciliation has to be the restoration of Indigenous women's roles in our communities and our nations. Reconciliation also has to be about addressing the issues that prevent Indigenous women from taking up our roles and responsibilities. A key challenge for Indigenous women is that we are exposed to a level of racialized violence and lack of safety that is unprecedented in our country. The RCMP [Royal Canadian Mounted Police] 2015 report named over 1,000 Indigenous women and girls who were murdered and missing. Since 2015, we know of sixteen more Indigenous women and girls that are missing or murdered. Many of these girls represented in those numbers were part of the child welfare system.

Trust is the fundamental premise of our original relationship as Indigenous people, and [it] is key to reconcil[ing] relationships. Trust will never be achieved until violence against Indigenous women and girls is eradicated within our communities and beyond. As RCAP clearly stated twenty years ago, in order for this fundamental covenant relationship to be restored, before Aboriginal and non-Aboriginal people can get on with the work of reconciliation, a great cleansing of the wounds of the past must take place. Part of that cleansing is the embedded gender discrimination that is part of colonization. Twenty years after RCAP, not all the wounds have been cleansed. Indigenous women are still dealing with gender-based inequities in health and most underlying systemic issues.

A key challenge for Indigenous women is the direct attack on our ability to engage as Canadian citizens and as Indigenous women with specific human and inherent rights, as noted under the UNDRIP [United Nations Declaration on the Rights of Indigenous Peoples]. These attacks do not come only from our government but [also] from our own community and leaders. When the Canadian government adopted the UNDRIP, it affirmed that Indigenous women have the right to lead and centrally participate in the decision-making processes that impact our lives, as outlined in Article 18 of the UNDRIP. It states: "Indigenous peoples have the right to participate in decision-making in matters which would affect their rights through representatives chosen by themselves in accordance with their own procedures, as well as to maintain and develop their own indigenous decision-making institutions."[3] Yet NWAC finds itself in a difficult situation. First, 60 percent of our core funding that the previous federal government removed has not been restored. Second, despite being the lead organization to bring national and global attention to missing and murdered Indigenous women and girls, we received no funding to respond to this issue, including supporting families or monitoring the Inquiry [into Missing and Murdered Indigenous Women].

The interpretation of [a] nation-to-nation [relationship] by the federal government has meant that Indigenous women through NWAC have been excluded at federal tables, including climate change and the environment and health, where three national Indigenous organizations have eagerly endorsed our removal and have been ready to speak on our behalf. This goes against the spirit of reconciliation. When there was zero funding for the environment, it was women, like Ojibway grandmother Josephine Mandamin, who walked around the Great Lakes each year; the women of Elsipogtog First Nation who first protested the fracking of New Brunswick; Ta'Kaiya Blaney of Tla'Amin First Nation in BC [who] spoke out as a thirteen-year-old girl to the UN about environmental concerns.

As stated last night by keynote speaker Dr. Dockstator, [a] nation-to-nation [relationship] means closing the gap between mainstream and displaced people. Issues facing Indigenous people today cannot be solved without Indigenous women being central to the solution. We care for our children, our families, our communities. We are the knowledge keepers and teachers who carry culture and tradition to future generations. We have specific governance roles to fulfill. While definitions of, and mechanisms for, Indigenous self-determination were described throughout RCAP as flexible and community driven, the reconstitution of Aboriginal nationhood in RCAP lost its flexibility and entrenched itself in stationary land bases and non-Indigenous federalism. That appears to be the understanding of [the] nation-to-nation [relationship] with this new federal government. This restrictive model for Aboriginal nations does not make provisions for self-determined Indigenous collective and individual identity, nor does it address Indigenous women's experiences of gender discrimination. This model has further left the federal government with control over who constitutes a nation.

In many ways, RCAP repeated the positioning of Indigenous women both as a special needs group and as rights-bearing citizens. RCAP broadly recognized Indigenous women's leadership and entitlement to full participation in their own governance, while at the same time situating the bulk of the consultation with Indigenous women as additive perspectives and concerns, a special interest along with Elders, youth, Métis, and off-reserve Indigenous people. Specific provisions and policy recommendations for Indigenous women's housing, education, role in governance, and economic development were sparse, if [not] non-existent, while the bulk of recommendations regarding Indigenous women were collected under the heading of "family." Although RCAP's formal recognition of Indigenous women's existing rights to leadership and self-determination were bold and inclusive statements, it [RCAP] ultimately relegated specific recommendations to family issues that prioritize Indigenous women's domestic work and experiences of family violence over the need for systemic changes to restore Indigenous women's leadership and voice in nation-to-nation relationships.

Systemic change at all levels, from community infrastructure to federal policy, that restores the legitimacy and value of Indigenous women's leadership is a critical factor in addressing violence, healing, and reconciliation. As RCAP stated, women are providing leadership in many community-based projects, and they are often in the front line of service provision. The importance that Indigenous women attach to healing cannot be overstated. And our role in achieving wellness needs to be acknowledged and incorporated in all aspects of the design, development, and implementation of health and social services.

Lastly, we cannot achieve a shared future where reconciliation and restoration [are] possible without ending systemic and interpersonal violence against Indigenous women. A nation cannot exist without the hearts of women. Nation-to-nation relations cannot be reconciled until Indigenous women are restored to their positions as decision makers for the life and well-being of our communities.

In summary, as Indigenous women, we carry a sacred inheritance. What we carry and how we fulfill those responsibilities must be based on our own self-determined, principled accountability. But not all the wounds have healed. Until we end the ongoing violence towards Indigenous women, we will continue to carry the wounds that prevent us from reconciling the fundamental premise of our original covenants. Trust must be actively demonstrated in all our endeavours. We are committed to a vision for a future where reconciliation and restoration become reality, and that includes Indigenous women in Canada. We know that nation-to-nation relations cannot be reconciled until Indigenous women are fully restored in their place as decision makers in life and for the well-being of our communities. Thank you, and *kuk'shun*.

NOTES

1   Francyne Joe, address to Sharing the Land, Sharing a Future: A National Forum on Reconciliation, Winnipeg, 2–4 November 2016.

2   Canadian Press, "Saganash's Remarks to the House of Commons on Murdered, Missing Native Women,"19 September 2014, http://www.680news.com/2014/09/19/saganashs-remarks-to-the-house-of-commons-on-murdered-missing-native-women/.

3   United Nations General Assembly, United Nations Declaration on the Rights of Indigenous Peoples, adopted 2 October 2007, A/RES/61/295, 8, http://www.un.org/esa/socdev/unpfii/documents/DRIPS_en.pdf.

CHAPTER 10
ADDRESS BY CAROLYN BENNETT[1]

Minister of Indigenous and Northern Affairs Canada

Thank you all so much. This is so exciting that this day has finally arrived, so thank you. *Merci. Miigwetch. Qujanamiik. Nakumiik. Maarsii. Mahsi Cho.*

It is amazing to be able to acknowledge the significance of this twentieth anniversary taking place here in the territories of Treaty 1 and in the homeland of the Métis people as well as the home to many Inuit here in Winnipeg. As we all know, the canoe routes of the Assiniboine and Red Rivers have been travelled by Indigenous people for thousands of years. And the rivers represent the meeting point and thousands of years of community. We look forward, as was said, not only to the dialogue and discussion but [also] to the work that we will all get to do together as we go forward from this event.

I think this conference represents a truly critical milestone on our journey of reconciliation as we work on the forum's theme: encouraging sharing the land [and] sharing a future. The conversations and dialogue, discussions and questions, will all play a key role in advancing the vital work of renewal and healing but also of tackling the tough questions and challenging us all to be better.

As Marlene [Brant Castellano] and Fred [Wien] know, I was really hoping that this conference would be truly disruptive in helping us to really have a look at what [a] nation-to-nation [relationship] means, what Inuit-to-Crown means, and what it would look like if we were getting that right. So I encourage you all to be disruptive, that we don't want the same old, same old. We actually want to be shooting for where we need to be.

Je veux en particulier saluer le travail extraordinaire de Marlene et de Fred dans le cadre de CRPA. Marlene, as you know, was the co-director of research, and Fred [was] the deputy director of research [with the Royal Commission]. I think as we see [by the] snowflakes on their lapel[s] that they exemplify the motto of the Order of Canada: *desiderantes meliorem patriam* ("they desire a better country"). They are national treasures. Your ongoing efforts, paid and unpaid, as you explained, to further Indigenous rights have been shining an important light on these issues over the past twenty years and long before that... as successive governments have been challenged to keep pace and demonstrate real change.

I think all of us today want to acknowledge the commissioners [of] the Royal Commission on Aboriginal Peoples [RCAP] as well as the Truth and Reconciliation Commission [TRC]. As for the RCAP, ... Co-Chairs René Dussault [and] Georges Erasmus and Commissioners Paul Chartrand, Peter Meekison, Viola Robinson, Mary Sillett, and the late Bertha Wilson that you spoke so beautifully about. For the TRC, Commissioners Wilton Littlechild, Marie Wilson, and now Senator Murray Sinclair. Your reports were so credible because of the way that you listened to people and communities. As you know, you set a gold standard in true citizen engagement. The reason people remind me that I need to dust off and read the report again wherever I go [is] because they listened to the people.

Il y a vingt ans le rapport de la CRPA était le premier de son genre. As the report came out, critics and ministers alike had the common refrain "RCAP had it right." For the first time, Canadians heard clearly and in depth about the history of the relationship between Canada and Indigenous peoples. For example, Canadians heard [that], "after some 500 years of a relationship that has swung from partnership to domination, from mutual respect and cooperation to paternalism and attempted assimilation, Canada must now work out fair and lasting terms of coexistence with Aboriginal people."[2]

As commissioners, you provided a different version of Canadian history than the one taught in schools, from the Royal Proclamation of 1763 onward: a history of broken treaty promises of the Indian Act, the policies of assimilation; of the suppression, even criminalization, of Indigenous culture; and the horror of residential schools. The report was scathing. Your central conclusion was that the main policy direction pursued for more than 150 years, first by colonial and then by Canadian governments, has been wrong.

It was bold at a time when bold words were needed. You stated that the concepts such as *terra nullius* and the doctrine of discovery are factually, legally, and morally wrong. The report spoke truth to power. It has been said that once you know the truth you can't unknow the truth. The Canadian embarrassment at our country's history created a growing desire for change.

Le rapport était également le premier à examiner les fondations de la guérison et la volonté d'entretenir une relation plus juste et honorable. The commission's co-chair, Georges Erasmus, saw the commission as a beacon of hope for our collective peoples when he said "what an enterprise with which to enter the new millennium. What a wasteful burden to be able to leave behind and what possibilities of peace and harmony await if together we get to work now to realize this new national dream."[3]

My colleague at the time, the Honourable Jane Stewart, responded to RCAP with ... *Gathering Strength: [Canada's Aboriginal] Action Plan* and a statement of reconciliation. When I read the statement of reconciliation, I find it eerily familiar. For example, it states [that] "reconciliation is an ongoing process. In renewing our partnership, we must ensure that the mistakes which marked our past relationships are not repeated."[4]

It seems like we're still saying the same thing. [The] *Gathering Strength Action Plan* had four objectives to support the renewal. First, to renew the Crown-Indigenous partnership and engage all possible partners so that the relationship will be a catalyst to better the lives of Aboriginal people in Canada. Second, to strengthen Aboriginal governance so that communities have the tools to guide their own destiny and to exercise their inherent right of self-government. Third, to design a new fiscal relationship that provides a stable flow of funds in support of transparent and accountable community development. And fourth, to sustain the growth of strong, healthy Aboriginal communities fuelled by economic development and supported by a solid basic infrastructure of institutions and services.

Beyond these objectives, Minister Stewart also outlined [that] the Crown's commitment to this partnership was to work out solutions together beforehand instead of picking up the pieces after the fact, a commitment to negotiate rather than litigate, a commitment to communication, a commitment to meaningful consultation, and a commitment to prompt action to address concerns before positions get too polarized to move.

In conclusion, she quoted the simple and profound statement of Chief Justice [Lamer] in the *Delgamuukw* case: "Let us face it. We're all here to stay."[5] So I am here to say "let's face it, twenty years from now things better be different." As [Wilton] Littlechild said in the first meeting with the prime minister last December, "what we need is reconcili-action." So I hope by your silver twenty-fifth anniversary that I am committed that we will be well on the way to sharing the land and sharing a future.

As a new member of Parliament, RCAP exposed me in the *Gathering Strength* event to understand my total ignorance of this shameful, shameful history of our country. I remember the *Gathering Strength* event at the Native Canadian Centre in Toronto. I remember the smudge ceremony. I'd never seen one before or knew what it was. I remember thinking how long is this going to take? I remember thinking, well, this is—I was just mortified and embarrassed that I knew so little about it. I was forty-seven years old and a very good student, and I knew nothing. Today we have an opportunity to look back over the past twenty years, take stock of our progress towards this new, new national dream.

The RCAP commissioners were clear, writing [that] "there can be no peace or harmony unless there is justice."[6] In May of 2006, the [Indian] Residential School Settlement Agreement (IRSSA) was signed by all parties, including the late Honourable Jim Prentice, whose recent tragic passing shocked and saddened us all. IRSSA became the largest class action lawsuit in Canadian history. This led to the 2008 apology by former prime minister Stephen Harper for a moral policy to forcibly remove children from their homes and into residential schools, a policy that has left a painful legacy and untold consequences in its wake. IRSSA also brought us the Truth and Reconciliation Commission and the road map for reconciliation that is laid out in their calls to action.

Of the ninety-four Truth and Reconciliation Commission calls to action, over forty of them overlap with the calls from RCAP, which is a clear sign that we haven't moved far or fast enough. We still don't even have the publication of a general history of Indigenous people that we can all agree on, which was an RCAP recommendation. In fact, in volume 1 it said [that] "the Government of Canada will commit to a publication of a general history of aboriginal peoples of Canada in a series of volumes reflecting the diversity of nations to be completed within 20 years."[7]

It is twenty years now. I don't think we have it. As RCAP said, "as we delved deeper, we came to appreciate the Commission's unique opportunity to approach the relationship between Canada and First Peoples in a new way, holistically. We realized that the usual strategy, tackling the problems one at a time, independently, is tantamount to putting a band aid on a broken leg instead of propos[ing] a comprehensive agenda for change."[8]

So here we are twenty years later, and we're not even close to being done. There has been some visible, concrete change but way too slowly. It's always been clear that not acting is disrespecting all of the people who spoke with the commissioners. Cynicism, passivity, despair are the results of nothing changing. We must look back and acknowledge our failures, but we are also given the responsibility and the opportunity to look ahead.

One of the things that inspires me every day is Christi Belcourt's beautiful stained glass window over the members' entrance [to the House of Commons] which commemorates the 2008 apology. It is with the beautiful Ojibway word *Giniigaaniimenaaning*, which is about looking forward. It means that we are, and as it said in the commission, we are thinking seven generations out, and we're dealing with seven generations back, but we need to look forward in this next seven generations by listening to the youth as well as listening to wise women and Elders.

This Friday will be one year since my swearing-in ceremony. I'm proud to say that some important steps have been taken, and I thank Claudette Commanda for making sure there was sage in my boots that day.

Dans ma lettre de mandat le Premier ministre a indiqué qu'aucune relation n'est pas plus importante pour lui et pour le Canada que celle qu'il entretient avec les peuples autochtones, et je suis tout à fait d'accord avec lui. As you know as well, one year ago in the mandate letter to every minister it stated it's time for a renewed nation-to-nation relationship with Indigenous peoples based on the recognition of rights, respect, cooperation, and partnership. We think that was huge in that it is a whole-of-government approach. This is not only the responsibility of one minister. It's the responsibility of every minister, and that is tough sledding in a government that has been so siloed forever. That's the work that we're trying to do together. So we are steadfast in our commitment to nation-to-nation, Inuit-to-Crown, government-to-government [relationships], invoking what Georges Erasmus called the "human underpinnings of a new relationship."[9]

We have promised early signs of reconciliation by Canada's 150th anniversary, where we will celebrate a Year of Reconciliation. We have made some progress on the ninety-four calls to action of the TRC, and thirty-five of them are well under way for the federal-led areas. The top priority was setting up the commission into the tragedy of Missing and Murdered Indigenous Women and Girls. *J'était honorée de participer à ce processus,* but as we heard in the pre-inquiry so many of the causes of that tragedy were well there in the RCAP report, well there in the TRC. It's a matter of "we just need to get on and do this" now.

We also know that in the recent budget we've begun to close those gaps that have been identified for so long; [we are addressing] the needed changes [and] the calls for infrastructure changes from the original RCAP report. As you know, we made the historic investment of $8.4 billion to improve the conditions of Indigenous people in their communities. I was just at the Infrastructure Conference of the AFN [Assembly of First Nations, committing to] funding [of] $4.6 billion over five years to help with housing and water, and wastewater, and education in First Nations and Inuit communities.

As the finance minister reminds me wherever he gives a speech, the biggest, most positive response is on drinking water on First Nations and the fact that everybody should be able to turn on the tap in this country and be able to drink from the tap. I believe that we won't be able to truly renew our nation-to-nation relationship until every family in every First Nations community in Canada is able to turn on the tap and drink the water.

Nous savons également maintenant qu'il est nécessaire d'offrir aux enfants un environnement d'apprentissage qui respecte leur culture. We need to close the shameful gap of 62 percent of Indigenous young adults on reserve not finishing high school compared to only 13 percent of non-Indigenous kids, but we need to listen to the youth. When you listen to the youth, it's totally inspiring. What the youth want [are] language and culture. What the youth want is on-the-land programming, and whether it's the Inuit Youth Council or the Youth Council in Attawapiskat the kids are asking for the same thing. They want to have an attachment to the land. They want to know their language and culture, and that is how they are going to succeed in education, in health outcomes, and [in] economic outcomes. They need a secure personal cultural identity that will lead to their resilience, their self-esteem, and their sense of control over their lives. They need Indigenous pedagogy that is learning by doing.

We have to stop the colonial approach of having kids copy off black-boards at the front of a room. That is not working. The kids are learning physics by trying to get their canoe forward in a wind. The kids are learning biology by cleaning a fish. The kids are learning chemistry by using the brain of a deer and tanning the hides. This is so disturbing that we still have in way too many classrooms in this country teachers standing at the front reading off a clipboard. None of us could do well that way, and ... we need to get back to the Indigenous way, which was learning by doing. Murray Sinclair has said that, in reminding us of the RCAP legacy, ... we have described for you a mountain, and we have shown you the path to the top, and we call on you to do the climbing.[10]

We need to speak the words of apology in humility, and ... those words are needed to start healing the shameful acts of the past. But we also need to deal with all Canadians right now. [There is an] unacceptable level of racism in this country. [Reconciliation] is not going to work until we name it, until we deal with it, and [when] every Canadian is prepared to correct misinformation and correct the attitudes that are holding everyone back.

I believe in acknowledging and repairing the injustices of the past but also acknowledging and repairing the injustices of the present. We will mark an opportunity to look forward together towards the brighter future into the next 150 years of Confederation. We need to bring all Canadians with us, and this conference is a very important tool to help with that goal. *La réconciliation s'adresse à tous les Canadiens.* We need to be speaking to the 96 percent of Canadians who are non-Indigenous. We have to climb that mountain together. It is going to be really important for us to recognize some of the successes.

I think that, with the RCAP push and hearing from the universities today, Indigenizing universities is not going to be easy, but we're seeing it happen. Universities here in [Winnipeg] are really leading the way in terms of Indigenous knowledge and Indigenous ways of knowing. We've got the commitment of all provinces and territories to actually change their curricula.

As the Elder said [in the opening], we not only have APTN [Aboriginal Peoples Television Network], but we actually have mainstream media beginning to take note of these stories of injustice but also these stories of success. I hope that again in this fortunate position that I have as minister and as member of Parliament ... every Canadian should have the advantage I have of new friends who are First Nations, Inuit, and Métis. You shouldn't have to be a member of Parliament to have this amazing window on what was this amazing culture and language before the settlers arrived. To have those friends correct you as you go forward—that's what friends do.

It is so important that, as you look to the subjects that have been chosen [at this conference], the six themes of nation-to-nation, closing the gap, youth engagement, citizen engagement, powerful communities, and healthy communities and moving to action, . . . we will read the papers, and we will learn from the thoughtful ideas and important work.

But together we're going to have to work with all Canadians to do this work. It means next year this great party in my riding will include the men from the Native men's residence and that transitional housing at the end of their street. We actually have to do this business of work together. We actually need the scholars to be asking the tough questions and putting really, really important solutions out on the table.

I was interested in reading the nation-to-nation piece, the "Completing Confederation" paper of the Transitional Governance Project. If the history of Indigenous-Crown relations teaches us anything, it is that, as much as the Crown must honour its promises, it cannot have more than an enabling and an accommodating role in Indigenous social, political, and economic development. This is not a call for benign neglect. Rather, we urge federal, provincial, and territorial governments at the political and bureaucratic levels to embark on their own critical self-examination of where their policies and actions continue to maintain the colonial mindset and hinder progress for Indigenous people and [whether they] better long-term relationships between Indigenous and other Canadians.

Next year, as we celebrate Canada 150 and the Year of Reconciliation, it is my sincere hope that we will have made progress [and] that the progress is in part because of the conversations that we've had at this forum. We have this year ahead with the four themes. One of them is reconciliation, one is youth, one is the environment, one is diversity. In some ways, they're all about reconciliation and that we actually have to take that work forward. As Gord Downie said in his concert two weeks ago, we have 150 years behind us that we need to learn from, and we've got 150 years ahead, and we'd better just get to work.

On the day of the TRC ceremony in Ottawa in June of 2015, Hereditary Chief Ray Jones reminded us of the Gitxsan phrase *shed dim amma gauu dingu mel*, meaning the canoe must be uprighted. So in closing I want to tell you a little story about a canoe I almost dumped. I had to do this interview for *BBC Hard Talk*, which is well named, but thankfully I'd just come off the North Saskatchewan River in Batoche with a group of kids from La Loche. I was asked by the interviewer "Why do you think this is any better time? Everybody's failed. Why do you think that this can be any better?" I said, "Well, you know, when I was paddling with these kids from one of the challenged communities in our country yesterday, we hit this huge rock. We got into water so shallow we had to get out and walk the canoe through. But the current was with us, and we got where we were going, and we're going to get it done this time." So thank you. *Merci. Miigwetch. Qujanamiik. Nakumiik. Maarsii. Mahsi Cho.*

NOTES

1   Carolyn Bennett, address to Sharing the Land, Sharing a Future: A National Forum on Reconciliation, Winnipeg, 2–4 November 2016.

2   Indigenous and Northern Affairs Canada, "Highlights from the Royal Commission on Aboriginal Peoples," September 2010, http://www.aadnc-aandc.gc.ca/eng/110010001 4597/1100100014637.

3   Indigenous and Northern Affairs Canada, "Address for the Launch of the Report of the Royal Commission on Aboriginal Peoples," September 2010, https://www.aadnc-aandc. gc.ca/eng/1100100014639/1100100014640.

4   Indigenous and Northern Affairs Canada, "Address by the Honourable Jane Stewart, Minister of Indian Affairs and Northern Development, on the Occasion of the Unveiling of *Gathering Strength: Canada's Aboriginal Action Plan,*" September 2010, http://www. aadnc-aandc.gc.ca/eng/1100100015725/1100100015726.

5   Antonio Lamer, C.J., in *Delgamuukw v. British Columbia,* [1997] 3 S.C.R. 1010 at para. 186.>
    Indigenous and Northern Affairs Canada, "Highlights from the Royal Commission on Aboriginal Peoples," September 2010, http://www.aadnc-aandc.gc.ca/eng/110010001 4597/1100100014637.

6   Indigenous and Northern Affairs Canada, "Highlights from the Royal Commission on Aboriginal Peoples," September 2010, http://www.aadnc-aandc.gc.ca/eng/110010001 4597/1100100014637.

7   Royal Commission on Aboriginal Peoples, *Report,* Volume 1, 1996. Recommendation 1.7.1.

8   Indigenous and Northern Affairs Canada, "Highlights from the Royal Commission on Aboriginal Peoples."

9   Georges Erasmus, Address for the Launch of the Royal Commission on Aboriginal Peoples, Hull, Quebec, 21 November 1996, www.rcaanc-cirnac.gc.ca (accessed 18 February 2021).

10 Justice Murray Sinclair, "Remarks on the Truth and Reconciliation Report," *Macleans,* 15 December 2015. https://www.macleans.ca/news/canada/justice-murray-sinclairs-remarks-on-the-truth-and-reconciliation-report/.

PART 3
POWERFUL COMMUNITIES, HEALTHY COMMUNITIES

CHAPTER 11

THUNDERBIRD IS RISING:
INDIGENIZING EDUCATION IN CANADA

Jo-ann Archibald Q'um Q'um Xiiem and Jan Hare

> Indigenizing education means that every subject at every level is examined to consider how and to what extent current content and pedagogy reflect the presence of Indigenous/Aboriginal peoples and the valid contribution of Indigenous knowledge.
>
> —Marlene Brant Castellano, 2014

Over the past twenty years, the Royal Commission on Aboriginal Peoples (RCAP) has been the focus of review, research, and dialogue concerning its policy implications for Indigenous people's lives and Indigenous-settler relations. Mi'kmaw scholar Marie Battiste's commentary on the educational recommendations of RCAP made in *Aboriginal Education: Fulfilling the Promise*, released in 2000, still holds currency: "Anyone who has read the chapter on education in Volume 3 of the report [*Gathering Strength*] will recognize the stories of how Aboriginal peoples are using education to make concrete changes in their lives."[1] Concrete changes are brought about by centring Indigenous cultures, knowledges, and beliefs at the core of learning.

As we consider the goal of Indigenizing education, we are motivated by the opening quotation from Marlene Brant Castellano, the former RCAP co-director of research, who identifies complex and important criteria for what constitutes the notion of Indigenizing education. In fact, her directive gives both purpose and structure to this chapter. RCAP presented a challenge for all involved in lifelong education to improve learning for Aboriginal learners through positive working relationships between educators and Aboriginal people and by using forms of Indigenous knowledge (IK) to provide relevant, respectful teaching and learning approaches. Ultimately, the recommendations recognized the importance of local control of education and family/community engagement that formed the basis of the 1972 Indian Control of Indian Education Policy. Aligning with these approaches, this chapter addresses the following questions. What does Indigenizing education mean? Why is it important? What does it look like? What are the issues?

Indigenizing education is a concept that has gained ground through the work of scholars seeking systemic changes to universities so that policies, practices, curricula, teaching, and research are responsive and relevant to Indigenous ways of knowing and Indigenous priorities.[2] From these emerging conversations about Indigenizing education, we come to understand that the priorities of RCAP are aligned with Indigenizing principles, practices, and policies. Sharing the lessons that she has learned from this scholarship and her own experiences in the academy, Indigenous scholar Jackie Ottmann summarizes that Indigenizing education is about transformational but sustainable change that requires strong and enduring leadership.[3] In this chapter, we draw on this theme of transforming educational institutions, recognizing that themes of decolonization, self-determination, and reconciliation are related and necessary parts of Indigenizing education. Transformation shapes the questions about Indigenizing education that we address.

RCAP presented a conceptual framework of lifelong learning. Using a circle framework with four quadrants, similar to the Plains Medicine Wheel, each stage of the life cycle is represented within it: child, youth, adult, and Elder.[4] Bringing this holistic framework together with Castellano's vision for the educational spaces where Indigenizing should occur, we align the life stages with an examination of major RCAP educational recommendations within educational contexts associated with these phases: early childhood education represents the child, K–12 education reflects youth, postsecondary education signals adulthood, and community education considers the Elder phase of life (see Figure 11.1). We focus on actions advancing RCAP's educational recommendations that have occurred in the past twenty years. In each educational context, we highlight significant policy, program, and curriculum initiatives occurring at national, provincial, and territorial levels, and then we discuss the successes and challenges of these initiatives in relation to the Indigenization questions framing this chapter.

FIGURE 11.1. LIFELONG LEARNING CONCEPTUAL FRAMEWORK.

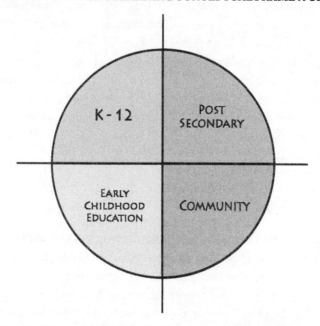

INDIGENIZING EARLY CHILDHOOD EDUCATION

Indigenous early childhood education and care services, in which Indigenous children learn from and are cared for by centre-based and/or program-based settings designed and operated by Indigenous peoples and communities, are central to the recommendations of RCAP. Recognizing the significant developmental outcomes achieved in these early stages of life, RCAP's primary recommendations focus on (1) extending early childhood services to all Aboriginal children regardless of residence; (2) encouraging programs that foster the physical, social, intellectual, and spiritual development of children, reducing distinctions among child care, prevention, and education; (3) maximizing Aboriginal control over service design and administration; (4) offering one-stop accessible funding; and (5) promoting parental involvement and choice in early childhood education options.[5]

RCAP draws attention to the emergence of culturally specific early childhood programs, highlighting federally funded programs, including the First Nations Inuit Child Care Initiative and the Aboriginal Head Start in Urban and Northern Communities program, as giving rise to strategic early interventions available to Aboriginal families and communities. In addition, the report draws attention to Indigenous languages as a basis for care and learning in early childhood programs. Indigenous scholar Margo Greenwood, who has traced the evolution of culturally specific early childhood education and care services in Canada, tells us that the focus on Aboriginal children's identities, embedded in Indigenous knowledges, has resulted in "the refocusing and transformation of many existing programs and the establishment of additional programs and services."[6] Following are exemplary Indigenous early learning programs at national and provincial levels.

NATIONAL PROGRAMS

ABORIGINAL HEAD START IN URBAN AND NORTHERN COMMUNITIES

Since 1995, the Aboriginal Head Start in Urban and Northern Communities (AHSUNC) program has been providing early intervention programming for First Nations, Inuit, and Métis children, ages three to five, and their families living off reserve. The program is funded by the Public Health Agency of Canada and currently supports nearly 4,800 children and their families at 133 project sites across the country.[7] A community AHSUNC program is supported by a sponsor, which can include a First Nations organization, a host agency, a non-profit organization, or an educational authority.

The program is federally funded yet locally delivered to ensure that other services directed at children and families can complement it, allowing for family support workers, health services, or child welfare and other community programs to be integrated. The program was developed in national consultation with Aboriginal families, communities, leaders, and organizations in urban and northern centres, resulting in six guiding program components: (1) Aboriginal culture and language; (2)

education and school readiness; (3) health promotion; (4) nutrition; (5) social support; and (6) parental involvement. It operates three to four half days per week nine months per year.

ABORIGINAL HEAD START ON-RESERVE

The Aboriginal Head Start On-Reserve (AHSOR) program was extended to Aboriginal children and families living on reserve in 1998, centred on the same six program components of AHSUNC as well as the same emphasis on building relationships with community members, programs, and services. ASHOR is a federally funded intervention by First Nations and Inuit Health. It serves over 9,000 children in over 300 First Nations communities across Canada. Unique to this program are its locally controlled delivery models, which allow for centre-based, outreach, and home-visiting versions.

FIRST NATIONS AND INUIT CHILD CARE INITIATIVE

In an effort to increase parental access to licensed child care, thereby ensuring that parents can prepare for and take part in employment, education, and training, the First Nations and Inuit Child Care Initiative (FNICCI) was established in 1995 through funding by Human Resources and Skills Development Canada. After 2011, FNICCI has been managed through the Aboriginal Skills and Employment Training Strategy, which falls under the mandate of Employment and Social Development Canada. FNICCI creates child-care spaces for Aboriginal children up to six years of age. Equally important to this initiative is the goal that children experience child-care services that reflect their values, beliefs, cultures, and languages.

PROVINCIAL AND TERRITORIAL INITIATIVES

ABORIGINAL INFANT DEVELOPMENT PROGRAM

Supporting Aboriginal families and children in British Columbia who are at risk for or have been diagnosed with developmental delays, the Aboriginal Infant Development Program (AIDP) provides home visits, appropriate activities, and assessments that are culturally sensitive and relevant to families. Established in 2002, the program responds to the need for culturally based programs. It is voluntary and family centred, and it focuses on children ages birth to three years old. Consultants assist families to access other health, social, and community services. The need for

AIDP services is steadily increasing as Aboriginal communities establish comprehensive child-care services. A provincial advisor for the program guides the twenty-nine AIDPs operating in British Columbia.

INUIT EARLY CHILDHOOD DEVELOPMENT WORKING GROUP

The Inuit Early Childhood Development Working Group (IECDWG) is a subcommittee of the Inuit Tapiriit Kanatami (ITK). Its role is to bring together regional Inuit organizations that are signatories to the agreements under the Aboriginal Skills Education and Training Strategy to develop and implement a vision for Inuit children, which is to ensure happy, healthy, and safe Inuit children and families. The IECDWG has been meeting formally each year since 2004, when an Inuit Early Childhood Development Strategy was finalized. This strategy, reviewed and updated annually, provides a vision, principles, and goals for Inuit early childhood development (ECD). The strategy and the working group support culturally specific services and address local needs of programs.

TRIPARTITE AGREEMENT ON FIRST NATIONS HEALTH GOVERNANCE

In response to RCAP recommendations, there has been a shift to maximize control over service design and administration of Aboriginal early learning programming. Authority for health programs in British Columbia, which include early childhood development services for First Nations children living on reserve, has been transferred to the First Nations Health Authority (FNHA). The FNHA plans, designs, funds, delivers, and manages programs previously administered by Health Canada. This unique agreement brings together BC First Nations, the federal government, and the provincial government to give communities greater control over delivery of a broad range of early childhood and development services that meet locally defined needs.

IMMERSION IN ABORIGINAL EARLY CHILDHOOD PROGRAMS

With the onset of Aboriginal early childhood programs grounded in the cultural traditions and languages of local Aboriginal communities, emphasis on Indigenous language preservation, revitalization, and use has become a priority. Early childhood programs in Canada have established learning settings in which young children are immersed in the culture and language of the community. RCAP highlighted the Splatsin Daycare in British Columbia as an example of how Aboriginal languages in early childhood programs give these programs a distinctly Aboriginal character. Since then, early immersion programs have expanded across Canada, including the Kihew Waciston Cree Immersion School in Onion Lake, Saskatchewan; the multiple classes of kindergarten at the Opaskwayak Cree Nation; the Nhiyawak Cree Immersion Kindergarten at St. Frances School in Saskatoon; the Eskasoni Mi'kmaq Immersion Program; and the Cseyseten language nest at Adam's Lake, British Columbia.

DISCUSSION: SUCCESSES AND CHALLENGES

School Readiness and Positive Identity Development through Culturally Grounded Programs and Services. AHS programs located on reserve and off reserve across Canada are proven examples of the positive impacts that culturally based early childhood programs have on the linguistic and cultural restoration of Indigenous communities and on school readiness. Program performance studies of the AHSUNC (2012) showed that children with prior participation in the program had significantly higher school readiness scores at the beginning of a school year than children of the same age new to the program. In an ASHOR survey, kindergarten teachers reported that they see a difference in the children who have attended an AHS program compared with children who did not attend one. Teachers report that children in the program have better basic skills, are more independent and confident, and have enhanced self-esteem. Furthermore, a review of eight selected Aboriginal Human Resources Development Agreements (AHRDAs) that include a FNICCI reveals that daycare centres funded through this initiative have had impacts on children's development and the local economy by enabling parents to pursue employment and training.[8]

Local Control of Early Learning Programs and Services. Another positive development in response to RCAP recommendations has been the shift to maximize control over service design and administration of Aboriginal early learning programming. AHS programs and the BC tripartite agreement are demonstrations of how programs and services can be delivered through flexible and responsive approaches. The ability of programs to decide on local priorities means that culturally enriched ECD programs can also contribute to the health and well-being of Indigenous children.[9] Furthermore, locally developed delivery models demonstrate how programs and services can meet the diverse needs of Indigenous children and families.

Professional Learning. The paucity of Aboriginal early childhood educators presents a major challenge for Aboriginal communities and programs.[10]
Reports suggest that the shortage of qualified Aboriginal early childhood
teachers is the result of stringent early childhood licensing requirements,
the high costs of developing and delivering local training programs, the vast
distances between postsecondary institutions and Aboriginal communities
(requiring potential educators to relocate from their families and communities), and formal academic requirements for acceptance into training
programs.[11] These factors are compounded by the need for increased funding to support professional learning.[12] Jessica Ball points out the need for
"federal investment in professional education to substantially increase the
skilled Aboriginal labour force for operating programs for young Aboriginal
children and families, including early childhood education[; such invest-
ment] is long overdue and could work to overcome the challenges of staff
recruitment, retention, and on-going improvement."[13]

Decline of Federal Support for Aboriginal Early Childhood Development.
According to a 2014 British Columbia Aboriginal Child Care Society
report, federal interest in the early 2000s in closing the gap in life chances
between Aboriginal children and other children in Canada through early
childhood education has receded. The report points to numerous changes
in policy direction that directly affect funding for Aboriginal early childhood education, including the shelving of the Kelowna Accord,[14] the delay
in accepting the United Nations Declaration on the Rights of Indigenous
Peoples (UNDRIP), and the Liberal government's intention to replace
plans for a national child-care program with the Universal Child Care
Benefit. Ball recommends a mechanism for monitoring Canada's commitments to Aboriginal children by drawing attention to a legal framework
and an independent national children's commission as means to monitor
conditions for Aboriginal children.[15]

Reports concerning Aboriginal early childhood education consistently call for increased and sustained funding to allow organizations
and communities to develop their own capacities and culturally appropriate early learning models.[16] The Public Policy Forum recommends a
comprehensive analysis of funding levels in non-Indigenous communities compared with First Nations, Inuit, and Métis communities because
there are significant funding disparities per capita for similar programs
that target different population groups.[17]

*Need to Increase Access to and Coordination of Aboriginal Early Learn-
ing Programs and Services.* Despite the emergence two decades ago of
federally funded programs, such as AHS, FNICCI, and others, as well as
many innovative provincial and local programs, there is an urgent need to
increase accessibility to Aboriginal early childhood education programs
for children and families. The 2012 First Nations Regional Health Survey
found that only a third of children living on reserve attended a formal-
ized child-care program. In urban and northern communities, there is a
growing demand for culturally relevant early childhood services that has
led to an annual average of 1,300 Aboriginal children on waiting lists for
AHSUNC programs.[18] As the Indigenous population continues to increase,
the demand for locally developed services grows. This is significant for
young Métis children and families for specific services not available at
the federal level.[19]

INDIGENIZING K–12 EDUCATION

RCAP's major K–12 educational recommendations discussed in this
section include (1) ensuring that education is recognized as a critical
component of Aboriginal self-government; (2) enacting aspects of Aboriginal control over Aboriginal education; (3) establishing system-wide
approaches such as a school board strategy; and (4) increasing culture-
based curricula and programs, including Aboriginal languages.[20]

EDUCATION AND ABORIGINAL SELF-GOVERNMENT

Across Canada, many tripartite educational agreements in the form of
memorandums of understanding among First Nations, the federal government, and provincial/territorial governments for kindergarten–postsecondary education of First Nations learners have been signed since 2008.
These agreements indicate approaches for the partners to work cooperatively to improve educational outcomes for First Nations students and to
support them if they move from on-reserve to off-reserve schools.[21] There
are a few modern-day BC treaties, other self-government agreements, and
educational laws that have been developed since RCAP that enable First
Nations to make laws concerning education provided on their reserves
and for educational institutions that they might develop. Very little information exists about how these agreements or laws have been enacted.

However, the Mi'kmaq Education Act, enacted in 1999 between the federal government and the Mi'kmaw[22] bands in Nova Scotia, is noteworthy. Under this act, Mi'kmaw communities may make laws about K–12 and post-secondary education as well as provide educational services and programs. The Mi'kmaw-Kina'matnewey, the official name for the Mi'kmaq Education Authority (MK) was established as a corporation under this act to support and deliver the act's services for twelve Mi'kmaw communities in Nova Scotia. The MK collects data on its students and works with universities on teacher education and master's degree programs. The following high school graduation rates for Mi'kmaw students were reported: 2010–11, 75 percent; 2012–13, 88 percent; 2013–14, 92 percent.[23]

PROVINCIAL/TERRITORIAL POLICY FRAMEWORKS

Some provincial ministries of education—such as in British Columbia, Alberta, Saskatchewan, Ontario, and Nova Scotia—have comprehensive Indigenous educational policy frameworks that include the expectation that school districts will work cooperatively with Aboriginal communities/organizations, the identification of goals for Aboriginal student academic success, and the inclusion of Aboriginal content and curricula. Others—such as in Manitoba—have a framework for K–12 curricular outcomes for teaching Aboriginal languages and cultures. The territorial governments of the Yukon, Northwest Territories, and Nunavut have approaches relevant to their specific contexts, such as agreements with Indigenous communities, an Aboriginal student educational achievement plan, and an Inuit culture-based curricular framework with teaching resources.

A noteworthy comprehensive framework is the five-year Aboriginal Education Enhancement Agreement (AEEA) of the BC Ministry of Education that started in 2000. Each of the province's sixty school districts works in partnership with Aboriginal peoples/communities to develop and implement an AEEA that sets improvement goals and carries out strategies for Aboriginal student success. School boards are expected to report annually on the progress of the AEEA. Since 2004, the BC Ministry of Education has undertaken the task of self-identification of Aboriginal students attending public schools so that their academic progress can be tracked throughout their schooling and into postsecondary education.[24] Schools/districts and stakeholder groups may use these data for assessing student progress on an annual basis and for planning future AEEA improvement goals. British Columbia is the only province that has collected and reported many different types of student data over a lengthy time period. Ontario began a voluntary Aboriginal student identification process in 2007; however, no student data on academic progress are evident on the provincial website.

ABORIGINAL CURRICULA AND RESOURCES

In this section, we highlight two national organizations that have created useful Indigenous curriculum and resource repositories and other exemplars of province-wide or territorial Indigenous curricula. Indspire, a national Indigenous-led registered charity, serves First Nations, Inuit, and Métis students through partnerships with Indigenous, private, and public sectors. Indspire's K–12 projects include a K–12 institute that is a virtual educational resource centre, national conferences, research assistance to schools and communities, and student career programs and activities.[25] The Martin Family Initiative "is committed to improving not only K–12 education for Indigenous children, but also the wider determinants that influence their educational outcomes, including health and well being."[26] Some projects include Promising Practices in Aboriginal Education, established in 2009, which includes K–12 curricular resources and practices, policies and research, and other topics such as parent/community engagement and early childhood education. Indspire and the Martin Family Initiative continue to add curricular and other educational resources to their websites.

In Nunavut, three foundational documents were published in 2007–8 that focused on Ilitaunnikuliriniq assessment, Inuglugijaittuq inclusive education, and Inuit Qaujimajatuqangit Nunavut curriculum. The foundation of the Nunavut 2008 Education Act includes Inuit values, Inuit language and bilingual education, inclusive education, and local control by district education authorities. Of note is the Elders in Schools program mandated in Nunavut's Education Act. In 2012–13, ninety-four certified Elders were teaching language and culture (traditional land-based, environmental knowledge and navigational skills).

In 2008, the Saskatchewan government made treaty education mandatory for K–12 grades and worked with the Saskatchewan Office of the Treaty Commissioner (OTC) to develop curricular materials and teacher training workshops with the project title We Are All Treaty People.[27] This project influenced the revision of the Saskatchewan provincial curriculum. As well, Saskatchewan universities have begun to make treaty education a mandatory part of their teacher education programs. The premise of this project is that "a Treaty takes at least two parties/peoples to enter into an agreement[;] if someone enjoys the fruits of this land known as Canada, then they must recognize that it was built on agreements/Treaties between its original inhabitants and the Crown."[28]

In 2015–16, the BC Ministry of Education completed a K–9 curricular redesign that has Aboriginal perspectives and resources embedded in each subject area and each grade level from kindergarten to grade nine. The First Nations Education Steering Committee (FNESC), a province-wide First Nations organization that provides second-level educational services, has led the development of provincial high school Aboriginal courses and resources.[29]

There has been an increase in school curricula that addresses the history and impact of Indian residential schools in Canada in response to the TRC recommendation that all K–12 students learn about this aspect of Canadian history. What follows are examples of residential school curricular resources that have been used in various territories and provinces. *Residential Schools Education*, a grade ten teaching resource, became mandatory in 2012 for grade ten northern studies in the Northwest Territories and social studies in Nunavut. One additional FNESC resource is the *Indian Residential Schools and Reconciliation Teacher Resource Guides* (2015) for grades five, ten, and eleven/twelve developed in response to the TRC call to action to develop age-appropriate curricula about these schools and their impacts for use in public education (and other systems).[30] Another resource that has been used widely across Canada is Project of Heart,[31] cooperative, inquiry-based school projects about the impacts of Indian residential schools.

DISCUSSION: SUCCESSES AND CHALLENGES

Some Progress in Local Control. RCAP's recommendation that emphasizes Aboriginal parental involvement and local control through legislation and school policies has been addressed to varying degrees across the country, though the quality and impact of such engagement is not consistently reported in publicly accessible documents on provincial and territorial websites. The three territorial governments of the Yukon, Northwest Territories, and Nunavut have their own educational acts that address Aboriginal education. Since the release of the RCAP report, provincial Ministries of Education have developed province-wide Aboriginal education strategies that include policy frameworks, action plans, and agreements. The Mi'kmaq Education Act in Nova Scotia has demonstrated substantial Mi'kmaq academic success, as noted above.[32]

More Provincial and School District Frameworks. Another RCAP recommendation related to the one above is a comprehensive school board Aboriginal education strategy developed with Aboriginal people to include hiring Aboriginal teachers; creating positions for Aboriginal administrators/leaders and counsellors/liaison workers/speech therapists; developing Aboriginal curricula; increasing Elder involvement; implementing Aboriginal language classes; including family/community involvement mechanisms; and reducing stereotypes/racism.

British Columbia's Aboriginal Education Enhancement Agreements for school districts appear to have consistent student academic growth patterns when there is a vibrant relationship between Aboriginal people (families, communities, organizations) and school/district staff and leadership.[33] Kitchenham, Fraser, Pidgeon, and Ragoonaden conducted research for the BC Ministry of Education on how AEEAs have helped to improve Aboriginal education and which improvements were needed for these agreements. The results of twenty-two participating school districts indicated that trust and relationship building are essential, that academic success is achieved through Indigenous inclusion, and that cultural alliances are beneficial.[34]

Increase in Aboriginal Curriculum. Another RCAP recommendation that has a systemic action implication is the development of innovative curricula that reflect Aboriginal cultures and community realities. This recommendation has been taken up across Canada at local levels, especially where public, independent, and First Nations schools have worked with First Nations, Métis, and Inuit family and community members to develop curricula, programs, and services based on local Indigenous knowledges. Some of these resources are for province-wide use as well. School districts, ministries of education, and other national educational association websites include information and web links to these numerous teaching/learning resources.

Indigenous K–12 teaching resources are at all grade levels and in all subject areas, including math and science. The latter (culturally responsive math and science) was only being introduced twenty years ago.

Today Indigenous knowledge and culturally responsive approaches to teaching math, science, and all other subjects are gaining momentum, though their use and impact need to be addressed through research. What is not evident is the uptake of these innovative curricula. Ministries of Education indicate that Aboriginal content and perspectives will be integrated more into the provincial curriculum; however, only two provinces have this system-wide inclusion, Saskatchewan with its 2007 mandatory K–12 treaty education and British Columbia with its 2015–16 redesigned curriculum. The ongoing challenge of meaningful implementation throughout the school system remains for Aboriginal curriculum.

Aboriginal Languages Require More Attention. Other ongoing challenges that have not been given sufficient attention and action are the recommendations that an Aboriginal Languages Act be developed and that Aboriginal language education be a priority in all educational systems.[35] Except for the territorial governments and Nova Scotia through the Mi'kmaq Education Act, Aboriginal language education does not appear to be a priority in all educational systems, nor has it received as much attention or support as Indigenous knowledge-based curricula.

Be Cautious with the Closing the Gap Discourse. Targets for improvement often focus on reducing the achievement gap between Aboriginal and non-Aboriginal students, which can be interpreted to mean that Aboriginal students have a deficit of ability to succeed and are vulnerable to being labelled/designated as special needs. Other important goals for success that counter this discourse of deficit reflect a more positive or holistic approach, such as a sense of belonging (emotional), student empowerment/leadership (physical), and knowledge and appreciation of Indigenous culture and history (social/emotional, spiritual, intellectual).

INDIGENIZING POSTSECONDARY EDUCATION

In this section, we address two key areas of postsecondary education: teacher education and colleges and universities.

TEACHER EDUCATION

Teachers are very important makers of change for K–12 education. RCAP made a number of recommendations related to preparing effective teachers, both Aboriginal and non-Aboriginal: (1) expand and fund existing Aboriginal teacher education programs contingent on evidence of Aboriginal support for the programs, involvement in program governance, use of Aboriginal content and pedagogy, and periodic evaluations; (2) increase the number of Aboriginal people through teacher education programs and career laddering opportunities delivered directly in communities and ensure that students in each province and territory have access to such programs; and (3) include courses on Aboriginal education for both Aboriginal and non-Aboriginal education students.[36]

A set of Indigenous teacher education programs established in the 1960s–80s and offered in Indigenous communities was mentioned in the RCAP report.[37] A few of them are still offering their programs, although the communities have changed and their programs have been revised. NITEP (Native Indian Teacher Education Program) with regional field centres is sponsored by the University of British Columbia; McGill University offers community-based programs throughout Quebec in partnership with First Nations and Inuit education authorites; and SUNTEP (Saskatchewan Urban Native Teacher Education Program) is offered by the Gabriel Dumont Institute, the University of Saskatchewan and the University of Regina. In 2016, we identified nineteen Indigenous teacher education programs that culminated in a Bachelor of Education degree.

Each province has at least one Indigenous teacher education program that includes preparation for elementary, middle, and high school teaching. The programs have many Indigenous education courses that constitute a specialization in this area, and many are community based or offer some parts of the programs at community sites. The range of courses includes Aboriginal history, Indigenous knowledge, math/science and Aboriginal culture, Aboriginal curriculum and pedagogy, and Indigenous languages.

To ensure Aboriginal language revitalization, a few Bachelor of Education degree programs provide programming to develop language educators with some educational laddering opportunities whereby learners can complete diplomas that lead to degrees. Examples include the following:

- The University of Victoria's Aboriginal Language Revitalization program and laddering certification culminate in a Bachelor of Education degree. The University of Victoria also offers a Master's in Indigenous Language Revitalization, the only such degree in Canada.

- Lakehead University has a Bachelor of Education in Aboriginal Education and a Native Language Instructors Program/Specialization in Native Language.
- There is a joint Aboriginal Language Specialist/Bachelor of Education degree with Red River College and the University of Winnipeg.
- Nipissing University offers a Diploma in Anishnaabemowin as a Second Language Program.

COLLEGES AND UNIVERSITIES

In reference to public postsecondary institutions, RCAP recommended that they have a comprehensive strategy to increase participation and retention of Aboriginal learners that includes Aboriginal curricula, meeting spaces, Aboriginal appointments to boards of governors, Aboriginal student unions, support services, and cross-cultural sensitivity training for faculty and staff.[38] RCAP also recommended that Elders have an active role in education throughout levels and systems and be compensated as professionals and that educational institutions facilitate exchanges among Elders.[39] Three provincial Ministries of Advanced Education have acted on the first recommendation.

PROVINCIAL ABORIGINAL POSTSECONDARY POLICY FRAMEWORKS

In British Columbia, an *Aboriginal Post-Secondary Education and Training Framework and Action Plan: 2020 Vision for the Future* (framework) was launched in 2012 with a vision, goals, strategies, and targets for 2013, 2016, and 2020. The framework was developed in partnership with many Indigenous communities and organizations. It includes systemic changes such as Aboriginal representation on boards of governors, capital funding projects for Aboriginal student gathering spaces, funding for students, support for community-based programs, and increased transition from K–12 to postsecondary education.[40]

Saskatchewan does not have a separate Aboriginal education policy framework, but it has goals of increasing First Nations and Métis student postsecondary enrolment and completion. The province funds various postsecondary institutions and programs to achieve this goal.[41]

Ontario developed the *Aboriginal Postsecondary Education and Training Policy Framework, 2011,* in consultation with many people. One common outcome is that all publicly funded colleges and universities have

Aboriginal Education Councils. There are many examples of programs and initiatives related to the plan's goals. In 2015, the Ontario government announced $97 million over three years for Indigenous postsecondary education and training.[42]

COLLEGE AND UNIVERSITY ABORIGINAL POSTSECONDARY STRATEGIES

Colleges and universities appear to have specific Aboriginal plans and/or include Aboriginal postsecondary education in their respective strategic plans. National publications such as *University Affairs*[43] and repositories such as Universities Canada indicate growing interest in and descriptions of programs and actions to Indigenize the academy through Indigenous programs/courses; Aboriginal admissions policies; spaces for students to gather and learn; support services that reflect Indigenous architecture and/or culture; Indigenous leadership positions; and Indigenous advisory councils. For example, the BC Ministry of Advanced Education provided funding for Indigenous student gathering spaces, which resulted in twenty-four postsecondary institutions receiving such funding.

Building or refurbishing existing facilities for Indigenous gathering spaces requires much institutional, government, and private sector funding and commitment. Some examples of new cultural spaces include

- the First Peoples House (longhouse style) at the University of Victoria, opened in 2010;
- the Gordon Oakes Red Bear Centre at the University of Saskatchewan, opened in 2015; and
- the First Peoples Pavilion at the University of Quebec, Val-d'Or campus.

Universities Canada (UC), with a membership of ninety-seven universities, released its thirteen principles on Indigenous education, which focused on the commitment to improve Indigenous education in member universities.[44] One useful UC project has been to create a database of 350 Indigenous-oriented programs and student services at universities across Canada. UC also released some data from a 2013 survey of its members, with a 90 percent rate of return, that indicated the following:

- Sixty-one universities (two of three) offer transitional programs for Indigenous students.
- Twenty-five Indigenous languages are taught.

- More than 75 percent of the universities offer cultural activities for Indigenous students.
- Seventy-one percent have a partnership with local Indigenous communities.
- Thirty-three percent of Indigenous programs are offered off campus.[45]

One area of innovation has been the establishment of Elders-in-Residence programs at colleges and universities. Trent University, the first Canadian university to establish a Department of Indigenous Studies, has had Elder tenure track positions since 1975.[46] Trent sponsors an annual Elders and Traditional Peoples Gathering and celebrated the fortieth anniversary of this gathering in 2016. Vancouver Island University (VIU) includes a university-wide Elders-in-Residence program that began in 1992. Recently, VIU acknowledged the significance of their contribution with the signing of a new faculty agreement that accords them faculty status.[47] Elders' roles have further expanded to include advising university governance bodies at institutions such as St. Mary's University, Simon Fraser University, and Lakehead University.

DISCUSSION: SUCCESSES AND CHALLENGES

Systemic Advancements. There have been some major advances and innovations in Indigenous postsecondary education since 1996. These innovations require system-wide cooperation and commitment from institutional leaders. Long-standing programs such as Indigenous teacher education, Indigenous law, and Indigenous studies began in the late 1960s and 1970s. To continue offering such programs requires immense effort, commitment, and leadership, often carried out by Indigenous faculty and staff and non-Indigenous allies. Indigenous teacher education programs that address the RCAP recommendations include community-based relationships and sites, Indigenous knowledge that shapes teaching and learning, and the introduction of Aboriginal language revitalization courses and programs.

In Canada, faculties of education have increased their course and content offerings in Indigenous education. Teaching and learning through Indigenous knowledge frameworks are helping pre-service teachers to be better equipped to respond to Indigenous education policy and curricular reform. These frameworks draw from Indigenous learning approaches that include storytelling, mentorship, experiential and intergenerational learning, holistic approaches, and land/place-based learning, and they present opportunities to advance and shift teacher candidates' understanding of Indigenous education in schools.[48] Studies underscore the significant shift in pre-service teachers' attitudes toward engaging in the practices of Indigenous education.[49]

Compulsory Aboriginal Courses or Approaches. RCAP recommended that Aboriginal education courses be included for all teacher education learners. The Indigenous teacher education programs have many such courses that constitute an Indigenous education specialization. In the past number of years, teacher education programs have responded to national and provincial policies that call for compulsory instruction in Indigenous education for their pre-service teachers. The Association of Canadian Deans of Education expressed its commitment to increasing future teachers' knowledge about and understanding of Indigenous education in its 2010 Accord on Indigenous Education. The 2015 TRC report has a number of recommendations that call on postsecondary institutions to require all students in the fields of nursing, medicine, legal studies, social work, and education to take courses dealing with Aboriginal history; the legacy of residential schools; Aboriginal rights; and Indigenous teachings, practices, and worldviews.

Sustaining Change. There appears to have been an increase in Indigenous postsecondary educational programs and services in recent years. Universities Canada notes that from 2013 to 2015 there was a 33 percent increase in programming and student services for Indigenous students.[50] The growth of Indigenous-oriented learning programs and student services might seem to be recent; however, to develop Indigenous community relationships, secure funding, and acquire university approval for new programs take years. The next challenge is to sustain these programs and services. Many postsecondary institutions are facing budget deficits and challenges, and more Indigenous people are interested in pursuing postsecondary education, so student funding remains a big challenge. It might appear that postsecondary institutions as systems have made some recent systemic changes to make their learning environments and processes more culturally relevant and safer for Indigenous learners.

Holistic Approaches. Constant vigilance to monitor the changes discussed above and to make improvements to them as needed is necessary to ensure that educational systems are more successful for Aboriginal learners. There is no quick fix, nor is there a single answer. The holistic approaches or strategic plans that seem to have promise or have demonstrated some success include establishing partnerships with Indigenous communities/organizations; using Indigenous knowledge systems for learning and creating student support programs; expanding the number of Indigenous faculty and staff, including Elders; increasing non-Indigenous student, faculty, and staff awareness and knowledge of Indigenous history, culture, and current situations; and monitoring progress consistently over time.

INDIGENIZING COMMUNITY EDUCATION

Local First Nations and Aboriginal communities have led innovation in the development of Aboriginal-controlled postsecondary institutions. RCAP recommendations related to Aboriginal postsecondary institutions include: (1) federal, provincial, and territorial governments work with Aboriginal governments to facilitate integrated delivery of adult literacy, basic education, academic upgrading, and job training under the control of Aboriginal people; (2) federal, provincial, and territorial governments collaborate with Aboriginal governments and organizations to establish and support postsecondary educational institutions controlled by Aboriginal people, including core and program funding, capital costs for new institutions, improvements in facilities for community learning centres, and fulfillment of treaties and modern agreements related to education; and (3) Aboriginal-controlled postsecondary institutions work cooperatively to establish working relationships with national accreditation bodies, develop regional boards and/or a Canada-wide board to create standards of accreditation for programs, facilitate the transferability of courses between institutions, and pursue matters of common interest.[51]

Indigenous institutions began offering programs in the 1970s in response to the high unemployment of Indigenous community members and the failure of public educational institutions to provide relevant and quality education to community members. Aboriginal-controlled institutions could ensure that traditional knowledge, methods, and courses were the basis of programming.[52] Furthermore, the authority of community-controlled institutions is consistent with the goals of Aboriginal jurisdiction over and self-determination of education. RCAP noted that "Aboriginal institutions delivering post-secondary education, like American tribal colleges, have their roots in the determination of communities and nations to see relevant education services offered close to home."[53]

Four categories of Aboriginal postsecondary institutions are outlined in the RCAP report: (1) a college affiliated with one or more (usually public) postsecondary institutions; (2) a small affiliated institution serving members of a tribal or regional area; (3) a community-based learning centre offering mainly adult education; and (4) a non-profit independent institution (local, provincial, and/or national) that offers programs in communities and to groups of communities.[54] Many examples of these four types of Aboriginal-controlled postsecondary institutions are still operating today, and many more have been established since 1996.[55] What follows are examples of Aboriginal-controlled postsecondary institutions that respond to the RCAP recommendations.

ACCREDITED FIRST NATIONS INSTITUTIONS

First Nations University of Canada

Formerly Saskatchewan Indian Federated College, First Nations University of Canada (FNUC) is a First Nations–controlled university that offers programs with Indigenous knowledge bases to both Indigenous and non-Indigenous students from across Canada and other countries. Its name change occurred in 2003 at the same time that its new magnificent building was completed. FNUC has campuses in Regina, Saskatoon, and Prince Albert. It enrols approximately 3,000 students annually in a wide array of degree programs. Lighting the Path, FNUC's 2013–18 strategic plan, outlines four major goals that address Indigenous languages, cultures, and traditions; innovative student learning experiences; sustainable growth; and enhanced stakeholder engagement.[56] FNUC continues to have a partnership with the University of Regina, which awards the certificates, diplomas, and degrees for programs offered by FNUC. It was the first Indigenous postsecondary institution to achieve university accreditation in Canada, and it is the only Aboriginal postsecondary institution to receive federal funding on a regular basis rooted in legislation.[57] Seventy-four First Nations communities in Saskatchewan support FNUC through the Federation of Saskatchewan Indian Nations. For a few years, FNUC had major political difficulties, but it appears that these issues have been resolved, and FNUC is gaining momentum and strength with its comprehensive set of university programs and courses.

Nicola Valley Institute of Technology

Nicola Valley Institute of Technology (NVIT) was formed by local First Nations communities in the Merritt area of British Columbia in 1983 to serve the postsecondary educational needs of Indigenous people in the area. In 1995, NVIT became a publicly recognized postsecondary institution funded by the provincial government. The main campus is in a fairly new facility in Merritt that includes classroom and administrative space, a student residence, a child-care facility, and a new trades building. Its second campus, much smaller, is located in Burnaby. NVIT's governance includes an Indigenous board of governors and an eighteen-member Elders' council. NVIT offers a diverse range of courses at its campuses and in many Indigenous communities, and it has many partnerships and affiliation agreements with Indigenous communities for programs and with colleges/universities for articulation and transferability of courses and programs.[58]

CONSORTIUMS

Advancing the goals of Aboriginal postsecondary institutions through sharing, collaborating, and lobbying are Aboriginal consortiums.[59] Examples include the Aboriginal Institutes' Consortium, the First Nations Adult and Higher Education Consortium, the National Association of Indigenous Institutes of Higher Learning, and the Indigenous Adult and Higher Learning Association. One international association is the World Indigenous Nations Higher Education Consortium.

Aboriginal Institutes' Consortium

The Aboriginal Institutes' Consortium (AIC) was established in 1994 for advocacy of and cooperation on the development of resources for postsecondary education with seven institutes in Ontario that engage nearly 4,000 learners each year. Developing a system of accreditation and achieving recognition and capacity development of Aboriginal institutions are among the objectives of the consortium. If it can achieve these goals, then "it would surely be a significant act of decolonization since it would allow Indigenous peoples to access colonial coffers and use those funds toward the betterment of Indigenous communities through postsecondary education programs constructed within Indigenous cultures and knowledges."[60]

World Indigenous Nations Higher Education Consortium

The World Indigenous Nations Higher Education Consortium (WINHEC) was launched in Calgary during the World Indigenous Peoples Conference on Education in 2002. Members include Australia, the United States, Canada, the American Indian Higher Education Consortium, Wanaga of Aotearoa of New Zealand, and Saamiland of North Norway. WINHEC provides an international forum and support for Indigenous people to access and complete postsecondary education in Indigenous institutes of higher education. WINHEC also serves as an accreditation authority for its members.

DISCUSSION: SUCCESSES AND CHALLENGES

Increasing Accessibility to Postsecondary Education for Indigenous Learners. Studies indicate that Aboriginal postsecondary institutions are contributing to increased enrolment of Aboriginal students.[61] Local programs allow Aboriginal students to develop skills and confidence needed for postsecondary participation. For students who might not have completed high school, Aboriginal postsecondary programs and services can offer supports that include study skills and upgrading to prepare students better for public institutions.[62] With transitional programs at these institutions, students can ladder in to provincial postsecondary schooling. Having attended a tribal college, Native American students were less likely to drop out when they transitioned to a mainstream institution.[63]

Funding Inequities. Aboriginal postsecondary institutions do not have access to equitable funding compared with provincial postsecondary institutions. Since there is no federal legislation that recognizes Aboriginal postsecondary institutions, the federal government provides discretionary, short-term funding generally obtained through competitive application,[64] with the exception of FNUC. Otherwise, Aboriginal institutions must partner with accredited provincial postsecondary institutions to access operating grants.[65] These funding restraints have implications for staffing, curricular development, physical space, and student services at Aboriginal institutions.

Recognition and Accreditation. Despite the efforts to meet the needs of Aboriginal learners and communities through Aboriginal-controlled institutions, Aboriginal students continue to be disadvantaged by policy restraints that prevent most Aboriginal-controlled postsecondary institutions from granting degrees. This positions them as "second-class" institutions, resulting in unfair judgments of Aboriginal students by potential employers.[66] In order that students can have their credentials valued and transferred, Aboriginal institutions must partner with provincial postsecondary institutions. For example, the Gabriel Dumont Institute, the only Métis-controlled institute in Canada, must have affiliations with the University of Saskatchewan and Saskatchewan Polytechnic (formerly Saskatchewan Institute of Applied Sciences and Technology) for students to receive accreditation of their degrees.[67] Mandated partnerships reduce the autonomy of Aboriginal institutions. To date, government policies and programs have not evolved to recognize the contributions and economic benefits of Aboriginal-controlled postsecondary institutions.[68]

CONCLUSION: THUNDERBIRD RISING

An Indigenous figure, Thunderbird, common to many Indigenous cultures across Canada, enters this concluding section to reinforce some of the successes discussed throughout the chapter and to pose some continuing challenges. Thunderbird is the most powerful supernatural being in Indigenous traditional stories. It can represent the power to change through its acts of bravery, persistence, and great strength. The movement in Indigenous education could be one of Thunderbird's key challenges and opportunities. The Royal Commission on Aboriginal Peoples provided a comprehensive set of recommendations for improving lifelong aspects of education for Indigenous learners and for learning about Indigenous history, culture, and contributions to Canadian society, for which the term "Indigenous education" is used in this chapter.

How educational systems have addressed Indigenous education at all levels and how they have created structural changes in governance, policies, programs, and curricula became the meaning of this chapter's subtitle, "Indigenizing Education in Canada." The progress on RCAP's educational recommendations since 1996 can be viewed as getting these systems ready for transformation, which is where Thunderbird comes into the story. The ongoing efforts of many people across Canada to Indigenize education are like the movements of Thunderbird, which make it rise. Indigenous education is improving, but it could rise even higher with greater cooperation and continued commitment.

What does Indigenizing education mean? It involves transforming educational systems through Indigenous knowledge approaches to include Indigenous values, philosophies/teachings, ways of knowing, pedagogies, content, and assessment. IK approaches are brought together with Western and other forms of knowledge, but they are not subservient to them. In fact, IK must be a core component of all educational levels and systems that serve Indigenous learners, and it must have a meaningful place in educational systems for all learners. Indigenous people must be engaged in decision-making and teaching roles that include policy, curricular, and program development, implementation, and evaluation. Indigenous community members, especially Elders and cultural knowledge holders at local levels, form the nucleus of the Indigenizing process. Without this expertise, Indigenizing education would be impossible. At the same time, community leaders, parents and family members of Indigenous learners, and educators, both Indigenous and non-Indigenous, have important roles in ensuring that Indigenous education is meaningful, relevant, and of high quality. The process of Indigenizing education has a role for all involved in education. At the same time, particular groups have been effective at driving systemic changes.

DRIVERS OF CHANGE

Indigenous people and non-Indigenous allies working in local community, provincial, national, and international contexts are the main drivers of change when they form coalitions and partnerships. The formation of regional, provincial, and national educational associations has resulted in some remarkable achievements. Indigenous organizations such as the First Nations Education Steering Committee, Indigenous Adult and Higher Learning Association in British Columbia, the First Nations Education Council in Quebec,[69] the Manitoba First Nations Education Resource Centre,[70] and the Mi'kmaw Kina'matnewey corporation in Nova Scotia have created strong partnerships with Indigenous communities and other educational professional associations to work with both provincial and federal governments on jurisdictional matters, curricula, policies, increasing the number of Indigenous teachers, and improving school facilities. Other professional national associations, such as the Association of Canadian Deans of Education, through its 2010 Indigenous Education Accord, and Indspire have created many opportunities for educators across Canada to work together to initiate systemic educational change.

ACHIEVEMENTS, BARRIERS, AND POLICY CHALLENGES

Two major areas of educational achievement in the past twenty years have been IK approaches and Indigenous local control of and engagement in education. However, the achievements have not been consistently spread across Canada, and some phases of lifelong education need much more attention and support. In this section, we first highlight the two major achievements and then Thunderbird's view of policy challenges.

Indigenous knowledge approaches are integral to early childhood programs both on and off reserve, especially Aboriginal-specific early childhood education and development programs that are holistic. In K–12 education, IK is often a natural part of First Nations schools. Public K–12 systems now include an Indigenous curriculum, but it is not an integral part of learning, except in the territories, British Columbia, and Saskatchewan. A number of other provinces are working on or plan to increase Indigenous curricula, especially after the TRC report in 2015. Certainly, Indigenous curricular resources have mushroomed in the past twenty years at all levels of education. The resources can be stand-alone, multimedia projects, units/lessons, and courses developed by or in partnership with Indigenous people. In postsecondary education, Indigenous teacher education programs continue to offer Indigenous education concentrations, with many programs offered in a community or region with options for study at university campuses. Teacher education programs across Canada are increasingly implementing a required Indigenous course for all pre-service teachers. Although not addressed in this chapter, more disciplines, such as law and social work, are requiring Indigenous course learning. Of note are three universities. The University of Winnipeg and Lakehead University, in the fall of 2016, required their students to complete an Indigenous course, and Trent University did the same in the spring of 2017.

Indigenous local control and engagement in education are vibrant in the following Indigenous early childhood education programs: Aboriginal Head Start in Urban and Northern Communities, Aboriginal Head

Start On-Reserve, and First Nations and Inuit Child Care Initiative. These three national programs have had positive impacts on the cultural identity development of young Aboriginal children and their subsequent readiness for K–12 schooling. Central to these programs are local Aboriginal community control and engagement of parents/family members. However, they are limited in their programming because of restricted federal funding. Despite funding issues, the Aboriginal children who experience these early childhood programs will have stronger Indigenous identities that they should be able to build upon as they enter the K–12 school system.

At the K–12 educational phase, Indigenous local control is strongest in First Nations schools. Provincial school systems might have local agreements and district-wide strategic plans developed in partnership or cooperation with First Nations, Métis, and Inuit communities and families of Indigenous children. This area of legislation still requires much attention since few Indigenous education acts exist.

In postsecondary education, Indigenous educational institutions are prime exemplars of local community control and governance. However, they have continual funding concerns because the majority do not receive core funding from either the federal government or provincial governments. Colleges and universities have increased Indigenous representation on their boards of governors and have Indigenous councils and advisory committees. The phrase "Indigenizing the academy" is often used in postsecondary education across Canada to signal intention and action in this area.

THUNDERBIRD'S VIEW OF EDUCATIONAL POLICY CHALLENGES

Thunderbird wonders what Indigenizing education in Canada will look like in the next twenty years. To build upon the educational successes since the RCAP report in 1996, Thunderbird suggests that some key policy challenges will need to be addressed.

Strengthening and sustaining systemic changes to Indigenous education continue to be key policy challenges and opportunities at all levels of education. Indigenous curricula, programs, and teaching approaches, along with the engagement of Indigenous people, have been introduced in some educational systems. However, these approaches are not consistently implemented throughout all educational levels, nor are they province-wide. Indigenous language revitalization is another area that requires more policy attention.

Limited government core funding continues to hinder the progress of Indigenous education across Canada. The achievements noted in each educational phase have resulted in some form of educational success that will need continued funding. The growing population of First Nations, Métis, and Inuit children, especially of preschool age, means that much more core funding will be required, and that increased funding will become a higher priority for K–12 and postsecondary education.

Action on Indigenous education legislation needs to be a priority at provincial and federal levels. Many of the current agreements enable First Nations and Inuit to develop laws, policies, and programs for their children who reside on Indigenous lands; however, they often do not have any authority to enter into legal agreements with provincial governments concerning the education that their children receive in the public school system. Métis and urban Indigenous people have not been involved in education legislation, another area needing attention.

Thunderbird is often visually characterized as having three tail feathers, with each feather representing the Indigenous past, present, and future. As we have revealed in this chapter, Indigenous knowledge and local control have always been at the heart of education for Indigenous peoples. The leadership of early Indigenous educators is acknowledged and remembered. Their efforts to make educational changes within systems that had very strong assimilationist goals were difficult; however, they persisted so that educators today can continue to strengthen IK in education. The impacts of these knowledges and core values are making significant differences in programs, practices, and policies that support Indigenous students, families, and communities for schooling/education today. With the power of Thunderbird, we are learning from the successes how to address the challenges presented so that future generations of learners, both Indigenous and non-Indigenous, can experience good-quality Indigenous education that prepares them for life in the twenty-first century.

NOTES

1 Quoted in Castellano, Davis, and Lahache, Aboriginal Education, viii.

2 Corntassel, "Insurgent Education and the Roles of Indigenous Intellectuals"; Kuokkanen, *Reshaping the University*; Mihesuah and Wilson, *Indigenizing the Academy*; Pidgeon, "Moving beyond Good Intentions."

3 Ottmann, "Indigenizing the Academy."

4 Royal Commission on Aboriginal Peoples (RCAP), Volume 3: Gathering Strength, 446.

5 RCAP, *Volume 3: Gathering Strength*, 422–23.

6 Greenwood, *BC First Nations Children*, 1; see also Greenwood, *An Overview of the Development of Aboriginal Early Childhood Services* and "Children Are a Gift to Us."

7 Public Health Agency of Canada, *Aboriginal Head Start*.

8 Human Resources and Skills Development Canada (HRSDC), *Summative Evaluation of the Aboriginal Development Human Resources Agreements*.

9 British Columbia Aboriginal Child Care Society (BCACCS), *Training, Recruitment, and Retention*.

10 Greenwood, de Leeuw, and Fraser, "Aboriginal Children and Early Childhood Development."

11 BCACCS, *Training, Recruitment, and Retention*; Preston, Cottrell, Pelletier, and Pearce, "Aboriginal Early Childhood Education in Canada."

12 Inuit Tapiriit Kanatami (ITK), *Understanding the Training Needs*.

13 Ball, *Improving the Reach of Early Childhood Education*, 2.

14 See http://www.thecanadianencyclopedia.ca/en/article/kelowna-accord/.

15 Ball, *Improving the Reach of Early Childhood Education*.

16 Ball and Moselle, *Contributions of Culture and Language in Aboriginal Head Start*; BCACCS, *Training, Recruitment, and Retention*; Nguyen, "Closing the Education Gap"; Preston, "Aboriginal Early Childhood Education."

17 Public Policy Forum, *Building Leaders*.

18 Public Health Agency of Canada, *Evaluation of the Aboriginal Head Start Urban and Northern Communities Program*.

19 Métis National Council, "Towards a Métis Nation Education Strategy."

20 RCAP, *Volume 3: Gathering Strength*, 444–87.

21 See https://www.aadnc-aandc.gc.ca/eng/1308840098023/1308840148639.

22 Following Mi'kmaw scholar Marie Battiste's (2013) usage, we use Mi'kmaw when it is an adjective preceding a noun.

23 Simon, *Mi'kmaw Kina'matnewey Supporting Student Success*.

24 Each student attending BC K–12 public schools is given a personal education number (PEN) used to track his or her progress throughout public school education and transition to postsecondary education. Aboriginal students are identified through a school process and verified with a student's family.

25 See https://indspire.ca.

26 See http://www.themfi.ca.

27 See https://www.crrf-fcrr.ca/en/news-a-events/articles/item/25199-2014-we-are-all-treaty-people.

28 Office of the Treaty Commissioner, Saskatchewan. See http://www.otc.ca/.

29 Examples are Aboriginal Math Resources 8, 9; English First Peoples 10, 11, and 12; and First Peoples Principles of Learning that have influenced the overall curricular redesign.

30   See http://www.fnesc.ca/about-the-project/.

31   See http://projectofheart.ca/what-is-project-of-heart/.

32   Battiste, *Decolonizing Education*.

33   Kitchenham, Fraser, Pidgeon, and Ragoonaden, *Aboriginal Education Enhancement Agreements*.

34   See *Aboriginal Education Enhancement Agreements: Complicated Conversations as Pathways to Success* at https://www.bced.gov.bc.ca/abed/research/AEEA-Final_Report_June_2016.pdf.

35   Galley, Gessner, Herbert, Thompson, and Williams, *A Report on the National Dialogue Session on Indigenous Languages*; Truth and Reconciliation Commission of Canada (TRC), *Honouring the Truth*.

36   RCAP, *Volume 3: Gathering Strength*, 490–500.

37   RCAP, *Volume 3: Gathering Strength*, 495–96. Only the Indigenous teacher education programs that RCAP mentioned in this section and those that still operated in 2017 are discussed here.

38   RCAP, *Volume 3: Gathering Strength*, 478–89.

39   RCAP, *Volume 3: Gathering Strength*, 491.

40   See http://www2.gov.bc.ca/gov/content/education-training/post-secondary-education/aboriginal-education-training.

41   See https://publications.saskatchewan.ca/#/products/87113.

42   See https://news.ontario.ca/maesd/en/2015/06/ontario-investing-in-aboriginal-postsecondary-education-and-training.html.

43   Macdonald, "Indigenizing the Academy."

44   Universities Canada, *Enhancing Indigenous Student Success*.

45   Universities Canada, *Enhancing Indigenous Student Success*.

46   See https://www.uwinnipeg.ca/index/cms-filesystem-action?file=pdfs/conferences/2007/trent-university.pdf.

47   Universities Canada, *Enhancing Indigenous Student Success*.

48   Archibald, *Indigenous Storywork*; Brayboy and Maughan, "Indigenous Knowledges and the Story of the Bean"; Canadian Council on Learning, *The State of Aboriginal Learning in Canada; Chambers*, "The Land Is the Best Teacher I Have Ever Had"; Deer, "Integrating Aboriginal Perspectives in Education"; Hare, "All of Our Responsibility"; Iseke-Barnes, "Pedagogies for Decolonizing"; Kitchen and Raynor, "Indigenizing Teacher Education" ; Williams and Tanaka, "Schalay'nung Sxwey'ga."

49   Deer, "Integrating Aboriginal Perspectives"; Kitchen and Raynor, "Indigenizing Teacher Education"; Martineau et al., "Alberta's Aboriginal Teacher Education Program"; Williams and Tanaka, "Schalay'nung Sxwey'ga."

50   Universities Canada, *Enhancing Indigenous Student Success*.

51   RCAP, *Volume 3: Gathering Strength*, 504, 522.

52   Aboriginal Institutes' Consortium, *Aboriginal Institutions of Higher Education*.

53   RCAP, *Volume 3: Gathering Strength*, 517.

54   RCAP, *Volume 3: Gathering Strength*, 517–19.

55   See Stonechild, *The New Buffalo*, for a comprehensive examination of Aboriginal history and policy in postsecondary education across Canada.

56   See http://fnuniv.ca/images/factsfigures/fnuniv_stratplan_2013_2018.pdf.

57   Jenkins, "Indigenous Post-Secondary Institutions."

58   Billy Minnabarriet, "Aboriginal Post-Secondary Education in British Columbia"; see also http://www.nvit.ca/about/default.htm.

59 Browning, "Aboriginal Post-Secondary Institutions in Canada."

60 Jenkins, "Indigenous Post-Secondary Institutions," 13.

61 *Aboriginal Institutes' Consortium, Aboriginal Institutions of Higher Education*; Browning, "Aboriginal Post-Secondary Institutions in Canada."

62 Browning, "Aboriginal Post-Secondary Institutions in Canada."

63 Jenkins, "Indigenous Post-Secondary Institutions."

64 Jenkins, "Indigenous Post-Secondary Institutions"; Madeleine MacIvor, "Aboriginal Post-Secondary Education Policy Development"; J. Paquette and G. Fallon, *First Nations Education Policy in Canada*.

65 Aboriginal Institutes' Consortium, *Aboriginal Institutions of Higher Education*.

66 Aboriginal Institutes' Consortium, *Aboriginal Institutions of Higher Education*.

67 J. Dorion and K.R. Yang, "Métis Post-Secondary Education."

68 Aboriginal Institutes' Consortium, *Aboriginal Institutions of Higher Education*.

69 See http://www.cepn-fnec.com/index-eng.aspx.

70 See https://mfnerc.org.

REFERENCES

Archibald, Jo-ann. *Indigenous Storywork: Educating the Heart, Mind, Body, and Spirit.* Vancouver: UBC Press, 2008.

Association of Canadian Deans of Education (ACDE). "Accord on Indigenous Education." 2010. https://csse-scee.ca/acde/wp-content/uploads/sites/7/2018/02/Accord-on-Indigenous-Education_Summary.pdf.

Ball, Jessica. *Improving the Reach of Early Childhood Education for First Nations, Inuit, and Métis Children: Moving Child Care Forward Project (a Joint Initiative of the Childcare Resource and Research Unit, Families and Well-Being at the University of Guelph, and the Department of Sociology at the University of Manitoba).* Toronto: Moving Child Care Forward, 2014. Movingchildcareforward.ca.

Ball, Jessica, and Kenneth Moselle. *Contributions of Culture and Language in Aboriginal Head Start in Urban and Northern Communities to Children's Health Outcomes: A Review of Theory and Research.* Ottawa: Public Health Agency of Canada, 2013. http://cahr.uvic.ca/nearbc/media/docs/cahr51f0ade9a51cf-phac-ashunc-language-and-culture-report.pdf.

Battiste, Marie. *Decolonizing Education: Nourishing the Learning Spirit.* Saskatoon: Purich Publishing, 2013.

Billy Minnabarriet, Verna. "Aboriginal Post-Secondary Education in British Columbia: Nicola Valley Institute of Technology—An Eagle's Gathering Place." PhD diss., University of British Columbia, 2012.

Brayboy, B.M., and E. Maughan. "Indigenous Knowledges and the Story of the Bean." *Harvard Educational Review* 79 (2009): 1–21.

British Columbia Aboriginal Child Care Society (BCACCS). *Training, Recruitment, and Retention in the First Nations ECE Sector: Background Paper.* Vancouver: BCACCS, 2014.

Browning, Kim. "Aboriginal Post-Secondary Institutions in Canada: A Struggle for Recognition." Paper presented at the University of Manitoba Faculty of Education Graduate Student Symposium, Winnipeg, March 2013. https://umanitoba.ca/faculties/education/media/2013-Browning-Kim.pdf.

Canadian Council on Learning. *The State of Aboriginal Learning in Canada: A Holistic Approach to Measuring Success.* Ottawa: Canadian Council on Learning, 2009.

Castellano, Marlene Brant. "Indigenizing Education." *Education Canada Magazine*, 10 June 2014. https://www.edcan.ca/articles/indigenizing-education/.

Castellano, Marlene Brant, Lynne Davis, and Louise Lahache. *Aboriginal Education: Fulfilling the Promise*. Vancouver: UBC Press, 2000.

Chambers, Cynthia. "'The Land Is the Best Teacher I Have Ever Had': Places as Pedagogy for Precarious Times." *Journal of Curriculum Theorizing* 22 (2006): 27–37.

Corntassel, Jeff. "Insurgent Education and the Roles of Indigenous Intellectuals." In *Transforming the Academy: Essays on Indigenous Education, Knowledges, and Relations*, edited by M. Smith, 47–51. Edmonton: University of Alberta Press, 2013.

Deer, Frank. "Integrating Aboriginal Perspectives in Education: Perceptions of Pre-Service Teachers." *Canadian Journal of Education* 36 (2013): 175–211.

Dorion, J., and K.R. Yang. "Métis Post-Secondary Education: A Case Study of the Gabriel Dumont Institute." In *Aboriginal Education: Fulfilling the Promise*, edited by M.B. Castellano, L. Davis, and L. Lahache, 176–89. Vancouver: UBC Press, 2000.

First Nations Education Steering Committee (FNESC) and First Nations Schools Association. *Indian Residential Schools and Reconciliation: Teacher Resource Guide* 5, 10, 11/12. West Vancouver: FNESC and First Nations Schools Association, 2015.

Galley, V., S. Gessner, T. Herbert, T. Thompson, and L. Williams. *A Report on the National Dialogue Session on Indigenous Languages*. Victoria: First Peoples' Cultural Council, 2016. http://www.fpcc.ca/files/PDF/General/FPCC__National_Dialogue_Session_Report_Final.pdf.

Greenwood, Margo. *An Overview of the Development of Aboriginal Early Childhood Services in Canada*. Washington, DC: Distributed by ERIC Clearinghouse, 2001. http://www.eric.ed.gov/contentdelivery/servlet/ERICServlet?accno=ED456954.

——. *BC First Nations Children: Our Families, Our Communities, Our Future*. Vancouver: Health Canada, First Nations and Inuit Health Branch, 2004.

——. "Children Are a Gift to Us: Aboriginal-Specific Early Childhood Programs and Services in Canada." *Canadian Journal of Native Education* 29, no. 1 (2006): 12–28.

Greenwood, Margo, Sarah de Leeuw, and Tina Fraser. "Aboriginal Children and Early Childhood Development and Education in Canada: Linking the Past and the Present to the Future." *Canadian Journal of Native Education, Special Issue on Early Childhood* 30, no. 1 (2007): 5–18.

Hare, Jan. "'All of Our Responsibility': Instructor Experiences with Required Indigenous Education Courses." *Canadian Journal of Native Education* 38, no. 1 (2015): 101–20.

Human Resources and Skills Development Canada (HRSDC). *Summative Evaluation of the Aboriginal Development Human Resources Agreements. Final Report*. Ottawa: HRSDC, 2009. http://publications.gc.ca/collections/collection_2011/rhdcc-hrsdc/HS28-165-1-2010-eng.pdf.

Inuit Tapiriit Kanatami (ITK). *Understanding the Training Needs of Early Childhood Educators across Inuit Nunangat*. Ottawa: ITK, 2010. https://www.oise.utoronto.ca/atkinson/UserFiles/File/Policy_Monitor/NU_01_07_14_-_UnderstandingTraining_Needs-FINAL.pdf.

Iseke-Barnes, Judy. "Pedagogies for Decolonizing." *Canadian Journal of Native Education* 31, no. 1 (2008): 123–48.

Jenkins, A.L. "Indigenous Post-Secondary Institutions in Canada and the US." *Higher Education Perspectives* 3 (2007): 1–27.

Kitchen, J., and M. Raynor. "Indigenizing Teacher Education: An Action Research Project." *Canadian Journal of Action Research* 14 (2013): 40–58.

Kitchenham, A., T. Fraser, M. Pidgeon, and K. Ragoonaden. *Aboriginal Education Enhancement Agreements: Complicated Conversations as Pathways to Success*. Victoria: BC Ministry of Education, 2016. http://www2.gov.bc.ca/assets/gov/education/administration/kindergarten-to-grade-12/aboriginal-education/research/aeea_report.pdf.

Kuokkanen, R. *Reshaping the University: Responsibility, Indigenous Epistemes, and the Logic of the Gift*. Vancouver: UBC Press, 2007.

Macdonald, M. "Indigenizing the Academy: What Some Universities Are Doing to Weave Indigenous Peoples, Cultures and Knowledge into the Fabric of Their Campuses." *University Affairs*, 6 April 2016. https://www.universityaffairs.ca/features/feature-article/indigenizing-the-academy/.

MacIvor, Madeleine. "Aboriginal Post-Secondary Education Policy Development in British Columbia, 1986–2011." PhD diss., University of British Columbia, 2012.

Martineau, C., E. Steinhauer, R. Wimmer, E. Vergis, and A. Wolfe. "Alberta's Aboriginal Teacher Education Program: A Little Garden Where Students Blossom." *Canadian Journal of Native Education* 38, no. 1 (2015): 121–48.

Métis National Council. "Towards a Métis Nation Education Strategy." 2014. http://www.Métisnation.ca/index.php/news/toward-a-Métis-nation-education-strategy.

Mihesuah, D.A., and A.C. Wilson. *Indigenizing the Academy: Transforming Scholarship and Empowering Communities*. Lincoln: University of Nebraska Press, 2004.

Nguyen, M. "Closing the Education Gap: A Case for Aboriginal Early Childhood Education in Canada: A Look at the Aboriginal Head Start Program." *Canadian Journal of Education* 34 (2011): 229–48.

Ottmann, Jacqueline. "Indigenizing the Academy: Confronting 'Contentious Ground.'" *Morning Watch: Education and Social Analysis* 40 (2013): 8–24.

Paquette, J., and G. Fallon. *First Nations Education Policy in Canada: Progress or Gridlock?* Toronto: University of Toronto Press, 2010.

Pidgeon, Michelle. "Moving beyond Good Intentions: Indigenizing Higher Education in British Columbia Universities through Institutional Responsibility and Accountability." *Journal of American Indian Education* 53, no. 2 (2014): 7–28.

Preston, J.P., M. Cottrell, T.R. Pelletier, and J.V. Pearce. "Aboriginal Early Childhood Education in Canada: Issues of Context." *Journal of Early Childhood Research* 10 (2012): 3–18.

Public Health Agency of Canada. *Evaluation of the Aboriginal Head Start Urban and Northern Communities Program at the Public Health Agency of Canada*. Ottawa:Public Health Agency of Canada, 2012. http://www.phac-aspc.gc.ca/about_apropos/evaluation/reports-rapports/2011-2012/ahsunc-papacun/index-eng.php#toc.

——. *Aboriginal Head Start in Urban and Northern Communities*. 15 November 2016. http://www.phac-aspc.gc.ca/hp-ps/dca-dea/prog-ini/ahsunc-papacun/index-eng.php.

Public Policy Forum. *Building Leaders: Early Childhood Development in Indigenous Communities*. Ottawa: Public Policy Forum, 2015. http://www.ppforum.ca/sites/default/files/Building%20Leaders%20-%20Final%20Report_0.pdf.

Royal Commission on Aboriginal Peoples (RCAP). *Volume 3: Gathering Strength*. Ottawa: Canada Communications Group, 1996.

Simon, L. *Mi'kmaw Kina'matnewey Supporting Student Success*. Toronto: Indspire, 2014.

Stonechild, Blair. *The New Buffalo: The Struggle for Aboriginal Post-Secondary Education in Canada*. Winnipeg: University of Manitoba Press, 2006.

Truth and Reconciliation Commission of Canada (TRC). *Honouring the Truth, Reconciling for the Future: Summary of the Final Report of the Truth and Reconciliation Commission of Canada*. 2015. http://www.trc.ca/websites/trcinstitution/File/2015/Honouring_the_Truth_Reconciling_for_the_Future_July_23_2015.pdf.

Universities Canada. *Enhancing Indigenous Student Success at Canada's Universities*. 2015. http://www.univcan.ca/wp-content/uploads/2016/06/enhancing-indigenous-student-access-at-canadian-universities.pdf.

Williams, Lorna, and Michelle Tanaka. "Schalay'nung Sxwey'ga Emerging Cross-Cultural Pedagogy in the Academy." *Educational Insights* 11, no. 3 (2007). http://einsights.ogpr. educ.ubc.ca/v11n03/articles/williams/williams.html.

CHAPTER 12
INSIGHTS INTO COMMUNITY DEVELOPMENT IN FIRST NATIONS:
A POVERTY ACTION RESEARCH PROJECT[1]

Jennifer S. Dockstator, Jeff S. Denis, Frederic Wien, Gérard Duhaime, Mark S. Dockstator, David Newhouse, Wanda Wuttunee, Charlotte Loppie, John Loxley, Warren Weir, Eabametoong First Nation, Misipawistik Cree First Nation, Opitciwan Atikamekw First Nation, Sipekne'katik First Nation, and T'it'q'et

BEFORE ALL OTHER WORDS

We first extend our gratitude to the five First Nations that are part of the Poverty Action Research Project (PARP): Eabametoong First Nation, Misipawistik Cree First Nation, Opitciwan Atikamekw First Nation, Sipekne'katik First Nation, and T'it'q'et. The PARP research team is committed to ensuring these First Nations' collaboration and consent on the content of this chapter. Without their participation in the project, however, this knowledge learning and sharing would not even be possible. In the spirit of Indigenous research, the entire PARP research team wishes to acknowledge the participation of the five First Nations communities in the project: Breaking from the conventions of academic authorship and introducing how the practice of mutually beneficial Indigenous research extends to publications, we acknowledge the five First Nations as equal partners in the preparation and content of this chapter, and they appear as co-authors. In addition, we are acknowledging the nature of Indigenous political organizations as governments, so political terms such as Chief and Council and Band Council are capitalized throughout this chapter.[2]

INTRODUCTION

From 2011 to 2017, the Poverty Action Research Project was on a dynamic and creative journey for community development with five First Nations across Canada. The research teams, over this time, experienced first-hand and gained a deep respect for the many strengths and resilience of First Nations peoples. As well, we learned about obstacles that they continue to face as they strive to provide for and ensure the well-being of their people and build healthy, thriving communities.

The purpose of this chapter, therefore, is to raise awareness of these First Nations' strengths as well as to appreciate their great capacity and fortitude in light of the challenges that they continue to face. As noted by Dr. Marlene Brant Castellano and Dr. Frederic Wien, one of the "fundamental requisites of reconciliation" is "removing impediments to a healthy, empowered future for successive generations" of Indigenous peoples in Canada.[3] The 1996 report of the Royal Commission on Aboriginal Peoples (RCAP) provides an honest account of how these impediments have arisen. The 2015 report of the Truth and Reconciliation Commission (TRC) builds on RCAP recommendations and calls for immediate action to restructure relationships in all sectors of society, reconciling past wrongs by investing time and energy to build truly mutually respectful relationships. Given its longitudinal nature, PARP is in a key position to contribute to this conversation, advancing the process of reconciliation by revealing insights into these "impediments" and offering perspectives grounded in trusting relationships and first-hand experiences. Some of these impediments are internal, but a significant number are external to communities, imposed on them by an outdated understanding by present-day institutions, reinforced by media, of the capacity, education, and experience of First Nations.

Toward this objective, this case study will first introduce the PARP project and the five participating communities. Summaries highlighting some of the "action research" pursued through PARP are also presented. One of the main findings of the project relates to Indigenous perspectives on *poverty*, seeing as this word sits prominently in the name of the project. So in this chapter we discuss how First Nations reject the label, preferring to frame PARP in a holistic context related to community health, cultural vitality, and other factors that contribute to well-being in First Nations. As well, we explore the value of community-driven research in the context of crediting First Nations with a great deal of experience, capacity, and resourcefulness in the face of resource scarcity (e.g., human and capital), inequitable funding, and burdensome government bureaucracies. Finally, we discuss impediments that hinder the empowerment of First Nations toward health and well-being, and we offer observations based on PARP experiences as a contribution to the discussion about reconciliation and relationship building. Although PARP researchers worked solely with First Nations communities, much of what is shared in this chapter relates to many Indigenous peoples across Canada, even though the chapter has a focus on First Nations.

Having said that, we acknowledge the distinctness of each First Nation, the Inuit and Métis, as well as Indigenous peoples living in urban settings. PARP thus unfolded differently for each community that took part in the project. What we share here are threads that have been picked up from experiences in each First Nation, which when woven together present a tapestry. These threads, or elements, hold insights and observations that we believe are important to share as all sectors of society discern how to make transformative change for reconciliation and relationship building between Indigenous peoples in Canada and non-Indigenous Canadians.

Most of the communities described here are some distance removed from urban centres, sometimes hundreds of kilometres away and in one case accessible only by air or ice road. Commentators from the south are quick to dismiss the prospects for development of First Nations communities, jumping to the conclusion that the only rational solution is to relocate the communities (meaning to disperse individuals) to more "promising" southern locales.

In this chapter, we take a different view, one that emerges naturally from close and sustained interactions with community members. It is a point of view that emphasizes the long history of inhabitants in their regions, their deep spiritual and cultural attachments to the lands and waters, their strengths and resilience, especially because of their ties to place. It is also a point of view that does not accept the status quo as a given; rather, it emphasizes the possibilities that exist if Aboriginal and treaty rights to lands and resources are recognized and if self-determination is supported. Nevertheless, developmental challenges are significant, and it is instructive to learn how the First Nations communities themselves, with assistance from external resources, approach the task of improving community health and well-being through deliberate actions.

BACKGROUND

PARP had its roots in the Assembly of First Nations (AFN) 2006 campaign to "Make Poverty History" and was first conceptualized through a joint partnership between the AFN and university researchers from across North America. The six-year research project was funded through a grant from the Canadian Institutes of Health Research, specifically the Institute of Aboriginal Peoples Health and the Institute of Population and Public Health. The overall aim of PARP was to work with First Nations communities to develop and begin implementing long-term strategies to reduce poverty, create a sustainable economic base, and provide the foundation for community health and well-being.

At the outset, sixty-one First Nations communities across Canada expressed interest in participating in the project. Five volunteer communities were selected to reflect the diversity of First Nations across the country. These five communities are Sipekne'katik in Nova Scotia, Opitciwan in Quebec, Eabametoong in northern Ontario, Misipawistik Cree at Grand Rapids, Manitoba, and T'it'q'et at Lillooet in British Columbia.

**FIGURE 12.1. LOCATIONS OF THE FIVE
COMMUNITIES PARTICIPATING IN PARP.**

RESEARCH PROCESS

As in any research undertaking, the work plan outlined a general process for all research teams to follow. In addition to researchers travelling to and building positive working relationships with the communities (if they did not already exist), a Community Advisory Committee (CAC) was to be established to guide and approve the researchers' activities, with regular reports to Chief and Council. When the project got under-way, however, research teams deferred to the direction of each community. In Opitciwan, Quebec, for example, the Nikaniw Committee was established (in Atikamekw, *nikaniw* can be translated as "go forward") and included representation from all interest groups in the community, including Band Council, health and social services, education, employment, youth association, women's association, and Elders. In Manitoba, the Misipawistik Cree Advisory Committee was called E'Opinitowak, which means "giving a hand up," and was composed of several community members and two external representatives (from Manitoba Hydro and the provincial government), both of whom were trusted by the community. Although other First Nations also formed CACs, Chiefs and Councils for some communities preferred to serve as the coordinating bodies, and no CAC existed. Both approaches were effective to varying degrees, and both raised challenges. An article in the *Engaged Scholar Journal*[4] explores these and other issues related to the process that each PARP team followed and the lessons learned, not only for researchers to consider when engaging with First Nations in community-driven participatory research, but also for government and industry personnel when developing policies and programs or building relationships for development ventures.

A community coordinator was also hired by PARP to assist the research team with various tasks. These tasks included, but were not limited to, undertaking a community assessment to identify salient characteristics, strengths, challenges, and opportunities; collaboratively preparing an economic development strategic plan; working with the community on its implementation; and eventually undertaking research to measure project outcomes. Every community hired at least one coordinator. In at least one instance, however, the First Nation and project team opted to work together in a different way (e.g., dealing directly with the Band Council and Administration or with the CAC).

The project unfolded differently for each community. PARP collaborated with the five First Nations to pursue numerous undertakings, ranging from research and strategic plan development and implementation to capacity building, policy development, and governance initiatives within the Band Administration. Initiatives also included cultural and economic development programs to engage youth and people of all ages interested in seeking employment or setting up a local business. What follows is a brief summary from each of the research teams and communities highlighting some of the major research and action initiatives pursued through PARP.

RESEARCH IN ACTION

SIPEKNE'KATIK FIRST NATION IN NOVA SCOTIA
Sipekne'katik First Nation is the second largest Mi'kmaq band in Nova Scotia and includes the communities of Indian Brook Indian Reserve 14, New Ross, Pennal, Dodd's Lot, Wallace Hills, and Grand Lake.

Sipekne'katik First Nation has 2,588 band members, with approximately 1,244 members residing in the community and 1,344 members residing outside of it. The land area of Sipekne'katik First Nation spans just over twelve square kilometres and is located sixty-eight kilometres from Kijipuktuk (Halifax) and twenty-nine kilometres southwest of Truro.[5]

FIGURE 12.2. SIPEKNE'KATIK COMMUNITIES.

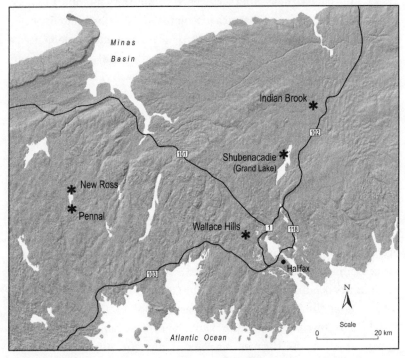

Source: http://povertyaction.ca/community/indian-brook-ns.

The PARP project in Sipekne'katik had a large Advisory Committee composed of persons from both within and outside the community. It included the Chief and several Band Council members as well as an Elder, agency heads, and others. External members included academics, senior federal and provincial government personnel, and representatives of First Nations governments and organizations.

An initial activity was the development of a strategic plan, ultimately called "Building Our Community Together: The Poverty Action Plan of the Shubenacadie First Nation." It was grounded in historical research, in a large number of key informant interviews, secondary data analysis, input from Advisory Committee members, and meetings with agency and department heads. Several open community meetings were also held.

Once developed, the strategic plan was approved in principle by Chief and Council, but further input from community members was mandated. Thus, a household survey of community members was conducted.

Of particular concern to the community's leaders was a more integrated approach to providing services to community members in need, in a bid to get away from a pattern of isolated and uncoordinated service provision. In response to this need, PARP developed and implemented a project in which community members, especially social assistance recipients, were invited to take part in a pilot in which each volunteer met with a group of relevant service providers who pooled their knowledge and services in support of the individual and his or her particular needs. The hope was that this holistic approach would be more successful in helping individuals to make the transition from dependence to self-reliance.

OPITCIWAN FIRST NATION IN QUEBEC

Opitciwan is an Atikamekw nation composed of three communities: Manawan, Wemotaci, and Obedjiwan-Opitciwan. Atikamekw means "whitefish" and refers to the species of fish that the people have eaten for ages. Opitciwan was formerly located at the tip of Mékiskan, a site that is accessible by water and is one hour by canoe from the spot that the community occupies today. In 1920, the Gouin Dam flooded the community, causing the families to move closer to the bay. The people settled slowly in the territory where the rising rivers meet, hence the name Opitciwan, which means "the meeting place of the rising rivers."

FIGURE 12.3. NITASKINAN TERRITORY.

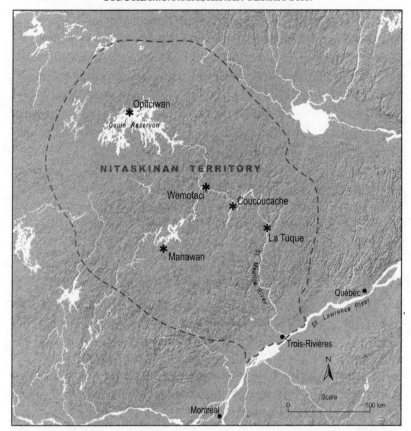

Source: http://povertyaction.ca/community/opitciwan-qc.

Opitciwan is located in the heart of Quebec north of the Gouin Reservoir in the region of La Mauricie. It is accessible by a logging road 166 kilometres long, linking the reserve to Highway 167 in Lac-Saint-Jean. Opitciwan is also accessible by La Tuque (Logging Road 10) and by Chibougamau (Logging Road Barrette-Chapais). Based on the 2011 census, the community has a population of 2,031 people.[6]

Early in its existence, Opitciwan's Nikaniw Committee decided to rally the largest possible number of people and organizations in the community in activities relevant to the fight against poverty. The committee directed its actions toward the well-being of children, family support, and the transmission of traditional knowledge. Toward this goal, it pursued activities, not without difficulty, by mobilizing human, material, and financial resources. Two activities are highlighted here.

The Family House had been under the supervision of the Women's Association of Opitciwan. However, it was not operational since the facility did not meet building standards, and no activities had been organized. The Women's Association and the Nikaniw Committee worked together on the project. With the collaboration of the Opitciwan Atikamekw Council, the building was brought up to code and the status cleared. Thanks to a financial arrangement involving the PARP project and a program called Child Future, a coordinator was hired to prepare and implement a program. The activities of the Family House have included, to date, a community kitchen that brings parents together, a room equipped with children's toys, conference luncheons, breakfasts for children, and a day nursery. The luncheons, held monthly, have been particularly popular. Up to fifty parents gather at a time and determine the topics for discussion. The program contributes to the well-being of children and supports families.

The Nikaniw Committee also established the Ocki Magadan program. Based on the active teaching of traditional knowledge, the program was initially intended for young adults who had dropped out of school; it has since been redirected toward youth in high school. In its different phases, Ocki Magadan has been made possible thanks to the resources of PARP, the Youth House, the Québec en forme program, the Quebec Social Initiatives Fund, and the education sector of the Opitciwan Atikamekw Council. The program holds activities in which young people learn traditional skills such as making tents or other utilitarian objects (e.g., canoes, baskets, etc.), beginning with the harvesting and processing of the base materials (e.g., moose hide, birch bark, etc.) and ending with the sales of products. The program contributes to the retention of students in Mikisiw High School, the transmission of traditional knowledge, and family support through generational bridging.

EABAMETOONG FIRST NATION IN ONTARIO

The community of Eabametoong First Nation (EFN, also known as Fort Hope) is located on the north shore of Eabamet Lake, 360 kilometres north of Thunder Bay. EFN is a member of the Nishnawbe Aski Nation and the Matawa Tribal Council and a signatory to Treaty 9.[7]

Eabametoong is a traditional name, which in Anishinaabemowin (the Ojibway language) means "the reversing of the water place." Each year, because of runoff, the flow of water from Eabamet Lake into the Albany River temporarily reverses. The name Fort Hope comes from the Hudson's Bay Company fur-trading post built by the lake in 1890. Nothing remains of the old trading post; however, two churches at the old bay site still stand, and the cemetery remains in use today. The site, referred to as Old Bay or Old Fort Hope, is six kilometres southwest of the community's current location across Eabamet Lake.

Today EFN has approximately 2,400 band members, about 1,300 of whom live on reserve, with the balance living in Thunder Bay, Geraldton, and other surrounding communities. EFN is accessible year round only by air with flights operated by two airlines. In recent years, the "winter ice road season" has been shortening because of climate change. Residents maintain these roads, which enable them to travel to Thunder Bay (sixteen hours), Pickle Lake (nine hours), and other surrounding First Nations.

The PARP research team took its direction from EFN's Chief and Council. When community input was required, individuals formed ad hoc committees to provide and coordinate public input. Several initiatives were undertaken and received PARP support, two of which are summarized here.

Previous attempts by EFN to establish an economic development corporation ended unsuccessfully. Since one PARP team member had corporate experience, Chief and Council sought PARP's assistance in establishing a new development corporation to separate Band politics from business yet remain consistent with the First Nation's vision and strategic goals. After a number of Band-wide meetings and surveys to gather community input on the proposal, Chief and Council passed Band Council Resolutions (BCRs) authorizing the start-up and affirming the corporation's overall direction to establish external sources of revenue for the Band. Board directors were selected, the first board meetings were held, and a strategic planning retreat was scheduled to set the direction for the corporation.

In February 2015, Chief and Council asked PARP to pursue a local economic development project with and for Eabametoong. After consultation with external resource people, the PARP research team proposed a Cultural Tourism Showcase Capacity Building Project to the Chief and Council, the economic development officer, and then the community in an October 2015 Band-wide meeting. Receiving EFN's approval for the concept, the PARP researcher began applying for grants from funding agencies. By August 2016, 100 percent funding was secured from the Ontario Aboriginal Economic Development Fund, the Northern Ontario Heritage Fund Corporation, the Ontario Tourism Development Fund, Kiikenomaga Kikenjigewen Employment and Training Services, and EFN, raising over $110,000 for the project.

The Cultural Tourism Showcase Project was a community-wide project with three phases:

1. *Training:* augmented previous training of the EFN tourism group; neighbouring communities were invited to participate in the training sessions.

2. *Learning through doing:* provided on-the-job experience to the tourism group in planning, advertising, and hosting a pilot Cultural Tourism Showcase Project in Eabametoong in the summer of 2017.

3. *Post-event review and analysis:* assessed the undertaking and determined its feasibility and the next steps for a variety of tourism ventures in EFN territory and northern Ontario.

MISIPAWISTIK CREE NATION, MANITOBA

The Misipawistik Cree Nation (MCN) is located on the northwestern shore of Lake Winnipeg where the mouth of the North Saskatchewan River enters the lake. Traditionally, people from the Misipawistik Cree Nation have considered their community the geographic centre of Manitoba. Misipawistik Cree Nation is approximately 400 kilometres north of Winnipeg and is accessible by Provincial Highway 6, by air, and by water. As of 2012, the total membership was 1,753, with 34 percent under the age of fifteen, of whom 20 percent were under the age of five.

PARP's team of two research co-leaders worked with a CAC throughout the project. This advisory group set the name and vision for the group. E'Opinitowak, "giving a hand up," was chosen instead of a reference to poverty, which the advisory group strongly objected to since they did not think that it would be an accurate depiction of the state in which they live. The advisory group determined that youth should be the focus of their collaborative efforts with PARP to help the community increase employment and improve living standards. The youth in MCN, as in other First Nations, include teenagers as well as those in their twenties and sometimes in their early thirties. As a result of the group's vision, the PARP research co-leaders secured donations of computers for the adult education computer lab as well as hockey equipment for use by youth so that they could enjoy their refurbished arena. Both were secured from provincial programs that, until then, were unknown to the community.

Other initiatives that E'Opinitowak pursued in collaboration with PARP included projects oriented toward youth that were locally designed and delivered. Although small in scale and low in cost, these projects were cost-shared and reached large numbers of community members. Deepening the revival of culture was important, as was a focus on employment and strengthening the resource economy of the community. Examples of projects include a life skills/canoe adventure course, the Lake Keepers program, and an initiative to help community members obtain a driver's licence.

T'IT'Q'ET, BRITISH COLUMBIA

The community of T'it'q'et (formerly Lillooet Indian Band), situated adjacent to the town of Lillooet, is approximately 254 kilometres northeast of Vancouver on Highway 99. T'it'q'et is one of eleven communities within the St'át'imc Nation that share a common language, culture, history, and territory. T'it'q'et currently has 394 registered members. The Band has seven reserves, including the main reserve, Lillooet Indian Reserve 1, and a shared reserve with the Bridge River Indian Band.

Through PARP, T'it'q'et undertook a number of projects, one of which was the preparation of a community health survey report to understand further the health and well-being of the community, to acquire information and data relevant to the development of the community's profile, and to improve health and well-being while concurrently reducing poverty by contributing to the development of an economic strategic plan for the community.

The research assistant designed questionnaires for adults (eighteen and older), youths (from twelve to seventeen), and children (up to eleven), and they were the primary tool for data collection. The development of these questionnaires was based on the national First Nations Regional Health Survey (conducted from 2008 to 2010) and a list of priority health indicators (identified by the T'it'q'et Regional Advisory Community). Using the questionnaires, two data collectors administered the house-to-house health survey in the community in November 2014.

The baseline data collected from the health surveys, once analyzed, will be an important tool for the community to use as a basis for comparison after future initiatives are implemented (in economic development and other pursuits) to determine the impacts of activities on various health indicators and, by extension, the health and well-being of the community.

A second project undertaken through PARP was a synthesis of the impacts of climate change and an introduction to management strategies used by First Nations communities in response to climate change. People across Canada, including First Nations communities, have noticed changes in their local environments and have been learning to adapt in order to survive. First Nations are strongly connected to natural environments for subsistence and for the preservation of their cultures. However, because of the frequency of fluctuations in weather patterns and the intensity of natural disasters (as consequences of climate change), communities are unable to make predictions using traditional knowledge with previous degrees of confidence; as a result, they have become vulnerable to the impacts of climate change. People in the Upper St'át'imc Territory, in particular T'it'q'et, have expressed concerns about the effects of climate change on their lifestyle, specifically on agriculture (or farming) and food security, fishing, hunting, logging, food gathering, and community traditions and culture.

HIGHLIGHTING FIRST NATIONS STRENGTHS

One of the many benefits that PARP team members enjoyed during the project was the meaningful relationships forged and strengthened. PARP's long-term nature fostered trust in new and ongoing friendships across the country. Team members saw first-hand the inherent strengths of communities as a whole and among band members of all ages—from political as well as non-elected leaders to Elders to youth. Many First Nations across Canada have rebounded from the impacts of colonialism-capitalism and residential schools, building on their connections with the land, their resilience, and their unremitting pursuit of their visions under strong leadership. Many are still struggling. The five communities that participated in PARP are at different points along this spectrum of health and well-being, and, in their own ways, they are working hard to achieve a healthy balance in community life. In this section, we shine a spotlight on the strengths underlying their tenacity in this quest in spite of ongoing adversities.

The six years during which PARP worked with the five First Nations across Canada showed us, as researchers, a perspective that few in Canadian society are aware of or few researchers attain, as nowhere in the literature have we come across what is highlighted here. That is, the picture that emerges from PARP's experiences and relationships shows the incredible capacity of leaders, the expertise in the community, and the exceptional education of workers in the community. Mainstream media and many non-Indigenous Canadians often assume that these attributes are deficient in many First Nations communities. For example, assumptions exist that the leaders and communities lack capacity, that few possess expertise, and that the majority lack the formal education required to address issues and/or solve problems.

With these assumptions firmly in place, generally speaking, the predominantly accepted approach to solving community problems has been to adhere to a prevailing system in which a First Nation is given little freedom or flexibility and is subjected to rigid controls. From the perceived lack of internal education, expertise, and thus capacity of the community to address effectively its issues, deferring to outsiders (i.e., outside the First Nation or non-Indigenous expertise) has been the default strategy of federal and provincial governments. First Nations have been given insufficient independence or power either to make their own decisions or to implement them.

From the experience of PARP, however, we learned that the leaders are able to deal with a multitude of incredibly complex, interconnected, and personally challenging issues simultaneously. They illustrate a high degree of capacity to move issues forward in a difficult, bureaucratic environment. With resilience and perseverance, despite the innumerable challenges that they face on a regular basis, First Nations communities demonstrate their expertise, responding to often simultaneous and interconnected challenges in pursuing a brighter, more positive future. Additionally, in spite of the need for more practical professional training and the requirement to learn on the job, the workers in the communities show a high degree of education and effectively integrate a number of disparate job functions with demanding and excessive funding and reporting requirements all within a challenging work environment.

The point that we want to emphasize, from the insider perspective offered by PARP, is that Western-based conceptions of capacity, expertise, and education take on a whole different meaning in and among First

Nations. From the perspective of the PARP team, there are leaders in every First Nation community with which we worked (elected officials, staff workers, and members of the community) who have the education, expertise, and capacity to work together to solve their problems. The workers and community members have the ability, desire, and motivation to move issues forward and seek a better future. What will enable them to do so is the provision of ample and equitable resources and the acknowledgement of their independence so that they can make and implement their own decisions.

The perspective offered by PARP researchers is that First Nations communities are not given the credit that they deserve. They consistently demonstrate that they are able to succeed despite incredibly difficult circumstances (take, for example, the list below of interconnected and complex issues with which many First Nations have to cope). We even speculate that few highly educated and experienced people from the rest of Canada, if thrown into the situations in which many First Nations find themselves (especially in remote communities), would be able to succeed as First Nations have been able to do.

To illustrate, PARP researchers can verify the challenges imposed on First Nations that seek funding and a green light to proceed with any given project. Granted, good planning is essential. However, a few issues have arisen in these approval processes that present unique challenges for First Nations. These issues include any one of the following or a combination of them: (1) when government forms, procedures, and deadlines shift midstream, requiring the completion of even more forms and steps before a file is considered ready; (2) when an agency fails to receive a report from one project, affecting the approval of another project seeking funding from the same agency; or (3) when one project requires multiple funders in order to proceed and, in turn, each funder requires separate expense reimbursement procedures and different templates for reporting. Workers in any agency can become stressed and frustrated with these fluid and complex circumstances. Keeping all of the forms, deadlines, and reporting requirements straight for several projects simultaneously places a significant burden on Band staff, especially when core funding is inadequate to support sufficient staffing levels and the few staff members carrying the load are stretched to the maximum.

We can throw into the mix additional complexities that First Nations face, not to mention emergencies and crises that occur all too frequently.

Consider the following (some of which are recounted in the media, whereas others are less publicized but still present significant challenges):

- population explosion among youth (up to the age of twenty-nine) with a high percentage of teenage parenthood;
- underfunding of schools, educational programs, and social programs;
- understaffed medical facilities;
- inadequate housing and infrastructure (water, sewer, electricity, fire protection);
- food insecurity and lack of affordable, healthy food options;
- environmental contamination;
- high expense of everyday living complicated by high unemployment rates;
- health issues (diabetes, etc.);
- high rates of violent death, suicide, prescription drug and other substance abuse;
- multigenerational echoes of residential school experiences;
- stitching together from twenty to thirty different funding programs every year;
- two-year election cycle mandated under the obsolete Indian Act (unless a First Nation has held a referendum to increase election terms), suspending Band activity during the campaign and causing delays or stoppages when new Chiefs and Councillors take office.

If thrown into these conditions, would many other Canadians be able to handle the demands and pressures? First Nations have proven to be resourceful in the face of historical and ongoing hardships and restrictions. They have developed the knowledge and skills to adapt to their changing environments and survive. Whereas most non-Indigenous Canadians have lived in very different conditions, developing knowledge and skills that might be good fits for "mainstream" society, such advantages might not help them to survive under conditions found on reserve that Indigenous peoples must endure, cannot escape, and rightly choose not to because of their strong connection to place. So it is inappropriate for outsiders to believe that they can turn up like saviours with the answers. Given this reality, this is why research projects such as PARP must be community driven and why Indigenous peoples deserve more credit for their knowledge, expertise, and capacity.

Indigenous perspectives, PARP also found, embrace a different understanding of success. Through PARP, we came to understand that a First Nations view of success includes a broader view compared with that of mainstream society.[8] First Nations success operates, in part, in an administrative environment that few others experience. It is where First Nations leaders, workers, and community members continue to move issues forward given on-the-ground realities arising from a long-endured bureaucratic regime under the Indian Act that has perpetuated repressive federal, provincial, and corporate mindsets and actions. Despite these circumstances, the resilience and adaptability of First Nations have prevailed, and they are still here.

One might question the plausibility of this stance given the tragedy of youth suicide; high unemployment rates; gaps in education, health, and housing; and ongoing addictions, among other news stories that make media headlines on a regular basis. But these headlines only scratch the surface. To accept the veracity of our point of view in this chapter, one must appreciate First Nations from a perspective of strength as opposed to that of deficit. And, in order to appreciate First Nations strengths, long-term respectful relationship building is a prerequisite—one that the TRC mandated in its calls to action for all sectors of society. One must take the time to learn to see beyond the headlines. The members of PARP had the privilege of gaining this insight over six years.

With this new perspective, as realized through the PARP research project, a totally different paradigmatic approach to solving the problems in a First Nations community is possible. From this point of view, the community is capable of solving its own problems. If given the resources to mitigate the overall challenges of the operating environment, the community has the experience, expertise, and capacity to succeed on its own terms. All that it requires is the independence to make its own decisions, and equitable resources will help to support and implement those decisions.

RESPECT FOR FIRST NATIONS CHALLENGES

This is not to dismiss each people's distinct cultural lens (recognizing that common ground exists between peoples) or to minimize the real challenges that First Nations continue to face (as noted above). What was reported in 2016 in the media about Attawapiskat, Ontario; Lac La Ronge, Saskatchewan; and other communities is not happening in isolation. First Nations across Canada are experiencing, to varying degrees, hardship and crisis. Their challenges are compounded by a number of issues that PARP explored in detail in an article published in the *Engaged Scholars Journal*.[9] The article also discusses several distinctive cultural protocols, perspectives, and other considerations especially relevant to academic and other external groups wishing to work or partner with a First Nation or in some way contribute to a community's development (on its terms). The article's main points follow.

RESPECT FOR DIFFERENT WORLDS

An overarching theme from PARP is the acknowledgement that core differences exist between mainstream Canadian society and all five communities involved in the project (and by extension other First Nations, Inuit, and Métis across the country). Our differences are not to be seen as negative, for our combined strength lies in the diverse nature of all our peoples. To ignore our differences and engage with First Nations insensitive to the histories and cultural traditions that make Indigenous peoples distinct is unacceptable in this new era of reconciliation.

RESPECT FOR DIFFERENT LANGUAGES

This has already been discussed in relation to Western and Indigenous understandings of words such as *poverty, success, capacity, education,* and *expertise.* Where English or French is not the original language of the people, and where different worldviews exist, special consideration must be given to word choice and communication strategies.

SPENDING TIME TAKING CARE OF RELATIONSHIPS

The building of a positive relationship serves as the central foundation for working with First Nations. When working with First Nations communities and organizations, taking time at the outset to establish respectful, trusted relationships is crucial, and taking care of these relationships over time is vital. People who wish to conduct research or business with First Nations must take into consideration and budget for the increased amount of time required in such undertakings. Those who seek to work with a community must realize that trust is not given overnight but earned.

RESPECTING FIRST NATIONS' PRIORITIES WITH TIME

Part and parcel with the above distinctions are the implications for time management. Many factors affect the pace of work:

- Weather: for fly-in and remote communities, bad weather will undoubtedly cause flight cancellations or poor driving conditions (if road accessible), causing project delays.
- Process: many, if not all, communities wish to ensure community-wide support for a particular "action" being contemplated. Chief and Council might call for Band meetings to seek broad endorsement of an initiative.
- Respect: many Chiefs and Councils and Band Administrations, unfortunately, are simply too busy at times with the demands of their positions. In addition, seasonal hunts require people to be absent for a few weeks each spring and fall. Unforeseen circumstances or planned absences can cause meeting deferrals and delays in the overall process.
- Emergencies: throughout PARP's tenure, all First Nations had to cope with deaths because of illness as well as suicide, with losses of the old as well as the young. In many if not all communities, when a death occurs, the Band observes the tradition of closing the Band office; all work halts so that everyone can pay respects to the family and honour the individual who has passed.

RESPECT FOR DIFFERENT PRESSURES AND SOCIAL FORCES

In addition to frequent requests to listen to proposals or participate in socio-environmental assessments, First Nations have had numerous obligations to Indian and Northern Affairs Canada (INAC) (now known as Indigenous Services Canada) and other federal departments and ministries. As already highlighted, extensive reporting and disclosure requirements, along with application deadlines and forms that sometimes change midstream, create a dynamic and demanding environment in which Band staff have to navigate.

As well, First Nations rely on federal transfer payments for their core funding, and until recently they have been operating in a budgetary reality in which federal funding increases had been restricted to 2 percent per year since 1996, despite higher rates of inflation and population growth.[10] With efforts by the current Liberal government to lift the funding cap, the creation of Indigenous Services Canada, and the dissolution of INAC, it is hoped that shortfalls will be eliminated and that cumulative impacts because of inequitable funding will be redressed.[11]

The short electoral cycle of two years as mandated by the Indian Act has caused its own set of pressures. Some communities are pursuing the change to three- or four-year terms, but this takes time.[12] With a two-year term, after acclimatizing to the job, before they know it, Chief and Council realize that only one year remains before the next election, so time is short to get anything accomplished before thoughts turn to the next campaign.

HUMAN RESOURCES

Depending on the community, grade eight might be the average level of formal, Western-based education attained by Band members. Fewer high school diplomas are offset by all of the learning on the job and life experiences of the Chief and Council and senior staff. Although formal postsecondary education might be limited, especially in more remote settings, as already discussed, First Nations have a great deal of experience and have adapted their skills and knowledge to navigate the complex bureaucracies of provincial and federal governments:

- Professional development programs for staff and management in Band Administrations are constantly needed. Additional training in various fields is sought, but this depends on the availability of funds, time, and coverage for those away on training. Distance learning might be a possibility, but in remote communities, such as Eabametoong First Nation, slow internet connectivity can be a limiting factor.
- Staff turnover is another issue. Job vacancies are common, and some First Nations struggle to retain people in key positions. Although not only an issue for remote communities, being a fly-in community exacerbates the challenge, for the population is isolated and might be comparatively smaller. The remoteness might not entice qualified people to apply and, once there, stay long term. Housing shortages also affect people's ability to commit to a position.

INFORMATION TECHNOLOGY (IT)

It may be likely that for some communities, such as those closer to urban areas, bandwidth speed is fast, and technology is available, facilitating effective communications via email and videoconferencing. Also, distance learning and online professional development courses may be readily available (but these assumptions may still be unfounded for some First Nations, even if they are closer to urban areas). For more remote First Nations, however, IT problems persist. In bad weather, often the internet and telephone lines disconnect. In Eabametoong First Nation, for example, limitations on bandwidth have restricted internet speeds and access to online instruction. Also, capabilities that others take for granted, such as sending email attachments, using programs such as DropBox to transfer larger files, and sharing calendars, fail. Downloading monthly bank statements and exploring websites for resources and information take too much time. Troubleshooting problems remotely is not possible given the limited bandwidth speed. For remote communities such as Eabametoong, these problems have significant impacts on staff productivity and impede information sharing and timely communication.

ADDITIONAL INSIGHTS INTO A FIRST NATIONS HOLISTIC DEVELOPMENT PROCESS

In this section, we describe a number of additional insights gleaned from PARP's long-term association with the five First Nations. As in other sections of this chapter, our intention is not to be prescriptive, for each community's distinctness necessitates an individualized process. We offer these insights in the spirit of sharing what PARP research teams learned during the six years of the project, contributing to the discussion on reconciliation and relationship building between Indigenous peoples and non-Indigenous peoples in Canada.

ACCEPTING COMMUNITIES WHERE THEY ARE
AND WHERE THEY WANT TO GO

An important task for us in the first year of the project was to select the five volunteer communities with which we would work. Two considerations influenced the selection process. First, we did not want to be accused of cherry-picking—that is, choosing communities that had the best prospects for development and leaving aside those in more challenging circumstances. Second, consistent with the first consideration, we wanted to include communities from across the country, a French-language community as well as an English-speaking community, at different stages in the process of development, and in a range of geographic locations, from urban or close to urban to rural and to northern fly-in. With these criteria in mind, we took direction from the AFN to ensure that all 633 communities had an equal opportunity to be considered. Sixty-three First Nations replied to the initial invitation, of which half provided additional information related to location, size, on- and off-reserve populations, and development challenges and opportunities. The final selection was made based on the aforementioned criteria.

During the decision-making process, we were advised by knowledgeable individuals that we should avoid including the community that had the most challenging development prospects on the ground, as it would be difficult to work under crisis conditions. The First Nation had recently declared a state of emergency because of prescription drug abuse. We ignored that advice partly because the need for assistance was so clear. We also had the idea that we should take the communities where they were at and where they wanted to go and try to provide assistance to move the yardstick along on each chosen journey.

The process of selection that we followed reinforced the community-driven nature of PARP as we worked to ensure that the First Nations chosen were representative of different environmental/geographic regions of the country as well as a range of socio-economic circumstances and stages of community development. With respect to the most challenged community, our experience was that it took longer to establish a proper relationship and to determine where we could be most helpful, but in the end the collaboration between the community and PARP yielded a strong relationship and significant project outcomes, which included establishing an economic development corporation and hosting a cultural tourism showcase, among other projects.

Significant projects were also undertaken in the other communities based on their priorities and directions. For example, the E'Opinitowak Committee in MCN noted that many youth did not have a driver's licence, a qualification for the majority of employment opportunities. PARP facilitated a process for youth to obtain their licences. T'it'q'et community members chose to do a health survey to understand better baseline pictures and health needs. They also pursued a study on food security and anticipated impacts of climate change. These were only a few of the many projects undertaken with PARP, illustrating the diversity in directions that the five First Nations chose to take with their respective PARP teams.

CULTURE IS EVERYWHERE

In earlier decades, writing about the economic development of disadvantaged communities or nations tended to emphasize the importance of having certain narrowly defined technical requirements for success. They included factors such as location in relation to markets, availability of natural resources, human capital, transportation networks, technology, and funds for capital investment.

Culture tended not to be an important part of these development models unless it was argued that the culture of the community or nation was all wrong—too tied to tradition, too present oriented, too much emphasis on extended families, and so on. In more recent times, culture has come into the picture in another way—as a product or experience that can be marketed, such as handicrafts or cultural tourism. Indeed, with PARP, one of the more isolated communities in the project, Eabametoong, developed a cultural tourism experience that brought southern visitors to the North, exposing them to a rich cultural experience in the broadest sense.

It was one of the major contributions of the Harvard Project on American Economic Development to bring forward another way in which culture plays a role, the concept of cultural congruence. This refers to American Indian Tribes or Canadian First Nations that have had a particular institutional structure imposed on them by colonial authorities in a one-size-fits-all manner (e.g., an elected Chief and Council system). Rarely have such structures matched the culture and traditions of the community, leading to a situation in which decisions made by the imposed institutions lack legitimacy and contribute to internal conflict. First Nations going back to their own traditions and reshaping their institutions accordingly as part of a nation-building process are addressing this lack of fit. T'it'q'et, for example, and the St'át'mic Nation of which it is a part, have written their own constitution, delineating relationships and responsibilities for present and future generations with respect to the lands and resources, people, language, and culture. The constitution is grounded in St'át'mic beliefs and values and reflects a holistic view of community self-governance, outlining principles related to St'át'mic title and rights, the economy, trade relations, justice, and spirituality. T'it'q'et's governance structure includes individual mandates for a Traditional Council and an Elders Council that collaborate with each other as well as with the Band Council. In fact, the Band Chief and Council report and answer to both the Traditional Council and the Elders' Council, the latter of which holds veto power over decisions, based on community direction.

What became evident over the six years that PARP worked with all five First Nations, and what we have tried to emphasize through this chapter both directly and indirectly, is that culture is central to how the communities prioritize their daily responsibilities and how they operate. For example, the First Nations involved in PARP taught the research teams how their cultures inform their processes of development in the conception of what constitutes a good life or in the culturally based protocols by which relationships are established between the communities and outside groups. In addition to the foundational principles that we followed, culture informed many of the project choices undertaken with PARP, such as Lake Keepers (already mentioned) and *Awakening the Spirit* (a video project for self-esteem among youth) in MCN, a birch bark course that can be taken for credit in the Opitciwan school, and a Cultural Tourism Showcase Project in Eabametoong, to name just a few. The conclusion that we have drawn is that culture is everywhere in First Nations, not only to be acknowledged but also to be respected in all aspects of the work at hand.

COMMUNITY-LEVEL DETERMINANTS OF HEALTH AND WELL-BEING
In our proposal to the Canadian Institutes of Health Research (CIHR) for funding, our initial thinking was to undertake research and action, in conjunction with the chosen communities, to address poverty as a social determinant of health. As noted above, in relation to community perspectives, we were too focused on the economic dimension. Our causal argument was that improvements in areas such as jobs, incomes, and business development would have direct, positive impacts on the health and well-being of individuals and families, though we were worried that the impacts might not be visible during the life of the project.

Our thinking changed as the project evolved and for reasons already discussed in this chapter. We began to see ourselves as contributing in a modest way to a process of nation building by undertaking a variety of initiatives following from community strategic plans

—activities such as creating an economic development corporation (EFN), improving communication capacity and training for Band staff (EFN), undertaking surveys so that leaders can be better informed to guide decision making (T'it'q'et), developing a food preservation and food security project (T'it'q'et and MCN), piloting an integrated services model to support persons seeking to exit social assistance (Sipek'nekatik), and, in MCN, engaging youth and Elders in learning traditional life skills, learning how to drive, and applying traditional knowledge as Lake Keepers. The idea was that, by supporting communities in projects of their choosing that reflect a holistic approach to "living well" (one of the terms that communities preferred to "poverty"), we would make a contribution to strengthening those communities. That in itself would have positive benefits for the health and well-being of community members.

THE ROLE OF EXTERNAL SUPPORTS

In the introductory sections of this chapter, we noted that all First Nations communities involved in PARP shared the common aspiration that the project contribute to improving community health and well-being. They sought to travel farther along the roads that they defined. Could they do it on their own? Our experience suggests that government supports are essential in the early stages even if communities are later able to generate significant own-source revenues. The driver's licence initiative that the E'Opinitowak Committee launched in MCN is a case in point; PARP team members coordinated with the government of Manitoba to facilitate the program so that community members could get their licences, which in turn increased their eligibility for employment.

Also, grants for training, infrastructure, communication, travel, and of course salaries are critical. The other requirement for government programs is that they be flexible and supportive, that they not seek to implement a centrally determined agenda but be available to support the strategic plans that the communities have set out. There would be little point in undertaking the development of strategic plans if support for their implementation were unavailable.

A related question is whether the academic sector can make a contribution, and here we are at risk of being self-serving. Suffice it to say that we were able to support relevant research (e.g., undertaking key informant interviews in MCN, T'it'q'et, and Sipek'nekatik or surveying the population to measure health status in T'it'q'et). We contributed our knowledge of the literature as well as specific academic expertise (e.g., in legal matters, in economics/business, or in the social determinants of health). Additionally, we helped to connect First Nations to other academics or to governments when requested. Importantly, in both Sipek'nekatik and Eabametoong, we provided a respite for the leaders to break away from crisis management and created opportunities to consider longer-range plans for the community. At the end of PARP, all five communities indicated a desire for the project to continue.

THE BENEFITS OF BRIDGING SOCIAL CAPITAL

Related to the above discussion is the usefulness of "bridging social capital," the social ties that connect people across divides such as race or class[13] to foster economic development and community well-being in geographically remote First Nations communities. As noted above, Indigenous peoples have many creative ideas, abilities, and talents, but as a result of colonization they do not always have access to the material resources necessary to implement them. A key role that PARP played was to connect First Nations to individuals, organizations, and municipalities that have abundant resources and are committed to reconciliation and social justice but do not themselves have the knowledge or connections to make good on their intentions. For example, PARP researchers working with Eabametoong First Nation helped to facilitate a unique partnership between EFN and Markham, Ontario.[14] As per this agreement, Eabametoong students now have access to Markham's online library system, the Band Administration can seek professional advice from Markham's municipal management on various issues, and the city and Markham citizens donated sports and fitness equipment to the First Nation.[15] Meanwhile, Markham's mayor and two city and regional councillors visited EFN to meet in person with the Band Council as well as community members at a PARP-sponsored dinner and community-wide breakfast. Finally, several Markham citizens travelled to EFN to participate in a Cultural Showcase in which they learned about EFN history, culture, and living conditions. This inaugural trip was part of a larger project that PARP fundraised for to build economic development capacity in tourism and related businesses. The point here is that such mutually beneficial connections do not necessarily emerge spontaneously; they often require deliberate bridging by a trusted third party. Investing in social infrastructure, and not just individually targeted policies and programs, is therefore critical to reducing poverty and enhancing well-being in First Nations and beyond.

POLITICAL AND ADMINISTRATIVE LEADERSHIP AND STABILITY

Although there is considerable debate in the literature about the importance of leadership in the process of development, our observations in the five communities were that it is of considerable significance. The challenges of development facing the communities are considerable, and both strong and visionary leadership is required for everything from dealing with crises to managing internal divisions, developing a vision for the community and related strategic planning, and dealing with external governments and private interests. Indeed, a strong case can be made that the leadership displayed is not fully recognized and appreciated by outsiders, governments, and businesses, and supports for leaders and leadership development are inadequate.

In addition to the quality of leadership is its stability. Most of the five First Nations involved in PARP are still bound by the two-year election cycle mandated by the Indian Act, which interferes significantly with longer-range planning. Over the life of our project, we experienced three elections in those communities with the two-year time frame, not to mention resulting changes in leadership.

To increase leadership stability, it appears that communities have two main options. The first option is to elect the same people repeatedly, a pattern that depends on many variables but works best when given leaders have outstanding abilities and community support.[16] The second option is to break away from the two-year cycle and choose a longer term between elections (e.g., four years) under the authority of the recently enacted First Nations Elections Act.

We found that leaders in these communities were well aware of the advantages of a longer period in office, and indeed one of the five communities does have elections every four years. It is difficult, however, to build community consensus for a longer term because of concerns about the ability to change leadership in short order if the people elected turn out not to be the best as viewed by a significant proportion of the community. This uncertainty is especially likely to arise if there are strong divisions within a First Nation.

Re-establishing a traditional system of governance, as in T'it'q'et and the other St'át'mic Nations (described above), is an approach that some communities are beginning to explore to address shortcomings of the election provisions in the Indian Act. The annual PARP gatherings, at which representatives from all five First Nations were present, were opportunities for them to learn from each other and gather ideas that they could take back to their respective communities for further discussion. Having been introduced to what the St'át'mic Nations were doing, other communities became curious about its potential for them.

POLITICS AND BUSINESS

One often hears in "Indian country" the refrain that politics and business need to be separated in order for development efforts to succeed. This point of view is often attributed to the Harvard Project, but in fact it represents a misreading and an oversimplification of what the project has to say.[17]

We found in the five communities that in fact the elected leaders play a crucial and necessary role in the development process. Although patterns vary from one community to the next, political leaders play a central role in defining community visions, developing strategic plans, putting in place a qualified civil service, enacting bylaws (BCRs), policies, and regulations, and dealing with external governments and private sector interests such as resource development or hydro companies. It is a very demanding role, placing considerable stress on both leaders and Council agendas.

Not everything can or should come to the table, however, and a strong case can be made for the formation of a separate but accountable structure such as a community economic development corporation. It can assemble the staff expertise required to deal with economic development initiatives, including the management of community-owned ventures, as well as provide a degree of separation from political considerations in decision making. Indeed, in Eabametoong, that is what we were asked to help establish, with a key project team member assisting in laying the legal and organizational groundwork. He was also asked to serve as a board member for the corporation. The Chief and Council represent all the shareholders of the corporation (the whole community) and play a key role, ensuring that the corporation complies with the strategic vision and plan for the community.

ACADEMIC TENSIONS

The kind of action research that we undertook in this project is a long way from mainstream practices and leads to significant tensions as a consequence. Even the language of mainstream research is problematic. For example, we responded to an opportunity for funding billed as "intervention research," a term that we abandoned quickly because the concept of (external) intervention does not have a happy history in the First Nations context.

Since the competition for grants from national funding agencies has become more competitive,[18] the expectation is high for proposals to be incredibly detailed about the research and how it will be implemented. This is at odds with the expectations of community-based research in the First Nations context, in which community engagement throughout the research process is a highly valued expectation. We have already noted the community-driven nature of PARP and how its original focus was substantially altered for a number of the communities. In our original proposal, we handled this tension to some extent by specifying only the common *process* that would be followed in each community (e.g., an Advisory Committee, research to develop a community profile, etc.). We avoided setting out a specific model of the development process or articulating required elements of a strategic plan.

Given the expectations of peer review committees, we might not have been successful in obtaining a grant were it not for the fact that CIHR had in place a mechanism whereby proposals in Indigenous health research could be reviewed by a special committee composed of persons who had knowledge of and experience in Indigenous health research and who inherently knew, as a result of their experience, that room for community influence had to be part of the research design.[19]

A similar tension exists with ethics reviews in which the mainstream practice is to require at the outset detailed specifications concerning how the work will be implemented before the research process begins. Requirements include having appendices with the actual questions to be used in the interview during the selection process and details on how participants (in this case, entire First Nations) will be recruited. In a related project submitted by one member of our research team, the ethics submission came to some 120 pages, and this was all before the research could actually begin. Our only recourse was to be specific but also not to hesitate in adapting research instruments as we went along, a process that required going back to the relevant ethics boards for amendments to the original application.

Other tensions arise with financial administrators in university settings who are reluctant to approve expenditures outside the norm, such as providing funds for feasts in the communities, paying for child care so that parents can participate in meetings, honorariums for Elders, or door prizes at community events. Their reluctance is rooted in a fear of being audited by the national granting councils, which suggests that a resolution of these tensions lies in changing practices and expectations at the national level.[20]

The granting councils and university-based ethics boards are far more comfortable and practiced when it comes to the *research* component of a project and much less geared to handle the *action* or *intervention* component. Ethics applications, for example, relate to matters such as research design, informed consent, and the risks/benefits of the research; nowhere do they ask for information assessing ethical practices and potential risks from the action part of the project. Yet it is more likely to be the action components that represent risks to participants than being asked a few questions by an interviewer or participating in a small group discussion.

A final point regards conventional approaches to knowledge arising from the research, most often deemed the property of an academic institution, and knowledge transfer, which typically has included requirements for publication and presentations at conferences. Recognizing that the knowledge shared by First Nations is *their* knowledge, the academy needs to adjust its policies on knowledge ownership and knowledge transfer to honour the principles of ownership, control, access, and possession (OCAP).[21] At the beginning of the project, PARP developed a written policy in partnership with AFN to ensure that permissions from the five First Nations were obtained before any article was published and that the principles embodied in OCAP were followed. One of PARP's practices, as a result, was to include all of the First Nations as authors of this chapter.

As this discussion shows, there is a lack of fit between the institutionalized requirements of mainstream research and the demands of community-based research in a First Nations context. Academic research ethics boards (REBs) and their ethics approval requirements are not set up for the type of action research that PARP pursued, a project that needed to be community driven: that is, based on what the communities wanted, not on what the researchers or academic institutions wanted. In response to the TRC Calls to Action and in this era of reconciliation, REBs have the potential to become increasingly responsive both to First Nations' expectations for any proposed research project and to community-driven action research protocols for developing good relations and working with First Nations partners.

RESPECTING TRADITIONAL KNOWLEDGES

The mainstream model of knowledge transfer typically shows that knowledge is generated by a research-oriented organization such as a university, hospital, or government laboratory and then transferred or applied to grateful recipients at the community level. Although this is a simplistic description even within the bounds of the mainstream model, historically it has been the prevailing orientation, with knowledge defined in Western scientific terms and collected accordingly.

Working with First Nations, a different perspective emerges. Since such research ideally involves the full engagement of the community in all phases, there is more of a sense that the community itself provides much of the knowledge, assembled and to some extent interpreted by the research partner. Furthermore, Indigenous knowledge is part of the picture in both conscious and subconscious ways, though it struggles to be recognized on par with Western science.[22]

For example, many of the projects that PARP researchers engaged in with their First Nations partners involved sharing traditional knowledge, seen by community members as integrally linked with improving health and well-being. Two projects illustrate this point. The first project was a culture-based credit course in the Opitciwan high school that involved harvesting birch bark and making baskets and canoes and that counted toward earning a high school or graduate-equivalent diploma (GED). The second project was a culture camp held around the summer solstice in MCN involving a fish fry (starting with setting the nets and catching the fish), learning food preparation, cooking, and preservation, sharing traditional teachings, and more. In these and other projects, PARP researchers observed and listened to both instructors and participants, reflecting on their experiences with increased senses of self-esteem, wellness, and connection to their roots and the land.

A further insight is that many First Nations in British Columbia have the traditional knowledge and applied skills to keep suicide levels low, so First Nations have much to learn from each other on how to tackle this important issue.[23]

NATION-TO-NATION LEARNING

PARP attempted to incorporate opportunities for nation-to-nation learning into the project design, with mixed results. The formal mechanism used was an Advisory Committee for the work in each community, leaving the details of its composition to be worked out in each case but providing some general guidance. In one community, for example, the Advisory Committee included community members such as the Chief, several councillors, an Elder, and others. It also included senior provincial and federal government representatives, on the ground that the design and implementation of a strategy to address poverty would benefit from government perspectives and funding. There were two academic members from the national project team and leaders from two First Nations in the same province who were widely recognized as having made great strides in achieving economic self-reliance and reduced government dependence.

The idea of having such an advisory body was outstanding in principle but less successful in practice. In this particular case, for example, though the Advisory Committee met several times and provided some useful guidance, there was resistance from some Councillors in recognizing that neighbouring communities, having made great progress in achieving self-reliance, had much to offer the First Nation involved in PARP. An element of intercommunity competitiveness came into play and impeded collaboration and opportunities to learn from each other's experiences. In other locations, either an Advisory Committee was not formed or, if it was, it contained key members from the community itself, such as the directors of various programs employed by the Band.

More informal mechanisms for intercommunity learning seemed to work better. There was great interest among community representatives to attend our annual national meetings, for example, and they showed considerable interest in hearing about the range of challenges that the communities faced and how they set out to address them. For instance, the other four First Nations were interested in learning more about the traditional governance structure in T'it'q'et and the childen-centred approach to family and child services in MCN, among other issues. Another mechanism for intercommunity learning involved the sharing and collaboration within Tribal Councils that brought together communities in the same geographic area that shared the same history and culture. Outside our project, learning also takes place at the annual meetings of organizations such as CANDO (Council for the Advancement of Economic Development Officers), which gives annual awards for excellence and offers multiple workshops on specific issues that delegates are free to attend if they so choose.

RECOMMENDATIONS FOR NATION-TO-NATION POLICY AND INSTITUTIONAL CHANGE

As Canada moves to interpret and act on the TRC Calls to Action, building upon RCAP and defining nation-to-nation relationships, a number of recommendations for policy and institutional change can be drawn from the preceding discussion. First, First Nations, and by extension Indigenous peoples across Canada, have a strong sense of their policy priorities and needs, requiring little outside help, if any, to know what is best for their communities. Allowing First Nations to direct processes promises to yield positive results, as it did for the communities that participated in PARP. In MCN, for example, setting the priority to increase opportunities for youth led to successful initiatives for this largest demographic of the community, providing training (e.g., to get a driver's licence) and employment (e.g., establishing a local seafood processing plant) as well as programs in life skills, culture, and recreation (e.g., the Lake Keepers program). Carrying out these programs in a comprehensive and holistic way, again taking direction from the community, was the key to success. In a number of instances, low-cost investments with minimal reporting requirements yielded significant, positive results; the driver's licence program is a case in point. So community-driven action research projects that build on community strengths and incorporate First Nations expertise, capacity, and knowledge are strongly recommended.

The same can be said when federal and provincial governments set their priorities. Rather than governments establishing Indigenous-focused initiatives for their various departments, a nation-to-nation relationship means that First Nations, Métis, and Inuit peoples, respecting that they know their needs best, are consulted and have a say in setting directions and deciding funding levels. In other words, federal and provincial governments ought to take their cues from First Nations, Métis, and Inuit governments rather than imposing one-sided decisions.

Second, strengthening ties to land and water is important for community well-being on economic, cultural, spiritual, mental, and emotional levels. A holistic approach to research for community health and well-being is therefore essential. This needs to translate into government funding that applies to all aspects of this holistic approach to health in support of physical wellness, mental strength, emotional balance, and spiritual freedom. Current funding envelopes, for example, tend to focus on the treatment of physical addiction, economic development, or infrastructure, with little or no funding for the mental, spiritual, and emotional dimensions of community wellness (aside from temporary supports given after specific emergencies and crises). For lasting improvements to health and well-being (on both individual and community levels), a holistic approach to funding that addresses all four dimensions is needed.

Third, important projects need not be large and costly. PARP funding, in various amounts, contributed to several successful community initiatives. Collaborating with the community and leveraging the external connections of PARP team members kept costs down in a number of initiatives, and the First Nations appreciated these lower costs. This project, however, though both timely and important, came to an end. Although all five communities expressed interest in continuing the association with the PARP teams, funding for such long-term collaborations does not exist. How can this approach to partnering in community-driven action research be supported in the future?

Fourth, the demand for project funding exceeds the supply, even with outside leveraging. Communities have developed sharp skill sets for prioritizing projects and reworking budgets, but ultimately there is a shortage of funds for small but effective projects as well as larger ones. Having to secure external funding on a project-by-project basis is onerous and time consuming, often with stringent limitations and reporting requirements. Equitable funding is essential, as is changing the bureaucratic maze and streamlining government funding processes to be in accordance with priorities set by First Nations. Although this will be challenging, it nevertheless needs to be done.

Fifth, hand in hand with ensuring equitable funding is the need to give First Nations autonomy and decision-making control over the use of the funds. One way to translate this recommendation into practice involves releasing First Nations from onerous reporting requirements on a per project basis in favour of one annual audit and report to be made available to all funding sources at the same time each year (rather than having one or more reports per project per funding agency throughout the year).

Finally, for granting agencies and academic REBs, policies need to reflect Indigenous priorities, protocols, and customs. What are First Nations ethics, and how can they be honoured in academic research application and approval processes? Rather than adhering to strictly

Western conventions, adaptations are needed to reflect the distinctness of collaborative research with First Nations. For example, terminology and customs need to be contemplated from Indigenous viewpoints and changed accordingly (e.g., the inappropriateness of intervention research, restrictions on honorariums, expectations to acknowledge the collaboration at a project's end with a gift exchange, etc.). REBs and granting agencies have an opportunity to learn from Indigenous peoples and, in the spirit of reconciliation, make their mandates flexible enough for the diversity that exists among Indigenous peoples and their protocols and customs.[24]

CONCLUSION

From 2011 to 2017, the Poverty Action Research Project was on a dynamic and creative journey for community development with five First Nations. The purpose of this chapter has been to raise awareness about the many strengths of First Nations peoples and to understand better a number of impediments that present challenges to them as they work for their communities' health and well-being.

Toward these objectives, this case study has

- described the Poverty Action Research Project;
- raised awareness about our different worlds and explored how poverty is perceived by First Nations, preferring instead to frame issues in holistic terms of health and well-being;
- highlighted First Nations strengths and acknowledged the credit due for their resilience and creativity in the face of significant and ongoing challenges;
- outlined distinctive cultural and other characteristics of First Nations especially relevant to academic and other external groups that wish to contribute to a holistic, collaborative, and community-driven process of development;
- discussed additional observations and insights based on PARP experiences; and
- suggested recommendations for policy and institutional change in light of the experiences of the PARP research team with the five First Nations that participated in the project.

Acknowledging the distinctness of each First Nation, how PARP unfolded differently for each community, and that this account is by no means exhaustive and all-encompassing given the diversity among Indigenous peoples across Canada, our intentions here have been to inform work in all sectors of society as together we discern how to progress toward reconciliation and strengthen relationship building between Indigenous peoples of Canada and non-Indigenous Canadians.

NOTES

1   As with any group effort in writing, it is extremely difficult to arrange the order of authorship since everyone's experiences and contributions to the research and writing processes are invaluable. Jennifer Dockstator and Frederic Wien co-wrote the "Introduction," "Background," and "Research in Process" sections. The various authors contributed to their respective sections in "Research in Action," describing PARP activities in the communities with which they worked. Jennifer and Mark Dockstator co-wrote the section "Highlighting First Nations Strengths." Jennifer summarized some of the challenges that each community faced in the section "Respecting First Nations Challenges." Frederic authored the section on "Additional Insights." Jennifer and Wanda Wuttunee contributed to the "Policy and Institutional Recommendations" section. Jennifer wrote the "Conclusion." And Jennifer and Frederic co-edited the chapter based on input from the research team.

2   The precedent for the practice of listing First Nations as authors can be found in Lonczak et al., "Navigating the Tide Together," and Smylie et al., "Indigenous Knowledge Translation."

3   Brant Castellano and Wien, "Sharing the Land, Sharing a Future."

4   Dockstator et al., "Pursuing Mutually Beneficial Research."

5   See http://sipeknekatik.ca/community-profile/.

6   See http://povertyaction.ca/community/opitciwan-qc.

7   For information presented in the first part of this community profile, see http://eabametoong.firstnation.ca/.

8   See, for example, Cornell, "American Indians, American Dreams."

9   Dockstator et al., "Pursuing Mutually Beneficial Research."

10 See http://www.cbc.ca/news/canada/how-does-native-funding-work-1.1301120.

11 See http://www.cbc.ca/news/aboriginal/first-nations-funding-cap-lifted-1.3359137.

12 Lengthening terms is now possible after the First Nations Elections Act came into effect April 2015, requiring the development of a community election code, adoption by a majority vote of the membership, and passage of a BCR. See http://www.aadnc-aandc.gc.ca/eng/1407356680075/1407356710099.

13 Baron, Field, and Schuller, *Social Capital: Critical Perspectives*; Halpern, *Social Capital*; Lin, Cook, and Burt, *Social Capital Theory and Research*.

14 See http://www.yorkregion.com/news-story/7095569-markham-signs-partnership-accord-with-eabametoong-first-nation/.

15 See http://www.cbc.ca/news/canada/thunder-bay/first-nations-girls-Ohockey-1.4091247.

16 Wien, "Profile of the Membertou First Nation, Nova Scotia."

17 For more information on the Harvard Project, see http://hpaied.org/.

18 Our grant came from CIHR.

19 Subsequently, CIHR did away with the special peer review committee and moved to a format in which reviewers would no longer meet face to face for much of the peer review process and with no guarantee that a given panel was composed of people with experience

in the field. In response to protests, CIHR is moving back to the original model.

20 Moore, "Implementing Chapter 9"; Stiegman and Castleden, "Leashes and Lies."

21 Schnarch and First Nations Centre, "Ownership, Control, Access, and Possession."

22 Bartlett, Marshall, and Marshall, "Two-Eyed Seeing."

23 Chandler and Lalonde, "Transferring Whose Knowledge?"

24 Fortunately, significant progress in adapting ethics requirements to meet the needs of research with Indigenous populations has been made; see Canadian Institutes of Health Research, Natural Sciences and Engineering Research Council of Canada, and Social Sciences and Humanities Research Council of Canada, "Tri-Council Policy Statement," Chapter 9.

REFERENCES

Baron, Stephen, John Field, and Tom Schuller, eds. *Social Capital: Critical Perspectives*. New York: Oxford University Press, 2000.

Bartlett, Cheryl, Murdena Marshall, and Albert Marshall. "Two-Eyed Seeing and Other Lessons Learned within a Co-Learning Journey of Bringing Together Indigenous and Mainstream Knowledges and Ways of Knowing." *Journal of Environmental Studies and Sciences* 2, no. 4 (2012): 331–40.

Brant Castellano, Marlene, and Frederic Wien. "Sharing the Land, Sharing a Future: Marking the 20th Anniversary of the RCAP Report." Concept paper, second draft, 1 May 2016.

Canadian Institutes of Health Research, Natural Sciences and Engineering Research Council of Canada, and Social Sciences and Humanities Research Council of Canada. "Tri-Council Policy Statement: Ethical Conduct for Research Involving Humans – TCPS 2." 2018. https://ethics.gc.ca/eng/policy-politique_tcps2-eptc2_2018.html

Chandler, Michael, and Christopher Lalonde. "Transferring Whose Knowledge? Exchanging Whose Best Practices? On Knowing about Indigenous Knowledge and Aboriginal Suicide." In *Aboriginal Policy Research: Setting the Agenda for Change*, vol. 2, edited by J. White, P. Maxim, and D. Beavon, 111–123. Toronto: Thompson Educational Publishing, 2004.

Cornell, Stephen. "American Indians, American Dreams, and the Meaning of Success." *American Indian Culture and Research Journal* 11, no. 4 (1987): 59–70.

Dockstator, Jennifer S., Eabametoong First Nation, Misipawistik Cree First Nation, Opitciwan Atikamekw First Nation, Sipekne'katik First Nation, T'it'q'et, Lillooet, BC, GerardDuhaime, Charlotte Loppie, David Newhouse, Frederic Wien, Wanda Wuttunee, JeffreyS. Denis, and Mark. Dockstator. "Pursuing Mutually Beneficial Research: Insights from the Poverty Action Research Project." *Engaged Scholar Journal* 2, no. 1 (2016): 17–38.

Halpern, David. *Social Capital*. Cambridge, UK: Polity Press, 2004.

Lin, Nan, Karen Cook, and Ronald S. Burt, eds. *Social Capital Theory and Research*. New York: Routledge, 2001.

Lonczak, Heather, Lisa Rey Thomas, Dennis Donovan, Lisette Austin, Robin L.W. Sigo, Nigel Lawrence, and Squamish Tribe. "Navigating the Tide Together: Early Collaboration between Tribal and Academic Partners in a CBPR Study." *Pimatisiwin: A Journal of Aboriginal and Indigenous Community Health* 11, no. 3 (2013): 395–409.

Moore, Carla. "Implementing Chapter 9 of the Tri-Council Policy Statement on the Ethics of Research Involving Aboriginal Peoples." In "Canada: How's It Going?" (MA thesis, Dalhousie University, 2015). http://hdl.handle.net/10222/64699.

Schnarch, Brian and First Nations Centre. "Ownership, Control, Access, and Possession (OCAP) or Self-Determination Applied to Research: A Critical Analysis of Contemporary First Nations Research and Some Options for First Nations Communities." *Journal of*

Aboriginal Health 1, no. 1 (2004): 80–95. http://www.naho.ca/jah/english/jah01_01/journal_p80-95.pdf.

Smylie, Janet, Nili Kaplan-Myrth, Kelly McShane, Métis Nation of Ontario-Ottawa Council, Pikwakanagan First Nation, and Tungasuvvingat Inuit Family Resource Centre. "Indigenous Knowledge Translation: Baseline Findings in a Qualitative Study of the Pathways of Health Knowledge in Three Indigenous Communities in Canada." *Health Promotion Practice* 10, no. 3 (2009): 436–46.

Stiegman, Martha L., and Heather Castleden. "Leashes and Lies: Navigating the Colonial Tensions of Institutional Ethics for Research Involving Indigenous Peoples in Canada." *International Indigenous Policy Journal* 6, no. 3 (2015): 1–10. https://ojs.lib.uwo.ca/index.php/iipj/article/view/7465/6109

Wien, Frederic. "Profile of the Membertou First Nation, Nova Scotia." In *Growth of Enterprises in Aboriginal Communities*, S. Loizides and R. Anderson, eds., 19-20. Ottawa: Conference Board of Canada, 2006.

——. "A Poverty Reduction Approach to Improving the Health and Well-Being of First Nations Communities" (unpublished research proposal summary), 2010.

CHAPTER 13
INDIGENOUS ECONOMIC
DEVELOPMENT WITH TENACITY

Wanda Wuttunee, Frederic Wien, and David Newhouse

The transformation of Aboriginal economies from dependence
on government transfers to interdependence and self-reliance
is fundamental to the development of self-government. It is now
widely accepted that Aboriginal nations and communities must be
able to generate sufficient wealth to provide an acceptable quality of life for their members. Without this capacity to generate
wealth and to use it for their own development, dependency will
continue, and the economic and social costs of maintaining it will
continue to rise.

—Royal Commission on Aboriginal Peoples, 1996[1]

The detailed analyses and recommendations for improved economic
health in the Indigenous community outlined in the work of the Royal
Commission on Aboriginal Peoples (RCAP) twenty years ago are still
entirely relevant and on track today. The expressed vision is still incomplete, however, with much work left outstanding.

Some supportive changes that occurred over the twenty-year period
are noted in this chapter, and we explore the diversity of perspectives

held by Indigenous communities across this country looking for the "good life" on their own terms. Working with capitalism in their own ways if at all was accurately predicted in the RCAP report. The requirements to move forward include understanding the diversity of goals within Canada's Indigenous communities. Although legal decisions in recent years support the definition of Indigenous rights and Crown responsibilities, it is important to realize that part of that process includes Indigenous communities themselves. Resource and labour force development and business dynamics built upon a foundation of educational opportunity are all being taken up by Indigenous communities at their own pace, within a context of growing awareness in Canada of the state of Indigenous peoples in this country.

ABORIGINAL ECONOMIES

If you listen to our Elders talk, they talk about us as part of everything, a part of the cycle of life, the cycle of the environment and our seasons, we're a part of it all.... We were people of the land and we were hunters and gatherers and we were conservationists and making sure there was also something for our tomorrow, for our children and our grandchildren.

—Mike Sutherland[2]

Attention must be paid to the ways in which Indigenous communities face the challenges of economic development. They are experiencing large demographic shifts, significant challenges with unemployment and poverty, changes in political structures (e.g., moving toward self-government), new opportunities for financial resources (e.g., the Ring of Fire, treaty land entitlement payments), and increased policy influence. Yet numerous studies over the past twenty years have shown widening gaps between Indigenous and non-Indigenous Canadians on indicators of well-being.[3] Indigenous people's quality of life continues to fall short of the quality of life enjoyed by the rest of Canada's population. The epigraph above from Mike Sutherland finds one way that holds for generations of community members, but it is too simplistic to assume that there is only one path for what is important today to Canada's Indigenous peoples and only one vision for the future. Diversity must be recognized for its importance in inspiring Indigenous communities and this country. Although there are many obstacles facing Indigenous peoples today, there are a number of areas in which positive change is taking place.

Historically, legislation (including the Indian Act) was enacted for the benefit of settler Canadians while failing to improve the lives of Indigenous Canadians. Treaty lands were small, removed from markets in most cases, generally of poor quality, and with limited opportunities for meaningful participation in the Canadian economy. Although charged with introducing agriculture as an alternative to self-sufficiency, government agents often did a poor job of providing farming implements and supporting marketing possibilities. If anything, many agents undermined the efforts of the government and Indigenous peoples. When opportunities to participate in the Canadian economy did arise, often non-Indigenous Canadians were unwilling to conduct business with Indigenous Canadians.[4]

However, the picture is not entirely bleak. The 2009 State of the First Nations Economy report identified significant growth in community and private businesses since the early 1970s and acknowledged that breakout communities in each region of the country are "successful in providing a viable economic base for their own communities and generating significant opportunities for their surrounding areas."[5] Research in the emerging field of Indigenous entrepreneurship has begun to explore macro-level economic and entrepreneurial frameworks for community development and other lines of inquiry that make up the study of Indigenous economic development.[6] The focus has been primarily on community-based Indigenous enterprises and the growth environment for band-owned businesses. Pedero and colleagues observed differences and similarities between Indigenous and non-Indigenous enterprises. They noted the choice by Indigenous enterprises to claim relevant mainstream business strategies without sacrificing cultural values or economic success. Integrating a particular culture and values in their businesses is what makes Indigenous businesses and entrepreneurs unique.[7] Although understanding the macro-level community approach to Indigenous entrepreneurship is critical, it is also important to explore the issue from the micro-perspective of individual business leaders.

Many Indigenous business leaders work in mainstream urban centres. It would be easy to assume that community connections are severed and that their activities have no impact on Indigenous communities. In fact, research shows that urban-based Indigenous people maintain strong connections to their cultures.[8] Academic research on understanding Canadian Indigenous entrepreneurs is sparse, with little theoretical development. From this framework, we can conclude that some individuals and communities are prepared to work in the mainstream economy. Questions about capitalism are still important in order to enrich decisions about engaging in the mainstream.

As more Indigenous scholars enter the academy, they question the relevance and impact of, and the relationship to, capitalism. In 2000, a member of the RCAP team, David Newhouse (Onondaga, Trent University), wrote a chapter on the topic "Resistance Is Futile: Aboriginal Peoples Meet the Borg of Capitalism." He examined the transformation of Aboriginal peoples living in a capitalist world. Economic development might be the key to progress, but it comes with an inevitable cost: "What capitalism does ultimately is redefine the nature of society. It creates a moral system which is used for valuing ends and means. Society then becomes a collection of individuals; each of us is allowed to pursue our own needs on the basis that this will result in the greatest good for all."[9] This flies in the face of the central tenets of traditional Aboriginal life, according to Newhouse, who pointed out that one missing element is that wealth accumulation for its own sake in order to spawn more wealth was not common.[10] He concluded that the cost might be minimized if Aboriginal people are mindful, cautious, and clear about the costs to their values and work to protect what is critical by transforming "these values ... into institutional actions."[11]

More recently, Indigenous authors have re-examined the nexus of capitalism and Aboriginality. For example, Clifford Atleo concludes that investigating alternatives to capitalism, along with recentring Indigenous values and principles where boundaries are crossed and Indigenous conceptions of health and wealth are not integrated but stand alone, comprise the step that follows from an initial examination of narrow socio-economic indices.[12] He believes that resistance is not futile but fertile. This research demonstrates the diversity of approaches to economic development, even to the point of critically reflecting on embracing capitalism uncritically. Practically, the range of economic activities reflects the spectrum of choices, from focusing on land-based activities in line with Sutherland's quotation to fully taking advantage of development opportunities, understanding that it is the particular mix of elements that guarantees peace with the results.

FAIR SHARE: INDIGENOUS RIGHTS
AND THE DUTY TO CONSULT

RCAP recognized that transforming the Canadian economy to the extent determined necessary for self-reliance in Indigenous communities required commitment, innovation, and creativity. Making space for Indigenous peoples in all their diversity still requires Canadians to buy in to freedom of choices and to give support for the implications of those choices. An inclusive society acknowledges the room for difference that should have been maintained in this country for Indigenous peoples since the beginning and by opening up will make for a stronger, more resilient country today and in the future.

The courts have considered Aboriginal rights, and their decisions have changed the Canadian landscape for many stakeholders since the RCAP report was published in 1996. In *Delgamuukw* (1997), the Supreme Court of Canada confirmed that Aboriginal title continued to exist in British Columbia and that it is a right to the land itself. Oral history must be relied on in future cases examining Indigenous title to the land. The court also urged negotiation rather than litigation to settle these questions in the future. This decision significantly moved the focus from site-specific rights to territorial rights.

More recently, in *Tsilhqot'in Nation* (2014), the Supreme Court relied on the *Delgamuukw* decision to declare, for the first time, that a specific group has Aboriginal title to Crown land. This was a significant decision that affects Indigenous groups and Canadians, most importantly in regard to increased certainty of Aboriginal title.

Crown obligations were meaningfully expanded in the *Haida Nation* (2004) decision when the Supreme Court confirmed that the Crown has a duty to consult with Indigenous communities and, where appropriate, accommodate claimed or proven Aboriginal rights where Crown action might adversely affect those rights. Clarity and certainty are important for all stakeholders, and the duty to consult keeps Indigenous communities in the decision-making loop despite not having a veto over proposed development projects or being required to prove their rights.

This duty to consult was defined more fully in the Supreme Court decision in *Little Salmon/Carmacks* (2010), which held that a duty to consult exists in respect of modern treaty rights. Modern treaties are included in the Crown's duty to consult with First Nations that represent the individual interests of community members. *Tsilhqot'in Nation* also made new law regarding this duty.

Another momentous decision focused on the rights of Non-Status Indians and Métis. In *Manitoba Metis Federation Inc.* (2013), the Supreme Court held that the honour of the Crown requires it to implement diligently the constitutional obligations to Aboriginal people. A narrow interpretation points to a declaration that the Crown wronged the Métis people historically. However, *Manitoba Metis Federation* proclaims their rights to lands in Manitoba, requiring the Crown to include them on the basis of the duty to consult in treaty land entitlement negotiations.

In summary, the courts have played a pivotal role in defining Aboriginal title and rights and clarifying the obligations of the Crown. Certainty means that Indigenous rights will not be so easily trampled on, with opportunities leading to economic self-reliance now existing in a better environment than twenty years ago. How have those opportunities transformed the well-being and self-governance of Indigenous peoples post-RCAP?

SEALING THE DEAL

Indigenous peoples have survived because of their well-honed adaptability skills. Resilience differs for each Indigenous community as wisdom flows from values, spirit, relationships infusing stances on critical issues by Elders, leaders, and community members. These features are at the core of Indigenous survival. The ways in which to accomplish meaningful individual and community well-being are as diverse as languages, locations, and dreams, making Indigenous Canadians, broadly speaking, similar to other Canadians with a multiplicity of opinions. To seal the deal, a community and its leaders must be convinced of project efficacy and share a vision before an opportunity is realized. We showcase this diversity of position in the next section.

RESOURCE DEVELOPMENT

Indigenous communities are interested and have become involved in the business of developing resources. For twenty years, the Canadian Aboriginal Minerals Association (CAMA) has worked to inform community members, industry, and governments about ways to work together. According to Hans Matthews, the president of CAMA, "governments have only recently embraced the desires, aspirations and plans of Aboriginal communities to be decision makers in resource development. Aboriginal communities want to engage with mining companies to share in the potential wealth, share in benefits, share in decisions, and work together to discuss ways to allow projects to proceed with minimal or no negative impact on our communities."[13] Communities across the North are involved with mining initiatives, such as the Meadowbank mine located in the Kivalliq region of Nunavut. The Diavik Diamond Mine in the Northwest Territories has participation agreements with the Tlicho Government, Yellowknives Dene First Nation, North Slave Métis Alliance, Kitikmeot Inuit Association, and Lutsel K'e Dene First Nation. Northern Ontario has increased mining activity as communities are inundated with opportunities to partner in the Ring of Fire resource development projects. For example, Wabun Tribal Council and Eabametoong First Nation in northern Ontario recognized the need for a development corporation through which to funnel all partnering invitations with an appropriate vetting procedure. This will give structure to a process that otherwise could be overwhelming to leaders already stretched thin.

The Canadian Council for Aboriginal Business (CCAB), the Aboriginal Human Resource Council, and the Council for Native Development Officers are bringing initiatives forward to support and encourage Indigenous businesses in activities that cross a wide range of economic sectors. Their efforts are also supported by the work of the National Aboriginal Economic Development Board (NAEDB), with research that points to the economic gaps between Indigenous peoples and the rest of Canadians. According to the 2015 Aboriginal Economic Development Report, more than $675 billion in future resource development projects will occur on Indigenous traditional lands, reserves, or land claim spaces: "As of 2014, there were over 260 active agreements between mining exploration and development companies and First Nations governments or organizations."[14]

Although having a seat at the table makes sense, especially when projects are going to proceed in any event, many communities are not interested in invasive projects on their lands. Key concerns[15] include the lack of voice in isolated communities in resource-rich lands as companies hover nearby. Courts and legislation have defined treaty and Aboriginal rights, which are not always acknowledged and honoured until Indigenous communities undertake expensive litigation. The loss of lands from industrial development threatens affected communities in terms of their histories, the future for their children, and their current well-being. Booth notes that studies demonstrate "the important connections between traditional lifestyle, access to traditional foods and indigenous well-being, including limiting the rise in diabetes and other diseases."[16] The loss of hunting and gathering locations irretrievably affects culture and Indigenous knowledge negatively as traditional use opportunities disappear.

Some Indigenous groups object vocally or through demonstrations and protests to proposed projects such as the Dakota Access Pipeline in North Dakota, where thousands joined in protest in the summer of 2016. In Canada, a Gathering of Nations focused on mega-pipeline projects and brought more than 160 First Nations signatories to Save the Fraser Declaration (2013) in opposition to Enbridge's Northern Gateway Pipeline project. The Indigenous groups conclude that the federal approval process contradicts ancestral laws, title, rights, and responsibilities. The signatories declare that "we will not allow the proposed Enbridge Northern Gateway Pipelines, or similar Tar Sands projects, to cross our lands, territories and watersheds, or the ocean migration routes of Fraser River salmon.... We have suffered enough.... We will not tolerate this great threat to us all and to all future generations."[17] Other communities have different views of the pipeline.

Aboriginal Equity Partners (AEP) is a coalition of thirty-one First Nations and Métis communities that have become owners of the Northern Gateway Pipeline.[18] An equity position means that they exercise rights to the development and execution of the project while reaping benefits for future generations. There are four stewards, drawn from the First Nations and Métis communities, who oversee AEP and liaise with the other owners and the pipeline company. The equity partnership is a new way of doing business with First Nations and Métis peoples in partnership with the resource industry.

AEP is making change from the inside out:

> As stewards of the land, we will have a direct and meaningful role in the environmental protection of lands along Northern Gateway's pipeline route and in marine operations. As project owners, we will ensure our Traditional Knowledge and Traditional Land Use knowledge is part of project decision-making and operations. We will be involved in identifying potentially affected areas and will be consulted on how to incorporate our traditional knowledge and

recommendations. Northern Gateway has committed to consult with us at every stage of the project and to minimize any impact on the land and ocean. Being partners in the project will allow us to ensure it is built to the highest safety and environmental standards while also providing our people with education, skills training and business opportunities. Northern Gateway is committed to building this important Canadian infrastructure project. They are open to change and recognize they have much more work to do with First Nations and Métis communities.[19]

The road to economic prosperity is clearly not straight, nor is it only one way.

EMPLOYMENT AND BUSINESS ACTIVITY

There are many other examples of diverse economic development strategies undertaken by Indigenous individuals and communities. National employment statistics[20] specify a range of employers that hired the 57 percent of Aboriginal people employed, including in the areas of health, social assistance, trades, construction, and manufacturing. The CCAB's recent report on Aboriginal entrepreneurs offers additional insights into the wide range of activity across industry sectors. Of the 42,100 self-employed, 34 percent were in the professional, scientific, and technical services, education, health, and social services; 19 percent were in construction; 10 percent were in primary manufacturing, wholesale/retail trade, and arts, entertainment, food, and cultural activities.[21]

The NAEDB focuses on shedding light on the gaps between Aboriginal peoples and the rest of Canadians. Although the foregoing statistics are important, the whole story is better understood if we ask "Why the disparity?" A series of benchmark socio-economic indicators covering 2006 to 2011 highlights the lack of change in "employment rate, participation rate and university completion.... Gaps between First Nations living on reserve and the non-Aboriginal population increased for employment and participation rates, reliance on government transfers, college and trades certification completion rates, [and] university completion rates."[22] The recommendations from the NAEDB speak to economic and social policy coordination as well as to strengthened efforts to support reserve communities that are really suffering.

The old saying "one step forward and two steps back" seems to characterize the rhythm of employment and business activity from the long view. It is incredible that communities that have suffered terrible hardships can

function at all. Gains have been made, but it is important
success along the road to parity as set forth by the NAEDB
wellness, which for some might require a different defini
Education and training were seen by RCAP to be key for bu
dence and employability.

EDUCATION

The key of education for many Indigenous families is hard to pick
they have suffered in residential schools, never completed high sc
want family members to stay in the community, which often does n
a school, college, or technical institute or one located nearby. Other
lies see the value in pursuing education outside the community. Yc
people go to high school or postsecondary institutions with the advic
remember where they come from and the teachings they know echoi
in their ears.

The NAEDB reports on gaps in education, recognizing that skills mean
"better labour market outcomes and stronger communities and businesses
in the 21st century knowledge-based economy."[23] In 2011, high school
completion rates in Aboriginal communities increased more quickly
than those in non-Aboriginal communities. Métis students followed by
First Nations students living off reserve achieved the higher completion
rates. A significant percentage of young Aboriginal women (64.4 percent)
completed high school, surpassing 59.4 percent of young Aboriginal men.
The conclusion is that, even with this increased completion rate, the overall completion rate gap of 18.5 percent compared with the non-Aboriginal
population was substantial.[24] Completion rates for colleges, trades, and
apprenticeships had only a 1.2 percent gap; the Métis student completion
rates drove the improvement over the 2006–11 period.[25] Finally, a growing gap between Aboriginal and non-Aboriginal university graduates
stands at 15 percent. This is despite increased completion rates for First
Nations, Métis, and Inuit living off reserve. Progress has been achieved,
but the number of non-Aboriginal graduates is increasing at a faster rate.

Educational achievement is part of the strategy for moving Indigenous communities forward, but it is a personal and individual choice
influenced by many factors, adding to the complexity of setting reasonable expectations. The current Trudeau government has laid out plans for
education that focus on new schools, improving numeracy, reading, and
writing K–12. Other plans focus on Indigenous languages and cultures,

infrastructure improvements to schools, and cash injections to support postsecondary school access.[26] In its annual special report, TD Economics takes a look at the long and winding road toward Aboriginal economic prosperity. In particular, the many steps taken to improve Aboriginal student success in schools are highlighted.[27]

Institutions are offering summer camps aimed at introducing middle and secondary students to university. Through fun activities and field trips, the memories are positive, and the dreams of returning after high school graduation are not so far away. These experiences continue with university staff and students building relationships with communities and supporting community schools through tutoring to improve completion rates.[28]

Without compromising standards, some university programs have addressed the lack of Indigenous students by broadening eligibility requirements. Funding issues still remain despite the support of communities, universities, governments, and the private sector. As more universities make Indigenous achievement a priority, resources are being directed at sharing role model stories of graduates and Elders who often mentor new students. There are many more issues that need to be addressed to draw Indigenous students onto the paths that they have selected for their futures.

PARTING THOUGHTS

Transformation is a challenge. In this case, sustainable prosperity is only possible if the opportunities stressed here for Canada's Indigenous peoples are supported and then multiplied and the challenges approached from all fronts to move to solutions that will work for everyone. We are truly mapping the unique journey to self-government as Indigenous people put their own marks on their destinies. It is a journey that cannot be completed without Canadians investing in the process as concluded in the RCAP report.

Finally, TD Economics notes in its seventh report on this topic that "too much is at stake for progress to stagnate.... We must all be part of the conversation and the solution. Analytics are one way to achieve greater understanding of the trends and progress made. Additionally, improved data can enable researchers and policymakers to appreciate the differences with the Aboriginal community itself. These same decision makers and persons of influence will then be equipped to permanently conquer the social challenges faced by the Aboriginal community."[29]

NOTES

1 RCAP, *The Report of the Royal Commission on Aboriginal Peoples*, 799.
2 Martens et al., "Understanding Indigenous Food Sovereignty," 31.
3 NAEDB, *The Aboriginal Economic Progress Report*; RCAP, *The Report of the Royal Commission on Aboriginal Peoples*; Salée, "Quality of Life."
4 Newhouse and Jetté, "CANDO Statement."
5 Assembly of First Nations, "The State of the First Nations Economy," 6.
6 Dana, "A Comparison of Indigenous and Non-Indigenous Enterprise"; Loxley, *Aboriginal, Northern, and Community Economic Development.*
7 Pedero et al., "Toward a Theory of Indigenous Entrepreneurship."
8 See United Way of Winnipeg, *Eagle's Eye View.*
9 Newhouse, "Resistance Is Futile," 150–51.
10 Newhouse, "Resistance Is Futile," 152.
11 Newhouse, "Resistance Is Futile," 154.
12 Atleo, "Aboriginal Capitalism."
13 Matthews, "Canadian Aboriginal Minerals Association."
14 NAEDB, *The Aboriginal Economic Progress Report*, 7.
15 Booth and Skelton, "You Spoil Everything."
16 Booth and Skelton, "You Spoil Everything," 688.
17 "Save the Fraser Declaration," 2013.
18 AEP, "AEP and Northern Gateway Pipeline."
19 AEP, "AEP and Northern Gateway Pipeline."
20 Statistics Canada, *Aboriginal Peoples.*
21 Statistics Canada, *Aboriginal Peoples*, 13.
22 NAEDB, *The Aboriginal Economic Progress Report*, 8.
23 NAEDB, *The Aboriginal Economic Progress Report*, 28.
24 NAEDB, *The Aboriginal Economic Progress Report*, 27.
25 NAEDB, *The Aboriginal Economic Progress Report*, 28.
26 Liberal Party of Canada, "First Nations Education."
27 Gulati and Burleton, *The Long and Winding Road.*
28 Gulati and Burleton, *The Long and Winding Road*, 10.
29 Gulati and Burleton, *The Long and Winding Road*, 16.

REFERENCES

Aboriginal Equity Partners (AEP). "AEP and Northern Gateway Pipeline." 2015. http://www.aepowners.ca/aep_and_ngp.

Assembly of First Nations. "The State of the First Nation Economy and the Struggle to Make Poverty History." A paper prepared for the Inter-Nation Trade and Economic Summit, Toronto, Ontario, 9–11 March 2009, by the Assembly of First Nations Make Poverty History Expert Advisory Committee.

Atleo, C. "Aboriginal Capitalism: Is Resistance Futile or Fertile?" *Journal of Aboriginal Economic Development* 9, no. 2 (2015): 41–51.

Booth, A., and N. Skelton. "'You Spoil Everything': Indigenous Peoples and the Consequences of Industrial Development in British Columbia." *Environment Development and Sustainability* 13, no. 4 (August 2011): 685–702.

Dana, Leo-Paul. "A Comparison of Indigenous and Non-Indigenous Enterprise in the Canadian Sub-Arctic." *International Journal of Business Performance Management* 9, no. 3 (2007): 278–86.

Delgamuukw v. British Columbia, [1997] 3 S.C.R. 1010.

Gulati, S., and D. Burleton. *The Long and Winding Road towards Aboriginal Economic Prosperity.* Toronto: TD Economics, 2015.

Haida Nation v. British Columbia (Minister of Forests), 2004 SCC 73, [2004] 3 S.C.R. 511.

Liberal Party of Canada. "First Nations Education." 2013. https://www.liberal.ca/realchange/first-nations-education-2/.

Loxley, John. *Aboriginal, Northern, and Community Economic Development: Papers and Retrospectives.* Winnipeg: Arbeiter Ring, 2010.

Manitoba Metis Federation Inc. v. Canada (Attorney General), 2013 SCC 14, [2013] 1 S.C.R. 623.

Martens, Tabitha, Jaime Cidro, Michael Anthony Hart, and Stéphane McLachlan. "Understanding Indigenous Food Sovereignty through an Indigenous Research Paradigm." *Journal of Indigenous Social Development* 5, no. 1 (2016): 18–37.

Matthews, H. "Canadian Aboriginal Minerals Association." 2016. https://www.aboriginalminerals.com/.

National Aboriginal Economic Development Board (NAEDB). *The Aboriginal Economic Progress Report.* Gatineau: NAEDB, 2015.

Newhouse, David, and Corinne Mount-Pleasant Jette. "CANDO Statement on the Economic Development Recommendations of the Royal Commission on Aboriginal Peoples." 1997. http://www.rbcroyalbank.com/RBC:olbopda_fq/aboriginal/rr_cando.html#top.

Newhouse, D. "Resistance Is Futile: Aboriginal Peoples Meet the Borg of Capitalism." In *Ethics and Capitalism,* ed. John Douglas Bishop, 141–55. Toronto: University of Toronto Press, 2000.

Peredo, Ana Maria, Robert B. Anderson, Craig Galbraith, and Benson Honig. "Toward a Theory of Indigenous Entrepreneurship." 2004. Conference of the Canadian Council for Small Business and Entrepreneurship. Regina, SK.

Peredo, Ana Maria, and Robert B. Anderson. "Indigenous Entrepreneurship Research: Themes and Variations." In *Developmental Entrepreneurship: Adversity, Risk and Uncertainty,* ed. C. Stile and C. Galbraith, 253–74. Oxford, 2006.

Royal Commission on Aboriginal Peoples (RCAP). *The Report of the Royal Commission on Aboriginal Peoples.* Ottawa: Ministry of Supply and Services, 1996.

Salée, Daniel, with the assistance of David Newhouse and Carol Lévesque. "Quality of Life of Aboriginal People in Canada: An Analysis of Current Research." *IRPP Choices* 12, no. 6 (2006).

"Save the Fraser Declaration." 2013. http://savethefraser.ca/.

Statistics Canada. *Aboriginal Peoples.* Ottawa: Statistics Canada, 2016.

Tsilhqot'in Nation v. British Columbia, 2014 SCC 44.

United Way of Winnipeg. *Eagle's Eye View: An Environmental Scan of the Aboriginal Community in Winnipeg.* 2nd ed. Winnipeg: United Way of Winnipeg, 2010. https://unitedwaywinnipeg.ca/wp-content/uploads/2017/03/UnitedWayEaglesEyeView-2010.pdf.

CHAPTER 14

POWERFUL COMMUNITIES, HEALTHY COMMUNITIES:
A TWENTY-FIVE-YEAR JOURNEY OF HEALING AND WELLNESS

Caroline L. Tait, Devon Napope, Amy Bombay, William Mussell, First Peoples First Person, and Canadian Depression Research and Intervention Network

Colonization, healing, and resilience reveal themselves to me. As Survivors, we ride waves of vulnerability for a lifetime and for generations. We were subjected to real risk factors including hunger, loneliness, ridicule, physical and sexual abuse, untimely and unseemly death. As we struggle to throw off the shackles of colonization we lean heavily toward healing, and resilience becomes our best friend.

—Madeleine Dion Stout[1]

FIGURE 14.1 KEVIN PEEACE, *SURVIVOR*,
USED WITH ARTIST'S PERMISSION.

Letter to My Family

My dear family, I know we love each other
I know we had some differences, my brothers
For that I'm sorry for what I put us through
Where do we go from here?
What do we do?
We're so lost, when does it all end?
I can't do this on my own, but I'll do what I can
Nothing ever changes, I don't like what I see
I feel so hurt, and I know it's not just me
I don't want to lose any of you,
And I don't want you to lose me too
I don't want to do this no more
I'm running out of tears, and my heart is sore
I fucking hate drugs and alcohol
But I hate seeing my family lost most of all
I can't fucking do this on my own
I know all we want is a happy home
I love these feelings when we're happy and together,
But nothing ever got better
Please pay attention to my letter
You all know how much I feel
You all know what I say is real
It's about time we faced the truth,
Break the cycle,
And build some deeper roots
I no longer want our kids to see us this way
I know it's hard, but we've got to find a better way
Please, my dear family, listen to what I say
Please, please

—Devon Napope

Twenty-five years is a mere whisper in the histories of the First Peoples of Canada. It marks the time required to see a new generation born and grow into adulthood, and it is a period long enough for societal change to be felt. A quarter of a century ago, the dream for positive societal change framed the release of the Royal Commission on Aboriginal Peoples (RCAP) final report in 1996. The commissioners and those who supported their work concluded that profound changes were required to repair the relationship between Canada and First Nations, Inuit, and Métis peoples. The commissioners began their work by asking, what would be the foundation upon which to build a fair and honourable relationship between Indigenous and non-Indigenous peoples of Canada? In talking and listening to Inuit, Métis, and First Nations peoples, the commission determined twenty years to be a reasonable time period over which much of the collective work that needed to be done by federal and provincial/territorial governments, First Nations, Inuit, and Métis peoples, and Canadians generally could be completed to meet this goal. The commissioners believed that a conceptual shift driven through sincere commitment by governments and hard work and perseverance by the entire country would bring about a renewed relationship between non-Indigenous Canadians and the First Peoples of this land.[2]

A focus on healing and wellness in Indigenous communities and Indigenous-led practices for addressing multigenerational trauma were central to the path forward as described by the Royal Commission. Also highlighted were the resilience, resistance, and determination of Indigenous peoples in the face of unthinkable adversity.[3] Twenty-five years later, we ask the following questions: How did this journey unfold for our people? What can we learn from RCAP and the past quarter century about addressing mental health, healing, and reconciliation? How can the past twenty-five years inform the implementation of the Calls to Action of the 2015 Truth and Reconciliation Commission (TRC) of Canada in areas of mental health and healing? What is our path today, and what will it be for the next generation?

Following an Indigenous path of healing and reconciliation, our discussion is driven by Indigenous passion for change and a better future and not by a Western academic voice. Although the architects of this chapter are located in universities and Indigenous organizations, it is written from the warm and embracing shadows of our Indigenous mentors—individuals such as Marlene Brant Castellano, Gail Valaskakis, William (Bill) Mussell, Ed Connors, Paul Hanki, Lorna Williams, Joseph Couture, Mary Simon, Gaye Hanson, Carol Hopkins, Brenda Restoule, Madeleine Dion Stout, Willie Ermine, Jo-ann Episkenew, Maria Campbell, Cindy Blackstock, Reg Crowshoe, Cynthia Wesley-Esquimaux, and Joan Glode, to name only a few. They have individually and collectively pushed Canada to think critically about the relationships that First Nations, Inuit, and Métis peoples have with Canadian health-care systems, health-care training, and Western medicine. Their work has drawn national and international attention to the intersections between historical oppression and social inequity experienced by Indigenous peoples. Specifically, they have drawn attention to the ways in which governments perpetuate deficit ideas of Indigenous peoples in order to deflect the legal and moral responsibilities that governments have to them. Our mentors have educated the country about the importance of Indigenous languages, healing practices, traditional medicines, and ways of knowing and being as central to healing and wellness. They have also brought to the tables that they have attended a raw honesty that refuses to devalue the diverse lived experiences of First Nations, Inuit, and Métis peoples, no matter how difficult these narratives are to hear and accept as truths. By privileging the lived experiences of our peoples, our mentors have supported younger generations of Indigenous thinkers to proceed in constructive and meaningful ways and to have the moral courage to speak at all times with strong Indigenous voices. It is the collective wisdom of our mentors, many of whom were deeply involved in and committed to RCAP and the healing movement, that shapes the ethos of this chapter.

In the following pages, we provide an overview of some of what has happened in the past twenty-five years as an "Indigenous healing movement" in Canada gained momentum after the release of the RCAP report and the launch of the Aboriginal Healing Foundation (AHF). We conclude that the past twenty-five years have been marked by periods of significant promise and change for First Nations, Inuit, and Métis peoples, but just as importantly the years have been marked by profound Indigenous struggle and loss, particularly for our most vulnerable individuals and families. The past quarter century saw an unprecedented outpouring of individual, family, and community accounts of survival in the face of government-sanctioned cultural genocide that occurred during the residential school era. These stories drove community-based healing across the country, with diverse forms of cultural-based healing emerging and expanding in urban, rural, remote, and reserve Indigenous communities. As healing began, contemporary forms of oppression (e.g., overrepresentation of Indigenous children in the child welfare system, Indigenous people involved in the criminal justice/prison system, and the number of missing and murdered Indigenous women and girls) were identified as extensions of colonization that grew out of the residential school era and systemic oppression of Indigenous peoples generally.

Our chapter weighs the work of RCAP and the TRC, asking the question of what happened during the two decades between the commissions that transformed the lives of our most vulnerable families. We conclude that, despite significant efforts by Indigenous peoples, high rates of multigenerational addiction and mental illness persisted, with rates of incarceration, involvement with child welfare services, unemployment, and school dropout being at unacceptably high levels. The promise of a better future outlined in the RCAP report is not reflected in our present-day realities, specifically for those living in poverty and experiencing multigenerational poverty and family crises. This is not to suggest, however, that Indigenous people have stood still over the past two and a half decades. Rather, there have been many notable gains, some of which have been lost; there were lessons learned, possibilities realized, and promises broken. For Indigenous peoples, the twenty-five-year journey has been full of government promises but largely marked by the ebb and flow of public opinion and the reluctance of governments to participate in real and meaningful change. Despite apologies by governments for the residential school system, both federal and provincial governments have curtailed real and sustainable change.

The optimism felt in 2015 by Indigenous peoples across Canada resulting from the release of the TRC's Calls to Action was overshadowed for many because of their striking resemblance to the RCAP recommendations. Both commissions provide compelling arguments for transformational change requiring government investment and commitment, and both commissions provide substantial evidence that government-sanctioned cultural genocide was responsible for the vast health and social disparities experienced today by First Nations, Métis, and Inuit peoples. When the respective reports were released, the commissions' conclusions were understood by Indigenous peoples across Canada to be foundational work upon which meaningful societal change could be built. In both instances, Indigenous peoples challenged governments and Canadian society generally to acknowledge what was in the reports and, in doing so, to implement the recommendations or calls to action that would result in transformative change.

To frame our analysis (to put it into the perspective of why it is important to look at the two commissions together), we privilege the "lived experiences" of Indigenous individuals who had the most to gain or lose by our country's response to RCAP and now the TRC: children and youth.

We draw from a single narrative of a young First Nations man, Devon Napope, who grew into adulthood over the twenty years between the release of the RCAP report and the TRC calls to action. Devon's writing gives us a glimpse of a reality that is unimaginable for most Canadians and for which our governments, even with direction from RCAP, largely failed to address for families such as the Napopes. Twenty-five years later, Devon's narrative continues to reflect life in Canada for far too many Indigenous children, youth, and families, and it directs us to what is at stake for Indigenous peoples, and Canada generally, if we fail to implement the TRC calls to action. This young man's narrative reminds us of the contradiction within the "work of society," in this case how quickly twenty-five years pass in the world of national commissions and inquiries while the same years are experienced as a lifetime of pain, grief, abuse, and brokenness for a child like Devon. Decision making for families like his is not informed by "recommendations" or "calls to action" but literally driven by the need to survive in the moment; decisions are driven by hunger, addiction, abuse, vulnerability, and unresolved trauma across generations. We invited Devon as a colleague to share his story as a form of resistance to the natural "objectification" of trauma and suffering to which critical analysis commonly falls prey. As Devon describes, there is nothing romantic or honourable in what he and his family have experienced, nor is there in the challenges that they continue to face. The lesson to be learned from his narrative is that Canadian governments and institutions, despite being provided with an achievable pathway by RCAP, failed to mobilize meaningful and sustainable changes that could have made Devon's childhood better. Ensuring that the TRC's work and calls to action do not suffer a similar fate in the next twenty-five years weighs heavily in our hearts and is the central unresolved question of our chapter.

"ALL BEFORE I WAS NINE YEARS OLD": DEVON'S STORY

By the time I was born, my hands were already bound. In a no-win situation, born to a family totally lost in poverty, drug and alcohol addiction, our house might as well have been adrift in a sea, hopes and dreams cast away, lost. My brothers and I had no choice about the broken homes we were born into, unaware of what types of dilemmas we were facing, or how to deal with racism in a merciless world. Us newborn babies were not good enough, our precious lives were not sufficient enough, for them to change their ways and overcome their addictions. I don't imagine my mother smiling down at me with all the despair her and my family have already been through. We were not enough, I was not enough, to overcome their brokenness, the pieces too far scattered.

No sunshine on this day, born to a father who already left, vanished, abandoned before birth. Born to a despondent mother who knew nothing about parenting. "What did I do for you to leave me, Father? What did I do for nobody to want me?" You see, I read my hospital records and felt dejected, disheartened. My mother, my mother's boyfriend, my auntie, and my granny, they all separately took me into the hospital, all before I was five years old. But the last one was my granny, who finally kept me, whose spirit was broken due to the beatings she received in kind from my grandfather. Eating at a restaurant with my brothers and family, playing duck duck goose in preschool, these are two of the few good memories that I can recall, but they were shattered, crushed by drunkenness, found under the influence of drugs, joints, and needles not hidden good enough for a curious child. Burnt popcorn, a hunger in my stomach, due to no food in the fridge. Loud, lewd, obscene, and immoral behaviour. Spanked by an electrical cord by an unknown person who was not my mother. Thrown across the kitchen by my uncle because I was already sick of everything I would catch a glimpse of. Everything that my young, innocent eyes were not supposed to gaze upon. Crying uncontrollably because I see my grandmother, my granny, in bed with a stranger. She was mine, the only woman whom I loved, who loved me back.

I was not about to see her be taken away. But nothing ever got better. From the day I was born, up until this very minute, these addictions are like a plague in our lives. That obliviousness and fear of the unknown, like a disease that no antidote can cure.

Being under the influence in mine and my family's lives is normal. I learned to accept these ways to live my life. What hurts the most is seeing my family lost, most of all. "Please stop drinking!" with tears in my eyes as I pour my granny's drink out on her. Different homes every year, different schools every year, no friends I remember except those I could relate to because I believed that I was not alone. This all before I was nine years old.

THE CONTRIBUTION OF RCAP TO MAJOR DEVELOPMENTS IN MENTAL HEALTH, WELLNESS, AND HEALING

Over its mandate, the Royal Commission on Aboriginal Peoples held 178 days of public hearings, visited ninety-six communities, consulted experts, commissioned research studies, and reviewed past inquiries and reports.[4] The five-volume report provided Canada with a comprehensive analysis of Métis, First Nations, and Inuit peoples' experiences of colonization, the contemporary realities in which they were living, and a set of recommendations that mapped a new and distinct path for the future of Indigenous and settler relations. Recognition of Indigenous self-determination and nation-to-nation relationships frame much of the report's analysis, including the commissioners' recommendation that "governments recognize that the health of a people is a matter of vital concern to its life, welfare, identity and culture and is therefore a core area for the exercise of self-government by Aboriginal nations."[5]

The recommendations in volume 3 under "Health and Healing" focused closely on infrastructure and government commitment to resources for the development of a system of Aboriginal healing centres and lodges across Canada that would foster holistic and culture-based health and wellness services. Along with this came an emphasis on Aboriginal human resources "compatible with the new system, its values and assumptions."[6] All of the recommendations included First Nations, Inuit, and Métis, with special emphasis on Métis, urban, rural, and settlement populations, First Nations treaties, and Aboriginal women's organizations.[7]

In its recommendations, RCAP began with the idea that Aboriginal self-government would be established across social, economic, and political spheres.[8] As such, health care would eventually be delivered under Aboriginal jurisdiction, with a framework developed in the interim "whereby agencies mandated by Aboriginal governments or identified by Aboriginal organizations or communities could deliver health and social services operating under provincial and territorial jurisdictions."[9] The Royal Commission spent considerable time in its recommendations on the establishment of policies, legislation, regulations, and funding to address gaps in the health-care system, break down jurisdictional barriers between and within governments, and pool resources and provide adequate funding to improve health outcomes across all

Indigenous communities. Aboriginal control, recognition of diverse Indigenous cultures and histories, an increase in Aboriginal human resources, and an extension of practices of traditional healing and their application to contemporary Aboriginal health and healing problems were woven throughout the recommendations.

Specifically, intergenerational trauma, addiction, and mental illness/distress were addressed by placing emphasis on holistic models of healing and the promotion of wellness and healthy lifestyle choices. Castellano, Archibald, and DeGagné point out that the hearings, research, and RCAP report specifically brought into public view the devastating effects of the residential school system. The commission wrote that

> no segment of our research aroused more outrage and shame than the story of the residential schools. . . . The incredible damage— loss of life, denigration of culture, destruction of self-respect and self-esteem, rupture of families, impact of these traumas on succeeding generations, and the enormity of the cultural triumphalism that lay behind the enterprise—will deeply disturb anyone who allows the story to seep into their consciousness and recognizes that these policies and deeds were perpetrated by Canadians no better or worse intentioned, no better or worse educated than we are today. . . . It is also evidence of the capacity of democratic populations to tolerate moral enormities in their midst.[10]

The accounts given by survivors of the residential school system to the commissioners not only brought to the forefront the intergenerational impacts of schools but also the devastating results of massive incursions by governments into the lives of Indigenous peoples across multiple generations. The commissioners argued for an extensive public inquiry into the residential school system and the effects of government policies generally on the health and well-being of Indigenous peoples. In fact, government policies, as described in the RCAP report, have arguably been the most harmful determinant of mental health, and health generally, for Indigenous peoples, with rates of addiction and mental illness/trauma directly related to government policies. The commissioners wrote that

> successive governments have tried—sometimes intentionally, sometimes in ignorance—to absorb Aboriginal people into Canadian society, thus eliminating them as distinct peoples. Policies

pursued over the decades have undermined—and almost erased—Aboriginal cultures and identities. This is assimilation. It is a denial of the principles of peace, harmony and justice for which this country stands—and it has failed. Aboriginal peoples remain proudly different. Assimilation policies failed because Aboriginal people have the secret of cultural survival. They have an enduring sense of themselves as peoples with a unique heritage and the right to cultural continuity. This is what drives them when they blockade roads, protest at military bases and occupy sacred grounds. This is why they resist pressure to merge into Euro-Canadian society—a form of cultural suicide urged upon them in the name of "equality" and "modernization." Assimilation policies have done great damage, leaving a legacy of brokenness affecting Aboriginal individuals, families and communities. The damage has been equally serious to the spirit of Canada—the spirit of generosity and mutual accommodation in which Canadians take pride.[11]

In the late 1990s and into the first decade of the new millennium, the RCAP report motivated and created momentum within governments to fund healing and wellness initiatives and to commit to reducing rates of addiction and mental illness/distress across Indigenous communities, be they reserve, settlement, remote, rural, or urban. As Wayne Spear writes in his documentation of the history of the Aboriginal Healing Foundation (AHF), the period following the release of the RCAP report up to 2007 was a unique, albeit brief, period when Indigenous people were involved at a high level in the design of policy instruments.[12] This was not business as usual in Ottawa. At the centre of this activity was the creation of Indigenous-led and -designed national bodies such as the AHF and the National Aboriginal Health Organization (NAHO). Although these organizations were not without their critics and were influenced by governments in setting their mandates, optimism and recognition that the country was taking a new direction spread across Indigenous nations. With the creation of these national organizations came funding for new mental health and healing initiatives, and Indigenous communities and organizations rose to the challenge, championing local community-based healing work.

Established Indigenous organizations such as the National Native Addictions Partnership Foundation (now Thunderbird Partnership

Foundation), Aboriginal Nurses' Association of Canada, National Association of Friendship Centres, Native Physicians Association of Canada, and Native Mental Health Association of Canada (now First Peoples' Wellness Circle) expanded their work with new resources and were driven in the direction described by RCAP. National and regional Indigenous political bodies, such as the Assembly of First Nations, Métis National Council, Inuit Tapiriit Kanatami, Native Women's Association of Canada, and Aboriginal Peoples Congress partnered with Indigenous organizations, creating significant momentum for improved mental health care and healing across Canada.

At the centre of mental health–care reform as advocated by Indigenous peoples was the need to address intergenerational trauma and to create sustainable healing and wellness supports.[13] Addressing addiction and suicide has persisted as a priority, but an increase in the diversity of illicit drugs and their associated risks, and increased gambling options (e.g., online gambling), present challenges in treating addiction and suicide, particularly among youth and young adults. Indigenous health-care leaders also advocate for improvements to health-care systems, including better access to mental health and addiction therapists and other care supports, and the need to address barriers and gaps in services, including reducing government jurisdictional barriers to care.

The Indigenous concept of "cultural safety" and its application to everyday mental health care and addiction highlighted the need for Indigenous languages and traditional healing practices and medicines to be entwined in mental health and healing pathways for Indigenous peoples. It also pointed to the need for greater awareness among non-Indigenous health-care providers of historical Indigenous-settler relations and the intergenerational trauma resulting from colonization.[14] Addressing acts of racism and systemic racial discrimination was a battle that Indigenous peoples fought, and continue to fight, across the human service sector; racism is directly correlated with inadequate patient care and poor health outcomes for our people.[15]

Indigenous artists, writers, actors, and musicians were also influenced by the release of the RCAP report, and over the past twenty-five years they have been instrumental through their creativity and activism in inspiring the country's thinking about healing and reconciliation.[16] Specifically, they have explored ideas and issues related to identity, colonization, healing, land, language, intergenerational trauma, resilience, and racism.

Their work has changed the national landscape, including raising public awareness both within and beyond Indigenous communities, drawing attention to injustices and inequities, and challenging government policies and treatment of Indigenous peoples.[17]

Drawing on their diverse voices and vantage points as activists, leaders, traditional knowledge keepers, health-care providers, innovators, researchers, and educators, First Nations, Inuit, and Métis peoples have woven new narratives for community, family, and individual healing, self-determination, and cultural revitalization. The voices of Indigenous activists have been particularly strong and effective, with Idle No More being a recent example of the mobilization of Indigenous voices that challenge systemic racism and neocolonial practices in government and business sectors. Despite these efforts, twenty-five years later, it is clear that the structural, legislative, policy, political, economic, and social changes described in the RCAP report have largely been unrealized, and any sustainable gains made have often been because of successful, albeit lengthy, legal battles.[18] Disparities contributing to mental distress have not decreased in many Indigenous populations and continue to be driven by compounding and persisting negative social determinants such as poverty, unemployment, overcrowding, and the child welfare system.[19]

The past twenty-five years, however, have seen Indigenous peoples across generations and through their cultures, languages, art, political involvement, education, research, and national and international forums disrupt, resist, reinvent, and re-establish their relationship with the rest of Canada. Significantly more awareness exists across Canada about the intergenerational impacts of government policies on the lives of Indigenous peoples, specifically the impact of the residential school system. The strength, wisdom, and voices of survivors have truly transformed Canada, and we have crossed a threshold as a country where it is impossible for governments at all levels to ignore what happened and to disagree with calls from Indigenous leaders and activists that profound changes are necessary.

Canada has also adopted the United Nations Declaration on the Rights of Indigenous Peoples, and implementation of the TRC calls to action is occurring across the country among different levels of government, health authorities, educational institutions, child welfare systems, and arenas of justice. If reflecting on the work of RCAP teaches us anything as we move forward, it is that as Indigenous peoples we must be vigilant that shifts in political power (federal and provincial/territorial) can make positive movements forward (e.g., Indigenization, reconciliation) vulnerable to being dismantled or co-opted by governments and other institutions. New agreements between Indigenous leadership bodies and federal, provincial, and territorial governments concerning resource allocation for mental health and addiction services, community-based healing, and addressing intergenerational trauma must be based on reflection on the past twenty-five years and the successes of, and challenges faced by, Indigenous self-determined bodies such as the AHF, NAHO, and Thunderbird Partnership Foundation. All four national political parties represented in the House of Commons must agree that, when there is evidence of growing momentum in community healing, reduction of addictions, improvements to mental health and wellness, and mitigation of intergenerational trauma, and evidence of successful outcomes provided by self-determined Indigenous bodies, such gains should not be vulnerable to being dismantled and undermined when changes in federal leadership occur. Both RCAP and the TRC argue for Indigenous leadership and nation-to-nation relationships as necessary for Canada to address its destructive colonial legacy. We now turn our attention to the work of the Aboriginal Healing Foundation and lessons learned from our recent past.

THE ABORIGINAL HEALING FOUNDATION

The AHF began its work in 1998 and was the largest funded healing initiative created to address the RCAP recommendations. The AHF was created through a contribution agreement of $350 million between a nationally representative board of directors composed of Métis, First Nations, and Inuit peoples and the federal government. The foundation was set up as a not-for-profit organization that operated at arm's length from the government and the representative Aboriginal organizations. In describing its mission, the AHF wrote that

> we see our role as facilitators in the healing process by helping Aboriginal people and their communities help themselves, by providing resources for healing initiatives, by promoting awareness of healing issues and needs, and by nurturing a broad, supportive public environment. We help Survivors in telling the truth of their experiences and being heard. We also work to engage

Canadians in this healing process by encouraging them to walk with us on the path of reconciliation. Ours is a holistic approach. Our goal is to help create, reinforce and sustain conditions conducive to healing, reconciliation, and self-determination. We are committed to addressing the legacy of abuse in all its forms and manifestations, direct, indirect and intergenerational, by building on the strengths and resilience of Aboriginal peoples.[20]

At the end of its mandate, the AHF had funded over 1,500 community-based projects over a fifteen-year period.[21] The AHF adopted a two-pronged research program to demonstrate Indigenous community healing and to distribute to Indigenous communities, organizations, and governments across the country strong evidence for community-based healing and comprehensive reviews of important healing, mental health, and addiction topics. Castellano, Archibald and DeGagné describe the AHF as working as a liaison between mainstream resources and Aboriginal peoples with an Aboriginal board of directors steering its mandate.[22]

The AHF responded to RCAP's recommendation for "the development of a system of Aboriginal healing centres and healing lodges under Aboriginal control as the prime units of holistic and culture-based health and wellness services."[23] RCAP envisioned healing centres that followed a holistic vision of health rather than a traditional biomedical model emphasizing treatment of specific illnesses. The healing centre model advocated by the commissioners included traditional healers, Elders, community health representatives, interpreters, nurses, doctors, and other health professionals, and it could be modified to suit the needs of specific communities. RCAP also emphasized that many Indigenous peoples wanted access to healing services grounded in their traditional practices and delivered within their communities.[24] Funding community-driven healing initiatives was a core principle of the AHF.[25] From 1998 to 2014, the AHF was the primary national funder of initiatives aimed at promoting well-being and healing among residential school survivors and their families, including twelve healing centres across the country.[26] Residential adult and youth treatment centres for addiction also provided addiction and healing support during this time through programs such as the National Native Alcohol and Drug Abuse Program, National Youth Solvent Abuse Program, and Métis Addictions Council of Saskatchewan Inc. There is still a high need in all regions of Canada for addiction services for Indigenous peoples but particularly for residential mental health, healing, and addiction in Nunavut. With new highly addictive and lethal illicit drugs in urban, reserve, and rural Indigenous communities and increases in gambling across Indigenous communities, the demand for in- and out-patient addiction and healing services is still high.[27]

Despite its success, the AHF faced organizational challenges, particularly in regard to what some residential school survivors interpreted as its narrow mandate. Some survivors thought that the AHF should have provided funding to revitalize language and culture rather than focus so much of its mandate on projects that addressed the harms caused by physical and sexual abuse experienced by students who attended residential schools.[28] Despite political and institutional barriers that narrowed the scope of what the AHF could fund, numerous types of projects were eligible for AHF funding: healing services, prevention and awareness initiatives, healing capacity training, knowledge building, needs assessments, legacy funding, conferences, and project designs.[29] However, in recognition of the level of need for local community-based healing reported by frontline service providers, almost three-quarters (70.9 percent) of the AHF's funding was allotted to such projects.[30]

Over its fifteen-year mandate, the reach and impact of AHF projects were significant. For example, over 200,000 Indigenous people are estimated to have participated in AHF-funded programs between 2000 and 2004, about two-thirds of whom had never participated in any previous healing activities.[31] Residential school survivors who accessed AHF-funded projects were found to prefer traditional healing supports such as Elders and ceremonies and noted that these services were the most critical to their overall well-being.[32] One of the notable impacts reported in case studies of funded projects was that the silence and shame surrounding residential school abuses were being broken, creating safe community and family environments for healing. The wide spectrum of benefits reported by participants speaks to the innovative approach adopted by many of the AHF-funded community-driven initiatives. Reported individual impacts included improved family relationships, increased self-esteem and pride, achievement of higher education and employment, and prevention of suicide. Reported community impacts included growth in social capital indicators such as volunteerism, informal caring networks, and cultural events.[33]

A later assessment was undertaken on behalf of Indian and Northern Affairs Canada (INAC) by consulting firm DPRA Canada in collaboration with T.K. Gussman Associates. Twenty AHF community-based initiatives were evaluated for the period from April 2007 to May 2009.[34] This evaluation revealed that the AHF-funded healing programs were effective in contributing to both individual and community healing, with program enrolment averaging 40 percent more for AHF projects than non-AHF projects. The AHF healing initiatives were particularly successful in engaging hard-to-reach groups, including men and youth, leading evaluators to conclude that the availability of culturally relevant healing motivated individuals to seek help.[35] Indeed, 62 percent of program participants reported that AHF healing projects were either the most important factor in their healing or contributed "quite a bit," and a further 53 percent stated that their participation in AHF programming led them to connect with other sources of healing and/or therapeutic intervention.[36]

Despite the recognized successes of AHF-funded programs, the need in communities extended beyond the financial resources available. In this regard, by 1999 the AHF had received eligible applications from communities across Canada that would have cost over $1 billion to fund.[37] The number of AHF healing projects reached its peak at 249 in 2003–4,[38] at which time most of the resources were being allocated to healing initiatives. However, only 11 percent of service providers reported feeling confident that they were reaching individuals who had the greatest need for healing.[39] Approximately 36 percent of funded healing initiatives had waiting lists, and program staff stated that many survivors were unable to receive care because of this and other limitations.[40]

Based on the study conducted by INAC with the twenty AHF initiatives, 99 percent of those who participated in the assessment asserted that individuals and communities still required a great deal of healing.[41] The 2009 INAC report concluded that these projects were significantly under-resourced and able to address only a fraction of the issues faced by the populations that they were serving. The health and healing needs of individuals and families intergenerationally affected and of Indigenous youth were highlighted as not being addressed adequately. The assessment also called for continued funding support and further assessment of initiatives into the post–Indian Residential School Settlement Agreement era.[42]

When a government evaluation of AHF programs was completed in 2010, as required by the Settlement Agreement, its central recommendation was sustainable funding.[43] Despite this and other calls for continuation of AHF funding, a wind-down strategy was implemented. The closure of the AHF had devastating impacts on the healing journeys of survivors, their families, and their communities.[44] The work of the AHF, and more recently that of the TRC, clearly indicate a dire need across Canada for healing initiatives for residential school survivors, their families, and their communities. Expanding this argument, also required are targeted healing initiatives for survivors of the Sixties Scoop, individuals involved with child welfare systems or "Indian hospitals," for families of missing and murdered women and girls, and for families experiencing multigenerational trauma.

The nature of the relationship between the AHF and community healing projects was a key factor in the success of those projects. Similar to programs funded by federal and provincial/territorial governments, the AHF required all projects to provide activity, outcome, and financial reporting. However, the expertise within the AHF as an organization and the flexibility within its oversight of projects meant that it was able to work more effectively with the projects that it funded than could traditional government funding models. The AHF was able to work with communities to fine-tune and modify projects as required in order to maximize their impacts for participants and communities. This approach was different from traditional government funding approaches, which tend to be inflexible in dealing with programmatic and budgetary adjustments. Today Indigenous health-care leaders and providers argue not only that communities lack adequate resources (services and human resources) to address individual and community trauma associated with residential schools and other colonial impacts[45] but also that the funding they receive places inflexible parameters around the projects and cumbersome reporting requirements that work against the success of the projects. Social position and geographical location further complicate the challenge of providing adequate services to high-risk individuals, as do the vulnerabilities that healing programs experience as the result of inadequate and short-term funding practices of governments.

Even today many Indigenous people do not know—or only recently have found out—their family histories in relation to residential school attendance. The lack of knowledge of family and community histories related to the residential school system speaks directly to the importance of funding for educational initiatives on the historical and contemporary impacts of residential schools alongside direct therapeutic programs. In this regard, the AHF highlighted the critical need for legacy activities to assist communities to make sense of the history of and trauma associated with the residential school system. To identify the contemporary impacts of the residential school system on Indigenous communities, the "recovery of awareness" is integral.[46] Participants in the INAC study identified positive impacts of AHF projects, but they also expressed concerns about the implications of dealing with centuries of unresolved grief and the consequences of the end of AHF funding.[47]

The majority of AHF programs had no alternative funding sources and were forced to shut down with the closure of the foundation. Although the AHF recommended that healing initiatives receive, at a minimum, ten years of sustained core funding to begin adequately to address the needs of communities and ensure continuity of care,[48] current funding structures for mental health services and healing are most often designed as short-term, crisis-based interventions that limit the ability of Indigenous communities to offer services that address long-term healing goals.[49] In its final report, and after fifteen years of funding community-based programs, the AHF noted that "we are still living with the legacy of the residential school, as we knew we would."[50] The anticipated discontinuation of AHF community healing was described as "catastrophic" and "disastrous," with one participant succinctly stating that "we had 100 years of abuse and 12 years of healing."[51]

The challenges facing survivors, their descendants, and their communities are complex and varied. Indigenous peoples view individual and collective healing as an ongoing process that requires supports and services far beyond the fifteen-year mandate given to the AHF.[52] That mandate ended not because it did not justify the widespread benefits that it had achieved for Indigenous peoples. Rigorous scientific and community-based evaluations clearly demonstrated the effectiveness and potential of the AHF in its short mandate.[53] Rather, despite national lobbying by Indigenous peoples, the Harper Conservative government ignored the evidence supporting a renewal of the AHF mandate. Resources for mental health/healing once again fell under the administration of the First Nations and Inuit Health Branch of Health Canada, and the capacity, experience, and knowledge held within the AHF were set aside.

For many communities, a culture of silence surrounding residential school experiences persisted, and many survivors were still hesitant to share their experiences.[54] For some, the TRC hearings were the first time that they publicly discussed what had occurred within the schools that they had attended. Although the Settlement Agreement represents an important step in the healing process, aspects of it have been spiritually and emotionally difficult for survivors and their families.[55] The TRC has completed its mandate, but survivors and their communities are still working toward addressing the spiritual, emotional, physical, and mental harms stemming from residential schools. Whether the creation of a new national organization similar to the AHF is the right direction for our country is yet to be determined as we tackle the implementation of the TRC calls to action and the National Inquiry into Missing and Murdered Indigenous Women and Girls. What we do know is that First Nations, Inuit, and Métis peoples are best positioned to make decisions about what is best for their communities and families. If governments and political parties across Canada, especially the federal government and parties, are truly committed to reconciliation, then they must shed partisan divides and move quickly and efficiently with Métis, First Nations, and Inuit leaders toward the establishment of distinct Métis, First Nations, and Inuit self-determined path(s) forward, paths appropriately funded and protected against being dismantled.

"MISERY AND PAIN MY CONSTANT COMPANIONS": DEVON'S YOUTH

Today I know what victimization is, but do you know what's the worst? It is being a nine-year-old and not knowing. For the most part, you could conjure up, or envision, what a bogeyman, a bad man, looks like, right? But what about when he has a smile on his face? Friend of the family in the same apartment? Makes you smile, makes you laugh. I had no father figure, no role models in my life. I was not aware yet of ulterior motives. So he found his way into my adolescent mind, slowly working my underdeveloped brain by exposing me to videos I should not be watching. Manipulated me into waiting for him naked in his one-bedroom apartment for a toy gun I wanted so bad, just for him to steal my keys and sneak into my apartment numerous times. Granny happened to be gone to Taber, Auntie and Uncle upstairs in another apartment, they may have well been across the world. Would anybody know I was curled up in a ball, fully clothed, blanket after blanket wrapped around me so tight, black silhouette in my home, where it should not belong? Innocence gone, trust gone, vulnerability gone. You see, I was getting schooled, unknown to me, I was getting conditioned for things I didn't even know ... don't talk, don't feel, don't trust. From the day I was born, little did I know how cruel this world would be. Why put me in this world just to suffer?

By the time I was twelve years old, I perfected and utilized these skills: not talking, not feeling, and definitely not trusting. I never talked about what happened to me, I put that locked in a safe in the back of my mind along with my feelings. But my memories and emotions had so much control over me, always clawing their way to the surface, tormenting me, making me feel when I did not want to, and I just wanted to feel nothing. Lost in my haze. Not trusting was always in the front of my mind, a constant reminder to not be hurt or get hurt, to never get too close to anyone. People coming through my life just to leave like an unanswered prayer lost in the wind. But try as I might that seemed to be my fate, pain, misery, and a lot more tears.

My criminal activity started when my uncle used us as bait in a grocery store. If that ain't love ... then what is? I don't know. It started with candy, food, clothing, materialistic items.

Break and enters, robberies, or like my older brother Keith says "home invasions." My incarceration started one month after I was legally old enough to be locked up ... twelve years old. Me and my brother just wanted shoes, shorts, the things we were deprived of.

Filled with anger and pain, all we had was each other, the love for one another. We tried to fight our way out of there; we picked up three more assault charges. I started a never-ending snowball down the hill. For the next six years, I spent more than four years in these jails, Kilburn Home, North Battleford Youth Centre, Yarrow. But these feelings and memories still linger from my childhood, misery and pain my constant companions.

INDIGENOUS WAYS OF HEALING AND HELPING

Because of the effects of colonization and the history of chronic exposure to individual and collective traumatic events, healing is significant to the mental health and well-being of Indigenous peoples in Canada and abroad.[56] RCAP defined Indigenous healing as "personal and societal recovery from the lasting effects of oppression and systematic racism

experienced over generations."[57] It has similarly been described as a "journey" and an "ongoing process" by residential school survivors and Indigenous peoples generally.[58] Because the cultural genocide experienced by
Indigenous peoples has contributed to health inequities, activities that
strengthen and support various aspects of Indigenous cultures and identities are important components of healing and wellness.[59] Indigenous
healing is often concerned with the reparation of social relations, such
as familial and community bonds that have been affected by the legacy of
colonization, particularly the residential school system.[60]

For twenty-five years, Indigenous peoples across Canada have engaged
wholeheartedly in healing and helping activities. The "healing movement"
did not happen as the result of RCAP; however, the RCAP gatherings and
final report greatly contributed to national awareness and understanding that healing was central to Indigenous peoples and the country generally to move forward. In his assessment of the importance of Indigenous
healing work, Waldram argues that the Indigenous healing movement is
"perhaps the most profound example of social reformation since Confederation." He writes that "the potential impact of the movement—for all
Canadians and especially Aboriginal people—is profound. The efforts to
restabilize Aboriginal societies after centuries of damaging government
policies continue to revitalize individuals and communities that, in turn,
contribute to a healthy and vibrant future."[61]

The Indigenous healing movement is not, however, "pan-Indigenous,"
as some have suggested; rather, it is collective Indigenous awareness that
holds truth telling, acknowledgement, forgiveness, courage, and reconciliation as its foundation. The healing movement is uniquely complex
and cross-cultural and grounded in diverse Indigenous worldviews and
the hard work of dedicated Indigenous leaders, Elders, healers, frontline
workers, and volunteers. Over the years, national institutions such as the
Aboriginal Healing Foundation, Thunderbird Partnership Foundation,
Truth and Reconciliation Commission of Canada, First Peoples Wellness
Circle, Native Human Service Program, First Nations Family and Caring
Society, Aboriginal Nurses' Association, Native Women's Association
of Canada, and Indigenous Physicians Association have reinforced the
movement.[62] However, the movement draws its enduring energy from
grassroots dedication and local relevance. The essence and purpose of the
healing movement are wholly Indigenous, deriving their momentum from
the cultural, linguistic, and historical diversity of Inuit, First Nations, and

Métis peoples and the shared teachings provided by ancestors, the land, sentient beings, and the elements. The movement is self-determined, bold, loving, and embracing.

The distance between local healing and a national movement of healing is minimized by a shared understanding by First Nations, Métis, and Inuit peoples that collective healing for all Indigenous peoples must occur. The deep wounds of colonization require healing and reconciliation for First Nations and Métis and Inuit to be equally prioritized by governments and supported across the country. This is the direction given by RCAP and is fundamental to reaching the goals set out by both RCAP and the TRC. Both commissions also argue that non-Indigenous Canadians too must deal with Canada's colonial past if we are to move forward as a country. For over a century, the central goal of government policies on First Nations, Inuit, and Métis peoples was cultural genocide, with remnants of that era still entrenched in government systems across the human service sector. The coercive measures adopted by governments did not, however, destroy Indigenous cultures, and Inuit, Métis, and First Nations peoples have not surrendered their Indigenous identities and rights. They have been left, however, with a legacy of pain, damage, and trauma that requires national and local recognition and support by Indigenous and non-Indigenous Canadians alike for recovery to occur.[63] The TRC concludes that,

> for many Survivors and their families, this commitment is foremost about healing themselves, their communities, and [their] nations, in ways that revitalize individuals as well as Indigenous cultures, languages, spirituality, laws, and governance systems. For governments, building a respectful relationship involves dismantling a centuries-old political and bureaucratic culture in which, all too often, policies and programs are still based on failed notions of assimilation. For churches, demonstrating long-term commitment requires atoning for actions within the residential schools, respecting Indigenous spirituality, and supporting Indigenous peoples' struggles for justice and equity. Schools must teach history in ways that foster mutual respect, empathy, and engagement. All Canadian children and youth deserve to know Canada's honest history, including what happened in the residential schools, and to appreciate the rich history and knowledge of Indigenous nations who continue to make such a strong contribution to Canada, including our very name

and collective identity as a country. For Canadians from all walks of life, reconciliation offers a new way of living together.[64]

The present-day challenge, William Mussell argues, is that Indigenous peoples are diverse, and their lifestyles fit somewhere on a continuum between "somewhat traditional" and "mostly Western."[65] Mussell observes that, because acculturation over the past four and five generations emphasized materialism and individual rights, the sense of mutual aid and togetherness traditionally characteristic of Indigenous cultures and societies is greatly undermined.[66] It is largely recognized that most Indigenous families and communities cannot or might not want to return to life on the land and traditional subsistence activities to heal and recover. However, the corrosive effects of widespread poverty and economic marginalization mean that many Indigenous people and their communities are unable to participate fully in settler society either. As Kirmayer, Tait, and Simpson write, "the presence of mass media even in remote communities makes the values for consumer capitalism salient and creates feelings of relative deprivation and lack where none existed before. Even those who seek solidarity in traditional forms of community and ways of life find themselves enclosed and defined by a global economy that treats 'culture' and 'tradition' as commodities or useful adjectives in advertising campaigns."[67]

Diversity in religious beliefs and the complex relationship that Indigenous peoples have with Christianity and the Church, stemming from their experiences with the residential school system and other colonial involvement of the Church, further complicate Indigenous identities and ways of being "Indigenous" in contemporary Canadian society. Tensions between those who practise Indigenous spirituality and traditions and those who are faithful to Christianity can divide communities and create social barriers to collective healing. Government policies that impose various status identifiers on Indigenous identity—such as "Registered Indian," "Status Indian," "Non-Status Indian," and "Aboriginal"—also create confusion about identity and jurisdiction and further complications for those individuals and families seeking help.

The complexities that contribute to Indigenous identities and how individuals and groups choose to conceptualize and participate in forms of healing and recovery are exacerbated by health-care systems that generate prevention, treatment, and recovery models for mental illness and distress outside Indigenous communities, cultures, and languages. Across Canada, Indigenous peoples participate in biomedical and Indigenous forms of healing, and it is not uncommon for them to draw on healing approaches from a spectrum of culturally based healing practices. Hart argues that, for the helping professions (social work, psychology, nursing, counselling, and medicine) to support Indigenous peoples to address the intergenerational impacts of colonization, these professions must have a more nuanced understanding of how Indigenous peoples, like other Canadians, express themselves in diverse and complex ways, depending on where in the society they are located socially, culturally, and linguistically. He argues that, regardless of the apparent diversity across Indigenous groups, a deep-rooted Indigenous understanding of ways of being is present even when not apparent to outsiders.[68]

Considering the wide variations in rates of mental illness and addiction across Indigenous communities directs us to the importance of considering diverse local contexts and different ways that groups respond to the persistent and oppressive stresses of colonization, sedentarization, bureaucratic surveillance, and technocratic control.[69] Elevated rates of emotional distress and problems such as depression, anxiety, substance abuse, and suicide are intertwined with individual identity and notions of place and belonging, which in turn are strongly influenced by collective processes at the level of band, community, or larger political entity.[70]

Wesley-Esquimaux and Smolewski argue that a central theme of the healing movement has been the recognition by Indigenous peoples that they need to overcome learned social helplessness, commonly manifested as substance abuse, self-harm, violence, and disengagement:

> Today's Aboriginal people of North America, like many other dispossessed and colonized groups, constantly have to re-negotiate their cultural and political identities, and their historic memories, vis-à-vis a legal and economic context created for them by a non-Aboriginal government. . . . In this climate of revival and change, it is vitally important to understand the mechanisms by which practice (Aboriginal people's lives, today and in the past) and identities (how Aboriginal people interpret themselves and their positions in the world outside their communities) are linked with past events and past experiences. This understanding is far more important to the healing process necessary for Aboriginal people to regain lost social

and cultural selves than just finding a handy (albeit empty and dry) definition for the underlying fabric of these identities and practices used when dealing with their non-Aboriginal counterparts.[71]

A common understanding held by Indigenous peoples is that "healing" is a journey taken every day for life.[72] The "journey" or "path" undertaken is meant to be transformative, from a place of pain (and commonly resistance and resilience) to a better life. However, it is understood that the journey is difficult and without end, and every person must be vigilant in the care for self and others. Equally, healing is conceptualized as a shared journey, one in which individual healing blends with collective healing of family, community, and nation. This is commonly the misunderstanding among governments and Western-trained health-care providers about the experience of mental illness and addiction in Indigenous communities. Although one does not need to be mentally ill or addicted to choose a path of healing, for those who live with mental illness or addiction a shared journey—characterized by collective understanding and communal caring—is most often the most meaningful and efficacious. The tendency of Western medical systems and governments to marginalize the importance of collective healing speaks to a lack of understanding of intergenerational trauma, how it is experienced, and how individuals and families reconcile it to live meaningful lives.

In studies that examine healing across Inuit, Métis, and First Nations communities, there is pressure to recognize "best practices" as a way to identify approaches or interventions that work and can be transferred to other Indigenous groups. The Western concept of best practices is driven by several factors both within and outside Indigenous communities and organizations. For example, in discussing this concept, Kenn Richards states that "the problem with 'best practice' as I've been experiencing it . . . is that it comes out of research that is decidedly non Aboriginal. We have to convince academics and particularly funders that there are alternative forms of practice. . . . But best practices clearly need to be developed within the context in which you are going to apply them at the end of the day, and I think we have a long way to go with respect to that."[73] What Richards points out is an ongoing tension between Indigenous and Western approaches to healing. In Indigenous approaches, healing is both an individual and a collective journey, and therefore responses to individual and social suffering must be grounded in the everyday contexts in which people live. In contrast, the Western understanding of healing is that the treatment of an individual's mental distress and illness is approached through individualized care plans involving combinations of pharmacological intervention, institutionalization, and generic treatment outside the family proven to relieve symptoms and promote "recovery."

Over the past twenty-five years, this tension has not subsided. However, through Indigenous-led initiatives and evaluative processes, a much better understanding of what constitutes successful approaches to healing for Indigenous peoples exists (e.g., the work of the AHF, Thunderbird Partnership Foundation, or the First Nations Regional Health Survey). Indigenous peoples, as stated above, are adept at drawing from diverse approaches to healing, commonly thinking nothing of blending traditional, Western, and other forms of healing to create meaningful supports and interventions. This is particularly true in areas of mental health and addiction, in which the blurring of knowledge and practice boundaries over the past twenty-five years has occurred in favour of prioritizing the needs of individuals, families, and communities. Traditional healing, medicine, and spirituality commonly coexist in Indigenous communities with drug-based therapies, harm-reduction interventions, and psychiatric and mental health services. In some instances, "alternative" or "complementary" medicines and treatments are adopted or modified to fit with local healing methods, thereby expanding the options for people on their healing journeys.

PROMISING PRACTICES

Twenty-five years after the release of the RCAP report, elevated rates of mental and social distress across Indigenous communities persist and require local community–based treatment and healing. Despite diverse healing practices both within and between First Nations, Métis, and Inuit cultures and communities, some key healing approaches are shared among nations.[74] For example, First Nations, Métis, and Inuit perspectives on health and healing are generally grounded in ideas of holism, a concept that integrates a person's spiritual, physical, mental, and emotional states with physical and spiritual environments.[75] Ceremonies occupy a critical role in many Indigenous healing systems, with First Nations, Métis, and Inuit people drawing on their own healing beliefs and practices and those not specific to their cultures. According to Hart, healing ceremonies are important in addressing mental and social distress because they connect people to spirituality and promote healing as a lifelong journey.[76] Elders play an invaluable role in healing because they are the keepers of special knowledge and teachings, and they are able to provide guidance and counselling to community members.[77]

In an effort to bridge the local context of healing (and to identify which resources are required to facilitate it) with government intervention and funding approaches to mental health and addiction, the National Aboriginal Health Organization described a staged approach to determining "best" practices for healing. NAHO argued that healing interventions move through three phases: first, innovation and achievement; second, good ideas and better or improved practices; and third, best practices. The criteria for achieving a best practice include impact, sustainability, responsiveness, client focus (including gender and social inclusion), access, coordination and integration, efficiency and flexibility, leadership, innovation, potential for replication, health and policy issue identification or resolution, and capacity for evaluation.[78]

The AHF adopted the term "promising healing practices" in its research on and evaluation of community-based healing projects and identified the following key characteristics that make a healing practice successful: "values and guiding principles that reflect [an] Aboriginal world view; a healing environment that is personally and culturally safe; a capacity to heal represented by skilled healers and healing teams; an historical component, including education about residential schools and their impacts; cultural interventions and activities; and a diverse range and combination of traditional and contemporary therapeutic interventions."[79]

In discussing suicide, Bodnar argues that, "for an explanatory model to be effective as a basis for finding solutions, it must encompass an understanding of the multiple challenges for Aboriginal people and the risk and protective factors at both the individual and [the] community levels."[80] These three examples present ideas about how best to understand and support healing for Métis, Inuit, and First Nations people. Taking direction from the study and evaluation of multiple local healing approaches, all three are in agreement that the complexity of local histories across multiple generations is at the heart of understanding present-day healing and wellness needs. Rather than focus on individual healing only, they emphasize the need for holistic approaches that encompass individual and collective wellness work. To undertake this challenge requires culturally safe timelines, funding, human resources, and infrastructure that support robust and sustainable local healing and wellness strategies.

CHANGES TO RESEARCH ON MENTAL HEALTH AND HEALING

Indigenous peoples are generally conflicted about mental health and healing research, particularly the idea of outside academic or government researchers entering their private and communal spaces to collect data on local and traditional healing practices and the mental health status of individuals and communities. The idea that Western-trained academics have the required insight and experience to correctly interpret and analyze the data that they collect, and to recommend directions for positive changes that are meaningful and relevant to Indigenous peoples, elicits at best skepticism and more commonly outright hostility because of the association of Western research approaches with other forms of colonial oppression.

The creation of the Institute for Aboriginal Peoples' Health (IAPH) in 2001 as one of the thirteen Canadian Institutes of Health Research was therefore a notable gain for Indigenous peoples in mental health, addiction, and community healing research (this institute is now known as the Institute for Indigenous Peoples' Health – IIPH). Under the leadership of Dr. Jeff Reading, the IAPH created a network of provincial and regional university-based Indigenous health research centres under the Aboriginal Capacity and Developmental Research Environments and Network Environments for Aboriginal Health Research programs that supported Indigenous self-determination in research and drove the expansion of community-based research projects and training of Indigenous researchers across the country (according to IAPH reports). At the time, the IAPH was the first and only national institute in the world focused on improving the health of Indigenous peoples. Almost all of the centres identified Indigenous healing, mental health, and addiction as priority research areas, with one centre, the National Aboriginal Mental Health Research Centre, focused entirely on Indigenous mental health and addiction.

The First Nations Information Governance Centre also emerged as a result of fierce efforts by First Nations to gain national control over health data governance. Out of this effort emerged two important gains: the First Nations Regional Health Survey (FNRHS or RHS for short) and the First Nations Principles of OCAP® (Ownership, Control, Access, and

Possession).[81] The RHS and OCAP® are the cornerstones of First Nations self-determination in national data collection, analysis, and governance, and the RHS is the only First Nations–governed national health survey in Canada. Its cultural framework is a four directions framework and "embodies a 'total person' and 'total environment' model that includes the individual's spiritual, emotional, mental, and physical well-being; their culture's values, beliefs, identity, and practices; their community and their relationship to the physical environment; and . . . their connectedness to family."[82] The RHS is implemented explicitly in keeping with OCAP® principles and collects information about on-reserve and northern First Nations communities based on both Western and traditional understandings of health and well-being.[83] The RHS is currently in the third phase and brings to our national understanding a holistic analysis of individual and community wellness that guides mental health, addiction, and community wellness priorities for First Nations communities.

Similarly, Inuit and Métis have created their own ethical guidelines for research. This process was partially facilitated by NAHO; however, Inuit and Métis have not secured the same level of national funding, organization, and infrastructure as First Nations and appear to have their greatest strength in research ethics applied at regional and local levels. The Nipingit was a joint program of the Inuit Tuttarvingat of NAHO and Inuit Tapiriit Kanatami and set the foundation for Inuit-specific research guidelines. The Métis Centre at NAHO similarly developed promising practices for research ethics with Métis peoples, and in recent years some provincial Métis bodies, particularly in Manitoba, Ontario, and Saskatchewan, have developed and implemented their own guidelines.[84]

Heightened awareness of the importance of Indigenous self-determined research that puts Indigenous peoples at the centre transformed how mental health research was undertaken with them. Rather than focus on mental and social illnesses, deficits, diagnoses, and symptoms only, Indigenous communities called for research on the resilience and healing journeys of Indigenous peoples.[85] Reductionist studies documenting rates of maladaptive behaviour and symptoms of mental illness were rejected in favour of research studies grounded in a holistic understanding of the person and her or his connection to family, community, land, spirit, and history. Indigenous communities and academics also challenged Western research processes by advocating for Indigenous community members to be full partners on national research grants, employing and writing about

Indigenous research methodologies, and moving to innovative and more effective knowledge translation tools such as videos, published articles, presentations at conferences with community members and organizations, policy documents jointly written with Indigenous research partners, and social media to disseminate results. Momentum in transforming research was at its height in the first decade of this century, but the loss of NAHO and changes to the governance of the Canadian Institutes of Health Research (CIHR) diminished the abilities of Indigenous communities and leaders to argue for self-determination in health research. However, with recent reinvestment in research by the federal government and the Institute of Indigenous Peoples' Health pushing hard for research funds to be held by Indigenous organizations and communities, the pendulum appears to be shifting back toward increased Indigenous self-determination in health research.

Privileging large-scale national research initiatives, such as the CIHR's Strategy for Patient-Oriented Research and Network Environments for Indigenous Health Research, creates additional challenges for Indigenous community stakeholders and academics who find themselves on teams on which there is little or no understanding of accepted ethical practices for research with Indigenous peoples. These large-scale research initiatives are often led by researchers and universities ill equipped, and at times unwilling, to understand the complexities of Indigenous peoples' relationship with research. This has led to increased efforts by Indigenous organizations and communities, with the support of Indigenous academics, toward self-determination in research, specifically the ability of Indigenous organizations and communities to hold research grants. The rationale behind this push is both moral (to counter the negative and destructive history of research in Indigenous communities) and practical (to provide higher investment for and participation by Indigenous stakeholders) in order to produce research that directly contributes to the reduction of health disparities and improved services and care for Indigenous peoples. How this will play out over the next decade in healing, wellness, and mental health research is unclear, but the potential to mobilize innovative community-based ideas to foster culturally safe healing and wellness initiatives is obvious.

"IF ONLY I LIVED 150 YEARS AGO": DEVON'S STORY

Ever since I was young, I felt strange, out of place, like I don't belong, a gut instinct that carried me throughout my life. Something just didn't feel right. A knot in my stomach that consumed me with a flood of emotions, anxiety and worry for the most part. But emotions I absorbed and utilized to get where I am today. I've never known or acknowledged where anything manifested from, why this, why that, were barely, if ever, asked. A product of my environment I turned out to be, you might say. For what was wrong in my life, I was unaware. "Hope," "healing," "opportunity," "growth," non-existent. Never to be uttered or pieced together in my mind, and for which no seeds were ever planted.

As I recollect, and as a young boy, looking through my brown eyes, envisioning my future.... But let's not forget that I was surrounded by a mist of dysfunction, hazy eyes, slurred speech, abuse, abandonment, and hopelessness in our broken homes and family. That was so common, I needed to accept it, drilled to accept it, minus the love or goodnights for me or my brothers, sisters, friends. So back to those innocent brown eyes looking towards his future. He sees powerlessness, doom, trapped in a fog of irreversible decline that will ultimately lead him to fail. Fixed future, like handwriting on the wall that nobody can decipher, except those chosen. So it seemed I was destined to become a drug addict, an alcoholic. To be consumed by an evil presence, while I break as many rules as I can along the way as I fulfill my role as a gang member. Forget love, I never had time for that, a projection of my family. Yes, a product of my environment, I took hold of the choices I was given, moulded by the world I knew. Proud and arrogant I was, naive and proud of nothing.

If I could only ... if I could only look up and see my ancestors shake their heads and help me acknowledge our way is not the right way, I might have stopped. If only I lived 150 years ago, I would have a clear picture of what I lost and what I was fighting for. Today I am so fractured, shattered, and crippled inside. A way of life long lost to me, that has fallen through the cracks, like a kiss goodbye. But fate also allowed me to change with the weather and to flow with the wind. To adapt, to always rise a better man with the sun. To continue my search and never forget what was lost. For what was not lost, I am grateful. And for what is unseen is eternal. Faith.

CONCLUSION

In the past twenty-five years, Indigenous peoples across Canada have reinforced cultural understandings of wellness and healing as cornerstones for the future. Wellness and healing are related not only to individual and collective physical, emotional, psychological, and spiritual existence but also to the environment in which people live. The revitalization of Indigenous languages, cultural practices, and traditional worldviews has positively reinforced a strong sense of individual and collective healing and wellness that has given rise to transformation across the country. In this chapter, we have discussed how some of this process has unfolded, the gains made, the challenges faced, and the fact that so much more needs to be done. Our discussion touches only the surface of the complex healing journeys that First Nations, Métis, and Inuit peoples have been on over the past twenty-five years. Our intention was not to capture all that has happened but to point to where RCAP has had the most influence and to give some insight into what has unfolded. Although much has been accomplished and much has changed, we conclude that, in the end, RCAP was a missed opportunity for our country despite having the great potential to change our collective future for the better. We further conclude that Indigenous peoples were ready, at the time of the release of the RCAP report, to accept the challenges put forward; however, despite their tireless effort, dedication, and commitment, governments did little to engage the rest of the country to embrace the urgent changes required.

We also presented the narrative of Devon Napope, which holds little reference to the Indigenous healing movement and what was going on in Canada. Despite the multigenerational trauma experienced by his grandparents and parents in residential schools, only recently has Devon found out about their experiences and started to put together the narrative of why his childhood was the way it was. He and his siblings deserved better, not only from the adults around them, but also from the society in which they were born. His story illustrates something often diminished when people talk about multigenerational trauma, simply that children are not born understanding oppression, racism, or marginalization as explanations for why life hurts so much. Children are also not born knowing that the world around them could and should be different and that there is nothing normal or natural about abuse, abandonment, exploitation, or addiction. The story of Devon's childhood, lived during the time between the two commissions, speaks to the urgency and importance of the implementation of the TRC calls to action.

As we examine and consider a new set of actions (those of the TRC), we conclude by asking whether Canada is truly ready to embrace the ninety-four calls to action put forward by the TRC? The suicides of six young First Nations girls in northern Saskatchewan over the weeks that our chapter was drafted are a sobering and powerful message from our Indigenous youth that Canada is failing them and must take seriously the challenges before it. At all levels of government, leaders are needed who are not afraid to commit wholeheartedly, not afraid to support Indigenous peoples to be strong, and not afraid to walk into the future with Indigenous nations.

NOTES

1   Dion Stout, "A Survivor Reflects on Resilience," 47.
2   RCAP, Volume 1.
3   RCAP, Volume 2.
4   RCAP, Volume 1.
5   RCAP, Volume 2, Ch. 3, s. 2.
6   RCAP, Volume 2, ss. 5–6.
7   RCAP, Volume 2, ss. 9, 13, 15, respectively.
8   RCAP, Volume 1.
9   RCAP, Volume 2, Ch. 3, s. 3.
10   RCAP, Volume 1, 601–02, as quoted in Castellano, "A Holistic Approach to Reconciliation," 2.
11   RCAP, Highlights from the Report, 3.
12   Spear, Full Circle, 4.
13   Aguiar and Halseth, "Aboriginal Peoples and Historic Trauma."
14   Aguiar and Halseth, "Aboriginal Peoples and Historic Trauma."
15   Allan and Smylie, First Peoples, Second Class Treatment.
16   Cooley, "Hearing and Healing."
17   Episkenew, Taking Back Our Spirits.
18   Ralston Saul, The Comeback.
19   Anderson, The Social Determinants of Higher Mental Distress among Inuit; Canada, Parliament, House of Commons, Breaking Point.
20   See http://www.ahf.ca.
21   Spear, Full Circle.
22   Castellano, "A Holistic Approach to Reconciliation," 69.
23   RCAP, Volume 2, 214.
24   RCAP, Volume 2, 218.
25   DeGagné, "The Story of the Aboriginal Healing Foundation."
26   AHF, Aboriginal Healing Foundation 2014 Annual Report.
27   Fortin et al., "Temporal Trends of Alcohol and Drug Use."
28   Spear, Full Circle.
29   AHF, Measuring Progress.
30   AHF, Aboriginal Healing Foundation 2014 Annual Report, 17.

31 Castellano, "A Holistic Approach to Reconciliation," 201.

32 AHF, *Measuring Progress; Aboriginal Healing Foundation 2014 Annual Report.*

33 AHF, *Aboriginal Healing Foundation 2014 Annual Report.*

34 Indian and Northern Affairs Canada (INAC). *Final Report DPRA Canada.*

35 INAC, *Final Report DPRA Canada,* 23.

36 INAC, *Final Report DPRA Canada,* 26.

37 AHF, *Aboriginal Healing Foundation 2014 Annual Report.*

38 AHF, *Aboriginal Healing Foundation 2014 Annual Report.*

39 AHF, *Measuring Progress.*

40 AHF, *Measuring Progress.*

41 INAC, *Final Report DPRA Canada,* 44.

42 INAC, *Final Report DPRA Canada,* 44.

43 INAC, *Final Report DPRA Canada,* 44.

44 AHF, *Aboriginal Healing Foundation 2014 Annual Report.*

45 Bombay, Matheson, and Anisman, "The Intergenerational Effects of Indian Residential Schools," and "Origins of Lateral Violence in Aboriginal Communities"; McMillan and Glode-Desrochers, "Final Report: Urban Aboriginal Well-being, Wellness and Justice."

46 Wesley-Esquimaux and Smolewski, *Historic Trauma and Aboriginal Healing,* 78.

47 INAC, *Final Report DPRA Canada,* 44.

48 Castellano, "A Holistic Approach to Reconciliation."

49 Lane et al., "Mapping the Healing Journey."

50 AHF, *Aboriginal Healing Foundation 2014 Annual Report,* 4.

51 INAC, *Final Report DPRA Canada,* 49.

52 Bombay et al., "The Intergenerational Effects of Indian Residential Schools," and "Origins of Lateral Violence in Aboriginal Communities"; DeGagné, "Toward an Aboriginal Paradigm of Healing"; Reimer et al., *The Indian Residential Schools Settlement;* Waldram, "Healing History?"

53 AHF, *Aboriginal Healing Foundation 2014 Annual Report;* Graham and Mitchell, *A Legacy of Excellence.*

54 McMillan and Glode-Desrochers, "Final Report: Urban Aboriginal Well-being, Wellness and Justice."

55 Reimer et al., *The Indian Residential Schools Settlement.*

56 Robbins and Dewar, "Traditional Indigenous Approaches to Healing"; Wadden, Where the Pavements Ends; Waldram, "Introduction."

57 RCAP, Volume 1, 109.

58 Quinn, "Reflections on Intergenerational Trauma"; Reimer et al., *The Indian Residential Schools Settlement* ; Waldram, "Introduction"; Saner and Wilson, "Stewardship, Good Governance and Ethics."

59 Bombay, Matheson, and Anisman, "Decomposing Identity"; Lavallée and Poole, "Beyond Recovery; McCabe, "The Aboriginal Healing"; Morrissette, "First Nations and Aboriginal Counsellor Education."

60 Waldram, "Healing History?"

61 Waldram, "Introduction," 7.

62 Mussell, "Mental Health from an Indigenous Perspective," 193.

63 TRC, *What We Have Learned,* 8.

64 TRC, *What We Have Learned,* 126.

65 Mussell, "Mental Health from an Indigenous Perspective," 192.

66 Mussell, "Mental Health from an Indigenous Perspective," 192.

67 Kirmayer, Tait, and Simpson, "The Mental Health of Aboriginal Peoples in Canada," 14.

68 Hart, "Indigenous Ways of Helping," 81–82.

69 Kirmayer et al., "The Mental Health of Aboriginal Peoples in Canada," 20.

70 Kirmayer et al., "The Mental Health of Aboriginal Peoples in Canada," 20.

71 Wesley-Esquimaux and Smolewski, *Historic Trauma and Aboriginal Healing,* 83.

72   Fletcher and Denham, "Moving towards Healing," 101.

73   Quoted in AHF, *Measuring Progress*, 6.

74   AFN, *Aboriginal Healing Foundation 2014 Annual Report*.

75   Hunter et al., "Aboriginal Healing"; McCormick, "Culturally appropriate means and ends"; RCAP, Volume 1.

76   Hart, "Indigenous Ways of Helping," 81-82.

77   Flicker et al., "Research Done in 'A Good Way.'"

78   Cited in AHF, *Measuring Progress*, 5-6.

79   AHF, *Measuring Progress*, 15.

80   Bodnar, "Perspectives on Aboriginal Suicide: Movement Towards Healing," 287.

81   See First Nations Information Governance Centre (FNIGC), *First Nations Regional Health Survey*.

82   Regional Health Survey National Team, *First Nations Regional Longitudinal Health Survey*, 139.

83   See http://fnigc.ca/our-work/regional-health-survey/about-rhs.html.

84   University of Manitoba, *Framework for Research Engagement with First Nations, Métis and Inuit Peoples*.

85   Kirmayer et al., "Rethinking Resilience from Indigenous Perspectives."

REFERENCES

Aboriginal Healing Foundation. *Measuring Progress: Program Evaluation*. Vol. 2 of Final Report of the Aboriginal Healing Foundation. Ottawa: Aboriginal Healing Foundation, 2006.

Aboriginal Healing Foundation 2014 Annual Report. Ottawa: Aboriginal Healing Foundation, 2014.

Aguiar, William, and Regina Halseth. "Aboriginal Peoples and Historic Trauma: The Processes of Intergenerational Transmission." Prince George, BC: National Collaborating Centre for Aboriginal Health, 2015.

Allan, Billie, and Janet Smylie. *First Peoples, Second Class Treatment: The Role of Racism in the Health and Well-Being of Indigenous Peoples in Canada*. Toronto: Wellesley Institute, 2015.

Anderson, Thomas. *The Social Determinants of Higher Mental Distress among Inuit*. 17 November 2015. Catalogue No. 89 653 X2015007. http://www.statcan.gc.ca/pub/89-653-x/89-653-x2015007-eng.pdf.

Bodnar, Ann. "Perspectives on Aboriginal Suicide: Movement Towards Healing." In *Journey to Healing: Aboriginal People with Addictions and Mental Health Issues*, edited by Peter Menzies and Lynn F. Lavallée, 285-99. Toronto: Centre for Addictions and Mental Health, 2014.

Bombay, Amy, Kimberley Matheson, and Hymie Anisman. "Decomposing Identity: Differential Relationships between Several Aspects of Ethnic Identity and the Negative Effects of Perceived Discrimination among First Nations Adults in Canada." *Cultural Diversity and Ethnic Minority Psychology* 26, no. 4 (2010): 507-16.

——. "The Intergenerational Effects of Indian Residential Schools: Implications for the Concept of Historical Trauma." *Transcultural Psychiatry* 51, no. 3 (2014a): 320-38.

——. "Origins of Lateral Violence in Aboriginal Communities: A Preliminary Study of Student-to-Student Abuse in Indian Residential Schools." Ottawa: Aboriginal Healing Foundation, 2014b.

Canada. Parliament. House of Commons. *Breaking Point: The Suicide Crisis in Indigenous Communities*. Report of the Standing Committee on Indigenous and Northern Affairs,

42nd Parliament, 1st Session, June 2017. http://www.ourcommons.ca/Content/ Committee/421/INAN/Reports/RP8977643/inanrp09/inanrp09-e.pdf.

Castellano, Marlene Brant. "A Holistic Approach to Reconciliation: Insight from Research of the Aboriginal Healing Foundation." In *From Truth to Reconciliation: Transforming the Legacy of Residential Schools*, ed. Marlene Brant Castellano, Linda Archibald, and Mike DeGagné, 383–400. Ottawa: Aboriginal Healing Foundation, 2008.

Cooley, Stephan. "Hearing and Healing: Indigenous Artists Talk Music and Reconciliation at the 2017 Global Forum Breakfast." 7 June 2017. https://www.iposgoode.ca/2017/06/ hearing-and-healing-indigenous-artists-talk-music-and-reconciliation-at-the-2017-global-forum-breakfast/.

Degagné, Michael. "Toward an Aboriginal Paradigm of Healing: Addressing the Legacy of Residential Schools." *Australasian Psychiatry* 15, Suppl. 1 (2007): S49–S53. https://doi.org/10.1080/10398560701701114.

———. "The Story of the Aboriginal Healing Foundation." In *Journey to Healing: Aboriginal People with Addictions and Mental Health Issues*, edited by Peter Menzies and Lynn F. Lavallée, 425–39. Toronto: Centre for Addictions and Mental Health, 2014.

Dion Stout, Madeleine. "A Survivor Reflects on Resilience." In *From Truth to Reconciliation: Transforming the Legacy of Residential Schools*, edited by Marlene Brant Castellano, Linda Archibald, and Mike DeGagné, 179–80. Ottawa: Aboriginal Healing Foundation, 2008.

Episkenew, Jo-Ann. *Taking Back Our Spirits: Indigenous Literature, Public Policy, and Healing*. Winnipeg: University of Manitoba Press, 2009.

First Nations Information Governance Centre (FNIGC). *First Nations Regional Health Survey (RHS) 2008/10: National Report on Adults, Youth and Children Living in First Nations Communities*. Ottawa: FNIGC, 2012.

Fletcher, Christopher, and Aaron Denham. "Moving towards Healing: A Nunavut Case Study." In *Aboriginal Healing in Canada: Studies in Therapeutic Meaning and Practice*, edited by James Waldram, 93–129. Ottawa: Aboriginal Healing Foundation, 2008.

Flicker, Sarah, Patricia O'Campo, Renée Monchalin, Jesse Thistle, Catherine Worthington, Renée Masching, Adrian Guta, Sherri Pooyak, Wanda Whitebird, and Cliff Thomas. "Research Done in 'A Good Way': The Importance of Indigenous Elder Involvement in HIV Community-Based Research." *American Journal of Public Health* 105 (2015): 1149–54. https://doi.org/10.2105/AJPH.2014.302522.

Fortin, Marilyn, Richard E. Bélanger, Olivier Boucher, and Gina Muckle. "Temporal Trends of Alcohol and Drug Use among Inuit of Northern Quebec, Canada." *International Journal of Circumpolar Health* 74, no. 1 (2015): 29146. https://doi.org/10.3402/ijch.v74.29146.

Graham, John, and Laura Mitchell. *A Legacy of Excellence: Best Practices Board Study*. Ottawa: Aboriginal Healing Foundation, 2009.

Hart, Michael Anthony. "Indigenous Ways of Helping." In *Journey to Healing: Aboriginal People with Addictions and Mental Health Issues*, edited by Peter Menzies and Lynn F. Lavallée, 73–85. Toronto: Centre for Addictions and Mental Health, 2014.

Hunter, Linda. M., Jo Logan, Jean-Guy Goulet, and Sylvia Barton. "Aboriginal Healing: Regaining Balance and Culture," *Journal of Transcultural Nursing* 17, no. 1 (2006): 13–22.

Indian and Northern Affairs Canada (INAC). *Final Report DPRA Canada and T.K. Gussman Associates: Evaluation of Community Based Healing Initiatives Supported through the Aboriginal Healing Foundation*. Ottawa: INAC, 2009. http://www.ahf.ca/downloads/ inac-evaluation.pdf.

Kirmayer, Laurence J., Stéphane Dandeneau, Elizabeth Marshall, Morgan Kahentonni Phillips, and Karla Jessen Williamson. "Rethinking Resilience from Indigenous Perspectives." *Canadian Journal of Psychiatry* 56, no. 2 (2011): 84–91.

Kirmayer, Laurence J., Caroline L. Tait, and Cori Simpson. "The Mental Health of Aboriginal Peoples in Canada: Transformations of Identity and Community." In *Healing Traditions: The Mental Health of Aboriginal Peoples in Canada*, edited by Laurence J. Kirmayer and Gail Valaskakis, 3–35. Vancouver: UBC Press, 2009.

Lane Jr., Phil, Michael Bopp, Judie Bopp, and Julian Norris. "Mapping the Healing Journey: The Final Report of a First Nation Research Project on Healing in Canadian Aboriginal Communities." Ottawa: Solicitor General Canada and the Aboriginal Healing Foundation, 2002. https://www.publicsafety.gc.ca/cnt/rsrcs/pblctns/mppng-hlng/mppng-hlng-eng.pdf.

Lavallee, Lynn F., and Poole, Jennifer M. "Beyond Recovery: Colonization, Health and Healing for Indigenous People in Canada." Aboriginal Policy Research Consortium International (APRCi), 2009. https://ir.lib.uwo.ca/aprci/254.

McCabe, Glen H. "The Aboriginal Healing: Regaining Balance and Culture. Journal of Transcultural Nursing-Derived Indigenous Therapy Model." *Psychotherapy: Theory, Research, Practice, Training* 44 (2007): 148–60.

McCormick, Rod. "Culturally appropriate means and ends of counselling as described by the First Nations People of British Columbia." *International Journal for Advancement of Counselling* 18 (1996): 163–72.

McMillan, L. Jane, and Pamela Glode-Desrochers. "Final Report: Urban Aboriginal Well-being, Wellness and Justice: A Mi'kmaw Native Friendship Centre Needs Assessment Study for Creating a Collaborative Indigenous Mental Resiliency, Addictions and Justice Strategy." Ottawa: UAKN Atlantic Regional Research Centre, 2014.

Morrissette, Patrick J. "First Nations and Aboriginal Counsellor Education." *Canadian Journal of Counselling and Psychotherapy* 37, no. 3 (2007): 205–15. https://cjc-rcc.ucalgary.ca/article/view/58719/44208.

Mussell, William. "Mental Health from an Indigenous Perspective." In *Journey to Healing: Aboriginal People with Addictions and Mental Health Issues*, edited by Peter Menzies and Lynn F. Lavallée, 187–99. Toronto: Centre for Addictions and Mental Health, 2014.

Quinn, Ashley. "Reflections on Intergenerational Trauma: Healing as a Critical Intervention." *First Peoples Child and Family Review* 3, no. 4 (2007): 72–82.

Ralston Saul, John. *The Comeback*. Toronto: Penguin Books, 2014.

Regional Health Survey National Team. *First Nations Regional Longitudinal Health Survey (RHS)*. Ottawa: AFN/First Nations Governance Committee, 2007. http://www.rhs-ers.ca.

Reimer, Gwen, Amy Bombay, Lena Ellsworth, Sara Fryer, and Tricia Logan. *The Indian Residential Schools Settlement Agreement's Common Experience Payment and Healing: A Qualitative Study Exploring Impacts on Recipients*. Ottawa: Aboriginal Healing Foundation, 2010.

Robbins, Julian, and Jonathan Dewar, J. "Traditional Indigenous Approaches to Healing and the Modern Welfare of Traditional Knowledge, Spirituality and Lands: A Critical Reflection on Practices and Policies Taken from the Canadian Indigenous Example." *International Indigenous Policy Journal* 2, no. 4 (2011): Article 2.

Royal Commission on Aboriginal Peoples (RCAP). *Highlights from the Report of the Royal Commission on Aboriginal Peoples*. Ottawa: Minister of Supply and Services, 1996a.

——. *Report of the Royal Commission on Aboriginal Peoples, Vol. 1: Looking Forward, Looking Back*. Ottawa: Minister of Supply and Services, 1996b.

——. *Report of the Royal Commission on Aboriginal Peoples, Vol. 3: Gathering Strength*. Ottawa: Minister of Supply and Services, 1996c.

Saner, Marc, and Jake Wilson. "Stewardship, Good Governance and Ethics." 1 December 2003. Institute on Governance Policy Brief No. 19. https://ssrn.com/abstract=1555815.

Spear, W.K. *Full Circle: The Aboriginal Healing Foundation and the Unfinished Work of Hope, Healing and Reconciliation.* Ottawa: Aboriginal Healing Foundation, 2014. http://www.ahf.ca/downloads/full-circle-2.pdf.

Truth and Reconciliation Commission (TRC) of Canada. *What We Have Learned: Principles of Truth and Reconciliation.* Ottawa: TRC, 2015.

University of Manitoba. *Framework for Research Engagement with First Nations, Métis and Inuit Peoples.* Winnipeg: University of Manitoba, 2013.

Wadden, M. *Where the Pavements Ends.* Vancouver: Douglas and McIntyre, 2009.

Waldram, James. "Introduction." In *Aboriginal Healing in Canada: Studies in Therapeutic Meaning and Practice,* edited by James Waldram, 1–8. Ottawa: Aboriginal Healing Foundation, 2008.

——. "Healing History? Aboriginal Healing, Historical Trauma, and Personal Responsibility." *Transcultural Psychiatry* 51 (2014): 370–86.

Wesley-Esquimaux, C.C., and M. Smolewski. *Historic Trauma and Aboriginal Healing.* Ottawa: Aboriginal Healing Foundation, 2004.

CHAPTER 15
CULTURAL SAFETY

Carrie Bourassa, Eric Oleson, Sibyl Diver, and Janet McElhaney

"Cultural safety" is a broad term. It was developed in the 1980s in New Zealand in response to the Indigenous Māori people's discontent with nursing care. Māori nursing students and Māori national organizations supported the theory of cultural safety, which upheld political ideas of self-determination and decolonization. Cultural safety was developed by non-dominant Māori people in response to negative experiences in the health and nursing system.[1] Cultural safety analyzes power imbalances (throughout society and throughout health-care practice); addresses institutional discrimination, colonization, and relationships with colonizers as they apply to health care; requires an examination of how personal bias, authority, privilege, and territorial history can influence the relationships between health-care providers and Indigenous people; and relies on both self-reflection and critical reflection. A key element of culturally safe practice is establishing trust with the patient. Culturally safe care empowers people because it reinforces the idea that each person's knowledge and reality are valid and valuable.[2]

It is well documented that race-based disparities in health exist in Canada.[3] Racism, oppression, historical legacies, and government policies continue to maintain health inequities in many Indigenous communities.[4] Indigenous peoples carry a disproportionately high burden of health issues compared with non-Indigenous populations and, in fact, suffer the worst health of any group in Canada. Moreover, Indigenous peoples in Canada experience the poorest living conditions and inequitable access to education, food, employment, and health care/health services, in a country that reliably ranks in the top ten on the United Nations Human Development Index.[5] It is not surprising that inequitable access leads to the worst health outcomes.[6] But it is most important to note that racism has been identified as the major factor in creating and reinforcing these disparities.[7] Such racism is rooted in our colonial history and the processes that have disconnected—and continue to disconnect—Indigenous communities from their lands, languages, and cultures.[8]

Current research demonstrates that racism affects the health and well-being of Indigenous people. Studies conducted among university students in Alberta in 2007 and recent studies in the United States and Australia have revealed that experiences of racism "were indicative of racial battle fatigue."[9] A study cited by Allan and Smylie using data from the 2003 Canadian Community Health Survey revealed that some of the health disparities experienced by racialized groups in Canada cannot be explained by socio-economic status alone. This study suggests that health disparities are evidence of the deterioration that occurs from experiencing racism and discrimination over time within social institutions and daily life. Racism is seen as a chronic stressor linked to the ill health of both African Americans and Indigenous Australians.[10] After hosting a series of seven regional discussions across Canada with Indigenous stakeholders, the Health Council of Canada released a report in 2012 on this topic. Indigenous participants did not favour using mainstream health services because they experienced stereotyping, discrimination, and racism and often felt marginalized, judged, and ignored. They also noted that most health-care practitioners were often unaware that they were being racist or judgmental and thought that most of the issues were systemic in nature. The report also documented that health-care systems valued and prioritized "Western" health systems and values over traditional medicine, and it noted communication issues between patient and practitioner (e.g., complicated terminology, not acknowledging traditional, holistic values or medicines).

Racism can be lethal. There have been documented cases across Canada regarding the deadly impacts of racism, including within the health-care system. One such fatal incident was the death of Brian Sinclair, a forty-five-year-old disabled First Nations man who sought treatment in a Winnipeg emergency room for a bladder infection. It is important to note that he was referred there by a community physician, and while he waited for treatment he vomited on himself several times. This prompted other emergency room patients, who saw that he was in obvious distress, to ask hospital staff to help him. After waiting thirty-four hours for treatment, Sinclair died from complications from an untreated bladder infection without ever seeing a physician, an unlikely outcome had he received proper and timely treatment. Although a provincial inquest was launched to investigate whether Sinclair's race or disability (or both) had anything to do with the lack of care and treatment, it was withdrawn by the family "due to frustration with its failure to examine and address the role of systemic racism in his death, and in the treatment of Indigenous Peoples in health care settings more broadly."[11] There were many assumptions made about Sinclair, including that he was intoxicated and homeless. These assumptions ultimately played a role in his death.

We begin this chapter by presenting a definition of cultural safety in the Indigenous health-care context, which distinguishes this concept from related terms based on a political commitment to equity. We then review the recommendations of the 1996 Royal Commission on Aboriginal Peoples (RCAP) regarding Indigenous health care, recommendations that align with the main tenets of cultural safety, and articulate a strong commitment to addressing the poor health and socio-economic status of Indigenous people in Canada. Unfortunately, current statistics indicate that most recommendations for achieving Indigenous-centred care have not been implemented, and a severe shortage of Indigenous physicians and health-care providers remains. Finally, we discuss how multiple health-care organizations have recently incorporated aspects of cultural safety into their "core competencies" for professional training. These approaches are far from comprehensive, however, and we conclude by calling for a renewed effort to include cultural safety, Indigenous self-determination, and other Indigenous-centred principles of care in health research and practice.

UNDERSTANDING CULTURAL SAFETY

Cultural safety is based on the understanding of power differentials in the health-care system. It exposes the social, political, and historical contexts of health care and enables practitioners to consider difficult concepts such as racism, discrimination, and prejudice. Colonization has contributed, and continues to contribute, to the health disparities faced by Indigenous people today.[12] Culturally safe practices seek to minimize the power differentials between health professionals and clients (or communities) by recognizing a patient-practitioner partnership that reflects a determining voice for the person or persons seeking care.

Cultural safety is an outcome, defined and experienced by those who receive the service. Patients feel safe based on respectful engagement that can help them to find paths to well-being. This concept requires both acknowledgement that we are all bearers of culture and self-reflection on one's own attitudes, beliefs, assumptions, and values.[13] *Culturally safe* care then requires building trust with Indigenous patients; recognizing, acknowledging, and responding to the roles of socio-economic conditions, history, and politics in determining health; communicating respect for a patient's beliefs, behaviours, and values; and ensuring that the client or patient is a partner in decision making.

Cultural safety recognizes health inequities and acknowledges without shame, through critical thinking and self-reflection, that oppression is the main cause of such inequities. Critical and self-reflection are teachable skills. Self-reflection can nourish cultural safety as the provider becomes better able to understand the upstream barriers (e.g., structural, interpersonal, and internalized racism, discriminatory laws, historical legacies, uneven distribution of economic opportunities, etc.) and their connection to the downstream effects (e.g., person-to-person mediated racism, classism, cycles of poverty, etc.), which influence the health and healing of those recognized as being under threat.[14]

Although health researchers and practitioners frequently use similar-sounding terms (e.g., "cultural awareness," "cultural sensitivity," and "cultural competence"), these terms lack the *political commitment* of "cultural safety" to equity in health-care research and delivery. Acknowledging this point is necessary in addressing health inequities between Indigenous and non-Indigenous peoples.[15] It is important to note that cultural safety does include the concepts of cultural awareness, cultural sensitivity, and cultural competence.[16]

Diffey and Lavallee point out that, despite the name *cultural safety,* it is not *cultural* but *power* inequities that are considered. Furthermore, the decision about whether a clinical encounter between a patient and a clinician is *safe* lies with the Indigenous patient. They argue that issues of race and social difference should be explicitly identified as originating in colonial power struggles and not as matters of *culture* or *ethnicity*.[17] Thus, by addressing colonial-based racism at these more structural levels, safety in clinical encounters is ensured.

Cultural safety, in fact, takes us beyond cultural awareness, the acknowledgement of differences between cultures. It also surpasses cultural sensitivity, which recognizes the importance of respecting difference. Cultural safety also helps us to understand the limitations of cultural competence, which focuses on the skills, knowledge, and attitudes of practitioners. For example, one major limitation of cultural competence is the reduction of culture to a set of skills that practitioners can gain by increasing their knowledge. Furthermore, cultural competence focuses on learning rather than on action.[18] In contrast, cultural safety is predicated on understanding power differentials inherent in health service delivery and redressing these inequities through educational processes.[19] It is a patient-centred approach and encourages self-reflection among health-care practitioners, which is seen as an essential skill, fundamental to the relationship between patient and physician.[20] Cultural safety focuses on systemic issues, including colonial-based racism.[21] Moreover, the concept emphasizes that the patient is not a "passive receiver" but a "powerful player in the relationship. Its success therefore cannot be evaluated as a function of knowledge of the practitioner, but is an outcome in and of itself that the practitioner can only help facilitate."[22]

In practice, cultural safety focuses on concepts of respect, dignity, attention, learning together, and shared knowledge and meaning. Practitioners are asked to examine the underlying social determinants of health and to reflect on how colonization has affected, and continues to affect, Indigenous peoples through legislation and policy. The patient-practitioner relationship is redefined using a cultural safety model that endorses a shared power paradigm and ensures that the patient is perceived as a person of value.[23]

Despite the evident resilience of Indigenous communities, health disparities between Indigenous and non-Indigenous people remain high. Much work is needed in health-related fields to narrow and ultimately close the gap between the health status of Indigenous and non-Indigenous people. One way to achieve this is to identify practices in both health *research* and health *practice* that bridge knowledge systems between these communities. This work requires the promotion of community-based participatory research, Indigenous sovereignty, and practices that are considerate to and respectful of Indigenous peoples—that is, those practices that support cultural safety. For Yeung, "cultural safety therefore extends beyond clinical practice to become a moral discourse for informing policy analysis. It is necessarily coupled with application at systemic levels, including consideration of whether mainstream health policies put Indigenous peoples' health at risk, or whether they fail to address gaps in health in Indigenous populations, thereby also producing a lack of safety."[24]

Cultural safety, at its core, is highly political. As noted earlier, the concept arose as a political response by Māori people to discontent with nursing care. According to Brascoupé and Waters, "the concept of cultural safety becomes a challenge to the power establishment in wider society, defined not just as a measure of the effectiveness of policy and delivery, but as a very real part of a political power struggle for control over one's own life. Cultural safety becomes a means of changing broad attitudes and deep-seated conceptions, on an individual and community-wide basis."[25] Given the history of Canada's policies of assimilation, this is particularly powerful and a central tenet of cultural safety in Canada. Not only are there historical policies that have intergenerational impacts on Indigenous people's health and well-being, but also there are current neocolonial policies that continue to affect Indigenous peoples through legislation, including the Indian Act. As the Truth and Reconciliation Commission (TRC) notes, "for over a century, the central goals of Canada's Aboriginal policy were to eliminate Aboriginal governments; ignore Aboriginal rights; terminate the Treaties; and, through a process of assimilation, cause Aboriginal peoples to cease to exist as distinct legal, social, cultural, religious, and racial entities in Canada."[26]

REMEMBERING THE ROYAL COMMISSION ON ABORIGINAL PEOPLES

It is striking that Chapter 3 ("Health and Healing") of RCAP's *Gathering Strength* volume begins by outlining the poor health and socio-economic status of Indigenous peoples in Canada—a situation that, as Indigenous scholars, we continue to lament today. The chapter also notes that this ill health and poor socio-economic status can be linked to the colonial policies and experiences since the time of contact. Moreover, RCAP speaks to the need for access to services "sensitive to their unique history and needs."[27]

Five themes emerged from RCAP's discussions with Indigenous peoples across Canada:

1. the demand for equal outcomes (equity for all in health care);
2. the belief in interconnectedness (holistic concepts of health);
3. the transition from dependency to autonomy;
4. the need for culture-based programming; and
5. a new role for traditional healing.

Based on these themes, RCAP made several health-related recommendations, most of which have never been implemented in mainstream policy, legislation, or programming. The first set of recommendations from Section 2.4, "Characteristics of a New Strategy," includes

1. pursuit of equity in access to health and healing services and in health status outcomes;
2. holism in approaches to problems and their treatment and prevention;
3. Aboriginal authority over health systems and, where feasible, community control over services; and
4. diversity in the design of systems and services to accommodate differences in culture and community realities.

RCAP also recommended a health strategy based on

- equitable access to health services and equitable outcomes in health status;
- holistic approaches to treatment and preventive services;
- Aboriginal control of services; and
- diversity of approaches that respond to cultural priorities and community needs.

These recommendations are strongly aligned with the main tenets of cultural safety. In practice, it promotes the integration of holistic approaches to health; Indigenous control of services; equitable access to health services (with the hope of equitable outcomes in health status); and the creation of culturally safe care using diverse approaches. Thus, though the model of cultural safety was in its infancy when the RCAP report was drafted, the recommendations in the report remain relevant today. Unfortunately, little progress has been made since the report was released in 1996. In fact, the gap in terms of ill health and poor socio-economic status between Indigenous and non-Indigenous Canadians has grown.[28]

In addition to advocating for self-government and self-sufficiency, in Section 3.1 RCAP recommended the following elements of a strategy:

1. the reorganization of health and social service delivery through a system of healing centres and lodges under Aboriginal control;
2. an Aboriginal human resources development strategy;
3. adaptation of mainstream service, training, and professional systems to affirm the participation of Aboriginal people as individuals and collectives in Canadian life and to collaborate with Aboriginal institutions; and
4. initiation of an Aboriginal infrastructure program to address the most pressing problems related to clean water, safe waste management, and adequate housing.

One recommendation from RCAP was the "equitable access to appropriate services by all Aboriginal people,"[29] yet twenty-five years later many Indigenous peoples do not have access to a primary care physician.[30]

Moreover, RCAP emphasized the need for more Indigenous health-care practitioners, particularly physicians, yet we continue to grapple with a shortage of Indigenous physicians, nurses, and other health-care providers. The 2012 Health Council of Canada (HCC) report, entitled *Empathy, Dignity and Respect: Creating Cultural Safety for Aboriginal People in Urban Health Care*, emphasized the systemic racism faced by Indigenous peoples in hospital settings. As a result, study participants indicated that they felt more comfortable and safe when they saw Indigenous staff and clinicians. The report also recommended an Aboriginal human resource strategy in addition to *cultural safety training*.[31]

Not only do we need more Indigenous physicians and health-care providers, but also we need to ensure that allied, non-Indigenous physicians and health-care providers are offering culturally safe services. We urgently need more Indigenous physicians. It is difficult to obtain their actual number in Canada, but various estimates provide a general sense of the problem. In 2005, there were 61,622 physicians in Canada, and of those an *estimated* 100 to 150 were Indigenous.[32] In 2004, the Aboriginal Health Human Resource Initiative announced a plan to spend $100 million over five years to increase the number of Aboriginal people working in health careers; however, this did not seem to translate into higher numbers of Indigenous physicians or Indigenous peoples working in other health professions. More recent data estimate that, while 3,000 Indigenous physicians are needed across Canada, a "best guess" offered by experts in the field is that there are only 300.[33] Based on graduation rates in medical schools, Dr. Alika Lafontaine, past president of the Indigenous Physicians' Association of Canada (IPAC), estimates that the country has graduated approximately 1,000 Indigenous physicians since the late 1990s.[34] To put this in context, the Canadian Medical Association reported over 80,000 physicians serving in Canada as of January 2017.[35] Indigenous peoples remain well underrepresented in the profession.

Given this gap, there is a clear need to provide additional training to existing physicians and health-care workers to ensure that they are providing culturally safe care. The HCC report was clear on this point: "A frequently repeated theme in the regional discussions was the importance of training activities that fill in the considerable gaps in knowledge, understanding, and experience that most Canadians have in relation to First Nations, Inuit, and Métis people, cultures, and communities."[36] The report also noted that cultural safety training must develop knowledge about both colonial history and present experiences of Indigenous peoples. The training must also incorporate activities that assist participants in understanding the impacts of their perceptions of Indigenous peoples on their practice and, ultimately, on the health outcomes for Indigenous patients. Finally, such training must develop a set of understandings and skills, including self-reflection and critical reflection, that will assist health-care professionals to engage with Indigenous peoples in ways that provide cultural safety.[37] In 2013, the National Collaborating Centre for Aboriginal Health (NCCAH) compiled an *Environmental Scan of Cultural Competency and Safety in Education, Training and Health Services*. It listed seven professional cultural training programs across the country. Most of the content of those programs addresses the themes of communication, leadership, health, and/or wellness; understanding the differences among cultural awareness, competence, sensitivity, and safety; as well as understanding the history of colonization, Indigenous or traditional knowledge, and concepts of oppression, racism, and discrimination.[38]

More recently, the Truth and Reconciliation Commission made several recommendations specific to health recruitment and training on Indigenous health:

23. We call upon all levels of government to:
i. Increase the number of Aboriginal professionals working in the health care field.
ii. Ensure the retention of Aboriginal health care providers in Aboriginal communities.
iii. Provide cultural competency training for all health care professionals.

24. We call upon medical and nursing schools in Canada to require all students to take a course dealing with Aboriginal health issues, including the history and legacy of residential schools, the United Nations Declaration on the Rights of Indigenous Peoples, Treaties and Aboriginal rights, and Indigenous teachings and practices. This will require skills-based training in intercultural competency, conflict resolution, human rights and anti-racism.[39]

After over twenty years of repeated calls for mandatory cultural competence or safety training, and after millions of dollars were poured into Aboriginal Health Human Resource plans, another multi-million-dollar commission in the form of the Truth and Reconciliation Commission issued recommendations eerily similar to the RCAP recommendations. Yet the reality in Indigenous communities, whether northern, on reserve, off reserve, urban, or rural, from coast to coast, is that our health remains poor; our economic, employment, and education opportunities are still bleak; and by all accounts not much has changed despite a Royal Commission that held such promise and hope and despite so many incredible opportunities for change. In Chapter 3 of the third volume of the 1996 report, we can see many recommendations that have still to be implemented twenty-five years later. Even after a formal national apology by the prime minister and ninety-four calls to action made by the Truth and Reconciliation Commission, not much has changed. Why are we holding out hope that this idea or theory of cultural safety might transform our health-care system? If not much has changed, and indeed given that the gaps in almost every health determinant measure are widening, then why are we focusing on this?

We do so because reconciliation is only beginning. We needed twenty-five years to wake up and understand what RCAP was really all about. RCAP still has something to teach us. We should not miss the theme of self-determination. It is at the core of Chapter 3 of Volume 3 of the report. We must shake up the system and rebalance it. We live in a system of power and control—one in which, for centuries, Indigenous peoples have had no power and no control. Cultural safety is based on the understanding of power differentials in the health-care system; it exposes the social, political, and historical contexts of health care and enables practitioners to consider difficult concepts such as racism, discrimination, and prejudice. Colonization has contributed and continues to contribute to the health disparities faced by Indigenous peoples today.[40] As we are able to balance the power differentials and become self-determining peoples through cultural safety, we can begin to address the inequities that have plagued us for centuries: "Taking a cultural safety approach to dealing with inequities enables physicians and other care providers to improve health care access for patients, aggregates, and populations; acknowledge that we are all bearers of culture; expose the social, political, and historical context[s] of health care; and interrupt unequal power relations."[41]

The Indigenous Physicians Association of Canada, Aboriginal Nurses Association of Canada, Canadian Nurses Association, College of Family Physicians of Canada, and Royal College of Physicians and Surgeons of Canada have all called for cultural safety training for their members. Requests for such training have ranged from recommending short workshops at conferences, to integrating more content into medical school curricula, to advocating for mandatory accreditation for physicians and surgeons. Indigenous practitioners, organizations, and communities need to be involved in determining how the training is structured to ensure that the difficult issues regarding systemic racism, white privilege, stigma, discrimination, and ongoing impacts of colonization, for example, are included in any cultural safety training. It is also important to include positive topics in training sessions as well, such as leadership, resilience, accountability, and Indigenous knowledge—but not at the expense of glossing over the uncomfortable issues that must be addressed in order for us to move forward together.

As the IPAC describes, cultural safety is the embodiment of two concepts: challenging privilege and addressing power imbalance.[42] Culturally safe practice is predicated on critical self-reflection that seeks to interrupt racism and oppression. Reflecting on one's privilege and how it translates into the power differential within the patient-provider relationship is a first step. The health-care provider then moves from reflection to active practices of care that challenge stereotypes, address inequities, and facilitate self-determination with Indigenous patients. Although responsibility for ensuring cultural safety rests with the provider, evaluation of whether cultural safety is achieved lies with the Indigenous patient. Thus, it is imperative for any cultural safety training to include these topics and to have both Indigenous and non-Indigenous facilitators who have the skills to walk participants through this process.

RECOMMENDATIONS: WHERE ARE WE?

In 2015, the Truth and Reconciliation Commission made several calls to action specific to health and healing. Four of them (18, 19, 22, and 23) are directly related to improving patient care, training, and transforming the health-care system. Cultural safety can promote reconciliation by supporting research that addresses patient care, structural racism, systemic inequalities, socio-economic inequities, intergenerational trauma, spiritual healing, as well as capacity building and training for both Indigenous and non-Indigenous health professionals. The TRC recommended the following:

18. We call upon the federal, provincial, territorial and Aboriginal governments to acknowledge that the current state of Aboriginal health in Canada is a direct result of previous Canadian government policies, including residential schools, and to recognize and implement the health care rights of Aboriginal people as identified in international law, constitutional law and under the Treaties.

19. We call upon the federal government in consultation with Aboriginal peoples, to establish measurable goals to identify and close the gaps in health outcomes between Aboriginal and non-Aboriginal communities, and to publish annual progress reports and assess long-term trends. Such efforts would focus on indicators such as:

infant mortality, maternal health, suicide, mental health, addictions, life expectancy, birth rates, infant and child health issues, chronic diseases, illness and injury incidence, and the availability of appropriate health services.

22. We call upon those who can effect change within the Canadian health-care system to recognize the value of Aboriginal healing practices and use them in the treatment of Aboriginal patients in collaboration with Aboriginal healers and Elders where requested by Aboriginal patients.[43]

In essence, the TRC recommended that research be undertaken to track appropriate health indicators in partnership with Indigenous peoples to identify and close the gaps in health outcomes. Acknowledging the link between colonization and the ill health of Indigenous people, and the link between the benefits of traditional healing practices and an increased number of Indigenous healing practitioners, would be extremely beneficial, both in research and in practice.

Research must inform practice, and practice must inform research. It is essential for research with Indigenous communities to follow community-based participatory research principles and to employ Indigenous research methodologies. Browne and colleagues outline ten strategies, based on ethnographic research studies, that can serve as health equity guidelines for organizations and providers.[44] These strategies are aligned with recommendations from the 2012 HCC report. These strategies include the following:

1. Explicitly commit to fostering health equity in partnership with Indigenous peoples in mission, vision, or other foundational policy statements.
2. Develop organizational structures, policies, and processes to support the commitment to health equity.
3. Optimize use of place and space to create a welcoming milieu.
4. Re-vision the use of time.
5. Continuously attend to power differentials.
6. Tailor care, programs, and services to local contexts, Indigenous cultures, and knowledge systems.
7. Actively counter systemic and individual experiences of racism and intersecting forms of discrimination.

8. Tailor care, programs, and services to address interrelated forms of violence.
9. Ensure opportunities for meaningful engagement of patients and community leaders in strategic planning decisions.
10. Tailor care to address the social determinants of health for Indigenous people.

Similarly, the 2012 HCC report recommended that health-care providers do the following:

1. Provide patient-centred care that meets patient-identified needs.
2. Look for and create opportunities for partnership and collaboration that will enhance cultural safety for First Nations, Inuit, and Métis people.
3. Look for and create opportunities for partnership and collaboration that will increase your organization's capacity to provide culturally competent services and enhance cultural safety for First Nations, Inuit, and Métis people who engage with your organization.
4. Take leadership from First Nations, Inuit, and Métis people and acknowledge their expertise with respect to the identification of their individual and collective needs, capabilities, strengths, and opportunities.
5. Value and acknowledge the knowledge, expertise, and skills of traditional healers, counsellors, teachers, and other traditional knowledge keepers and practitioners.
6. Develop policies and initiatives that will support the recruitment and retention of Aboriginal employees at all levels of your organization.
7. Develop methodologies that can be used to assess qualitative outcomes of activities that enhance cultural competency and cultural safety.
8. Use collaboration and partnership opportunities to enhance the cultural competency of urban health systems and cultural safety for First Nations, Inuit, and Métis community members using those systems.

9. Build capacity within communities through research that enhances accountability and understanding.[45]

There are several community-based Indigenous health research projects across Canada that are led by Indigenous health researchers and communities and directly related to cultural safety. Many of them are funded through the CIHR. These are positive, albeit slow, steps toward enhancing capacity, accountability, and leadership as well as building models of care. Conducting research with, by, and for Indigenous peoples is but one recommendation, though it is an important one.

The National Collaborating Centre for Aboriginal Health[46] identified five organizations that provided Indigenous core competencies, which apply both to general public health and to specific Indigenous health needs; however, few of these organizations identified a comprehensive framework for Indigenous health care.

As an example, in 2009 the Aboriginal Nurses' Association of Canada published *A Framework for First Nations, Inuit and Métis Nursing*, which describes core competencies for nursing education. The competencies outlined include postcolonial understanding, communication, respect, and inclusivity. Implementation of this competency model is achieved through program support, engagement with Indigenous communities, as well as accreditation and program approval.[47]

The Public Health Agency of Canada indicates that it has no Indigenous-specific competencies but that all competencies listed are "relevant" to Indigenous health. Its seven core competencies, contained within Core Competencies for Public Health in Canada, 2007, are public health sciences; assessment and analysis; policy and program planning, implementation, and evaluation; partnership, collaboration, and advocacy; diversity and inclusiveness; communication; and leadership.

The Association of Faculties of Medicine of Canada and the Indigenous Physicians Association of Canada established a partnership to develop core competencies for undergraduate medical education in First Nations, Inuit, and Métis health. In 2009, they developed a set of core competencies for undergraduate medical students that address the physician's role in Aboriginal health care as a medical expert, communicator, collaborator, manager, health advocate, scholar, and professional.[48]

The last competency framework of note is the National Indian and Inuit Community Health Representatives Organization, which began the Road to Competency project in 2006. The National Aboriginal Health Organization also developed competencies, but this organization is no longer in existence because of funding cuts.

We put forward an alternative not included in the NCCAH document. We think that this might be a viable option that could be considered. Working in consultation with the Aboriginal Health Advisory Committee, in 2011 the Royal College of Physicians and Surgeons developed an additional framework for consideration that could be widely applied. It is called the CanMEDS Physician Competency Framework. It describes the knowledge, skills, and abilities that specialist physicians require to deliver effective health care. With the move toward competency-based education, most health professional education programs (e.g., nursing, physiotherapy, etc.) have now adopted a similar framework.

After engagement with academics, practitioners, and various Indigenous stakeholders, the Royal College has developed a set of competencies, including Indigenous health and primary health care; empowerment, community relations, and cultural competence; prevention, promotion, and protection; emergency care; communication; ethics, leadership, and teamwork; and administration. In reality, many of the CanMEDS framework tenets extend beyond the specific challenges of serving Indigenous communities and can easily apply to other health-care professionals in their practices (nursing, physiotherapy, etc.).

The framework is based on seven "roles" that health professionals need to be competent in performing. By mapping Indigenous health values against each role (see Figure 15.1), providers can begin to reflect on their personal biases as well as the effects that their clinical skills and interpersonal relations have on patient relationships. Providers who embrace these values can also embrace and integrate Indigenous knowledge and ways of being into their practices, and they can offer welcoming environments in which Indigenous patients feel safe and respected.[49]

As shown in Figure 15.1, interpreting Indigenous health values through the CanMEDS framework results in seven principles that can guide culturally safe interventions, such that patients can realize their full potential as Indigenous peoples without feeling threatened in a health-care setting. It is also helpful to note that the 2015 revision to the CanMEDS framework changed the term "manager" to "leader." This shift reflects a philosophy of practice that physicians must be equipped with the training, knowledge, experience, skills, and tools needed to lead culturally safe improvements in

Indigenous health. In this context, the concept of "patient safety" includes the idea of cultural safety and considers core issues of justice, efficiency, and effectiveness in the allocation of health-care resources.

FIGURE 15.1. INDIGENOUS HEALTH VALUES AND PRINCIPLES FOR CULTURALLY SAFE INTERVENTIONS.

'Mapping' Indigenous Health Values as Interpreted Through the CanMEDS Framework

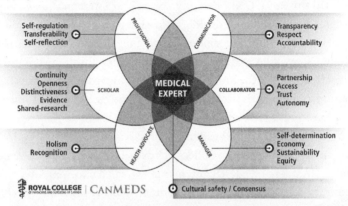

Source: Indigenous health values and principles for culturally safe interventions (Royal College of Physicians and Surgeons of Canada, 2011). Copyright held by Royal College of Physicians and Surgeons of Canada. Reproduced here with permission.

Following guiding principles that emanate from Indigenous values is essential because it serves to deconstruct the power differentials at systemic and personal levels and to support culturally safe partnerships based on respect and understanding between health providers and the Indigenous communities that they serve. The use of culturally safe methods fosters personal and professional development and makes change possible. In addition, viewing culturally safe practices through competency-based frameworks, such as the Indigenous adaptation of the CanMEDS physician roles, brings stronger attention to Indigenous health, facilitates transference into education and practice, and provides additional direction for leadership.

What is most important in applying such frameworks, however, is that the patient remains in control (patient-centred care). One of the overarching principles reflecting this concept is stated in the college's statement on Indigenous health values and principles: "The [health] care of an Indigenous person reflects the dimensions of quality for patient-centred care that resonate with his/her culture in all stages of that person's life. The physician demonstrates empathy, open-mindedness, consensus and understanding of the issues facing Indigenous peoples and the social determinants of health that contribute to their health status. The decision-making process recognizes the value of Indigenous peoples' self-determination through the principles of ownership, control, access and possession and the benefits of making unencumbered and informed choices to promote health-sustainability and equity."[50]

CONCLUSION: WHERE DO WE NEED TO GO?

Elders often remind us that "we don't know what we don't know." As we are reflecting on the magnitude of the work that has been done by some of the most amazing people we know, we are overwhelmed with joy and gratitude. On the other hand, we know there is so much more to do, and as we ponder on what we must "recommend" we are similarly overwhelmed but in a different way. There is so much that we don't know and so much to do. Yet we are strong people. We are resilient. We are survivors. Much has been done, yet it seems as if little has been accomplished. Or maybe we are being too harsh. Maybe our expectation of changing a colonial system over the course of twenty years or less is too high. Well, if you don't have expectations, no one will ever meet them. Someone very wise told us that.

We have learned much from those who have gone before us—those who have paved the way and done the hard work. We have a path to follow now, a path that was not there before. We have similar, if not the same, recommendations that are being made over and over again. Why is this important? Because we know what we need in our communities. We always have known. We must continue to demand what we know we need and what we want. Our relatives said it in RCAP, they said it through the TRC, and they are saying it through all of our important community-based research projects. So, to summarize, this is what we need:

1. self-determination;
2. more Indigenous physicians, health-care providers, and researchers;
3. culturally safe allied physicians, health-care providers, and researchers (i.e., individuals who are appropriately trained in culturally safe approaches that address the tough topics of white privilege, systemic racism, discrimination, etc.);
4. more research to document poor health outcomes related to the racism and stereotyping faced by Indigenous communities and research to evaluate culturally safe interventions;
5. culturally safe models of care for health services offered to Indigenous people, regardless of location;
6. self-determination (Wait, did we say that already? Well, it's worth stating again.);
7. to acknowledge and value Indigenous knowledge and the expertise and skills of traditional healers and counsellors;
8. better ways of developing partnerships and collaborations with Indigenous communities and organizations so that they can determine the nature of such partnerships/collaborations;
9. to prioritize and provide patient-centred care;
10. to challenge privilege and practise self-reflection daily;
11. allies and champions of culturally safe practices; and
12. research and theory that can translate into policy at all levels.

NOTES

1   National Aboriginal Health Organization (NAHO), *Fact Sheet: Cultural Safety*.
2   NAHO, *Fact Sheet: Cultural Safety*.
3   Lasser, Himmelstein, and Woolhandler, "Access to Care, Health Status and Health Disparities."
4   Virginia Department of Health, *What Is Health Inequity?*
5   Allan and Smylie, *First Peoples, Second Class Treatment*; Lavallee, Diffey, and Anderson, "Community Needs Assessment Study"; Reading and Wien, *Health Inequities and Social Determinants*.
6   Aboriginal Health Advisory Committee, *Indigenous Health Values and Principles Statement*, 2013; Reading and Wien, *Health Inequities and Social Determinants*.
7   Allan and Smylie, *First Peoples, Second Class Treatment*; Diffey and Lavallee, "Is Cultural Safety Enough?"; Hart and Lavallee, "Colonization, Racism, Social Exclusion and Indigenous Health"; Loppey, Reading, and de Leeuw, *Aboriginal Experiences with*

Racism and Its Impacts.

8   Commission on Social Determinants of Health, "Closing the Gap in a Generation"; Lavallee, Diffey, and Anderson, "Community Needs Assessment Study"; King, Smith, and Gracey, "Indigenous Health Part 2."

9   Allan and Smylie, *First Peoples, Second Class Treatment,* 9.

10   Allan and Smylie, *First Peoples, Second Class Treatment,* 9.

11   Allan and Smylie, *First Peoples, Second Class Treatment,* 9.

12   Aboriginal Nurses' Association of Canada, *Cultural Competence and Cultural Safety.*

13   Health Council of Canada (HCC), *Empathy, Dignity and Respect.*

14   Royal College of Physicians and Surgeons of Canada, *Indigenous Health Fact Sheet,* July 8, 2013.

15   Darroch et al., "The United States Does CAIR about Cultural Safety."

16   Brascoupé and Waters, "Cultural Safety."

17   Lavallee, Diffey, and Anderson, "Community Needs Assessment Study."

18   Lavallee, Diffey, and Anderson, "Community Needs Assessment Study."

19   Aboriginal Nurses' Association of Canada. *Cultural Competence and Cultural Safety.*

20   Indigenous Physicians Association of Canada (IPAC), *First Nations, Inuit and Métis Health Core Competencies.*

21   Diffey and Lavallee, "Is Cultural Safety Enough?"

22   Yeung, "Conceptualizing Cultural Safety," 3–4.

23   Yeung, "Conceptualizing Cultural Safety," 3–4.

24   Yeung, "Conceptualizing Cultural Safety," 4.

25   Brascoupé and Waters, "Cultural Safety," 12–13.

26   Truth and Reconciliation Commission (TRC) of Canada, *Honouring the Truth,* 1.

27   Royal Commission on Aboriginal Peoples (RCAP), *Report of the Royal Commission on Aboriginal Peoples, Vol. 3,* 184.

28   Hole et al., "Visibility and Voice; Yeung, "Conceptualizing Cultural Safety."

29   RCAP, *Vol.3,* Ch. 3, s. 12.

30   Royal College of Physicians and Surgeons of Canada, *Indigenous Health Fact Sheet.*

31   HCC, *Empathy, Dignity and Respect.*

32   Anderson and Lavallee, "The Development of the First Nations."

33   Many Guns, "Aboriginal Graduates Praise UBC Medical Program."

34   Lafontaine, correspondence with the authors, 31 October 2016.

35   Canadian Medical Association (CMA), "Canadian Physician Resources–2017 Basic Facts."

36   HCC, *Empathy, Dignity and Respect,* 37.

37   HCC, *Empathy, Dignity and Respect,* 37.

38   Baba, *Cultural Safety in First Nations, Inuit and Métis Public Health.*

39   TRC, *Honouring the Truth.* See also http://aptn.ca/news/2015/06/02/read-94-recommendations/.

40   Aboriginal Nurses' Association of Canada, *Cultural Competence and Cultural Safety.*

41   IPAC, *First Nations, Inuit and Métis Health Core Competencies,* 10.

42   IPAC, *First Nations, Inuit and Métis Health Core Competencies,* 10.

43   TRC, *Honouring the Truth,* 160–63.

44   Browne, et al., "Enhancing Health Care Equity."

45   HCC, *Empathy, Dignity and Respect,* 64–65.

46   Baba, *Cultural Safety in First Nations, Inuit and Métis Public Health.*

47   Baba, *Cultural Safety in First Nations, Inuit and Métis Public Health.* Aboriginal Nurses Association of Canada, *Cultural Competence.*

48   Baba, *Cultural Safety in First Nations, Inuit and Métis Public Health.*

49   IPAC, *First Nations, Inuit and Métis Health Core Competencies.*

50   Royal College of Physicians and Surgeons of Canada, *Indigenous Health Fact Sheet,* 3.

REFERENCES

Aboriginal Health Advisory Committee. Royal College of Physicians and Surgeons of Canada. *Indigenous Health Values and Principles Statement,* 2013. Ottawa: Royal College of Physicians and Surgeons of Canada, 2013. http://www.royalcollege.ca/portal/page/portal/rc/common/documents/publications/dialogue/2013/aboriginal_health_e.pdf.

Aboriginal Nurses Association of Canada. *Cultural Competence and Cultural Safety in Nursing Education: A Framework for First Nations, Inuit and Métis Nursing.* Ottawa: Aboriginal Nurses' Association of Canada, 2009.

Allan, Billie, and Janet Smylie. *First Peoples, Second Class Treatment: The Role of Racism in the Health and Well-Being of Indigenous Peoples in Canada.* Toronto: Wellesley Institute, 2015. http://www.wellesleyinstitute.com/wp-content/uploads/2015/02/Summary-First-Peoples-Second-Class-Treatment-Final.pdf.

Anderson, Marcia, and Barry Lavallee. "The Development of the First Nations, Inuit and Métis Medical Workforce." *Medical Journal of Australia* 186 (2007): 539–40.

Baba, Lauren. *Cultural Safety in First Nations, Inuit and Métis Public Health: Environmental Scan of Cultural Competency and Safety in Education, Training and Health Services.* Prince George, BC: National Collaborating Centre for Aboriginal Health, 2013. http://www.nccahccnsa.ca/Publications/Lists/Publications/Attachments/88/CIPHER_report_EN_web_updated2.pdf.

Brascoupé, Simon, and Catherine Waters. "Cultural Safety: Exploring the Applicability of the Concept of Cultural Safety to Aboriginal Health and Community Wellness." *Journal of Aboriginal Health* 5, no. 2 (2009): 6–41. http://www.naho.ca/documents/journal/jah05_02/05_02_01_Cultural.pdf.

Browne, Annette J., et al. "Enhancing Health Care Equity with Indigenous Populations: Evidence-Based Strategies from an Ethnographic Study." *BMC Health Services Research* 16, no. 544 (2016): 1–17. https://doi.org/10.1186/s12913-016-1707-9.

Canadian Medical Association (CMA). "Canadian Physician Resources—2017 Basic Facts." 2017. https://www.cma.ca/En/Pages/basic-physician-facts.aspx.

Commission on Social Determinants of Health. "Closing the Gap in a Generation: Health Equity through Action on the Social Determinants of Health." World Health Organization, 2007. http://apps.who.int/iris/bitst eam/10665/43943/1/9789241563703_eng.pdf.

Darroch, Francine, et al. "The United States Does CAIR about Cultural Safety: Examining Cultural Safety within Indigenous Health Contexts in Canada and the United States." *Journal of Transcultural Nursing* 28, no. 3 (2016): 1–9. https://doi.org/10.1177/1043659616634170.

Diffey, Linda, and Barry Lavalle. "Is Cultural Safety Enough? Confronting Racism to Address Inequities in Indigenous Health." Office of Educational and Faculty Development newsletter, University of Manitoba, 2016. https://umanitoba.ca/faculties/health_sciences/medicine/education/ed_dev/media/June10-OEFD_Newsletter_2016_spring.pdf.

Hart, Michael, and Barry Lavallee. "Colonization, Racism, Social Exclusion and Indigenous Health." In *The Social Determinants of Health in Manitoba,* 2nd edition, ed. Lynne Fernandez, Shauna Mackinnon, and Jim Silver, 145–59. Canadian Centre for Policy Alternatives: Winnipeg, 2015.

Health Council of Canada (HCC). *Empathy, Dignity and Respect: Creating Cultural Safety for Aboriginal People in Urban Health Care,* December 2012. https://healthcouncilcanada.ca/files/Aboriginal_Report_EN_web_final.pdf.

Hole, Rachelle, et al. "Visibility and Voice: Aboriginal People Experience Culturally Safe and Unsafe Health Care." *Qualitative Health Research* 25, no. 12 (2015): 1662–74. https://doi.org/10.1177/1049732314566325.

Indigenous Physicians Association of Canada (IPAC). *First Nations, Inuit and Métis Health Core Competencies: A Curriculum Framework for Undergraduate Medical Education,* April 2009. Association of Faculties of Medicine of Canada. https://afmc.ca/pdf/CoreCompetenciesEng.pdf.

King, M., A. Smith, and M. Gracey. "Indigenous Health Part 2: The Underlying Causes of the Health Gap." *Lancet* 374 (2009): 76–85. https://doi.org/10.1016/S0140-6736(09)60827-8.

Lasser, Karen E., David U. Himmelstein, and Steffie Woolhandler. "Access to Care, Health Status and Health Disparities in the United States and Canada: Results of a Cross-National Population-Based Survey." *American Journal of Public Health* 96, no. 7 (2006): 1300–1307. https://doi.org/10.2105/AJPH.2004.059402.

Lavallee, Barry, Linda Diffey, and Marcia Anderson. "Community Needs Assessment Study for Planning the Indigenous Health Curriculum in Indigenous Medical Education at the University of Manitoba: CC–E–OC4-3." *Medical Education* 48 (2014): 52–53.

Loppie, Samantha, Charlotte Reading, and Sarah de Leeuw. *Aboriginal Experiences with Racism and Its Impacts.* National Collaborating Centre on Aboriginal Health, 2014. http://www.nccah-ccnsa.ca/Publications/Lists/Publications/Attachments/131/2014_07_09_FS_2426_RacismPart2_ExperiencesImpacts_EN_Web.pdf.

Many Guns, Kelly. "Aboriginal Graduates Praise UBC Medical Program." *First Nations Drum,* 21 July 2016. http://www.firstnationsdrum.com/2016/07/aboriginal-graduates-praise-ubc-medical-program/.

National Aboriginal Health Organization (NAHO). *Fact Sheet: Cultural Safety.* 31 January 2006. http://www.naho.ca/documents/naho/english/Culturalsafetyfactsheet.pdf.

National Collaborating Centre for Aboriginal Health. "The State of Knowledge of Aboriginal Health: A Review of Aboriginal Public Health in Canada." Prince George, BC: NCCAH, 2012. https://www.nccih.ca/docs/context/RPT-StateKnowledgeReview-EN.pdf.

Public Health Agency of Canada. "Core Competencies for Public Health in Canada Release 1.0." Ottawa: Public Health Agency of Canada, 2007.

Reading, Charlotte, and Fred Wien. *Health Inequities and Social Determinants of Aboriginal Peoples' Health.* 2009. http://www.nccah-ccnsa.ca/docs/social%20determinates/NCCAH-Loppie-Wien_Report.pdf.

Royal College of Physicians and Surgeons of Canada. *CanMEDS: Better Standards, Better Physicians, Better Care. The CanMEDS Roles.* Ottawa: Royal College of Physicians and Surgeons of Canada, 2011. http://www.royalcollege.ca/rcsite/documents/health-policy/cultural-safety-poster.pdf.

——. *Indigenous Health Fact Sheet,* July 8, 2013. Ottawa: Royal College of Physicians and Surgeons of Canada, 2013. http://www.royalcollege.ca/rcsite/documents/health-policy/indigenous-health-fact-sheet-july-8-2013-e.pdf.

Royal Commission on Aboriginal Peoples (RCAP). *Report of the Royal Commission on Aboriginal Peoples, Vol. 3: Gathering Strength.* Ottawa: Minister of Supply and Services, 1996.

Truth and Reconciliation Commission (TRC) of Canada. *Honouring the Truth, Reconciling for the Future: Summary of the Final Report of the Truth and Reconciliation Commission of Canada,* 2015. http://nctr.ca/assets/reports/Final%20Reports/Executive_Summary_English_Web.pdf.

Virginia Department of Health. *What Is Health Inequity?* 2013. http://www.vdh.virginia.gov/health-equity/unnatural-causes-is-inequality-making-us-sick/what-is-health-inequity/.

Yeung, Sharon. "Conceptualizing Cultural Safety: Definitions and Applications of Safety in Health Care for Indigenous Mothers in Canada." *Journal for Social Thought* 1, no. 1 (2016): 1–13. http://ir.lib.uwo.ca/jst/vol1/iss1/3/.

CHAPTER 16

WHAT WILL IT TAKE?
ENDING THE CANADIAN GOVERNMENT'S CHRONIC FAILURE TO DO BETTER FOR FIRST NATIONS CHILDREN AND FAMILIES WHEN IT KNOWS BETTER

Cindy Blackstock

> Another picture that reappears too frequently is the disparity in the treatment of Canada's Indigenous peoples. My predecessor, Sheila Fraser, near the end of her mandate, summed up her impression of 10 years of audits and related recommendations on First Nations issues with the word "unacceptable." Since my arrival, we have continued to audit these issues and to present at least one report per year on areas that have an impact on First Nations. . . . When you add the results of these audits to those we reported on in the past, I can only describe the situation as it exists now as beyond unacceptable.
>
> —Michael Ferguson, Auditor General of Canada, 2016[1]

What will it take to get the government of Canada, primarily represented by the Department of Indigenous and Northern Affairs (INAC) and Health Canada (HC), to implement available solutions so that First Nations children have an equitable chance to grow up safely with their families? Whatever it is, no one has found it yet. Academic research, internal and external government reviews (including the Royal Commission on Aboriginal Peoples [RCAP][2]), media reports dating back many years, and more recent legal orders have not been enough to pierce through the department's inertia. Focusing on Canada's relationship with First Nations children, in this chapter I present two confronting proposals. First, the government of Canada perpetuates discrimination toward First Nations children by deliberate choice and/or its failure to identify and correct colonialism within INAC/HC philosophies and systems. Second, we (academics, the media, and the public) have largely let the government get away with it.

If Canada were fully committed to addressing the long-standing inequities in public services, then frankly it would take monolithic incompetence to achieve such a perfect record of failure. Additionally, a contrite government would logically launch wide-scale internal departmental reform to fix its approach in the wake of past failures. Canada has not. Instead, successive Canadian governments have avoided ending the discrimination toward First Nations children through strategies of denial, deflection, deferral, and the use of official procedures such as study and consultation to mask inaction. These tactics are often nested in colonial narratives questioning the "capacity" of First Nations peoples to care for their children or manage their money.

The themes that emerge from this case study are likely familiar to Métis and Inuit communities and are echoed in many First Nations relationships with provincial governments. I use a case study approach not to exclude these experiences but to dive deep into one example of a government relationship with Indigenous children in the hope that new ideas about how to implement meaningful reforms for all Indigenous children and families will emerge.

I begin the chapter by setting out INAC/HC's response to the long list of reports and the growing list of legal rulings confirming its discriminatory treatment of First Nations children before identifying issues in federal government politics, INAC/HC bureaucracy, the media, and the public requiring attention and action. Unravelling Canada's puzzling failure to do better when it knows better for First Nations children is key to the full and proper realization of the Royal Commission on Aboriginal Peoples[3] and the Truth and Reconciliation Commission (TRC).[4] I then make recommendations for further study and reform.

CANADA'S WON'T DO/CAN'T DO RELATIONSHIP WITH FIRST NATIONS CHILDREN AND FAMILIES

> The appalling reality is that everyone involved believed they were doing their best and stood firm in their belief that the system was working well. . . . The miracle is that there are not more children lost in this system run by so many well-intentioned people. The road to hell was paved with good intentions and the child welfare system was the paving contractor.
>
> —RCAP, 1996[5]

On 15 November 1907, the front page of the Ottawa *Evening Citizen* featured this chilling headline: "Schools Aid White Plague: Startling Death Rolls Revealed."[6] The article referred to a report by Dr. Peter Henderson Bryce, the chief medical health officer for Indian Affairs, who found that children in residential schools were dying at rates of 24 percent per year from preventable diseases.[7] In one school that Bryce studied, for every three children who walked in, only one walked out alive. Bryce called for increased ventilation in the schools and equitable health-care treatment for First Nations children.[8] In particular, he pointed out that First Nations across Canada received less funding for tuberculosis prevention and treatment than did the less populated city of Ottawa.[9] The cost of Bryce's reforms was estimated to be $10,000 to $15,000. Canada refused to pay.[10]

No one knows for sure who leaked the report to the *Evening Citizen*, but Bryce has been the main suspect. After reading his report, Samuel Hume Blake, a lawyer and judge, said that "doing nothing to obviate the preventable causes of death . . . brings the Department within unpleasant nearness to the charge of manslaughter."[11] As Bryce and Blake demonstrate, some prominent people of the period could clearly see that what Canada was doing was immoral, if not illegal, but too many were silent, and the children continued to die.

Bryce continued to press for reform inside the public service and experienced retaliation as a result before being pushed out of the public service in 1921—the year that Duncan Campbell Scott was serving his term as president of the Royal Society of Canada. A year later Bryce took another stab at awakening the slumbering people of the period to the reckless defiance of the Canadian government. He walked out of the publishing house of James Hope and Sons with his manuscript *The Story of a National Crime*, which detailed the horrendous death rates of children in the residential schools and Canada's failure to act. It cost thirty-five cents. Bryce circulated it to all MPs, to the clergy, and to community members, in the hope that they would be outraged and force the government to act. They were not outraged, and the deaths continued to happen. Bryce died in relative obscurity in 1932. The Truth and Reconciliation Commission estimated that at least 4,000 children died in the schools, and that is likely a gross underestimate.[12]

As historian John Milloy and the final report of the TRC note, Bryce and Blake were not exceptions. Reports of wrongdoing toward children in the schools regularly flowed into Ottawa and were often ignored or minimized. Although occasionally Canada would take some action, it was often perfunctory and inadequate to address the scale of the harm.

In 1946, the Canadian Association of Social Workers (CASW) called on a Special Joint Committee of the Senate and the House of Commons to address the inferior child welfare services provided to "Indian" children and families. Although the official CASW position unfortunately supported assimilation of First Nations children, the association clearly called on Canada to remedy inequities in family support services and living conditions on reserves.[13]

The need to address inequities in services for First Nations children was picked up again during Canada's centennial year. INAC commissioned social worker George Caldwell to report on the conditions of 454 children in nine residential schools in Saskatchewan. He found that 80 percent of children placed in the residential schools that he studied were there for child welfare reasons, yet there was no evidence of services for families so that the children could stay at home.[14] His key recommendation called for INAC "to direct more resources and energy into services for children in their own homes. . . . Where substitute care is required, homes in the Indian community should be helped to provide this service."[15]

The family supports that Caldwell called for were not provided, and few were available in the child welfare systems operated by provinces/territories,[16] resulting in mass removals of First Nations children in what

Patrick Johnston termed "the Sixties Scoop."[17] Noting that in some provinces First Nations, Métis, and Inuit children comprised as much as 60 percent of children in care, even though they accounted for less than 5 percent of the overall child population, Johnston said that "the real problem, in my opinion, is situated in the child welfare system and not in Indigenous families. Given that assumption, where are the shortcomings in child welfare and what changes are needed? To begin, one of the major problems that must be addressed is the issue of culturally inappropriate services and standards."[18] Johnston argued that child welfare standards, based on Western values and experiences, failed to adapt to the cultures and experiences of Indigenous peoples. This mismatch contributed to the failure of Western social workers to account for cultural differences in parenting and the multigenerational impacts of colonization in their assessments of child risk.[19] According to Johnston, the problem was magnified by the federal government's inadequate, and uneven, provision of child and family services to First Nations families on reserves, particularly in regard to the family support services to keep children safely at home that Caldwell had called for twenty-four years earlier.[20]

The cultural identity disruption experienced by children subjected to the non-culturally based services and placements in non-Aboriginal homes during the Sixties Scoop is being borne out in more recent research.[21] It is also being heard in Canadian courts. Sixties Scoop survivors are seeking damages from Canada to pay for services to reclaim their Indigenous identities, family connections, and languages.[22] Although none of the Sixties Scoop class action cases filed by survivors has culminated in a final decision, the courts have ruled that evidence of cultural identity loss can be brought by the plaintiffs in the *Brown v. Attorney General of Canada* case.[23]

Johnston also foreshadowed the problem that would give rise to Jordan's Principle[24] when he described the detrimental effects of jurisdictional squabbling between federal and provincial/territorial governments over First Nations children. Pursuant to the Indian Act, R.S.C., c. 1-5, the federal government has responsibility for "Indians" and "lands reserved for Indians." However, Section 88 of the Indian Act allows for the application of provincial/territorial "general laws of application," including child welfare on reserves. In practice, this means that the federal government funds child welfare and other public services on reserves but that the provinces hold jurisdiction. This jurisdictional split opened the door for a great deal of government buck-passing to avoid costs related to service provision to First Nations children. As Johnston noted, the consequences of these jurisdictional disputes can be linked to the deaths of children deprived of basic child welfare services as provinces refused to provide the services unless the federal government paid for them.[25] As he wrote, "the most appalling aspect of the situation is the fact that those children died essentially because of the quibbling and bickering of the federal and some provincial governments about which one was responsible for providing child welfare services. It is yet another black mark against this country for its treatment of Indigenous people."[26]

In 1981, Johnston made it clear that no further studies were needed—the problems were well known, and so were the solutions: Indigenous peoples must be provided with the support necessary to design and deliver equitable and culturally based services.[27]

Fifteen years after Johnston penned his article, RCAP called on the federal and provincial/territorial governments to provide Aboriginal child and family service agencies with adequate resources and more flexibility.[28] As a child protection worker on the frontlines working with First Nations families dealing with the multigenerational consequences of Canada's residential school policy, I breathed a sigh of relief. It was clear to me and many of my colleagues that child welfare urgently required more culturally based family support services to tackle the problems of poverty, poor housing, and addiction driving First Nations children into foster care at overrepresented rates. The response of INAC to the RCAP child welfare recommendations came in 1997 when it partnered with the Assembly of First Nations to study INAC's First Nations child and family services program (FNCFSP). Under this program, INAC provided funding to First Nations to deliver child welfare services subject to a host of INAC requirements, including that First Nations must use provincial child welfare legislation and standards. Concerned about the mass removals of children by provincial child welfare authorities during the Sixties Scoop, First Nations began operating their own child welfare agencies pursuant to provincial legislation and federal funding as early as the 1970s, and by 2000 there were over 100 such agencies operating across Canada. INAC's funding approach under the FNCFSP has been driven by child population versus service need or child welfare statutory requirements.[29]

INAC and the Assembly of First Nations released a report entitled *First Nations Child and Family Services: Joint National Policy Review (NPR)* in June 2000. It confirmed that First Nations children on reserves received about seventy-eight cents on the dollar in child welfare services compared with children off reserves, despite the higher needs of First Nations children and families owing to the multigenerational impacts of residential schools.[30] The *NPR's* seventeen recommendations for reform echoed those made by Caldwell and Johnston decades earlier, including the need to recognize First Nations jurisdiction in child welfare, create additional funding for prevention services to stem the overrepresentation of First Nations children in care, and address jurisdictional disputes that barred First Nations children from accessing the full range of government services available to other children in Canada.[31] Canada, as represented by INAC, acknowledged the report but failed to act meaningfully on its recommendations, claiming that a more detailed study was required. First Nations children and their families paid the price. According to Brad McKenzie, the number of First Nations children entering child welfare care on reserves increased a staggering 71.5 percent between 1995 and 2001.[32]

In 2004, the Assembly of First Nations and INAC began the more detailed study that INAC said was necessary to implement reform. Completed by over twenty leading experts, including several economists, the *Wen:de* reports were released in 2005.[33] The *Wen:de* reports confirmed that the funding envelope for prevention and agency operations fell about 30 percent below what was needed. Among the specific problems identified was that INAC did not provide funding based on community needs or statutory requirements. INAC also failed to adjust the formula to adapt to best practices and stopped providing an inflation adjustment in 1995, meaning that agencies had 21 percent less purchasing power for services than they had in 1989, when the formula driving the FNCFSP program, named Directive 20-1, was launched. *Wen:de* provided detailed economic reforms on both the level and the structure of funding and warned against piecemeal implementation of the approach given the wide-scale inequities in the FNCFSP program.[34]

Wen:de also recommended the adoption of Jordan's Principle. It is named in memory of Jordan River Anderson of Norway House Cree Nation. He was born in 1999 with complex medical needs, so he had to stay in the hospital until age two, when doctors approved a discharge plan. The plan included his placement with medically trained foster parents near the hospital until his condition further stabilized and he could live with his family in Norway House Cree Nation. If Jordan were a non-Aboriginal child, then the province would have paid for the supports that he needed in the foster home and eventually in his own home. However, he was a First Nations child, so Manitoba took the position that Canada (as represented by INAC and Health Canada) should pay for those supports. The resulting dispute meant that federal officials decided to leave Jordan in the hospital for over two years while they argued over who should pay. Sadly, Jordan died in the hospital at age five, never having spent a day at home. Jordan's Principle is a child-first principle for resolving jurisdictional disputes that aims to ensure that First Nations children can access the government services that they need without adverse differentiation related to their race. The government body of first contact pays for the service and seeks reimbursement of costs after the child gets the service. The House of Commons unanimously passed Motion 251 in support of Jordan's Principle in December 2007, and then federal officials narrowed it so significantly that no child in the country ever qualified. The federal response to Jordan's Principle required that First Nations children have a complex medical need and multiple service providers to receive equitable access to government services. For children who met this narrow definition, Canada applied a nebulous and non-transparent vetting process that required the deputy minister of INAC to proclaim the case a Jordan's Principle case so that a child could receive the services. As of 2016, the government's official position was that no Jordan's Principle case existed, but the *Wen:de* reports revealed 393 cases in a sample of twelve First Nations child and family services agencies.[35]

In 2007, Canada's failure to implement the *Wen:de* report sparked the Assembly of First Nations and the First Nations Child and Family Caring Society of Canada (Caring Society) to file a legal case alleging that Canada's failure to provide equitable child welfare funding and properly to implement Jordan's Principle contravened the Canadian Human Rights Act, R.S.C. 1985, c. H-6. Over the next nine years, Canada, as represented by the attorney general, spent over $10 million on eight[36] failed attempts to have the case dismissed on jurisdictional grounds.

Even as Canada tried to get the case dismissed, evidence of the inequalities in its provision of First Nations child welfare continued to pile up. The auditor general and the Standing Committee on Public Accounts found Canada's provision of First Nations child and family services to be flawed and inequitable.[37] The government's internal documents obtained via access to information or filed as evidence during the tribunal hearings linked the inequalities to the growing overrepresentation of First Nations children in child welfare care. According to government officials, inequitable funding for child welfare created "circumstances that were dire," resulting in growing numbers of children in care and First Nations child and family service agencies being unable to meet provincial child welfare legal standards.[38]

The documents also countered Canada's official position that there were no Jordan's Principle cases,[39] as government officials tracked numerous cases in which First Nations children were being denied public services available to other children.[40] For example, one government document prepared by officials in INAC and Health Canada detailed how First Nations children with disabilities would be able to access only one piece of mobility equipment every five years, whereas their non-Aboriginal peers received the equipment as needed.[41] In another tragic case, federal government officials reviewed a physician's request for a hospital bed for a child so that she would not suffocate. The request passed through the hands of over a dozen officials before someone in Health Canada wrote "absolutely not."[42] The physician bought the bed using his own funds. Stunningly, the federal government held to its public claim that there were no Jordan's Principle cases, even after the Federal Court found Canada's denial of at-home care services to a youth in Nova Scotia to be a Jordan's Principle case.[43]

It is reasonable to assume that the accumulation of convincing evidence would spark the government to fix the inequities. It did not. Instead, Canada appears to have framed the problem as an unfavourable public relations matter and launched a scorched earth litigation approach to silence the complaint. The Canadian Human Rights Tribunal found that the Department of Justice and INAC unlawfully withheld records highly prejudicial to its case,[44] resulting in a pending judgment on obstruction of justice.[45]

In a disturbing echo of Canada's retaliation against Dr. Bryce, Canada also engaged in wilful and reckless retaliation against me by blocking my participation in a meeting between the Chiefs of Ontario and INAC officials.[46] The Office of the Privacy Commissioner of Canada also found that Canada violated the Privacy Act when it deployed over 180 public servants to monitor me with the aim of discrediting the child welfare case.[47]

Despite Canada's vigorous opposition, the Canadian Human Rights Tribunal began hearing the merits of the case in 2013. Over the next eighteen months, twenty-five witnesses, including four experts, testified to over 500 documents. Canada planned on calling an expert witness, KPMG, but dropped it after its expert report found insignificant differences in the calculations of the shortfall in First Nations child and family services funding identified in the *Wen:de* reports.[48]

On 26 January 2016, the Canadian Human Rights Tribunal issued its landmark decision substantiating the complaint by finding INAC's provision of First Nations child and family services and failure to properly implement Jordan's Principle to be discriminatory on the basis of race and national ethnic origin.[49] Specifically, the tribunal found that Canada's inequitable provision of child welfare services incentivized the removal of First Nations children and that Canada's narrow approach to Jordan's Principle ignored cases in which children were denied services because of jurisdictional disputes within the federal government and between the federal government and other governments.[50] The tribunal noted that Canada had failed to fix the flaws in its approaches to child and family services and Jordan's Principle, despite having been aware of them for many years. Overall, the tribunal summed up Canada's defence as "unreasonable, unconvincing and not supported by the preponderance of evidence in this case."[51]

The tribunal ordered Canada to cease immediately its discriminatory conduct in the provision of First Nations child and family services and Jordan's Principle. Canada did nothing until March 2016, when, without consultation with First Nations, it announced $71 million for child and family services in Budget 2016. This amount fell $38 million short of what federal officials had thought was necessary in 2012 and over $130 million short of what the Caring Society said was needed immediately while longer-term reform and equity were implemented. The government was unmoved by the critiques and dug in to defend the $71 million as its response to the tribunal orders even after federal legal submissions to the tribunal revealed that Budget 2016 had been prepared in 2015—months *before* the tribunal delivered its ruling. Following Budget 2016, Canada issued another unilateral announcement, this time on Jordan's Principle. Health Canada and INAC announced "up to" $382 million for Jordan's Principle and then limited the definition to children with "critical short-term illnesses and disabilities." When challenged about why the definition narrowed equitable access to government services to First Nations children with disabilities and short-term illnesses, Canada failed to reply. Instead, it has relied on public relations strategies of seeking commendation for the "over 900" children whom the government is now supposedly helping.[52] None of these public statements mentions anything about the over 162,000 children left out of the government's approach to Jordan's Principle or clarifies that the government is "helping" because it is being forced to do so by legal order.

The public relations approach appears to be unchanged despite evidence of the horrendous impacts of lingering inequitable access on First Nations children. For example, in evidence before the tribunal, federal officials confirmed that Canada does not fund mental health services required under Ontario's Child and Family Services Act, R.S.O. 1990, c. 11, meaning that First Nations children, at higher risk of suicide than other children, are denied mental health services available to other children. This is a clear-cut case of Jordan's Principle in that in sworn testimony the federal government admits that First Nations children are denied a statutory service available to other children. Yet, when the tribunal issued its decision in January 2016, Canada did not take immediate action to remedy the discrimination, even though youth suicides on reserves continued to happen. In its compliance report of 31 October 2016 to the tribunal, Canada explained its failure to provide statutory mental health services in Ontario by saying that "related issues with respect to First Nations children's mental health and funding for Band Representatives are being examined as a part of this review process and also as part of a longer-term engagement and reform process involving national and regional discussions."[53] On 11 January 2017, the ministers of health and Indigenous affairs issued a joint statement sending their condolences to the families of two twelve-year-old girls from the Wapekeka First Nation in Ontario who had died by suicide.[54] In response, Wapekeka released a $376,000 funding proposal for mental health that it had made to Health Canada in July 2016 citing the urgent need to respond to a suicide pact among children in the community. According to Porter and Tasker,[55] a Health Canada official acknowledged receiving the mental health proposal and said that it had come at an "awkward" time in the federal government budget cycle, when all available funds had been allocated. Upon learning of Health Canada's statement, Wapekeka First Nation Band Council member Joshua Frogg said "Awkward? . . . It was awkward to break ground in the permafrost so that we could bury these children. It was awkward for our youth to cry at the funeral."[56] Frogg went on to demand that Health Canada immediately provide mental health services to address the suicidal ideation of other children in the community. Prime Minister Justin Trudeau met with First Nations leaders to listen to their concerns; however, according to Nishnawbe Aski Nation Grand Chief Alvin Fiddler, Trudeau made no commitment to provide services.[57]

Although the condolences of the government of Canada must be acknowledged when First Nations children die, they should not distract from a full and proper assessment of Canada's role in such tragedies. Canada does not kill First Nations children, but the federal government's negligence in remedying public service inequalities means that children are put in situations in which they are more likely to die. A 2017 report by Quebec coroner Bernard Lefrancois found that five suicide deaths among members of the Innu Nations could have been prevented if services to address the factors contributing to suicide were provided: "De l'avis du coroner, le problème majeur de base réside dans le régime d'apartheid dans lequel les Autochtones sont plongés depuis 150 ans sinon plus."[58] Meanwhile, CBC reported that the prime minister dismissed a First Nations chief's question about youth suicide at a town hall meeting indicating that he would talk to her later.[59]

Unsatisfied with Canada's response to its January 2016 order, the Canadian Human Rights Tribunal issued three non-compliance orders against Canada.[60] After the second non-compliance order was issued, in September 2016, Canadian Press journalist Kristy Kirkup asked Prime Minister Trudeau why the federal government was not complying with three legal orders to stop the discrimination. The prime minister said that "no government in history has done more for repairing the relationship with indigenous Canadians and indeed investing in positive outcomes for indigenous Canadians and their communities—$8.4 billion over five years in the last budget," and he went on to say that the government should do better for First Nations kids but didn't take any action.[61]

On 26 October 2016, the Manitoba Legislative Assembly passed a unanimous motion condemning the federal government for its failure to comply with the decisions of the tribunal.[62] A day later MP Charlie Angus (NDP) tabled a motion in the House of Commons to urge the government to abide by the tribunal's orders and stop fighting in court First Nations families trying to get services that their children needed. Dr. Bryce was mentioned in the House of Commons for the first time in decades as First Nations MP Romeo Saganash said that deliberate inaction on the part of [the] government to prevent the deaths of children amounts to manslaughter. Those are not my words. Those are the words of a respected lawyer who examined Dr. Bryce's report in the 1920s. There are key elements to Dr. Bryce's story that are instructive in the case of the 163,000 kids today. First, the government knows about the preventable deaths of children. Second, they have the solutions to fix it. Third, they have chosen not to obey the order of the tribunal to prevent further harm, and in fact [the government] retaliates against and resists those who demand better. Fourth, it can get away with it if members of Parliament allow it. We cannot make the same mistake twice.[63]

After the governing Liberal Party debated against the motion, Senator Murray Sinclair, the former TRC chair, urged all parliamentarians to vote in favour of it since child welfare equity and reform are the top TRC call to action. The moral weight of his call contributed to the Liberal change in position, and on 1 November 2016 the non-binding motion passed unanimously.[64] Three days later the government was back in court fighting a First Nations teenager who required $6,000 in medical treatment so that she could eat and talk without chronic pain. Prior to the hearing, the federal government had spent at least $32,000 fighting her.[65] The $155 million in additional funding called for in the motion never materialized, nor did the proper implementation of Jordan's Principle to ensure that First Nations children can access all government services on the same terms as other children. The whole matter prompted the *Toronto Star* editorial board to note that, "if the government is going to make good on its historic commitment to reconciliation, it will not be enough to rely on its current recipe: promise respect, provide hope, turn the page, repeat."[66]

Repeat indeed. In the wake of the unilateral decision by Canada on Budget 2016 and later on the Jordan's Principle announcement made in July 2016, Canada suggested that its non-compliance can be explained by the need to consult with First Nations peoples. First Nations peoples were saying to implement the tribunal orders immediately, but Canada was not listening. On 31 October 2016, Prime Minister Trudeau stood up in the House of Commons and said that "one of the challenges this House has always faced, that government has always faced, is the fact that dictating the solutions from the government side upon indigenous peoples hasn't worked. Indeed, that has continued to fail."[67] A month later the INAC minister unilaterally appointed a special representative to consult with First Nations while INAC continued to stall on implementation of the tribunal orders and the establishment of a consultation process for child welfare reform proposed by First Nations.[68] In December 2016, the Chiefs in Assembly, representing the vast majority of First Nations across Canada, passed a unanimous resolution at their Special Chiefs Assembly expressing concern about the lack of accountability for the ministerial special representative.[69] The resolution also called on Canada to implement the tribunal orders and the House of Commons motion and to honour First Nations proposals for consultation.[70] The resolution further required the minister to stop making unilateral decisions and to reorient the ministerial special representative's mandate toward reforming INAC internally.[71] Weeks later the minister apparently ignored the resolution—there was no sign of compliance with the tribunal orders, and she continued to send the ministerial representative out to meet with First Nations to find "best practices." Overall, it appears that Canada's use of "consultation with First Nations" varies depending on the aims of the government. INAC has demonstrated an unbridled capacity for unilateral decision making when it suits the government and then uses "consultation" to shield it from acting on directions from First Nations and tribunals/courts. Frustrated by Canada's failure to comply, the Assembly of First Nations, Chiefs of Ontario, Nishnawbe Aski Nation, and Caring Society all filed formal motions of non-compliance with the Canadian Human Rights Tribunal, and they were heard on 22–24 March 2017.[72] These hearings resulted in a further non-compliance order against Canada regarding Jordan's Principle. The tribunal linked Canada's failure to provide equitable services with the deaths of the two twelve-year-old girls in the Wapekeka First Nation, thus thwarting any possibility of preventing the tragedies.[73] Although recently there has been some progress toward compliance with Jordan's Principle at Health Canada, it is important to note that the government has chosen to appeal the parts of the order obliging the government to respond to Jordan's Principle cases in a timely way. INAC continues to dig in to defend its actions toward First Nations children and families despite the mounting legal orders, evidence, and tragedies of its failure to comply. All of this has prompted the United Nations Committee on the Elimination of Racial Discrimination to say that "the Committee is alarmed that despite its previous recommendation (CERD/C/CAN/CO/19-20, para. 19), and multiple decisions by the

Canadian Human Rights Tribunal, less money is reportedly provided to Indigenous children than in other communities and that this gap continues to grow."[74] The tribunal issued a non-compliance order on Canada's implementation of the child and family services matters and an order in 2019 finding Canada's "wilful and reckless" discrimination to be ongoing and worthy of maximum amount of compensation per victim allowable under the Canadian Human Rights Act. Canada has sought a judicial review in Federal Court of the compensation order seeking to quash the tribunal's compensation order.

The foregoing historical overview shows a consistent pattern of recommendations to improve the safety and well-being of First Nations children and families. First coming into sharp focus in Dr. Bryce's 1907 report, the need for service equity has been on the agenda for over a century.[75] Recommendations for Canada to recognize First Nations child welfare jurisdiction date back more than thirty-five years, and calls to increase community-driven prevention services that address poverty, poor housing, and substance abuse have been on the books for over seventy years.[76] Canada has repeatedly either not implemented the recommended reforms or implemented them in a piecemeal fashion. The action nerve centre of the Canadian government has been impervious to repeated reports of the preventable deaths of children in the past and in the present linked to its inequitable treatment of First Nations children. Despite this repeated pattern, Canada has never launched an independent and comprehensive review of INAC's internal operations to pinpoint and address how the department has failed on such a grand scale. In fact, INAC has resisted any attempt to explore its role in the historical and contemporary colonization of Indigenous children by obscuring the factual record using a public relations approach intended to mitigate the department's wrongdoing and withholding of documents.[77] Even during the Truth and Reconciliation Commission, it took an Ontario Superior Court of Justice order to compel Canada to release its records so that the commissioners could better describe Canada's role in residential schools.[78]

Instead, Canada is more apt to view evidence of government wrongdoing as a public relations challenge that warrants one or more of the following responses: (1) minimization of the problem; (2) reframing of the inequity to make government actions appear benevolent; (3) use of official procedures such as studies or alleged consultations to mask inaction; and (4) projection of responsibility for the problem onto others, including First

Nations themselves. Although there is no doubt that First Nations have the ultimate responsibility to care for their children, this responsibility cannot be exercised reasonably when Canada piles on trauma via discriminatory services while rejecting First Nations–driven recommendations for change. Nor can meaningful progress be made toward implementing available solutions mapped out in the RCAP report or other studies on First Nations, Métis, or Inuit children until academic and public attention places INAC's conduct squarely in focus. In the next sections, I touch on the political, bureaucratic, academic, media, and public domains of Canada's conduct that require further scrutiny in order to unravel why Canada perpetuates discrimination against First Nations children.

THE POLITICAL AND BUREAUCRATIC DOMAIN

Justin Trudeau is often viewed as the most Aboriginal-friendly prime minister since Confederation, having committed to full implementation of the TRC calls to action, of which child welfare equity and reform comprise the top recommendation. Yet his response to federal government wrongdoing toward First Nations children is similar to responses offered by generations of politicians before him: protect the government and downplay the harm to children without making any commitment to take the action needed. This approach was evident in the responses by the ministers of INAC and Health Canada to the suicides of the two twelve-year-old girls in northern Ontario described earlier in this chapter. In a similar vein, the minister of INAC appeared on a CBC Radio show in January 2017 to say that she accepted the tribunal's finding that Canada has discriminated against First Nations children but defended, indeed lauded, Canada's response to the decision.[79] In this interview, she attributed the non-compliance orders rendered by the tribunal to miscommunication. When asked when the $155 million promised by Parliament in the November 2016 motion would appear, she refused to pinpoint a date, saying only that the government wants to ensure that the money is spent in the right way before releasing it.[80]

This political narrative is deeply embedded in what Native American legal scholar Robert Williams calls the colonial "civilized" and "savage" dichotomy.[81] The government invokes this dichotomy to create a refined colonial cloak of stereotypes, misinformation, and distraction that enables the systematic violation of Aboriginal peoples' rights in

Canada, including their right to raise happy and healthy children. The cloak does not hide discrimination per se. Rather, it mutes it in plain sight by making the government's conduct seemingly normal, even benevolent. It directs public discourse and government policy away from the government and onto First Nations "capacity building" and "accountability." The INAC minister's suggestion that the government is holding back more money to comply with the tribunal's orders because it wants to ensure that it is well spent is a hallmark of the "civilized" and "savage" dichotomy. It is absurd, and indeed colonial, that the government responsible for racially discriminating against 165,000 children proclaims the right to determine when First Nations are up to spending the money to end the discrimination responsibly.

This type of political cognitive dissonance and government amnesia allows governments to act unethically while proclaiming to be benevolent. Sociologist Zygmunt Bauman suggests that politically headed bureaucracies bend toward unethical conduct by segmenting responsibility for tasks, distancing themselves from the consequences of their dire actions, reframing their wrongdoing as achieving some higher purpose, and placing a high premium on loyalty to the organization.[82] Another enabling feature is hiring people at the top of the organization who are not part of the affected group. INAC has all of these features. It is a large hierarchical bureaucracy nested in colonialism and headed primarily by non-Aboriginal people largely immune from the direct consequences of their actions. INAC and Health Canada documents also tend to detract from the humanity of the children and their families through the use of antiseptic bureaucratic terms, such as "eligible" or "ineligible" child, and by framing the task as program administration instead of service delivery.

The minister is not the first to claim that government financial stewardship requires deferral of equality and justice for First Nations, Métis, and Inuit peoples. In their book *Accounting for Genocide: Canada's Bureaucratic Assault on Aboriginal People*, Neu and Therrien explore INAC's use of funding agreements as a colonial tool.[83] They set out how deeply engrained the stereotype of financial mismanagement as a cultural trait of Indigenous peoples is within INAC and how the department has fed this misconception to its advantage. It is absurd, but this type of discourse works when the public is uninformed. And for decades the Canadian public has been uninformed; however, that is starting to change.

RCAP provided Canada's political leaders with a road map to move away from these colonial philosophies and actions. The failure of Canada to act on those recommendations is played out in its contemporary relationships with First Nations, Métis, and Inuit children. In the absence of sustained, wide-scale, internal reform of the Canadian government, Canada's proclamations of reconciliation will not be backed by action. It is unlikely that the federal government will choose to do this on its own; academics, the media, and the public must therefore demand it, using peaceful direct action.

THE ACADEMIC DOMAIN

We are unique also in this, that two languages have equal recognition and authority in our literature sections, and that the premier place is occupied by the first civilized language heard by the natives of this country, which is forever the pioneer language of ideals in freedom and beauty and in the realm of clear logic, criticism and daring speculation.

—Duncan Campbell Scott, Presidential Address,
Royal Society of Canada, 1922[84]

Academics have a mixed record when it comes to First Nations children and families. On the positive side, Caldwell, Johnston, and RCAP played important roles in identifying the disadvantages faced by First Nations children and their families and pointing to the need to affirm First Nations jurisdiction and provide equitable services to keep children safely at home.

However, scholars charged with studying human rights, law, politics, divinity, social work, and a host of other disciplines either ignored or enabled the residential schools and the diminishment of Indigenous peoples and knowledge. Pointedly, Duncan Campbell Scott was elected president of the Royal Society of Canada in 1922, the same year that Peter Henderson Bryce released his *National Crime* leaflet documenting Scott's refusal to save the lives of children dying in residential schools.[85] Scott's election reflects the cognitive dissonance in the academic community of the period in that there is no evidence, that I am aware of, that his presidency was challenged because of Bryce's revelations. Scott was lauded as the children died. As Ian Mosby notes, researchers were also sometimes directly responsible for harming children in residential schools by depriving them of essential nutrients to determine their effects on the body.[86]

Governments have also used research in the furtherance of their colonial agendas by engaging in unnecessary studies to mask inaction on known problems. This has been true in the case of Canada's relationship with First Nations children. Over the past fifty years, non-Indigenous and Indigenous researchers and consulting groups have accepted government contracts to study First Nations child welfare even when the government has failed to act on known harms documented in previous studies on the same issue. Academics are often willing actors in this government masquerade given the scholastic tendency to discount historical knowledge and the professional rewards for attaining research grants and publishing articles and books.[87] Although Indigenous research codes of ethics[88] help to prevent the type of egregious research that Mosby documented, there is still a need to develop stronger safeguards to prevent the government from using academic research that it commissions to mask its own inaction on known harms. Even more concerning is the absence of any ethical review of Indigenous program evaluations/research activities tendered by the federal government. In my experience, all government-sponsored research and program evaluations would strongly benefit from an independent ethics review mechanism designed and operated by Indigenous peoples. Such mechanisms can ensure alignment of government research/evaluation tenders with the self-determining interests of First Nations peoples and coherence with Indigenous research ethics and methods.

Overall, the academic community must delve into its own complicity with Canada's past and present colonial ideologies and practices and develop safeguards and accountability mechanisms to ensure that it is responsive to, and supportive of, the efforts of Indigenous peoples to care for their children and restore their communities.

THE MEDIA AND PUBLIC DOMAINS

In this particular matter, he [Duncan Campbell Scott] is counting upon the ignorance and indifference of the public to the fate of the Indians; but with the awakening of the health conscience of the people, we are now seeing on every hand, I feel certain that serious trouble will come out of departmental inertia, and I am not personally disposed to have any blame fall upon me.

—Peter Henderson Bryce, 1922[89]

Although Bryce's report was covered in the media briefly, public attention was not sustained, and the children continued to die. Bryce's faith in his fellow citizens was largely, and tragically, misplaced, yet over 100 years later I agree with the authors of the RCAP and TRC reports that his strategy of educating and engaging Canadians in change is essential to pressure governments to improve the safety and well-being of Indigenous children and families.

More than 100 years after Bryce's report was released, has the public awakened to the situation of First Nations children? Somewhat, but not to the degree required to force government compliance with the Canadian Human Rights Tribunal decisions. The rise of Indigenous media has made an important contribution in ensuring that Canada's relationship with Indigenous children is featured regularly, and it has spurred the interest of non-Indigenous media in stories affecting First Nations children.[90] In fact, the Aboriginal Peoples Television Network (APTN) successfully argued in Federal Court for the right to broadcast the Canadian Human Rights Tribunal hearings.[91] APTN's broadcasting of the hearings ensured that low-income First Nations children, youth, and families at the centre of this case could watch the proceedings and participate in an online educational campaign for the case called I Am a Witness.[92] Coverage in mainstream media is critical to expanding public awareness, and directing action, to end the crosscutting inequalities affecting First Nations children. Although the number of mainstream journalists covering Canada's discriminatory conduct toward First Nations children has increased, the coverage, and the public attention, are not proportionate to the harm. When the tribunal ruling was handed down, Indigenous and mainstream media focused on the story for a couple of days, but then it was dropped in favour of frivolous matters such as heckling in Parliament.[93] Indigenous journalist Jorge Barrera suggests that improved media coverage of Indigenous peoples requires journalists to look past "issues" to the underlying and interconnected themes.[94] I agree entirely, and, because many journalists were deprived of a good education on Aboriginal peoples in school, it is essential that professional development programs led by Indigenous media experts be provided to build the capacity of mainstream media to cover these stories.

While progress is made in the media, it is essential that Indigenous organizations reach out to the public directly to provide accurate information on the harms that First Nations children experience, and the available solutions, and to engage the public in peaceful direct action to set things right. Public engagement strategies must be structured in ways that allow a broad cross-section of society, including children themselves, to support First Nations–designed solutions. The First Nations child welfare case inspired the development of a public education and engagement online campaign called I Am a Witness. The campaign website includes legal documents and expert reports by all of the parties to the tribunal, and it invites the public to register to witness the case. Registered witnesses are not asked to take a side in the case; rather, they are left to make up their own minds about whether Canada's conduct toward First Nations children is acceptable or not. To date, there are over 15,000 registered witnesses, making it the most watched human rights case in Canadian history.[95]

Although the public has played an important role in the case, increased public pressure will be required to prompt the government into compliance with the tribunal's orders. The challenge for the Caring Society in both the short term and the longer term will be to leverage the I Am a Witness campaign into a stronger movement. Just as in Dr. Bryce's time, so too it is the people of the period who can ultimately force the government to make the changes needed. The historical record reveals that, absent public pressure, it is highly unlikely that the Canadian government will take meaningful action on its own.

CONCLUSION

World Health Organization Director-General Dr. Margaret Chan said that "social injustice is killing on a grand scale,"[96] and it is not an overstatement to suggest that Canada's flawed and inequitable provision of public services to First Nations children and families on reserves exemplifies the tragedy.[97] Moreover, the continuance of these inequalities places First Nations children in positions in which their safety and well-being are impoverished and they are more likely to die.

The federal government's conscious decision to perpetuate inequitable public services on reserves undermines the safety and well-being of First

Nations children and their families. The deaths of children related to service denials have not been enough to spur governments of the past[98] or present[99] fully to implement available solutions and stop this wave of devastation. Governments have rarely helped the children, yet they have consistently protected themselves, and academics, the media, and the public have let them get away with it. We need to up our game collectively and hold the government accountable for its conscious refusal to expand jurisdictional models to affirm First Nations jurisdiction, provide equitable and flexible funding for culturally based services that target family poverty, housing, and addiction, and account for historical trauma. Although continued study of First Nations interventions is encouraged, if we are serious about reforming child welfare, then it is time to place federal/provincial/territorial governments that fail to do better when they know better in the crosshairs of investigations, debates, and social movements.

As Dr. Bryce warned in 1907, public ignorance and indifference feed wayward government policy. An aware and engaged public is this generation of First Nations children's best hope. Let's not let them down.

NOTES

1   Auditor General of Canada, *Fall Reports*.
2   RCAP, *Children Are Our Future*.
3   Erasmus and Dussault, *Report of the Royal Commission on Aboriginal Peoples*.
4   TRC, *Honouring the Truth*.
5   Erasmus and Dussault, *Report of the Royal Commission on Aboriginal Peoples*, Vol. 3, 2.2, 26.
6   "Schools Aid White Plague: Startling Death Rolls Revealed," *Evening Citizen* [Ottawa], 15 November 1907, 1.
7   Bryce, *Report on the Indian Schools*.
8   Bryce, *Report on the Indian Schools*, 18–19.
9   Bryce, *The Story of a National Crime*, 13.
10   Titley, *A Narrow Vision*, 83.
11   Quoted in Milloy, *A National Crime*, 77.
12   TRC, *Honouring the Truth*, 93.
13   Special Joint Committee, 1946, 158–59.
14   Caldwell, *Indian Residential Schools*, 67.
15   Caldwell, Indian Residential Schools, 149.
16   Aboriginal Justice Implementation Commission, 2001.
17   Johnston, *Native Children*, 47.
18   Johnston, "Indigenous Children," 48.
19   Johnston, "Indigenous Children," 48.
20   Johnston, "Indigenous Children," 48.
21   Carrière, "Community and Culture"; Sinclair, "Identity Lost."
22   *Brown v. Attorney General of Canada*, 2014 ONSC 6967.
23   *Brown v. Attorney General of Canada*, 2014 ONSC 6967.

24   Jordan's Principle is a child-first principle for resolving jurisdictional disputes within
      and between federal and provincial governments to ensure that all First Nations children
      can access government services on the same terms as other children. It applies to Inuit
      and Métis children to the extent that they receive services from the federal government
      as well.

25   Johnston, "Indigenous Children," 49.

26   Johnston, "Indigenous Children," 49.

27   Johnston, "Indigenous Children," 49.

28   RCAP, *Children Are Our Future.*

29   Auditor General of Canada, *First Nations Child and Family Services Program.*

30   Macdonald and Ladd, *First Nations Child and Family Services,* 92.

31   Macdonald and Ladd, *First Nations Child and Family Services,* 92.

32   McKenzie, *Block Funding,* 19–20.

33   Blackstock et al., *Wen:de;* Loxley et al., *Wen:de.*

34   Blackstock et al., *Wen:de;* Loxley et al., *Wen:de.*

35   Loxley et al., *Wen:de,* 16.

36   Department of Justice invoices, Access to Information Requests A-2013-00464, A-2014-
      01467.

37   Auditor General of Canada, *Programs for First Nations on Reserves,* Ch. 4; Standing.
      Committee on Public Accounts, "First Nations Child and Family Services Program,"
      Ch. 4.

38   INAC, "First Nations Child and Family Services." ·

39   CBC News, "First Nations Children Still Face Delays."

40   Blackstock, "Social Movements and the Law."

41   INAC and Health Canada, "Terms of Reference."

42   Canada, "Jordan's Principle."

43   *Pictou Landing Band Council and Maurina Beadle v. Attorney General of Canada,* FC
      342 (2013).

44   *First Nations Child and Family Caring Society of Canada et al. v. Attorney General of
      Canada,* 2013 CHRT 16.

45   *First Nations Child and Family Caring Society of Canada et al. v. Attorney General of
      Canada,* 2016 CHRT 2.

46   *First Nations Child and Family Caring Society of Canada et al. v. Attorney General
      of Canada,* 2015 CHRT 14.

47   Office of the Privacy Commissioner of Canada, *Securing the Right to Privacy.*

48   KPMG LLP, "Indian and Northern Affairs Canada."

49   *First Nations Child and Family Caring Society of Canada et al. v. Attorney General of
      Canada,* 2016 CHRT 2.

50   *First Nations Child and Family Caring Society of Canada et al. v. Attorney General of
      Canada,* 2016 CHRT 2, paras. 349, 391.

51   *First Nations Child and Family Caring Society of Canada et al. v. Attorney General of
      Canada,* 2016 CHRT 2, para. 460.

52   Canada, "Government of Canada."

53   INAC, "Statement on the Canadian Human Rights," 9.

54   Kirkup, "Libs to Support Angus Motion."

55   Porter and Tasker, "Wapekeka First Nations."

56   Quoted in Talaga and Ballingall, "Trudeau Meets with Ontario Indigenous Leaders."

57   Talaga and Ballingall, "Trudeau Meets with Ontario Indigenous Leaders."

58   Bureau du coroner Québec, "Dépôt du rapport d'enquête publique du coroner." English
      translation: In the opinion of the coroner, the major problem resides with the apartheid
      regime which Aboriginal peoples have been immersed in for over 150 years.

59   Margison, "Trudeau Gets an Earful."

60   *First Nations Child and Family Caring Society of Canada et al. v. Attorney General of Canada*, 2016 CHRT 10; *First Nations Child and Family Caring Society of Canada et al. v. Attorney General of Canada*, 2016 CHRT 16.

61   Quoted in Kirkup, "Libs to Support Angus Motion."

62   Manitoba Legislative Assembly, *Debates and Proceedings*, 41st Legislature, 1st Session, 26 October 2016, https://www.gov.mb.ca/legislature/hansard/41st_1st/hansardpdf/50.pdf.

63   Canada, House of Commons, *House of Commons Debates*, 42nd Parliament, 1st Session, 148 (99), 6247, para. 1650.

64   Kirkup, "Libs to Support Angus Motion."

65   Department of Justice, Access to Information A-2016-00627/SH.

66   *Toronto Star* Editorial Board, "On Indigenous Child Welfare."

67   Quoted in Galloway, "Liberals to Support NDP Motion."

68   AFN, Special Chiefs Assembly, Resolution 83/2016.

69   AFN, National Advisory Committee on INAC's Child Welfare Reform Engagement Strategy, Resolution 83/2016.

70   AFN, National Advisory Committee on INAC's Child Welfare Reform Engagement Strategy, Resolution 83/2016, 3.

71   AFN, National Advisory Committee on INAC's Child Welfare Reform Engagement Strategy, Resolution 83/2016, 4.

72   *First Nations Child and Family Caring Society of Canada et al. v. Attorney General of Canada*, 2017 CHRT 14.

73   *First Nations Child and Family Caring Society of Canada et al. v. Attorney General of Canada*, 2016 CHRT 10; *First Nations Child and Family Caring Society of Canada et al. v. Attorney General of Canada*, 2017 CHRT 14, paras. 88–92.

74   United Nations Committee on the Elimination of Racial Discrimination, *Concluding Observations*, 8, para. 27.

75   Bryce, *Report on the Indian Schools.*

76   Johnston, "Indigenous Children at Risk"; Macdonald and Ladd, *First Nations Child and Family Services*; RCAP, *Children Are Our Future*; Special Joint Committee of the Senate and the House of Commons, 1946, 158–59.

77   *First Nations Child and Family Caring Society of Canada v. Attorney General of Canada*, 2013 CHRT 16.

78   *Fontaine v. Canada*, 2013 ONSC 684.

79   CBC News, "First Nations Child Welfare."

80   CBC News, "First Nations Child Welfare."

81   Williams, *Savage Anxieties.*

82   Bauman, *Modernity and the Holocaust.*

83   Neu and Therrien, *Accounting for Genocide.*

84   Scott, "Poetry and Progress," xlix.

85   Bryce, *Report on the Indian Schools.*

86   Mosby, "Administering Colonial Science," 147.

87   Blackstock, "The Emergence of the Breath of Life Theory."

88   CIHR, "CIHR Guidelines."

89   Bryce, *The Story of a National Crime*, 6.

90   Journalists for Human Rights, *Buried Voices.*

91   *APTN v. Canada (Human Rights Commission)*, 2011 FC 810, para. 3.

92   Blackstock, "Social Movements and the Law," 13.

93   Blackstock, "Social Movements and the Law," 13.

94   Barrera, "Expert Opinion," 11–12.

95 Blackstock, "Social Movements and the Law," 6.

96 Chan, "Inequities Are Killing People."

97 Bryce, *The Story of a National Crime*; Milloy, *A National Crime*; TRC, *Honouring the Truth*.

98 Bryce, *Report on the Indian Schools*.

99 Porter and Tasker, "Wapekeka First Nations."

REFERENCES

Aboriginal Justice Implementation Commission. "Child Welfare." Chapter 14 of *Aboriginal Justice Inquiry*, 487–526. Winnipeg: Statutory Publications, 2001. http://www.ajic. mb.ca/volume.html.

APTN v. Canada (Human Rights Commission), 2011 FC 810.

Assembly of First Nations (AFN). National Advisory Committee on INAC's Child Welfare Reform Engagement Strategy. Resolution 83/2016, passed 2016.

Auditor General of Canada. *First Nations Child and Family Services Program—Indian and Northern Affairs Canada: 2008 May Report of the Auditor General of Canada*.

——. *Programs for First Nations on Reserves: 2011 June Status Report of the Auditor General of Canada*. http://www.oag-bvg.gc.ca/internet/English/parl_oag_201106_e_35354.html.

——. *Fall Reports: Auditor General of Canada*. 2016. http://www.oag-bvg.gc.ca/internet/English/parl_oag_201611_00_e_41829.html.

Bauman, Zygmunt. *Modernity and the Holocaust*. New York: Cornell University Press, 1989.

Barrera, Jorge. "Expert Opinion: Jorge Barrera." In *Buried Voices, Changing Tones: An Examination of Media Coverage of Indigenous Issues in Ontario, Media Monitoring Report 2013–2016*, 11–12. Toronto: Journalists for Human Rights, 2016.

Blackstock, Cindy. "The Emergence of the Breath of Life Theory." *Journal of Social Work Values and Ethics* 8, no. 1 (2011).

——. "Expert Analysis: Cindy Blackstock." In *Buried Voices, Changing Tones: An Examination of Media Coverage of Indigenous Issues in Ontario, Media Monitoring Report 2013–2016*, 13–15. Toronto: Journalists for Human Rights, 2016a.

——. "Social Movements and the Law: Addressing Engrained Government-Based Racial Discrimination against Indigenous Children." *Australian Law Review* 19, no. 1 (2016b): 6–19.

Blackstock, C., T. Prakash, J. Loxley, and F. Wien. *Wen:de: We are Coming to the Light of Day*. Ottawa: First Nations Child and Family Caring Society of Canada, 2005.

Brown v. Attorney General of Canada, 2014 ONSC 6967.

Bryce, Peter Henderson. *Report on the Indian Schools of Manitoba and the North-West Territories*. Ottawa: Department of Indian Affairs, 1907.

——. *The Story of a National Crime: Being an Appeal for Justice for the Indians of Canada*. Ottawa: James Hope and Sons, 1922.

Bureau du coroner Québec. "Dépôt du rapport d'enquête publique du coroner: 14 janvier 2017." https://www.coroner.gouv.qc.ca/medias/communiques/detail-dun-communique/depot-du-rapport-denquete-publique-du-coroner-1.html.

Caldwell, George. *Indian Residential Schools: A Research Study of the Child Care Programs of Nine Residential Schools in Saskatchewan*. Ottawa: Department of Indian Affairs and Northern Development, 1967.

Canada. "Jordan's Principle: Case Conferencing to Case Resolution." Federal/Provincial Intake Form, 2012. Canadian Human Rights Commission Exhibit 420, CHRT 1340/7008.

——. "Government of Canada Focused on Making a Difference for First Nations Children and

Families." 2016. http://news.gc.ca/web/article-en.do?nid=1143619&tp=980.

——. House of Commons. *House of Commons Debates*, 148 (99), 42nd Parliament, 1st session, 2016.

——. Canada, Special Joint Committee of the Senate and the House of Commons Appointed to Examine and Consider The Indian Act. *Minutes of Proceedings and Evidence*. Ottawa, 1946–1949.

Canadian Institutes for Health Research (CIHR). "CIHR Guidelines for Health Research Involving Aboriginal People (2007–2010)." 2013. http://www.cihr-irsc.gc.ca/e/29134. html.

Carrière, Jeannine. "Community and Culture: The Heart of the YTSA Open and Custom Adoption Program." In *Aski Awasis: Children of the Earth—First Peoples Speaking on Adoption*, edited by Jeannine Carrière, 125–28. Winnipeg: Fernwood Publishers, 2010.

CBC News. "First Nations Children Still Face Delays in Accessing Health Care: Report." 2015. https://www.cbc.ca/news/canada/manitoba/first-nations-children-still-face-delays-in-accessing-health-care-report-1.2951750

——. "First Nations Child Welfare." 2017. http://www.cbc.ca/news/canada/ottawa/programs/ottawamorning/first-nations-child-welfare-1.3927221.

Chan, Margaret. "Inequities Are Killing People on a Grand Scale Reports WHO Commission." 2008. http://www.who.int/mediacentre/news/releases/2008/pr29/en/.

Department of Indian and Northern Affairs Canada (INAC). "First Nations Child and Family Services (FNCFS) Q's and A's." N.d. Access to Information request 2365-70.

——. "Fact Sheet: First Nations Child and Family Services." 2006. https://fncaringsociety.com/sites/default/files/docs/Fact-Sheet-FN-Child-Family-Services-Indian-Northern-Affairs.pdf.

Department of Indigenous and Northern Affairs and Department of Justice. "Statement on the Canadian Human Rights Tribunal Decision on First Nations Child and Family Services." 2016. http://news.gc.ca/web/article-en.do?nid=1029679.

Department of Justice. Access to Information request A-2016-00627/SH, 2016.

Erasmus, Georges, and Réne Dussault. *Report of the Royal Commission on Aboriginal Peoples*. Ottawa: The Commission, 1996.

First Nations Child and Family Caring Society of Canada et al. v. Attorney General of Canada, 2013 CHRT 16.

First Nations Child and Family Caring Society of Canada et al. v. Attorney General of Canada, 2015 CHRT 14.

First Nations Child and Family Caring Society of Canada et al. v. Attorney General of Canada, 2016 CHRT 2.

First Nations Child and Family Caring Society of Canada et al. v. Attorney General of Canada, 2016 CHRT 10.

First Nations Child and Family Caring Society of Canada et al. v. Attorney General of Canada, 2016 CHRT 16.

First Nations Child and Family Caring Society of Canada et al. v. Attorney General of Canada, 2017 CHRT 35.

Fontaine v. Canada, 2013 ONSC 684.

Galloway, Gloria. "Liberals to Support NDP Motion on First Nations Child Welfare." *Globe and Mail*, 31 October 2016.

INAC and Health Canada. "Terms of Reference: Officials Working Group, May 2009." *CHRC Tab 302, First Nations Child and Family Caring Society of Canada et al. v. Attorney General of Canada*, CHRT 1340/7008.

Johnston, Patrick. "Indigenous Children at Risk: Child Welfare Services Need Radical Changes." *Ipolitics*, November–December 1981. http://policyoptions.irpp.org/magazines/july-2016/revisiting-the-sixties-scoop-of-indigenous-children/.

——. *Native Children and the Child Welfare System*. Toronto: James Lorimer, 1983.

Journalists for Human Rights. *Buried Voices, Changing Tones: An Examination of Media Coverage of Indigenous Issues in Ontario, Media Monitoring Report 2013–2016*. Toronto: Journalists for Human Rights, 2016.

Kirkup, Kristy. "Libs to Support Angus Motion on First Nations Child Welfare." *Ipolitics*, 31 October 2016. http://ipolitics.ca/2016/10/31/libs-to-support-angus-motion-on-first-nations-child-welfare/.

——. "Ontario Grand Chief Urges Federal Action after Suicides of Two Girls." *Globe and Mail*, 11 January 2017. https://beta.theglobeandmail.com/news/national/ontario-grand-chief-urges-federal-action-after-suicides-of-two-girls/article33590643/?ref=http://www.theglobeandmail.com&.

KPMG LLP. "Indian and Northern Affairs Canada: Review of *Wen:de: The Journey Continues*." Exhibit 249 filed at the Canadian Human Rights Tribunal for T-1340/7708.

Loxley, John, et al. *Wen:de: The Journey Continues*. Ottawa: First Nations Child and Family Caring Society of Canada, 2005.

Macdonald, Rose-Alma, and Peter Ladd. *First Nations Child and Family Services: Joint National Policy Review*. Ottawa: AFN and Department of Indian and Northern Affairs Development, 2000.

Manitoba Legislative Assembly. *Legislative Assembly of Manitoba: Debates and Proceedings*, LXIX, 50, 26 October 2016.

Margison, Amanda. "Trudeau Gets an Earful from Veteran, Chiefs, Disabled Participant in London, Ont." CBC News, 14 January 2017. http://www.cbc.ca/news/canada/windsor/trudeau-townhall-politics-1.3935973.

McKenzie, Brad. *Block Funding Child Maintenance in First Nations Child and Family Services: A Policy Review*. Report prepared for Kahnawake Shakotiia'takehnhas Community Services, Winnipeg, 2002.

Milloy, John. *A National Crime: The Canadian Government and the Residential School System—1879 to 1986*. Winnipeg: University of Manitoba Press, 1999.

Mosby, Ian. "Administering Colonial Science: Nutrition Research and Human Biochemical Experimentation in Aboriginal Communities and Residential Schools, 1942–1952." *Social History* 46, no. 91 (2013): 145–72.

Neu, Dean, and Richard Therrien. *Accounting for Genocide: Canada's Bureaucratic Assault on Aboriginal People*. Blackpoint: Fernwood Publishing, 2003.

Office of the Privacy Commissioner of Canada. *Securing the Right to Privacy: Annual Report to Parliament 2012–2013*. Ottawa: Office of the Privacy Commissioner of Canada, 2013.

Pictou Landing Band Council and Maurina Beadle v. Attorney General of Canada, 2013 FC 342.

Porter, Jody, and John Paul Tasker. "Wapekeka First Nations Asked for Suicide-Prevention Months before Deaths of 2 Girls." CBC News, 19 January 2017. http://www.cbc.ca/news/canada/thunder-bay/wapekeka-suicides-health-canada-1.3941439.

Royal Commission on Aboriginal Peoples (RCAP). *Children Are Our Future*. 1996. https://www.aadnc-aandc.gc.ca/eng/1100100014597/1100100014637#chp5.

Saganash, Romeo. "Indigenous Affairs." In *House of Commons Debates*, 148(099), 42nd Parliament, 1st Session. http://www.parl.gc.ca/HousePublications/Publication.aspx?Language=E&Mode=1&DocId=8546490.

Scott, Duncan Campbell "Poetry and Progress." In *Royal Society of Canada Annual Report (1922)*, L–LXVII. Ottawa: Royal Society of Canada, 1922.

Sinclair, Raven. "Identity Lost and Found: Lessons from the Sixties Scoop." *First Peoples Child and Family Review* 3, no. 1 (2007): 65–82.

Standing Committee on Public Accounts. "Chapter 4: First Nations Child and Family Services Program—Indian and Northern Affairs Canada." In *May 2008 Report of the Auditor General: Report of the Standing Committee on Public Accounts.* http://www.fncaringsociety.com/docs/402_PACP_Rpt07-e.pdf.

Talaga, Tanya, and Alex Ballingall. "Trudeau Meets with Ontario Indigenous Leaders in Wake of Girls' Suicides." *Toronto Star,* 19 January 2017. https://www.thestar.com/news/canada/2017/01/19/trudeau-meets-with-ontario-indigenous-leaders-in-wake-of-girls-suicides.html.

Titley, Brian *A Narrow Vision: Duncan Campbell Scott and the Administration of Indian Affairs in Canada.* Vancouver: UBC Press, 1986.

Toronto Star Editorial Board. "On Indigenous Child Welfare: The Liberals' Symbols Are Souring." *Toronto Star,* 6 November 2016. https://www.thestar.com/opinion/editorials/2016/11/06/on-indigenous-child-welfare-the-liberals-symbols-are-souring-editorial.html.

Truth and Reconciliation Commission (TRC) of Canada. *Honouring the Truth, Reconciling for the Future: Summary of the Final Report of the Truth and Reconciliation Commission of Canada.* Winnipeg: TRC, 2015.

United Nations Committee on the Elimination of Racial Discrimination. *Concluding Observations on the Twenty-First to Twenty-Third Periodic Reports of Canada.* Geneva: United Nations Committee on the Elimination of Racial Discrimination, 2017.

Williams, Robert. *Savage Anxieties: The Invention of Western Civilization.* New York City: St. Martin's Publishing Group, 2012.

CHAPTER 17

THE ART OF HEALING AND RECONCILIATION:
FROM TIME IMMEMORIAL THROUGH RCAP, THE TRC, AND BEYOND

Jonathan Dewar

> I've always believed that the art object itself cannot heal. For me, the process of creating art is a process of healing for myself. The object itself, the result, is not a healer, but it could be a trigger, a trigger for somebody else to consider their own situation, in their own context.
> —Adrian Stimson[1]

INTRODUCTION

October 2016 saw the fiftieth anniversary of the death of twelve-year-old Chanie Wenjack and with it the release of a handful of creative responses, including Gord Downie's album *Secret Path*, Joseph Boyden's novella *Wenjack*, illustrated by Kent Monkman, and Terril Calder's short animated film *Snip*. It was a season of anniversaries. The June and November 2016 Sharing the Land, Sharing a Future forums (Calgary and Winnipeg, respectively) celebrated the twentieth anniversary of the release of the report of the Royal Commission on Aboriginal Peoples (RCAP) "and our experience of the intervening twenty years to advance good relations and develop a shared responsibility for the future."[2] The context at that forum also built on the unprecedented attention that residential schools and the broader colonial context received during the recently concluded mandate of the Truth and Reconciliation Commission (TRC) of Canada, which released its ninety-four calls to action on 2 June 2015 and its final report on 15 December 2015. These, too, are dates that we will mark. Through RCAP and the TRC, we have been able to argue at each step that the spotlight on residential schools, truth, healing, and reconciliation was arguably never brighter. And, throughout, there has been a compelling argument that artists and curators have been the principal wielders of that spotlight. But they did not start this work in 1996. Or in 1990 in the wake of the Oka resistance, which spawned the 1991–95 Royal Commission on Aboriginal Peoples.

Or in response to the 1969 White Paper.

Or. . . .

In truth, there is no starting point. Indigenous peoples have been engaged in truth, healing, and reconciliation (this one is more complicated) since time immemorial, and "art" has always been an integral part.

This chapter is only an entry point into the subject of First Nations, Inuit, and Métis art and creativity. It should go without saying that this broad topic is really a book, a course, a multiyear study. And even then they are mere entry points. A full exploration of Indigenous art and creativity in Canada is a life's work, and here I humbly defer to the many artists, curators, scholars, and other cultural producers living that work; I mention a handful within this chapter but implore readers to follow the trail back to their works, the contexts in which they practise, and the worlds that they inhabit—wherein one will discover many more makers and knowledge holders—and beyond.

ART AND HEALING: FROM TIME IMMEMORIAL

In 2009, I was privileged to work with Linda Archibald to develop a research project for the Aboriginal Healing Foundation (1998–2014)[3] that explored how community-based healing initiatives (projects) funded by the foundation incorporated art and/or creative practices; this work spawned numerous publications with several other collaborators, from which I draw for this section. We had this assumption—"Indigenous approaches include arts and culture in a holistic model of healing that encompasses the physical, emotional, intellectual, and spiritual world"[4]—in mind when we asked "What happens when art, music, dance, storytelling, and other creative arts become a part of community-based Aboriginal healing programs?"

Both the literature and our respondents overwhelmingly indicated that Indigenous societies have acknowledged the healing power of art, dance, music, dramatic re-enactment, and storytelling for millennia—and they continue to do so today because "Indigenous approaches include arts and culture in a holistic model of healing that encompasses the physical, emotional, intellectual, and spiritual world."[5] As one respondent said, "For Aboriginal people, arts and crafts have always been an intrinsic part of our communal culture. We used art in every part of our daily lives; from making clothing to decorating ceremonial objects."[6]

Although our focus was on what communities were choosing in a contemporary context, part of that context, and thus a focus within their approaches, was the notion of "historical trauma." The term is used to describe the impacts of serious and painful losses on a people over time and across generations. It is a collective form of post-traumatic stress disorder embedded in the history of what Aboriginal people in North America have experienced and endured.[7] According to Cynthia Wesley-Esquimaux and Magdalena Smolewski, historical trauma can be defined as follows: "A new model is being introduced for trauma transmission and healing, citing the presence of complex or endemic post-traumatic stress disorder in Aboriginal culture, which originated as a direct result of historic trauma transmission (HTT). A variety of disciplines, including history, anthropology, psychology, psychiatry, sociology and political science, are called upon to illuminate the model of historic trauma transmission and provide different perspectives and information on how historic trauma can be understood as a valid source of continuing dis-ease and reactivity to historical and social forces in Aboriginal communities."[8] Many respondents drew parallels between the traditional knowledge held by individuals and communities and the knowledge expressed by contemporary practitioners of various healing modalities. Respondents acknowledged that art can be a tool for creatively transforming pain and trauma into something new and, in the process, contributing to feelings of personal mastery, self-esteem, and resilience and that art making provides an indirect means of addressing experiences too painful to approach directly.[9] Mohawk artist and activist Ellen Gabriel spoke about art as "a non-threatening form of expression that can spark discussion, curiosity.... [It] can convey a message which can introduce an issue without necessarily overwhelming the audience."[10]

Our major findings were as follows. When given the opportunity to design their own initiatives, Aboriginal communities overwhelmingly chose to include the arts, and those approaches can be characterized as follows: (1) acknowledging the innate healing power of creativity (creative arts as healing); (2) using the arts in the therapeutic process (creative arts in therapy); and (3) understanding that a holistic approach to healing includes creative arts, culture, and spirituality within its very definition (holistic healing includes creative arts).

RECONCILIATION

Charles Hauss wrote that in the past few years "reconciliation has become one of the 'hottest topics' in the increasingly 'hot' field of conflict resolution."[11] To be sure, one need only conduct a simple Google search of scholarly works that feature *reconciliation* and *Canada* as keywords to see that there has been a recent proliferation of new works focusing on reconciliation in the Canadian context. But how did we get *here*, and more importantly, what exactly are we doing *here*? It is the *doing* that is essential—and Canadian artists and theorists are at the forefront of engaging with both the theory and, much more importantly, the practice of reconciliation. This is not to say that the arts offer the definitive answers; rather, artists are highlighting the complexities of asking how one practises reconciliation, since many, including T.A. Boer[12] and David Gaertner,[13] argue that reconciliation is difficult—if not impossible—to define. Gaertner and I, along with other colleagues, also problematized this notion in research that we conducted for the Truth and Reconciliation Commission. As we noted, "the act of reconciliation is itself deeply complicated, and that success should not be measured by *achieving* a putative reconciliation but by movement toward these lofty goals. Indeed it could be proposed that full reconciliation is both mercurial and impossible, and that the efforts of theorists, artists, Survivors, and the various publics engaged in this difficult process are best focused on working collaboratively for better understanding of our histories, our traumas and ourselves."[14]

In this chapter, I present an overview of how artists and scholars are challenging the very definition of reconciliation as well as inviting others to reflect critically on the meanings of and relationships between art and healing, commemoration, and memorialization. The findings discussed throughout the chapter arise from a substantial literature review that led to conversations with a number of artists and scholars who have engaged the themes at play within the context of the TRC work and all that preceded it in and through their art.

WHERE ARE WE?

The intense spotlight of RCAP and the TRC should forever have removed any notion that the history and legacy of Indian residential schools and the tremendous damage that they did to Canada's Indigenous peoples between the early 1800s and 1996[15] are in any way hidden. Whereas Trudy Govier observed that Canada has tended to turn away from residential schools and other events of its colonial history because the stories "are unpleasant and incompatible with the favoured picture we have of ourselves, and they imply a need for restitution and redress, threatening our rather comfortable way of life,"[16] we have seen more recently unprecedented coverage in the mainstream media and in educational curricula. Govier's point was that we all must acknowledge that, "through patterns of colonization, land use, racism, disregard for treaties, and the residential school system, we are linked significantly to the institutions that are responsible.... We share responsibility for these things," and we "are beneficiaries of the injustices."[17] Although the latter cannot be said to have been definitively established, the conversation is well under way, and it is robust, with many new voices joining in and challenging our notions of what it means to inhabit this space/place that we call Canada.

The legacies of residential schools were first meaningfully illuminated at the grassroots level during the late 1970s and early 1980s. During that time, former students, or survivors, came together in support of health and healing, and over time much broader social movement support grew as Aboriginal communities began to demand and receive apologies from churches that had run particular schools.[18] As Emma LaRocque notes in her book *When the Other Is Me: Native Resistance Discourse, 1850–1990*, while engagement with residential schools became more and more prominent in art, literature, and scholarship from the 1980s onward, concepts of healing and reconciliation began to develop and evolve alongside political and personal activism.[19] Healing, in particular, became well defined in grassroots efforts as well as government initiatives. Needless to say, the various healing initiatives and movements have become inextricably woven into the experiences of individuals as well as the institutional and societal efforts to address the legacies of residential schools. In fact, one can argue that healing initiatives and movements are among the few positive legacies of residential schools often overshadowed by the many more painful and destructive legacies.

The issue of residential schools came to unprecedented national prominence in 1996 with the release of the RCAP report, which raised deep and sometimes deeply troubling questions about the past and present experiences and realities of Canada's Aboriginal peoples.[20] The negative impacts of the residential school experience for survivors and their descendants loomed large throughout the RCAP report, and the many shocking details led to a federal policy document entitled *Gathering Strength: Canada's Aboriginal Action Plan.* It supported the creation of the Aboriginal Healing Foundation (AHF), a national, Aboriginal-managed, not-for-profit corporation. The AHF was established through a government grant of $350 million in 1998 and given an eleven-year mandate to encourage community-based, Aboriginal-directed healing initiatives that would address the legacy of physical and sexual abuse suffered in the residential school system and its intergenerational impacts.[21]

By 2005, survivors and groups representing their interests were taking legal action to force the federal government to offer an official apology and to compensate survivors. Individual lawsuits against the government, churches, and perpetrators grew in number, as did class action lawsuits. This wave of activity led to negotiations that culminated in 2007 with a finalized agreement for the multi-billion-dollar Indian Residential Schools Settlement Agreement (IRSSA). Two components of the IRSSA in particular received significant (and often negative) mainstream attention: compensation[22] and the creation of a Truth and Reconciliation Commission.[23] There were two funds within the IRSSA: the Commemoration Fund ($40 million), to be distributed through a process of proposal adjudication by the TRC and Aboriginal Affairs and Northern Development Canada, and the Healing Fund, which directed an additional $125 million to the AHF to continue funding existing projects until 31 March 2012.[24] Despite these developments, the legacy of residential schools rose to national

prominence only on 11 June 2008 when Prime Minister Stephen Harper
delivered an official apology in the House of Commons:

> For more than a century, Indian Residential Schools separated over
> 150,000 Aboriginal children from their families and communi-
> ties. In the 1870's, the federal government, partly in order to meet
> its obligation to educate Aboriginal children, began to play a role in
> the development and administration of these schools. Two primary
> objectives of the Residential Schools system were to remove and
> isolate children from the influence of their homes, families, tradi-
> tions and cultures, and to assimilate them into the dominant culture.
> These objectives were based on the assumption [that] Aboriginal
> cultures and spiritual beliefs were inferior and unequal. Indeed,
> some sought, as it was infamously said, "to kill the Indian in the child."
> Today, we recognize that this policy of assimilation was wrong, has
> caused great harm, and has no place in our country.... The Govern-
> ment of Canada built an educational system in which very young
> children were often forcibly removed from their homes, often taken
> far from their communities. Many were inadequately fed, clothed
> and housed. All were deprived of the care and nurturing of their
> parents, grandparents and communities. First Nations, Inuit and
> Métis languages and cultural practices were prohibited in these
> schools. Tragically, some of these children died while attending resi-
> dential schools and others never returned home.... The burden of
> this experience has been on your shoulders for far too long. The
> burden is properly ours as a Government, and as a country. There
> is no place in Canada for the attitudes that inspired the Indian Resi-
> dential Schools system to ever prevail again. You have been working
> on recovering from this experience for a long time and in a very real
> sense, we are now joining you on this journey. The Government of
> Canada sincerely apologizes and asks the forgiveness of the Aborig-
> inal peoples of this country for failing them so profoundly.[25]

Also profound was the silence regarding residential schools, and
the breaking of that silence is still a recent phenomenon. For survivors
and those affected intergenerationally, this silence was and is deeply
personal as well as communal since it has been felt across and within
families and Aboriginal communities and within the body politic for

decades. For others, ignorance and deliberate silence continue to exist on all sides of this issue.

It is obvious now as we look back at the 1970s and 1980s that residential schools remained in the proverbial shadows, even as artists were lauded for their frank depictions of "Native life" and their works were described as *seminal* and *influential*, words often associated with Maria Campbell's *Halfbreed* (1973) and Jeannette Armstrong's *Slash* (1985). Tomson Highway's plays *The Rez Sisters* (1988) and *Dry Lips Oughta Move to Kapuskasing* (1989) also received national prominence. We are now certain that residential schools and related realities such as day schools,[26] the Sixties Scoop,[27] and off-reserve as well as urban struggles lurk in the backgrounds of these works. Visual artists also began to break ground, though most of their art provided the same kind of subtle and coded messages found in literary works of the time. Norval Morrisseau's 1975 canvas *The Gift*, for example, is not overtly about residential schools but about the "gift" of Christianity and smallpox. It was not until Joane Cardinal Shubert's 1989 installation *The Lesson* and Jim Logan's early 1990s acrylic on canvas series on residential school abuse, *A Requiem for Our Children*, that the mould of subtle and coded art was broken in a shocking way.

If, in the recent past, virtually no one was addressing residential schools in art, more and more Aboriginal artists are now doing so. We can now see that watershed "moments" centrally concerned with health and healing, such as RCAP and the TRC, have enabled First Nations, Inuit, and Métis authors, poets, playwrights, and scholars to explore these and many other related issues front and centre in their work, though many have noted that Aboriginal peoples have been passing on their storied life lessons through many forms of cultural expression from time immemorial.

The concept of reconciliation, "restoring good will in relations that have been disrupted,"[28] also existed prior to the TRC and will exist well beyond its mandate. It is thus important that we pay attention to the role of Aboriginal artists and their art in reconciliation pre-TRC and outside the context of residential schools.

In 2009, I embarked on a five-year study to explore the role that First Nations, Inuit, and Métis[29] artists and art play in reconciliation generally and specifically within the context of the TRC process as it has been envisioned, defined, and/or experienced by established Aboriginal artists across various disciplines and media. Although I quote many scholars here, the study focuses on the perspectives of artists, curators, and/or scholars that I gleaned from one-on-one interviews and public comments made at a series of events that addressed questions about art, artists, and reconciliation.

It is essential for Aboriginal artists to speak to this issue, so I appreciate Gayatri Chakravorty Spivak's notion of speaking to[30] when talking about art that has been produced, is in production, or is being envisioned. Linda Alcoff, in her article "The Problem of Speaking for Others," nicely describes the concept of *speaking to* after deconstructing the academic postures of *listening* to and *speaking for*: "To promote *listening* to as opposed to *speaking for* essentializes the oppressed as non-ideologically constructed subjects. But Spivak is also critical of speaking for which engages in dangerous re-presentations. In the end Spivak prefers a speaking to in which the intellectual neither abnegates his or her discursive role nor presumes an authenticity of the oppressed but still allows for the possibility that the oppressed will produce a *countersentence* that can then suggest a new historical narrative."[31] And, as Aboriginal peoples in Canada have rightly come to expect a participatory role in research involving them and their communities, researchers working with Aboriginal artists must help to create space for them to speak for themselves both in their art and through the research in which they participate. Furthermore, to understand Aboriginal perspectives on reconciliation, we must respect traditional ways of knowing. Consequently, in my study I attempted to understand and represent knowledge that is personal, oral, experiential, holistic, and conveyed through narrative expression.[32]

As Allan Ryan notes in the introduction to his 1999 work, *The Trickster Shift: Humour and Irony in Contemporary Native Art*, the artists whom he references "constitute a loose alliance of socially active, politically aware, and professionally trained individuals ... who have ... exhibited with one another, written about one another, lectured on one another, curated exhibitions for one another, and to varying degrees influenced one another."[33] This was certainly the case with the art and commemoration initiatives that developed out of the IRSSA Commemoration Fund. I explored the artists and their art in my study in a similar fashion, for I sought to make sense of how networks and/or communities of artists engage and interact with each other within the particular policy framework presented by the IRSSA and TRC—or in resistance to it.

Since 2008, the TRC has organized seven mandated national events and numerous community events, which have included authors such as Basil Johnston, Beatrice Mosionier, and Joseph Boyden[34] as part of the artistic programming. The TRC also made an open call for submissions from artists, initially placing the call firmly on the testimony side of its mandate: "One of the main roles of the Commission is the gathering of statements and experiences of those impacted by the Residential School System. This is often done through written, audio, video and recorded statements. Artistic expressions are another way to make a statement about the residential school experience. All statements will be archived at the National Research Centre on the Residential School System [National Centre for Truth and Reconciliation]. This Centre will act as the country's largest and most complete record of the Residential School System and the experiences of survivors."[35] A more refined and detailed description followed, saying that the TRC

> believes that artists have a profound contribution to make in expressing both truth and reconciliation. The TRC invites all artists to submit works that relate to experiences at Indian Residential Schools or that relate to the legacy and impact of those experiences on former students, parents, future generations, communities, and on relationships within families and between communities. In addition, the TRC invites artists to submit works relating to apology, truth, cultural oppression, cultural genocide, resistance, resilience, spirituality, remembrance, reconciliation, rejuvenation and restoration of Aboriginal culture and pride. Why is the Truth and Reconciliation Commission of Canada gathering artistic works? The TRC believes that collecting artistic works is an important and meaningful way to express the truth, impact and legacy of the Residential School experience and to assist with reconciliation.[36]

COMMUNITY AND RESPONSIBILITY

The convergence of truth-telling, reconciliation efforts, and commemoration also presented a unique opportunity to test and build critically upon the notion that Aboriginal peoples have a responsibility to build their own Aboriginal communities. I highlight Jace Weaver's theory of *communitism* (a combination of *community* and *activism*)[37] as a way into this aspect of the study because his is a theory to which I have long subscribed and with which I have engaged in past scholarly work; it also reflects my positioning both as a scholar and as a professional in that I have chosen to dedicate my efforts to Aboriginal issues and work that serves Aboriginal communities.

Communitism is a theory that supports the artist's "proactive commitment to native Community."[38] There are many related theories about the importance of community to Aboriginal artists and their obligations to their communities. For example, Jeannette Armstrong has written and spoken at length about *En'owkin*: "This idea of community, as understood by my ancestors, encompassed a complex holistic view of interconnectedness that demands our responsibility to everything we are connected to."[39] Interestingly, En'owkin is the name given to the Indigenous cultural, educational, and creative arts institution with which Armstrong has long been affiliated in Penticton, British Columbia. She defines the concept as an "Okanagan conceptual metaphor which describes a process of clarification, conflict resolution and group commitment. We focus on coming to the best solutions possible, through respectful dialogue [sic] literally through consensus."[40] She wrote to me in 2012 to say that her concern

has mostly been about the broader effects [on] our Indigenous Nations (as opposed to the heinous effects on individuals which other experts are engaged in) in regard to the decline and extinctions of original languages and cultures as a result of the subtractive (to indigenous culture) and submersi[ve] (in colonial culture) education process that the schools were about. The loss of language is a loss of a way to see and experience the world from within an Indigenous perspective unique to each specific place each language and culture is indigenous to. The concept has been the subject at the centre of all of my arts, my writing, my activism in arts and culture as well as indigenous rights, and my work in culture and language revitalization, for living indigenous language renewal, for authentic indigenous arts practice recovery, for the revival in education pedagogy, of indigenous philosophy . . . and science perspectives. I believe that the role of reconciliation in a broader sense must provide ways and means to assist in the remedy of what has been destroyed. . . . Truth, from the perspective above, must not just include personal testimonials of abuse and loss, but attempt to display the depth and breadth of effects [on] all strata of

Indigenous Nations—social, psychological, intellectual, economic and so on, as well as to attempt to display the truth about the depth and breadth of the meaning to the rest of [the] world of the loss of even a single language and a single way of perceiving life. Understanding the whole picture is the first step to reconciliation. It seems to me [that] . . . only an artist might attempt to make these visible whether through formal or informal response as [an] artist.[41]

Since reconciliation for Armstrong is arguably about the bigger picture, the larger Canadian community, Weaver's and Armstrong's notions of an Aboriginal person's obligation to serve his or her community's needs do not account for this healing or breach-repairing paradigm per se, unless one acknowledges that a healthy community—that is, the artist's community—requires healthy contexts and relations.

Thus, reconciliation is an effort that might be essential to communitism and to another of Armstrong's concepts, *people without hearts*,[42] which means "people who have lost the capacity to experience the deep generational bond to other humans and to their surroundings. It refers to a people's collective disharmony and alienation from their land. It refers to those whose emotion is narrowly focused on their individual sense of well-being without regard to the well-being of others in the collective."[43] Although it seems as if she is speaking about the disharmony within Aboriginal communities that has resulted from the many disruptions caused by residential schools, in fact Armstrong is relating an anecdote involving her father's use of the term to characterize the neighbouring non-Aboriginal Penticton community of her childhood. She uses the Okanagan term deliberately to envelop her neighbours in her worldview and, in this sense, can be said to be characterizing "the collective" as the broader Canadian community.

The changing landscape of efforts to address the legacy of residential schools has significantly influenced the conversation about reconciliation in Canada. As I embarked on my journey to interview artists across the country, I wondered whether their pre-IRSSA engagements with this conversation through their art would be markedly different from their post-IRSSA engagements, particularly given the exclusive, legal nature of the agreement and the emotional and social impacts of its components.

I wondered how to address the concept of *community* when my intention was to interview a diverse and potentially disparate group of individuals who self-identified as both *Aboriginal* and *artist*. Which is the community, Aboriginal or artist? There are problems with the first conception of community because of the diversity across and within First Nations, Inuit, and Métis. The problems with the latter conception result from the fact that, though the concept of *artist community* is broadly accepted among those involved in the arts, that understanding of community is not addressed in generally accepted research guidelines. Furthermore, Aboriginal artists understand that their responsibility to the community—to "give back"—refers specifically to each individual's Aboriginal community. The study thus presented an opportunity to explore notions of community from the perspectives of individual Aboriginal artists as well as to examine the intersections between and/or barriers to their First Nations, Inuit, Métis, or other identities and their identities as artists. Finally, the study provided a significant opportunity to explore not only the artist's responsibility to give back to her or his community but also what it meant for me to give back to my community through my work.

Maria Campbell helped me to begin to find the answer. She said, "I am familiar with concepts of truth and reconciliation from the place of a community activist because I work with community and I work with families in community, so I see them on the front lines, so to speak. And I'm an artist on the front lines."[44] She added that

> it's always been my work, because of my own background. In order for myself to heal and to find some semblance of sanity in my life, I went to work with other people who were going through what I had gone through. So most of my work for the last 40-some years has been with women and children in crisis, so I work a lot with youth and with families. And that's even in my teaching; when I was teaching at university it was geared to that. And my work as a writer and as a playwright, you know, it's all about healing family, because I feel if families are not healed and helped, then we don't have anything; we don't have any kind of future, no matter how many apologies, no matter what, we have nothing if we can't.[45]

But not all paint the special responsibility to community in the same way. Alex Janvier's 2001 canvas *Blood Tears* has been featured prominently in the past few years—as the cover of the 2008 Aboriginal Healing Foundation's volume *From Truth to Reconciliation: Transforming the Legacy of Residential Schools* and within the major 2013 exhibition *Witnesses:*

Art and Canada's Indian Residential Schools. When Janvier was asked if he considered himself an activist or activator, he said, "None of those two descriptions. We were just acting as people who wanted to move forward as artists and wanted to be recognized as artists, not as curio-makers. I didn't want to be qualified as a curio-maker, I was doing serious work and the others were doing serious work in their own style."[46] But of painting residential school–themed or -inspired works Janvier did say that "I had to heal too. I'm a sick person from all that. [And if others] could see that [work], then they could chime into it on their own terms."[47] Janvier's *Blood Tears* further contributes to the creation of opportunities for sharing by including on the verso of the canvas his own terms of loss:

- Language of Denesu'line targeted, forbidden to speak was to be strapped, and severely punished!
- Loss of culture, custom
- Loss of parenthood, parents and extended families
- Loss of grandparents
- Loss of Elder's knowledge
- Loss of traditional belief, told that it was evil
- Told the Indian ways was the work of the devil . . .
- Many, many died of broken bodies, of twisted conflicting mental difference
- Most died with "Broken spirit"
- Some lived to tell about it
- The rest are permanently, "Live in fear"
- The rest will take their silence to their graves as many have to this day.[48]

Of course, not "every artwork is about a specific historical event that happened to Aboriginal peoples. . . . Sometimes the reference is muted, indirect; other times more obvious, more critical."[49]

DEFINING/DEFYING RECONCILIATION

The RCAP through TRC years (1990s through 2015) saw a considerable amount of scholarship as well as theoretical and practical focus on reconciliation between aggrieved parties within nation-states, notably the vast but still recent body of literature spawned by the South African Truth and

Reconciliation Commission experience. There is a large body of international literature concerning the role of art and artists in truth and reconciliation processes, which often come in the form of formal commissions. There is a similarly expansive body of literature on the role of art and artists in commemoration, another core component of the IRSSA and one that will be administered by the TRC following its final report. And there is a considerable body of literature, including a growing literature specific to Canada and Aboriginal North America, on the role of art in healing and the therapeutic nature of art. The notion of "art as witness" has considerable importance here and provides a fascinating way to explore the relationship between art and reconciliation.

I also acknowledge that concept(s) of "reconciliation" might or might not be influenced and/or affected by the changed landscape introduced through Canada's Truth and Reconciliation Commission. This landscape is necessarily specific to residential schools and, arguably, exclusive insofar as the settlement agreement adheres to an approved list of schools and therefore an approved list of "members" of the experience.

We can begin with a simple dictionary definition since the word *reconciliation* is fairly common. *Webster's Revised Unabridged Dictionary* defines the word as "1. The act of reconciling, or the state of being reconciled; reconcilement; restoration to harmony; renewal of friendship. 2. Reduction to congruence or consistency; removal of inconsistency; harmony."[50]

In contrast, Brian Rice and Anna Snyder understand the word *reconciliation* in the context of truth and reconciliation commissions, so they define it in terms of the five general aims of a TRC: (1) to discover, clarify, and formally acknowledge past abuses; (2) to respond to specific needs of victims; (3) to contribute to justice and accountability; (4) to outline institutional responsibility and recommend reforms; and (5) to promote reconciliation and reduce conflict over the past.[51]

Similarly, the mandate of Canada's Indian Residential Schools Truth and Reconciliation Commission, known as "Schedule N," defines reconciliation as "an ongoing individual and collective process, and [it] will require commitment from all those affected including First Nations, Inuit and Métis former Indian Residential School (IRS) students, their families, communities, religious entities, former school employees, government and the people of Canada. Reconciliation may occur between any of the above groups."[52] Of course, reconciliation between peoples, in the context of wrongs done in a colonial past (and present), is much more complicated.

Although it is not possible to capture all that complexity in one study, the following are some key areas of focus.

Jennifer Llewellyn, in her article "Bridging the Gap between Truth and Reconciliation: Restorative Justice and the Indian Residential Schools Truth and Reconciliation Commission," nicely encapsulates the task ahead of the TRC, saying that it is "well positioned to paint a comprehensive picture of the residential school system and its legacy. This will provide the necessary context to give meaning and legitimacy to the common experience payments and independent assessment process parts of the settlement. From this picture of the past, the commission will be able to recommend the way through to a future marked by new, reconciled relationships within Aboriginal communities and between Aboriginal and non-Aboriginal peoples."[53] She also highlights the key challenge to TRCs in Canada and elsewhere: "As the TRC [in Canada] begins its journey, it must figure out how to navigate the complex and difficult road of 'truth' and map a course toward reconciliation. In doing so, it will face the substantial challenge that others who have travelled this path before have encountered: bridging the gap between truth and reconciliation."[54] She also highlights the South African Truth and Reconciliation as the most telling example:

> The South African slogan ["Truth. The road to reconciliation."] does serve as an important and necessary temper on unrealistic expectations. It cautions that truth and reconciliation are not one and the same. Distinguishing the two also makes clear that while truth may be necessary for reconciliation, it alone is not sufficient. There is a road toward reconciliation, and truth is a fundamental part of the journey, but there are other steps to be taken along the way. The lesson of this slogan for the South African commission was clear. They could not promise nor be expected to produce reconciliation. Indeed, no one process or institution could achieve this goal. This same conviction underpins the description of reconciliation in the Indian Residential Schools TRC's mandate as an ongoing process.[55]

Llewellyn makes an essential point here; there is no generally applicable road map to reconciliation—and certainly not one that can be copied from other commissions. The point is that there will be truth telling along with other steps. Therefore, is art itself truth telling, and/or is it some other step on the path of truth and reconciliation? I invited Aboriginal artists to speak more generally to theories of reconciliation, particularly those with dissenting opinions. I present a short discussion of some of these theories and the views that artists hold toward them.

Taiaiake Alfred and Jeff Corntassel argue that the discourse on reconciliation is flawed, in fact, at its very roots: "Far from reflecting any true history or honest reconciliation with the past or present agreements and treaties that form an authentic basis for Indigenous-state relations in the Canadian context, 'aboriginalism'[56] is a legal, political and cultural discourse designed to serve an agenda of silent surrender to an inherently unjust relation at the root of the colonial state itself."[57] Alfred further calls reconciliation an "emasculating concept," saying that "reconciliation as a concept or process is not as compelling, factually or logically speaking, as resurgence because, being so embedded in the supposedly progressive discourses on Onkwehonwe-Settler [Aboriginal-non-Aboriginal] relations . . . it is almost unassailable from within established legal and political discourses, thus presenting a huge obstacle to justice and real peacemaking."[58] Without "massive restitution . . . for past harms and continuing injustices committed against our peoples," he writes, "reconciliation would permanently enshrine colonial injustices and is itself a further injustice."[59] He argues that we must place the discourse within the broader colonial context of Canada's history and present; otherwise, Indigenous-settler relations will continue to be built on a foundation of "false decolonization,"[60] which according to Alfred continues to be immoral. He also challenges the notion of Indigenous peoples being "victims of history,"[61] arguing that the discourse has been too conciliatory on the Indigenous side, with Indigenous people seeking only to "*recover* from the past" and settling for white notions of reconciliation. This is not resistance or "*survivance*."[62] Rather, it is acquiescence to "a *resolution* that is acceptable to and non-disruptive for the state and society that we have come to embrace and identify with."[63]

John Paul Lederach writes about conflict, resolution, and transformation at social and societal levels in situations of persistent and ongoing violence in *The Moral Imagination: The Art and Soul of Building Peace*. His titular concept of moral imagination is "the capacity to imagine and generate constructive responses and initiatives that, while rooted in the day-to-day challenges of violent settings, transcend and ultimately break the grips of those destructive patterns and cycles."[64] His use of the word *moral* is key here. It refers to integrity, allowing for the use of imagination, where dogmatic, ideological positioning cannot: "Moral . . . appeals to something great . . . beckon[ing] us to rise toward something beyond those things that are immediately apparent and visible. The quality of this phrase I most wish to embrace reverberates in this potential to find a way to transcend, to move beyond what exists while still living in it."[65] Lederach also offers a strategy for moral action: "This is the challenge of restorying: It continuously requires a creative act. To restory is not to repeat the past, attempt to recreate it exactly as it was, nor act as if it did not exist. It does not ignore the generational future nor does it position itself to control it. Embracing the paradox of relationship in the present, the capacity to restory imagines both the past and the future and provides space for the narrative voice to create."[66] Lederach writes that "the real challenge of authenticity and the moral imagination is how to transcend what has been and is now, while still living in it. For the moral imagination to make the journey across this terrain it will need to address complexity and support change over time."[67] It is in this moral space that Lederach writes about that Alfred might be arguing for Indigenous peoples to "us[e] words, symbols and direct non-violent action as the offensive weapons of our fight . . . [and] seek to contend, to inform our agitating direct actions with ideas, and to use the effects of this contention to defeat colonialism by convincing people of the need to abandon the cycle of subjugation and conflict and join us in a relationship of respect and sharing."[68] That might be the change that Lederach calls for and that Alfred places in a Canadian context, which Lederach's work does not (cannot yet) do.

Alfred's call for "words" and "symbols" might well be art, as both Martha Minnow's[69] and Jill Bennett's[70] books allow. In the chapter "Facing History" in *Between Vengeance and Forgiveness: Facing History after Genocide and Mass Violence*, Minnow highlights a number of elements that truth commissions cannot offer, including vengeance and closure through prosecution: "Disappointments with truth commissions are likely to erupt over the reliability and completeness of the reported facts, over interpretations, and over the apparent trade of truth for punishment."[71] Outside the necessary reports that relay such information, there are other avenues, and Minnow moves in the direction of memorials that often accompany or are integral to the formal reporting of commissions. She also notes that, within these initiatives, "more literal and concrete forms of commemoration and monuments use sculptures and paintings, museums, plays, and poems."[72] Minnow believes that art can indeed be a most useful tool that goes well beyond commemoration since the "art of the unthinkable should disturb as well as commemorate."[73] Bennett's *Empathic Vision: Affect, Trauma, and Contemporary Art* follows this line of thought, though Bennett examines it within the context of "trauma art" and deconstructs it along with notions of political art and the political in art. As Dora Apel writes, "art illuminates traumatic experience through the sideways glance, allowing the viewer to apprehend what can only be shown indirectly, allusively and in sometimes surprising ways."[74]

Dian Lynn Million goes in yet another direction, rightly placing the reconciliation dialogue within a healing paradigm: "*Healing* from trauma and historical trauma is now an international discourse on social 'collateral damage' among those who have suffered the fate of History as the subjugated, linked to demands for justice from the perpetrators of their distress. Across a spectrum, at the level of the International, community and individual, healing is the reaffirmation of boundary; of holism from fragmentation. Canada has attempted to handle the material/physical outcome of its colonialism in Native communities through institutionalization, and now increasingly through therapeutic interventions that are often self-administered bureaucracies."[75] Million engages reconciliation dialogue from the perspective of a healing paradigm and places the dialogue in a larger colonial context: "The residential school survivor's abuse discourse continuously struggles to articulate a something else larger. It is the struggle to make Canada hear: that Canada recognize not only their past acts but their present ones; acts whose resonance and material outcome are a continuation of their colonization, 'not a psychological problem to be defused in a therapist's room.'"[76]

That said, the healing paradigm and the healing movement within, which can include or lead into reconciliation, are intimately connected to trauma and the extensive body of literature that focuses on it. For example, Marlene Brant Castellano writes about historical trauma in the context of the multiple assaults suffered by Aboriginal people: "Memories of family networks and whole communities reach back through generations, repeating themes of loss and powerlessness, relocation, epidemics and residential school."[77]

When I interviewed Métis artist, curator, and scholar David Garneau in November 2011, he initially said of the concepts of truth and reconciliation that "I haven't been deeply involved, but I've been paying attention, reading, puzzling over things."[78] And indeed he did puzzle over these issues in the coming months. In 2011, he said that

> I remember when South Africa Truth and Reconciliation was going on, there was one leader, a flower painter, who was a great speaker. When asked why he made such beautiful and political[ly] innocuous works in this time of crisis, he said that he was not drawn to make work about the inequities and horrors but about the good things in life; after all, they were fighting for a change, to move away from those horrors and toward what, well, toward the sort of things he was painting. Bob Boyer also said, "the people I hang out with, non-artists, they like beautiful things, that's why I want to make my things beautiful." He did make very agitated things at certain times, and then he did very personal work. It was all coded though, sometimes very hard to read, the titles usually helped. But there's some people who want to make their way through the world, and be healthy people. How long can you be angry? How long can you be damaged and make that? You know, imagine being in a room like this and making unhappy art all the time. I mean that's gotta be part of it. Part of it too is that, [if an artist is] making a living off his work, he's got to make some things that people can live with.[79]

But something that Garneau could not live with is the concept of reconciliation as he sees it defined by the TRC and those reading its report. By the summer of 2012, Garneau had further defined the landscape in which he now found himself operating:

> The colonial attitude, including its academic branch, is characterized by a drive to see, to traverse, to know, . . ., to translate (to make equivalent), to own, and to exploit. It is based on the belief that everything should be accessible, is ultimately comprehensible, and a potential commodity or resource, or at least something that can be recorded or otherwise saved. Primary sites of resistance, then, are not the occasional open battles between the minoritized, oppressed, or colonized and the dominant culture, but the perpetual, active refusal of complete engagement: to speak with one's own in one's own way; to refuse translation and full explanations; to create trade goods that imitate core culture without violating it; to not be a Native informant.[80]

So Garneau called for "irreconcilable spaces of Aboriginality" and challenged the very choice of the word *reconciliation,*

> a synonym [of *conciliation*] with a difference. *Re*-conciliation refers to the repair of a previously existing harmonious relationship. This word choice imposes the fiction that equanimity is the status quo between Aboriginal peoples and Canada. [However, i]nitial conciliation was tragically disrupted and will be painfully restored through the current process. In this context, the imaginary the word describes is limited to post-contact narratives. This construction anaesthetizes knowledge of the existence of pre-contact Aboriginal sovereignty. It narrates halcyon moments of co-operation before things went wrong as the seamless source of harmonious origin. And it sees the residential school era, for example, as an unfortunate deviation rather than just one aspect of the perpetual colonial struggle to contain and control Aboriginal people, territories, and resources.[81]

ART AND HEALING: CONTEMPORARY PRACTICES

Many survivors and others affected by the legacy have submitted artworks to the TRC. It goes without saying, of course, that Aboriginal writers have been exploring the above themes for decades and that a call from the TRC in 2009 was not *the* catalyst for residential school–related writing. It was *a* catalyst, however. Aboriginal Healing Foundation funding certainly was a major incentive for poet and playwright Armand Garnet Ruffo, who used an early call put out by the AHF to begin work on the screenplay that would eventually become his award-winning film *A Windigo Tale* (released in 2010). He, too, noted the silence: "[In the 1960s, 1970s, and 1980s] nobody talked about it.... We played right by the residential school. When I'd ask my mother what's that building, she'd say, don't worry about that and then eventually it was torn down."[82] But *A Windigo Tale* is very much about healing:

> What struck me is that [Armstrong and Highway] were dealing with [residential schools] in an oblique way, not hitting it dead on. But really talking about the impact of it more, and that's what I was interested in, as well, loss of culture ... and language. So that

became a big issue and of course residential schools did come up, because that's why most of us have lost [our culture], either directly or indirectly, because of that. So I wanted to talk about those issues as well, like we were all doing [at the Enowkin Centre in Penticton, British Columbia, in the 1980s and early 1990s].[83]

However, it is important to keep in mind LaRocque's cautionary note about an "aesthetic of healing": "As constructive as [it might sound], we must be careful not to squeeze the life out of native literature by making it serve, yet again, another utilitarian function. Poets, playwrights, and novelists, among others, must also write for the love of words. Healing is fast becoming the new cultural marker by which we define or judge Aboriginal literature."[84]

Picking up from Bennett's *Empathic Vision*, and the suggestion that the TRC process allows for a unique opportunity to test her theories in this context, there is a much larger but obviously related field that Aboriginal artists might be engaged in (or resisting): art therapy and its use in healing and reconciliation in Canada. The following is a brief overview of this field. My intention is to identify avenues for interrogating whether or not artists are connected to or see themselves as connected to notions of therapy or the therapeutic through their art making.

Art therapy and the expressive arts exist within the healing landscape in Canada, and the recent literature that focuses on or acknowledges its use by and for Aboriginal peoples in Canada often notes a natural relationship between the practice of art therapy and Aboriginal culture, particularly traditional healing and shamanism. As Stephen Levine says, "shamen are the prototype of the artist as therapist."[85]

In a chapter titled "From Shamanism to Art Therapy," Shaun McNiff describes the shaman as an archetype and includes a useful discussion of the similarities between art therapy and shamanism: "The parallels between shamanism and the field of art therapy seem to lie in the commitment of both to work with psychological conflict and struggle through creative action and enactment."[86] In *Poiesis: The Language of Psychology and the Speech of the Soul*, Levine delves into Western and Indigenous philosophical traditions in the search for a theoretical basis to explain why and how creative processes contribute to healing: "In turning to the arts for healing, we are re-discovering an ancient tradition. In early societies and in indigenous cultures, all healing takes place through ceremonial means. Music, dance, song, story-telling, mask-making, the creation of visual imagery and the ritual re-enactment of myth are all components of a communal process in which suffering is given form."[87] He goes on to note that professionals now do what shamen once tended to do in traditional healing: "Today, the various roles of the shaman are divided among different professional groups—physicians, psychotherapists, artists, and priests. With regard to the creative transformation of emotional conflict, this role fragmentation has diffused the shaman's source of power, which lay in the integration of body, mind, spirit, and art."[88]

There is also resistance in art. Linda Tuhiwai Smith, in *Decolonizing Methodologies: Research and Indigenous Peoples*, writes that, "for indigenous people, the critique of history is not unfamiliar, although it has now been claimed by postmodern theories."[89] She explains that the "idea of contested stories and multiple discourses about the past, by different communities, is closely linked to the politics of everyday contemporary indigenous life.... These contested accounts are stored within genealogies, within the landscape, within weavings and carvings."[90] Charlotte Townsend-Gault acknowledges that Western notions of "art" might be, for some Aboriginal peoples, "a colonizer's term, a restriction and distortion of the cultural expressions of the past which fails to do justice to the visual culture of the present," but asks if "the conflict between aboriginal and Euro-American aesthetics [has] been both productive and extending."[91] To that end, she writes that since at least the mid-1980s it has been evident that the aim of many works by Aboriginal artists is "to remember, to condemn, to overturn, to instruct, to translate across cultural boundaries, and yet to withhold translation, to make beautiful things, according to various ideas of beauty and, sometimes, riotously and discomfitingly, to entertain."[92]

COMMEMORATION

How do we remember? As with art therapy, some artists are involved formally or informally in efforts to commemorate and memorialize, whereas others are not or resist the notion. A key question is what role, if any, does reconciliation play in commemorative art and vice versa?

Because the Commemoration Fund existed within a settlement agreement, is it then bound to what John Torpey calls "reparations politics,"[93] which encompass all those things that we do to address historical wrongs and misdeeds, such as apologies, monetary compensation, revising historical narratives, and commemoration? If so, then is this the ground upon which resistance can be built? As Govier writes, "collective acknowledgement is especially important because strategies such as the construction of museums and memorials and the amending of educational policy are more available to collectives than to individuals."[94] This, however, then feeds into what Brian Osborne has postulated, that "national mythologies and symbols are manipulated to encourage identification with the state and reinforce its continuity and ubiquity. Through various devices, otherwise detached individuals are implored to recognize one another as being members of a larger group sharing a common historical metanarrative ... on the foundations of a 'should have been' past, rather than an actual history."[95]

There is certainly already ground for resistance. Residential schools, it can be said, represent a mass atrocity that the Canadian state committed in concert with Christian denominations (Chrisjohn and Young,[96] Haig-Brown,[97] Milloy[98]) against fellow citizens (though this can certainly be problematized across the decades given the large body of literature contesting the rights and citizenship of Aboriginal people). Memories of the schools cannot be collective memories of Aboriginal people alone. All Canadians must share the burden of recollection of residential school history.

Interpretations of commemoration vary greatly between community and individual, Aboriginal and non-Aboriginal. Cultural and spiritual or religious beliefs about grieving, for instance, inform how people choose to commemorate. Similarly, worldview shapes how people remember and how their remembering affects their physical, spiritual, emotional, and mental well-being. In *Lakota Grieving: A Pastoral Response*, Stephen Huffstetter writes about a rudimentary exchange between Lakota and non-Aboriginal grieving practices:

> A Lakota worldview questions why western culture tries to dichotomize civil and religious practice anyway. Both are a part of life.
> ... An elderly Lakota woman recounted the first time she went to a "white" funeral. After the rosary, the altar society served cake and coffee. Just as she was settling into conversation, people started leaving and sons and daughters of the woman being waked started gathering their belongings to leave. "I could not believe they were

going to leave their mother alone by herself in the church all night! Didn't they know how lonely she would feel and how much she needed them around to help her through this hard time of death?" Her relationship with the spirit of her dead friend was still very real and tangible for her.[99]

Aboriginal communities have sacred ceremonies, customs, and spiritual connections to their dead. Commemorative practices for honouring the dead and the missing and to commemorate the deaths of children are entered into Aboriginal collective memory in specific and sacred ways. National commemoration of residential schools cannot presume to replace community customs; it must seek to expand the collective memory of those who will be remembered. Huffstetter describes an oral culture of memorialization at Lakota wakes: "The real work of the wake went on with the gathering, the sharing of the meal, renewing family ties and remembering. People use the time to talk and tell stories about the one who had died, as a way of beginning to memorialize them."[100]

If residential schools are placed within a broader Canadian context—a colonial history—then the history can be rationalized as a shared Canadian history, whether former student, perpetrator, bystander, or descendant of one or more of those identities. But each of those experiences spawns its own memories or forgettings, as John Gillis has written: "National memory is shared by people who have never seen or heard of one another, yet who regard themselves as having a common history. They are bound together as much by forgetting as by remembering."[101] This is particularly true if the forgetting is in response to trauma; to that end, Joachim Wolschke-Bulmahn links identity and memory: "Identity and memory are not stable and objective things, but representations or constructions of reality. The members of a particular nation, for example, share a specific history, but do they necessarily have the same identity? The way humans see themselves as a member of a particular group depends also on their own interpretation of history, their own ideas about the future, and their political, moral and other ideals. Identity and memory have to do with particular interests, such as class, gender, or power relations."[102] As well, "the concepts of memory and identity are related to each other," and identity is "inconceivable without history and without the remembrance and commemoration of history, however much such remembrance may distort historical events and facts."[103] Gillis writes that "memory and identity are two of the most frequently used terms in contemporary public and private discourse."[104] Regardless, "the parallel lives of these two terms alert us to the fact that the notions of identity depend on the idea of memory and vice versa. The core meaning of any individual or group identity, namely, a sense of sameness over time and space, is sustained by remembering; and what is remembered is defined by the assumed identity."[105] He also says that, "at this particular historical moment, it is all the more apparent that both identity and memory are political and social constructs, and should be treated as such."[106] Richard Handler in "Is 'Identity' a Useful Cross-Cultural Concept?" does just that, arguing that "cultures are not individuated entities existing as natural objects with neat temporal and spacial boundaries"[107] and that "groups are not bounded objects in the natural world."[108] "'Who we are,'" he writes, "is a communicative process . . . that includes many voices and varying degrees of understanding and, importantly, misunderstanding."[109] He is critical, suggesting that "to deconstruct notions of cultural identity at precisely the moment when the disempowered turn to them may aid in the reactionary social forces who seek to reassert the validity of homogeneous 'mainstream' collective identities against proponents of 'multicultural' diversity."[110] However, "to support without criticism identity claims is to aid in the reproduction of an ideology that is both hegemonic and, I believe, oppressive."[111] To combat this, "our critiques of identity [must] focus on those mainstream claims that too often go unchallenged . . . rather than writing exclusively about the 'invention' of minority identities, traditions, and cultures."[112]

Gillis, like Wolschke-Bulmahn, says that "memories and identities are not fixed things, but representations or constructions of reality," and "we are constantly revising our memories to suit our current identities."[113] He, too, argues that memory and identity operate within a social framework, noting that "'memory work' is, like any other kind of physical or mental labour, embedded in complex class, gender and power relations that determine what is remembered (or forgotten), by whom, and for what end."[114] Whereas Gillis focuses, in part, on "collective amnesia,"[115] writing that "new memories requir[e] concerted forgettings,"[116] Maurice Halbwachs places collective memory in a social context in *On Collective Memory*. He writes that the "individual calls recollections to mind by relying on the frameworks of social memory,"[117] which means that social groups influence individual identity and memory. Although "the various groups that compose society are capable at every moment of reconstructing their past ... they most frequently distort that past in reconstructing it."[118] He also says that "a remembrance is in very large measure a reconstruction of the past achieved with data borrowed from the present, a reconstruction prepared, furthermore, by reconstructions of earlier periods wherein past images had already been altered."[119]

Noa Gedi and Yigal Elam question the usefulness of the term "collective memory," writing that so-called experts ("memoriologists") have simply taken an old, familiar term, "myth," and reinvented it.[120] For historians, collective memory is only useful metaphorically: that is, it stands in for myth. They reject Halbwachs's argument that "there is really no room for history as a science, that is, as a methodological effort aimed at reconstructing actual past events by means of conventional methods of verification ... and finally ... proposing theoretical models which would explain them."[121] Claiming that his "notion of history writing ... is rather an intentional formation of the past without any obligation to 'historical truth,'" Gedi and Elam write that, for Halbwachs, history "thus becomes a tool for the ideological and moralistic needs of society." As they write, "collective memory"

> has become the predominant notion which replaces real (factual) history ... and real (personal) memory. ... Indeed, "collective memory" has become the all-pervading concept which in effect stands for all sorts of human cognitive products generally. ... What is lost ... is the dialectical tension between the old simple personal memory as a questionable source of evidence, and history as a corroborated version of past events. Instead we now have history as "collective memory," that is, as a fabricated narrative (once called "myth") either in the service of social-ideological needs, or even expressing the creative whim of a particular historian. Not all of those who have adopted "collective memory" and use it profusely necessarily embrace the theory behind the term.[122]

Like Halbwachs, Pierre Nora places collective memory in a social context but argues that it has changed because of changes in social structures:

> The conquest and eradication of memory by history, then, confronts us with the brutal realization of the difference between real memory—social and unviolated, exemplified in but also

retained as the secret of so-called primitive or archaic societies—
and history, which is how our hopelessly forgetful modern societies, propelled by change, organize the past. On the one hand, we
find an integrated, dictatorial memory—unself-conscious,
commanding, all-powerful, spontaneously actualizing, a memory
without a past that ceaselessly reinvents tradition, linking the
history of its ancestors to the undifferentiated time of heroes,
origins, and myth—and on the other hand, our memory, nothing
more in fact than sifted and sorted historical traces.[123]

What was once a more holistic environment of memory is now an arti-
ficial archival form of memory. Where memory "is life, borne by living
societies...in permanent evolution, open to the dialectic of remembering
and forgetting, unconscious of its successive deformations, vulnerable to
manipulation and appropriation," history is "the reconstruction, always
problematic and incomplete, of what is no longer."[124] Essentially, we have
moved away from living with and experiencing memory to letting static
sites of memory, such as museums and monuments, do all the work. Gedi
and Elam, though, call Nora's view "radical," writing that Nora "substi-
tut[es] the monument for living memory, thereby turning it into the actual
location of 'collective memory.' The end result is that because history
and memory stand in opposition to one another, he has to declare *lieux
de memoire* as 'another history.' We thus no longer deal with events but
with sites."[125]

Kirk Savage, in "The Politics of Memory: Black Emancipation and the
Civil War Monument," writes that "all shared memory requires mediating devices to sustain itself."[126] The mediating devices are archives and
monuments. When combined with rituals of remembering, they define
collective memory and identity, since "the public monument represents
a kind of collective recognition—in short, legitimacy—deposited there."[127]
Brian Osborne also considers monuments, focusing on Canadian identity, calling the Cartier monuments an example of how a monument can
become a "dynamic site of meaning."[128] But that does not mean there are
not challenges, as he writes in another article, that monuments be seen
as "spatial and temporal landmarks; they were loaded with memory; they
performed a didactic function; they were signs of national progress; they
were heroic figures (men, of course!) who represented the anonymous
masses; symbols of rights and liberties."[129]

This is not a new concept. Gillis, in his Introduction to the collection that he edited in 1994, itself a seminal piece, presents a wide-ranging overview of the history of commemoration in the West, identifying "the pre-national, . . . the national (from the American and French revolutions to the 1960s), and the present, post-national phase[s]."[130] Gillis notes that in the pre-national phase only the elites of society institutionalized memory, separate from the popular memory that existed within the living memory of regular people. The national phase, however, saw a wider institutionalization by agents of the state. Although he calls these commemorations more democratic, they were almost always of notable men of historical significance. The post-national phase, though, represents a "tendency toward the personalization of memory,"[131] away from the collective and toward a "plurality of pasts."[132] Gillis also references the contested terrain of collective memory and identity and notes that "class, region, gender, religion, [and] race"[133] contest a sense of common identity because of the subjective nature of any representation within a public commemorative monument. Osborne, too, highlights this, noting that "each group [has] its own lists of heroes and villains." Thus, "rather than being sites of consensus building, public space and its population of carefully selected monuments and statuary become contested terrains."[134]

Gillis also writes that the "relationship between memory and identity is historical; and the record of that relationship can be traced through various forms of commemoration."[135] He notes that commemorative activity is "by definition social and political, for it involves the coordination of individual and group memories, whose results may appear consensual when they are in fact the product of processes of intense contest, struggle, and, in some instances, annihilation."[136] There are conscious and unconscious decisions to include and exclude. Daniel Levy explores the relationship between revisionism and collective memory. Citing examples from Germany and Israel, he notes that the "histories of nations are increasingly problematized and have become a realm of commemorative combat"[137] or competing memories. Levy acknowledges that, "in contrast to the state-supportive role of historians during the formative phase of nationalism, collective memory is increasingly a contested terrain on which groups self-consciously struggle to shape and re-shape their national past to suit their present political views of the future."[138] So he asks "whose past is it? What image of the past nation prevails in the public sphere?"[139] He concludes that the "contested nature of the nation and the multiplication of other identity options are thus reflected in the proliferation of struggles over collective memory."[140]

Alan Gordon defines public memory as "conceptions of history enshrined in historic sites and public monuments in the streets, parks, and squares of a city."[141] He argues overtly that public memory, like collective memory, is contested terrain, but he does not confine collective memory to the above, noting that it is also made up of more nebulous things such as customs and cultural practices. The choices of whom and how to commemorate through monuments "reveal much about the sense of history of the men and women who select them, and in this respect, commemoration is closely related to power: it reveals an ongoing contest for hegemony. The subjects people choose to commemorate illustrate and teach idealized social conventions. . . . Public memory, then, works to turn history into a shared experience in the interest of broadly and loosely defined political goals."[142] This notion of "teaching" is of critical importance, says Roger Simon, "particularly if we take public memory as a sphere for developing a historical consciousness—not as an individual awareness and attitude but as a commitment to and participation in a critical practice of remembrance and learning."[143] He argues that public memory would then "become a time of interminable and exacting learning not where one is just informed through remembrance but where one learns to remember anew."[144] Similarly, Osborne ends his article by asking "is there a need for a new paradigm of heritage commemoration? . . . The classical allegorical forms of didactic statuary and monuments no longer resonate with the modern world. Rather than being declarative sites of conceptual closure, perhaps they should be ambiguous sites of pondering and reflection."[145]

As with the truth-telling component of the TRC, commemoration initiatives potentially face the similar challenge of reaching those who might have difficulty hearing or listening to the stories of others. Just as there is diversity across First Nations, Inuit, and Métis experiences of residential schools, so too there will be diversity across the non-Aboriginal public that will listen to these stories. A goal, as Simon says, should be the transformation of those willing to listen, view, and ponder.[146]

This is precisely what Métis artist Christi Belcourt asks of viewers of *Giniigaaniimenaaning (Looking Ahead)*, the stained-glass window that she was commissioned to design after a 2011 national competition.

The window sits prominently in the Centre Block on Parliament Hill. She describes it as follows:

> The story begins in the bottom left corner of the glass, with your eye moving upwards in the left panel to the top window, and flowing down the right window to the bottom right corner. The glass design tells a story. It is a story of Aboriginal people, with our ceremonies, languages, and cultural knowledge intact; through the darkness of the residential school era; to an awakening sounded by a drum; an apology that spoke to the heart; hope for reconciliation; transformation and healing through dance, ceremony, language; and resilience into the present day. The title of the piece is "Giniigaaniimenaaning" [which] ... translated into English means ... "Looking Ahead." The title is in Anishinaabemowin (Ojibway) and includes, within the deeper meaning of the word, the idea that everyone is included and we are all looking ahead for the ones "unborn."[147]

Viewers are invited on a journey, from a precontact history in which traditions are intact, through the 150 years of Indian residential schools, culminating with survivors breaking their silence. At its peak, the window includes a banner referencing 2008, the year of Prime Minister Stephen Harper's official apology. The right panel depicts dancing and drumming, healing as well as traditional activities, a mother holding a baby, the words *I love you* in Cree, Anishinaabemowin, Inuktitut, and Mi'kmaq. And then the circle is complete, with a return to the earth, to the lodge, and to traditional ways.

That journey alone is powerful. But perhaps viewers should also know the stories behind such pieces. For, as Belcourt told me in 2014, survivors have a specific message to convey. One survivor whom Belcourt went to for advice underlined the idea of hope: "So I offered tobacco and I said 'What do you think about this, should I do it? And if I do it, what should be in there?' And that's when she told me, 'Yes, do it.' She said, 'Make it about hope. ... She said, 'I don't have hope because I've been affected so badly ... but I want to have hope for the future generations. I want them to have hope.' She said, 'I can't, but I want them to have it.'"[148]

CONCLUSION

There are numerous conclusions to draw from the work that many artists and scholars have done over the past several years pre- and now post-TRC. These conclusions build upon the work that many others did pre- and post-RCAP. I will focus on a few key themes. The first is the important framing of what it means to "witness." This term is certainly not new, but it became central to the work of the TRC and to artists and curators during those years.

There are many definitions of the term. It means, most commonly, to "see an event, typically a crime or accident, take place"[149] or to be the person who does the seeing. In a legal sense, of course, it also refers to the person called on to act as a witness—a "person giving sworn testimony to a court of law or the police,"[150] whether simply, as described above, or in an expert sense. This concept is closely related to the notion of testimony: that is, to deliver one's witness account. I make no claim that what I write here is in any way testimony. Instead, I argue that I am playing a role that David Gaertner described recently as follows: "A witness in this sense becomes a living archive—a repository of history guaranteed by mutual consensus."[151] But its use as a mass noun was perhaps most useful to my project: that is, the idea of some "thing" being "evidence" or "proof." *English Oxford Living Dictionaries* provides an example: "The memorial service was *witness* to the wide circle of his interests."[152] I like this example because the editors (inadvertently) chose an example that incorporates the notion of memorial and the notion of a publicly accessible performance of sorts, which resonates with the concept of the various art and curatorial practices discussed herein. And I continue to be guided by something that my co-editor on *Reconcile This!*, Ayumi Goto, wrote in our Introduction to that special, art-focused issue of the journal *West Coast Line*: "When understood as a socially engaged activity, witnessing incites creative collaboration. It provokes dialogical intercessions that push up against imposed projections of reconciliation."[153]

Collaboration, a theme that I will come back to shortly, would also prove to be a key finding in this work, and the concept resonated when, in 2009, the Truth and Reconciliation Commission provided a more detailed definition of "the Aboriginal principle of witnessing" than its passing reference in Schedule N of the IRSSA:

The term witness is in reference to the Aboriginal principle of witnessing, which varies among First Nations, Métis and Inuit peoples. Generally speaking, witnesses are called to be the keepers of history when an event of historic significance occurs. Partly because of the oral traditions of Aboriginal peoples, but also to recognize the importance of conducting business, building and maintaining relationships in person and face to face.

Through witnessing the event or work that is undertaken is validated and provided legitimacy. The work could not take place without honoured and respected guests to witness it.

Witnesses are asked to store and care for the history they witness and most importantly ... to share it with their own people when they return home.[154]

Over the past several years were many fascinating presentations, conversations, and displays of powerful artwork that played with these two themes, such as the 2013 *Witnesses* show at UBC (witness Skeena Reece's collaboration with Sandra Semchuk in the haunting video installation *Touch Me*) and Carey Newman's *Witness Blanket*, which I was introduced to in an appearance by the artist during the TRC's national event in Edmonton in March 2014. There Newman introduced the project to the audience through an inspiring talk, asking us, as he does through the project website, "to bear witness, or to show by your existence that something is true, ... to pay tribute to all who have been directly or indirectly affected by Canada's Indian Residential Schools."[155] And he described this project as follows (here my notes mirror the words from the website, so I quote directly from that source):

Strewn in the wake of the Indian Residential Schools are an immeasurable number of broken or damaged pieces. These fragmented cultures, crumbling buildings, segments of language, and grains of diminished pride are often connected only by the common experience that created them. Imagine those pieces, symbolic and tangible, woven together in the form of a blanket. A blanket made from pieces of residential schools, churches, government buildings, and cultural structures.

A blanket where the story of each piece is as important to its construction as the wood and screws that hold it together.

A blanket with the sole purpose of standing in eternal witness to the effects of the Indian Residential School era—the system created and run by churches and the Canadian government to "take the Indian out of the child." Left alone, these pieces may be forgotten, lost, buried, or worse—be uncomfortable reminders that leave painful impressions on the minds and hearts of those who recognize what they represent. Individually, they are paragraphs of a disappearing narrative. Together they are strong and formidable, collectively able to recount for future generations the true story of loss, strength, reconciliation and pride.[156]

I kicked myself that day for not renewing my ethics approval, which might have allowed me to interview Newman and ask all the questions that were now rambling through my mind. I had to make do with an inspiring chat and a commitment to seek out the *Witness Blanket* at one of its forthcoming installation sites, where I could witness it and bear witness as Newman asked. I finally had the opportunity at the TRC's final event, on 2 June 2015, in Ottawa.

But there were three foundational projects that speak to what I have learned through this project: community and responsibility come together through collaboration, trust, and protocol. The first was a small, two-day artist and scholar gathering hosted 7–8 October 2011 by the Centre for Innovation in Culture and the Arts at Thompson Rivers University, Kamloops, British Columbia, where project team member Ashok Mathur was Canada Research Chair in Cultural and Artistic Inquiry. As part of a project funded in part by a TRC research grant and the AHF, a small group of artists and curators joined a research team of which I was a part to help think through possible approaches and avenues to effective and ethical research practice, not only grounded as necessary in reconciliation theory but also contributing to reconciliation practice. One of the key themes from this discussion was complexity. How could we work through all the complexities of history, legacy, and trauma, all of which exist simultaneously within the residential schools issue and art history in Canada?

One suggestion was to acknowledge that reconciliation is a *work in progress*, a theme that I and my fellow editors of the Aboriginal Healing Foundation's *Response, Responsibility, and Renewal: Canada's Truth and Reconciliation Journey* (Gregory Younging and Mike DeGagné) titled one of the volumes, "Reconciliation: A Work in *Progress*."[157] Other participants in the discussion noted, with some mirth, how familiar artists and curators are with the concept of a work in progress. It was at this point that the group hit on the concept of incubation (an intense form of residency) as a way to approach these complexities. What if, the group concluded, we invited artists, curators, and other thinkers to come together equipped with works in progress of their own that would touch, in some fashion, on any of the themes and/or complexities within the question "what is the role of art and the artist in reconciliation?" The incubation would combine artistic, curatorial, and research practice and question if and/or how any one or all of these things, or the interplay itself, can contribute to reconciliation practice. Essentially, the advice was that taking "a residency approach … rather than an exhibition approach to these topics might also be more healthy as it plays less on the public display of pain and more on private exploration and study."[158] Leah Sandals interviewed many of the artists whom I have worked with over these years, including David Garneau, who told her that "I have a lot of anxiety about shows that are basically a display of Aboriginal pain. … Why are we—Aboriginal and non-Aboriginal curators—presenting Aboriginal pain to a primarily non-Indigenous audience? What do we hope to achieve?"[159] As such, the group that I was working with advised that we would need to bring together people and ideas in some way to provide a foundation for the eventual physical and intellectual gathering, a "pre-catalogue" of ideas. The *catalogue*, of course, is another play on words/concepts, turning on its head the straightforward arc of artist/curator/space/exhibition/catalogue with which so many of the artists in attendance were familiar.

Reconcile This! became, as I wrote in 2011, "a pre-catalogue of an 'exhibition' that may or may not one day materialize post–*Reconcile This!* For all intents and purposes, this event will lead into Reconciliation: Work(s) in Progress, a two-day symposium followed by a five-day incubation artistic residency, hosted by the Shingwauk Residential Schools Centre (SRSC) at Algoma University in Sault Ste. Marie, Ontario."[160] I hosted this event in my capacity as director of the Shingwauk Residential Schools Centre, 27 September–3 October 2012. This was followed in 2013 by a month-long artist residency at Thompson Rivers University in partnership with the SRSC called Reconsidering Reconciliation and culminated in the publication of *The Land We Are: Writers and Artists Unsettle the Politics of Reconciliation*, edited by Gabrielle Hill and Sophie McCall.

On 2 June 2015, the TRC released its ninety-four calls to action, a few of which speak specifically to the arts under the subheading "Commemoration":

79. We call upon the federal government, in collaboration with Survivors, Aboriginal organizations, and the arts community, to develop a reconciliation framework for Canadian heritage and commemoration....

81. We call upon the federal government, in collaboration with Survivors and their organizations, and other parties to the Settlement Agreement, to commission and install a publicly accessible, highly visible, Residential Schools National Monument in the city of Ottawa to honour Survivors and all the children who were lost to their families and communities.

82. We call upon provincial and territorial governments, in collaboration with Survivors and their organizations, and other parties to the Settlement Agreement, to commission and install a publicly accessible, highly visible, Residential Schools Monument in each capital city to honour Survivors and all the children who were lost to their families and communities.

83. We call upon the Canada Council for the Arts to establish, as a funding priority, a strategy for Indigenous and non-Indigenous artists to undertake collaborative projects and produce works that contribute to the reconciliation process.[161]

It is this last call to action that underscores the major finding from this work: collaboration. I had always envisioned my project as one in which I would create space to feature the words and works of artists, curators, and other cultural producers, but I had not originally envisioned it as a collaboration. The question of responsibility was one of the core questions that I wanted to ask. But it was not until I began to encounter the artists whom I would go on to interview that I realized how essential collaboration was to pushing intellectual and creative boundaries.

The Canada Council for the Arts (in partnership with the J.W. McConnell Foundation and the Circle on Philanthropy and Aboriginal Peoples in Canada) also announced a new program in 2015, {Re}conciliation,[162] described as "a groundbreaking initiative which aims to promote artistic collaborations that look to the past & future for new dialogues between Aboriginal and non-Aboriginal peoples in Canada."[163] Although it is obvious that this program speaks directly to Call to Action 83 (above), the council and its partners were already way out in front with their initiative when the TRC released its calls, as the council makes clear in this announcement:

> This initiative aims to promote artistic collaborations between Aboriginal and non-Aboriginal artists, investing in the power of art and imagination to inspire dialogue, understanding and change. The Canada Council administers the {Re}conciliation initiative, which was developed by Canada Council, the J.W. McConnell Family Foundation and The Circle *in anticipation* of the Truth and Reconciliation Commission's final report and recommendations. A first call for proposals was issued in May 2015. A second will be issued in 2016. Interested artists and arts organizations will be invited to submit proposals for project funding up to $75,000. Applicants who submitted a proposal in 2015 but did not receive funding are eligible to re-submit to future deadlines.[164]

How were these partners able to anticipate such a thing? They were able to do so in the same way that the many artists, curators, and scholars engaged in these issues were able in 2008 to anticipate that there would be an explosion of art making and art scholarship related to residential schools, healing, and reconciliation: engagement with the Indigenous community in general and the Indigenous arts community in particular. The council and its partners engaged with these communities likely, in many cases, seeking the advice and expertise of the same people whom I and many others were engaging with to explore the many questions about the role(s) of art and the artist in reconciliation. Although the idea of profound silences and the efforts over decades to break those silences comprised an important theme to explore in this work, and since it is clear that this effort is still needed (as many of the contemporary works that I reference make clear, as does the Canada Council's new program), it also became clear that collaboration was a principal finding in my work, which fed into the collaborative research that my colleagues and I were doing for the TRC itself in *Practicing Reconciliation: A Collaborative Study of Aboriginal Art, Resistance and Cultural Politics*. The TRC was listening, as evidenced in volume 6 of its final report, *Canada's Residential Schools: Reconciliation*, in which such work is cited and the theme of collaboration—indeed the very word—features prominently throughout the volume and the calls to action. The Canada Council for the Arts was listening, too, and arrived at the same conclusion that we reached, even before the TRC called for it. All because the community had told us (itself, really) that collaboration, particularly across cultures, was a tool—perhaps *the* tool—for taking reconciliation from theory to practice: art practice, curatorial practice, institutional/organizational support practice, and even the practice of witnessing through art.

France Trépanier and Chris Creighton-Kelly tied all the themes that I have explored in this chapter together nicely when they wrote that "Aboriginal artists, even those living in an urban environment, have both a connection and a strong sense of responsibility to their community. These artists will create their work in collaboration with members of their community, even if those people are not 'professional' artists in the Western sense of that term. When that respect is given, honour is given back."[165] In my own work, and with collaborators on those other projects, I have sought to practise this as our research and creative approaches. We know that, as Trépanier and Creighton-Kelly write, "this relationship is deepened when artists actually listen to community members. The artist seeks not just information for the content of their work, but a more profound understanding of how their work connects to history and knowledge."[166] And, clearly, the practices of individuals, collectives, and communities are changing how others do business: "For some Aboriginal artists, implicating their community is an essential part of their work. Even the most professional of these artists will insist that they are not just making art, but involving their community in that process. In this way, art that is made in collaboration with a community can be part of a healing process that actually strengthens that community. *This aspect of Aboriginal art making is often misunderstood and ignored by funding agencies and other mainstream organizations.*"[167] Of the latter, given the Canada Council development, perhaps we can say "no more."

And yet....

If I were asked to make a recommendation to whoever will spearhead the creation of the monuments that the TRC calls for across the country, then it wold be to implore the creative people behind the work to ensure that their efforts create community and, ideally, ongoing collaboration between peoples. They cannot be static. They cannot be merely symbolic.

They must be substantive as well. Maria Campbell had the most arresting argument for the subjectivity of symbolism when we spoke:

MC: For me, a good commemoration, I mean we had a commemoration ceremony in Batoche two years ago, they called it a commemoration ceremony and it was a battle between the Canadians and the Métis and they brought these people together and they sang songs and they did all kinds of nice things and the commissioners came, I don't know who all else was there but all of those people from opposing sides were there, for this commemoration ceremony. Well, for me, they went away and there's a plaque, but the people still have no land. Nobody ever talked about what did the people die for? What was this war about?

JD: Louis Riel is still a traitor.

MC: And I hope to God he stays that way. The next horrible thing they could decide to do is pardon him.

JD: People are arguing that.

MC: That's right and some people, I absolutely wonder where their common sense is, are fighting to have him pardoned. Why? I mean why would you do that to him? He gave his life so that at least he would give us something to hang onto forever and to pardon him is to say he didn't do anything wrong. Well, fine then we're all going to go away happy? Well, excuse me, what happened to the land? There was never any land settlement given.

JD: So what if the pardon is as the first step in those other things?

MC: To me that would be a really evil thing to do, but I wouldn't be surprised if it is. But it won't change anything, pardoning Riel, if it doesn't change what he died for. I think they think by pardoning him no one will talk about it, it's taking the martyr away from the cause. I would certainly never support anything like that, nor would I ever let anybody forget what he died for and that the pardoning was done so that we would say, "OK, we forgive you." And then it's OK for them to haul the resources away and for them to....

JD: Now, only the state can do that so, as objectionable as that is to you, that is an act by the state....

MC: It was also an act by the state to charge him with treason and hang him.

JD: What if a commemoration of Riel or another historical figure also included your vocal opposition to the state's ... like is there a way to have it reflect multiple perspectives? Or can we just not see eye to eye...?

MC: I couldn't see me seeing eye to eye, maybe somebody else could, I can't. I can't see that I could sit across the table from somebody that pardoned him and I don't believe in the pardon and we're going to have some kind of commemoration together. What is that doing? It's not doing anything. For me everything for me is to make things easier for the state.[168]

Although fellow Métis artist David Garneau did not make the same point about Riel, he did offer a thought in *Reconcile This!* that might speak to Campbell's concern. He wrote that "art is not healing in itself, but it can be in relation. Art is a stimulant and a balm when taken internally, but dangerous if mistaken for experience. There is a profound difference between reading signs and being engaged by a symbol. Sharing in a discourse about histories, responsibility, and transformation among artworks and with other human beings is a corrective to the colonial desire for settlement."[169] As a curator, he and others might well have the solution to how to commemorate Riel beyond symbolism, in stone, song, line/form/colour, rather than law.

Commemorative efforts—as Candace Hopkins stated at the Stronger than Stone: (Re)Inventing the Indigenous Monument symposium 21 to 24 November 2014 at Alberta College of Art and Design in Calgary and at Wanuskewin Heritage Park in Saskatoon—must ensure that "we will move from a place of resistance to a place of ownership."[170] This certainly reminds me of my conversation with Alex Janvier and his use of the descriptor *landlord*. Before our one-on-one interview, in which he repeated similar themes, Janvier spoke to the small group of us gathered at Thompson Rivers University in 2011. His words were rendered in free verse from the transcript by Ayumi Goto in *Reconcile This!* That text reads, in part,

> I've painted about most things that anyone can talk about
> the younger people can really start painting
> and be the real people in the arts
> go into the best galleries in Canada and the world
> China, Japan, Germany, they want to see our work, they think it's
> really something that we're surviving
> eventually we'll be able to conquer the art world
>
> we're in the forefront of a powerful movement,
> asserting ourselves as the landlords
> we may not get it all back, but we will get something, psychologically
> even if you have a small reserve, it's important to know that you're
> the landlord.[171]

Janvier was clearly calling for change, and he alluded to the importance of community, albeit across generations. The change that he called for is undeniably substantive. But how can it be systemic? This last idea goes far beyond Call to Action 83's specific reference to the Canada Council for the Arts and funding for reconciliation projects. And, interestingly, in going beyond we actually have to go back to 1996 and the RCAP report. That commission made a very different recommendation, one that has not been realized. Although it spoke of the need to change Canada's institutions (in ways that we would now refer to as decolonization and/or Indigenization), it also called for something new: "3.6.19: Federal, provincial, territorial and Aboriginal governments co-operate to establish and fund an Aboriginal Arts Council, with a minimum 20-year life span and an annual budget equivalent to five per cent of the Canada Council budget, to foster the revitalization and development of Aboriginal arts and literature."[172] My 2011 conversation with Armand Garnet Ruffo[173] contained the most precise return to this idea, which encompasses all three elements of symbolism, substance, and systemic change:

JD: So, do you have any misgivings around the idea of the TRC's $20 million fund for commemoration initiatives? They've said they're going to look at everything from the tried-and-true monument—if that's what someone proposes—to a community that wants to have a Sunday afternoon gathering of some sort. So it could be permanent or it could be ephemeral.

AGR: Well, again, I have no problem with it. I guess it depends on the community, it depends on what one means by commemoration. Not that we shouldn't think about it critically. I mean there was an Elder on CBC radio, asking what has all this stuff accomplished. He was saying that he went through residential school, and his people are still being locked up and thrown in jail. And we still have the lowest educational attainments in the country. Many of our First Nations languages are on the verge of extinction and government after government has done little, if anything, about it. There's not even a repository, a library, of Indigenous languages in the country. To put up a statue, yes, it's important to commemorate what happened, and I think there's a place for that, but we can't stop there. We want to memorialize so we don't forget it, but let's also celebrate the future. Let's celebrate the things that we can do now to make things better, not only focus on what happened.

JD: I like that idea: a statue's okay, but also build the institutions.

AGR: Exactly. Our own institutions—that's what we need now! When we started this conversation, we talked about healing, and we talked about the role of the artist. Well, the role of the artist for me is to prod and poke society in whatever form that may take. So where are we as a people in this society? Where do we stand? At the end of the twenty-first century, will we even be here? Is all this stuff currently going on just lip service? Isn't the agenda still really about assimilation into capitalism and ultimately taking control of what little land we have left, by whatever means? Before long Aboriginal politicians will be sitting in the House of Commons working for the government of Canada, and then what?

JD: Back to the activism.

AGR: Yeah, right now we are basically being legislated out of existence. That's happening now, and so healing, yes, being healthy is critical, but we better also take the next step, and soon. . . . For me it's important also to show our potential. We need the vision of where we can be, before we can get there. I think right now, we know the present, we know the near past, in terms of residential school[s], and we're learning about our distant past, but we still don't know our future—where we can go. I'm concerned about our children seven generations from now. Will our beautiful cultures and languages survive another hundred years? I'd like to see a vision of us with our cultures intact, playing an active and positive role in Canada. So, yeah, that's the kind of artistic call I'd like to see. How do artists envision a positive future for us on this land? I think right now we need that vision more than ever. Louis Riel knew this when he said that his people would sleep for a hundred years and when they awoke, the artists would give them their spirit back. Let's look forward to another hundred years.[174]

In 2017, Canada celebrated 150 years of Confederation. This project taught me that many contemporary artists are still focusing their beams of light, to illuminate their existences and those of their community members still in the shadows, either because the stories have not yet been (permitted to be) told or are (perceived as) ignored or even relegated to "sad chapters" that we have now left behind. I have suggested in the public education work that I've done over many years that perhaps one element of reconciliation is knowing that the story of this space/place is the story of diverse First Nations and Inuit from time immemorial . . . through contact with Europeans . . . through centuries of cooperation and conflict, trade, treaty, and colonization, love and friendship, hardship, betrayal . . . through fair and forced settling, immigration, and (many forms of) migration . . . through the birth, marginalization, and resurgence of the Métis Nation . . . through relationship with, resistance to, and suppression by the Crown . . . through the privileged negotiation of the terms of Confederation for the establishment of the modern nation state that is Canada . . . through its reliance on/reluctance about (non-white) immigration . . . through and toward many individual, community, and national accomplishments across the wonderful diversity of languages and cultures of this land.

That picture (painted here with words, my medium of choice) is not perfect, but it has allowed me to engage many different people in conversations about reconciliation, conversations that have allowed people to recognize enough of a connection to a story, a feeling, to want to interrogate it further. In doing so, people invariably place themselves within the narrative, sometimes sheepishly (as I did in my youth, grasping for connections to notions of culture and community) and sometimes defiantly, as we have seen with the resistance by some to the Canada 150 narrative.[175]

Creating opportunities for others to explore how they position themselves within the story/stories of Canada has proven to be, particularly in my experience as an educator, one of the most useful tools in transformative learning. As John Paul Lederach wrote, "the capacity to restory imagines both the past and the future and provides space for the narrative voice to create,"[176] and what I have seen audiences create for themselves is a space where position(s) and the concept of intersectionality allow individuals to be witnesses of the fact that it is impossible to tell our collective histories without many voices woven together. That is where Maria Campbell's notion of reciprocity is so essential. When I asked Campbell if she would ever separate this interest in being on the front lines from artistic sensibility, she said that it's all grassroots:

> My concern and my sole purpose as an artist [are] to heal my community. And to help myself.... I get my power from the community, so I give it back. There's reciprocity. Reciprocity is a big teaching in our community, that what you take ... you have to give back. And there are responsibilities to taking people's power to heal yourself, whether it's their stories or their friendship, or just making a place in the community.... You can't just go and take that power. You'll get sick.... I can talk about myself as an artist because over the years I've come to terms [with the fact] that the artist is a community worker.... That's my definition of an artist. I get power from the people and I give it back to them. And how it affects them and what happens is not up to me. I go in there with truth and with kindness, and whatever is supposed to happen will happen.[177]

It's not just a matter of "you tell me your story, and I'll tell you mine," but a requirement for acts of respect and humility to create this new "work."

It should be clear that RCAP and the TRC and the many truths that they have asked us to witness might be behind us in one sense but that they must also be our future—in the form of *doing*, of intellectual and emotional *work* that contributes to the collective, often collaborative, work of symbolic gestures and substantive and systemic changes. In 1996, these were recommendations; in 2015, they were calls to action. Today and tomorrow they must be what we *practise*.

NOTES

1   Quoted in Dewar, "'Dance with Us,'" 169.
2   Sharing the Land, Sharing A Future Conference, https://www.queensu.ca/sps/rcap20.
3   The importance of the Aboriginal Healing Foundation is discussed in a subsequent section.
4   Archibald and Dewar, "Creative Arts, Culture, and Healing," 1.
5   Archibald et al., *Dancing, Singing, Painting*, 7.
6   Archibald et al., *Dancing, Singing, Painting*, 8.
7   Archibald et al., *Dancing, Singing, Painting*, 1.
8   Wesley-Esquimaux and Smolewski, *Historic Trauma*, iii.
9   Archibald and Dewar, "Creative Arts, Culture, and Healing," 8.
10 Quoted in Archibald and Dewar, "Creative Arts, Culture, and Healing," 9.
11 Hauss, "Reconciliation," 1.
12 Boer, "Reconciling South Africa."
13 Gaertner, "'The Climax of Reconciliation.'"
14 Dewar et al., *Practicing Reconciliation*, 7.
15 Indian residential schools is the "official" term used by the government of Canada, with some variants, including Inuit as a descriptor. Hereafter, I will use the broader, more inclusive, term "residential schools" to ensure that all of Canada's Aboriginal peoples are included. Residential schools refer to all government-funded, church-run "schools" where children were in residence, including industrial schools, boarding schools, student residences, hostels, billets and even Inuit tent camps in the North. First Nations, Inuit, and Métis children were all subject to the assimilatory goals of the government and the proselytizing efforts of the various church entities through schooling; however, the government of Canada has only apologized formally for the residential school experience. The "day school" experience, which affected many more Métis students proportionally, as well as some First Nations and Inuit students, has not been formally addressed. For more information on the Métis experience, not covered in great detail here, see TRC, *Canada's Residential Schools: The Métis Experience, Volume 3. The Final Report of the Truth and Reconciliation Commission of Canada*. A short description of the unique experiences of Inuit and Métis is also featured in the "Where Are the Children?" website content discussed in this chapter.
16 Govier, "What Is Acknowledgement," 78.
17 Govier, "What Is Acknowledgement," 78–79.
18 The first to apologize was the United Church of Canada in 1986. Other apologies and statements followed: the Oblate Missionaries of Mary Immaculate (Roman Catholic) in 1991, the Anglican Church in 1993, and the Presbyterian Church in 1994. See "Timeline" in *From Truth to Reconciliation*, 64–65.
19 LaRocque, *When the Other Is Me*.
20 The Royal Commission on Aboriginal Peoples was born in a time of ferment when the future of the Canadian federation was being debated passionately. It came to fruition in the troubled months following the demise of the Meech Lake Accord and the confrontation, in the summer of 1990, between Mohawks and the power of the Canadian state at Kanesatake (Oka), Quebec.

21   AHF, "FAQs."

22   There are two compensation elements: (1) the Common Experience Payment (CEP), a process through which all former students who can prove their residency at a school on the government-approved list could apply for compensation based on a formula of $10,000 for the first year of attendance and $3,000 for each additional year; and (2) the Independent Assessment Process for specific abuse claims. The media attention in 2007 was decidedly negative, focusing on speculation that survivors would not or could not handle an influx of money responsibly, which would lead to drug and alcohol abuse, violence, and financial predation. The AHF conducted two studies that explore these issues: see AHF, *Lump Sum Compensation Payments*; AHF, *The Indian Residential Schools*.

23   An interim executive director was appointed in September 2007 to set up the TRC Secretariat in advance of the process that would name Harry LaForme as commission chair and Claudette Dumont-Smith and Jane Brewin Morley as the two commissioners. The TRC began its work on 1 June 2008. On 20 October 2008, LaForme resigned as chair when he and the commissioners could not reconcile their differences. Dumont-Smith and Brewin Morley's resignations followed shortly thereafter. The TRC was reconstituted on 10 June 2009, with Justice Murray Sinclair appointed chair and Marie Wilson and Wilton Littlechild as commissioners.

24   The AHF had also received $40 million in 2005 from the federal government, bringing the total amount of funds received by the AHF through the two mandates to $515 million. The AHF's mandate under the IRSSA officially ended 31 March 2012, but the AHF remained open with a small operational staff managing monies from the Catholic entities, parties to the IRSSA, who chose to commit a portion of their obligated financial commitment within the IRSSA to the AHF. The AHF continued to fund twelve of its longer-term healing centres until 2014, at which time it wound down and dissolved.

25   Harper, "Statement of Apology."

26   Day schools were just that—schools that students attended without being "in residence." They might have been schools located within a reserve community or residential schools, which for some students did not include residing at them; those students might have been billeted in white homes or returned home each night. Nonetheless, the experiences of students in day schools have been described as similar if not identical in terms of the assimilationist and proselytizing aims.

27   The Sixties Scoop refers to the alarming number of Indigenous children removed from their homes by various Children's Aid or social services bodies during this decade and beyond.

28   AHF 2008, 3.

29   In a Canadian context, Aboriginal refers to *First Nations, Inuit, and Métis* (FN/I/M) individuals and/or peoples and may be used interchangeably, as I do here, though there is some political positioning to the choice of FN/I/M over Aboriginal to underscore separate identities and diversities. Native, too, can be used interchangeably with *Aboriginal*, though its use has fallen out of favour since it has often been used to refer exclusively to *First Nations* or *Indians* without being explicit. It is therefore ambiguous, and I use it only when referring to another author's use of the term; I treat Indian in a similar fashion. I will highlight problematic issues if they arise in that context. Indigenous is equally valid but used primarily to refer to Indigeneity in an international context, and that is how I will use the term.

30   Spivak, "Can the Subaltern Speak?"

31   Alcoff, "The Problem of Speaking for Others."

32   Castellano, "Updating Aboriginal Traditions."

33   Ryan, *The Trickster Shift*, xi.

34   The reader can go online to explore the late-2016 and early 2017 controversies over Boyden's identity and early work. I will not cover them here.

35   TRC, Open Call for Artistic Submissions. http://www.trc.ca/assets/pdf/mroom_TRC_
     Art_Submissions_en_p6.pdf.
36   TRC, Open Call for Artistic Submissions.
37   Weaver, *That the People Might Live*, 1997.
38   Weaver, *That the People Might Live*, xiii.
39   Armstrong, "En'owkin."
40   Armstrong, "En'owkin."
41   Quoted in Dewar, "'Dance with Us,'" 158–59.
42   Armstrong translates this from the original Okanagan, which is not reproduced in print.
43   Armstrong, "Sharing One Skin," 1997.
44   Quoted in Dewar, "'Dance with Us,'" 130.
45   Dewar, "'Dance with Us,'" 130.
46   Dewar, "'Dance with Us,'" 133.
47   Dewar, "'Dance with Us,'" 133.
48   "Timeline," in *From Truth to Reconciliation*, viii.
49   Trépanier and Creighton-Kelly, *Understanding Aboriginal Arts*, 57.
50   *Webster's Revised Unabridged Dictionary, Dictionary.com*, dictionary1.classic.reference.
     com/browse/reconciliation.
51   Rice and Snyder, "Reconciliation," 46.
52   TRC, Our Mandate. Schedule N of the Indian Residential Schools Settlement Agreement
     http://www.trc.ca/about-us/our-mandate.html.
53   Llewellyn, "Bridging the Gap," 185.
54   Llewellyn, "Bridging the Gap," 186.
55   Llewellyn, "Bridging the Gap," 187.
56   The authors reject the term "aboriginal" outright in favour of "Indigenous," arguing that
     "this identity is purely a state construction that is instrumental to the state's own attempt
     to gradually subsume Indigenous existences into its own constitutional system and body
     politic." Alfred and Corntassel, "Being Indigenous," 598.
57   Alfred and Corntassel, "Being Indigenous," 598.
58   Alfred, *Wasáse*, 152.
59   Alfred, *Wasáse*, 152.
60   Alfred, *Wasáse*, 112.
61   Alfred, *Wasáse*, 130.
62   This is Gerald Vizenor's concept that blends notions of survival and resistance.
63   Alfred, *Wasáse*, 128–30.
64   Lederach, *The Moral Imagination*, 29.
65   Lederach, *The Moral Imagination*, 27–28.
66   Lederach, *The Moral Imagination*, 149.
67   Lederach, *The Moral Imagination*, 59.
68   Alfred, *Wasáse*, 77.
69   Minnow, *Between Vengeance and Forgiveness*.
70   Bennett, *Empathic Vision*.
71   Minnow, *Between Vengeance and Forgiveness*, 129.
72   Minnow, *Between Vengeance and Forgiveness*, 138.
73   Minnow, *Between Vengeance and Forgiveness*, 142.
74   Apel, *Memory Effects*, 3.
75   Million, "Telling Secrets," 73.
76   Million quotes from LaRocque, "Preface," 74.
77   Castellano, *Final Report*, 160.
78   Quoted in Dewar, "'Dance with Us,'" 117.
79   Dewar, "'Dance with Us,'" 118.
80   Garneau, "Imaginary Spaces," 32.
81   Garneau, "Imaginary Spaces," 35.

82 Quoted in Dewar, "'Dance with Us,'" 81.

83 Dewar, "'Dance with Us,'" 81–82.

84 LaRocque, *When the Other Is Me*, 168.

85 Levine, *Poiesis*, 11.

86 McNiff, *Art Heals*, 186.

87 Levine, *Poiesis*, 10.

88 Levine, *Poiesis*, 188.

89 Smith, *Decolonizing Methodologies*, 33.

90 Smith, *Decolonizing Methodologies*, 33.

91 Townsend-Gault, "Hot Dogs," 113.

92 Townsend-Gault, "Hot Dogs," 113.

93 Torpey, "Introduction," 5–7. Torpey defines the word *reparations* narrowly to mean "a response to past injustices" and the words *reparations politics* as "a broader field encompassing 'transitional justice,' 'apologies,' and efforts at 'reconciliation' as well" (3).

94 Govier, "What Is Acknowledgement," 79.

95 Osborne, "Landscapes, Memory, Monuments, and Commemoration," 41–42.

96 Chrisjohn and Young, *The Circle Game*.

97 Haig-Brown, *Resistance and Renewal*.

98 Milloy, *A National Crime*.

99 Huffstetter, *Lakota Grieving*, 28.

100 Huffstetter, *Lakota Grieving*, 29.

101 Gillis, "Memory and Identity," 3.

102 Wolschke-Bulmahn, *Places of Commemoration*, 2.

103 Wolschke-Bulmahn, *Places of Commemoration*, 2.

104 Gillis, "Memory and Identity," 3.

105 Gillis, "Memory and Identity," 3.

106 Gillis, "Memory and Identity," 5.

107 Handler, "Is 'Identity' a Useful Cross-Cultural Concept?" 29.

108 Handler, "Is 'Identity' a Useful Cross-Cultural Concept?" 30.

109 Handler, "Is 'Identity' a Useful Cross-Cultural Concept?" 30.

110 Handler, "Is 'Identity' a Useful Cross-Cultural Concept?" 38.

111 Handler, "Is 'Identity' a Useful Cross-Cultural Concept?" 38.

112 Handler, "Is 'Identity' a Useful Cross-Cultural Concept?" 30.

113 Gillis, "Memory and Identity," 3.

114 Gillis, "Memory and Identity," 3.

115 Gillis, "Memory and Identity," 7.

116 Gillis, "Memory and Identity," 7.

117 Halbwachs, *On Collective Memory*, 182.

118 Halbwachs, *On Collective Memory*, 182.

119 Halbwachs, *On Collective Memory*, 69.

120 Gedi and Elam, "Collective Memory," 40.

121 Gedi and Elam, "Collective Memory," 40.

122 Gedi and Elam, "Collective Memory," 40–41.

123 Nora, "Between Memory and History," 8.

124 Nora, "Between Memory and History," 8.

125 Gedi and Elam, "Collective Memory," 49.

126 Savage, "The Politics of Memory," 146.

127 Savage, "The Politics of Memory," 135–36.

128 Osborne, "Constructing Landscapes of Power," 431.

129 Osborne, "Landscapes, Memory, Monuments, and Commemoration," 50.

130 Gillis, "Memory and Identity," 5.

131 Gillis, "Memory and Identity," 14.

132 Gillis, "Memory and Identity," 18.

133 Gillis, "Memory and Identity," 18.

134 Osborne, "Landscapes, Memory, Monuments, and Commemoration," 54.

135 Gillis, "Memory and Identity," 5.

136 Gillis, "Memory and Identity," 5.

137 Levy, The Future of the Past," 65.

138 Levy, The Future of the Past," 64.

139 Levy, The Future of the Past," 65.

140 Levy, The Future of the Past," 65.

141 Gordon, *Making Public Pasts*, xv.

142 Gordon, *Making Public Pasts*, xv.

143 Simon, "The Pedagogical Insistence," 197.

144 Simon, "The Pedagogical Insistence," 198.

145 Osborne, "Landscapes, Memory, Monuments, and Commemoration," 72.

146 Simon, "The Pedagogical Insistence," 197–98.

147 Belcourt, "Artist Description of 'Giniigaaniimenaaning.'"

148 Quoted in Dewar, "'Dance with Us,'" 165.

149 "Witness," in *English Oxford Living Dictionaries*, www.oxforddictionaries.com/
     definition/english/witness.

150 "Witness."

151 Gaertner, "'Aboriginal Principles of Witnessing,'" 138.

152 "Witness."

153 Dewar and Goto, *Reconcile This!*, 10.

154 TRC, "Honorary Witness."

155 Newman, "Inspiration."

156 Newman, "Inspiration."

157 Younging, Dewar, and DeGagné, *Response, Responsibility, and Renewal.*

158 Sandals, "Art, Residential Schools and Reconciliation."

159 Sandals, "Art, Residential Schools and Reconciliation."

160 This text is a lightly edited version of the introduction that I wrote for *Reconcile This!* It
     was a special art-focused issue of the journal *West Coast Line* that I co-edited with Ayumi
     Goto, available free as a download from http://reworksinprogress.ca/wp-content/
     uploads/2012/08/wcl74h.pdf, a website to support a follow-up iteration of this ongoing
     work. See 6.

161 TRC, *Calls to Action*, 9.

162 I was privileged to serve as a member of the jury for what was at the time a one-time,
     special initiative that now appears likely to be sustained in ongoing fashion under the
     council's new programming.

163 Canada Council for the Arts, "{Re}conciliation." https://canadacouncil.ca/initiatives/
     reconciliation.

164 Canada Council for the Arts, "Discover the Programs," emphasis added. https://
     canadacouncil.ca/initiatives/reconciliation.

165 Trépanier and Creighton-Kelly, *Understanding Aboriginal Arts*, 62.

166 Trépanier and Creighton-Kelly, *Understanding Aboriginal Arts*, 62.

167 Trépanier and Creighton-Kelly, *Understanding Aboriginal Arts*, 61; emphasis added.

168 Quoted in Dewar, "'Dance with Us,'" 316–17.

169 Garneau, "Imaginary Spaces," 38.

170 Hughes, "Not Written in Stone."

171 Dewar and Goto, *Reconcile This!*, 15.

172 RCAP, *Report of the Royal Commission*, 602.

173 This text is from a version of the interview that Ruffo and I edited together for publication;
     see Ruffo, "'Our Roots Go Much Deeper.'"

174 Ruffo, "'Our Roots Go Much Deeper,'" 223–26.

175   Readers should familiarize themselves with the numerous threads that inform the Resistance 150 hashtag on Twitter: https://twitter.com/resistance150?lang=en.
176   Lederach, *The Moral Imagination*, 149.
177   Quoted in Dewar, "'Dance with Us,'" 198.

REFERENCES

Aboriginal Healing Foundation (AHF). *Lump Sum Compensation Payments Research Project: The Circle Rechecks Itself*. Ottawa: AHF, 2007.

——. *The Indian Residential Schools Settlement Agreement's Common Experience Payment and Healing: A Qualitative Study Exploring Impacts on Recipients*. Ottawa: AHF, 2010.

——. "FAQs." 2012. www.ahf.ca/faqs.

Alcoff, Linda. "The Problem of Speaking for Others." *Cultural Critique* 20 (1991–92) : 5–32.

Alfred, Taiaiake. *Wasáse: Indigenous Pathways of Action and Freedom*. Toronto: Broadview, 2005.

Alfred, Taiaiake, and Jeff Corntassel. "Being Indigenous: Resurgences against Contemporary Colonialism." *Government and Opposition* 40, no. 4 (2005): 597–614.

Apel, Dora. *Memory Effects: The Holocaust and the Art of Secondary Witnessing*. New Brunswick, NJ: Rutgers University Press, 2002.

Archibald, Linda, and Jonathan Dewar. "Creative Arts, Culture, and Healing: Building an Evidence Base." *Pimatisiwin: A Journal of Indigenous and Aboriginal Community Health* 8, no. 3 (2011): 1–26.

Archibald, Linda, Jonathan Dewar, Carrie Reid, and Vanessa Stevens. *Dancing, Singing, Painting, and Speaking the Healing Story: Healing through Creative Arts*. Ottawa: AHF, 2012.

Armstrong, Jeannette. "En'owkin: What It Means to a Sustainable Community." Center for Ecoliteracy, n.d. https://www.ecoliteracy.org/article/enowkin-what-it-means-sustainable-community.

——. "Sharing One Skin: Native Canadian Jeannette Armstrong Explains How the Global Economy Robs Us of Our Full Humanity." *New Internationalist Magazine* 287 (1997). https://newint.org/features/1997/01/05/sharing/.

Belcourt, Christi. "Artist Description of 'Giniigaaniimenaaning.'" http://www.aadnc-aandc.gc.ca/eng/1339417945383/1339418457202.

Bennett, Jill. *Empathic Vision: Affect, Trauma, and Contemporary Art*. Stanford, CA: Stanford University Press, 2005.

Boer, T.A. "Reconciling South Africa or South Africans? Cautionary Notes from the TRC." *African Studies Quarterly* 8, no. 1 (2004): 19–37.

Canada Council for the Arts. "[Re]conciliation." http://canadacouncil.ca/aboriginal-arts-office/reconciliation.

——. "Reconciliation Programs." http://canadacouncil.ca/council/news-room/news/2015/reconciliation-programs.

Castellano, Marlene Brant. "Updating Aboriginal Traditions of Knowledge." *Indigenous Knowledges in Global Contexts: Multiple Readings of Our World*, edited by G.J.S. Dei, B.L. Hall, and D.G. Rosenberg, 21–36. Toronto: OISE and University of Toronto Press, 2000.

——. *Final Report of the Aboriginal Healing Foundation, Volume I: A Healing Journey: Reclaiming Wellness*. Ottawa: AHF, 2006.

Chrisjohn, Roland, and Sherri Young. *The Circle Game: Shadows and Substance in the Indian*

Residential School Experience in Canada. Penticton, BC: Theytus Books, 1997.

Dewar, Jonathan. "'Dance with Us as You Can': Art, Artist, and Witness(ing) in Canada's Truth and Reconciliation Journey." PhD diss., Carleton University, 2017.

Dewar, Jonathan, David Gaertner, Ayumi Goto, Ashok Mathur, and Sophie McCall. *Practicing Reconciliation: A Collaborative Study of Aboriginal Art, Resistance and Cultural Politics: A Report Commissioned by the Truth and Reconciliation Commission on Indian Residential Schools*. Kamloops, BC: CiCAC Press, 2013.

Dewar, Jonathan, and Ayumi Goto, eds. *Reconcile This! West Coast Line* 74 (2012). http:// reworksinprogress.ca/wp-content/uploads/2012/08/wcl74h.pdf.

Gaertner, David. "'The Climax of Reconciliation': Transgression, Apology, Forgiveness and the Body in Conflict Resolution." *Journal of Bioethical Inquiry: An Interdisciplinary Forum for Ethical and Legal Debate* 1, no. 1 (2011). http://rmooc.ca/wp-content/ uploads/2013/07/gaertner.pdf.

——. "'Aboriginal Principles of Witnessing' and the Truth and Reconciliation Commission of Canada." In *Arts of Engagement: Taking Aesthetic Action in and beyond the Truth and Reconciliation Commission of Canada*, edited by Dylan Robinson and Keavy Martin, 135–55. Waterloo, ON: Wilfrid Laurier University Press, 2016.

Garneau, David. "Imaginary Spaces of Conciliation and Reconciliation." *West Coast Line* 74 *Reconcile This!* (2012): 28–38.

Gedi, Noa, and Yigal Elam. "Collective Memory: What Is It?" *History and Memory* 8, no.1 (1996): 30–50.

Gillis, John R. "Memory and Identity: The History of a Relationship." In *Commemorations: The Politics of National Identity*, edited by John R. Gillis, 3–24. Princeton, NJ: Princeton University Press, 1994.

Gordon, Alan. *Making Public Pasts: The Contested Terrain of Montréal's Public Memories, 1891–1930*. Montreal and Kingston: McGill-Queen's University Press, 2001.

Govier, Trudy. "What Is Acknowledgement and Why Is It Important?" In *Dilemmas of Reconciliation: Cases and Concepts*, edited by Carol A.L. Prager and Trudy Govier, 65–89. Waterloo, ON: Wilfrid Laurier University Press, 2003.

Haig-Brown, Celia. *Resistance and Renewal: Surviving the Indian Residential School*. Vancouver: Arsenal Pulp Press, 1988.

Halbwachs, Maurice. *On Collective Memory*. Trans. Lewis Coser. Chicago: University of Chicago Press, 1992.

Handler, Richard. "Is 'Identity' a Useful Cross-Cultural Concept?" In *Commemorations: The Politics of National Identity*, edited by John R. Gillis, 27–40. Princeton, NJ: Princeton University Press, 1994.

Harper, Stephen. "Statement of Apology—To Former Students of Indian Residential Schools." 2008. http://www.aadnc-aandc.gc.ca/eng/1100100015644/1100100015649.

Hauss, Charles (Chip). "Reconciliation." In *Beyond Intractability*, edited by Guy Burgess and Heidi Burgess. Boulder: Conflict Information Consortium, University of Colorado, 2013. http://www.beyondintractability.org/essay/reconciliation.

Hill, Gabrielle, and Sophie McCall. *The Land We Are: Artists and Writers Unsettle the Politics of Reconciliation*. Winnipeg: ARP Books, 2015.

Huffstetter, Stephen. *Lakota Grieving: A Pastoral Response*. Chamberlin, South Dakota: Tipi Press, 1998.

Hughes, Tarin. "Not Written in Stone: Propositions and Provocations from 'Stronger than Stone, (Re)inventing the Indigenous Monument.'" *BlackFlash*, 10 August 2015. blackflash. ca/stronger-than-stone/.

LaRocque Emma. "Preface or Here Are Our Voices—Who Will Hear?" In *Writing the Circle: Native*

Women of Western Canada, edited by Jeanne Perreault and Sylvia Vance, xv–xxx. Norman: University of Oklahoma Press, 1990.

——. *When the Other Is Me: Native Resistance Discourse, 1850–1990*. Winnipeg: University of Manitoba Press, 2010.

Lederach, John Paul. *The Moral Imagination: The Art and Soul of Building Peace*. Toronto: Oxford University Press, 2005.

Levine, Stephen K. *Poiesis: The Language of Psychology and the Speech of the Soul*. London, UK: Jessica Kingsley Publishers, 1997.

Levy, Daniel. "The Future of the Past: Historiographical Disputes and Competing Memories in Germany and Israel." *History and Theory* 38, no. 1 (1999): 51–66.

Llewellyn, Jennifer. "Bridging the Gap between Truth and Reconciliation: Restorative Justice and the Indian Residential Schools Truth and Reconciliation Commission." In *From Truth to Reconciliation: Transforming the Legacy of Residential Schools*, edited by Marlene Brant Castellano et al., 183–201. Ottawa: AHF, 2008.

McNiff, Shawn. *Art Heals: How Creativity Cures the Soul*. Boulder: Shambhala Publications, 2004.

Million, Dian Lynn. "Telling Secrets: Sex, Power and Narrative in the Rearticulation of Canadian Residential School Histories." PhD diss., University of California, 2004.

Milloy, John S. *A National Crime: The Canadian Government and the Residential School System, 1879–1986*. Winnipeg: University of Manitoba Press, 1999.

Minnow, Martha. *Between Vengeance and Forgiveness: Facing History after Genocide and Mass Violence*. Boston: Beacon Press, 1998.

Newman, Carey. "Inspiration." http://witnessblanket.ca/#!/inspiration/.

Nora, Pierre. "Between Memory and History: Les lieux de memoire." Trans. Marc Roudebush. *Representations* 26 (1989): 7–25.

Osborne, Brian S. "Constructing Landscapes of Power: The George Etienne Cartier Monument, Montréal." *Journal of Historical Geography* 24, no. 4 (1998): 431–58.

——. "Landscapes, Memory, Monuments, and Commemoration: Putting Identity in Its Place." *Canadian Ethnic Studies* 30, no. 3 (2001): 39–86.

"Reconciliation." In *Webster's Revised Unabridged Dictionary*. dictionary1.classic.reference. com/browse/reconciliation.

Rice, Brian, and Anna Snyder. "Reconciliation in the Context of a Settler Society: Healing the Legacy of Colonialism in Canada." In *From Truth to Reconciliation: Transforming the Legacy of Residential Schools*, edited by Marlene Brant Castellano et al., 43–61. Ottawa: AHF, 2008.

Royal Commission on Aboriginal Peoples (RCAP). *Report of the Royal Commission on Aboriginal Peoples*. 1996. Ottawa: Canada Communications Group. https://www.bac-lac. gc.ca/eng/discover/aboriginal-heritage/royal-commission-aboriginal-peoples/Pages/ final-report.aspx

Ruffo, Armand Garnet. "'Our Roots Go Much Deeper': A Conversation with Armand Garnet Ruffo." With Jonathan Dewar. In *Arts of Engagement: Taking Aesthetic Action in and beyond Canada's Truth and Reconciliation Commission*, edited by Dylan Robinson and Keavy Martin, 215-26. Waterloo, ON: Wilfrid Laurier University Press, 2016.

Ryan, Allan J. *The Trickster Shift: Humour and Irony in Contemporary Native Art*. Vancouver: UBC Press, 1999.

Sandals, Leah. "Art, Residential Schools and Reconciliation: Important Questions." *Canadian Art*, 14 November 2013. canadianart.ca/features/art-and-reconciliation/.

Savage, Kirk. "The Politics of Memory: Black Emancipation and the Civil War Monument." In *Commemorations: The Politics of National Identity*, edited by John R. Gillis, 127–49.

Princeton, NJ: Princeton University Press, 1994.

Simon, Roger I. "The Pedagogical Insistence of Public Memory." In *Theorizing Historical Consciousness*, edited by Peter Seixas, 181–201. Toronto: University of Toronto Press, 2004.

Smith, Linda Tuhiwai. *Decolonizing Methodologies: Research and Indigenous Peoples*. London: Zed Books, 1999.

Spivak, Gayatri Chakravorty. "Can the Subaltern Speak?" In *Marxism and the Interpretation of Culture*, edited by Cary Nelson and Lawrence Grossberg, 271–316. Champaign: University of Illinois Press, 1988.

"Timeline." In *From Truth to Reconciliation: Transforming the Legacy of Residential Schools*, edited by Marlene Brant Castellano et al., 64–65. Ottawa: AHF, 2008.

Torpey, John. "Introduction: Politics and the Past." In *Politics and the Past: On Repairing Historical Injustices*, edited by John Torpey, 5–7. Lanham: Rowman and Littlefield, 2003.

Townsend-Gault, Charlotte. "Hot Dogs, a Ball Gown, Adobe, and Words: The Modes and Materials of Identity." In *Native American Art in the Twentieth Century*, edited by W. Jackson Rushing III, 113–33. Abingdon, United Kingdom: Routledge, 1999.

Trépanier, France, and Chris Creighton-Kelly. *Understanding Aboriginal Arts in Canada Today: A Knowledge and Literature Review*. Ottawa: Canada Council for the Arts, 2011.

Truth and Reconciliation Commission (TRC) of Canada. "Call for Artist Submissions." http://www.trc.ca/websites/trcinstitution/index.php?p=200.

——. "Honorary Witness." http://www.trc.ca/websites/reconciliation/index.php?p=331.

——. "Open Call for Artistic Submissions." http://www.trc.ca/websites/trcinstitution/index.php?p=194.

——. "Schedule N." http://www.trc.ca/websites/trcinstitution/File/pdfs/SCHEDULE_N_EN.pdf.

——. *The Truth and Reconciliation Commission of Canada: Calls to Action*. 2015. http://www.trc.ca/websites/trcinstitution/File/2015/Findings/Calls_to_Action_English2.pdf, 9.

Weaver, Jace. *That the People Might Live: Native American Literatures and Native American Community*. Toronto: Oxford University Press, 1997.

Wesley-Esquimaux, Cynthia, and Magdalena Smolewski. *Historic Trauma and Aboriginal Healing*. Ottawa: AHF, 2004.

"Witness." In *English Oxford Living Dictionaries*. http://www.oxforddictionaries.com/definition/english/witness.

Wolschke-Bulmahn, Joachim, ed. *Places of Commemoration: Search for Identity and Landscape Design*. Dumbarton Oaks: Dumbarton Oaks Research Library and Collection. 2001.

Younging, Gregory, Jonathan Dewar, and Mike DeGagné, eds. *Response, Responsibility, and Renewal: Canada's Truth and Reconciliation Journey*. Ottawa: AHF, 2009.

PART 4
MOVING TO ACTION

CHAPTER 18
ENGAGING CITIZENS IN INDIGENOUS–NON-INDIGENOUS RELATIONS[1]

Lynne Davis and Chris Hiller

In this chapter, we address the complex processes of engaging and involving diverse Canadians in efforts to bring about changes in Indigenous–non-Indigenous relations. Many initiatives aimed at prompting such changes and fostering reconciliation have emerged recently in Canadian society, particularly in the wake of the report of the Truth and Reconciliation Commission (TRC) in 2015. Here we consider the myriad discourses on which these initiatives draw and the ways in which these discourses in turn shape and constrain how Canadians construct their identities and envision a path forward. Although these forms of engagement provide Canadians with significant opportunities for learning and growth, it remains a challenge to bring general public understandings into conversation with Indigenous aspirations. In our review of the educational intent, content, and impact of a range of initiatives, we conclude that Canadians need more than just information about past wrongs and current inequities to sustain the difficult work of bringing about just relations based on respect for the self-determination, land repatriation, and sovereignty of Indigenous peoples.

THE TRC CALLS TO ACTION

In its ninety-four calls to action, the TRC challenged different sectors of Canadian society to step up efforts to bring about changes in the lives of Indigenous peoples and in Indigenous–non-Indigenous relationships.[2] Through its recommendations, the TRC calls on various levels of government, as well as faith communities, educational institutions, and professional groups in the sectors of education, health, child welfare, and justice, to work in concert with Indigenous peoples and organizations to challenge the structural, cultural, and attitudinal fabric of Canadian society. As outlined in Calls to Action 43 and 44, this broad program of public education centres on the 2007 United Nations Declaration on the Rights of Indigenous Peoples (UNDRIP)[3] as the appropriate framework for reconciliation.

These calls to action echo the findings of the Royal Commission on Aboriginal Peoples (RCAP), which, in its final report released two decades earlier, concluded that a new relationship between Aboriginal and non-Aboriginal people must be built upon mutual recognition, mutual respect, sharing, and mutual responsibility.[4] In the words of the TRC, "in 1996, the *Report of the Royal Commission on Aboriginal Peoples* urged Canadians to begin a national process of reconciliation that would have set the country on a bold new path, fundamentally changing the very foundations of Canada's relationship with Aboriginal peoples. Much of what the Royal Commission had to say has been ignored by government; a majority of its recommendations were never implemented. But the report and its findings opened people's eyes and changed the conversation about the reality for Aboriginal people in this country."[5] In their specificity, the TRC calls to action have provided concrete starting points for different parties to mobilize around particular goals. Indeed, it might be said that the TRC has issued a challenge to which institutions and organizations have felt a moral imperative to respond. As we will discuss in this chapter, there has been a surge in initiatives from governments, educational institutions, arts organizations, faith communities, and NGOs that have seen this invitation to action as a critical and perhaps redemptive moment in a history marked by cultural genocide, stolen lands, ignored sovereignty, broken treaty promises, and racism. At the same time, despite the careful analyses underlying these calls to action, and despite burgeoning initiatives that now seek to heed them, many scholars question the transformative potential of these recommendations themselves, especially as they are enacted through mainstream initiatives.

In reflecting on the present moment, we must recognize that the TRC report—like the RCAP report before it—stands in a long history of political mobilization by Indigenous peoples to assert their sovereignty and rights and to shape and change relationships with non-Indigenous peoples.[6] In response to that sustained resistance, Indigenous peoples have often been met with settler Canadian ignorance, racism, and active denigration of their rights. At the same time, some settlers have worked as allies under the leadership of Indigenous peoples or through collaborative processes in support of specific issues or in defence of Indigenous territories.[7] Through relationships of joint action, significant learning has emerged over time and provides a foundation for the citizen engagement being mobilized in the wake of the TRC report.

"Citizen engagement," or the related term "civic engagement," has numerous definitions, but a common thread is the idea that citizens are actively engaged in organizing for change in their communities.[8] In contemporary understandings such terms are often used to encourage direct involvement in learning, deciding, and acting[9] and often in efforts to promote forms of citizen participation generally sanctioned by the liberal democratic state (e.g., voting, signing petitions, demonstrating, participating in organizations). Thus, these terms are appropriate for describing many of the activities in which Indigenous and non-Indigenous people come together. At the same time, in discussing Indigenous–non-Indigenous solidarities, it is also important to include those relationships and forms of engagement that challenge the legitimacy of Canada's unilateral imposition of Crown sovereignty over Indigenous sovereignty in the context of settler colonialism. Thus, our discussion here seeks to be as inclusive as possible in assessing citizen engagement in Indigenous–non-Indigenous relations.

This assessment is marked by our own locations as non-Indigenous academics and settler Canadian activists engaged in an ongoing journey to understand what it means to work with Indigenous peoples in alliance and solidarity and what our responsibilities are as persons of settler heritage on Indigenous lands. Born at Unama'ki on the East Coast and of Eastern European Jewish ancestry, Lynne now lives in the territories of the Michi Saagig Anishinaabeg, more specifically the Mississaugas of Curve Lake, in territories shared with settlers by the Treaty 20 Nations. At Trent University, where she works in the Chanie Wenjack School for Indigenous

Studies, Lynne teaches courses in Indigenous–non-Indigenous alliance building and in "transforming settler consciousness." Chris's German, Scottish, and English ancestors settled on the traditional territories of the Haudenosaunee, Anishinaabe, and Huron Wendat peoples and never left. She now lives and works as an anti-colonial researcher and educator on Anishinaabe, Haudenosaunee, and Attawandaron territories (Guelph, Ontario), on lands supposedly "surrendered" to settlers as part of the Upper Canada Land Surrenders. The question of how to change the way in which settler Canadians think is central to our shared research interests.

The chapter is divided into three parts. The first part outlines a set of issues related to efforts to engage Canadians in the work of shifting Indigenous-settler relations, including the discourses most often targeted and mobilized through recent examples of such efforts, and the multiple and at times contradictory effects that these circulations of discourse produce. The second part of the chapter provides a sampling and overview of the kinds of citizen mobilizations that have emerged over the past decade. The third part offers a critical assessment of how these mobilizations and discourses work together and considers implications for a critical approach to Indigenous–non-Indigenous citizen engagement. While we draw on diverse literatures, we recognize there are many other important scholars, commentators, and leaders of initiatives whose work would enrich the discussion. We offer regrets for omissions in our brief treatment of issues that have many layers and complexities.

THE IMPORTANCE OF ANALYZING DISCOURSES AND NARRATIVES

Before considering examples of the diverse mobilizations currently unfolding in Canada, it is important to reflect on a number of critical issues that shape the intent, conditions, and impacts of these diverse forms of engagement in the present. We will address three here. First, initiatives must contend with how Canadians continue to be shaped by, and continue to respond intellectually and affectively to, dominant national narratives and settler mythologies—fables so often presented commonsensically by politicians in phrases such as "Canadians believe that...." Second, initiatives draw on multiple and competing discourses that intersect in locally and temporally specific ways to provoke, shape,

and limit responses to the TRC calls to action, leading to markedly different destinations in relation to decolonization and Indigenous–non-Indigenous relationships. Third, clashing and converging discourses precipitate diverse conceptions of what "reconciliation" means, what it entails
or demands, and where it might lead. We will discuss each of these issues
briefly insofar as they shape an understanding of citizen engagement in
Indigenous–non-Indigenous relations.

ENGAGING HOW CANADIANS UNDERSTAND THEMSELVES

Drawing from scholarship in anti-colonialism, anti-racism, critical
whiteness, Indigenous studies, and feminist studies over the past three
decades, a number of scholars have analyzed narratives that shape how
Canadians understand themselves. Settler scholar Paulette Regan deconstructs Canada's "benevolent peacemaker" myth, the contours of which
continue to structure Canadians' understandings of history and self-image in the present.[10] The benevolent peacemaker myth guides Canadians to
the familiar storyline that Canada brought peace, neutral law, order, and
good government to Indigenous peoples and, through treaties, avoided
the massacres that occurred as American society unfolded. Here Regan
echoes the work of many scholars who highlight the myth of Canada as
a benevolent, tolerant, and more "civilized" peacemaker nation as the
"historical myth of choice"[11] in current versions of Canadian popular
history.

This pervasive mythology manifests in the persistent investment of
Canadians in thinking of themselves as helpers and upholders of the rule
of law.[12] Governments and other social actors at times can mobilize this
investment to different ends; the Liberal federal government elected in 2015,
for example, drew on these narratives of national identity in its response
to the Syrian refugee crisis, galvanizing the support of many Canadians
who desired to "help."[13] At the same time, the benevolent peacemaker
myth accounts in part for the difficulty that Canadians continue to have
in acknowledging and addressing the structural violence at the foundation
of their relationships with Indigenous peoples, including broken treaty
promises, the residential school system and cultural genocide, theft of Indigenous lands, and pervasive racism. Regan points out that "the peacemaker
myth lies at the heart of the settler problem; it informs, however uncon-
sciously, the everyday attitudes and actions of contemporary politicians,

policy makers, lawyers, and negotiators, and it remains an archetype of settler benevolence, fairness and innocence in the Canadian public mind."[14]

In spite of the striking number of public inquiries in Canada regarding the lived realities of Indigenous peoples, beginning with the 1996 Royal Commission on Aboriginal Peoples and continuing into the present with the 2017 Public Inquiry into Missing and Murdered Indigenous Women and Girls, and despite the recent upsurge of media coverage following publication of the TRC final report in 2015, it is still not unusual to hear Canadians say "I didn't know." Lenapé-Potawatomi scholar Susan Dion comments on how classroom teachers often say that they know nothing about Indigenous peoples. She calls this claim "the perfect stranger," describing it as a complicated position shaped by what people know, what they do not know, and what they *refuse* to know. What they *do* know, argues Dion, includes stereotypical representations that are produced by and reinforce dominant narratives.[15]

In contemplating citizen engagement in Indigenous–non-Indigenous relations, then, it is important to acknowledge and attend to how different forms of engagement either draw on and reinforce, or challenge and disrupt, the dominant settler narratives through which Canadians come to understand themselves. In this regard, there is an important political and pedagogical distinction to be made between forms of engagement that, through the mobilization of such narratives, continue to position Canadians to perceive themselves as "helpers" of Indigenous peoples and those that provoke Canadians' self-perception as settlers occupying Indigenous lands.

Furthermore, in assessing how dominant national narratives play out in current efforts to engage diverse non-Indigenous people, there are critical questions to be explored with respect to the historical and emerging relationships among Indigenous peoples and racialized peoples, recently arrived immigrants, and refugees. In a rich collection of essays edited by Mathur, Dewar, and DeGagné, Malissa Phung poses the important question "Are People of Colour Settlers Too?"[16] Indigenous and Black Lives Matter activists have found common ground in their struggles and have initiated deeper conversations about how they are similarly affected by white supremacy, police violence, and other impositions of state surveillance.[17] Recent scholars and activists also surface questions regarding how both the circulation and contestation of national narratives are mediated by relations of power related to gender, class, and sexuality.[18] Within the seams of these conversations, complexities emerge from layers of intersecting histories of racism, colonialism, and heteropatriarchy, all the while pointing to the foundational reality that all non-Indigenous Canadians inherit benefits from living on Indigenous homelands right here, right now.[19]

COMPETING DISCOURSES

As many scholars have noted, discourses are related to power; they are fundamental to structuring how we think about and act in the world. The French philosopher Michel Foucault deeply explored the interplay of discourse and power, and his concept of discourse is well described by Yellowknives Dene scholar Glen Coulthard in *Red Skin, White Masks*:

> Here I employ "discourse" in a Foucauldian manner to refer to the myriad of ways in which the objects of our knowledge are defined and produced through the languages we employ in our engagement with the world and with others. Discursive formations, in other words, are not neutral; they "construct" the topic[s] and objects of our knowledge; they govern "the way that a topic can be meaningfully talked about and reasoned about." They also influence how ideas are "put into practice and used to regulate the conduct of others." Just as a discursive formation can legitimize certain ways of thinking and acting, they can also profoundly limit and constrain "other ways of talking and conducting ourselves in relation to the topic or constructing knowledge about it."[20]

Given the ways that they produce, shape, and constrain our capacities for thought and action, discourses have profound implications for efforts to engage people in shifting Indigenous–non-Indigenous relations. To begin, Canadians are often positioned to respond to discourses in alignment with their understandings of themselves, the narratives by which they define their identities as Canadians, and the stories that they have learned to tell about Canada. Thus, choosing how issues are "framed" discursively is an important dimension of social and political mobilization, and organizers of current forms of Indigenous–non-Indigenous engagement make strategic choices about which discourse is likely to draw the most supporters into new identities, positions, and forms of action.[21]

At the same time, no discourse operates independently, but each mixes and competes with other discourses in ways that have multiple and even contradictory effects. These clashes among discourses can affect how problems are defined, how identities are constructed, and how possibilities for action and change are enacted or even imagined.

For example, the discourse of equality continues to play an important role in shaping the political and social landscape in Canada and serves as a key driver of civil discourse and engagement, despite the reality of ongoing inequities and discrimination. Indigenous peoples strategically deploy this discourse in the public sphere in a number of ways. For example, in its 2015 materials outlining federal election priorities for First Nations and Canada, the Assembly of First Nations drew on the notion of "closing the gap" to shame the federal government into making more funds available for First Nations education. In this case, the federal underfunding of First Nations education relative to provincial jurisdictions was something that the public could readily grasp as unfair. The same can be said in relation to the underfunding of First Nations child welfare on reserves, a struggle relentlessly pursued by Dr. Cindy Blackstock of the First Nations Child and Family Caring Society in a legal battle with Canada that began in 2007 and was ostensibly won in 2016 when the Canadian Human Rights Tribunal ruled in favour of Blackstock's action.[22]

At the same time, the discourse of equality has been used in other contexts to challenge Indigenous or treaty rights. In British Columbia, for example, Conservative politicians drew on discourses of equality to buttress their call for a provincial referendum on the BC Treaty Process in 2002, arguing that the treaties "contravene the Canadian ideals of equality, democracy, and individualism by perpetuating a division of Canadians along racial lines by setting up racially based territorial enclaves and by granting special rights and status to Indian people."[23] In land disputes such as the 2006 Haudenosaunee land reclamation at Caledonia, Ontario, opponents called on the police to remove the blockade holding that there should be "one law for all."[24] Such protests mobilize equality discourse in combination with other neoliberal and individualist discourses to claim a violation of settler rights. The same refrain has been used when Indigenous peoples have asserted their rights to resources, such as in the case of the 1995 Saugeen Ojibway's assertion of fishing rights at Cape Croker.[25]

Liberal social justice discourse also continues to appeal broadly to mainstream Canadians. Within this discursive framework, social justice itself is understood as equality and respect for difference in the context of a multicultural society; discrimination is recognized as systemic, and the historical wrongs against Indigenous peoples can be seen as spilling into the present. Within current manifestations of this framework, outstanding land and treaty issues need to be resolved; Indigenous rights need to be respected; legacies of residential schools such as family impacts, cultural alienation, social disruption, and lower educational levels need to be addressed; and racism needs to be challenged. Especially when crossed with (human) rights discourse, social justice discourse opens up possibilities for building bridges between Indigenous peoples and others who experience inequities in Canadian society, including anti-poverty groups, people of colour, immigrants, those experiencing gender-based and sexual violence, and other groups in civil society.

Again, Indigenous peoples and their supporters have mobilized social justice discourse in a number of effective ways. For example, when the Coalition for a Public Inquiry into Ipperwash lobbied the provincial government to call an inquiry into the 1995 death of Stoney Point activist and land defender Dudley George at the hands of the Ontario Provincial Police, coalition members drew on liberal discourses of social justice in claiming their right as concerned citizens to know what their government had done to influence the killing. Framing the issue in this way engaged a larger segment of the public than if the coalition had been focused on expediting a land dispute between First Nations and the government, allowing the coalition to draw broad support from unions, municipalities, churches, human rights groups, political parties, and many NGOs.[26]

At the same time, many Indigenous and anti-colonial scholars have critiqued liberal social justice discourse and its preoccupation with equality for the way in which it fails to challenge the underlying legitimacy of the settler state or to call into question how settlers continue to benefit from past and present forms of colonization.

Conversely, anti-colonial, anti-racist, and decolonizing discourses that have emerged over the past three decades, while highly heterogeneous, share a common critical stance in relation to the settler colonial state and its interests. Indigenous and non-Indigenous scholars draw on these discourses to figure settler colonialism as being fundamentally about the land.[27] Together, these discourses construct Canada as a settler colonial state with well-developed structural mechanisms to access and extract Indigenous lands and resources, assimilate Indigenous peoples, and preserve settler privileges. These discourses situate the nation-state and its institutions (e.g., the courts) as acting to bring Indigenous peoples and Indigenous sovereignties under Canadian sovereignty. Within these discursive frameworks, racism, heteronormative and gender-based conformity, and the regulation of populations through Indigenous status definitions and immigration policies are perceivable as dimensions of a targeted agenda to eliminate Indigenous relationships with their lands and to force conformity to state and corporate interests. At the same time, anti-colonial, anti-racist, and decolonization discourses differ with regard to the extent to which they centre questions of Indigenous land, dispossession, and sovereignty; such differences at times precipitate tensions that play out in coalition-building efforts involving Indigenous peoples and other racialized and minoritized communities.[28]

Indigenous knowledge holders, scholars, leaders, and communities also draw on long-standing discourses of Indigenous sovereignty as well as more emergent discourses of Indigenous resurgence in political, social, intellectual, and on-the-ground efforts to assert Indigenous sovereignty, protect Indigenous lands and life ways, and call for the honouring of treaties. Arising from Indigenous knowledges and customary laws, these diverse discourses come into play in everyday actions when Indigenous lands are threatened, such as when the duty to consult has been violated, and when Indigenous peoples are treated like just another "minority" or "multicultural group" rather than as sovereign Indigenous peoples. Currently, Indigenous peoples mobilize these discourses in countless ways, including through assertions of Indigenous laws and knowledge systems, efforts to rejuvenate languages and cultural practices, reassertions of traditional governance and jurisdiction, and reclamations of land and territory through blockades, occupations, and other direct actions.

Jeff Corntassel (Cherokee), Leanne Simpson (Michi Saagiig), and Glen Coulthard (Yellowknives Dene), as leading Indigenous theorists who draw extensively from emergent discourses of Indigenous resurgence, share a critical analysis of settler colonialism and speak of pathways of decolonization based on Indigenous knowledges, relationships with lands, and core cultural principles. They caution against Indigenous peoples being subsumed by the politics of recognition that seeks to subvert Indigenous sovereignty and relationships with lands. They promote language recovery, cultural rejuvenation, and land-based practices. At times, resurgent discourses cross with or contest discourses of Indigenous rights, provoking discussions of "rights" versus "responsibilities" as a core epistemological challenge in framing rights-based conversations and actions.[29]

In 2012, for example, the Idle No More movement drew on the discourse of Indigenous resurgence effectively to galvanize Indigenous peoples and their supporters at the grassroots level to oppose the introduction of Bill C-45 into Parliament, legislation that removed environmental protections for water and fish habitats and affected Indigenous lands, waterways, and rights without consultation.[30]

The above discussion offers a brief outline of a few of the many discourses that currently come into play in Indigenous—non-Indigenous relations.[31] Although no discourse operates in isolation, and all are inflected with internal inconsistencies and contentions, we argue here that these discourses work in complex ways to bring people to different and at times conflicting or shifting destinations in relation to Indigenous—non-Indigenous relations. Some discourses are useful in encouraging a wide range of non-Indigenous people to become engaged in activities to improve relationships and to address inequities, but they do so at the cost of drawing on and reinforcing dominant self-perceptions or narratives. Other discourses, though more marginal, function to take non-Indigenous people out of their comfort zones by centring aspects of decolonization that are most unsettling to settler imaginaries and privileges.

UNDERSTANDINGS OF RECONCILIATION

Reconciliation bears particular attention, both as a complex discourse (or perhaps more usefully a discursive hub) and as a highly contested concept, in Canada generally and in Indigenous contexts specifically.[32] Aligned with notions of transitional justice and coming to ascendancy internationally over the past decade, reconciliation as a discourse circulates in many institutional sites and crosses with an array of discourses (legal, psychological, political, theological) to shape and constrain important conversations about what it means to "reconcile" knowledges, legal systems, nations, peoples, and sovereignties.

Since the 2008 federal apology to residential school survivors and the attendant establishment of the TRC, and particularly since the publishing of its final report in 2015, reconciliation has evolved into a widespread discourse in Canadian society. In that final report, the TRC offers this definition: "To the Commission, 'reconciliation' is about establishing and maintaining a mutually respectful relationship between Aboriginal and non-Aboriginal peoples in this country. For that to happen, there has to be awareness of the past, acknowledgement of the harm that has been inflicted, atonement for the causes, and action to change behaviour."[33] Although the mandate of the TRC was to address Canada's history of residential schools, the definition above offers latitude to look at other aspects of Canada's settler colonial nature, such as those pertaining to the economy, governance, and land. As the TRC report states, "in the face of growing conflicts over lands, resources, and economic development, the scope of reconciliation must extend beyond residential schools to encompass all aspects of Aboriginal and non-Aboriginal relations and connections to the land."[34]

Coulthard traces how, in the aftermath of the 1996 RCAP report, the federal government strategically mobilized reconciliation discourse in such a way as to carefully separate the colonial actions of the past from Canada's actions today. In drawing this clear temporal line, colonial violence and injustice are relegated to the distant past, and Canada is positioned as no longer a settler colonial state.[35] Coulthard argues that in this discursive frame, Canada's task in reconciliation becomes one of "repairing the psychologically injured or damaged status of Indigenous people themselves" rather than addressing embedded structural injustices.[36] In a similar vein, Simpson warns of the risk that notions of reconciliation as conceived by the TRC, with its focus on residential schools, might lead non-Indigenous people to believe that the "wrong" has now been "righted" and that there is no further need to address either other historical wrongs or the many dimensions of ongoing colonialism, including Canada's continued refusal to embody treaty relationships or address the dispossession of Indigenous lands.[37]

Although the TRC final report does highlight the need for Canada to renounce the Doctrine of Discovery and to recognize land rights, Indigenous critiques of reconciliation as a guiding framework point to a relative lack of sustained attention to questions of land and the absence of discussion about sovereignty and reparation. Simpson worries about whether there is political will on the part of the government to make genuine change:

> If reconciliation is to be meaningful, we need to be willing to dismantle settler colonialism as a system. Our current government needs to move beyond window dressing and begin to tackle the root causes of Indigenous oppression in Canada. This means respecting when Indigenous peoples say no to development on our lands. It means dismantling land claims and self-government processes

that require us to terminate our Aboriginal and treaty rights to sit at the table. It means repealing the most damaging aspects of the *Indian Act* and respecting First Nations political systems, governance, and ability to determine who belongs in our communities. It means being accountable about the collective damage that has been done and is being done, and supporting the regeneration of languages, cultures, and political systems. It means stop fighting us in court. It means giving back land, so we can rebuild and recover from the losses of the last four centuries and truly enter into a new relationship with Canada and Canadians.[38]

Such skepticism about the dubious and potentially recolonizing effects of reconciliation discourse remains a cautionary reminder to pay close attention to the nuances of citizen engagement initiatives, how they are shaped and constrained, what they reiterate, and what results might flow from them. It is also a warning that notions of reconciliation can be used to deflect attention away from or to dilute more threatening discourses, such as those pertaining to Indigenous lands, treaties, and sovereignty.

FORMS OF ENGAGEMENT

In this section, we offer examples of what "citizen engagement," as called for by the TRC, looks like at this moment. There are many projects, initiatives, and ongoing actions by diverse parties, including

- formal curricula;
- informal education directed at the general public;
- workshops—professional, online, experiential;
- corporate training;
- arts, performing arts and literature publications, performances, festivals, and gatherings;
- land defence and reclamation; and
- direct solidarity action.

The initiatives or engagements that we consider here are organized by an array of actors, including Indigenous peoples, governments, NGOs, faith communities, grassroots organizations, and individuals. We will share a scan of these engagements, based on information from websites, under the headings "Reconciliation: Promoting Relationships," "For the Earth," "Widespread Mobilization," and "Education." We chose these headings because they appeared to be significant themes and/or represent different kinds of public participation. Because the websites vary in their level of detail, we offer no comparative evaluation of individual engagements. Also, we make no claim about the comprehensiveness of this representation of the many engagements that have arisen, except to say that we have attempted to provide an interesting variety.

RECONCILIATION: PROMOTING RELATIONSHIPS

Since the TRC issued its calls to action in 2015, there has been a groundswell of actions bearing the word *reconciliation* in their names, organized by governmental, non-governmental, public, church, and educational institutions. These initiatives appear almost daily. Many are new and one-time events, but some are long-standing educational and social justice initiatives that now emphasize reconciliation as an aspect of their work. The examples offered below, though not comprehensive, reflect the various engagements flowing out of the TRC's discourse on reconciliation as expressed through its calls to action. Please keep in mind that the examples given here, while current when chosen, will be out of date by the time you read them. They are emblematic of the types of events being organized in the public sphere, including guest lecture series, one-time conferences and collaborations, as well as one-time reconciliation themes for regularly occurring events.

1. Reconciliation Canada was founded in 2012 by Chief Robert Joseph, a traditional chief from the Gwawaenuk First Nation and the organization's leading spokesperson.[39] The Reconciliation Canada website does not define the word *reconciliation* per se but starts from the residential school experience. The process of reconciliation is focused on building bridges at individual and collective levels. Reconciliation dialogue workshops bring small groups of people together to share their stories, to "discuss visions for a better future, and to develop individual and collective reconciliation action plans."[40] Reconciliation Canada works with many kinds of organizations and the corporate sector and has an "economic reconciliation" program.

In 2016, Reconciliation Canada received $1.8 million as a Canada 150 Signature Project. The organization assumed a leadership role in preparing a "national narrative on reconciliation" report, convening thought leaders on reconciliation, holding a national gathering of spiritual leaders and youth, mobilizing organizations that wish to pursue reconciliation, organizing walks for reconciliation, and celebrating multiculturalism in Canada. Since 2016, it has been hosting national gatherings that focus on the themes of "optimum potential, shared prosperity and social and systemic change."[41] In its "Reconciliation in Action: A National Engagement Strategy," it "will examine and document perceptions, actions and aspirations of Canadians in relation to reconciliation. This narrative will recognize our common history, highlight current achievements and create hope for the next 150 years."[42]

2. Reconciliation Saskatoon, a coalition of over ninety organizations, has organized events including ceremonies, performances, language learning, residential school–related activities, inspirational speakers, a school graduation pow wow, a four-week reading campaign, Indigenous awareness training, and an annual reconciliation walk. Coalition members include diverse organizations, including local and provincial political entities (e.g., City of Saskatoon and the Office of the Treaty Commissioner), Indigenous organizations (e.g., Indian and Métis Friendship Centre of Saskatoon and Saskatoon Tribal Council), local community and social services (e.g., Saskatoon Health Region and Saskatoon Police Service), school organizations (e.g., Saskatoon Public Schools and University of Saskatchewan), faith bodies (e.g., local Catholic and Anglican dioceses), and private sector groups (e.g., Affinity Credit Union and SaskTel).[43]

3. The National Arts Centre (NAC) in Ottawa sponsored eight events on the theme of Indigenous Story-Telling and Reconciliation in January and February 2016.[44] NAC has since instituted a national Indigenous Theatre to bring forward the works and talents of Indigenous artists and performers.

4. {Re}conciliation is an arts-funding program of the Canada Council for the Arts "to promote artistic collaborations that look to the past and future for new dialogues between Aboriginal and non-Aboriginal peoples in Canada." The program is a collaboration with the J.W. McConnell Family Foundation.[45]

One project funded by the {Re}conciliation program was O k'inadas// Complicated Reconciliations: An Artist Residency, an initiative held as part of a Summer Indigenous Art Intensive Program at the University of British Columbia, Okanagan. It was part of a larger continuing project called Art + Reconciliation to explore "how artistic practices can engage in questions of reconciliation" in the Canadian context. The residency project provided online resources generated through the artistic exchanges during the summer of 2016.[46]

Another {Re}conciliation-funded project was established by the Mi'kmaw Native Friendship Centre in Halifax. "This Is What I Wish You Knew" brought together fifty Indigenous community artists—youth, adults, and Elders—in Halifax to explore their individual and collective identities and develop the stories that they "wish you—the public—knew." A large interactive clay mural showcases the artists' journeys, through individually created tiles linked to films profiling each artist's story, "to build understanding, create a space for dialogue, and lay the foundation for reconciliation."[47]

5. Canadian Roots Exchange (CRE), is a national organization that brings together Indigenous and non-Indigenous youth in dialogue and leadership development.[48] They sponsor Indigenous and non-Indigenous youth exchange programs and an annual conference. They also organize Indigenous leadership development projects such as the Indigenous Policy School. In a collaborative research project, they are tracking attitudes of Canadian youth towards reconciliation.

6. Project of Heart, a national award-winning educational initiative developed by non-Indigenous Ottawa schoolteacher Sylvia Smith, engages learners in schools and universities with the history of residential schools. The project outlines a six-step process of reconciliation, including meeting with a residential school survivor and participating in arts-based and social justice components. Students in classrooms across Canada have participated in this initiative, which now lists its home as the National Centre for Truth and Reconciliation.[49]

7. Simon Fraser University in Burnaby, British Columbia, hosted its President's Dream Colloquium on "Returning to the Teachings: Justice, Identity, and Belonging." Nine prominent speakers, most of them Indigenous, addressed the theme in the context of Education for Reconciliation, in the fall of 2016. The theme was seen as a response to the TRC's call for Indigenous knowledge to contribute to a new way forward.[50]

8. Trent University in Peterborough, Ontario, hosted its fortieth annual Elders and Traditional Peoples Gathering on the theme of "Rekindling the Fire: Reconciliation and the Way Forward." The gathering brings together Elders and traditional peoples from Anishinaabe, Haudenosaunee, and other Indigenous Nations.[51]

9. Universities Canada, representing ninety-six universities in Canada, issued a set of thirteen principles in 2015 on Indigenous education and five commitments to action. Most were focused on "closing the gap" for Indigenous students and Indigenizing the academy.[52]

10. The Canadian Association of University Teachers published a list of territorial acknowledgements for over eighty universities and colleges that are members of the association. The intention was to assist members in properly acknowledging First Nations' territories as a first step in cultivating relationships with First Nations.[53] A critical analysis of this resource has been written by Métis lawyer Chelsea Vowel.[54]

11. The University of Toronto Faculty of Medicine's Continuing Professional Education office has been hosting two-day conferences on Indigenous Health, offered within an overall framework of education and reconciliation. The conferences aim to attract health professionals across a wide range of health sector roles.[55]

12. The Vancouver Dialogues Project, which operated between April 2010 and July 2011, brought together First Nations, urban Aboriginal organizations, and immigrant communities in Vancouver to engage in opportunities for cross-cultural understanding and relationship building. The project sought to engage both Indigenous and immigrant communities through dialogue circles, community research, cultural exchange visits, projects involving youth and Elders, and legacy projects. The project generated face-to-face discussions, artistic expressions, videos, and on-site visits. Extensive documentation can be found on its website.[56]

13. In response to a specific deadline named in the TRC's final report and calls to action, a number of national church, faith, and interfaith groups—

including parties to the Settlement Agreement—have issued statements on their specific plans for Call to Action 48, which entails implementing and upholding the principles of the UNDRIP.[57]

The engagements mentioned above are in no way exhaustive, but they do provide the grounds for some observations about the kinds of initiatives being organized in the name of reconciliation and the mobilization of Indigenous and non-Indigenous people:

- They are focused on a positive tone for creating a better future. They use words such as *respect, dialogue, relationship building,* and *opportunity*. However, guest speakers can draw on a range of discourses that do not reflect the framing by organizers.
- Many initiatives are time limited. That does not mean that organizations will not plan additional activities in the future, but they have specific boundaries for the events that they are hosting. We notice that some one-time events have become annual events.
- Organizations such as Reconciliation Saskatoon bring together diverse Indigenous and non-Indigenous parties to undertake a common goal. They are rich in the knowledge and expertise brought to the table.
- These initiatives reach out to targeted audiences, from the general public to professional members, and they include adults, youth, and children. The organizations have the capability and potential to reach different sectors of society and create different kinds of conversations.

FOR THE EARTH

The relationships of Indigenous peoples with their traditional territories, their place-based knowledges, and their holistic spiritual beliefs have positioned them on the frontlines of protecting Mother Earth. It should be remembered that the defence of Kanehsatà:ke traditional territories led to the Oka confrontation in 1990, which ultimately led to the establishment of the Royal Commission on Aboriginal Peoples. Indigenous actions to protect Mother Earth and traditional territories are diverse and may or may not involve non-Indigenous peoples.

From the frontlines of defending traditional territories, Indigenous peoples have found allies in other Indigenous Nations and among settler peoples. From sites of struggles from Kanehsatà:ke to Caledonia, from

Nawash to Muskrat Falls, Labrador, from Elsipogtog to Bella Bella, and from Site C dam in the Peace River area to Wet'suwet'en, Indigenous peoples have confronted, and continue to confront, the settler colonial state when their territories and their responsibilities to their lands and relations have been threatened. Following are a few examples of how Indigenous land defenders are engaging with non-Indigenous peoples and inviting them to stand with them in solidarity.

14. Water Walks. The Anishinaabe water walking movement began in 2003 when the late Grandmother Josephine Mandamin began her inaugural walk around Lake Superior to honour the water and to raise awareness of the importance of protecting water as sacred. Since then, a water walking movement has evolved under the leadership of Anishinaabe women. The annual events attract women, men, and families both Indigenous and non-Indigenous with the goal of bringing water issues to the fore. Each year local water walking organizations decide on a water walking route, usually circling a lake or walking along a river. This is a grassroots spiritual movement in which Indigenous women's leadership is recognized and non-Indigenous people come to learn and act in solidarity.[58]

15. Asubpeeschoseewagong First Nation (also known as Grassy Narrows First Nation), whose blockade in opposition to logging in its traditional territories was established in 2002, sponsored River Run, a walk to raise awareness of decades-old mercury pollution in the local river caused by industry and the Minamata disease that ensued. Grassy Narrows asked the Ontario government to conduct a cleanup of the river. River Run events in 2016 and 2019 included a 1,700-kilometre walk from Grassy Narrows to a family-oriented rally at Queen's Park in Toronto.[59] As a result of tireless activism, Grassy Narrows signed an agreement with the federal government in April 2020 that will see a long-promised treatment centre for mercury poisoning built in the community.

16. The Sacred Trust Initiative is empowered by the Tsleil-waututh Nation to stop the Kinder Morgan pipeline expansion in its traditional territories. In 2014, the Tsleil-waututh Nation made national headlines when it and allied supporters rallied on Burnaby Mountain. In November 2015, it held a one-day "learning for reconciliation" to celebrate the first anniversary of the Burnaby Mountain mobilization. The purpose was "to strengthen

Indigenous and settler alliances" in anticipation of their continuing opposition to the Kinder Morgan pipeline expansion, which has now morphed into active opposition to the Trans Mountain pipeline.[60]

17. The West Moberly First Nation and the Prophet River First Nation oppose the flooding of their Peace River territories to build the Site C dam. BC Hydro was approved to begin clearing for the dam by the Liberal BC government, and in 2016 the federal government issued the necessary permits despite a legal challenge that was before the courts. This constituted a serious breach of the duty to consult. Members of the two First Nations travelled to eastern Canada on their Justice for the Peace speaking tour to raise awareness of and support for their opposition and to attend federal court proceedings in Montreal. The First Nations are supported by the Union of BC Indian Chiefs, the Assembly of First Nations, local farmers, and NGOs such as RAVEN Trust,[61] Amnesty International, Leadnow, and Sierra Club of BC, among others.[62] In December 2017, the NDP-Green coalition BC government approved the Site C dam, although the First Nations continue to pursue legal challenges to end its construction.

18. The Unist'ot'en Clan of the Wet'suwet'en in northwestern British Columbia established a camp at the entrance to their traditional territories. The clan's traditional leaders had said no to the Enbridge Pipeline and continue to defend their land. Each summer they have welcomed diverse volunteers to join the Unist'ot'en Camp, where volunteers can contribute to priorities of the leaders, participate in land-based activities, and learn protocols that respect Indigenous sovereignty.[63] The Unist'ot'in resistance to pipeline construction through Wet'suwe'ten territories foreshadowed the refusal of Wet'suwe'ten Traditional Chiefs to the construction of the Coastal GasLink pipeline through their traditional territories in January and February, 2020, resulting in solidarity blockades in southern Canada.

These mobilizations led by Indigenous peoples reach across borders and, in an era of global communications, can bring Indigenous and non-Indigenous peoples into solidarity quickly, as demonstrated in the Standing Rock resistance in North Dakota that began in 2016 and the Wet'suwe'ten land protection in 2020. Anti-globalization activists, environmentalists, and non-Indigenous peoples engaged in challenging social and environmental relationships have found commonalities in different times and spaces.[64] Tuck and Yang point to the incommensurability of struggles and the contingent nature of Indigenous and non-Indigenous solidarities.[65] Certainly, there are networks forged on the frontlines of struggle that can be mobilized as new challenges appear.

WIDESPREAD MOBILIZATIONS

The mobilizations described in this section have been energized by the forces described above. They take advantage of the technological possibilities of the present moment, connecting diverse supporters and drawing on deep pools of talent. They are excellent examples of Indigenous-led citizen engagement.

19. Idle No More offers an outstanding example of the mobilization potential of Indigenous-led movements.[66] Organized in December 2012 using social media, Idle No More galvanized Indigenous peoples and their supporters across the country and, to some extent, around the world in peaceful gatherings to protest the oppressive and colonial actions of the federal government in all their manifestations, beginning with proposed legislation Bill C-45, which removed environmental protections for waters, fish, and natural habitats. While drawing heavily on the discourse of Indigenous resurgence, this inclusive movement mobilized a number of different discourses, creating a common platform for Indigenous peoples engaged in specific land-based struggles and those fighting against colonialism, capitalism, and a host of issues grounded in dispossession of Indigenous lands, racism, discrimination, environmental destruction, and violence such as the Missing and Murdered Indigenous Women and Girls (MMIWG) campaign. This "round dance revolution" gave presence to Indigenous peoples in urban and rural spaces and drew in thousands of non-Indigenous peoples who shared a frustration with the dictatorial style of the federal Harper government.

20. The Missing and Murdered Indigenous Women and Girls campaign is arguably one of the most successful mobilizations of Indigenous and non-Indigenous women. Violence against Indigenous women, girls, and Two-Spirit people has manifested in extraordinarily high rates of murder and disappearance.[67]

Establishing violence against Indigenous women and girls as a government policy priority came about only after more than fifteen years of organizing by the Native Women's Association of Canada (NWAC). NWAC established the Sisters in Spirit campaign and reached out to form partnerships with NGOs, including Amnesty International, KAIROS Canada, the Elizabeth Fry Society, the United Church of Canada, and the Anglican Church of Canada.[68] NWAC held its first October 4th vigil in 2006, an annual event prompting many grassroots organizations to organize local, spiritually based vigils. Missing and murdered Indigenous Women and Girls has been a cause around which church, social justice, anti-racist, and feminist organizations have rallied, under the leadership of Indigenous women. In Vancouver, the February 14th Annual Women's Memorial March is held in the Downtown Eastside.[69]

Arts-based responses to missing and murdered Indigenous women and girls have included Christi Belcourt's *Walking with Our Sisters* exhibit of 1,810 moccasin vamps and 118 children's moccasin vamps, created by Indigenous and non-Indigenous contributors from across the country.[70] Issues related to missing and murdered Indigenous women and girls include colonialism, sexism, oppression tied to gender and sexuality, racism, poverty, violence, and other forms of systemic discrimination. Elders and Indigenous scholars have drawn the parallel between how the land and the bodies of Indigenous women are treated in settler society.[71] The community-based mobilization to address missing and murdered Indigenous women and girls has brought together people who might have diverse analyses but find common ground in their understanding of injustice.

Given the intense campaign over many years, it is not surprising that the TRC called for a national inquiry. One of the first announcements of the new federal government in 2015 was a national inquiry to investigate root causes, to hear from the families, and to recommend strategies to bring about change.[72] The MMIWG Inquiry issued its final report in April of 2019.

EDUCATION

The need for widespread public education was recognized by the Royal Commission on Aboriginal Peoples as an indispensable element in bringing about change in Indigenous and non-Indigenous relationships. Dialogue, cross-cultural education, meaningful interaction, and public role modelling were identified by RCAP as parts of a strategy to transform

Canadian consciousness.[73] Nearly two decades later, the TRC similarly agreed that Canadians of all ages lack an understanding of Indigenous peoples. Call to Action 62 specifically addresses education in publicly funded institutions, calling for the residential school legacy, treaties past and present, and Indigenous contributions to this country to be mandatory parts of the curriculum in each province and territory.[74] The public school system, colleges, and universities are responding, as are NGOS, governments, professional organizations, and industries. Because of the wide range of initiatives that aim to educate, we will mention only a few examples in this section.

Improving public school education about Indigenous peoples and Indigenous–non-Indigenous relationships has been the incessant goal of Indigenous peoples for decades. There are important variations in each province/territory, and of course the content varies not only because of the differences in Indigenous territories but also because of the particular discourses reinforced by curricular designers. Although each province and territory could be represented here, this short overview simply points to the extensive work being undertaken in the field of education. We also offer a few examples of initiatives by Indigenous Nations to offer culture and place-based education for schools and the general public.

21. Both Saskatchewan and Manitoba have implemented treaty education throughout the grade levels, developing curricula in collaboration with Indigenous educators and Elders. Saskatchewan's Teaching Treaties in the Classroom program brings mandatory treaty education into the school system.[75] These two provinces have developed outcomes and indicators for each grade level, demonstrating that students will develop an increasingly complex understanding of treaties. In Manitoba, the K–12 treaty education curriculum has been supported with resource kits by the Treaty Relations Commission of Manitoba.[76]

22. Following the spirit of the Association of Canadian Deans of Education Accord on Indigenous Education in 2010,[77] compulsory Indigenous studies courses for teacher candidates have been introduced in some schools of education, including Trent University and Lakehead University. Lakehead, the University of Winnipeg and Trent are implementing mandatory courses in Indigenous studies for all undergraduates, and

other universities are looking for ways to follow suit without incurring backlashes from students.

23. KAIROS Canada, an ecumenical social justice organization representing eleven churches and church entities, is the latest manifestation of a forty-year trajectory of Indigenous solidarity work involving churches in Canada. At the time of release of the RCAP report in 1996, KAIROS Canada's predecessor, the Aboriginal Rights Coalition, created the Blanket Exercise, a two-hour experiential exercise designed to introduce Canadians to the history of colonization, land dispossession, and Indigenous resistance in Canada. Over the years, the exercise has been revised for youth and children and refined to involve Indigenous facilitators, to deepen Indigenous pedagogies, and to engage extensively with local Elders, and Knowledge Keepers. Since being showcased at national TRC events, the KAIROS Blanket Exercise has been facilitated for thousands of groups across the country including police and health authorities, government agencies, and educational institutions at every level.[78]

Since 2010, KAIROS Canada has also organized national education and action campaigns that relate specifically to the theme of reconciliation. It has worked with other organizations to call on governments to adopt and implement the UNDRIP as the framework for reconciliation.[79] Since 2016, as part of its multiyear Winds of Change campaign focusing on reconciliation, KAIROS Canada has led a national education and petition campaign to pressure governments to implement TRC Call to Action 62, that is, to implement education for reconciliation.[80]

24. The Secret Path project tells the story of Chanie Wenjack, a twelve-year-old Ojibway boy who escaped from the Cecilia Jeffery Residential School near Kenora and died as he tried to walk home over 400 miles in winter. The story, told with the permission of the Wenjack family by lead singer of The Tragically Hip, the late Gord Downie, and cartoonist Jeff Lemire, resulted in an animated documentary, a graphic novel, and a recorded album. Downie introduced this project in the last days of his life, and the publicity generated has elevated awareness of residential schools. *The Secret Path* book has been adopted in school curricula in some jurisdictions. The Gord Downie and Chanie Wenjack Foundation has initiated a number of projects that encourage Canadians to engage in conversations about reconciliation.[81]

25. Nk'mip Desert Cultural Centre showcases the history, culture, and art of the people of the Osoyoos Indian Band. Located in what is now southern British Columbia, the centre displays indoor and outdoor exhibits in its fifty-acre desert site. There is a primary museum, a reconstructed traditional village with a traditional pit house and sweat lodge, desert walking trails, and an outdoor sculpture garden. The centre conducts educational programming and group tours.[82]

26. The Woodland Cultural Centre, located in Brantford, Ontario, is located in the former Mohawk Institute Indian Residential School, known as the Mush Hole (1828–1970). The Centre offers public and school educational tours of the residential school and is restoring the school through its Save the Evidence campaign. The Centre provides cultural leadership through its museum, archives, art gallery, and library and offers exhibits, language and educational programs. It is governed by the Six Nations of Grand River, the Mohawks of the Bay of Quinte and the Mohawks of Wahta.[83]

27. Governments and industries are also sponsoring educational events for employees who need to build positive relationships with Indigenous peoples in order to carry out their work. Some governments have mandated compulsory training for public servants. Training can involve generic cultural awareness workshops or information-specific seminars on topics such as recent legal cases, regulatory frameworks, and the duty to consult. West Coast consultant Robert Joseph has developed workshops that have become important resources for learning relationship-building skills in government and industry contexts. The Ontario Federation of Indigenous Friendship Centres delivers custom-designed workshops for civil servants and other organizations. This kind of training reaches employees who make decisions affecting Indigenous peoples.[84]

28. The Transforming Relations website was created in 2014 by senior Indigenous studies undergraduate students at Trent University in the course called "Transforming Settler Consciousness." The website documents over 200 educational initiatives by Indigenous peoples, non-governmental organizations, educational institutions, faith communities, governments, and businesses to shift the awareness of Canadians. This collection has been a source for the discussion of initiatives in this chap-

ter. Readers are encouraged to learn about additional initiatives that can be found on the site.[85]

These few examples do not even begin to scratch the surface of action by Indigenous and non-Indigenous educators, leaders, communities, governments, teachers, NGOs, churches, and grassroots activists. However, they point to the different fronts on which there is movement towards transforming Canadian consciousness and the way in which Canadians understand their relationships with Indigenous peoples. Although the TRC has been a watershed moment in catalyzing citizen engagement, KAIROS Canada's educational initiatives and Indigenous-led initiatives such as the Woodland Cultural Centre are examples of engagements that predate the TRC. Ongoing public educational work by Indigenous peoples as well as by small groups of Indigenous and non-Indigenous activists and advocates has been part of efforts to improve Indigenous–non-Indigenous relations. Reconciliation provides a discursive opportunity to advance this agenda at this particular moment in history.

ASSESSMENT

In Part 1, we outlined a number of issues (e.g., Canadian narratives, dominant discourses, different conceptualizations of reconciliation) that influence citizen engagement and change. In Part 2, we offered diverse examples to illustrate what "citizen engagement" looks like at this time in Canada. Although these examples are in no way exhaustive, collectively they demonstrate that there is momentum for change in different sectors of Canadian society and that Indigenous peoples are choosing to partner with and/or educate non-Indigenous peoples.

In Part 3, we first present a brief review of what we know about learning and change in the context of Indigenous–non-Indigenous relations. Then we revisit the earlier argument that different discourses lead to different destinations. As citizen engagement initiatives draw on and reinforce different discourses, the results can be uneven in achieving the goals of Indigenous peoples, particularly in relation to Indigenous sovereignty, land rights, and self-determination.

WHAT WE KNOW ABOUT LEARNING AND CHANGE

Currently, there is an unprecedented amount and diversity of information produced by Indigenous peoples in the public domain. Academic

literature, creative written and visual works, movies, arts-based performances, interviews, research studies, oral histories, traditional teachings,
Facebook sites, language learning on the web, and apps can be found with
ease. Aboriginal Peoples Television Network broadcasts the national news
nightly from coast to coast to coast. The fact that Canadians still know so
little about Indigenous peoples and Indigenous-settler relations demonstrates that simply providing more information alone will not change how
Canadians think, a reality acknowledged by RCAP in its report.[86]

A number of studies shed light on the processes of learning and
change as they affect settler consciousness. Key research has been
conducted by Chris Hiller, who studied the experiences of twenty-two
settler activists engaged long term in issues related to Indigenous land
struggles.[87] For these activists, learning is described as an ongoing journey, not something that occurred immediately or once and for all. At the
same time, individuals described critical moments of insight or turning
points that helped or forced them to challenge entrenched Canadian
narratives and to understand themselves in a different light. Hiller
depicts two intersecting and at times competing learning spirals. One
spiral describes decolonizing one's own self, realizing that one's own
beliefs, assumptions, and identities have been shaped by colonialism and
that one has to learn to see Indigenous—non-Indigenous relationships in
a very different way. Understanding one's own settler history and realizing how one benefits personally from ongoing colonialism are important
components of this learning. One aspect of this process is learning one's
identity and responsibilities as a settler beneficiary of treaties, as they
are interpreted by Indigenous peoples; where there are no treaties, as in
most parts of British Columbia, or where treaties were disregarded or
used as a colonial tool to dispossess Indigenous peoples, it is also the deep
realization that one has made one's home on stolen land. The other spiral
is one of relearning or acquiring new knowledge, including Indigenous
knowledge and an understanding of land and history from Indigenous
perspectives. This spiral is also about non-Indigenous people witnessing
and confronting historical and ongoing colonial practices that dispossess
and displace Indigenous peoples; in other words, it is also about engaging
in action against ongoing forms of colonial encroachment in relation to
Indigenous peoples, their lands, and their sovereignty. These processes
of learning, unlearning, and relearning go on simultaneously. At the
same time, Hiller reports that these are not simply smooth processes

of growing insight and acquisition; rather, they involve contradictions as individuals encounter perspectives and knowledge that threaten settlers' identities and sense of well-being.

Discomfort arises when one recognizes that the narratives received as "truth" through socialization in family and school are social constructions that support settler interpretations of the world and hide the truth of ongoing colonialism and one's own complicity with it. Regan uses the phrase "unsettling the settler within" to describe the process of decolonizing oneself, embracing discomfort, and interacting differently with Indigenous peoples.[88] Battell Lowman and Barker describe the complex emotions, including fear and guilt, that surface when people see the larger picture of colonization, the occupation of Indigenous lands, and their own complicity with its continuance.[89] Eva Mackey analyzes settlers' "structures of feeling," including their sense of entitlement and anxiety, since their relations to land are built upon long histories of socially constructed and enforced "certainty" that Indigenous claims to their own lands disrupt, creating "uncertainty."[90] When faced with such disruptions, there is a rush among settlers toward what anti-racist and anti-colonial scholars have deemed "moves to innocence," which serve to re-establish a sense of comfort when cherished identities and forms of privilege are threatened.[91]

These moves to innocence are efforts by individuals to absolve themselves of any connection to historical and contemporary processes of colonialism, racism, racialized privilege and discrimination, and the personal benefit of occupying Indigenous lands.[92] They are readily identifiable in everyday speech: "My family has been here for many generations"; "My ancestors weren't here at the time"; "That happened a long time ago"; "I have Indigenous friends"; "My ancestors were escaping persecution." Tuck and Yang describe "settler moves to innocence" in particular as "those strategies or positions that attempt to relieve the settler of feelings of guilt or responsibility without giving up land or power or privilege, without having to change much at all."[93] They describe a number of these moves to illustrate how readily settlers, including the most well-meaning activists, resist shifts in the status quo.[94] Learning, then, is not simply a matter of absorbing information. It is a process that engages emotions and identities in complex ways.

The literatures on Indigenous–non-Indigenous alliances that have emerged over the past decade point to coalitions as important sites of learning, particularly for non-Indigenous peoples.[95] Working together with Indigenous peoples on land issues, racism, and other sites of joint action, and exposure to different cultural perspectives helps non-Indigenous individuals to see how their own (colonial) worlds are constructed. Those involved in Indigenous–non-Indigenous alliances and coalitions have outlined both opportunities and cautions in relationship building. Relationship tensions include different styles of working and planning, conflicts over goals, differences in the pace of decision making, non-Indigenous ignorance of cultural protocols and history, arrogance of non-Indigenous allies, and turnover of the parties for continuity of the relationship.[96] Some authors offer advice for non-Indigenous aspiring allies such as taking the time to build trust and respect, learning the history of relations, never assuming the voice of Indigenous peoples, always keeping promises, and embodying the stance of the learner.[97]

Despite the learning that can happen in alliances and coalitions, even the process of working in solidarity on various issues does not guarantee that non-Indigenous people will consider deeper questions of their own complicity with the ongoing processes of colonization. As noted previously, Dion has pointed to the individual knowledge of people as being composed of what they know, what they do not know, and what they choose not to know. Individuals can be wilfully blind[98] and turn away from what Deborah Britzman terms "difficult knowledge."[99] This returns to the question of how discourses are used to mobilize Canadians in becoming engaged in Indigenous–non-Indigenous relations and the effects these different discourses have in shifting or reproducing colonial relationships and structures.

CITIZEN ENGAGEMENT IN
INDIGENOUS-NON-INDIGENOUS RELATIONS

This brief review makes plain the fact that reconciliation as a concept is being embraced by an array of Indigenous and non-Indigenous peoples, even while some have misgivings. A multitude of different projects, initiatives, and engagements have been launched, many by grassroots Indigenous and non-Indigenous peoples. Whether focused on addressing past abuses (residential schools), inequality (closing the gap), cultural awareness and exchange, or social justice (missing and murdered Indigenous women and girls), Indigenous and non-Indigenous peoples are coming together to learn and to lobby for change in institutional and government policies that obstruct the lives and opportunities of Indigenous peoples. One also cannot underestimate the important relationship building of informal grassroots networks that have developed among artists, writers, musicians, environmentalists, and academics as well as those in community-based organizations and clubs. Idle No More made excellent use of such networks to bring forward a thunderous voice that rocked politicians and the Canadian public through its urgency and seemingly sudden emergence.

At the same time, understandings of and expectations for what reconciliation means and entails remain diverse and conflicting. As a discursive hub, reconciliation draws on related discourses for strength and appeal. "Equality," "mutual respect," "recognition," "walking forward together," and "social justice" are important ideas that have emerged in discussions about *reconciliation*, and they are evident in the many initiatives that bear the word in their names. This framing of reconciliation is consistent with, and serves to reinforce, the predominant way that many Canadians see themselves based on dominant settler narratives.

This framing of reconciliation also has implications for how Canadians understand the meanings, demands, and limits of allying with Indigenous peoples. Jeffrey Denis and Kerry Bailey asked forty settler Canadians attending TRC events about their understandings of reconciliation and allyship, and they noted some significant disconnects with broader Indigenous aspirations and struggles: "Although participants' visions of reconciliation generally aligned with core aspects of the TRC's vision, including an emphasis on respectful relationships, historical awareness, cultural understanding, healing, and 'closing the gap' on socioeconomic and health outcomes, most were strikingly disconnected from wider movements for decolonization and Indigenous land struggles."[100] Although most participants shared an understanding of allyship to include building relationships, educating others, lobbying for changes in policies, and confronting racism, few talked about supporting land rights, self-determination, and Indigenous sovereignty. Similar concerns were raised by Davis and colleagues when analyzing twenty-five initiatives from entries on the Transforming Relations website.[101] They observed a similar absence of engagement with Indigenous land issues, treaties, and sovereignty in most initiatives documented on the site.

Viewed through the lens of scholarship on settlers' moves to innocence, the fact that so many Canadians are mobilized by forms of reconciliation discourse detached from broader questions of Indigenous land

and sovereignty can be seen in part as a reflection of the desire of settlers to avoid discomfort and unsettlement. The umbrella of reconciliation allows settler Canadians to engage in relationship building without necessarily taking on the identity of "settlers" in understanding themselves in Indigenous-settler relations and in ways that do not necessarily shift the status quo. It is precisely this caution that is advanced by Indigenous resurgent theorists who warn that reconciliation is intended ultimately to absorb Indigenous peoples into settler society. Yet, through these very critiques, Indigenous scholars and activists also disrupt and push at the boundaries of the dominant discourse of reconciliation, crossing it with discourses of Indigenous sovereignty, rights, and resurgence in order to open up spaces for new critical conversations about restitution, jurisdiction, and the return of land.

CONCLUDING COMMENTS

We are in a time characterized by fluidity as governments reach toward commitments to advance agendas of reconciliation. In accordance with Recommendations 2.3.45, 2.3.46, and 2.3.47 of the RCAP report, the federal government moved to focus more on nation-to-nation relationships by creating a Department of Crown-Indigenous Relations and Northern Affairs, hiving off program and service delivery to a minister of Indigenous services.[102] The UNDRIP, with its many possibilities to move forward on issues of sovereignty, has not been central to public educational initiatives or policy discussions to date, except the more limited imperative of free, prior, and informed consent.[103] When a private member's bill to bring Canadian laws into harmony with the UNDRIP, Bill C-262, was advanced by then NDP MP Romeo Saganash and accepted by the House of Commons in 2019, the initiative encountered opposition in the Senate. In December 2020, federal ministers of justice and Crown-Indigenous relations introduced Bill C-15, which similarly proposes to begin a process of bringing Canadian law into alignment with UNDRIP.[104] If passed, this initiative will require exceptional leadership if the general public is to absorb the potentialities of Indigenous self-determination. Sovereignty is a difficult discourse in Canada, and the reality of Indigenous sovereignty serves as a direct challenge to the broader colonial agenda of bringing Indigenous peoples under Canadian sovereignty once and for all.[105] It disrupts the notion of "our Indigenous peoples," a phrase often heard in mainstream media. Indigenous and non-Indigenous leaders need to be able to articulate that it is just and fair for Indigenous peoples to determine what happens in their traditional lands and territories. They also need to help Canadians understand that Indigenous Nations agreed to share their lands to provide homes for settler Canadians and that the treaties were made with promises that must be kept. Of course, Canada also claims territories that Indigenous Nations have never agreed to share with Canada through treaties.

It cannot be ignored that settler Canadians have mobilized, and continue to mobilize, *against* Indigenous Nations on land and resource issues, as demonstrated in the watershed moment of Kanehsatà:ke (Oka) and in parallel challenges at Gustafson Lake, Ipperwash, Caledonia, and the Tyendinaga rail blockades. Mackey has done an in-depth analysis of the Caldwell First Nation's struggle in the late 1990s to secure a land base against concerted backlash from Chatham-Kent settlers in southwestern Ontario.[106] On Pigeon Lake in Michi Saagiig territories, cottagers continued to mobilize against Michi Saagiig wild rice harvesters in 2015.[107] There are numerous examples of land- and resource-based oppositions and tensions from coast to coast to coast.

Simpson has observed that "land is an important conversation for Indigenous peoples and Canada to have because land is at the root of our conflicts."[108] And Mackey has noted that "settler colonialism—including philosophy, settler jurisprudence, legislation and settler 'structures of feeling'—pivot on axiomatic assumptions about settler entitlement and certainty in land, property and settler futures, as well as on materializing 'settled expectations.' The question, then, is whether decolonization, for settlers and settler law, may entail embracing particular forms of (likely uncomfortable) uncertainty, in order to imagine and practice relationships and power in new and creative ways."[109] As we have noted, reconciliation is a discursive hub that can lead in different directions. Simply providing more information to Canadians about past and continuing colonization will not give them the foundational knowledge and experiential base to sustain the kind of deep and discomforting conversation about land and sovereignty essential to true decolonization.

In 1996, the RCAP report foresaw public education as an essential component of changing the relationship between Indigenous and non-Indigenous peoples in Canada. Twenty-five years after the report, "sharing the land and sharing a future" require a level of individual and collective self-awareness that settler Canadians in particular and Canadian society in general still do not possess. Citizen mobilization in Indigenous–non-Indigenous relations can make an important contribution if there is enough courage to recognize "O Canada, our home on Native land"—the contested truth, simply stated, on protest signs. There is work to be done in imagining what sharing the land will look like so that new imaginaries can form within the consciousness of Canadians. This historical moment has presented openings and possibilities that require real leadership—Indigenous and non-Indigenous—to realize.[110]

NOTES

1   The title of this chapter reflects the mandate of the assignment to prepare a contribution on citizen engagement in the context of Indigenous–non-Indigenous relations. Various terms used here flow from differences in ideological orientation and commitment. "Aboriginal" is the term used in relation to the Royal Commission on Aboriginal Peoples, but it has been critiqued by many Indigenous people who consider the term to be colonial since it is embedded in Canada's Constitution Act and responsibilities that arise from it. "Indigenous" is the term used to refer to Indigenous peoples in the United Nations Declaration on the Rights of Indigenous Peoples and is generally used in an international context. More problematic are the terms "non-Indigenous" and "settler." "Indigenous-non-Indigenous" is often critiqued because the binary oversimplifies complex identities. "Non-Indigenous" also masks the reality of settler colonialism in Canada as an ongoing set of practices and processes, including occupation of Indigenous lands, from which settlers benefit. Use of the term "settler" facilitates a conversation about settler colonialism in the present and the responsibilities to change Canadian society in structure and process. Emma Battell Lowman and Adam Barker make the case for using the term "settler" in Chapter 1 of their volume; see Battell Lowman and Barker, *Settler: Identity and Colonialism in the 21st Century*. Jeff Corntassel has suggested using the terms used in local Indigenous Nations to refer to settlers; see Corntassel, "Re-Envisioning Resurgence." Since this chapter is not specific to particular traditional territories, we use the term "settler" to reference non-Indigenous people in general but also to invoke the settler origins of the Canadian state and its ongoing practices of occupying Indigenous lands, trying to subsume Indigenous sovereignty, and asserting control over Indigenous peoples in a multitude of ways. For a deep analysis of settler colonialism, see Eva Mackey, *Unsettled Expectations*; Tuck and Yang, "Decolonization Is Not a Metaphor"; Veracini, *Settler Colonialism: A Theoretical Overview*; and Wolfe, "Settler Colonialism and the Elimination of the Native."

2   Truth and Reconciliation Commission (TRC) of Canada, *Truth and Reconciliation Commission of Canada: Calls to Action*.

3   United Nations General Assembly (UNGA), United Nations Declaration on the Rights of Indigenous Peoples.

4   Royal Commission on Aboriginal Peoples (RCAP), *People to People, Nation to Nation*, 20–21.

5   TRC, *Honouring the Truth, Reconciling for the Future*, 15.

6   Simpson, "First Words," xiii–xiv.

7   An exhaustive list of these collaborative alliances is beyond the scope of this chapter.

From the 1950s onward, forerunners of contemporary organizations included the Indian-Eskimo Association, Project North, Aboriginal Rights Coalition, and Canadian Association in Support of Native Peoples. There have been many issue-specific examples such as the Coalition for a Public Inquiry into Ipperwash and the Sisters in Spirit Campaign in relation to missing and murdered Indigenous women and girls. There have also been many place-based alliances.

8   There are many organizational definitions of citizen engagement, civic engagement, and citizen participation. According to the Canadian Institutes of Health Research, "*Citizen engagement* is the meaningful involvement of individual citizens in policy or program development. To put it simply, citizens are 'engaged' when they play an active role in defining issues, considering solutions, and identifying resources or priorities for action." CIHR, "Citizen Engagement." Recent trends in civic engagement emphasize the significant contributions that arise when collective or citizen intelligence is applied to solving policy and community issues. See Desouza and Smith, "Capturing the Wisdom of Crowds." There is a move away from one-way, government-controlled communications to highly dialogical and collaborative processes involving multiple networks. Dialogue and "deliberative democracy" are contemporary approaches to civic engagement, using a variety of tools and participatory technologies to bring citizens together in problem-solving and visioning processes. See Svara and Denhardt, "The Connected Community," 5, 34–38. The possibilities for meaningful processes of engagement have expanded exponentially with the advent of social media, and web-based platforms have emerged that empower citizens to engage in policy issues with or without government guidance or intervention. Desouza and Smith, "Capturing the Wisdom of Crowds."

9   Nabatchi and Leighninger, *Public Participation for 21st Century Democracy*, 15.

10   Regan, *Unsettling the Settler Within*, 83–110.

11   Culhorne, *The Pleasure of the Crown*, 369.

12   Davis et al., "Complicated Pathways."

13   This point was punctuated by Prime Minister Trudeau's first speech to the 71st Session of the United Nations General Assembly on 19 September 2016. He ended by saying that "we know it will be hard work. But we're Canadian. And we are here to help."

14   Regan, *Unsettling the Settler Within*, 87.

15   Dion, *Braiding Histories*, 178–79.

16   Phung, "Are People of Colour Settlers Too?," 289. See also Dua, "Thinking through Anti-Racism and Indigeneity in Canada"; Lawrence and Dua, "Decolonizing Antiracism"; and Sejdev, "People of Colour in Treaty."

17   Examples of Indigenous–Black Lives Matter conversations can be found in various web-based coverage, such as Democracy Now! "Occupied Canada: Indigenous and Black Lives Matter Activists Unite to Protest Violence and Neglect"; Simpson, "An Indigenous View on #BlackLivesMatter"; and Tallbear, "Badass (Indigenous) Women Caretake Relations." There is emerging scholarship on this. See, Maynard and Simpson, "Towards Black and Indigenous Futures on Turtle Island: A Conversation."

18   Morgensen, *Spaces between Us*.

19   Battell Lowman and Barker, *Settler: Identity and Colonialism in the 21st Century*, 136.

20   Coulthard, *Red Skin, White Masks*, 102–03. Coulthard draws on the explanation of Stuart Hall in outlining an understanding of discourse, as elaborated by Michel Foucault.

21   Snow et al., "Frame Alignment Process."

22   To date, despite nine non-compliance orders, the federal government has not responded by making appropriate funding available. In 2019, the federal government was also ordered to compensate First Nations children who were removed from their homes and placed into purposely underfunded care. Jackson, "Tribunal Orders Canada to Compensate Parents."

23   Furniss, *The Burden of History*, 141; see also Mackey, "Universal Rights in Conflict."

24   Keefer, "Contradictions of Canadian Colonialism," 80–83.

25   Wallace, Struthers, and Bauman, "Winning Fishing Rights."

26   For a case study of the Coalition for an Inquiry into Ipperwash, see Davis, O'Donnell, and Shpuniarsky, "Aboriginal-Social Justice Alliances."

27   Simpson, "Land as Pedagogy"; Tuck and Yang, "Decolonization Is Not a Metaphor." Although clustering diverse discourses in this discussion runs the risk of oversimplifying, it is beyond the scope of this chapter to discuss their differences in depth.

28   Dua, "Thinking through Anti-Racism and Indigeneity in Canada"; Lawrence and Dua, "Decolonizing Antiracism."

29   Even the UNDRIP—named by the TRC as the central framework for implementing reconciliation—is seen through this resurgence discourse as limiting because of its focus on attaining state recognition of rights rather than challenging state sovereignty.

30   See, for example, Corntassel, Chaw-win-is, and T'lakadzi, "Indigenous Storytelling"; Coulthard, Red Skin, White Masks, 160; and Simpson, "Land as Pedagogy."

31   Henderson and Wakeham, Reconciling Canada, 8.

32   As Henderson and Wakeham note, this global proliferation of reconciliation discourse is marked and sparked by the UNGA resolution to declare 2009 the International Year of Reconciliation. Henderson and Wakeham, Reconciling Canada, 3.

33   TRC, Canada's Residential Schools, 3.

34   TRC, Honouring the Truth, 190.

35   Coulthard, Red Skin, White Masks, 121.

36   Coulthard, Red Skin, White Masks, 121.

37   Simpson, Dancing on Our Turtle's Back, 22.

38   Simpson, "Land and Reconciliation," para. 30.

39   "Reconciliation Canada," Reconciliation Canada—A New Way Forward Society, http://reconciliationcanada.ca.

40   "Reconciliation Dialogue Workshops," Reconciliation Canada—A New Way Forward Society, http://reconciliationcanada.ca/programs-initiatives/dialogue-workshops/.

41   "National Reconciliation Gatherings," Reconciliation Canada—A New Way Forward Society, http://reconciliationcanada.ca/programs-initiatives/national-reconciliation-gatherings/.

42   "Reconciliation in Action: A National Engagement Strategy," Reconciliation Canada—A New Way Forward Society, http://reconciliationcanada.ca/programs-initiatives/reconciliation-in-action-a-national-engagement-strategy/.

43   "Reconciliation Saskatoon," Office of the Treaty Commissioner, http://www.otc.ca/pages/reconciliation_saskatoon.

44   "Spotlight on Indigenous Storytelling and Reconciliation," National Arts Centre, 28 November 2017, http://nac-cna.ca/en/stories/story/spotlight-on-indigenous-storytelling-and-reconciliation.

45   "Reconciliation," Canadian Council for the Arts, 30 April 2020, https://canadacouncil.ca/initiatives/reconciliation.

46   "2016 Summer Indigenous Intensive," RE 2017 Summer Indigenous Intensive, http://rmooc.ca/okinadas/2016-summer-indigenous-intensive/.

47   Mi'kmaw Native Friendship Centre, "This Is What I Wish You Knew," 2017, http://www.thisiswhatiwishyouknew.com/.

48   Canadian Roots Exchange, "Canadian Roots," 2017, http://canadianroots.ca.

49   Project of Heart, "Project of Heart," 1 July 2016, http://projectofheart.ca.

50   Simon Fraser University, "President's Dream Colloquium on Returning to the Teachings: Justice, Identity and Belonging," 2016, http://www.sfu.ca/dean-gradstudies/events/dreamcolloquium/DreamColloquium-Reconciliation.html.

51   Trent University, "Truth and Reconciliation Theme for 40th Annual Elders and Traditional Peoples Gathering at Trent University," Trent University Daily News, 23 February 2016, http://www.trentu.ca/newsevents/newsDetail.php?newsId=14861.

52 Universities Canada, "Universities Canada Principles on Indigenous Education," 29 June 2015, http://www.univcan.ca/media-room/media-releases/universities-canada-principles-on-indigenous-education/.

53 Canadian Association of University Teachers, "CAUT Guide to Acknowledging Traditional Territory," 2016, https://www.caut.ca/content/guide-acknowledging-first-peoples-traditional-territory.

54 Vowel, "Beyond Territorial Acknowledgements."

55 University of Toronto, "Indigenous Health Conference: Towards Health and Reconciliation," University of Toronto Faculty of Medicine, 2020, http://www.cpd.utoronto.ca/indigenoushealth/.

56 City of Vancouver, "The Dialogues Project," 24 October 2016, http://vancouver.ca/people-programs/dialogues-project.aspx.

57 For links to these various church responses, see Kairos Canada, "Indigenous Rights: Churches' Response to Call to Action #48," http://www.kairoscanada.org/what-we-do/indigenous-rights/churches-response-call-action-48.

58 For the Mother Earth Water Walk, see http://www.motherearthwaterwalk.com/?page_id=2788.

59 "River Run 2019: walk with Grassy Narrows for mercury Justice, Free Grassy Narrows, 30 April 2020. https://freegrassy.net/walk-with-grassy-narrows-for-mercury-justice/.

60 "Reconciliation in Action: One Year after Burnaby Mountain," Tsleil Waututh Nation Sacred Trust Initiative 2017, https://twnsacredtrust.ca/reconciliation-in-action-one-year-after-burnaby-mountain/.

61 RAVEN Trust, 28 November 2017, https://raventrust.com.

62 "Site C," Amnesty International, 2016, http://www.amnesty.ca/our-work/campaigns/site-c.

63 "Unist'ot'en Camp," 30 April 2020, https://unistoten.camp.

64 An excellent example can be found in the video by Idle No More on the Peoples' Climate March in New York City, 22 September 2014. As one speaker pointed out, Indigenous peoples led the march, an indication that environmentalists had come to understand that Indigenous peoples are on the frontlines of defending the planet. "Idle No More at the Peoples' Climate March," Idle No More, 22 September 2014, http://www.idlenomore.ca/idle_no_more_at_the_peoples_climate_march.

65 Tuck and Yang, "Decolonization Is Not a Metaphor," 28. See also Snelgrove, Dhamoon, and Corntassel, "Unsettling Settler Colonialism."

66 "Idle No More," 2017, http://www.idlenomore.ca.

67 Native Women's Association of Canada, "Missing and Murdered Indigenous Women and Girls—NWAC," 2017, https://nwac.ca/mmiwg/.

68 The National Coalition for Our Stolen Sisters was formed in 2002 with NWAC, KAIROS, Amnesty International, the Elizabeth Fry Society, the United Church of Canada, and the Anglican Church of Canada. Amnesty supported a pilot project to undertake research and documentation on MMIWG, produced an international report in 2004, and established a campaign called Stolen Sisters.

69 "Annual Downtown Eastside Women's Memorial March," Feb 14th Annual Women's Memorial March: Their Spirits Live within Us, last updated 13 February 2017, https://womensmemorialmarch.wordpress.com/.

70 "Walking With Our Sisters," 2020.

71 "Idle No More at the Peoples' Climate March," Idle No More, http://www.idlenomore.ca/idle_no_more_at_the_peoples_climate_march. A speaker in this video makes this point explicitly.

72 "National Inquiry into Missing and Murdered Indigenous Women and Girls," Missing and Murdered Indigenous Women and Girls, http://www.mmiwg-ffada.ca/en/about-us/background/.

73 RCAP, The Report of the Royal Commission on Aboriginal Peoples, Vol. 5: 91–116.

74 TRC, *Truth and Reconciliation Commission of Canada: Calls to Action*, 7, Call to Action 62 states that "we call upon the federal, provincial, and territorial governments, in consultation and collaboration with Survivors, Aboriginal peoples, and educators, to:
    i. Make age-appropriate curriculum on residential schools, Treaties, and Aboriginal peoples' historical and contemporary contributions to Canada a mandatory education requirement for Kindergarten to Grade Twelve students.
    ii. Provide the necessary funding to post-secondary institutions to educate teachers on how to integrate Indigenous knowledge and teaching methods into classrooms.
    iii. Provide the necessary funding to Aboriginal schools to utilize Indigenous knowledge and teaching methods in classrooms.
    iv. Establish senior-level positions in government at the assistant deputy minister level or higher dedicated to Aboriginal content in education."

75 "Teaching Treaties in the Classroom: Grades 7–12," Office of the Treaty Commissioner, http://www.otc.ca/resource/purchase/teaching_treaties_in_the_classroom. html?page=3.

76 "What Is the Treaty Education Initiative?," Treaty Education Initiative, Treaty Relations Commission of Manitoba, 2017, http://www.trcm.ca/treaty-education-initiative/what-is-the-treaty-education-initiative/.

77 "Accord on Indigenous Education," Canadian Society for the Study of Education, http://www.csse-scee.ca/docs/acde/ACDE_Accord_on_Indigenous_Education.pdf.

78 "Blanket Exercise Workshop," Indigenous Rights, KAIROS Canada, http://www.kairoscanada.org/what-we-do/indigenous-rights/blanket-exercise.

79 "Campaign on the UN Declaration on the Rights of Indigenous Peoples," Indigenous Rights, KAIROS Canada, https://www.kairoscanada.org/what-we-do/indigenous-rights/undrip-campaign.

80 "Winds of Change Campaign," Indigenous Rights, KAIROS Canada, http://www.kairoscanada.org/what-we-do/indigenous-rights/windsofchange-overview.

81 "Gord Downie's *The Secret Path*," The Secret Path, October 2016, http://www.secretpath.ca; "Gord Downie and Chanie Wenjack Foundation," 2017, https://www.downiewenjack.ca.

82 Nk'mip Desert Cultural Centre, https://nkmipdesert.com.

83 Woodland Cultural Centre, https://woodlandculturalcentre.ca.

84 "Indigenous Cultural Competency Training (ICCT)," Ontario Federation of Indigenous Friendship Centres, 2013, http://www.ofifc.org/indigenous-cultural-competency-training-icct.

85 "Transforming Relations: A Collaborative Collection," Transforming Relations, 2017, https://transformingrelations.wordpress.com.

86 RCAP 1996a, *People to People, Nation to Nation*, 144.

87 Hiller, "Tracing the Spirals of Unsettlement."

88 Regan, *Unsettling the Settler Within*.

89 Battell Lowman and Barker, *Settler: Identity and Colonialism*, 90.

90 Mackey, *Unsettled Expectations*, 7–9.

91 Battell Lowman and Barker, *Settler: Identity and Colonialism*, 99–105, describe a similar phenomenon as "moves to comfort."

92 Boler and Zembylas, "Discomforting Truths"; McWhiney, "Giving Up the Ghost"; Tuck and Yang, "Decolonization Is Not a Metaphor."

93 Tuck and Yang, "Decolonization Is Not a Metaphor," 10.

94 Tuck and Yang, "Decolonization Is Not a Metaphor," 10–28. Tuck and Yang's "moves to innocence" include settler nativism, settler adoption fantasies, colonial equivocation, "free your mind and the rest will follow," a(s)t(e)risked peoples, and reoccupation and urban homesteading.

95 See, for example, Davis, O'Donnell, and Shpuniarsky, "Aboriginal-Social Justice Alliances"; Davis, "The High Stakes of Protecting Indigenous Homelands"; and Wallace, *Merging Fires*.

96   For discussions of relationship tensions, see Davis, *Alliances* (case studies by Sherman, Richland, and Sekaquaptewa, and by Smith and Sterritt). See also Davis, "The High Stakes of Protecting Indigenous Homelands," and Davis, "Home or Global Treasure?"

97   Bishop, *Becoming an Ally*; Davis and Shpuniarsky, "The Spirit of Relationships," 340–43; Gehl, "A Colonized Ally meets a Decolonized Ally"; Hiller, "Placing Ourselves in Relation"; Regan, *Unsettling the Settler Within*, 228.

98   Lynne Davis wishes to acknowledge Cherokee scholar Eber Hampton for drawing her attention to the role of "willful blindness" in the process of transforming consciousness and for recommending Heffernan, *Willful Blindness*.

99   Britzman, *Lost Subjects, Contested Objects*.

100 Denis and Bailey, "You Can't Have Reconciliation without Justice," 138.

101 The results of this analysis are reported in Davis et al., "Complicated Pathways," 398–414.

102 RCAP, *The Report of the Royal Commission on Aboriginal Peoples*, 172.

103 The UNDRIP has been critiqued by some Indigenous scholars as inadequate because Article 46 excludes "any right to engage in any activity or to perform any act contrary to the Charter of the United Nations or construed as authorizing or encouraging any action which would dismember or impair, totally or in part, the territorial integrity or political unity of sovereign and independent States." UNGA, United Nations Declaration on the Rights of Indigenous Peoples, 11.

104 On 20 November 2017, Minister of Justice Jody Wilson-Raybould expressed the federal government's intention to back Bill-262, which recently passed second reading. See Tasker, "Liberal Government Backs Bill." See Jones, "Liberals Introduce Bill to Implement UN Indigenous Rights Declaration."

105 Coulthard does a thorough examination of the "politics of recognition"; see Coulthard, *Red Skin, White Masks*. He is not the only academic to raise these issues, but he gives a clear account of them.

106 Mackey, *Unsettled Expectations*, 78-100.

107 Jackson, "Canada's Wild Rice Wars."

108 Simpson, "Land and Reconciliation."

109 Mackey, *Unsettled Expectations*, 36.

110 We would like to extend sincere gratitude to Dr. Jeff Denis (McMaster University) for his critical and insightful feedback on a late draft of this chapter and to Amy Champagne for timely technical assistance. Miigwech!

REFERENCES

Battell Lowman, Emma, and Adam Barker. *Settler: Identity and Colonialism in the 21st Century*. Halifax: Fernwood Publishing, 2015.

Bishop, Anne. *Becoming an Ally: Breaking the Cycle of Oppression in People*. 3rd ed. Halifax: Fernwood Publishing, 2015.

Boler, Megan, and Michalinos Zembylas. "Discomforting Truths: The Emotional Terrain of Understanding Difference." In *Pedagogies of Difference: Rethinking Education for Social Change*, edited by Peter Pericles Trifonas, 110–36. New York: RoutledgeFalmer, 2003.

Britzman, Deborah. *Lost Subjects, Contested Objects: Toward a Psychoanalytic Inquiry of Learning*. Albany: State University of New York Press, 1998.

Canadian Institutes of Health Research (CIHR). "Citizen Engagement." Last modified 9 January 2012. http://www.cihr-irsc.gc.ca/e/41592.html.

Corntassel, Jeff. "Re-Envisioning Resurgence: Indigenous Pathways to Decolonization and Sustainable Self-Determination." *Decolonization: Indigeneity, Education and Society* 1, no. 1 (2012): 86–101.

Corntassel, Jeff, Chaw-win-is, and T'lakadzi. "Indigenous Storytelling, Truth-Telling, and Community Approaches to Reconciliation." ESC: *English Studies in Canada* 35, no.1(2009):137-59. doi:10.1353/esc.0.0163.

Coulthard, Glen Sean. *Red Skin, White Masks: Rejecting the Colonial Politics of Recognition.* Minneapolis: University of Minnesota Press, 2014.

Culhane, Dara. *The Pleasure of the Crown: Anthropology, Law and First Nations.* Burnaby, BC: Talonbooks, 1998.

Davis, Lynne. "The High Stakes of Protecting Indigenous Homelands: Coastal First Nations' Turning Point Initiative and Environmental Groups on the B.C. West Coast." *International Journal of Canadian Studies* 39 (2009): 137–59. doi:10.7202/040827ar.

——. "Home or Global Treasure? Understanding Relationships between Environmentalists and the Heiltsuk Nation." *BC Studies* 171 (2011): 9–36.

Davis, Lynne, ed. *Alliances: Re/Envisioning Indigenous–non-Indigenous Relationships.* Toronto: University of Toronto Press, 2010.

Davis, Lynne, Chris Hiller, Cherylanne James, Tessa Nasca, and Sara Taylor. "Complicated Pathways: Settler Canadians Learning to Re/Frame Themselves and Their Relationships with Indigenous Peoples." *Settler Colonial Studies* 7, no. 4 (2017): 398–414. doi: 10.1080/2201473X.2016.1243086.

Davis, Lynne, Vivian O'Donnell, and Heather Shpuniarsky. "Aboriginal-Social Justice Alliances: Understanding the Landscape of Relationships through the Coalition for a Public Inquiry into Ipperwash." *International Journal of Canadian Studies* 37 (2007): 95–119. doi:10.7202/040778ar.

Davis, Lynne, and Heather Shpuniarsky. "The Spirit of Relationships: What We Have Learned about Indigenous/non-Indigenous Alliances and Coalitions." In *Alliances: Re/Envisioning Indigenous–non-Indigenous Relationships,* edited by Lynne Davis, 334–48. Toronto: University of Toronto Press, 2010.

Democracy Now! "Occupied Canada: Indigenous and Black Lives Matter Activists Unite to Protest Violence and Neglect." 20 May 2016. https://www.democracynow. org/2016/5/20/occupied_canada_indigenous_black_lives_matter.

Denis, Jeffrey S., and Kerry A. Bailey. "'You Can't Have Reconciliation without Justice': How Non-Indigenous Participants in Canada's Truth and Reconciliation Process Understand Their Roles and Goals." In *The Limits of Settler Colonial Reconciliation: Non-Indigenous People and the Responsibility to Engage,* edited by Sarah Maddison, Tom Clark, and Ravi Da Costa, 137–58. London: Springer, 2016.

Desouza, Kevin, and Kendra L. Smith. "Capturing the Wisdom of Crowds: Combining Citizen Intelligence and Online Civic Platforms." Planning, December 2014. https://www. planning.org/planning/2014/dec/capturingwisdom.htm.

Dion, Susan D. *Braiding Histories: Learning from Aboriginal Peoples' Experiences and Perspectives.* Vancouver: UBC Press, 2009.

Dua, Enakshi. "Thinking through Anti-Racism and Indigeneity in Canada." *Ardent Review* 2, no.1 (2008): 31–35.

Feb 14th Annual Women's Memorial March. "Annual Downtown Eastside Women's Memorial March." 13 February 2017. https://womensmemorialmarch.wordpress.com/.

Furniss, Elizabeth. *The Burden of History: Colonialism and the Frontier Myth in a Rural Canadian Community.* Vancouver: UBC Press, 1999.

Gehl, Lynn. "A Colonized Ally meets a Decolonized Ally: This is What They Learn. 24 February 2014." https://www.lynngehl.com/black-face-blogging/a-colonized-ally-meets-a-decolonized-ally-this-is-what-they-learn.

Heffernan, Margaret. *Willful Blindness: Why We Ignore the Obvious at Our Peril.* Toronto: Doubleday Canada, 2011.

Henderson, Jennifer, and Pauline Wakeham, eds. *Reconciling Canada: Critical Perspectives on the Culture of Redress*. Toronto: University of Toronto Press, 2013.

Hiller, Chris. "Placing Ourselves in Relation: Euro-Canadian Narratives of Grappling with Indigenous Sovereignty, Territory, and Rights." PhD diss., Wilfrid Laurier University, 2014.

——. "Tracing the Spirals of Unsettlement: Euro-Canadian Narratives of Coming to Grips with Indigenous Sovereignty, Title, and Rights." *Settler Colonial Studies* 7, no. 4 (2017): 415–40. doi:10.1080/2201473X.2016.1241209.

Jackson, Kenneth. "Tribunal Orders Canada to Compensate Parents Who Lost Children in Care." APTN National News, 16 March 2020. https://aptnnews.ca/2020/03/16/tribunal-orders-canada-to-compensate-parents-who-lost-children-in-care/.

Jackson, Lisa. "Canada's Wild Rice Wars." 20 February 2016. https://www.aljazeera.com/indepth/features/2016/02/canada-wild-rice-wars-160217083126970.html.

Jones, Ryan Patrick. "Liberals Introduce Bill to Implement UN Indigenous Rights Declaration." *CBC News*, 3 December 2020. https://www.cbc.ca/news/politics/liberals-introduce-undrip-legislation-1.5826523.

Keefer, Tom. "Contradictions of Canadian Colonialism: Non-Native Responses to the Six Nations Reclamation at Caledonia." In *Alliances: Re/Envisioning Indigenous-non-Indigenous Relationships*, edited by Lynne Davis, 77–90. Toronto: University of Toronto Press, 2010.

Lawrence, Bonita, and Enakshi Dua. "Decolonizing Antiracism." *Social Justice* 32, no. 4 (2005): 120–42.

Mackey, Eva. "Universal Rights in Conflict: 'Backlash' and 'Benevolent Resistance' to Indigenous Land Rights." *Anthropology Today* 21, no. 2 (2005): 14–20. doi:10.1111/j.0268-540X.2005.00340.x 2005.

——. *Unsettled Expectations: Uncertainty, Land, and Settler Decolonization*. Halifax: Fernwood Publications, 2016.

Mawhiney, Janet. "'Giving Up the Ghost': Disrupting the (Re)production of White Privilege in Anti-Racist Pedagogy and Organizational Change." MA thesis, Ontario Institute for Studies in Education of the University of Toronto, 1998. http://www.collectionscanada.gc.ca/obj/s4/f2/dsk2/tape15/PQDD_0008/MQ33991.pdf.

Maynard, Robyn, and Leanne Betasamosake Simpson. "Towards Black and Indigenous Futures on Turtle Island: A Conversation." In *Until We Are Free: Reflections on Black Lives Matter in Canada*, edited by Rodney Diverlus, Sandy Hudson, and Syrus Marcus Ware, 75–94. Regina: University of Regina Press, 2020.

Missing and Murdered Indigenous Women and Girls (MMIWG). "National Inquiry into Missing and Murdered Indigenous Women and Girls." http://www.mmiwg-ffada.ca/en/about-us/background/.

Morgensen, Scott Lauria. *Spaces between Us: Queer Settler Colonialism and Indigenous Decolonization*. Minneapolis: University of Minnesota Press, 2011.

Nabatchi, Tina, and Matt Leighninger. *Public Participation for 21st Century Democracy*. Hoboken, NJ: Jossey-Bass, 2015.

Office of the Treaty Commissioner. "Reconciliation Saskatoon." http://www.otc.ca/pages/reconciliation_saskatoon.

——. "Teaching Treaties in the Classroom: Grades 7–12." http://www.otc.ca/resource/purchase/teaching_treaties_in_the_classroom.html?page=3.

Ontario Federation of Indigenous Friendship Centres. "Indigenous Cultural Competency Training (ICCT)." 2013. http://www.ofifc.org/indigenous-cultural-competency-training-icct.

Phung, Malissa. "Are People of Colour Settlers Too?" In *Cultivating Canada: Reconciliation through the Lens of Cultural Diversity*, edited by Ashok Mathur, Jonathan Dewar, and Mike DeGagné, 289–98. Ottawa: AHF, 2011.

RAVEN—Respecting Aboriginal Values and Environmental Needs. "RAVEN Trust." 28 November 2017. https://raventrust.com.

Reconciliation Canada. "National Reconciliation Gatherings." http://reconciliationcanada.ca/programs-initiatives/national-reconciliation-gatherings/.

——. "Reconciliation Dialogue Workshops." http://reconciliationcanada.ca/programs-initiatives/dialogue-workshops/.

——. "Reconciliation in Action: A National Engagement Strategy." http://reconciliationcanada.ca/programs-initiatives/reconciliation-in-action-a-national-engagement-strategy/.

Regan, Paulette. *Unsettling the Settler Within: Indian Residential Schools, Truth Telling, and Reconciliation in Canada.* Vancouver: UBC Press, 2010.

Royal Commission on Aboriginal Peoples (RCAP). *People to People, Nation to Nation: Highlights from the Report of the Royal Commission on Aboriginal Peoples.* Ottawa: Ministry of Supply and Services, 1996a.

——. *The Report of the Royal Commission on Aboriginal Peoples.* Vol. 5. Ottawa: Ministry of Supply and Services, 1996b.

Sejdev, Robinder K. "People of Colour in Treaty." In *Cultivating Canada: Reconciliation through the Lens of Cultural Diversity*, edited by Ashok Mathur, Jonathan Dewar, and Mike DeGagné, 263–74. Ottawa: AHF, 2011.

Simpson, Leanne Betasamosake. "First Words." In *Alliances: Re/Envisioning Indigenous-non-Indigenous Relationships*, edited by Lynne Davis, xiii–xiv. Toronto: University of Toronto Press, 2010.

——. *Dancing on Our Turtle's Back: Stories of Nishnaabeg Re-Creation, Resurgence and a New Emergence.* Winnipeg: Arbeiter Ring Press, 2011.

——. "Land as Pedagogy: Nishnaabeg Intelligence and Rebellious Transformation." *Decolonization: Indigeneity, Education and Society* 3, no. 3 (2014a): 1–25.

——. "An Indigenous View on #BlackLivesMatter." *Yes! Magazine*, December 2014. http://www.yesmagazine.org/peace-justice/indigenous-view-black-lives-matter-leanne-simpson.

——. "Land and Reconciliation: Having the Right Conversations." *Electric City Magazine*, 5 March 2016. http://www.electriccitymagazine.ca/2016/01/land-reconciliation/.

Snelgrove, Corey, Rita Kaur Dhamoon, and Jeff Corntassel. "Unsettling Settler Colonialism: The Discourse and Politics of Settlers, and Solidarity with Indigenous Nations." *Decolonization: Indigeneity, Education and Society* 3, no. 2 (2014): 1–32.

Snow, David, E.B. Rochford, S.K. Worden, and R.D. Benford. "Frame Alignment Process, Micromobilization and Movement Participation." *American Sociological Review* 51 (1986): 464–81.

Svara, James, and Janet Denhardt, eds. "The Connected Community: Local Governments as Partners in Citizen Engagement and Community Building. A White Paper Prepared for the Alliance for Innovation." Arizona State University, 15 October 2010. http://icma.org/en/icma/knowledge_network/documents/kn/document/301763/connected_communities_local_governments_as_a_partner_in_citizen_engagement_and_community_building.

Tallbear, Kim. "Badass (Indigenous) Women Caretake Relations: #NoDAPL, #IdleNoMore, #BlackLivesMatter." Cultural Anthropology Hot Spots, 22 December 2016. https://culanth.org/fieldsights/1019-badass-indigenous-women-care-take-relations-nodapl-idlenomore-blacklivesmatter.

Tasker, John Paul. "Liberal Government Backs Bill that Demands Full Implementation of UN Indigenous Rights Declaration." CBC News, 21 November 2017. http://www.cbc.ca/news/politics/wilson-raybould-backs-undrip-bill-1.4412037.

Truth and Reconciliation Commission (TRC) of Canada. *Truth and Reconciliation Commission of Canada: Calls to Action.* Winnipeg: TRC, 2015a. http://www.trc.ca/websites/trcinstitution/File/2015/Findings/Calls_to_Action_English2.pdf.

——. *Canada's Residential Schools: The Final Report of the Truth and Reconciliation Commission of Canada.* Vol. 6. Montreal and Kingston: McGill-Queen's University Press, 2015b.

——. *Honouring the Truth, Reconciling for the Future: Summary of the Final Report of the Truth and Reconciliation Commission of Canada.* Toronto: James Lorimer, 2015c.

Tuck, Eve, and K. Wayne Yang. "Decolonization Is Not a Metaphor." *Decolonization: Indigeneity, Education and Society* 1, no. 1 (2012): 1–40.

United Nations General Assembly (UNGA). United Nations Declaration on the Rights of Indigenous Peoples, adopted by the General Assembly, 2 October 2007, A/RES/61/295. http://www.refworld.org/docid/471355a82.html.

Veracini, Lorenzo. *Settler Colonialism: A Theoretical Overview.* Basingstoke, UK: Palgrave Macmillan, 2010.

Vowel, Chelsea. "Beyond Territorial Acknowledgements." In *Âpihtawikosisân/Law, Language, Life: A Plains Cree Speaking Métis Woman in Montreal.* 23 September 2016. http://apihtawikosisan.com/2016/09/beyond-territorial-acknowledgments/.

"Walking With Our Sisters." 2020. http://walkingwithoursisters.ca/.

Wallace, Rick. *Merging Fires: Grassroots Peacebuilding between Indigenous and Non-Indigenous Peoples.* Halifax: Fernwood Publishing, 2013.

Wallace, Rick, Marilyn Struthers, and Rick Cober Bauman. "Winning Fishing Rights: The Successes and Challenges of Building Grassroots Relations between the Chippewas of Nawash and Their Allies." In *Alliances: Re/Envisioning Indigenous–non-Indigenous Relationships,* edited by Lynne Davis, 91–113. Toronto: University of Toronto Press, 2010.

Wolfe, Patrick. "Settler Colonialism and the Elimination of the Native." *Journal of Genocide Research* 8, no. 4 (2006): 387–409. doi: 10.1080/14623520601056240.

CHAPTER 19
SSHRC AND THE CONSCIENTIOUS COMMUNITY:
REFLECTING AND ACTING ON INDIGENOUS RESEARCH AND RECONCILIATION IN RESPONSE TO CTA 65

Aaron Franks

My task in this short chapter is to provide an independent and critical perspective on the role of social sciences and humanities research in "advanc[ing] understanding of reconciliation" in Canada. I pay particular attention to the role of the Social Sciences and Humanities Research Council of Canada (SSHRC) in shaping the discourse of reconciliation and in supporting a research milieu and funding initiatives that reflect this vision.[1] This chapter is not a systematic review of existing initiatives and certainly not a policy paper, official or otherwise. This is a "think piece" intended to push the edges of accepted thinking outward a bit, and I feel both privileged and daunted by the opportunity.

OUTLINE

The think piece unfolds like this. You should know a bit about me, my positionality, and my relationship to SSHRC. And then how an ethic of decolonization frames my observations, deductions, and intuitions about practical action. I name some of the contradictions that we need to face to do this work and reflect on how the social sciences and humanities can address them in important ways.

In the next section, I delve into what SSHRC can do, as a prime agenda-shaping and of course funding agency, to advance understanding of reconciliation in concert with universities, Indigenous communities, and other actors. The section lays out two basic aims: promotion of autonomous research spaces in the long-term interest of genuine nation-to-nation collaboration and support for foundational research that develops Indigenous knowledge systems first by and for Indigenous people. I suggest five sets of actions:

- decentralization of SSHRC;
- Indigenization of university and regional-level research, learning, and community collaboration;
- support for undergraduate, non-academic, and other "unconventional" highly qualified personnel (HQP) and learners;
- institutional self-inquiry; and
- strengthened support for interdisciplinarity and research-creation.

I conclude with a summation of ideas and a reinforcement of hope.

MY POSITION

These reflections and proposals stem from my particular position. I am of mixed settler-Indigenous background (more specifically Métis, English [Lincolnshire], Irish [Drumcree], Norwegian [Stavanger], German [unknown], and Muskegowuk [around what became Fort Severn]) and do not have a landed community. I am an early career academic but had a first career in the theatre. I have done extensive participatory research but rarely with the sort of stable, bounded communities that still appear in many research texts. I have worked with Indigenous academics, artists, advocates, and students but have never taken an Indigenous studies course. In coming to know my positionality, including my Indigeneity, and my place in the Canadian story, I resist nostalgia and have come to depend instead on a materialist historical reading of the overlays between my family's journey and the enterprise of Canada, between myself and the colonial present.

I think that my position has encouraged me to think between Indigeneity "in and of itself" and Indigeneity as a reflection of the desires and apprehensions of broader, non-Indigenous society. I think that I can recognize (but not fully inhabit) the very different experiences of Indigenous resurgence as the recovery and enhancement of life and dignity in thousands, maybe millions, of local moments in what is now Canada, as a global project of territorial resistance and autonomous human development, and as a socio-political achievement framed nationally by a capitalist liberal democracy.

MY ROLE

For nearly two decades, SSHRC has solicited input, deliberated, and taken steps to implement research funding initiatives, reconsider grant review criteria, and support researcher, administrator, and student development in formal and informal ways, often in conjunction with other bodies. SSHRC has an Aboriginal Advisory Circle (AAC), has met with many faculty and administrators at geographically diverse universities, and engages with organizations such as the Canadian Indigenous/Native Studies Association (CINSA), Universities Canada, and the Canadian Federation for the Humanities and Social Sciences. There are also multiple conversational channels among the "TC3+"[2] and with federal agencies such as Indigenous and Northern Affairs Canada (INAC).

Through the Mitacs Canadian Science Policy Fellowship program, SSHRC invited me to work alongside it in 2016–17 as an independent researcher. From this unique (and privileged) position as a "critical friend," I assisted SSHRC in taking on and responding to current and past consultations and providing a transdisciplinary perspective that cuts across the complex ecology of SSHRC granting programs and related initiatives.

GLIMPSING RECONCILIATION

Of course, reconciliation is not resurgence; they mean different things and are used in discourse to do different things. But the current drive toward *reconciliation*, while powered through formal governance channels and embodied in the exhaustive work of the Truth and Reconciliation Commission (TRC) of Canada, owes much to Indigenous *resurgence(s)* even if the two are often in tension. Autonomy and accommodation agonistically—maybe antagonistically—make room for one another. Regardless of personal/political sympathies, there is a basic dialectical reasoning to this. The social sciences and humanities, far from being the poor relations to other kinds of inquiry that research funding levels might suggest, will be central to understanding what is required—after so many decades of failure—to transform the nation to the point where reconciliation is not an empty token.[3]

Reconciliation must be much more akin to decolonization than accommodation; truly living Eighth Fire teachings[4] will mean a fundamental reconsideration and reconfiguration of geopolitical relationships in Canada. The social sciences and humanities in Canada, not least through the actions and discourses of agenda-shaping organizations such as SSHRC, will be both continually informing and informed by this reconfiguration.

In fact, I have come to believe more and more that *decolonization is a prerequisite for reconciliation*. I think that we have to square up to the language we use. The authors of the 2015 TRC report are careful to note in the introduction to the executive summary that the term "reconciliation" itself has multiple meanings and risks serving romanticized political imaginaries: "To some people, reconciliation is the re-establishment of a conciliatory state. However, this is a state that many Aboriginal people assert never has existed between Aboriginal and non-Aboriginal people. To others, reconciliation, in the context of Indian residential schools, is similar to dealing with a situation of family violence. It's about coming to terms with events of the past in a manner that overcomes conflict and establishes a respectful and healthy relationship among people, going forward. It is in the latter context that the Truth and Reconciliation Commission of Canada has approached the question of reconciliation."[5]

The sense of reconciliation that I work from here is less concerned about definitions, as important as they might be, and more inspired by the TRC's own declaration of action: "To the Commission, reconciliation is about *establishing* and maintaining a mutually respectful relationship between Aboriginal and non-Aboriginal peoples in this country."[6] Establishing such relations requires decolonization as befits the progressive reconfiguration of a settler colonial society.

I don't think that there is a better word available than *decolonization*. It is a concept that, over the past decade or more, has been advanced in several consultations with SSHRC (e.g., some but certainly not all SSHRC interlocutors in CINSA, some members of the SSHRC AAC). It appears at times in the documents resulting from these consultations. It is not alien thinking, but it remains for most people opaque, threatening, and unactionable. But we are in a time when senior federal politicians such as former minister of justice Jody Wilson-Raybould publicly enjoined the Assembly of First Nations to pursue decolonization. As a SSHRC staff member recently described discussing reconciliation while avoiding mention of decolonization, *it's like gender, how can you discuss it without mentioning sexism?* At the same time ... "the easy absorption, adoption, and transposing of decolonization [are] yet another form of settler appropriation."[7]

GLIMPSES OF SSHRC

Building on its work since 2002 to develop and extend dedicated programming in Aboriginal research, as well as discussions on Call to Action (CTA) 65 with a cross-section of Indigenous, postsecondary, and federal partners started in 2016, SSHRC has been leading a joint effort with its sister agencies, the Canadian Institutes of Health Research (CIHR) and the Natural Sciences and Engineering Research Council of Canada (NSERC), to develop options for implementation of CTA 65.

In 2002, responding to concerted representation from Indigenous organizations and extensive support in the research community, SSHRC opened up a dialogue on research with Indigenous peoples that led in 2004 to its pilot program in Aboriginal research.[8] The main policy shift at the base of the new program was away from research "on and for" Aboriginal peoples and toward research "by and with" those peoples. This can be interpreted as a key (perhaps *the* key) principle for reconciliation in relation to research. In 2016, SSHRC invested an estimated $30 million of its annual program budget (about 10 percent) in research and research training conducted by and with Indigenous peoples.

In 2015, working with its Aboriginal Advisory Circle, SSHRC widened the application of the principles of Aboriginal research to all of its programming, adopting an enhanced definition of Aboriginal research and merit review guidelines that outline key reference points in the council's support for Aboriginal research: "Research in any field or discipline that is conducted by, grounded in, or engaged with, First Nations, Inuit or Métis communities, societies or individuals and their wisdom, cultures, experiences or knowledge systems, as expressed in their dynamic forms, past and present. Aboriginal research embraces the intellectual, physical, emotional and/or spiritual dimensions of knowledge in creative and interconnected relationships with people, places and the natural environment."[9] An in-depth analysis of SSHRC's mandate and structure is beyond my task. However, there are aspects of the organization that I believe are directly relevant to its capacity to fulfill CTA 65 in the transformative way befitting this historic opportunity.

SSHRC is highly centralized in Ottawa and is almost exclusively non-Indigenous in its staffing. It is heavily oriented to project and student/HQP funding rather than supporting ongoing operational costs for organizations or structural innovations in institutions. SSHRC also benefits from many committed professionals who want to engage with the task of fulfilling CTA 65. This call specifies that SSHRC work with "Aboriginal peoples, post-secondary institutions and educators and the National Centre for Truth and Reconciliation and its partner institutions."[10] It has been pointed out that, though several of the staff and management have PhDs, very few have extensive experience working in a university. This is not at all a reflection on competence or commitment; however, as with the lack of Indigenous staff and management, it necessitates a high level of translation between institutional cultures, in this case from university/research to government/policy.

STAKES AND OPPORTUNITIES

SSHRC management tasked with thinking through CTA 65 have been generous with their thoughts and concerns. In one instance, two perceived "existential" risks and obstacles were identified that I believe merit frank and wide-ranging discussion.

First is autonomy and accountability in the current state-patron relationship. Indigenous peoples and the organizations that represent them rightfully demand a much higher degree of self-determination in how they manage their affairs and advocate for their interests in their relationships with other levels of government, corporations, and other actors. This is equally true of greater Indigenous control over research that affects Indigenous communities, First Nations, and other stakeholders. The Assembly of First Nations, Inuit Tapiriit Kanatami, Métis National Council, and others say in various ways that "we need your help" and, in the same breath, "let us do it ourselves." Although on one level there is increased understanding within funding agencies why this should be so, there is little capacity within state institutions to facilitate peer-to-peer or nation-to-nation relations where it is perceived that most of the financial expenses are borne by one partner.

Second is the legitimacy of Indigenous knowledge and funded research. What is Indigenous knowledge, and who will accept its validity? What is at stake by admitting Indigenous knowledge systems (IKS) into the research paradigm (and consequent "credibility of our research and status in the community, here and globally")? The idea of IKS being brought into the "research tent" is a huge ask, especially when the social sciences and humanities are already seen as "soft" and hard to justify. When my placement at SSHRC began, my supervisors and I sat down and discussed our hopes for the year and the challenges and opportunities that addressing the call to action right in the DNA of the funding system presented. I was surprised by the sincerity behind the comment (and I paraphrase) *we are trapped because our mandate is Western paradigm, empiricist research.* The sense was that the primacy of Western enlightenment epistemology was being challenged.

GROUNDS FOR SUSPICION, HOPE, AND ACTION

Like research, research funding is not value neutral; likewise, in a world of boundaries and limits (often quite helpful ones), a hyper-pluralistic approach ("let a thousand flowers bloom") is not realizable in some pure form. Having laid out where I'm coming from, my present sense of reconciliation, and some of my observations while at SSHRC (a brilliantly generous host), I want to square my thinking up to the challenges by naming some contradictions. In general, we need to stop talking about first steps and beginnings. The colonial relationship that has oppressed Indigenous people is centuries old, the Indian Act is over 140 years old, individuals spoke out against the Indian residential school system 100 years ago, and RCAP reported its findings twenty-five years ago. The reality is that more facts might be helpful in addressing specific problems, but they are not the foundation for the change that has eluded us or, more accurately, the change that we have evaded.

Thinking deeply through reconciliation presents necessary challenges to *procedural* notions of dialogue and equity. I purposefully engage with the words of two prominent Indigenous social leaders respected within multiple Indigenous and non-Indigenous communities, Senator Murray Sinclair and Professor Cindy Blackstock.

DIFFERENCE IS REAL

Reconciliation is not an Aboriginal problem. It is a Canadian problem. It involves all of us.

—Murray Sinclair, 2015[11]

From this statement, I draw two directions: that reconciliation aimed at "fixing" Indigenous peoples and their problems while the state and non-Indigenous society remain unaltered is a perpetuation of oppression and violence and that, though this problem might indeed involve all of us, Indigenous and non-Indigenous people in Canada are differentially positioned. Furthermore, as recognized by Section 35 of the Constitution Act, 1982, and the United Nations Declaration on the Rights of Indigenous Peoples, to which Canada is a signatory, Indigenous people have the right to assert this difference.

In short, *yes, all people in Canada but not all together all of the time.* This is challenging. It challenges ideas of equity and federalism and deeply ingrained tenets of liberalism and pluralism. It challenges a prevailing (though not universally accepted) vision of "the academy" as a smooth space in which competing ideas jostle collegially on a level playing field. SSHRC is mandated to work on behalf of all Canadians, and it is the primary funding instrument for the social sciences and humanities in Canada. Excitingly, this increasingly involves partnerships between university-based researchers and a multitude of non-university actors—community groups, government agencies, businesses, and NGOs.

I thus argue that, for social sciences and humanities research to advance the understanding of reconciliation, *autonomous research spaces by and for Indigenous actors, and spaces for non-Indigenous reflection and self-inquiry, need to be facilitated.* Not without irony, effective dialogue and mutually beneficial human (and ecological) development will depend on not papering over difference. But there are options besides either essentialist separatism or relativist pluralism.

RECONCILIATION IS GOOD BUT COSTS

We're going to have to have some courage in research. We're going to have to have the courage to embrace what hurts as a country, and support those who are helping us do it.

—Cindy Blackstock, 2016[12]

Far from fetishizing suffering (be it from guilt, oppression, or both) or wallowing in it, reconciliation will require the conscious integration of enormous, permanent, material loss into our thinking and value systems. I think that this is required at the level of narratives of Canadian federalism and nation building, as I sense Blackstock implies above. To that process of "restorying," I would add the consequences of the specific violences of modernity. In other words, as social scientists, artists, researchers, commentators, educators, learners, and leaders, we need to reweave loss and absence into our thinking and lifeworld.

This too is challenging in that it rubs against the current paradigm of problem solving and risks (maybe) imposing some further colonial injustice, such as, *if Indigenous peoples are beginning to overcome violence and reassert themselves as vibrant societies, isn't it the wrong time to question a positive modernity and deny "them" the gifts of modern progress?*

Although research addressing excruciating levels of imposed violence, preventable illness, and environmental destruction is urgently needed, we should be wary of focusing on an "emergency first responder" approach if it sidelines "slow research," the theoretically rich, methodologically challenging, and socially risky research needed to advance understanding of reconciliation.

WHAT THE SOCIAL SCIENCES AND HUMANITIES CAN DO

Perhaps it's because I did my PhD in a discipline with both "physical" and "human" branches (geography) and frequently saw the institutional jostling between them, but too often I still sense the social sciences and humanities positioned as the "communications office" for the natural and applied sciences. So we must argue for the *independent* abilities of these disciplines, not least the qualitative fields, to explain phenomena, connect processes, and facilitate action toward reconciliation.

This must include targeted research aimed at meeting immediate needs but also less obviously instrumental research that, from my reading of these two quotes, explores differing experiences:

- What are the criteria of "success" and the pyrrhic victories of settlement processes, negotiation, and ultimately reconciliation?
- What is the cost not only of past injustices but also of the current and future process of reconciliation itself?
- Where are we when there is so much talk of "starting" and "new beginnings" and others are speaking from the middle of a centuries-old process?
- What is the legitimate place in the world of emotions, affect, and experiential knowledge as a core part of Indigenous, non-Indigenous, and relational (both within and between the two) governance and socio-economic relations?

Such research must combine the analytical and affective, the historical and personal, and the territorial and familial.

A major challenge to using the rhetoric of reconciliation in a sincere, good way, and to an organization such as SSHRC charged with advancing knowledge in a pluralistic yet focused way, is that it is easy to forget that reconciliation (with concomitant Indigenous recovery and resurgence) is not a mental project. It is material, fleshy, and real. The strong call from many critics of the discourse of reconciliation is that most often reconciliation is confined to a strictly individual/familial psychological process of recognition, grieving, and recovery without (conveniently) much or any attention to the material basis of national resurgence and autonomy: land.

Material-ecological and social-political conditions are changing, and advancing an understanding of reconciliation requires advancing an understanding of the future-facing conditions within which it will have to be achieved. Couldn't these conditions include . . . *everything?* In theory. But I argue that *climate change* and emerging *forms of governance* are focal points of academic and social interest worthy of funding calls and targeted programs that span any discipline enfolded within the social sciences and humanities. This includes the fine arts, literature, cultural studies, and the like alongside sociology, anthropology, geography, and other social sciences.

WHAT SSHRC CAN DO

It might be time for SSHRC to venture into new organizational territory by supporting the resourcing and self-organizing of Indigenous-led initiatives in addition to its more traditional activity of competitive, project-based research funding. I argue that SSHRC can and should engage more openly with the question of decolonization, specifically the relationship between decolonization and reconciliation and, in the specific world of research, meaningful collaboration.

In asking what SSHRC can do, I am also asking how SSHRC might need to change. When I think of "doing" activities, I think not only of programming, granting, outreach, and communications but also of developing the frameworks and working principles that underpin these tools. Similarly, change at SSHRC might mean shifts in its structure and in its sense of leadership and awareness of the importance of the social sciences and humanities to transformative, lasting reconciliation.

I suggest that focus can be shared between negotiating collaboration and autonomy and the (re)development of IKS.

BUILDING COLLABORATION THROUGH SUPPORTING AUTONOMY

We need an open and critical discussion on the theory and practice of making *autonomous Indigenous research space*. By this, I mean the possibilities for research that does not automatically presume partnership with non-Indigenous actors and in which benefits might not be readily apparent to non-Indigenous communities and institutions.

Collaboration is a necessary aim, but within existing structures collaboration can be inadvertently coercive. This is especially true when university-based academics (likely to be non-Indigenous) are increasingly charged with making an "impact" and governments, agencies, and other organizations working on behalf of Indigenous people face an incredible list of threats to survival and well-being.[13]

Similarly, we need critical discussion on the theory and practice of making *peer-to-peer spaces for non-Indigenous or settler research and education*. By this, I mean the possibilities for research, education, and outreach that do not demand that Indigenous academics and communities are responsible for educating their non-Indigenous peers. Collaboration by all means, but non-Indigenous partners must demonstrate reflexive knowledge of their positions, accountability for structural power imbalances, and willingness and capacity to investigate and query the historical, cultural, and socio-political bases for their circumstances and motivations for collaboration.

One of the persistent research tropes that these critical discussions could help to evolve is *community*, a concept that "has been problematized by about 100 years of research."[14] How to value meaningfully dispersed communities of place, interest, and practice? Brent describes community as the "continually reproduced desire to overcome the adversity of social life."[15] This definition allows for flexibility of place, scale, and identity and accommodates tangible relationships born of common cause.

CHAMPIONING THE (RE)DEVELOPMENT OF IKS

Family clans have been severed and because we are a relational people … our relationships to our environment and our cosmology … place us in a state of upheaval. It is almost like our bodies have been evacuated to somewhere foreign and unhealthy.
—Stan Wilson, Opaskwayak Cree Nation, 2016[16]

I suggest that not all but enough of us understand the above statement sufficiently to make it a basis for further inquiry and action, without having to ask "yes, but what does he *mean?*" and without having to translate Wilson's "diagnosis" of unhealth. If the academy is indeed pluralistic and sincerely seeks to Indigenize itself, then Wilson's evidence will be seen as illuminating, not confounding.[17] This does not mean not open to interpretation, or critique, but the ontological realities of relationality, embodiment, and interpellation of environment and cosmology should now be established as "credible."

One of the many tensions that an institutionalized academic engagement with Indigenous knowledge triggers is the legitimacy and transferability of land-based knowledge systems within the academy. It is an important discussion and one in which, without "discovering" and appropriating Indigenous epistemologies, the Western/Euro-American academy can learn much. And there are some resonances between "the spatial turn" in the social sciences and humanities and what Glenn Coulthard calls Indigenous land-based normativity.[18]

Above all, there is a great need to enable research that not only employs or instrumentalizes Indigenous knowledge but also asks what it is *now* and actively *builds* it. SSHRC and the academy writ large cannot expect fully formed and efficacious Indigenous inquiry and educational practice to enter into equitable peer-to-peer relations with Western/Euro-American counterparts entrenched in our institutions. A critical conversation on autonomous research spaces should also address how Indigenous knowledges, when encountering mainstream research, are almost invariably required to explain and justify themselves to their non-Indigenous counterparts in ways that prevailing systems are not.

SPECIFIC MEASURES

I will take a deep breath and respectfully suggest five (fairly) specific measures that SSHRC could take. Like the rest of this thought piece, they are intended to provoke discussion.

1. Decentralization

SSHRC could connect more effectively with diverse constituencies by moving, physically and virtually, some of its operations out of Ottawa and its centre on 350 Albert Street. This could happen in two ways. Certain core activities at SSHRC could be moved to a second urban centre in the west, and Indigenous research programming and academic, government, and community engagement could take place in both. Sound impossible? It has been floated that all of the tri-council funders be co-located in the old NRC Canada Laboratories Building at 100 Sussex Drive, though there are concerns that there would not be enough room for all three. Relocating certain operations to a second office could create this space.

A more likely scenario is a small number of SSHRC centres housed in regionally and culturally diverse universities and colleges. They could rotate to serve a new location every five to ten years. These centres would bring together the complementary capacities of Indigenous and allied researchers, educators, Elders, knowledge keepers and pathfinders,[19] administrators, Indigenous student and community organizations, and local and regional First Nations, Inuit, and Métis communities.

In the view of one speaker invited to SSHRC, representing an Indigenous community organization in a partnership grant (and I paraphrase), you've got to get out of this building, get out of Ottawa. Bring your expertise to other places to help incubate research.

2. Indigenization of Resources and Approaches

This ties in directly to the establishment of the regional centres described above. These nodes would provide distinctive self-organizing spaces for Indigenous faculty and, through intentional and extended engagement, deepen the understanding of Elders, knowledge keepers, and pathfinders and their unique hybrid roles in academia, student support, and community engagement and secure better resources for them as key parts of these horizontally organized nodes.

In case this seems to be wildly out of tune with the way that universities can work, I should point out that through much effort, foresight, and creative energy such "nodes" are already in the making. As an example, Nipissing University is a relatively small university in North Bay, Ontario, near several First Nations. It has a dynamic Aboriginal Initiatives office that integrates its teaching and learning functions with both its student support and community engagement activities. It works closely with faculty, deans, department heads, and undergraduate and graduate students, and it facilitates links with several local First Nations, the City of North Bay and its Reconciliation North Bay initiative, and multiple primary and secondary schools in the area.

In collaboration with the other funding councils, Canadian Foundation for Innovation, individual universities, and other actors, SSHRC could provide structural, multiyear funding to such a centre. The centre would organize to meet local needs relatively organically, as in the Nipissing example, but would have extra capacity to

- coordinate regional initiatives among multiple universities, colleges, First Nations, Inuit, and Métis, groups representing "unlanded" Indigenous communities, and other collaborators;
- in conjunction with other regional centres have a stronger, more proactive, advisory role than the current SSHRC Aboriginal Advisory Circle; this could take the form of multiple regional advisory circles;
- play a potential role in peer review and determining review criteria; and
- strengthen the resources available to Elders and knowledge keepers, create more reciprocal relationships with them, and practise respect for their complex and often hard-earned lived experiences.

These "centres plus" could act as regionally sensitive research coordinating hubs for fixed periods of time, with a handful of centres operating around the country at any given time and moving periodically.

On a final note, I envision that these centres will empower the growing cohort of Indigenous faculty working across many disciplines, with their own complex and evolving relationships to Indigeneity and reconciliation, to shape multiple agendas in advancing the understanding of reconciliation.

3. Expanding Training Opportunities

SSHRC should consider ongoing funding for training non-academic, secondary school, undergraduate, or otherwise "non-traditional" HQP (in grant speak) and learners. This is an area of keen interest for many SSHRC-funded researchers and Indigenous community organizations. Community-engaged research can benefit immeasurably from the contributions of these participants and partners, but for a variety of reasons such collaborators might not find it appropriate to enrol in a SSHRC-eligible higher education (HE) institution. The HE enrolment and completion rates for Indigenous students continue to be low, but some proposed improvements might be counterintuitive. For example, an Indigenous academic involved in a multipartner community research project with many HQP noted in discussion that, in her experience, Indigenous youth who participate in this work might not immediately see themselves as a fit for academic research and learning but can change their perspectives in their own time through involvement in the work and watching their peers do so as well.

4. Institutional Self-Inquiry

This involves increasing the capacity of mainstream institutions to play their part in reconciliation without imposing a double burden on Indigenous communities—that of being marginalized and then being required to educate and in a sense assuage the concerns of non-Indigenous partners.

This is difficult but not unprecedented work. The National Arts Centre of Canada (NAC) is preparing to establish an Indigenous Theatre division to work independently from and alongside the French and English Theatre divisions. Fundamental to this has been an extensive process of dialogue, reflection, and at times difficult encounter with Indigenous theatre makers of all kinds that the NAC and partners called The Indigenous Cycle. It consisted of several parts over 2014–15. First The Summit gathered twelve Indigenous leaders and ten institutional listeners over three days at the Banff Centre for the Arts. Then, a year later, strongly informed by the experience of The Summit, theatre company Debajehmujig/Storytellers hosted Indigenous theatre makers and NAC administrators at their home space on Manitoulin Island over eleven days for The Study and finally The Repast.

Of the many takeaways from this series of immersions, deep listening sessions, and dialogues, a key one for the NAC has been to acknowledge the space that needs to be made within its own structure not just for Indigenous voices and faces but also for Indigenous leaders and creative and organizational forms. On a personal level, those involved were able to come to this teaching through experiential learning and at times difficult self-reflection.[20]

5. Value Interdisciplinary, Qualitative, and Research-Creation Work
I confess to having little specific to suggest here at this point, but I am making it a priority to learn more. I would like to learn much more with SSHRC and other funders (from NSERC to the Canada Council) how they approach truly or "radically" interdisciplinary research[21] and hear the experiences of other students and faculty members (not to mention university research officers and Indigenous and community organizations that collaborate on such proposals and projects). I believe that it needs to be mentioned here, even as a place holder, because full-spectrum reconciliation will require this sort of research.

There might also be productive conversations to be had on the theme of "research creation" at SSHRC, specifically on the connections among research, material practice, culture, aesthetics, and "radical" interdisciplinarity. How can Indigenous work make use of the research creation frame, and how can non-Indigenous research creation respectfully learn from Indigenous approaches? In which ways could we understand an energetic commitment to research creation as a way of Indigenizing the academy?

CONCLUSION

All people in Canada must be clear, loud and united in expressing their heartfelt belief that reconciliation must happen in order for it to be effective.

—Senator Murray Sinclair, 2015[22]

This is a daunting enough step, but with respect I offer that the impulse for clarity and unity cannot be the basis for SSHRC efforts to "advance understanding of reconciliation," the TRC's direct charge to SSHRC.

The greatest threat to this moment is not dissensus or conflict but that reconciliation becomes a filter through which business-as-usual practices and policies are passed largely unaltered and legitimated "on the other side." Avoiding this will require the will, honesty, and courage to allow the most catalytic aspects of reconciliation to penetrate and transform a decolonizing Canada for First Nations as well as settlers and newcomers. Decolonization is deliberate here.

From a research perspective, I have advocated that SSHRC work to empower and reconfigure its Indigenous advisory and review bodies (e.g., the regional centres) and make room for established and emergent Indigenous leadership in the social sciences and humanities. Bolstering capacity is as much a requirement for mainstream, agenda-shaping institutions themselves (i.e., self-inquiry at SSHRC) as it is for beleaguered Indigenous communities. To make an imperfect analogy between the social sciences and humanities and health and well-being, social sciences and humanities research to advance transformative reconciliation will need not only to attend to urgent needs (the emergency room) but also to spend the time and resources needed to foster nation-to-nation relations and diverse academic engagements from the perspective of Indigenous resurgence and decolonization (lifelong holistic care and ecological health). This requires committing resources to non-traditional research contributors and learners (e.g., funding these HQP outside university structures), strengthening existing commitments to interdisciplinary work and research creation, and acknowledging in practice that Indigenous knowledges are coming into being and that distinct autonomous spaces are required for that to happen.

I close with a degree of humility and perspective. Indigenous people will continue to live, organize, and realize themselves in spite of historical efforts to assimilate or annihilate them. What SSHRC does now is important, but as an AAC member pointed out in an email, "I'm inclined to think in terms of emerging issues in addition to gap issues. We know very little about the *emerging* nature of Aboriginal society and how to support it beyond an examination of the problems: our assumptions have been that Aboriginal society will look very much like modern Canadian society (and while that *may* be true, it hasn't been tested). Public policy options I think need to flow from this understanding as much as the gap analysis" (emphasis added). We must be open to making a future that develops quite differently from the proscriptive and punitive relationships that too often we have settled on to date.

NOTES

1   TRC, *Honouring the Truth*, 293. Call to Action 65.

2   The three tri-council funders plus the Canadian Foundation for Innovation.

3   In keeping with the clarity demanded by transformative and lasting reconciliation, I note that many federal policies sought to eradicate—through assimilation or death—Indigenous people and that they came dangerously close to *succeeding* rather than *failing*. My point is that we are in an extremely delicate time, and it would be disingenuous and dangerous to suppose that there is a line marking a 180-degree turn between what the state and society at large consider "success" and "failure."

4   For a discussion of the Eighth Fire concept in contemporary Anishnaabek thought, see, among other sources, Nolan, *Medicine Shows*, Chapter 11.

5   TRC, *Honouring the Truth*, 7.

6   TRC, *Honouring the Truth*, 7.

7   Tuck and Yang, "Decolonization Is Not a Metaphor," 3.

8   The dialogue led to a summary report to SSHRC in October 2003, *Opportunities in Aboriginal Research*, http://www.sshrc-crsh.gc.ca/funding-financement/apply-demande/background-renseignements/aboriginal_backgrounder_e.pdf.

9   The full SSHRC definition of Aboriginal research can be found at http://www.sshrc-crsh.gc.ca/funding-financement/programs-programmes/definitions-eng.aspx#a0. CIHR's definition of Indigenous health research is comparable to SSHRC's definition of Aboriginal research: http://www.cihr-irsc.gc.ca/e/50340.html. SSHRC's Guidelines for the Merit Review of Aboriginal Research are found at http://www.sshrc-crsh.gc.ca/funding-financement/merit_review-evaluation_du_merite/guidelines_research-lignes_directrices_recherche-eng.aspx.

10   TRC, *Honouring the Truth*, 8.

11   Quoted in Fedio, "Truth and Reconciliation Report Brings Calls for Action."

12   Interview, SSHRC Knowledge Synthesis Grants: Aboriginal Peoples video, https://www.youtube.com/watch?v=9nOwOQbdSls.

13   See Coombes, Johnson, and Howitt, "Indigenous Geographies III."

14   This comment was made by a member of the SSHRC AAC as part of a discussion on the consistent and often generalized assertion of community rights, perspectives, and needs in Indigenous research guidelines.

15   Brent, "The Desire for Community," 221.

16   Quoted in "Effects of Hydroelectric Land Disruption: Reflections on the OCN Territory," Hydro Research Alliance newsletter, spring 2016.

17   If justification from a Western/Euro-American perspective is required, then consider American pragmatist philosopher C.S. Peirce's category of abductive reasoning in addition to deduction and induction.

18   Coulthard, *Red Skin, White Masks*.

19   I am thinking of diverse Indigenous practices and positionalities that often get conflated into the term "Elder." For example, Mary Ann Spencer, a Mohawk-Dutch Elder in Residence at Four Directions Aboriginal Student Centre at Queen's University, considers herself a *pathfinder* in a Mohawk cultural and intellectual mode. See http://www.queensu.ca/gazette/stories/pathfinder-knowledge-carrier-and-guide-life.

20   For in-depth description of and reflection on this journey, I encourage readers to go to http://nac-cna.ca/en/stories/story/the-summit-the-study and download the documents.

21   It's entirely subjective, but by "radically" interdisciplinary I mean work that fully integrates, for example, an epidemiologist, a poet, and a botanist as opposed to an epidemiologist, an oncologist, and a toxicologist.

22   Spoken at the ceremony marking the release of the TRC report, 2 June 2015, http://
      www.cbc.ca/radio/asithappens/as-it-happens-tuesday-edition-1.3096950/
      reconciliation-is-not-an-aboriginal-problem-it-is-a-canadian-problem-it-involves-
      all-of-us-1.3097253.

REFERENCES

Blackstock, Cindy. Video interview. SSHRC Knowledge Synthesis Grants: Aboriginal Peoples, 2016. https://www.youtube.com/watch?v=9nOwOQbdSls.

Brent, Jeremy. "The Desire for Community: Illusion, Confusion, Paradox." *Community Development Journal* 39, no. 3 (2004): 213–23.

Coombes, B., J.T. Johnson, and R. Howitt. "Indigenous Geographies III: Methodological Innovation and the Unsettling of Participatory Research." *Progress in Human Geography* 38, no. 6 (2014): 845–54.

Coulthard, Glen. *Red Skin, White Masks: Rejecting the Colonial Politics of Recognition.* Minneapolis: University of Minnesota Press, 2014.

Fedio, Chloe. "Truth and Reconciliation Report Brings Calls for Action, not Words." CBC News, 2 June 2015. http://www.cbc.ca/news/politics/truth-and-reconciliation-report-brings-calls-for-action-not-words-1.3096863.

Nolan, Y. *Medicine Shows: Indigenous Performance Culture.* Toronto: Playwrights Canada Press, 2015.

Truth and Reconciliation Commission (TRC) of Canada. *Honouring the Truth, Reconciling for the Future: Summary of the Final Report of the Truth and Reconciliation Commission of Canada.* 23 July 2015. http://www.trc.ca/websites/trcinstitution/File/2015/Honouring_the_Truth_Reconciling_for_the_Future_July_23_2015.pdf.

Tuck, Eve, and K. Wayne Yang. "Decolonization Is Not a Metaphor." *Decolonization, Indigeneity, Education and Society* 1, no. 1 (2012): 1–40.

CHAPTER 20

CANADA'S ABORIGINAL POLICY AND THE POLITICS OF AMBIVALENCE: A POLICY TOOLS PERSPECTIVE

Daniel Salée and Carole Lévesque

It is customary for public policy specialists to ponder whether the policy outcomes that they analyze meet the original policy objectives and to consider whether the tools used for policy implementation were appropriate or adequate or whether a different approach would have been likely to yield more significant results. They are also often expected to look forward and reflect on the practices that should be discontinued or maintained and to think of ways that will lead to improved policy outcomes and enhance policy capacity. Although we initially planned to conform to this conventional line of analysis in examining Canada's Aboriginal policy since the report of the Royal Commission on Aboriginal Peoples (RCAP) was released in 1996, we realized that it might be rather disingenuous to do so, for at least three reasons.

First, this type of analytical concern implicitly infers that all of the actors involved in the policy field under scrutiny exercise more or less equivalent sway in the formulation and implementation of policy, that they all pull together toward the same goals, and that they have a shared sense of what is beneficial for those toward whom policy is targeted. That is not the case in the field of Aboriginal policy. Although Indigenous organizations and individuals have had noticeable success over the past few decades in making their voices heard and in getting governments to accept their particular visions on certain issues, the historical, unequal division of power and influence between settler state and society and Indigenous peoples still operates. The socio-political hierarchy separating settler Canadians and Indigenous peoples is undeniable and lends little credence to the image of a policy community of relatively equal actors.

Second, asking what needs to be done to improve Aboriginal policy and Indigenous-state relations in the future suggests that as a society we do not know—or that we are not too sure—which course of action ought to be pursued and that more thinking is needed. The truth is we do know. RCAP and subsequent reams of scholarly and specialized literature have shown clearly that the way to positive, socially transformative change designed to better the social and economic conditions of Indigenous peoples is through a much greater measure of self-government than what they have been allowed to enjoy, and direct, unimpeded, and unconditional participation in any decision likely to affect them. Governments have been reluctant to make significant steps in that direction despite varied and conclusive evidence of the amelioration that it brought about when attempted. Setting out to explore avenues for improvement within an institutional and politico-administrative framework that is known to be problematic, but that the state is nevertheless disinclined to modify, seems to be rather pointless. Instead of trying to tweak existing arrangements, analytical efforts might be better spent on determining the motives behind the state's resistance to real change and on working to neutralize the blockages that it creates.

Third, we believe that what is fundamentally at stake at this juncture is whether or not Canada is prepared as a settler society to commit genuinely to reconfiguring the nature and content of its relationship with Indigenous peoples by accepting unreservedly their conception of what is important to them and by building anew *with* them an institutional edifice suitable for an authentic democratic and mutually respectful interface. Trying to devise new tools purportedly designed to enhance policy capacity or steer policy makers on the right track is of little use if the appropriateness of the whole framework within which Aboriginal policy is currently made is not questioned first.

These reservations inform the analytical perspective that we adopt in this chapter. Minister of Indian Affairs and Northern Development Jane Stewart declared in her address at the January 1998 unveiling of *Gathering Strength: Canada's Aboriginal Action Plan* that "the time has come to state formally that the days of paternalism and disrespect are behind us and that we are committed to changing the nature of the relationship between Aboriginal and non-Aboriginal people in Canada."[1] To what extent did the Canadian state make good on that vision? That is the main question that we explore in this chapter. *Gathering Strength* laid out a comprehensive action plan that garnered the support of key Indigenous stakeholders. It insisted on the importance of re-establishing the relationship between Indigenous peoples and the Canadian state and society on new and fairer grounds, on a true commitment to equality and partnership-driven initiatives. Policy makers have thus had an acceptable policy blueprint and a clear sense of what needs to be done for the past two decades. Yet the government's current rehashing of the same vision and the same vocabulary used in *Gathering Strength,* as if the government was putting forward entirely new notions and innovative actions,[2] suggests embarrassingly that the state's declared intention of twenty-five years ago has not been acted on satisfactorily. Yet, as we will see, the state has deployed an important array of tools and actions ostensibly in line with its action plan. Why, then, are we seemingly back to square one, feeling compelled to repeat promises already made, vowing once more to commit to reconciliation and partnership? Were the appropriate means to enact the policy package contained in *Gathering Strength* not taken? Were the tools of policy implementation not used properly? Did they simply fail to meet the challenge of the kind of political and institutional transformation that is called for? Or is it the plan itself that is at fault? These are important and relevant questions that must not be skirted. Before we consider how the process of implementation can be mended and which new policy tools might be designed to that end, it might be more useful and more productive to look critically at the pattern of implementation of the action plan so as to understand the reasons that the policy agenda set more than two decades ago still seems to be unaccomplished. The more analytically suitable question is not so much "what is to be done?" but "why was it not done?"

In this chapter, we purposely adopt a policy tool perspective to analyze and take stock of the evolution of Canada's Aboriginal policy since RCAP. Focusing on policy tools helps us to get a clearer sense of what the state actually does to reach the policy goals that it sets for itself and to make things happen in accord with the vision that it claims to put forward. Examining the instruments chosen to act on a given policy vision can lead to a better, more informed, appreciation of the nature of public action in a given policy area. It can also allow one to evaluate the appropriateness of the state's choice of approach to implement its policy objectives and can thus provide telling insights into the genuineness of the state's commitment to its declared aims. Finally, through a policy tools analysis, we can discern which way of doing things is most effective and likely to remain so over time. We conceive this chapter ultimately as a contribution to a reflection on the policy framework and institutional arrangements that preside over the conduct of Aboriginal policy in Canada.

In what follows, we first review the key elements of *Gathering Strength*. We then move on to set out the analytical framework that informs our analysis. In the third section, we examine critically the governments' choices over time of the various policy tools at their disposal and assess their impacts. We conclude in the final section with a general reflection on the way in which the Canadian state has handled its Aboriginal policy in light of the initial intentions of *Gathering Strength*.

GATHERING STRENGTH: THE FOUR PILLARS
OF CANADA'S ABORIGINAL POLICY

Gathering Strength was published fourteen months after the RCAP report was released. The commission had recommended that the federal government call a First Ministers' Conference within six months of the release of its report to discuss it and engage in immediate action, but the government did not follow this recommendation. Instead, it issued a document entitled "Aboriginal Agenda: Three Years of Progress," which outlined government achievements since 1993. In April 1997, the Assembly of First Nations staged a national day of protest to denounce the refusal of the prime minister to meet with Indigenous leaders to discuss the RCAP report.[3] The tardiness of the government's response did not go unnoticed and was seen by many in Indigenous circles as a sign of ill will and bad faith in the government.

In the end, *Gathering Strength* stayed relatively close to the broad notions that informed the RCAP report. The action plan rested on a four-pronged conception of what the government understood needed to be done to improve the quality of life of Indigenous people and to reorient their relationship with the state. It called for a new partnership between Indigenous people and Canadians that would enable them to work in tandem toward common goals; it insisted on the importance of financially viable Indigenous governments able to generate their own revenues and operate with secure, predictable government transfers; it vowed to help Indigenous governments to be reflective of, and responsive to, their communities' needs and values; and it promised to arrange for Indigenous people to enjoy standards of living equivalent to those that non-Indigenous Canadians take for granted.

Building upon this initial vision, the government set out a policy framework composed of four key objectives:[4]

- *Renewing the Partnership*. This commitment included, as noted above, an initial statement of reconciliation acknowledging the historical prejudice toward Indigenous peoples. It also came with the establishment of a $350-million "healing fund" to address the legacy of abuse in the residential school system. Other government promises under this objective included the preservation and promotion of Aboriginal languages; a public education campaign to enhance non-Indigenous Canadians' understanding of Indigenous traditions and issues; the inclusion of Indigenous partners in program design, development, and delivery; the examination by the government of possible ways to improve existing systems; and a more coordinated and more effective approach to dealing with the specific issues faced by Indigenous people living in urban settings.
- *Strengthening Aboriginal Governance*. This objective requires that the government work with Indigenous peoples, the provinces and territories, as well as other partners to develop practical, sustainable governance arrangements for Indigenous peoples built upon legitimacy, authority, and accountability. Under this heading, the government pledged to put forward initiatives that would develop the capacity of Indigenous peoples to negotiate and implement self-government, establish additional treaty commissions,

as well as Indigenous governance centres, create an independent claims body in cooperation with First Nations, develop a Métis enumeration program, fund Indigenous women's organizations to enhance women's participation in self-government processes, and explore the possibility of developing an instrument of recognition of Indigenous governments.

- *Developing a New Fiscal Relationship.* The government's goals in this area included working toward greater stability, accountability, and self-reliance; developing new financial standards with public account and audit systems that conform to accepted accounting principles; assisting First Nations governments to achieve greater independence through the development of their own revenue sources, enhanced data collection, and information exchange.

- *Supporting Strong Communities, People, and Economics.* Under this objective, the government stated its commitment to improving health and public safety, investing in people, and strengthening the economic development of Indigenous communities. It claimed to be ready to make use of approaches to strengthen the capacity of Indigenous people and organizations to design and deliver programs and services to meet the needs of Indigenous individuals and communities. Such approaches entailed devoting resources to improving living standards in Aboriginal communities with respect to housing and water and sewer systems; welfare reform to reduce dependence and focus on job creation; a five-year Aboriginal Human Resources Development Strategy; expansion of the Aboriginal Head Start program; education reform; increased focus on health-related needs and programs; improved access to capital; and establishment of urban youth centres.

On the whole, *Gathering Strength* endorsed at least two key points made by the RCAP report: "It committed the government of Canada to working with Aboriginal nations to enhance the exercise of their inherent right to self-government and to improve the services and infrastructure of their communities."[5] The federal government's action plan was greeted with guarded approval as "a good first step" by the leadership of the Assembly of First Nations.[6] National Chief Phil Fontaine in fact announced with Minister Stewart a number of joint initiatives designed to strengthen the government-to-government relationship between

Ottawa and First Nations.[7] To many people in Indigenous activist circles and communities, however, *Gathering Strength* missed the mark.[8] In part, as Peter Russell has noted, "the government did not respond specifically to the hundreds of detailed recommendations in the RCAP report. Nor was it phrased in language consistent with central tenets of RCAP. Nowhere did the government response use the language of colonialism and postcolonialism."[9] Indigenous scholar Kiera Ladner has argued that the federal policy directive disappointed largely because it "completely fail[ed] to create a framework for a renewed relationship based upon the principles of respect, recognition, responsibility, and sharing. Instead, it impose[d] a vision of a renewed relationship between *unequal* partner[s] in Confederation that is based upon a federal commitment to negotiate the inferiority of Aboriginal nations, Aboriginal governments, and their inherent right to self-government.... *Gathering Strength* assume[d] that Aboriginal peoples are not true nations but bodies of people that can be reorganized as Aboriginal nations that exercise the delegated powers and responsibilities of inferior governments, regardless of what treaties say."[10]

That *Gathering Strength* did not meet the expectations of those who wished for a fuller measure of self-government for Indigenous peoples or for a greater governmental willingness to engage sincerely and honestly with Canada's colonial past is hardly surprising. Although the Canadian state was prepared to make amends for the historical wrongs done to Indigenous peoples, it certainly did not mean to relinquish—either then or now—its constitutionally entrenched powers and prerogatives. With *Gathering Strength*, the Canadian state went as far as it saw fit to go in accommodating Indigenous claims and aspirations. That might not be far enough for those who are primarily motivated by ideals of administrative autonomy or political sovereignty for Indigenous peoples, but chastising the state for failing to move in that direction does not help much in understanding why the state chooses a given course of action rather than another. In this chapter, we are concerned less with the political intentions of the state and of those who resist it than with the ways and means that the state uses to implement the policy vision that it put forward after RCAP. We believe that this choice of analytical focus allows for a more detached examination of the state's concrete actions and of the nature and depth of its commitment to its own policy vision.

POLICY TOOLS: WHAT'S IN A NAME?

Interest in policy tools has a long history. Distinguished Oxford professor and policy scholar Christopher Hood has noted that "debating alternative possible ways of keeping public order, enforcing laws, or collecting revenue is a classical concern of political thought."[11] From the Enlightenment era's search for proper surveillance devices and crime prevention methods, to Benthamite preoccupations with the executive implementation of penal or welfare policy, to twentieth-century explorations by Robert Dahl and Charles Lindblom of the politico-economic instruments used by modern states, thinking about, devising, or examining policy tools has been an integral part of policy studies.[12] The literature on policy tools has expanded considerably over the past few decades.[13] It is wide ranging but generally consists of the analysis of the techniques and toolkits by which governments carry out their public policy goals as the main gateway to policy analysis.

Authors who tend to favour a more pragmatic approach often limit their examinations of policy instruments to their function as problem-solving techniques. They might also gauge their effectiveness and relevance or search for alternatives to existing instruments. But, by and large, they see policy tools primarily through their materiality only, as things to be understood in and of themselves or as choices of technique made by those responsible for the execution of given policies. Such a perspective can easily be uncritical. It informs analyses that are essentially descriptive of the tools—with little or no concern for the reasons or the processes that led to the choice of tools—or analyses that are focused mainly on adjusting existing tools or developing new ones to achieve maximum efficiency with respect to desired outcomes. Such analyses offer little insight into the political or administrative dynamics that might have led to the selection of the tools.

The work of Pierre Lascoumes and Patrick Le Galès transcends these analytical limitations by bringing into play considerations of the political and social construction of chosen tools. These authors emphasize the importance of situating policy tools in the broader socio-political contexts in which they emerge and on which they necessarily depend. They argue, first, that policy tools "reveal a [fairly explicit] theorization of the relationship between the governing and the governed: every instrument constitutes a condensed form of knowledge about social control and ways of exercising it" and, second, "that instruments at work are not neutral devices: they produce special effects, independently of the objective pursued [i.e., the aims ascribed to them], which structure public policy according to their own logic."[14] Lascoumes and Le Galès rightly stress power relations and the role that they play in determining both the materiality of the tool and the socio-political outcomes that it is expected to produce. "A public policy instrument," they contend, "constitutes a device that is both technical and social, that organizes specific social relations between the state and those it is addressed to, according to the representations and meanings it carries. It is a particular type of institution, a technical device with the generic purpose of carrying a concrete concept of the politics/society relationship and sustained by a concept of regulation."[15] Policy tools, therefore, are "bearers of values, fueled by one interpretation of the social and by precise notions of the mode of regulation envisaged."[16]

What does a policy tool actually look like? The panoply of instruments from which a government can choose is varied, and different typologies have been suggested to differentiate between policy tools.[17] In this chapter, we adopt the distinction that some authors make between three types of public policy tools:[18]

- *Substantive policy instruments* "are intended to directly change behavior on the part of individuals, households, communities and corporations. They can include the use of law and regulation to prohibit or control certain activities; the application of taxes, charges and incentives to activities the government wishes to discourage or encourage; public education and information campaigns intended to motivate action; encouraging voluntary action by companies, communities and individuals."[19]

- *Institutional instruments* involve strategies that dwell on the creation or use of specific agencies inside or outside governments to act as focal points for policy development, implementation, and evaluation or to provide specific services, such as the regulation of activities that pose risks to public safety and the environment, or to manage natural resources.

- *Procedural instruments* are focused on modifying decision-making processes with respect to policies and projects that might affect a given policy area (e.g., environment, education, health, etc.). Procedural policy instruments are the tools of choice when governments are concerned (or forced) to restructure their relationships with stakeholders within or outside the state. They might include government reorganization, support for specific interest groups, or the creation of quasi-independent advisory committees or commissions of inquiry. They involve civil society stakeholders and non-governmental representatives of policy networks in the policy-making process and are meant to alleviate their frustration with or resistance to the government.[20]

The factors that lead a government to opt for one type of instrument rather than another depend on a mixture of variables. Christopher Hood explains that "the array of policy tools looks different if we are concerned only with information-gathering and behavior modification between citizens and government than if we are concerned with the orchestration of action among different levels of government and different institutional forms. It may also look different if we take a 'change-agent' perspective than if we take a 'system' perspective."[21] One might also well imagine, in keeping with the analytical perspective propounded by Lascoumes and Le Galès, that the type of instrument chosen hinges on the position of social actors involved, their respective abilities to affect the prevailing power dynamics, and the determination of the government to enact its vision. Canadian political scientist Michael Howlett and his colleague M. Ramesh probably summed it up best. Decisions about tool selection look like "muddling through in which the choice is shaped by the characteristics of the instruments, the nature of the problem at hand, past experiences of governments in dealing with the same or similar problems, the subjective preference of the decision-makers and the likely reaction to the choice by affected social groups."[22] In more detailed iterations of his views, Howlett, one of the most significant and prolific contributors to the study of policy tools, insists on the importance of government legitimacy in influencing the types of instruments chosen. A government that faces discontent or experiences declining legitimacy is more likely to resort to procedural tools.

By its tone and orientation, the literature on policy tools can easily leave one with the impression that the choice of instruments is generally dictated by considerations of effectiveness, efficiency, and the likelihood of achieving the best results—not unlike a carpenter who has to choose between a hand saw, a jig saw, and a circular saw depending on the nature of the task. Howlett's focus on legitimacy suggests that tool selection is not as neutral as it might seem—not as strictly pragmatic or task dependent—but in the end Howlett nonetheless infers that the changing nature of contemporary governance has led governments to "experiment" with stakeholder participation and various forms of collaborative government and that the emergence of procedural policy instruments is a more or less natural evolution away from the command-and-control spirit of substantive tools.

We see things differently. Whether a government chooses substantive, procedural, or institutional policy tools has to do ultimately with the amount of coercion that it believes is necessary to exercise over stakeholders active in a given policy area. Governments are usually more likely to favour initial instruments that will allow their views and objectives to prevail. Whenever a government chooses to use instruments that would allow non-governmental actors to weigh in on the policy process and potentially change the outcome that it initially planned, it is either because it deems it politically profitable to do so or because it does not have a strong preference for the outcome and is willing to wait and see how things will naturally play out. All policy instruments are not created equal, and in particular some substantive ones are clearly meant to deliver a more robust punch and keep the government in total control of the agenda.

Using the typology described above, in the next section we take stock of the various policy tools that have been deployed since *Gathering Strength*. By doing so, we hope to get a clear sense of the tools that the Canadian state has favoured over time, shed light on the rationale behind the tool selection, and assess the dynamics of power relations at play in the ways in which the tools are chosen and utilized.

IMPLEMENTING CANADA'S ABORIGINAL POLICY: WHAT POLICY TOOLS REVEAL

Here we consider the main policy tools used by the Canadian state to implement the policy vision elaborated in *Gathering Strength*. We do so according to tool type (substantive, institutional, and procedural) and the action plan's policy pillars (Renewing the Partnership, Strengthening Aboriginal Governance, Developing a New Fiscal Relationship, and Supporting Strong Communities, People, and Economics).

One cannot avoid noticing the fact that several policy goals have been left aside and that no particular tool has been utilized or devised to ensure their implementation. Until Prime Minister Trudeau's promise in December 2016 to propose an Indigenous Languages Act, for example, the commitment to preserve and promote Indigenous languages never materialized, though it is an important objective of Renewing the Partnership. Similarly, next to nothing has been undertaken to increase public understanding of Indigenous traditions, another pledge made under Renewing the Partnership. On the goal of Strengthening Aboriginal Governance, much was done but not necessarily in keeping with the demands and expectations of Indigenous stakeholders. The same can be said of Developing a New Fiscal Relationship. With respect to Supporting Strong Communities, People, and Economics, the objective of reforming education, important within the purview of this policy pillar, was addressed only toward the end of the time period considered and rather unsuccessfully.

On closer examination, one is struck by the significant emphasis that governments have accorded to the question of Aboriginal governance. The issue, of course, is chief among Indigenous stakeholders' concerns and claims and a major bone of contention with the Canadian state. It has shaped the nature and dynamics of interaction between Indigenous people and settler Canadians since the nineteenth century and brings into play debates about the extent to which the state should recognize and accommodate Indigenous self-determination and self-government. It is hardly surprising, then, that nearly three of four interventions (70 percent) carried out with substantive policy tools in the past twenty-five years and almost half (49 percent) of all interventions, inclusive of all three instrument types, have been focused on the area of Aboriginal governance. In contrast, the other three policy pillars have received considerably less attention: Renewing the Partnership gets 16 percent of state actions; Developing a New Fiscal Relationship 7 percent; and Supporting Strong Communities, People, and Economics 28 percent. Hardly surprising, perhaps, but *Gathering Strength* gave equal importance to its four policy pillars; the fact that Aboriginal governance was the object of much more policy activity in the ensuing decades is a strong indication that, where issues related to Indigenous people are concerned, this one matters the most in the eye of the Canadian state.

We note finally that governments made limited use of procedural policy tools. In fact, they largely ignored them whenever Aboriginal governance was concerned.[23] Given the rhetoric of partnership renewal and reconciliation, which has pervaded the state's discourse since *Gathering Strength*, one might have expected to see a greater reliance on procedural tools. In part, this is because, as scholars of policy tools are inclined to suggest, the recourse to such tools is a deepening trend in contemporary state practices. It is also because notions of partnership and reconciliation imply in principle a greater willingness by governments to include non-governmental stakeholders in the design and development of policy and in the delivery of resultant programs affecting the latter directly—exactly what procedural policy tools are for.

Evidence of this trend, though, has not been strong in the field of Aboriginal policy in Canada over the past two and a half decades. Instead, the multiplication of legislation and regulations and the creation of several institutional tools designed to undergird and enforce them indicate that the Canadian state has more often than not favoured a command-and-control approach and resorted to tools more likely to maintain and enforce the traditional dynamics of power and social hierarchies that historically have shaped interactions between Indigenous peoples and settler society. Since *Gathering Strength* was released, all governments have engaged in actions and applied policy tools designed to enforce policies and regulations that contradict and disregard the spirit and objectives of the action plan. As the following suggests, in every area of public action targeted by *Gathering Strength* examples abound that ultimately raise doubts about the state's commitment to make amends, to stimulate more equitable and harmonious relationships with Indigenous peoples, or to empower and work collaboratively with them as equal partners.

GOVERNANCE ISSUES

In 2002, the Liberal government of Jean Chrétien introduced in the House of Commons the First Nations Governance Act, which aimed

(a) to provide bands with more effective tools of governance on an interim basis pending the negotiation and implementation of the inherent right of self-government;

(b) to enable bands to respond more effectively to their particular needs and aspirations, including the ability to collaborate for certain purposes; and

(c) to enable bands to design and implement their own regimes in respect of leadership selection, administration of government and financial management and accountability, while providing rules for those bands that do not choose to do so.[24]

Despite the language of community empowerment and self-government in which the bill was couched, it rapidly became clear to a number of observers[25] that the government's intent had little to do with giving Indigenous communities more political and administrative autonomy. The process of consultation was not designed to reach a large number of people and did not seek to establish the kind of meaningful dialogue that RCAP called for and *Gathering Strength* promised. Far from enhancing the latitude of communities to work toward self-government, the proposed legislation invested new executive authority in the minister and cabinet by allowing them to impose governance regimes on communities that would not comply with the requirements of the act. In the end, the law would have consolidated the municipalization of Indigenous communities, something that they had always strongly resisted. Opposition to the First Nations Governance Act was widespread and vocal. The government (then under Paul Martin) eventually gave it up in early 2004. Still, it is remarkable that the first inclination of the government was to seek ways to restrict First Nations' leeway to determine their governance regimes on their own.

The First Nations Governance Act was part of a legislative suite presented as a way to strengthen Indigenous governance. Although the objective sounded honourable, it did have one implicit caveat: to be acceptable, Indigenous governance had to conform to values, standards, and methods in line with the Canadian state's understanding of good governance. The vocabulary of the 2002 Speech from the Throne is telling in this regard. To strengthen Indigenous governance, the government announced that it was prepared "to support democratic principles, transparency and public accountability, and to provide the tools to improve the quality of public administration in First Nations communities."[26] The intention was high-minded, but the inference was clear: governance in many Indigenous communities is slack, inadequate, ineffective, and fails to abide by the basic rules of accountability. The government is not to give Indigenous communities *carte blanche* for them to determine freely their codes of governance. It will dictate instead new guidelines—only with a view, purportedly, to ensure the better good of all concerned in mind—and force the leaders of Indigenous communities to "clean up their act."

The 2005 First Nations Fiscal Management Act that created seemingly supportive instruments such as the First Nations Tax Commission, the First Nations Financial Management Board, the First Nations Finance Authority, and the First Nations Statistical Institute reflected the same spirit. Established under the guise of initiating a new fiscal relationship with Indigenous peoples and facilitating their integration into the administrative mainstream of the Canadian state, they are run by notable Indigenous community leaders whose presence lends an aura of legitimacy and an appearance of consensus. In fact, they were put in place to ensure that Indigenous communities toe the line and carry out the rules and procedures of accountability dictated by the government.

In 2012, the Harper government consolidated this containment of Indigenous managerial capacity by enacting its First Nations Financial Transparency Act. This legislation stemmed from the widespread belief—encouraged in part by government officials—that Indigenous leaders were inherently corrupt and spendthrift managers of public funds. Presented as an initiative conceived to improve financial management and to rationalize delivery of services to band members by band councils—again allegedly with the better good of communities in mind—it was clearly intended to force Indigenous elected officials, under pain of sanctions, to abide by strict, government-imposed rules of accountability. It interfered with First Nations jurisdictions and contravened their right to be self-determining as protected by international conventions.[27]

The notion that problematic practices of governance in some communities might be attributable to the very system imposed in the first place by the Canadian state was not part of the government's thought process. Instead, the state posed itself as saviour, as exemplar of managerial rectitude, and as having solutions to problems that it had actually created. The conceit inherent in such a stance is minimized through the recourse to a generally upbeat language and vocabulary, which, despite stressing the government's resolve to empower Indigenous communities and encourage the development of genuinely Indigenous modes of governance, only serve to mask the state's paternalistic and autocratic mindset.

The 1999 First Nations Land Management Act, for instance, though ostensibly designed to increase First Nations' control and authority over land management on Indian reserves, does not quite bestow on First Nations communities that avail themselves of its provisions all the autonomy that they might seek. The freedom that proponents[28] suggest the law lends to a community in determining the content of its land management regime is rather partial. First, the general framework within which the act operates is largely defined by the Canadian state's adherence to common law norms and concepts of property, ownership, and contract; Indigenous notions hardly figure in the mix. Second, those who opt in have to seek government approval to do so and must conform to state-imposed obligations insofar as management practices are concerned.[29] Their independence is ultimately contained within and constrained by the value system of the Canadian state and by its frequently imperious ways.[30]

A similar pattern marked the First Nations Control of First Nations Education Act, which the Harper government proposed in 2014. As its title suggests, the new bill was promoted as reflecting the government's commitment to enhance First Nations' control over the education of First Nations children (at primary and secondary levels) and to improve the quality and reliability of existing educational infrastructure on reserves. The government was also quick to claim it as an example of collaborative government, for it was the result of prior negotiations and agreements with the leaders of the Assembly of First Nations. In reality, as several sections of the act clearly indicate, the government had little intention of relinquishing any form of substantial control over education to First Nations communities. Despite the stated wish of Indigenous leaders that First Nations communities obtain full control of education in accord with inherent and treaty rights, and that there be no unilateral federal oversight,[31] the act rested entirely on the notion that the state was to continue to provide the standards, reporting, and other oversight mechanisms to ensure that First Nations communities meet state-imposed norms.[32] The proposed legislation faced widespread and intense opposition and was eventually abandoned by the government.[33]

ECONOMIC EMPOWERMENT

One of the explicit objectives of *Gathering Strength* was to help Indigenous communities build economic capacity so as to reduce their dependence on government handouts and to take better control of their collective agenda. Instruments such as the aforementioned First Nations Tax Commission, First Nations Financial Management Board, First Nations Finance Authority, and First Nations Statistical Institute—notwithstanding the reservations that one might entertain in regard to the degree of autonomy that they allow First Nations to enjoy—were created precisely for the purposes of leveraging capital for local economic and business development, supporting Indigenous entrepreneurship, and assisting communities through the process of gaining added economic capacity. Yet, though the state seems to be ready to lend a helping hand, it has had few qualms about restricting access to critical resources and tools that Indigenous communities need to ensure their economic viability, particularly if it thinks that somehow its interests are at stake. The specific claims issue is a telling case in point.

Land by most standards is an important and essential lever of economic development. Without it, opportunities for economic success are severely limited. Having been dispossessed of their ancestral territories and confined through the reserve system to tiny parcels of land, many of Canada's Indigenous communities are painfully aware of that fact. Since 1973, when the Supreme Court of Canada recognized in the *Calder* case that the precontact occupation of the land by Indigenous peoples entitled them to legal rights to the land that survived European settlement, most have been battling hard and with little success to regain possession and have the Canadian state recognize their ownership of and control over traditional territories. The mechanisms and the rules that the state was compelled to put in place in the wake of the *Calder* decision to address Indigenous land claims regularly proved to be unsatisfactory and the source of ever-increasing tensions between many Indigenous communities and the state. They generally made for a slow and cumbersome process in which the government was both judge of and party to land claims. Furthermore, settlements favouring Indigenous communities were not binding on the state.[34]

In 2003, the government adopted the Specific Claims Resolution Act in an apparent effort to appease the discontent of First Nations stakeholders. The new law created a commission to facilitate claims negotiation and dispute resolution along with a tribunal authorized to make binding decisions on the validity of claims and compensation awards. However, it capped the awards at a prescribed maximum of $10 million per claim and maintained the government as the sole authority over the appointment of commissioners and judges. This, unsurprisingly, led the Assembly of First Nations to take exception to the act. The legislation received royal assent but was never proclaimed in force. The approach to the adjudication of specific claims then in use, so disappointing to Indigenous communities, continued for several more years.

In 2007, the Harper government pledged to initiate a reform that would create a fully independent land claims tribunal and released an action plan promising impartiality and fairness, greater transparency, faster processing of claims, and better access to mediation.[35] A year later an act of Parliament instituted the Specific Claims Tribunal, which has been in operation since 2009 as an independent adjudication tribunal with the authority to make binding decisions on the validity of specific claims and to award settlements (to a maximum of $150 million administered from a dedicated fund, capped at $250 million per year). This new instrument of land claims resolution comes closer than any of the previous ones to addressing and satisfying the concerns that Indigenous communities have expressed for decades in regard to the unfair way in which their claims have been handled. The tribunal's annual reports lead one to believe that the backlog of claims has been noticeably reduced, and a number of band chiefs have indicated their support for the new approach. However, problems persist. Bands uninterested in trading a cash settlement for the formal surrender of territorial lands "find their desire for land return eclipsed by a system geared exclusively towards monetary compensation."[36] This has apparently given rise to a context in which "the government's practice of making 'take it or leave it' settlement offers, cancelling meetings, and arbitrarily terminating negotiations have become commonplace."[37] Another, more troubling, problem that results from the new land claims resolution framework is the double standard that it creates by excluding from expropriation (and therefore restitution to Indigenous communities) all lands owned by private third parties, even when a specific claim has been verified. As observers have noted, "whereas Indigenous lands have been subject to expropriation through historical land theft and 'allowable' infringements to this day, the lands of private Canadian citizens are off the table for negotiations even where those lands were illegally surrendered."[38]

The state's conduct over the years with respect to specific land claims raises doubts about the genuineness of its professed resolve to help Indigenous communities along the path of economic independence as the state seems repeatedly to be intent on hampering their access to and control over the one resource that more than anything else is vital to economic empowerment. The fact is the state may be genuine in its desire to help, but its genuineness is framed within a particular understanding of economic development,[39] which does not include unsettling Canada's existing colonial property regimes. Opening the door indiscriminately to the general reclaiming and restitution of Indigenous land poses what the state sees as the real danger of hindering the investment opportunities and the various projects of resource extraction entertained by the private settler interests that it supports. Hence, from the state's perspective, relinquishing full control over decision-making authority and control over land to Indigenous communities that might have a different view of sustainable or beneficial economic development on their territories constitutes an untenable risk. In other words, the state is probably sincere when it claims to facilitate the development of Indigenous communities' economic capacities as long as those communities agree to play by its rules.

QUALITY-OF-LIFE ISSUES

Governments are duly aware of the gaps that separate Indigenous people from settler Canadians in terms of social conditions. This has been well known and extensively documented for years. Improvements have been noted over the past two or three decades, but large segments of Indigenous peoples in Canada are still far from experiencing the high standards of living normally enjoyed by most settler Canadians.[40] Governments vow regularly to address the situation and tackle the unfairness of it all. But then again they also often proceed with measures and policies that seem to be ill fitted to ameliorate the quality of life of Indigenous peoples.

A glaring example is the Harper government's 2012 Jobs and Growth Act, Bill C-45, an omnibus bill ostensibly designed to implement the government's budget but containing significant modifications to several existing laws. Among them was the Navigation Protection Act, which removed the obligation of proponents of power line and pipeline projects to prove that their projects do not constitute environmental threats to the navigable waterways that they will cross. The act dropped protected waterways from 2.8 million to fewer than 100, thus exposing almost all Indigenous communities in the country to potential, significant damage to their immediate environments. The C-45 package also included the Environmental Assessment Act, which loosens the environmental assessment process and eases existing constraints. The act weakens the obligation to consult with or take into consideration First Nations communities affected by a development project. It limits their ability to prevent environmental mishaps and further destruction of their ways of life. The insistent support of the Trudeau government for the Kinder Morgan

Trans Mountain Pipeline project and the Site C dam in British Columbia, in spite of the disapproval of several Indigenous communities and the misgivings of experts about the environmental propriety of these projects, falls directly in line with the spirit and intent of those laws.

The First Nations Property Ownership Act put forward in 2013 by the Harper government is another example of a legislative proposal likely to countermand efforts to improve the quality of life in First Nations communities. The rationale behind this proposal was that it would cancel the dispositions of the Indian Act that restrict the acquisition of private property for First Nations people living on reserves, open up more possibilities for business entrepreneurship, and generally improve the socio-economic conditions of First Nations peoples. Although prominent Indigenous leaders called for and supported the initiative whole-heartedly,[41] it is far from clear that it would yield such outcomes. Similar designs enacted in the United States in the late nineteenth century led to the privatization of Indigenous communal land and facilitated instead the settlement of non-Indigenous people and the destruction of whole Indigenous communities.[42] The Harper government did not manage to introduce the First Nations Property Ownership Act in Parliament before it was electorally defeated in 2015, but it certainly intended to do so had it been returned to power. It is probable that a similar legislative proposal will be brought back before long, for the notion that private property must be introduced in all First Nations communities is becoming well entrenched in the state's understanding of things.[43] Critics are concerned that the eventual implementation of measures or legislation patterned after the First Nations Property Ownership Act will only exacerbate the housing crisis in Indigenous communities. The Harper years saw drastic cuts to the funding of First Nations housing, creating severe shortages of adequate accommodations in many places. Opening reserve lands to private property and the concomitant marketization of it would inevitably lead to several negative consequences. They include the further appropriation of Indigenous land by corporations and wealthy Canadians, the ensuing loss of Indigenous control over the use of reserve lands, and exclusion from ownership by most Indigenous people whose income is often insufficient to afford private property—this at a time when Indigenous homelessness in major Canadian cities is already significant.[44] It is difficult in such a context to look on the state's commitment to improving the quality of life of Indigenous peoples in a positive light.

THE POLITICS OF AMBIVALENCE

One might be easily led to conclude on the basis of this overview and the Canadian state's apparent predilection for substantive policy tools in the field of Aboriginal policy that the state has totally and purposely resisted efforts to include Indigenous stakeholders meaningfully in the policy process. It might also seem that notions of partnership and reconciliation that so readily pervade its official discourse are but rhetorical smokescreens meant to mask its true intention of not changing the existing dynamics of socio-political power between settler Canadians and Indigenous peoples. Reality, though, is not as clear-cut.

In several cases in which the state has preferred a more coercive approach through the use of substantive policy tools such as legislation and regulation, room was usually made for the direct participation of Indigenous stakeholders in the process leading to a legislative or regulatory outcome. Most of the legislation concerning Aboriginal governance was the result of negotiations that necessarily involved the participation of Indigenous stakeholders and communities. That is true particularly where the devolution of power, the granting of self-government or increased administrative autonomy, and the settlement of comprehensive land claims were at stake. Governments have even withdrawn legislative proposals that they strongly defended following a negative response from Indigenous stakeholders; notably, as we saw, the First Nations Governance Act (2002) and the First Nations Control of First Nations Education Act (2014).

For all that the Harper government sought to lessen the obligation to consult with Indigenous communities before initiating environmentally sensitive development projects, governments have nevertheless been compelled for more than a decade to abide by landmark Supreme Court rulings confirming the state's duty to consult.[45] Embarking on development ventures on Indigenous lands without first seeking the consent of the communities that might be affected by them (or including them as partners) is now practically unthinkable. The creation of the Consultation and Accommodation Unit in the Department of Indigenous and Northern Affairs in 2007 bears witness to the state's willingness to accept the imperatives of the duty to consult. In 2016, the Trudeau government's declared intention to support the United Nations Declaration on the Rights of Indigenous Peoples (UNDRIP) is an additional indication that the

Canadian state takes Indigenous participation in policy and decision making seriously, for it is one of the UNDRIP's key principles. The notion of free prior and informed consent contained in the UNDRIP—whereby states must consult and cooperate in good faith with Indigenous peoples and seek their approval before giving the green light to development projects on their lands or adopting and implementing laws or measures concerning them—might not yet be understood the same way by all, but governments and corporations know that it cannot be dismissed and have to act accordingly.[46]

On a number of occasions, governments clearly activated tools meant to enable the state to follow suit on the vision contained in the 1998 action plan, notably with respect to the Renewing the Partnership pillar. The Truth and Reconciliation Commission (TRC) and the National Inquiry into Missing and Murdered Indigenous Women and Girls (MMIWG) are good examples of this. As typical procedural tools, they involve Indigenous stakeholders in determining future policy orientations. Seemingly determined to implement the TRC recommendations, the Trudeau government pledged to support financially the work of the National Centre for Truth and Reconciliation based at the University of Manitoba, create a National Council for Reconciliation, and institute permanent bilateral mechanisms with the principal Indigenous organizations.[47] One could add to that list a number of similar interventions driven by the same spirit of appeasement: the Aboriginal Healing Foundation; the Kelowna Accord under the Martin government; the 2005 Indian Residential Schools Settlement Agreement; the 1998 Urban Aboriginal Strategy; and several land claims settlement and self-government agreements that are telling and remarkable examples of the appreciable latitude that the Canadian state is sometimes prepared to grant some Indigenous nations.[48] Finally, as a recent comprehensive review of policies and practices related to educational attainment in Indigenous communities has shown, partnerships and collaborative initiatives between governments and Indigenous communities have been the dominant approach in the field of education.[49]

What are we to make of this state of affairs? The choice of policy tools deployed by the Canadian state to enact the vision of Aboriginal policy in *Gathering Strength* reveals in fact that it has been, and continues to be, extremely ambivalent, and less consistent than one might hope, in dealing with Indigenous peoples.

On the face of it, the state's commitment to "renew the partner-ship," "support Indigenous communities," and "strengthen Aboriginal governance" does look sincere and real. The fact is the state is making strategic choices.

On issues loaded with a heavy symbolic and socio-psychological charge, the state readily availed itself of procedural policy tools. The governments that established the TRC (Harper) and the MMIWG (Trudeau) ultimately understood that it would be politically unwise to do nothing on these issues and that acting unilaterally would be counterproductive since the result would garner little or no legitimacy. Not involving Indigenous stakeholders in a clear and prominent way, particularly after they had lobbied so persistently for these commissions, was not an option. One might surmise that selecting these instruments was probably unprob-lematic even if these choices afforded Indigenous people a greater possi-bility to influence and participate in policy making. Nobody is against virtue, and the physical and psychological harm inflicted on residential school children and Indigenous women and girls is an intolerable notion to contemporary liberal sensitivity. Something meaningful had to be done, both to answer to that sensitivity and to preserve the integrity of the moral high ground that settler Canadians like to occupy.

Another factor likely played out even more compellingly in the deci-sion to opt for a procedural policy tool to address these issues: the "cost" of bringing in Indigenous people to shape policy on an equal footing with the state is low in these cases, particularly when one considers the appre-ciable "return on the investment." The public and participatory nature of commissions of inquiry or consultations such as the TRC and the MMIWG provides wronged individuals and communities with not only a liber-ating opportunity to vent their resentment and frustration but also the consoling impression of being heard and included and mattering at last. It showcases the state in a better, more compassionate, light, making it look prepared to listen and make amends; as long as the government of the day appears to be appropriately contrite, it can defuse, at least for a time, the bitterness of the injured and the protest of the angry. Policy discussions can then be diverted without much difficulty to the sanguine terrain of noble sentiments, thus allowing state authorities to dodge the more challenging debates about systemic injustice and the unfairness of path-dependent policies. In the realm of policy goals that have been framed in malleable, indefinite, and ultimately less demanding terms (e.g., "reconciliation" and "renewing the partnership"), where intangible good intentions prevail over steadfast commitments to actual structural and political reconfiguration, procedural policy tools might seem to be just the ticket. They make the state appear to be welcoming change by opening up the policy process to civil society stakeholders, but in the end they spare it the obligation to unsettle existing structures and dynamics of power.

On policy issues in which the state believes that a greater degree of direct involvement in the policy process by non-governmental actors might jeopardize its interests and lead to institutional and systemic change that it is not prepared to accept, it is a different matter altogether. Goodwill and sincere repentance will simply not suffice. The state is likely to feel justified in seeking and imposing policy tools that will keep it in command and in control of the agenda. The twin issues of Indigenous self-determination and Indigenous self-government are a case in point. Although *Gathering Strength*'s objective of "strengthening Aboriginal governance" is couched in a language that seems to call for increased governance latitude and political autonomy for Indigenous communities, the tools deployed in the area of Aboriginal governance are not meant to facilitate such goals.

It may well be that contemporary governments tend to favour procedural policy tools, as specialists of the question have observed, but the trend does not hold much sway yet insofar as Aboriginal policy in Canada is concerned. Procedural policy instruments may readily include Indigenous people in the policy process, but their use does not necessarily guarantee that policy outcomes will meet their expectations, nor does it automatically translate into a reconfiguration of the relations of power and social hierarchy that define Indigenous peoples' interface with the Canadian state.

NOTES

1 Stewart, "Address," 7 January 1998.

2 "It is time for a renewed, nation-to-nation relationship with First Nations peoples," said newly elected Prime Minister Justin Trudeau at a gathering of First Nations leaders on 8 December 2015, "one that understands that the constitutionally guaranteed rights of First Nations in Canada are not an inconvenience but rather a sacred obligation." Quoted in Mas, "Trudeau Lays Plan."

3 Institute on Governance, "Revisiting RCAP: Towards Reconciliation," 19.

4 As per the summary by Hurley and Wherrett, *The Report of the Royal Commission on Aboriginal Peoples*, 3.

5 Russell, "The Royal Commission on Aboriginal Peoples," 167.

6   Barnsley,"Cree Chief Slams *Gathering Strength*."

7   Barnsley, "Mixed Reviews."

8   Barnsley, "*Gathering Strength* Not Strong Enough"; Barnsley,"Cree Chief Slams *Gathering Strength*."

9   Russell, "The Royal Commission on Aboriginal Peoples," 167.

10   Ladner, "Negotiated Inferiority," 261.

11   Hood, "Intellectual Obsolescence," 128.

12   Hood, "Intellectual Obsolescence," 128–29.

13   See the special issue of *Governance* 20, no. 1 (2007) on the topic. See also Howlett and Mukherjee, "Policy Design."

14   Lascoumes and Le Galès, "Understanding Public Policy," 3.

15   Lascoumes and Le Galès, "Understanding Public Policy," 4.

16   Lascoumes and Le Galès, "Understanding Public Policy," 4.

17   Other typologies have been proposed. Lascoumes and Le Galès, "Understanding Public Policy," 12–14, for example, distinguish between legislative and regulatory instruments, economic and fiscal instruments, information/communication-based instruments and best practices, each type corresponding to a type of political relations and a type of legitimacy. Howlett and Ramesh, *Studying Public Policy*, 148, identify three types of policy instruments based on state capacity or the level of state involvement and the constellation of social actors involved in policy making. They differentiate among voluntary instruments (which involve little role for the government beyond advocacy and persuasion), mixed instruments (which involve a greater role for the state and include information, exhortation, subsidies, taxes, and user charges), and compulsory instruments (regulation, public enterprises, and direct provision of services). Quite a few more typologies are available in the literature on policy tools. See Lascoumes and Simard, "L'action publique," 14–16.

18   We borrow directly from Winfield, "Implementing Environmental Policy." His typology suits us, for it more clearly suggests the dynamics of coercion and authority inevitably at work in making choices among policy tools.

19   Winfield, "Implementing Environmental Policy."

20   Howlett, "Managing the 'Hollow State.'"

21   Hood, "Intellectual Obsolescence," 141.

22   Howlett and Ramesh, "Patterns of Policy Instrument Choice," 13.

23   One notable exception was the creation in 2005 of the National Centre for First Nations Governance as an independent, not-for-profit organization, funded by the federal government. The centre commissioned academics and lawyers specialized in Aboriginal governance to put together a body of research and knowledge destined to support the governance work required by First Nations. The centre also delivered numerous workshops to citizens and leaders. Its government funding was cut in 2013. It was later reinstituted as a fully independent, self-financed organization under the name Centre for First Nations Governance. See http://www.fngovernance.org/about/where_we_have_been.

24   Quoted in Ladner and Orsini, "The Persistence of Paradigm Paralysis," 189.

25   See, in particular, Ladner and Orsini, "The Persistence of Paradigm Paralysis," 189, and Elias, "An Assessment of the First Nations Governance Consultation Process."

26   Quoted in Ladner and Orsini, "The Persistence of Paradigm Paralysis," 186.

27   Palmater, *Indigenous Nationhood*, 162–68.

28   Some analysts welcomed it as a significant step toward the empowerment of Indigenous communities. See Alcantara, "Reduce Transaction Costs?" and Boutilier, "An Unsung Success."

29   Lajoie et al., "La réforme de la gestion."

30   Which most likely explains why, eighteen years later, hardly more than 10 percent of Canada's First Nations communities bought in to the act (72 of 615, according to the

figures of the First Nations Land Management Resource Centre at https://labrc.com/framework-agreement. Palmater, "Opportunity or Temptation?," has suggested that those who did pursued specific local projects or goals; the act does not reflect the actual needs of First Nations communities in general. In a recent MA thesis, "An Economic Analysis of Factors," Chen shows that participation in the act did not lead to significant evidence of economic gain.

31 Atleo, *Open Letter to the Minister of Aboriginal Affairs.*

32 Palmater, "Chief Shawn Atleo Should Tear Up First Nations Education Act"; Palmater, *Indigenous Nationhood*, 169–71.

33 Since then, the Trudeau government has pledged to implement the UNDRIP, which, as far as education is concerned, states that "Indigenous peoples have the right to establish and control their educational systems and institutions providing education in their own languages in a manner appropriate to their cultural methods of teaching and learning" (Article 14). During the 2015 electoral campaign, Trudeau also promised $2.6 billion for First Nations education and nation-to-nation negotiation about education. This has yet to materialize.

34 In 1974, the federal government set up the Office of Native Claims (ONC) at Indian and Northern Affairs Canada. Eight years later, of the 250 claims that had been submitted, only 12 were settled. The fact that the government was both judge and party in the claims process was a major point of contention. After the Oka crisis, which dramatically underscored the extent of the divide between Indigenous peoples and settler society and state over land claims, the government replaced the ONC with an interim Indian Specific Land Claims Commission (ICC) with powers limited to reviewing claims and making recommendations. In its 2000–01 report, the ICC acknowledged that, after a decade of existence, the specific claims process remained "painfully slow" and "in gridlock." See Butt and Hurley, *Specific Claims in Canada.*

35 Quoted in Pasternak, Collis, and Dafnos, "Criminalization at Tyendinaga," 68–69.

36 Pasternak, Collis, and Dafnos, "Criminalization at Tyendinaga," 69.

37 Pasternak, Collis, and Dafnos, "Criminalization at Tyendinaga," 70.

38 Pasternak, Collis, and Dafnos, "Criminalization at Tyendinaga," 70.

39 See Gombay, "'Oubliez la faune et la flore et vivez par l'argent.'"

40 For a good overview and summary of the gaps in quality-of-life standards between Indigenous peoples and settler Canadians, see http://www.thecanadianencyclopedia.ca/en/article/native-people-social-conditions.

41 The most ardent Indigenous advocate of this legislation is Manny Jules, former chief of the Kamloops Indian Band and chief commissioner of the First Nations Tax Commission.

42 Palmater, *Indigenous Nationhood*, 193. For an in-depth and reasoned critical analysis of the act, see Fabris, "Beyond the New Dawes Act."

43 Fabris, "Beyond the New Dawes Act," 107.

44 Crompton, "Dispossession under the First Nations Property Ownership Act."

45 *Haida Nation v. British Columbia (Minister of Forests)* [2004]; *Taku River Tlingit First Nation v. British Columbia (Project Assessment Director)* [2005]; and *Tsilhqo'tin Nation v. British Columbia* [2014].

46 See Papillon and Rodon, "Indigenous Consent and Natural Resource Extraction."

47 "Statement by the Prime Minister."

48 The Nisga'a Agreement (2000) and the Cree Nation Governance Agreement (2017) are exemplary in this regard.

49 Lévesque and Polèse, *Une synthèse des connaissances.*

REFERENCES

Alcantara, Christopher. "Reduce Transaction Costs? Yes. Strengthen Property Rights? Maybe: The First Nations Land Management Act and Economic Development on Canadian Indian Reserves." *Public Choice* 132, nos. 3–4 (2007): 421–32.

Atleo, Shawn. *Open Letter to the Minister of Aboriginal Affairs and Northern Development Canada.* Office of the National Chief, Assembly of First Nations, 25 November 2013. http://www.afn.ca /uploads/files/13-11-25_open_letter_to_minister_valcourt_final.pdf.

Barnsley, Paul. "Cree Chief Slams *Gathering Strength.*" *Windspeaker* 17, no. 1 (1999). www.ammsa.com/publications/windspeaker/cree-chief-slams-gathering-strength-0.

——. "*Gathering Strength* Not Strong Enough." *Windspeaker* 2, no. 5 (1998a). www.ammsa.com/publications/saskatchewan-sage/gathering-strength-not-strong-enough.

——. "Mixed Reviews to Canada's RCAP Response." *Windspeaker* 2, no. 5 (1998b). www.ammsa.com/publications/saskatchewan-sage/mixed-reviews-rcap-response.

Boutilier, Sasha. "An Unsung Success: The First Nations Land Management Act." *Policy Options*, 18 August 2016. http://policyoptions.irpp.org/magazines/august-2016/an-unsung-success-the-first-nations-land-management-act.

Butt, Emma, and Mary C. Hurley. *Specific Claims in Canada.* Ottawa: Library of Parliament, 2006. https://lop.parl.ca/content/lop/researchpublications/prb0618-e.htm.

Chen, Ying. "An Economic Analysis of Factors Influencing the Adoption of the First Nations Land Management Act and the Consequences of Adoption." Guelph University, 2015. https://atrium.lib.uoguelph.ca/xmlui/bitstream/handle/10214/8825/Ying_Chen_201505_Msc.pdf?sequence=1&isAllowed=y.

Crompton, Nathan. "Dispossession under the First Nations Property Ownership Act." *Rabble.ca*, 31 January 2013. http://rabble.ca/blogs/bloggers/mainlander/2013/01/dispossession-under-first-nations-property-act.

Elias, Peter Douglas. "An Assessment of the First Nations Governance Consultation Process." Paper prepared for the Chiefs of Ontario. http://www.turtleisland.org/news/critiquel.pdf.

Fabris, Michael P.C. "Beyond the New Dawes Act: A Critique of the First Nations Property Ownership Act." MA thesis, University of British Columbia, 2016.

Gombay, Nicole. "'Oubliez la faune et la flore et vivez par l'argent': Le Plan Nord et le développement nordique." *Géographie, économie, société* 15 (2013–14): 327–44.

Hood, Christopher. "Intellectual Obsolescence and Intellectual Makeovers: Reflection on the Tools of Government after Two Decades." *Governance* 20, no. 1 (2007): 127–44.

Howlett, Michael. "Managing the 'Hollow State': Procedural Policy Instruments and Modern Governance." Canadian Public Administration 43, no. 4 (2000): 412–31.

Howlett, Michael, and Ishani Mukherjee. "Policy Design: From Tools to Patches." *Canadian Public Administration* 60, no. 1 (2017): 140–44.

Howlett, Michael, and M. Ramesh. "Patterns of Policy Instrument Choice: Policy Styles, Policy Learning and the Privatization Experience." *Policy Studies Review* 12, nos. 1–2 (1993): 3–24.

——. *Studying Public Policy: Policy Cycles and Policy Subsystems.* Toronto: Oxford University Press, 1995.

Hurley, Mary C., and Jill Wherrett. *The Report of the Royal Commission on Aboriginal Peoples.* PRB99-2E, Parliamentary Information and Research Service. Ottawa: Library of Parliament, 2000. https://lop.parl.ca/content/lop/researchpublications/prb9924-e.htm.

Institute on Governance. "Revisiting RCAP: Towards Reconciliation: The Future of Indigenous Governance." Symposium discussion paper, Institute on Governance, Ottawa, 2014.

Ladner, Kiera L. "Negotiated Inferiority: The Royal Commission on Aboriginal Peoples Vision of a Renewed Relationship." *American Review of Canadian Studies* 31, nos. 1–2 (2001): 241–64.

Ladner, Kiera, and Michael Orsini. "The Persistence of Paradigm Paralysis: The First Nations Governance Act as Continuation of Colonial Policy." In *Canada: The State of the Federation 2003: Reconfiguring Aboriginal-State Relations*, edited by Michael Murphy. Montreal and Kingston: McGill-Queen's University Press for the Institute of Intergovernmental Relations, Queen's University, 2005.

Lajoie, Andrée, Eric Gélineau, Stéphanie Lisa Roberts, and Alisa Kinkaid. "La réforme de la gestion des terres des Premières Nations: Pour qui?" *Politique et sociétés* 23, no. 1 (2004): 33–57.

Lascoumes, Pierre, and Patrick Le Galès. "Introduction: Understanding Public Policy through Its Instruments—From the Nature of Instruments to the Sociology of Public Policy Instrumentation." *Governance* 20, no. 1 (2007): 1–21.

Lascoumes, Pierre, and Louis Simard. "L'action publique au prisme de ses instruments." *Revue française de science politique* 61, no. 1 (2011): 14–16.

Lévesque, Carole, and Geneviève Polèse. *Une synthèse des connaissances sur la réussite et la persévérance scolaire des élèves autochtones au Québec et dans les autres provinces canadiennes*. Research report, Cahiers DIALOG no. 2015-01. Montreal: INRS and DIALOG, 2015.

Mas, Susana. "Trudeau Lays Plan for New Relationship with Indigenous People." CBC News, 8 December 2015. http://www.cbc.ca/news/politics/justin-trudeau-afn-indigenous-aboriginal-people-1.3354747.

Palmater, Pamela. "Chief Shawn Atleo Should Tear Up First Nations Education Act." *Rabble. ca*, 30 April 2014. http://rabble.ca/blogs/bloggers/pamela-palmater/2014/04/chief-shawn-atleo-should-tear-first-nations-education-act.

——. *Indigenous Nationhood: Empowering Grassroots Citizens*. Halifax: Fernwood, 2015.

——. "Opportunity or Temptation? Plans for Private Property on Reserves Could Cost First Nations Their Independence." *Literary Review of Canada*, April 2010. Reviewcanada. ca/magazine/2010/04/opportunity-or-temptation.

Papillon, Martin, and Thierry Rodon. "Indigenous Consent and Natural Resource Extraction: Foundations for a Made-in-Canada Approach." *IRPP Insight* 16 (2017).

Pasternak, Shiri, Sue Collis, and Tia Dafnos. "Criminalization at Tyendinaga: Securing Canada's Colonial Property Regime through Specific Land Claims." *Canadian Journal of Law and Society* 28, no. 1 (2013): 65–81.

Russell, Peter. "The Royal Commission on Aboriginal Peoples: An Exercise in Policy Education." In *Commissions of Inquiry and Policy Change: A Comparative Analysis*, edited by Gregory J. Inwood and Carolyn M. Johns, 154–71. Toronto: University of Toronto Press, 2014.

"Statement by the Prime Minister of Canada on Advancing Reconciliation with Indigenous Peoples." 15 December 2016. http://pm.gc.ca/eng/news/2016/12/15/statement-prime-minister-canada-advancing-reconciliation-indigenous-peoples.

Stewart, Jane. "Address by the Honourable Jane Stewart Minister of Indian Affairs and Northern Development on the Occasion of the Unveiling of *Gathering Strength: Canada's Aboriginal Action Plan*." 7 January 1998. https://www.rcaanc-cirnac.gc.ca/eng/11001 00015725/1571590271585.

Winfield, Mark. "Implementing Environmental Policy in Canada." In *Canadian Environmental Policy and Politics: The Challenges of Austerity and Ambivalence*, 4th ed., edited by Debora VanNijnatten. Toronto: Oxford University Press, 2015.

CHAPTER 21
EXECUTIVE SUMMARY:
CANADIAN PUBLIC OPINION
ON ABORIGINAL PEOPLES[1]

Michael Adams

The Environics Institute

What does mainstream society know and think about Aboriginal peoples today? In recent years, a handful of media-sponsored public opinion polls have purportedly shown that the Canadian public is "hardening" to Aboriginal aspirations. Such results are not consistent with other research conducted by the Environics Institute and others, which found clear evidence of a more understanding and supportive perspective. Needed today is a current, balanced, and thoughtful understanding of non-Aboriginal Canadian public opinion about Aboriginal peoples and their relationships with broader society and institutions in Canada. Such research provides essential empirical evidence to inform the media, decision makers, opinion leaders, and others in both Aboriginal and non-Aboriginal communities. Such information can help to avoid a misreading of public sentiment that can lead to growing divisiveness and conflict that could take years to repair.

To address this need, the Environics Institute for Survey Research conducted a national public opinion survey to take a proper reading of non-Aboriginal public knowledge about and attitudes toward Aboriginal peoples. The objective of this research is to understand non-Aboriginal Canadians better in terms of what they know and do not know about Aboriginal peoples and the challenges that they face:

- perceptions of and attitudes toward Aboriginal peoples generally and specific issues (e.g., residential schools, reconciliation, economic disparities);
- how opinions about Aboriginal peoples have changed (or not) over the past decade; and
- how perspectives vary across the population, based on region, demographics, and social values.

The research consisted of telephone interviews conducted between 15 January and 8 February 2016, with a representative sample of 2,001 individuals eighteen years and older across Canada who did not self-identify as Aboriginal (i.e., First Nations, Métis, or Inuit). The survey was conducted in English or French (as per the respondent's stated preference). Approximately 40 percent of the interviews were conducted via respondents' cellphones.

MAIN CONCLUSIONS

CURRENT IMPRESSIONS AND
UNDERSTANDINGS OF ABORIGINAL PEOPLES

Most non-Aboriginal Canadians have at least some level of awareness and appreciation of Aboriginal peoples, and many acknowledge this community as a part of what defines the country, though by no means the most important part (much greater emphasis is given to symbols such as the health-care system, multiculturalism, and geography). The level of knowledge and understanding of Aboriginal peoples varies considerably across the population, but non-Aboriginal Canadians are increasingly paying attention to news and stories, and most express an interest in learning more about Aboriginal cultures. Awareness of the Indian residential schools experience and its consequences has grown significantly over the past decade, and a majority of non-Aboriginal

Canadians report at least occasional direct contact with Aboriginal peoples, whether in public settings, at work, or in social situations. At the same time, non-Aboriginal awareness of the Truth and Reconciliation Commission (TRC) and its conclusions is surprisingly low, even among those who claim to be following the issues.

Some people have positive impressions of Aboriginal peoples in terms of their traditions and cultures and their legacy as the first inhabitants of these lands. For others, the overall impressions are coloured by the tragedies and challenges of colonization, forced assimilation, poor living conditions, and missing and murdered Aboriginal women and girls. The increased profile given to Aboriginal issues in recent years appears to have had a positive effect on the impressions of some Canadians. One-quarter say that their impressions are now more positive than before because of what they have learned, compared with one in ten whose impressions have gotten worse. This growing appreciation notwithstanding, the public remains divided on whether Aboriginal peoples have unique rights and status as first inhabitants or are just like other cultural or ethnic groups in Canadian society.

ABORIGINAL PEOPLES AND BROADER CANADIAN SOCIETY

A majority of non-Aboriginal Canadians recognize and understand at some level the challenges and disparities that Aboriginal peoples face, and such awareness seems to have grown over the past decade. Many now seem to know that Aboriginal peoples live with the stigma of being Aboriginal, that they experience ongoing discrimination (both interpersonal and institutional), and that there are significant social and economic inequalities between Aboriginal peoples and other Canadians. Most Canadians also believe that the challenges that Aboriginal peoples face are not of their own making, and increasingly they appreciate that the current challenges are tied to the legacy of abuse and discrimination from the Indian residential school experience.

This public recognition of the challenges facing Aboriginal peoples notwithstanding, it is also evident that many believe that their mistreatment is not necessarily any more significant than that experienced by other marginalized groups in Canadian society, such as blacks and South Asians and especially Muslims. As well, Canadians are less sure that Aboriginal peoples experience systemic institutional discrimination, though they are more apt to believe that it happens in the educational and criminal justice systems than in health care or the workplace. Moreover, there is also ambivalence in public attitudes about the significance of the current challenges facing Aboriginal peoples: a majority rejects the idea that mainstream society continues to benefit from such ongoing discrimination and expresses the view that Aboriginal peoples have a sense of entitlement about receiving special treatment from governments and taxpayers.

This pattern of views on how Aboriginal peoples are treated reveals crisscrossing sentiments that counterbalance recognition and understanding of existing challenges with underlying questions about how serious a barrier discrimination and inequality are to Aboriginal peoples' success in building their communities and well-being.

RECONCILIATION AND THE PATH FORWARD

Despite this ambivalence about the place of Aboriginal peoples in broader society, the general public's understanding of and feelings about mistreatment and current challenges underlie a widespread belief in the importance of moving forward to find meaningful solutions. Non-Aboriginal Canadians express strong support for reconciliation and for taking actions to improve relations between Aboriginal peoples and other Canadians.

Which actions are non-Aboriginal Canadians prepared to support to develop more positive relationships with Aboriginal peoples? First and foremost, such development starts with education; there is broad public consensus on the importance of learning about the historical abuse and discrimination that Aboriginal peoples faced in Canada. Solid majorities also give strong backing to education-related recommendations of the Truth and Reconciliation Commission to include a mandatory curriculum in all schools to teach about Aboriginal history and culture and to ensure that funding for Aboriginal schools matches funding for other schools in the same province or territory. There is also strong public support for actions to mitigate the loss of Aboriginal culture through funding to ensure the preservation of Aboriginal languages and to improve the living conditions on reserves. Smaller majorities endorse steps to cede full control of lands and resources to Aboriginal peoples and to settle outstanding land claims at whatever the cost.

Reconciliation also strikes a chord of cooperation, relationship building, and inclusion. To further this goal, non-Aboriginal Canadians see a place for a strong Aboriginal voice in federal institutions, including guaranteed Aboriginal representation at first ministers' meetings, in the federal cabinet, and in Parliament.

The public embraces these actions from institutional actors, but a majority also sees a strong role for individual Canadians such as themselves in helping to bring about improved relationships with Aboriginal peoples, and this sentiment has strengthened significantly over the past decade. At the same time—perhaps because of the scope of the challenges, past failures, and slow pace of real change—members of the public are only cautiously optimistic about the prospects for achieving meaningful reconciliation with Aboriginal peoples in their lifetimes.

HOW OPINIONS VARY ACROSS THE COUNTRY

Although the conclusions about public opinion described above hold true for the non-Aboriginal population as a whole, there are important differences in viewpoints across the country, by region, socio-demographic characteristics, and other dimensions. The key variations follow.

Region. There is a general east-west divide in the degree to which non-Aboriginal Canadians hold specific perspectives on Aboriginal peoples, tied in part to the presence and profile of Aboriginal populations with whom non-Aboriginal people have first-hand contact. The notable exception to this pattern is British Columbia.

Canadians living in Ontario, Quebec, Atlantic Canada, British Columbia, and the territories hold the most consistently positive views of Aboriginal peoples across the various topics covered in the survey. More than elsewhere in the country, they perceive Aboriginal peoples as having unique rights as first inhabitants, and they express a stronger interest in learning more about Aboriginal cultures. The sense of relations between Aboriginal peoples and other Canadians in these regions is distinctly more positive, with larger proportions exhibiting favourable attitudes toward Aboriginal peoples when it comes to opinions on, among other things, realizing the negative impacts of Indian residential schools, acknowledging prejudice, and rejecting the idea that Aboriginal peoples have an unhealthy sense of entitlement.

Moreover, residents in these provinces and territories display greater levels of support for action to achieve reconciliation, including the TRC calls for action, and to strengthen Aboriginal peoples' voice and representation in federal institutions. And they express a greater commitment to a strong role for individual Canadians to help bring about reconciliation.

In contrast, non-Aboriginal Canadians living in the prairie provinces hold more ambivalent perspectives on Aboriginal peoples and are less sympathetic overall than others to the challenges that they face. Although they acknowledge a large standard-of-living gap between Aboriginal peoples and other Canadians, they are more likely than others to see Aboriginal peoples themselves as the main obstacle to achieving social and economic equality with other Canadians, and they are more likely to think that Aboriginal peoples have a sense of entitlement when it comes to support from governments.

For residents in these provinces, higher levels of direct contact with Aboriginal peoples, and greater awareness of issues such as Indian residential schools and the TRC, have not resulted in a more positive appreciation of, and feelings for, Aboriginal peoples.

Gender. Gender appears to be a defining factor in a modest but consistent pattern, with women generally more likely than men to share positive perspectives on Aboriginal peoples. Women consider Aboriginal history and culture a major aspect of what defines Canada, more readily acknowledge that Aboriginal peoples have unique rights as the country's first inhabitants, and express higher levels of interest in learning more about Aboriginal cultures. They are also more convinced of ingrained anti-Aboriginal prejudices among Canadians, and they connect the dots between Indian residential schools and the current challenges that Aboriginal peoples face, in comparison with men. And women more consistently voice support for recommendations from the Truth and Reconciliation Commission as well as strengthening Aboriginal representation in federal institutions.

Age. With the benefit of life experience and knowledge, older non-Aboriginal Canadians (notably those sixty years and older) are more aware of, and pay attention to, Aboriginal news and stories. Perhaps as a result, they are also more ready to acknowledge the challenges that Aboriginal peoples face, including the substantial gap in living standards compared with other Canadians and the frequent discrimination that they face, both interpersonal and institutional. Older Canadians, however, also place greater onus on Aboriginal peoples themselves as a key obstacle to their achieving social and economic equality, and they are more likely than younger Canadians to believe that Aboriginal peoples have a sense of entitlement to government support.

Although less informed, non-Aboriginal Canadians eighteen to twenty-nine years of age are more apt to express support for different aspects of reconciliation, including the need to appreciate the history of treatment of Aboriginal peoples and to acknowledge the long-term impacts of Indian residential schools. The youngest generation is also much more optimistic about the prospects for meaningful reconciliation in their lifetime (not surprising given that youth are often the most optimistic of generations).

Country of birth. Canadians who have immigrated to Canada demonstrate a small but consistently more positive orientation toward Aboriginal peoples in comparison with those who are Canadian born. Immigrants are more likely to consider Aboriginal history and culture to comprise a major aspect of what defines Canada and to believe that Aboriginal peoples have unique rights as first inhabitants. They are also more likely than Canadian-born citizens to have an interest in learning more about Aboriginal cultures and to perceive relations between Aboriginal peoples and other Canadians as positive. Given this perspective, it is not surprising that they give greater support to initiatives that make the teaching of Aboriginal history and culture mandatory components in provincial and territorial curricula as well as to funding to preserve Aboriginal languages.

Distinct worldviews about Aboriginal peoples. When the different strands of regional and demographic variations are considered together, what emerges are five groups of non-Aboriginal Canadians, each of which has a distinct worldview of Aboriginal peoples with respect to the topics and issues covered on the survey. The groups differ primarily across two dimensions: a positive versus negative orientation toward Aboriginal peoples and their place in society and the level of knowledge about this population and the challenges that it faces.

Two of the groups (making up 41 percent of the population) have a distinctly positive orientation, one of which is well informed (connected advocates) and one notably less so (young idealists). Two other groups (35 percent) are much more negative in their perspective, one of them being generally knowledgeable about many of the issues (dismissive naysayers) and the other mostly uninformed and disengaged (disconnected skeptics). The fifth and final group (informed critics, 23 percent of the population) includes some of the most informed non-Aboriginal Canadians when it comes to Aboriginal peoples, while their orientation is a mix of positive and negative opinions. This typology sums up the spectrum of non-Aboriginal perspectives on Aboriginal peoples and provides a valuable foundation for future communications and education initiatives.

NOTES

1   The full report was publicly released by the Environics Institute in June 2016. It can be found at https://www.environicsinstitute.org/projects/project-details/public-opinion-about-aboriginal-issues-in-canada-2016.

CONCLUSION
WHAT'S THE WAY FORWARD?

Katherine A.H. Graham and David Newhouse

The time has come for tears of sorrow to be wiped away and our throats to be cleared of dust, and for us to speak in a frank and open way about our future in this land we share.

It is essential to recognize and respect the common humanity of all people—to recognize and respect Aboriginal people as people who do matter and whose history matters, not only to them but to all Canadians.

—Royal Commission on Aboriginal Peoples[1]

The Commission defines reconciliation as an ongoing process of establishing and maintaining respectful relationships. A crucial part of this process involves repairing damaged trust by making apologies, providing individual and collective reparations, and following through with concrete actions that demonstrate real social change.

—Truth and Reconciliation Commission of Canada[2]

We accept their findings, including that what happened amounts to genocide.

—Prime Minister Justin Trudeau, on the Report of the Inquiry into Missing and Murdered Indigenous Women and Girls, 2019[3]

And so, by way of conclusion, we must ask a number of questions. Within Canada, are we actively recognizing our true history of the relationships between First Nations, Métis, and Inuit peoples and those who came from away? Are we collectively pursuing goals and projects that reflect the process of reconciliation? Are we able to claim that we are living up to the Royal Commission on Aboriginal Peoples (RCAP) four principles of recognition, respect, sharing, and responsibility so that we can be guided to a better future? Are we fostering institutional change that will bring First Nations, Métis, and Inuit people into Canada? Are we sharing the resources and bounty of the land in accordance with the original treaties? Have we been able to clear our tears and use our voices to good effect?

These are big and important questions that require constant reflection. This conclusion will not provide definitive answers. It cannot and should not. Instead, our intention is more modest: to examine some of the key recent developments since the RCAP twentieth-anniversary national forum in order to propel readers to begin their own assessments. We explore these questions by looking at developments related to three themes: addressing the colonial legacy, continuing Confederation through institutional change, and recognizing Indigenous governance. The questions of clarity of perspective and robustness of voice are relevant to all three of these themes. They also relate to the power of Indigenous cultures and creativity in helping everyone to move forward.

ADDRESSING THE COLONIAL LEGACY

The colonial foundation of the relationship between the Crown and Indigenous peoples within Canada is non-controversial. The relationship between Europeans and Indigenous peoples in the land rests on the *Sublimius Deus* of 1493, which came to be known as the doctrine of discovery. It set out a relationship of inferiority that required Indigenous peoples to be subsumed within the sovereignties of European powers: Spain, France, and England. The doctrine of discovery still reverberates through Canadian law and political institutions. One only needs to look at the Royal Proclamation of 1763, the intention and tyranny of the Indian Act, the historical treatment of the Métis in Rupert's Land, and the "opening" of the Arctic through forced relocation of Inuit for a basic map of this history. A cornerstone of the RCAP report was the recommendation that there be a new Royal Proclamation stating Canada's commitment to a new relationship. It would be accompanied by legislation setting out a new treaty process and recognizing Indigenous nations and governments, putting the doctrine of discovery aside for the first time in more than half a millennium.

There has been no such Royal Proclamation. The generally critical reaction of Indigenous political leaders to the Trudeau government's 2017 promulgation of ten principles respecting the government of Canada's relationship with Indigenous peoples is discussed in the introduction to this volume. In essence, the government of Canada was thought to have violated the RCAP principle of respect by unilaterally developing and announcing these principles. It is proving to be difficult to move away from the principle of unilateralism embodied in more than half a millennium of practice.

There is some evidence, however, that the government of Canada is intent on building new relationships. In his remarks to the RCAP forum, Clement Chartier, president of the Métis National Council, spoke of the aspiration for a framework for reconciliation of Métis Section 35 rights. In April 2017, the prime minister and the president of the Métis National Council signed a Canada–Métis Nation Accord, committing both parties to collaborative work to realize Métis self-government and self-determination. The 2017 federal budget allocated $84.9 million over the next five years and $28.3 million per year subsequently to support building governance capacity of the Métis National Council and collaborative work on Métis self-government and self-determination.[4]

The Inuit Nunangat Declaration on Inuit-Crown Partnership was signed in Iqaluit the same month. Signatories were the Inuit Tapririit Kanatami, Inuvialuit Regional Corporation, Makavik Corporation, Nunatsiavut government, Nunavut Tunngavik Incorporated, and government of Canada. It created an Inuit-Crown Partnership Committee "to collaboratively identify and take action on shared priorities and monitor progress going forward."[5]

Later the same year, the prime minister and the grand chief of the Assembly of First Nations signed a memorandum of understanding agreeing to a formal process of meeting three times a year, beginning in 2017, to co-develop policy and to discuss progress on agreed-upon priorities.

Between January 2017 and September 2018, the government of Canada signed a total of thirty-nine agreements with individual First Nations and other governments/organizations representing Indigenous peoples in Canada setting out new relationships and affirming the goal of reconciliation.[6] The actual level of functionality of these agreements, including the three with the national political organizations, undoubtedly varies. But the fact remains that they exist and form points of accountability for both parties in each case but, most particularly, for the federal government. This principle of mutual accountability is not dissimilar to the approach taken in the development of the 2005 Kelowna Accord. Although it was abandoned by the Harper government, the process of engagement and specific initiatives identified in that accord remain tantalizing. This was evident from some of the commentary at the RCAP national forum. The challenge remains regarding how to ensure that agreements for engagement continue past changes of government. The transformation of existing federal-provincial-territorial institutions and the creation of new ones, appropriate to fostering a long-term relationship of mutual engagement, accountability, and respect, is an important priority.

Furthermore, we have seen significant levels of federal spending on Indigenous needs. Successive federal budgets from 2016 ($8.4 billion) to 2019 ($4.5 billion) have totalled $21 billion in federal funding for "reconciliation." Much of this money has been allocated to "bridging the gap," the colonial legacy of underdevelopment, related to historical infrastructure needs on reserves. Some has also been allocated to child and family services. In addition, there have been funds devoted to governance capacity building and continuing education and dialogue on reconciliation. In this last instance, the National Centre for Truth and Reconciliation received long-term funding in Budget 2019.

There have been significant and positive initiatives by other public institutions in response to the TRC Calls to Action. Canada's national granting councils are collaborating with each other and with groups such as the Social Sciences and Humanities Research Council's Indigenous Advisory Circle to change their granting processes in ways that respond to the need for Indigenous peoples and communities to be full partners in research. The Councils have added new programs for Indigenous research and are exploring ways of encouraging new Indigenous scholars and researchers. Under the auspices of provincial governments, there has been significant progress in developing K–12 school curricula that promote understanding of Indigenous cultures and a more accurate history of Indigenous peoples in the evolution of Canada. Universities and colleges have also worked actively to serve Indigenous students better, to undertake curricular innovation to educate the broad student body on Indigenous cultures and histories, and to reflect historical and contemporary connections with the Indigenous peoples whose territories they now share.

Some terrible examples of the enduring legacy of colonialism remain. The 2019 report of the National Inquiry into Missing and Murdered Indigenous Women and Girls provided shocking findings about the continuing systemic oppression of Indigenous women, girls, and 2SLGBTQQIA (Two-Spirit, lesbian, gay, bisexual, transgender, queer, questioning, intersex, and asexual) people. Its 231 calls for justice reflect the breadth and depth of systemic change required to stem this horror. Also in 2019, the Canadian Human Rights Tribunal ordered reparations for every on-reserve First Nations child removed from their family. This follows and supports its 2016 finding of systemic and willful underfunding of child and family services discussed by Cindy Blackstock in this volume.

Looking beyond the public sphere, one can also see changes in the nature and level of engagement by Indigenous peoples and their representative organizations and governments in Canadian economic space. The first manifestations of this predate the Royal Commission and are represented by the development corporations established in the 1970s as a result of the first modern treaties with the Inuvialuit in the western Arctic and the Cree and Inuit of James Bay. Increasingly, Indigenous peoples and governments are players in the economy. They own enterprises, including but not limited to resource extraction and harvesting, airlines, casinos, hotels, traditional foods, wineries, and cannabis cultivation. They develop properties, especially in locations adjacent to growing cities. Some First Nations have established urban reserves as spaces for economic development. In addition, beyond the capital that some derive from modern treaty settlements, Indigenous individuals and businesses have access to banking services through the First Nations Bank of Canada, founded the year after the RCAP report, and through other chartered banks that have come to recognize the importance of Indigenous entrepreneurship and commerce.

The development of an Indigenous economy in today's world is sometimes accompanied by controversy. This is perhaps most acute in relation to proposed property development and participation in the resource economy. Recent disputes over Indigenous participation in pipeline development are an obvious case in point. There are differences of opinion about the processes of consultation used by resource companies (as well as governments) and about the benefits and negative implications of participating in proposed developments. These differences require attention and resolution through negotiations among First Nations, Inuit, and Métis representatives, corporations, and governments.

The character of Indigenous peoples' current participation in Canadian economic space is uneven. Indigenous governments and development corporations operate in the Canadian economy in different ways and in vastly different scales. Indigenous people living in urban areas often participate in the Canadian economy as individual employers or employees. For some, especially those embroiled in conflicts over resource development, this economic picture represents an extension of the colonial legacy. Over the past twenty-five years, Indigenous participation in Canadian economic space has broadened and exerted more of an impact since the RCAP report.

CONTINUING CONFEDERATION

The Royal Commission on Aboriginal Peoples recommended a new Royal Proclamation to acknowledge the mistakes of the past and to elaborate the Royal Proclamation of 1763. It was intended to put the doctrine of discovery in the past. In addition, it would recommend that a third order of Aboriginal government be added to the federal and provincial orders. Like the federal and provincial orders, this third order would be subject to the Charter of Rights and Freedoms. It would have authority over matters related to the good government and welfare of Indigenous peoples and their territories. The commission also recommended the creation of a third house of Parliament to reflect the existence of this third order (acknowledging that the Senate was originally intended to reflect the interests of the provinces and regions). The commission acknowledged that these changes to Confederation would ultimately require a constitutional amendment. However, it expressed the view that "the government of Canada can act now, in terms of public policy and legislation, by enacting an Aboriginal Parliament Act."[7] The commission further recommended that the provinces mirror the approach at the federal level.

To date, there has been no new Royal Proclamation, though there were some musings that it might occur during the 2015–19 Trudeau government. Furthermore, Canadian politicians have shown no appetite for constitutional change since the failure of the Charlottetown Accord in 1992, four years prior to the RCAP recommendations. At the time of writing, there appears to be no constitutional path for changing Confederation.

There has been one change, however, to federal government institutional arrangements that is significant. That is the 2017 split of the former Ministry of Indian and Northern Affairs into the Ministry of Crown-Indigenous and Northern Relations and the Ministry of Indigenous Services. After more than twenty years, it appeared that the government had adopted one of the Royal Commission's recommendations. The truth is that the government had gone partway only. The full RCAP recommendation[8] proposed a particularly strong role for the minister of Crown-Indigenous relations. The minister would chair a Cabinet Committee on Aboriginal Relations and have significant control over the entire fiscal envelope for federal funding related to Indigenous peoples and governments. The government was silent on these ideas in 2017.

Announcement of the split received a mixed reaction. Some wondered why it had taken over twenty years for the government to enact the original RCAP recommendation. Others were skeptical that the split was a mere chimera or would result in another layer of bureaucracy increasing the challenges for Indigenous governments and organizations seeking to have their voices heard.[9] One notable aspect of the new arrangement is that the First Nations and Inuit Health Branch was moved from Health Canada to Indigenous Services Canada, thus adding a significant component of Indigenous services in terms of federal personnel and finances to this new ministry. By 2019, at least one prominent commentator argued that the split, especially the creation of Indigenous Services Canada, actually provides an advantage to Indigenous peoples and their governments by placing explicit limits that did not previously exist on the scope of unilateral federal action.[10]

An essential part of reconciliation and continuing Confederation relates to treaties and treaty making. This is unfinished business. The interpretation of historical treaties remains contentious. The interpretation is now based on historical scholarship that foregrounds Indigenous understandings of them as well as Supreme Court decisions. It is becoming increasingly clear that the original agreement to share the land and its resources is gaining strong adherents. Resolution of specific claims related to individual First Nations territories is a work in progress. The question of a land base for Métis remains an open one. Canada is a signatory to twenty-six "modern treaties," beginning with the 1975 James Bay and Northern Quebec Agreement with the Cree and Inuit of northern Quebec. These treaties represent an important step forward in acknowledging the unceded rights to lands, resources, and self-government of each First Nation and Inuit co-signatory. Among other things, they are playing an important role in changing the political map of Canada. For example, we are seeing new governing relationships in the northern territories as the governments of the Yukon, Northwest Territories, and Nunavut evolve in their relationships with First Nations governments resulting from modern treaties and, in the case of Nunavut, the government of Nunavut.[11]

Implementation of the terms of modern treaties is also, however, stubbornly problematic. One result is that a number of Indigenous signatories to these agreements came together in 2003 to form the Land Claims Agreements Coalition. At the time of writing, there are twelve members collectively working to ensure that the nature and terms of modern treaties are understood by all Canadians and that the Crown lives up to its commitments under these treaties. This is serious work, and in 2016 the coalition was successful in receiving a large grant from the Social Sciences and Humanities Research Council of Canada to support its research. Managing the treaty relationship as part of continuing Confederation is an important part of the role of the minister of Crown-Indigenous relations and northern affairs.

Crown-Indigenous relations in British Columbia have taken a unique path. The entire territory of the province was historically unceded. In 1993, as RCAP was under way, the British Columbia Treaty Commission was established in an attempt to move treaty negotiations among Canada, British Columbia, and First Nations along. This did not result in significant progress, yielding only two treaties. In September 2019, Canada, British Columbia, and the BC First Nations Summit jointly announced a new policy to support treaty negotiations in the province. It bases treaty negotiations "on the recognition and continuation of rights without those rights being modified, surrendered or extinguished when a treaty is signed."[12] We have yet to see the results of this policy shift on the rights basis of negotiation, but it can be seen as a positive sign of real progress on treaty making in British Columbia and on implementation of UNDRIP principles within Canada.

What is the picture that emerges from these recent developments? In sum, they represent important steps in continuing the evolution of the Canadian Confederation. The actual outcomes and impacts of

institutional reform within the federal government, providing the Indigenous co-signatories to modern treaties with resources to press their
cases for fully implementating and restarting the BC treaty process with
a new and explicit statement of its rights base, have yet to be seen. But all
of these initiatives hold promise for a better relationship that serves all
people living in the Canadian Confederation well. The Royal Commission's recommendations for a new Royal Proclamation and constitutional
amendment, however, remain calls in the wind.

RECOGNIZING INDIGENOUS GOVERNANCE

Recognition is one of the four RCAP principles: "It requires both sides to
acknowledge and relate to one another as partners, respecting each other's
laws and institutions and co-operating for mutual benefit."[13]

Canada adopted the 2007 UNDRIP in 2016, promising to adopt and
implement the declaration in Canada in accordance with the Canadian
Constitution. The adoption of the declaration, according to the minister of Crown-Indigenous relations, "breathed life into Section 35 of the
Canadian Constitution and a full box of rights for Indigenous peoples in
Canada."[14] Implementing the declaration in Canadian law has proven to
be challenging. Despite the challenges, the declaration provides a strongly
held and believed-in blueprint for change. With strong support from
Indigenous leaders, desire for implementation of the UNDRIP is unlikely
to dissipate and will continue to shape their desire for political recognition and power to shape Indigenous peoples' futures.

Where do we stand? The modern treaties, as previously discussed, have
resulted in the establishment (or in some cases re-establishment) of Indigenous governments with mandates that co-exist with or, in some cases,
replace the statutory powers of other governments in Canada. This is most
commonly the case in terms of powers over lands and the management of
resources. These governments also have independent election systems.

In the case of First Nations, the Indian Act remains dominant, with
all of its prescriptions and restrictions on the authority of First Nations
governments. To be sure, there are some avenues for First Nations to opt
out of some key elements of the act. The government of Canada enacted the
First Nations Land Management Act in 1999. It enables First Nations that
sign on to make laws regarding reserve lands. Since 2014, First Nations
have been able to establish their own electoral systems under the First

Nations Elections Act. In 2013, the Harper government passed the First Nations Financial Transparency Act, requiring First Nations governments to provide annual public reports of their financial statements and promising to withhold funds from those that do not. This legislation was controversial, and the withdrawal of funds from non-compliant governments was ended by the Trudeau government soon after coming to office. In 2018, that government announced that it would move to a new funding regime for First Nations governments, extending the time limit for the contributions agreements that fund many activities in First Nations to ten years. Each of these initiatives provides some additional autonomy to First Nations governments. They do not, however, signify a fundamental new relationship since they essentially delegate powers from the federal level or, in the case of the financial transparency legislation, require adherence to federally imposed requirements.

At present, is there a path out from under the Indian Act? There is an important First Nations–led initiative in this regard. A number of First Nations from across Canada are working with the Centre for First Nations Governance, a non-profit organization that focuses on First Nations governance, to build their own governance systems. Their work is based on five pillars: the people, the land, laws and jurisdictions, institutions, and resources.[15] Participating First Nations are working independently based on their own traditions and priorities. At the same time, they are strongly networked through the centre and its allied researchers. This Transformational Governance Project is already yielding positive results and holds the potential for new forms of recognition of First Nations governments that have chosen their own paths forward, more than availing themselves of opportunities for discretion made possible by federal legislation.

"Indian control over Indian education" has been a mantra for First Nations for decades. Almost fifty years ago, the National Indian Brotherhood (now the Assembly of First Nations) published a report using that phrase as its title. That report spoke of the need to end the assimilationist intention and reality of education: "Integration viewed as Aboriginal one-way process is not integration and will fail. In the past, it has been the Indian student who was asked to integrate: to give up his identity, to adopt new values and a new way of life. This restricted integration of education must be radically altered if future education programs are to benefit Indian children."[16]

First Nations children living off reserve, as well as Métis and Inuit children, receive education through provincial and territorial systems. Indian control of Indian education for the majority of Indigenous people who receive their primary and secondary education through provincial systems remains elusive. On reserve, realizing the goal of appropriate curriculum and self-governance of education has been a struggle. One exacerbating factor has been the growing gap between funding for First Nations education on reserve and public systems resulting from the 2 percent cap on federal funding increases imposed in the 1990s.

There have been some recent positive developments. First, the 2 percent cap on First Nations program funding was lifted by the federal government in 2016. Second, and more important, the federal government has begun to engage with First Nations to formally devolve jurisdiction over education. In 1997, the governments of Canada and Nova Scotia signed the Mi'kmaq Education Agreement providing thirteen Mi'kmaq First Nations in that province with jurisdiction over education K–12 on reserve and with management responsibilities for postsecondary education. Funding to support this agreement was provided in five-year increments. The record speaks for itself. High school graduation rates have gone from 30 to 90 percent in the intervening period. In 2019, the federal government recognized the success of this agreement by extending it for a ten-year period, twice the length of the previous five-year agreements.[17] In 2018, Canada and the Nishnawbe Aski Nation (NAN) concluded an Agreement-in-Principle on Education that would provide similar jurisdiction to NAN on behalf of its forty-nine First Nations communities in northern Ontario. Work continues on the specifics of a final agreement. Arising from the death of Jordan River Anderson, a severely disabled First Nations child from Manitoba who died amid a jurisdictional stand-off between the Canadian government and the Manitoba government over who would pay for his care, Jordan's Principle was promulgated as the result of a 2016 Canadian Human Rights Tribunal finding that the government of Canada had behaved in a discriminatory way in Jordan's case. Since that time, the government of Canada has provided almost $700 million to help with the health, social services, and educational needs of First Nations children. The emphasis has been on quick response and flexibility. For example, in northwestern Ontario, responsibility for the Choose Life Program was vested in NAN, which then engaged with individual First Nations that identified their particular needs for support.

These examples suggest that the federal government can depart from past tendencies to micromanage First Nations programs and recognize the value of Indigenous governance. In the case of the Mi'kmaq Education Agreements, the positive outcomes show the potential of this approach.

Recognition of Indigenous governance has extended to the international domain as well. The International Joint Commission, which manages waterways that flow between Canada and the United States, has engaged First Nations, Métis, and American tribes who have cultural connections with and use watersheds where the commission works. These watersheds, such as the Great Lakes Basin and the Lake of the Woods–Rainy River Watershed, have had Indigenous members on their respective management boards. But in 2019 the commission began an engagement process to determine how it could further improve its relationships with Indigenous governments, considering active collaboration on watershed management.[18]

Since the RCAP report and particularly since the TRC report, there has been a significant rise in awareness of the importance of Indigenous peoples to the true history of urban Canada. We have seen the adoption of territorial acknowledgements by municipal governments and efforts to commemorate Indigenous peoples and cultures in public places. One domain in which there has been little activity is in developing or recognizing Indigenous governance in urban areas. The Royal Commission devoted a chapter in its final report to urban issues. It explored a number of potential models of urban governance whose applicability and practicality would vary depending on the characteristics of the Indigenous population in any particular city. Since the RCAP report, there has been additional research on the urban context and governance.[19] However, the essence of organizing urban Indigenous life remains with Indigenous service organizations. They are often vital and provide crucial services to First Nations, Métis, and Inuit people living in cities. However, their dependence on relatively short-term, project-related funding from federal and sometimes provincial/territorial sources remains high. This renders their longer-term viability tenuous. Urban Indigenous governance, therefore, is an unopened path of change.

KEEPING UP THE MOMENTUM: THE POWER OF INDIGENOUS CULTURES AND CREATIVITY

Readers will make their own conclusions about contemporary progress on building a new relationship within Canada. It is obvious from the previous commentary and the full contents of this volume that there have been some positive developments and some setbacks since the RCAP report in 1996. As we now look at the completed reports of the Royal Commission on Aboriginal Peoples, the Truth and Reconciliation Commission, and the National Inquiry into Missing and Murdered Indigenous Women and Girls, some might wonder if "the Indigenous moment" has passed as a focus of public and public policy attention and whether governments, in particular, will move on to other things.

We strenuously argue that this is impossible. As this volume attests, the voices of Indigenous peoples, their governments, their representative organizations, and their allies are persistent. They are accustomed to struggle. In our view, they now have a source of energy that was relatively unknown, until recently, to others in Canada. It is the power of Indigenous creativity and the arts to show the strength and dynamism of Indigenous cultures and to draw others in. It affects us all. We now have a national Indigenous theatre program as part of the National Arts Centre. Canada is the only country that has a national Indigenous broadcasting network. First Nations, Métis, and Inuit artists, musicians, and writers are receiving wide recognition, not just as personalities but also for the substance of their work. They are drawing us all in, making us aware of the past and prompting us to think about the future. Equally important, they are inspiring the young generation. They provide strong role models for Indigenous youth. They also animate new cultural and creative relations between Indigenous and settler youth, fostering a better future. The power of the arts and cultural vibrancy to catalyze action in other domains is strong. The arts can bring us to tears or to laughter. The dynamism of Indigenous arts and cultures will contribute to our knowledge that we need to be clear voiced and persistent in thinking about our future in this land we share. Louis Riel might have been prescient when he is reputed to have said, "My people will sleep for 100 years, but when they awake it will be the artists who give them their spirit back."

NOTES

1   RCAP, "Volume 1: Looking Forward, Looking Back," xxv.
2   TRC, Honouring the Truth, 16
3   Stueck and Woo, "Trudeau Accepts Indigenous Inquiry's Findings of Genocide."
4   See http://www.rcaanc-cirnac.gc.ca.
5   See http://www.pm.gc.ca.
6   See http://www.raanc-cirnac.gc.ca.
7   RCAP, Volume 2, 378.
8   RCAP, Volume 2, s. 4.3.
9   Coburn, "Splitting INAC."
10 Metallic, "Making the Most Out of Canada's New Department."
11 DeLancey, "Indigenous Evaluation in the Northwest Territories."
12 CIRNAC news release, 5 September 2019.
13 Hear Our Voice, 2.
14 Fontaine, "Canada Officially Adopts UN Declaration."
15 See http://www.fngovernance.org.
16 NIB, Indian Control over Indian Education, 25.
17 See http://www.nationalobserver.com.
18 Chiasson, "Historic Workshop."
19 See, for example, Abele and Graham, "Federal Urban Aboriginal Policy"; Newhouse and
    Peters, Not Strangers in These Parts.

REFERENCES

Abele, Frances, and Katherine A.H. Graham. "Federal Urban Aboriginal Policy: The
    Challenge of Viewing the Stars in the Urban Night Sky." In Canada in Cities: The
    Politics and Policy of Federal-Local Governance, edited by Katherine A.H. Graham
    and Caroline Andrew, 250–69. Kingston and Montreal: McGill-Queen's University
    Press, 2014.

Chiasson, Chrissy. "Historic Workshop Marks First-Ever Gathering of Indigenous Board
    Members, Partners." International Joint Commission, 19 August 2019. https://www.ijc.
    org/en/historic-workshop-marks-first-ever-gathering-indigenous-board-members-
    partners.

Coburn, Veldon. "Splitting INAC: Coercive Fiscal Federalism in the Disguise of 'Reconciliation.'"
    Yellowhead Institute, 2018.

DeLancey, Debbie. "Indigenous Evaluation in the Northwest Territories: Opportunities
    and Challenges." Canadian Journal of Program Evaluation, special issue on Indigenous
    Evaluation 34, no. 3 (2020): 492–512.

Fontaine, Tim. "Canada Officially Adopts UN Declaration on Rights of Indigenous Peoples."
    CBC News, 10 May 2016. https://www.cbc.ca/news/aboriginal/canada-adopting-
    implementing-un-rights-declaration-1.3575272.

Hear Our Voice: Sharing the Land, Sharing a Future. Report on a National Forum on
    Reconciliation—Marking the 20th Anniversary of the Royal Commission on Aboriginal
    Peoples. Winnipeg: National Forum Steering Committee, 2016.

Metallic, Naomi. "Making the Most Out of Canada's New Department of Indigenous Services
    Act." Yellowhead Institute, 2019.

National Indian Brotherhood (NIB). Indian Control over Indian Education. Ottawa: NIB, 1973.

Newhouse, David, and Evelyn J. Peters. Not Strangers in These Parts: Urban Aboriginal Peoples.
    Ottawa: Policy Research Initiative, 2003.

Royal Commission on Aboriginal Peoples (RCAP). *Volume 1: Looking Forward, Looking Back.* Ottawa: Minister of Supply and Services, 1996.

——. *Volume 2: Restructuring the Relationship.* Ottawa: Minister of Supply and Services, 1996.

Truth and Reconciliation Commission (TRC) of Canada. *Honouring the Truth, Reconciling for the Future: Summary of the Final Report of the Truth and Reconciliation Commission of Canada.* 2015. http://www.trc.ca/websites/trcinstitution/File/2015/Honouring_the_Truth_Reconciling_for_the_Future_July_23_2015.pdf.

Stueck, Wendy, and Andrea Woo. "Trudeau Accepts Indigenous Inquiry's Findings of Genocide." *Globe and Mail*, 4 June 2019. https://www.theglobeandmail.com/canada/british-columbia/article-trudeau-accepts-indigenous-inquirys-finding-of-genocide/.

APPENDIX
THE SHARING THE LAND, SHARING A FUTURE FORUM OVERSIGHT COMMITTEE

- Michèle Audette, Native Women's Association of Canada
- Marlene Brant Castellano, Trent University (Co-Chair)
- Simon Brascoupé, Institute of Aboriginal Peoples' Health (Canadian Institutes of Health Research)
- Caroline Davis, Queen's University
- Jennifer Dockstator, Trent University
- Mark Dockstator, First Nations University of Canada
- Elizabeth Ford, Inuit Tapiriit Kanatami
- Lynn Freeman, School of Policy Studies, Queen's University
- Irving Leblanc, Assembly of First Nations
- Marion Lefebvre, Institute on Governance
- Ry Moran, National Centre for Truth and Reconciliation
- Amy Nahwegahbow, Native Women's Association of Canada
- Scott Serson, Canadians for a New Partnership
- Gauri Sreenivasan, Federation for the Humanities and Social Sciences
- Eduardo Vides, Métis National Council
- Frederic Wien, Dalhousie University (Co-Chair)
- Harry Willmot, Circle on Philanthropy and Aboriginal Peoples in Canada

CONTRIBUTORS

Frances Abele is Chancellor's Professor in the School of Public Policy and Administration at Carleton University. She was deputy director of research at the Royal Commission on Aboriginal Peoples and is the principal investigator of the Rebuilding First Nations Governance Project.

Michael Adams is President of the Environics Institute for Survey Research. He is the author of seven books, including *Fire and Ice: The United States, Canada and the Myth of Converging Values* (2003). He holds an Honours BA in Political Studies from Queen's University (1969) and a MA in Sociology from the University of Toronto (1970). In 2009, he received an honorary Doctor of Letters from Ryerson University. In 2016, he was awarded the Order of Canada, the country's highest domestic honour.

Erin Alexiuk is a PhD Candidate in the School of Environment, Resources, and Sustainability at the University of Waterloo in Ontario, Canada. She is also a Research Associate at the Waterloo Institute for Social Innovation and Resilience (WISIR), and a Fellow of the Transformations Systems Mapping and Analysis Working Group.

Jo-ann Archibald Q'um Q'um Xiiem, PhD, OC, is from the Stó:lō Nation and has kinship in St'át'imc First Nation in British Columbia. She is Professor Emeritus in the Faculty of Education at University of British Columbia. Over a forty-five-year educational career, Jo-ann has been a school teacher, curriculum developer, researcher, university leader, and professor. Archibald's scholarship relates to Indigenous knowledge systems, storywork/oral tradition, transformative education at all levels, Indigenous teacher and graduate education, and Indigenous methodologies.

Cindy Blackstock, PhD, is a member of the Gitxsan First Nation. She is honoured to serve as the Executive Director of the First Nations Child and Family Caring Society and as a Professor at McGill University. Consistent with RCAP, she combines human rights litigation and social movements to address long-standing inequalities in First Nations public services so that First Nations children and their families have an opportunity to thrive in ways they self-define.

Amy Bombay is an Ojibway (Rainy River First Nation) Associate Professor in Department of Psychiatry and the School of Nursing at Dalhousie University. Her primary areas of inquiry explore the relationships between historical trauma, contemporary stressor exposure, and stress-related pathology among Indigenous peoples in Canada.

Carrie Bourassa, BA, MA, PhD, is the Scientific Director of the Canadian Institutes of Health Research—Institute of Indigenous Peoples' Health (CIHR-IIPH) and a Professor, Community Health and Epidemiology, University of Saskatchewan. She is the Principal Investigator for the Canada Foundation for Innovation funded Morning Star Lodge as well as the Cultural Safety, Evaluation, Training and Research lab. Dr. Bourassa has nearly twenty years' experience as a professor in the field of Indigenous health studies. Through her role as Scientific Director of IIPH, she leads the advancement of a national health research agenda to improve and promote the health of First Nations, Inuit, and Métis Peoples in Canada.

The Honourable Yvonne Boyer, LLD, LLM, JD, LLB, was appointed to the Senate of Canada on 25 March 2018 to represent the province of Ontario, and she is the first Indigenous person to serve as a senator for the province. Prior to this appointment, she was the Associate Director of the Centre for Health Law, Policy, and Ethics at the University of Ottawa and part-time Professor. Yvonne Boyer is a member of the Métis Nation of Ontario.

Marlene Brant Castellano is Professor Emerita and former chair of the Department of Native Studies, Trent University. She served as Co-Director of Research for the Royal Commission on Aboriginal Peoples.

Lynne Davis is a settler Canadian of Eastern European heritage who lives in Michi Saagiig Nishnaabeg Aki (Treaty 20 and Williams Treaties). She teaches Indigenous-settler relations and alliances in the Chanie Wenjack

School for Indigenous Studies at Trent University. She worked for the Royal Commission on Aboriginal Peoples on the education research and policy teams and helped draft the final RCAP report on education.

Jeffrey S. Denis is an Associate Professor of Sociology at McMaster University. His research examines the dynamics of racism and colonialism, Indigenous solidarity activism, and social determinants of health. He is engaged in multiple community-based participatory research (CBPR) projects with Indigenous communities and recently published a book on Anishinaabe-settler relations in northwestern Ontario titled *Canada at a Crossroads: Boundaries, Bridges, and Laissez-Faire Racism in Indigenous-Settler Relations.*

Jonathan Dewar, PhD, has spent most of his twenty-plus-year career directing research and knowledge translation initiatives on behalf of Indigenous-governed non-governmental organizations (NGOs). Jonathan is of mixed heritage, descended from French-Canadian, Scottish-Canadian, and Huron-Wendat grandparents. He received a doctorate from the School of Indigenous and Canadian Studies at Carleton University, where his research focused on the role of the arts in health, healing, and reconciliation. He is the Chief Executive Officer of the First Nations Information Governance Centre.

Sibyl Diver is an interdisciplinary environmental scientist, a lecturer at Stanford University in the Earth Systems Program, and co-lead for the Stanford Environmental Justice Working Group. She does community-engaged research on Indigenous water governance, focusing on Pacific Northwest salmon watersheds. This includes research on co-management (or collaborative management) arrangements between Indigenous communities and state agencies. She received her PhD from Berkeley's Department of Environmental Science, Policy and Management, where she helped build the Karuk-UC Berkeley Collaborative, a group supporting the Karuk Tribe's eco-cultural revitalization strategy in Northern California. For the past twenty years, Sibyl has worked in partnership with community leaders on issues of Indigenous peoples and salmon around the North Pacific—in the Russian Far East, Alaska, Canada, and the United States.

Jennifer S. Dockstator has a PhD in Environmental Studies from York University. Her dissertation is titled, "Widening the Sweetgrass Road:

Re/Balancing Ways of Knowing for Sustainable Living with a Cree-Nishnaabe Medicine Circle." Through Trent University and First Nations University of Canada, she has been the Project Director for the National Centre for Collaboration in Indigenous Education (NCCIE), a project aimed at amplifying community voices about Indigenous education and sharing teaching resources created with an Indigenous lens.

Mark S. Dockstator, Haudenosaunee of the Oneida Nation of the Thames, is an Associate Professor of Indigenous Studies at Trent University. He is a former President of the First Nations University of Canada. Other positions he has held include Chair of the First Nations Statistical Institute and Special Advisor to the Royal Commission on Aboriginal Peoples.

Gérard Duhaime is a Professor of Sociology at Université Laval (Quebec), and Canada Research Chair in Comparative Aboriginal Conditions since 2002. He is the author of several books and papers in the fields of economic sociology specially related to the circumpolar Arctic and Indigenous peoples' living conditions.

Eabametoong First Nation (EFN) is located on the north shore of Eabamet Lake, 360 kilometres north of Thunder Bay, Ontario. EFN is a member of the Nishnawbe Aski Nation and the Matawa Tribal Council and is a signatory to Treaty 9. Eabametoong is a traditional name, which in Anishinaabemowin (the Ojibway language) means "reversing of the water place." The community has a population of approximately 2,500 people (about 1,600 of whom live in Eabametoong).

Aaron Franks is a Senior Advisor at the First Nations Information Governance Centre. He holds a PhD in Human Geography from the University of Glasgow and has worked for many years as a formal and informal educator, a researcher, and an artist. Originally from Treaty Six territory (Edmonton), Aaron is of British, Northern European, Anglo-Métis (Birch Hills, Saskatchewan, and Red River, Manitoba), and Cree descent and lives on unceded Algonquin territory in Ottawa.

First Peoples-First Person is a national research and intervention network focused on improving the wellness and mental health of Indigenous peoples. It is part of the Canadian Depression Research and Intervention Network (CDRIN), http://cdrin.org/.

Katherine A.H. Graham is Professor Emerita in the School of Public Policy and Administration at Carleton University. She has done research and taught in the fields of Indigenous and Northern policy and administration for over forty years. She served on the research staff of the Royal Commission on Aboriginal Peoples for the duration of its existence, initially as Coordinator of the Urban Aboriginal Working Group and later as Co-Director of Governance. She is a settler, originally from Treaty 1 and Red River Métis Territory.

Jan Hare is Anishinaabe from the M'Chigeeng First Nation. She is Professor and Associate Dean for Indigenous Education in the Faculty of Education at the University of British Columbia, where she also serves as Director of NITEP – UBC's Indigenous Teacher Education Program. Her research is concerned with centring Indigenous knowledge systems in early learning and kindergarten to grade twelve schooling, through to post-secondary education. She has been recently awarded a Canada Research Chair in Indigenous Pedagogy.

Chris Hiller is a settler Canadian of mixed European heritage who lives in Haudenosaunee, Anishinaabe, and Attawandaron territories (Guelph, Ontario) and is an Assistant Professor in Social Development Studies at Renison University College at University of Waterloo. Her research explores pedagogical strategies for transforming settler consciousness, recognizing Indigenous sovereignty, and working towards decolonized futures.

Derek Kornelsen holds a PhD in Political Science from the University of British Columbia, an MA in Political Studies from University of Manitoba, and a BAH in Psychology from the University of Winnipeg. He is currently working with the Manitoba First Nations Centre for Aboriginal Health Research. He is involved in developing a number of local, national, and international research projects and partnerships, as well as working to develop a research program exploring Indigenous peoples' connections to land as a social determinant of cultural/social well-being and health.

Josée Lavoie is a Professor with the Department of Community Health Sciences in the Faculty of Health Sciences at the College of Medicine at the University of Manitoba, and Director of Ongomiizwin Research at the University of Manitoba. Dr. Lovoie's program of research is located at the interface between policy and Indigenous health services, with a focus on contracting, accountability, and responsiveness. She is particularly interested in how Western and Indigenous knowledge systems interface in the provision of health services in Indigenous communities.

Carole Lévesque is a Professor at Institut national de la recherche scientifique (Montreal). She is the founder and director of DIALOG, an Indigenous peoples research and knowledge network. She is also Co-Director of the ODENA Research Alliance dedicated to the study of Aboriginal peoples in Quebec's cities.

Charlotte Loppie is a Professor in the School of Public Health and Social Policy in the Faculty of Human and Social Development at the University of Victoria. She is also Associate Dean Research in the Faculty of Human and Social Development (UVIC).

John Loxley served as a Professor of Economics at the University of Manitoba.

Catherine MacQuarrie's career comprises a range of experience and expertise—in media, public service, and Indigenous governance. Over twenty-three years as a public servant, she held increasingly senior leadership positions in a number of departments and central agencies in the Government of Canada and the Government of the Northwest Territories. Recently retired from government, she is now pursuing a life-long ambition to help advance First Nations' self-government through the Rebuilding First Nations Governance Project.

Janet E. McElhaney, MD, FRCPC, FACP, is Professor of Medicine at the Northern Ontario School of Medicine, the HSN Chair in Healthy Aging, and Scientific Director, Health Sciences North Research Institute. She received her MD degree and completed residencies in internal medicine and geriatric medicine at the University of Alberta. Dr. McElhaney's research interests are in the prevention of disability in older adults, which in recent years has included First Nations communities and the design of community-based interventions to support healthy aging. She has received a total of $2,406,628 as the Nominated Principal Investigator for Indigenous Health Research grant awards from the Canadian Institutes of Health Research (CIHR), Ontario Health Research Fund, AGE-WELL, and the Northern Ontario Academic Research Fund. In addition, she has been Co-Investigator on grants focused on Indigenous persons living with dementia funded by the Canadian Consortium on Neurodegeneration in Aging and CIHR.

The Misipawistik Cree Nation (MCN) is located on the northwestern shore of Lake Winnipeg where the mouth of the North Saskatchewan River enters Lake Winnipeg and has a population of approximately 720 people. Traditionally, people from the Misipawistik Cree Nation have considered their community the geographic centre of Manitoba. Misipawistik Cree Nation is approximately 400 kilometres north of Winnipeg.

William Mussell, a Stó:lō educator and mental health advocate, is currently the Chair of First Peoples Wellness Circle and Vice President of Thunderbird Partnership Foundation. He has held roles as Executive Director of the Union of British Columbia Indian Chiefs, founding Chair of the Coqualeetza Cultural Education Centre, Co-founder of the Sal'i'shan Institute, President and Co-chair of the Native Mental Health Association of Canada, and Chair of the First Nation, Inuit, and Métis Advisory Committee to the Mental Health Commission of Canada.

Devon Napope was born and raised in Saskatoon, Saskatchewan. He is a member of One Arrow First Nation. Devon is a board member/director of STR8 UP an organization that works with individuals who are trying to leave the gang life. Since his involvement with STR8 UP, Devon has spoken to many youth, adults, and professionals, across the province of Saskatchewan. Devon is currently completing an Indigenous social work degree and is the proud father of four children.

David Newhouse is Onondaga from the Six Nations of the Grand River near Brantford, Ontario. He is Professor of Indigenous Studies, Director of the Chanie Wenjack School for Indigenous Studies, and Professor in School of Business Administration at Trent University. He has been Chair of the Department of Indigenous Studies, now the Chanie Wenjack School for Indigenous Studies, since 1993. His research examines the emergence of modern Aboriginal society. His publications include *In the Words of Elders: Aboriginal Cultures in Transition; Hidden in Plain Sight: Aboriginal Contributions to Canadian Development and Identity, Volumes I and II; Not Strangers in These Parts: Urban Aboriginal Peoples;* and *Well-Being in Urban Aboriginal Communities.*

Eric Oleson, MPA, BA, is a graduate of the public policy school at the University of Regina, an activist, and the founder of multiple businesses based in Regina, Saskatchewan. He lives in Regina with his wife and their pets.

Opitciwan is an Atikamekw nation comprised of three communities: Manawan, Wemotaci, and Obedjiwan-Opitciwan. "Opitciwan" means "the meeting place of the rising rivers" and is located in the heart of the Province of Quebec north of the Gouin Reservoir in the region of La Mauricie. It is accessible by a 166-kilometre logging road, linking the reserve to Highway 167 in Lac-Saint-Jean. Based on the 2011 census, the community has a population of 2,031 people.

Jeff Reading is a Professor in the Faculty of Health Sciences at Simon Fraser University and the inaugural British Columbia First Nations Health Authority Chair in Heart Health and Wellness at St. Paul's Hospital. He is also Director of the Indigenous Health Education Access Research and Training (I-HEART) Centre in Vancouver. Reading holds MSc and PhD degrees in community health sciences from the University of Toronto. From 2000 to 2008, he served as founding Scientific Director of the Institute of Aboriginal Peoples' Health at the Canadian Institutes of Health Research and chaired CIHR's Indigenous Peer Review Committee from 2016 to 2018. Reading is a volunteer with the Heart and Stroke Foundation of Canada's national advisory council (CoMPASS). He also serves on the board of directors of Genome British Columbia.

Daniel Salée teaches in the Department of Political Science and in the School of Community and Public Affairs at Concordia University. He is one of the main initiators of Concordia's First Peoples Studies program and a founding member of DIALOG, Quebec's research and knowledge mobilization network devoted to the advancement of Indigenous Studies. Professor Salée has published extensively on issues related to Indigenous peoples-settler relations in Quebec and Canada.

Satsan (Herb George) is a Wet'suwet'en Hereditary Chief of the Frog Clan, a long-time Speaker for the Wet'suwet'en Nation, and a key figure and strategist in the 1997 Delgamuukw-Gisdayway decision. Satsan is President of the Centre for First Nations Governance, a role he has held for over fifteen years. More recently, he co-founded and is the visionary leader of the Transitional Governance Project and is Co-Director of the Rebuilding First Nations Governance Project, a SSHRC Partnership Project.

Sipekne'katik First Nation is the second largest Mi'kmaq band in Nova Scotia and includes the communities of Indian Brook Indian Reserve (IR) #14, New Ross, Pennal, Dodd's Lot, Wallace Hills, and Grand Lake. Sipekne'katik First Nation has 2,588 band members, with approximately 1,244 members residing in the community and 1,344 members residing out of the community. Sipekne'katik First Nation is located 68 kilometres from Kjipuktuk (Halifax, Nova Scotia).

Caroline L. Tait holds a PhD in medical anthropology from McGill University and is a Professor in the Department of Psychiatry at University of Saskatchewan. She is a member of the Métis Nation-Saskatchewan from MacDowall, Saskatchewan. She is the nominated principal investigator of the Canadian Institutes of Health Research (CIHR)-funded Saskatchewan First Nations and Métis Health Research Centre, the Network Environments for Indigenous Health Research (NEIHR) National Coordinating Centre, and the Saskatchewan Indigenous Mentorship Network.

The T'ít'q'et community (formerly Lillooet Indian Band), situated adjacent to the town of Lillooet is approximately 254 kilometres northeast of Vancouver, British Columbia on Highway 99. T'ít'q'et is one of eleven communities within the St'át'imc Nation that share a common language, culture, history, and territory. T'ít'q'et currently has 394 registered members. The band has seven reserves, including the main reserve Lillooet IR #1 and a shared reserve with the Bridge River Indian Band.

Warren Weir is the Cowichan Campus Academic Administrator at Vancouver Island University. He specializes in Aboriginal organization and management, First Nation education, strategic management, and Indigenous community economic development.

Frederic C. Wien has an Honours BA in Political Studies and Spanish from Queen's University (1962–66), and an MA and PhD in Development Sociology, Government and Latin American Studies from Cornell University (1966–71). He served as Deputy Director of Research at the Royal Commission on Aboriginal Peoples, and currently holds an emeritus appointment in School of Social Work at Dalhousie University.

Wanda Wuttunee is Professor in Native Studies at the University of Manitoba. She is Cree from Red Pheasant Cree Nation in Saskatchewan. Dr. Wuttunee focuses her teaching and research on future Indigenous business leaders and their efforts to benefit home communities. She also is interested in mainstream business/community partnerships that work to enhance vibrant, sustainable, and healthy Indigenous communities in Canada.

INDEX

A

Aboriginal Arts Council, 348

Aboriginal Education Enhancement Agreement (AEEA), 142, 145

Aboriginal Equity Partners (AEP), 213–14

Aboriginal Head Start in Urban and Northern Communities (AHSUNC), 136–37, 139, 141

Aboriginal Head Start On-Reserve (AHSOR), 137, 139

Aboriginal Healing Foundation (AHF): accomplishments of, 232–38; and addiction, 233–34; art funding of, 309, 328, 341; defunded, 55; effect of its closing, 236, 237; founding of, 41, 229, 313; history of, 353n24; research into healing by, 246; residential school survivors and, 234, 236–37

Aboriginal Health Human Resources Initiative (AHHRI), 55–56, 266

Aboriginal Infant Development Program (AIDP), 137–38

Aboriginal Institutes' Consortium (AIC), 154

Aboriginal Languages Act, 146

Aboriginal Peoples Television Network (APTN), 299, 389

aboriginalism, 324

addiction, 230, 233–34, 243–44

Alfred, Taiaiake, 324, 325

Anderson, Jordan River, 52, 286–87, 471

Angus, Charlie, 291

Armstrong, Jeannette, 315, 318–19

art therapy, 329–30

art/artists: and activism, 230–31, 349; AHF funding of, 309, 341, 382; collaborative work of, 343–45; collected by TRC, 317; as commemoration, 332, 337–38; and community, 317–21, 345, 348, 351; healing properties of, 309–11, 328–29; influence of residential schools on, 315, 317, 328–29, 340–41, 343; influenced by RCAP, 230–31; initiatives on reconciliation, 315–16, 319, 341–42, 377–78; inspired by Missing and Murdered Indigenous Women and Girls campaign, 384; TRC recommendations for, 343

Assembly of First Nations (AFN): and 2015 election, 370; and decolonization, 409; opposition to Specific Claims Resolution Act, 440; and PARP, 170; partners with INAC on child welfare report, 285–86; protest on lack of response to RCAP, 427; and reciprocal accountability, 62; signs memorandum of understanding with federal government, 463

Awakening the Spirit, 191

B

Barrera, Jorge, 299

Belcourt, Christi, 125, 337–38, 384

Bellegarde, Perry, 7–8

benevolent peacemaker myth, 367–68

J